THE SERMONS
AND
LITURGY
OF
SAINT JAMES

Pope Calixtus writing the *Codex Calixtinus*. *Codex Calixtinus*, Santiago de Compostela, Cathedral Archive, s.n., f. 1r.

THE SERMONS
AND
LITURGY
OF
SAINT JAMES

Book One of the
Liber Sancti Jacobi
A Translation, with Introduction,
Commentaries and Notes by
Thomas F. Coffey and
Maryjane Dunn

Italica Press
New York & Bristol
2021

Copyright © 2021 by Thomas F. Coffey & Maryjane Dunn

Italica Press Medieval and Renaissance Texts Series

Italica Press, Inc.
99 Wall Street
Suite 650
New York, New York 10005

All rights reserved. No part of this publication may be reproduced, stored in a retrieval system, or transmitted, in any form or by any means, electronic, mechanical, photocopying, recording, or otherwise, without prior permission of Italica Press. For permission to reproduce selected portions for courses, please contact the Press at inquiries@italicapress.com.

Library of Congress Cataloging-in-Publication Data
Names: Coffey, Thomas F., translator, writer of introduction, writer of added commentary. | Dunn, Maryjane, translator, writer of introduction, writer of added commentary.
Title: The sermons and liturgy of Saint James : book one of the Liber Sancti Jacobi / a translation, with introduction, commentaries and notes by Thomas F. Coffey and Maryjane Dunn.
Other titles: Liber Sancti Jacobi. Book 1. English.
Description: New York : Italica Press, 2021. | Series: Italica Press medieval and Renaissance texts series | Includes bibliographical references and index. | Summary: "The first English translation of Book One of the Liber Sancti Jacobi or Book of Saint James based on the Codex Calixtinus and the Salamanca Manuscript 2631. Includes introduction, commentaries, notes, bibliography, and addenda from the end of the manuscript of liturgical materials, hymns, and miracle tales"-- Provided by publisher.
Identifiers: LCCN 2021007292 (print) | LCCN 2021007293 (ebook) | ISBN 9781599103266 (hardcover) | ISBN 9781599103273 (trade paperback) | ISBN 9781599103280 (kindle edition) | ISBN 9781599104133 (adobe pdf)
Subjects: LCSH: Liber Sancti Jacobi. Book 1. | James, the Greater, Saint--Cult--Spain--Santiago de Compostela. | Christian pilgrims and pilgrimages--Spain--Santiago de Compostela. | Sermons, Latin--Translations into English. | Catholic Church--Liturgy--Texts--Early works to 1800.
Classification: LCC BT685.5 .L5313 2021 (print) | LCC BT685.5 (ebook) | DDC 264/.020094611--dc23
LC record available at https://lccn.loc.gov/2021007292
LC ebook record available at https://lccn.loc.gov/2021007293

Cover Illustration: "Saint James," Salamanca, University Library, MS 2631, f. 2v.

For a Complete List of Titles in Italica Press Medieval & Renaissance Texts
Visit our Web Site at
http://www.italicapress.com/index003.html

ABOUT THE EDITORS

THOMAS F. COFFEY holds a B.A. in French and an M.A. and Ph.D. in Medieval Romance Philology, with German, Greek, and Spanish as support languages. He has taught various levels of French, German, and Spanish at Creighton University in Omaha, Nebraska and English and French in Nordrhein-Westfalen, Germany. He has published in English, French, and Latin and has worked extensively on medieval texts in the areas of rhetoric, French history, and the Inquisition.

MARYJANE DUNN is an associate professor of Spanish at Henderson State University. She has followed the pilgrimage to Santiago de Compostela both personally (first walking the Camino Francés in 1979) and professionally in her scholarly work, focusing on the realities of medieval pilgrimage as well as on its medieval allegorical and nineteenth-century literary depictions. She has published two annotated bibliographies of pilgrimage, and her recent research delves into the pedagogy of the Camino as the basis for university courses in Spanish, history, sociology, and literature.

Contents

About the Editors	V
Illustrations	IX
Acknowledgments	XI
Abbreviations	XII
Introduction	XIII
Prologue	XIII
Saint James the Greater in the New Testament	XV
Saint James in Early Christian Writings	XVI
Saint James in Spain	XVII
The *Codex Calixtinus* and Other Manuscripts	XX
The *Liber Sancti Jacobi*	XXII
The Introduction to the *Codex Calixtinus*	XXVIII
Liturgy in the Roman Catholic Church	XXX
Book I of the *Liber Sancti Jacobi*	XXXVII
The Addenda Material of the *Codex Calixtinus*	XLII
Twentieth-Century Editions and Translations of the *Liber Sancti Jacobi*	XLV
Notes on the Translation	XLVII
The Sermons	LI
The Letter of Pope Saint Calixtus	1
Chapter 1	14
Chapter 2	23
Chapter 3	63
Chapter 4	64
Chapter 5	70
Chapter 6	85
Chapter 7	105
Chapter 8	144

Chapter 9	153
Chapter 10	168
Chapter 11	175
Chapter 12	179
Chapter 13	197
Chapter 14	201
Chapter 15	205
Chapter 16	220
Chapter 17	227
Chapter 18	291
Chapter 19	295
Chapter 20	306
The Liturgy	315
Abbreviations	316
Chapter 21	317
Chapter 22	321
Chapter 23	343
Chapter 24	363
Chapter 25	369
Chapter 26	371
Chapter 27	382
Chapter 28	387
Chapter 29	403
Chapter 30	405
Chapter 31	415
Addenda	429
Bibliography	483
Index of Biblical Citations	491
General Index	503

ILLUSTRATIONS

Pope Calixtus writing the *Codex Calixtinus*. *Codex Calixtinus*, Santiago de Compostela, Cathedral Archive, s.n., fol. 1r.
                                Frontispiece

Colophon, Book One. *Codex Calixtinus*, Santiago de Compostela, Cathedral Archive, s.n., f.139v.   x

"Dum Pater Familias." *Codex Calixtinus*, Santiago de Compostela, Cathedral Archive, s.n., f.193r.   XIV

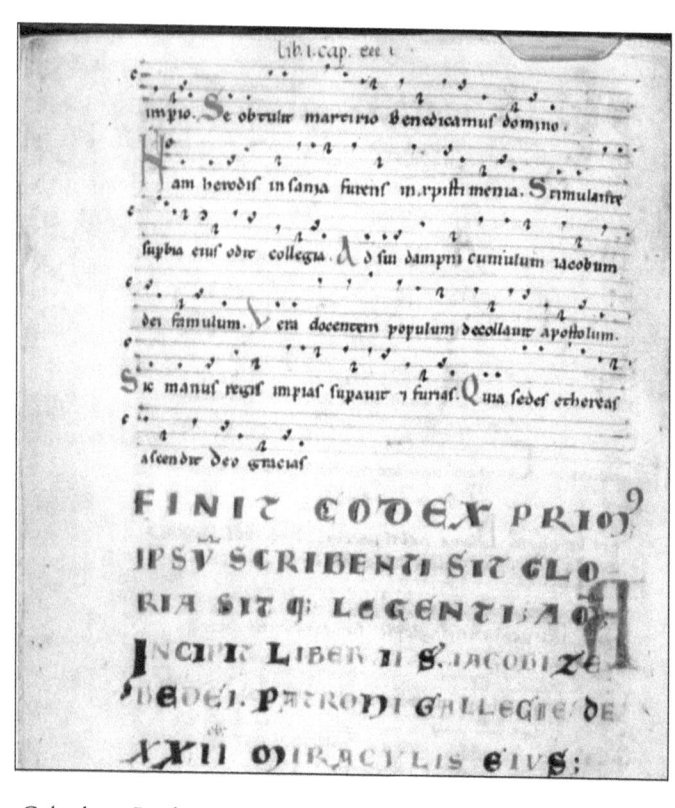

Colophon, Book One. *Codex Calixtinus,* Santiago de Compostela, Cathedral Archive, s.n., f.139v.

ACKNOWLEDGMENTS

We wish to thank Beth Farwell, Associate Director for Central Libraries, Baylor University, for access to the facsimile copies of both the *Codex Calixtinus* and the Salamanca Manuscript 2631, which are housed in the Central Libraries Special Collections at Moody Memorial Library, as well as the Baylor University's Digital Projects Group, Electronic Library, which provided scans of important pages of both facsimiles.

We are also grateful to the staff of the Reinert Alumni Memorial Library at Creighton University, the staff of the Huie Library at Henderson State University, and the Pius XII Memorial Library and Vatican Film Library at Saint Louis University for their help in providing materials.

Much of our introduction and final edits were completed while under social distancing and quarantine during the spring 2020. As libraries around the world closed, we relied heavily on colleagues, friends, and social media contacts to help us track down necessary information. We greatly appreciate George Greenia's generous sharing of his time, books, and scans of articles. We are also grateful to Terence J. McGovern for providing extensive information on liturgical matters found in Book I and the addenda. José Anguita Jaén graciously emailed us copies of his articles. Surprisingly, Google Books and Facebook groups became valued resources. A sincere thank you to several members of Facebook's "Teaching the Middle Ages" group — Courtney Thomaselli, Olivia Holmes Moroni, Katherine Mersch, and Richard Newhauser — for quickly tracking down page numbers for Ovid quotes. We also appreciate members of the Facebook "International Medieval Sermon Studies Society" for sharing their ideas and observations about obtuse questions we posted and for their help in deciphering the paleography of several marginal notes. We are thankful that so many on-line resources and databases, such as JSTOR and HathiTrust, waived their membership fees to allow free access to their collections during the initial months of the pandemic.

We are indebted to Gene McCullough, for his assistance in proofing early drafts of the translation and offering ideas for making the text more accessible to non-scholarly readers.

ABBREVIATIONS

AH   *Analecta hymnica medii aevi.* Edited by Guido M. Dreves. Leipzig: O.R. Reisland, 1907.

CC   *Codex Calixtinus.* Manuscript. Santiago de Compostela, Cathedral Archives, s.n.

CCA   *Codex Calixtinus Addenda.* Manuscript, folios 185–96. Santiago de Compostela, Cathedral Archives, s.n.

Herbers   *Liber Sancti Jacobi: Codex Calixtinus.* Edited by Klaus Herbers and Manuel S. Noya. Santiago de Compostela: Xunta de Galicia, 1998. Latin transcription.

LSJ   *Liber Sancti Jacobi.*

Moralejo   *Liber Sancti Jacobi: Codex Calixtinus.* Translated by A. Moralejo, C. Torres, and J. Feo. Santiago: Consejo Superior de Investigaciones Científicas, Instituto Padre Sarmiento de Estudios Gallegos, 1951. Spanish translation.

PG   *Patrologiae cursus completus: Series graeca.*

PH   *Pasionario hispánico.* Edited by Angel Fábrega Grau. Madrid: Consejo Superior de Investigaciones Científicas, 1953–55.

PL   *Patrologiae cursus completus: Series latina.*

S   *Codex Calixtinus.* Universidad de Salamanca, MS 2631.

Whitehill   *Liber Sancti Jacobi. Codex Calixtinus.* Edited by Walter Muir Whitehill, Germán Prado, and Jesús Carro García. 3 vols. Santiago: Consejo Superior de Investigaciones Científicas, Instituto Padre Sarmiento de Estudios Gallegos, 1944. Latin transcription.

Xunta   *Liber Sancti Jacobi: Codex Calixtinus.* Revised edition by María José García Blanco. Santiago de Compostela: Xunta de Galicia, 2014. (Translated by A. Moralejo, C. Torres, and J. Feo. [Santiago: Consejo Superior de Investigaciones Científicas, Instituto Padre Sarmiento de Estudios Gallegos, 1951]).

INTRODUCTION

Prologue

In the archives of the Cathedral of Santiago de Compostela is found a manuscript known as the *Codex Calixtinus* (CC), an indispensable source of information on Saint James the Greater. It dates from the twelfth century, and its text contains a work generally known as the *Liber Sancti Jacobi* (LSJ) or "Book of Saint James." In fact, the LSJ consists of five books. These are: Book I, the Sermons and Liturgy; Book II, the Miracles of Saint James; Book III, the Great *Translatio*; Book IV, the Chronicle of Pseudo-Turpin; and Book V, the Guidebook.[1] Outside of these five books the CC opens with an introductory letter, a table of contents for Book I, and ends with several folios of addenda material. The original name of this particular manuscript, as well as those that have been copied from it, is not necessarily *Codex Calixtinus*. The first words of the CC, immediately prior to the introductory letter, purportedly written by Pope Calixtus, are: "From the material it is titled: this book is called 'James,'"[2] giving rise to the long-standing confusion between

---

1. All of these individual books have now been published by Italica Press (New York): Book V, *The Pilgrim's Guide* by William Melczer (1993), Book II, *The Miracles of Saint James* by Thomas Coffey, Linda Davidson, and Maryjane Dunn (1996), Book IV, *Chronicle of Pseudo-Turpin* by Kevin Poole) 2014), Books II and III, *The Miracles and* Translatio *of Saint James* by Thomas Coffey and Maryjane Dunn (2018), and Book I, (this present volume). The first translation of Book II (1996) also included the opening letter of the CC and the *Veneranda dies* sermon from Book I; its translation was based solely on the CC.

2. In Latin, the CC begins: *Ex re signatur: liber iste Iacobus vocatur;* the form *vocatur* is not absolutely clear, as the expected abbreviation is not there, but rather a single, otherwise unexplained, vertical line that resembles an "I"; the context clearly requires the passive ending "ur" as we have interpreted it. The Salamanca (S) manuscript has a large lacuna here, where what is believed to have been an initial miniature of Calixtus writing, similar to that in the CC, (Frontispiece) has been cut out. One can read only the last few letters of the opening lines at the edge of the cut, though it is clear that the words relevant to the title are not there. The missing letters are supplied in brackets

the name of the Compostela manuscript, *Codex Calixtinus*, (a name based on its supposed author, Pope Calixtus II)[3] and the name for its contents, *Liber Sancti Iacobi*.[4] Some scholars prefer to call the work simply the *Iacobus*, taking that title from the instructions in the statement in the manuscript itself.[5]

Much about the origin of the CC/LSJ still remains a mystery. When was it composed? Why was it composed? Who really composed it? Where was it written? About these we can only conjecture.[6] However, we know that the CC is considered the earliest

---

here from CC: *[Cal]ixtus // [episcopu]s servus // [ser]vorum // [Dei] sanc[tissimo] con // [ve]ntui // [Clu]niacen // [si]s basili // [ce] sedis // apostolice sue electionis, heroibusque fammosissimis....*

3. Calixtus, formerly Guy of Burgundy, was born c.1065, was made Archbishop of Vienne in 1088 by Pope Urban II, and was elected pope in 1019, with his papacy lasting from 1119 to 1124. Throughout we use the name "Calixtus" — as does the manuscript — to refer to the person or persons who authored, recorded, and/or compiled the CC/LSJ.

4. Joseph Bédier was the first to propose that the manuscript housed in Compostela be denominated *"Codex Calixtinus,"* while the compilation itself be called the *Liber Sancti Jacobi* ("La Chronique de Turpin et le pèlerinage de Compostelle," *Annales du Midi* 24 (1912): 18, n.1). Manuel Díaz y Díaz, "El texto y la tradición textual del Calixtino," in *Pistoia e il cammino di Santiago: Una dimensione europea nella Toscana medioevale,* ed. Lucia Gai (Naples: Edizione Scientifiche Italiane, 1984): 23–55) furthers this argument.

5. In earlier days, the Latin "i" was used for both the semivowel "j" and the vowel "i." In the Renaissance, the practice arose to use "i" for the vowel and "j" for the semivowel. In general, we have returned to the practice of using "i" in both cases for modern transcriptions; however, the use of *Jacobus* and *Jacobi* are firmly fixed in the Renaissance convention.

6. The study made by Díaz y Díaz, María Araceli García Piñeiro and Pilar del Oro Trigo, *El* Códice Calixtino *de la Catedral de Santiago: Estudio codicológico y de contenido* (Santiago de Compostela: Centro de Estudios Jacobeos, 1988) is indispensable for information about the LSJ and the CC. Also useful are Klaus Herbers, *Der Jacobuskult des 12. Jahrhunderts und der* Liber Sancti Jacobi, *Studien über das Verhältnis zwischen Religion und Gesellschaft im Hohen Mittelalter,* Historische Forschungen 7 (Wiesbaden: F. Steiner, 1984) and the collection of articles based on the 1985 conference on the *Codex Calixtinus* at the University of Pittsburgh, *The* Codex Calixtinus *and the Shrine of St. James,* ed. John Williams and Alison Stones (Tübingen: Gunter Narr Verlag, 1992).

INTRODUCTION

surviving complete manuscript of the LSJ and that subsequent copies were made directly from it. This is not a hagiographic work, a simple saint's life for James. It is a highly diverse compilation of lore, verse, and music that had developed over time and space. From the scant materials of the New Testament era to the time when the LSJ was composed, from the Eastern to the Western early Christian traditions, it is helpful to summarize the development of these traditions to give context to the LSJ.

SAINT JAMES THE GREATER IN THE NEW TESTAMENT

The earliest and most widely accepted Christian writings about James are found in the three synoptic Gospels (Matthew, Mark, and Luke) and the Acts of the Apostles. With the exception of the story of Herod's beheading of James (Acts 12:1–2), his brother John is always present with him. In Luke 5:1–11, we read that James and John were fishermen on Lake Gennesaret (the Sea of Galilee) and were partners of [Simon] Peter; after experiencing the miracle of the great catch, they "left everything and followed Him [Jesus]." The story of James's calling differs slightly in Mt 4:21–22 and Mk 1:19–20, which say that he and his brother John were mending their nets in their father Zebedee's boat when Jesus saw them and called them into His service. James, along with his brother John as well as Peter, was specifically named as witnessing the transcendental moments of Jesus's life: His Transfiguration,[7] His raising of Jairus's daughter,[8] and His agony in the Garden of Gethsemane.[9] James and John — or their mother on their behalf — boldly asked a favor of Jesus: that they be allowed to sit in glory at his right and at his left, a request denied by Jesus who said it was not in his power to grant.[10] James was outspoken in at least one other instance, when he entreated Jesus to let him call down fire to punish a Samaritan

---

7. Mt 17:1–13, Mk 9:2–13, and Lk 9:28–36.
8. Mk 5:21–42 and Lk 8:40–56.
9. Mt 26:36–46 and Mk 14:32–42.
10. Mk 10:35–45 (the brothers' request) or Mt 20:20–28 (their mother's request).

village that would not welcome them on their way into Jerusalem.[11] It is not surprising that Jesus gives James and John the sobriquet "Boanerges" (Sons of Thunder) for their impetuous and imperious natures.[12] In the end, however, James was to be counted among the most faithful; Luke specifically names him as present along with the other disciples at the post-Ascension gathering during which the apostles voted for Matthias to replace Judas to complete their group.[13] Finally, Luke tells us that James became the first of the apostles to be martyred, in Jerusalem by Herod Agrippa, in 44CE.[14]

Saint James in Early Christian Writings

During the early centuries of Western Christendom, Saint James was not a particularly important figure. Confusion, or ambiguity, about where James preached and where he was buried is apparent from the earliest writings. Adding to the uncertainty is the confusion among the several Saint James of the Christian New Testament and the Early Church — James the Greater (the apostle and brother of John), James the Lesser (the apostle also known as James, son of Alpheus), and James the Just (also named by some as the brother of Jesus and apocryphally as the first bishop of Jerusalem and to whom is attributed the New Testament Epistle of James). However, the story of Saint James evolved over nine centuries, as it was created and embellished by various authors whose work, intentionally or not, served to increase his significance in medieval religion, history, and culture. James first appears outside the New Testament in Eusebius' *Ecclesiastical History* (c. 315), where we read the beginnings of the story of Josias (although he is not given a name) who was converted by James and martyred alongside him.[15] Eusebius borrowed this story from Clement of Alexandria's (d.c.215) now lost work called

11. Lk 9:51–56.
12. Mk 3:14–17.
13. Acts 1:12–26.
14. Acts 12:1–3.
15. Eusebius of Caesarea, *Ecclesiastical History* 2.9 (PG 20:157–58).

INTRODUCTION

The Outlines.[16] This very early story of the converted guard weaves in and out of the Saint James legend across the centuries. Some early Arabic or Coptic texts say that James traveled with Peter to "the country of Lydia" (modern day Turkey)[17] or "the city of India,"[18] and James is also described as having preached to the Twelve Tribes of Israel.[19] Although these events do not appear in the LSJ, some elements of the Eastern tradition managed to enter the West through a collection of saints' lives credited to Pseudo-Abdias, a supposed bishop of Babylonia, who narrated the now-famous story of the conversion of the magician Hermogenes and his pupil Philetus, as well as the conversion of the guard (this time named Josias) by Saint James, and the story of Saint James's beheading in the time of Abiathar the priest.[20] None of these works in any way link Saint James to the Iberian Peninsula.

Saint James in Spain

The development of the story of Saint James as it is connected to the Iberian Peninsula prior to the compilation of the LSJ began slowly with a half dozen shorter mentions. They can be summarized as follows. First, in the sixth century, an anonymous author in a *Breviary of the Apostles* linked Saint James with the Iberian Peninsula

---

16. Often referred to by its Greek name *Hypotyposes* [ὑποτύπωσες] or *Outlines*. Only fragments, such as those written down by Eusebius, remain.
17. S.C. Malan, trans., *The Conflicts of the Holy Apostles, an Apocryphal Book of the Early Eastern Church, Translated from an Ethiopic MS* (London: D. Nutt, 1871), 172.
18. Agnes Smith Lewis, *The Mythological Acts of the Apostles, Translated from an Arabic MS in the Convent of Deyr–es–Suriani, Egypt, and from MSS in the Convent of St. Catherine on Mount Sinai and in the Vatican Library* (London: C.J. Clay and Sons, 1904), 30.
19. Malan, *Conflicts,* 172–78. Also, Lewis, *Mythological Acts,* 30–34.
20. The text is found in Johann Albert Fabricius, *Codex apocryphus Novi Testamenti,* 2 ed. (Hamburg: Schilleri & Kisneri, 1719); and Richard A. Lipsius, *Die Apokryphen Apostelgeschichten und Apostellegenden* (Braunschweig: C.A. Schwetschke und Sohn, 1883). For a translation of the text relevant to James, see Coffey and Dunn, *Miracles,* 97–105.

and mentioned his feast day and tomb.[21] Second, Isidore of Seville (c.560–636), in his work *On the Birth and Death of the Fathers*, announced that James had preached the Gospel in Spain.[22] Third, Aldhelm of Malmesbury (c.639–709), in the *Song on the Altars of the Twelve Apostles*, acknowledged the connection between Saint James and the Iberian Peninsula.[23] Fourth, a poem ascribed, although probably falsely, to Beatus de Liébana (c.730–c.800) was an acrostic of which the initials yield, in part, the name of King Mauregatus of Asturias (r.783–88, d.789), and which linked James with the Feast of his *Translation*.[24] Fifth, Usuard (d.877), in his *Martyrology*, told of James's Feast on July 25 and of his *translation* to and burial in "the Spains."[25] Sixth, Notker Balbulus (c.840–912), in his *Martyrology*, demonstrated that the legend of Saint James had acquired most of its elements: James preached both in Palestine and Spain, he died in Jerusalem at the hands of Herod, his body was brought for burial to Galicia, and there a cult of followers was established and miracles took place.[26]

Beginning in the ninth or tenth century, there is a marked increase in the details surrounding the emerging cult of Saint James. First, an anonymous writer produced a *Letter of Pope Saint Leo* that presented the circumstances, laden with lore, of Saint James's

---

21. *Breviarium apostolorum*, found in Theodor Schermann, *Prophetarum vitae fabulosae* (Leipzig: Teubner, 1907), 208.
22. Isidorus Hispalensis, *De ortu et obitu patrum*, ch. 71, sect.125 (PL 83:151).
23. The hymn exists in two manuscripts — from Toledo and Santo Domingo de Silos. Jan van Herwaarden provides a detailed explanation of the differences between these two manuscripts, as well as describing the connection between this version and earlier Eastern texts via the imagery of the twelve precious stones and their connection to Syrian elements; see his *Between St. James and Erasmus: Studies in Late Medieval Religious Life* (Leiden: Brill, 2003) 320-27. For the English translation of this poem, see Coffey and Dunn, *Miracles*, 106.
24. *O Dei verbum Patris ore proditum*, PL 1306–07. For an English translation of this text, see Coffey and Dunn, *Miracles*, 107–109.
25. Usuardus, *Martyrologium*, PL 124:295–96.
26. Notker Balbulus, *Martyrlogium*, PL 131:1125–26.

INTRODUCTION

martyrdom, the *translation* of his body, the actions of his disciples, and his subsequent burial in what is now Santiago de Compostela.[27] Second, prior to the eleventh century, an anonymous writer produced the *Pasionario Hispánico* that recounts stories of the early saints of the Iberian Peninsula and contains elements of the Eastern tradition, such as the story of Hermogenes and Philetus, as well as of Josias, and of Saint Torquatus and his followers.[28] This work parallels the Pseudo-Abdias's "Passion of Saint James" mentioned above, but mixes in additional elements — such as the Twelve Apostolic Men and the name of a Christian woman, Luparia, who appears in a miracle in Guadix, Spain — that have become tangled into the Saint James legend. Third, an anonymous writer produced (c.1077) the *Agreement of Antealtares*[29] in which negotiations relative to the *translation* of James and land matters related to Saint James's tomb dated to the time of Alfonso II the Chaste of Asturias (c.760–842, r.783 and 791–842). In the *Agreement* the legend appears with most of its elements and describes the revelation of the location of the tomb by angels to the hermit Pelayo who lived nearby. Fourth, there exists a work known as the *Historia Compostelana* ascribed to Munio, Hugo, and Girardo, canons of the cathedral under Diego Gelmírez, archbishop of Compostela, that spans the years 1100–1139. This work begins with two chapters describing the life

27. The text of this letter forms chapter 2 in the *Translatio*. See Coffey and Dunn, *Miracles*, 85–88.
28. Angel Fábrega Grau published a two-volume Latin study and edition of the *Pasionario Hispánico* (Madrid: Consejo Superior de Investigaciones Científicas, 1953–55). An excellent, newer critical edition with a Spanish translation is *Pasionario Hispánico* by Pilar Riesco Chueca (Seville: Universidad de Sevilla, 1995). This edition, however, does not contain the *Passion of Saint James,* although it does contain that of Torquatus. For an English translation of this, see Coffey and Dunn, *Miracles,* 110–21.
29. For an English translation of the complete agreement, see Coffey and Dunn, *Miracles,* 122–26.

of Saint James, his martyrdom, his *translation,* and the discovery of his body by Teodomiro.[30]

THE *CODEX CALIXTINUS* AND OTHER MANUSCRIPTS

The twelfth-century manuscript of the *Liber Sancti Jacobi,* the *Codex Calixtinus,* has been at the Compostela Cathedral since its compilation. It was "discovered" in the cathedral archives in 1879 by Fidel Fita y Colomé during a period of renewed international interest in Santiago de Compostela and the art and architecture of the pilgrimage route.[31] It apparently has never left Compostela.[32] It is made up of 225 folios. There are 184 folios of text for Books I, II, III and V that are numbered sequentially, plus 29 folios of Book IV, the Pseudo-Turpin, that are numbered separately.[33] At the end of the codex there are eleven folios of miscellaneous additional material.

---

30. Munio Nindoniensis, Hugo Portugalensis in Gallaecia, and Geraldus Presbyter, *Historia Compostellana,* PL 170:889–1236. An English translation of Chapters 1 and 2 on the discovery of Saint James's tomb and his *translation* is found in Coffey and Dunn, *Miracles,* 127–31.

31. Sasha Pack, "Revival of the Pilgrimage to Santiago de Compostela: The Politics of Religious, National, and European Patrimony, 1879–1988." *The Journal of Modern History* 82 (June 2010): 355. This was the era of the creation of the replica castings of the Portico de la Gloria for the Victoria and Albert Museum in London. During this period Spanish interest was also aroused with the initial studies of the Compostela Cathedral by José Villa-Amil y Castro, *Descripción histórico-artístico-arqueológica de la Catedral de Santiago* (Lugo: Soto Freire, 1866), as well as Lopez Ferreiro's eleven-volume church history, *Historia de la Santa A.M. Iglesia de Santiago de Compostela* (Santiago: Seminario Conciliar Central, 1898–1911). Fita, with Julien Vinson, published the first Latin edition of the Book V Guide: *Le codex de Saint-Jacques de Compostelle (Liber de miraculis S. Jacobi): Livre IV* (Paris: Maisonnueve, 1882). At that point it was called "Book Four" because the *Pseudo-Turpin* had been removed in the seventeenth century.

32. It did, however, go missing from the cathedral archives for a year (July 2011–July 2012), when it was stolen by, and later recovered from, a disgruntled cathedral employee.

33. The separate numbering is due to a rebinding of the manuscript when Book IV, the *Pseudo-Turpin,* was removed. There is no remnant of the original folio numbers, and those that are today visible reflect a later addition. Díaz y Díaz, et al., *El Códice Calixtino,* covers the physical aspects of the CC in detail.

INTRODUCTION

This addenda includes liturgical materials, hymns, five additional miracle tales, and the famous hymn *"Dum Pater Familias."* There are references within Book I to some of these materials (most notably the musical pieces). The colophon of the work proper is found on folio 184v (the end of Book V) and reveals the French monastic influence on the compilation: "This book has first been diligently received by the Church of Rome; it was written in various places, that is to say, in Rome, in the lands of Jerusalem, in France, in Italy, in Germany, in Frisia and mainly in Cluny."[34]

The Salamanca manuscript (S) of the LSJ, housed at the Biblioteca Histórica de la Universidad de Salamanca (MS 2631)[35] was copied c.1325 in Compostela and is one of the four complete (long) versions of the LSJ, containing all five books of the CC. The Salamanca manuscript has five illuminations, marginal decorations, and decorated capitals; it has a very compact two-column layout. It generally incorporates the marginal entries of the CC into the body of its text. While S has spread out the text that in CC has musical annotation, as if notes might be added later, only single lines and a space are seen where the staves would appear, and there would barely be enough room to add even a helpful layout of the notes on these staves. Apart from the lack of the addenda material and musical notation, S is a complete copy of the CC with some similar illustrations. The other complete (long) copies of the CC are the Vatican San Pietro C 128 and the London, British Library, Additional 12213. The Ripoll manuscript and other copies of the CC are not complete.[36]

---

34. Melczer, *The Pilgrim's Guide*, 133. The Latin (f.214v) reads *Hunc Codicem prius Ecclesia Romana diligenter suscepit. Scribitur enim in compluribus locis: In Roma scilicet, in Hierosolimitanis horis, in Gallia, in Ytalia, in Theutonica et in Frisia, et Precipue apud Cluniacum.*

35. The manuscript is available as a downloadable pdf at https://gredos.usal.es/handle/10366/128808. (Accessed 6/8/2020.)

36. Descriptions of these manuscripts as well as page photos may be found in Alison Stones, Jeanne Krochalis, Paula Gerson, and Annie Shaver–Crandell, trans. and eds., *The Pilgrim's Guide: A Critical Edition* (London: Harvey Miller, 1998, 2 vols.) I: 109–13, 114–16, 153–68. Díaz y Díaz, et al., *El* Códice

The *Liber Sancti Jacobi*

The LSJ contains five books, each with a different focus. Book I, the longest, contains the liturgical material and music for the saint's feast days. This book consists of two major sections: the first contains sermons and readings on Saint James and the second contains a compendium of liturgical prose, poetry, and musical material suitable for the Feasts of Saint James. Book II, divided into twenty-two chapters, narrates the miracles worked by the saint after his death. These miracles take place in a wide geographic area; none take place at the tomb itself within the cathedral. Book III, the shortest, narrates the miraculous *Translatio* of James's body after his martyrdom in the Holy Land to his final resting place in Galicia. It also confirms the dates and celebrations of Saint James's three feast days — his Passion (July 25), his *Translation* and Calling (December 31), and his Miracles (October 3). Book IV, commonly referred to as the "Pseudo-Turpin Chronicle," links Charlemagne to the Compostela pilgrimage, as it describes Charlemagne and Roland in battle against the Moors on the Iberian Peninsula, instigated by Charlemagne's dream vision of Saint James. Finally, Book V provides the famous twelfth-century guide to the four French routes that lead toward Compostela, describing its perils and intermediary destinations. It also names the monuments and necessary practices both along the route and once at Compostela and includes cautions about bad food and water found, as well as warnings about and colorful descriptions of local inhabitants.[37]

Calixtino, gives extensive information about the different manuscripts and has a thorough listing and discussion of the various complete and partial copies of the LSJ, including a sixteenth–century copy on paper by Juan de Azcona. Díaz y Díaz's Appendix I (327–34) contains a succinct and clear chart showing the disposition of the folios of the LSJ as they are found in twelve manuscript copies.

37. In addition to the English translation by William Melczer, published by Italica Press, there is also a critical study of Book V with a facing page Latin/English text available in Stones, et al.

INTRODUCTION

Several questions were posed earlier about the mysteries surrounding the origin of the LSJ: Why was it written? When was it written? Who really wrote it? Where was it written? To these questions we have only hints of answers. The question of why the LSJ/CC was written seems obvious: one can assume that it was intimately tied to the celebration and promotion of the shrine to Saint James in Compostela. It served as an early form of advertisement for the saint's shrine in Compostela in an age when pilgrimage was an important religious devotion. Yet scholars' opinions vary widely about the purpose of the LSJ. Some view it as an exaltation of the saint's cult and propaganda for the pilgrimage route and the aggrandizement of Compostela. Others have pointed to the complex twelfth-century political-religious alliances and relationships on the peninsula, including the pervasive role of the French religious order of Cluny in the establishment of monasteries along the road. Another reading of the text centers on a recurring concern about the Reconquest efforts on the Iberian Peninsula. This argument is less persuasive as only Chapter 1 (the siege of Zaragoza by the Christians) and Chapter 19 (the fall of Coimbra to the Christians) of the Miracles speak directly to events of the Reconquest. Saint James's appearance to Charlemagne and his help in the fall of Pamplona in Book IV, the *Pseudo-Turpin Chronicle*, seem a more important link to Spanish–French relations than to the actual battles between the Moorish and Christian kingdoms on the Iberian Peninsula. The importance of feast days and concern for the proper liturgy provide yet another possible purpose.

It is generally believed that each of the LSJ's five books was originally written at a different time. As to when the CC itself was composed and assembled, this can be established within certain parameters: between 1139 and 1172. From a letter found in the addenda material of the CC and ascribed to Pope Innocent II (pope 1130–43), although likely a forgery, one could posit a date of about 1139–40, basing the dating on the signatories to the letter. While a forgery may present a plethora of historical and moral issues, the nature of a forgery necessitates the use of as many accurate facts as possible in its production thus creating a single time-frame by selecting signatories who would have been both cardinals (as claimed) and alive (as necessary). Additionally, the last of the miracles of Book II is datable to 1139, and that would be in line with a date of around 1140. The next firmly datable event relative to the manuscript occurred in the year 1172, when a monk named Arnaud du Mont from the monastery in Ripoll wrote to his house asking permission to stay in Compostela to copy a portion of a manuscript, which he thought worth having in the Ripoll monastery, now known as MS Ripoll 99 and housed in the Archivo de la Corona de Aragón in Barcelona. This manuscript gives us a certain fixed date for the CC's completion.[38] It appears, therefore, that the CC was probably assembled into its final form sometime between 1140 (immediately after the latest dated element) and 1172 when Arnaud du Mont made his copy.

Who wrote and/or compiled the LSJ/CC is even more complex. Several chapters of Book II's Miracles are ascribed to authors other than "Calixtus" (Bede, Hubert, and Saint Anselm[39]); Book III's *Translatio* is clearly a compilation of apocryphal stories surrounding Saint James's Passion and *Translation* and his disciples in both Jerusalem and Spain, as well as long detailed passages about the celebration and dating of his feasts. Book IV's *Chronicle of Pseudo-Turpin* draws on a wide range of literary genres and was ostensibly written by Turpin, archbishop of Reims and warrior-priest under Charlemagne. Book V's Guide is presented as the work of Pope Calixtus, but parts are ascribed to Aimery the Chancellor, who is also signatory to the authentication letter in the addenda material.[40] Likewise, Book I includes material by "Pope Calixtus" and "Pope Leo," names which may both be used as pseudonyms

---

38. Díaz y Díaz, "El *Codex Calixtinus:* Volviendo sobre el Tema" in Williams and Stone, *Codex Calixtinus,* 1–9.

39. Venerable Bede (672/3–735), an English Benedictine, author of the *Ecclesiastical History of the English People;* St. Hubert (656–727), bishop of Liège; St. Anselm (1034–1109), Italian Benedictine and archbishop of Canterbury.

40. Melczer, *Pilgrim's Guide,* 140, n. 31.

INTRODUCTION

for the otherwise anonymous compiler of the work. Book I also includes known sermons by Bede, Gregory the Great, Jerome, and Augustine,[41] but the identity of several of the authors of the individual hymns, sermons, and miracles is doubtful. Many pieces are attributed to historical figures, but the attribution in the CC is the only (or earliest) known source. The CC opens with a letter from "Calixtus" addressed to Diego Gelmírez[42] in Compostela and William, patriarch of Jerusalem.[43] Although the letter is ascribed to Pope Calixtus II, he had died some sixteen years before the first possible compilation date.[44] On folio 192 within

---

41. St. Gregory the Great (c. 540–604), pope (590–604); St. Jerome (c. 347–420), translator of the Bible into Latin; St. Augustine (354–430), North African theologian, author of his *Confessions* and *The City of God*.

42. Diego Gelmírez (c. 1069–1140) was bishop of Compostela (c.1100–1121), and later archbishop (1121–40) until his death. His see was raised to archdiocesan status in 1121 and subsequently to metropolitan status by Pope Calixtus II. The metropolitan status was contested and even lost on a number of occasions. There are several pieces of correspondence between Gelmírez and Pope Calixtus in PL 163. For a detailed biography, see R.A. Fletcher, *Saint James's Catapult: The Life and Times of Diego Gelmírez of Santiago de Compostela* (Oxford: Clarendon Press, 1984); and Anselm Gordon Biggs, *Diego Gelmírez, First Archbishop of Compostela* (Washington DC: Catholic University of America Press, 1949).

43. There are at least three people with the name William to whom this letter might have been directed in the Holy Land. Given the compilation date of the mid–twelfth century, the most likely candidates are the first patriarch who served 1128–30 or William of Messina, who served 1130–45 (and died in 1185); Dreves (AH 17:193) identifies him as this last figure: William of Messina.

44. Pope Calixtus II (1119–24). Before his election as pope, Guy (or Guido) was archbishop of Vienne. A noble by birth and a reformer by inclination, he is probably best known for attempting reconciliation with the Holy Roman emperor and for his role in effecting the Concordat of Worms. His works are contained in PL 163:1073–1414 and consist primarily of 282 letters from him (columns 1093–1338) and of six letters to him (columns 1338–60). Among the letters, there are several sent to Cluny and several to Gelmírez; the opening letter of the CC is not among them. There is also other biographical and bibliographical information as well as a discussion of Calixtus relative to the LSJ at columns 1365–68. Among the dubious

the addenda material of the manuscript, in the introduction to the aforementioned letter ascribed to Innocent II, the names of Aymeric Picaud and a companion named Giberga are mentioned as having been the one(s) to carry the manuscript to Compostela. Some scholars ascribe to Aymeric Picaud authorship of the entire work, some just of Book V, while others consider him to be only the scribe or the person who delivered the manuscript to Compostela.[45] The compiler's identity may never be determined.

As to where the CC was written, indications are that it was at least heavily influenced, if not fully directed, by the abbey of Cluny. There was an ongoing relationship between the abbey and Compostela, and a good deal of correspondence between Calixtus and Diego Gelmírez, Compostela's archbishop. The colophon at the end of the Guide specifically mentions Cluny as one of the primary places of composition. The numerous mentions of things French, such as places and people, and some linguistic slips that are remarkably French, show that this was not an idle comment. Cluny had become an important center for the papacy from the time when Gelasius II (1118–19) escaped from Rome and headed to France, where, after stays in various southern cities, he died at the monastery of Cluny in 1119. He had been named a cardinal in 1088, along with the future pope Innocent II. Gelasius had been chosen for the learning that he had acquired at the monastery of Monte Cassino — a center of renewed interest and a part of the

---

works at the end of the PL section, there are four sermons and the miracles as recorded by Vincent of Beauvais. For detailed information on Calixtus, see Ulysse Robert, *Bullaire du pape Calixte II* (Paris: Imprimerie Nationale, 1891; rpt. Hildesheim: G. Olms, 1979) and his *Histoire du pape Calixte II* (Paris: Alphonse Picard, 1891). The collection of bulls contained in the *Bullaire* exceeds 500 letters.

45. For an overview of the historical scholarship on authorship, see Díaz y Díaz et al., *El Códice Calixtino*, 81–87. Stones et al. in *The Pilgrim's Guide* (I, 18–22) offer background on Aymericus the Chancellor and Aymeric Picaud as traditionally depicted, but also consider whether they could be the same person, and how Book V, the papal letter, and the hymn "To the Honor of the Highest King" *(Ad honorem Regis summi)* of the addenda are related.

INTRODUCTION

Gregorian reform movement — where he had been a pupil of, among others, the renowned rhetorician Alberic the Deacon.

Calixtus, who is best known for his defense of the Jews in his bull *Sicut Judeis* (1120) and for his work in securing the agreement known as the Concordat of Worms (1122), was pope from 1119 to 1124. While the CC and LSJ are attributed to Calixtus, it is not possible that he was the compiler of the work, nor is it likely that he was even partially responsible for its content. However, Calixtus was interested in Compostela and likely also in having a foothold in Spain that might over time be expanded. His successor, Honorius II (1124–30), was sympathetic to Compostela, but less enthusiastic than his predecessor. Finally, Innocent II (1130–43) showed a general interest in the Iberian Peninsula though not the particular interest in James that Calixtus had. In fact, the likely forged letter of Innocent in the addenda material of the CC would, if taken at face value, point to a date for the Codex of approximately 1140, during the reign of Innocent II. This was also the year in which Diego Gelmírez died, after his long association with Compostela. In the end, though, the genesis of the CC remains open to speculation.

Establishing authority for the document seems generally limited to choosing important authors for the sermons, such as Bede, Jerome, Gregory I, John Chrysostom,[46] and Augustine. This was augmented by sermons attributed to Pope Calixtus and an unidentified Pope Leo. (Regnal numbers were not regularly supplied to distinguish the various popes, emperors, kings and others prior to the late thirteenth and early fourteenth century.[47]) Additionally, the letter of Innocent II contained in the addenda

---

46. St John Chrysostom (c. 347–407), archbishop of Constantinople.
47. Michel-André Lévy laid out the problems associated with the lack of numbering for French kings and with subsequent attempts to rectify it in his *Louis I, II, III…XIV…, L'Étonnante histoire de la numérotation des rois de France* (Paris: Jourdan, 2014). While popes, including Innocent, used regnal numbering long before kings did, the practice was not firmly established, and the absence of an identifying regnal number for Calixtus or Leo is not remarkable.

material served to bolster the authority of the book. Finally, works attributed to Fulbert of Chartres and other authors are not found in documents prior to the CC. The author also displayed on several occasions some transliterated Greek that was reasonably accurate. He presents a multi-lingual (Latin–Greek–Hebrew) hymn. He further demonstrates a global awareness with his use of geographical terms, especially in *Veneranda dies* sermon of Book I, chapter 17. He also includes references to German, Arab, and vernacular Romance languages, which he retrofits to his medieval Latin. Finally, he exhibits a flowing style that effortlessly incorporates rhetorical devices into the prose that leads one to continue reading.

The Introduction to the *Codex Calixtinus*

The introductory letter of Pope Calixtus is often considered an introduction to the entire *Liber Sancti Jacobi*, however, it is likely this letter was intended primarily as an introduction to Book I. The letter notes that the material contained in both Book I (Sermons and Liturgy) and Book II (Miracles) should be considered important edifying stories: "what is contained in the first two books is quite sufficient for reading at matins. And if all the sermons and miracles of Saint James that are contained in this book cannot be read on his feast days because of their length, they may be read afterward at least throughout each week in the refectory, and certainly on such a day as was once his feast."[48] The compiler of the entire work, said to be Pope Calixtus, explains the basis for the book:

> For when I was a young scholar who had loved the apostle from childhood, I walked through barbarian lands and provinces for a period of fourteen years and wrote down diligently whatever I found, even on a few vile and ragged sheets of parchment, so that I might be able to compile them into a single volume, so that those who are devotees of Saint James might very aptly find all

---

48. Below p. 6.

together the things that are necessary for reading on feast days.[49]

This statement offers a clue to the purpose of at least Books I, II, and potentially III and the addenda materials. While this does not explain the inclusion of Books IV and V, it does indicate the existence of material in the overall codex that is of a nature considered too secular for liturgical or even more general reading in refectories. Moreover any attribution of authorship for the CC to Calixtus is further undermined by this statement. He was born around 1065 and made archbishop of Vienne in 1088 at approximately the age of 23. This in itself would likely rule out a fourteen-year period when he would have been free to walk "through barbarian lands and provinces." His age and training would have precluded this prior to his appointment as archbishop, and his duties as an archbishop would have prevented this after that time.

This introductory letter ends with (or is followed by) an index for the chapters of Book I. In addition, a later hand has entered the folios for the beginning of Books II, III, and IV and the letter of Pope Innocent. From the numbering of the folios, it is apparent that the present folio numbers in the index to Book I and on the folios of the present Books I, II, III, and V were added after the Pseudo-Turpin book was removed from the CC. When it was reinserted, Arabic numbers appear to have been added from folio 164 onward through the Guide (now again becoming Book V) and through the addenda material. In fact, all five books begin with an introduction and an index of chapters in the original hand.

Within the index for Book I, the title is recorded for each chapter, and the incipit is given for most chapters. There is no incipit for chapters 27, 28, 30, and 31. In chapter 27, the entry is for the fourth item in the chapter; in chapter 29, for the third item. The incipit of the Latin does not, however, generally match the incipit of the English translation, as the initial Latin words often end up in a non-initial position within the English text. There is good

---

49. Below p. 6.

rapport between the index titles of the chapters of Book I and the titles of the headers to these chapters in the body of the work. In eight cases, however, (chapters 2, 7, 10, 12, 13, 16, 18 and 20) the index title uses *Expositio* or "Explanation," while the body of the text uses *Sermo* or "Sermon." Among the chapters of the liturgical section (21–30), the titles in the index are paraphrased to some extent, though they clearly reflect the material indexed. The most significant deviation from the index and the actual chapter headers arises with chapters 15 and 16. In the index, the sermon of chapter 15 is attributed solely to "Maximus," presumably referring to the bishop of Turin, who was a prolific writer in the early fifth century,[50] but the sermon of chapter 15 is attributed to Pope Leo. Again in the index, the sermon of chapter 16 is attributed to Jerome and to Maximus, but the actual sermon of chapter 16 is attributed to Jerome and John Chrysostom. In fact, the wording of chapter 16 is found to be an amalgam of Jerome and Chrysostom.

LITURGY IN THE ROMAN CATHOLIC CHURCH

Book I is unique in having no title assigned to it. However, it is clearly "Sermons, Readings, and Liturgy of Saint James" as suggested by the codex's introductory letter. The sermons, of course, stand as self-contained units that fit into many liturgies. The liturgical material, however, is a compendium of material suitable for reading on various James-related occasions, though they are expected to be used in appropriate places in services, which are unspecified but no doubt familiar to those living at the time. The texts of Book I, along with Book II containing the Miracles, are suitable for official reading, as for example, by a lector in refectories during meals, when silence was often observed. As mentioned above, Calixtus singles out Books I and II as suitable for inclusion with liturgical readings, distinguishing them from the less liturgically-appropriate material: the story of the *translation* in Book III, the Charlemagne story of Book IV, and the Guide Book of Book V, although they are not

---

50. See Letter of Calixtinus, p. 4, n. 20.

INTRODUCTION

named, described, or specifically designated. Since Books I and II were not only suitable for refectories but were principally intended for the Mass and the Divine Office, we have provided a general description of them, as ceremonies central to Book I.

THE MASS

The Mass in the Roman Catholic Church began as a ceremony of the breaking of the bread. In fact, the Mass is a ceremonial commemoration of the Last Supper, and the words that are central to this commemoration are "This is My body" and "This is My blood," words of consecration, which are expressed in the most simple manner in Mark 14:22–24, with the standard wording of the Canon of the Mass coming more from the longer version of Matthew (26:26–28) and Luke (22:19–20). The Gospel of John (13) discusses other aspects of the Last Supper, and Paul (1 Corinthians 11:23–26) refers to the words in longer form. Over the centuries, additional prayers and formulae became associated with this Mass and at times incorporated into the Mass; at times items were varied or removed. The father of canon law, Gratian (mid-twelfth-century), in his *Decretals*,[51] gave a detailed account of the development of the Mass from its beginning up until his time, although it is spread out over the course of his book on canon law *(Concordia discordantium canonum)*. In the early fourteenth century, Bernard Gui (c.1262–1331), who was not only an inquisitor but also an historian with a deep interest in compendia and who later became the bishop of Lodève, France, assembled a treatise on the Mass, largely gleaned from the disparate references in Gratian, into a single work: *La Messe* (The Mass).[52] Some of the formulae were a part of every Mass or of almost every Mass and for this reason are called the Ordinary of the Mass. Examples of the Ordinary are the *Kyrie*, the Creed, the Canon, the Consecration, and the Our Father,

---

51. Gratianus, *Decretum*, PL 187 (all).
52. Thomas F. Coffey and Terrence J. McGovern, *"La Messe,"* in *A Middle French Translation of Bernard Gui's Shorter Historical Works* by Jean Golein (Lewiston: The Edwin Mellen Press, 1993), 443–55.

to name but a few. Other prayers, which varied with the progress of the liturgical year beginning with Advent and culminating with the end of the season of Pentecost, were particular to different days or seasons and, as a result, they were called the Proper of the Mass. Special feasts, whether on a Sunday or other day of the week, also had a Proper. Each Sunday had its own Proper. Saints were commemorated throughout the year and in some cases had a Proper specific to them or else a Proper specific to their group, such as for a martyr, virgin, or confessor, among other distinctions. The unique prayers that were specific to a group were known as the Common, for example, the Common for Confessors.

Finally, feasts were ranked in order of importance and when two feasts coincided, for example a Sunday and saint's feast day, one had to supersede the other. The system was complex, with solemnities outranking feasts, feasts outranking commemorations, and commemorations outranking memorials. Within the feast category, for example, there were double first class, double major, double, simple, and other designations. Sundays were similarly ranked. These classifications denoted complex differences, not only in prestige but in the form of the liturgy itself, such as the adding of a sequence for certain Sundays of the highest rank (such as Easter or Pentecost), or the inclusion of additional readings or prayers, such as the use of a collect, gradual, or alleluia. Calixtus explains how to proceed with the Octaves of the Passion of Saint James that could coincide not only with the feast of Saint Peter in Chains, but also with a Sunday, if they fell on that day of the week.[53] Although he does not discuss rankings explicitly, there have long been such rankings.

Over time, the Mass continued to evolve, with accretions and deletions and geographic variations,[54] until the time of the Council of Trent in 1570. Faced with extreme variations in the rites proliferating at the time of the Reformation, the Church instituted,

---

53. See below ch. 23.29.
54. Examples include the Gallican Rite in the Frankish lands and the Mozarabic Rite in the Iberian Peninsula.

INTRODUCTION

in its view once and for all, a single service for the entire Catholic Church, with few exceptions. The Mass that came from the Council of Trent was called the Tridentine Mass. This configuration remained largely intact until the Second Vatican Council (1962–65) when the Latin Mass was replaced in most cases by Mass in the vernacular languages. While missals containing the full service as approved by the Vatican are abundant from the time of the Council of Trent onward, they have not been found in the period of the LSJ. Until the promulgation of the Tridentine Mass, Masses were largely designated "rites" usually according to geographical region. Various rites could have different prayers, a different order of the ceremony and often readings independent of the more common Roman Rite, the main rite of the Latin church.[55]

The Tridentine Mass could be celebrated in its fullness as Solemn High Mass, with deacons and subdeacons carrying out varied roles and with many of the parts (*Gloria,* Creed, Psalm, etc.) sung, often in Gregorian chant. It could also be celebrated as a High Mass, in a somewhat abbreviated form, with no deacon or subdeacon, with many parts still sung. The Low Mass was largely unsung without deacon or subdeacon. Especially in the Solemn High Mass, there was the use of incense and holy water aspersions, washing of hands, the use of distinctive vestments, making the sign of the cross, spreading of hands for prayer, clasping of hands for prayer, the singing of various parts from the altar area and the choir, while congregational singing was limited, as well as ceremonial movements of the hand for blessings and prayers. An overview of the Mass is found in Chart 1.

---

55. For example: Alexandrian Rite, Armenian Rite, Byzantine Rite, East and West Syriac Rites, and Latin Rite.

SERMONS AND LITURGY OF SAINT JAMES

Chart 1 – The Mass		
Tridentine	In LSJ	Notes
Prayers at Foot of Altar	No	Ordinary – Not customary at this time but a Psalm is indicated at times
Confession / Absolution	No	Ordinary – Not customary at this time
Introit	Yes	Proper
Kyrie Eleison	Yes	Ordinary
Gloria	Yes	Ordinary with exceptions
Oration / Prayer / Collect	Yes	Proper – As Oration and Collect
Epistle / Reading	Yes	Usually "Reading" with Epistle only once
Gradual / Alleluia / Tract	Yes	Proper – As Gradual, Alleluia and Tract
Sequence	Yes	As "Prosa" in Latin
Gospel	Yes	Proper
Sermon	Yes	Book I is "Sermons"; not mentioned in Liturgy
Creed	Yes	Ordinary with exceptions
Offertory Prayers	No	Ordinary
Offertory	Yes	Proper
Washing of Hands	No	Ordinary
Secret	Yes	Proper
Preface	Yes	Ordinary, but with variations
Sanctus / Benedictus	Yes	Ordinary
Prayers of the Canon	No	Ordinary
Consecration & Elevation	No	Ordinary
Commemoration Prayers	No	Ordinary
Minor Elevation	No	Ordinary
Our Father	No	Ordinary
Communion Prayers	No	Ordinary
Agnus Dei	Yes	Ordinary
Communion of Priest	No	Ordinary
Communion of Faithful	No	Ordinary (if present)
Ablutions	No	Ordinary

INTRODUCTION

Communion	Yes	Proper
Post Communion	Yes	Proper
Dismissal	Yes	Ordinary, but only *Benedicamus Domino*. No evidence of *Ite missa est*
Blessing	No	Ordinary

The Divine Office

The Divine Office, also known as the Liturgy of the Hours or the Breviary, consists of prayer sequences that are spread out over the course of the day. It usually begins in the very early hours of the morning (Matins) and ends with the final hours of the evening (Compline). Since the time of Saint Benedict (6th c.), the prayers for certain hours have been an important part of the monastic life. They consist of a variety of Psalms, hymns and readings. Matins (about 3:00 a.m.) can contain Nocturns and Vigil prayers, presumably because they occurred so early as to obscure night with morning. Nocturns and Vigils seem to be connected with Sundays and major feasts rather than with the weekdays or lesser feasts. After Matins come Lauds (about 5:00 a.m.), followed closely by Prime (first hour of the day, that is 6:00 a.m.), Terce at the third hour (9:00 a.m.), Sext at the sixth hour (noon), None at mid–afternoon (3:00 p.m.), and Vespers at the twelfth hour (6:00 p.m.). Three of these — Prime, Sext and Vespers — coincide with the more modern observance of the Angelus, with the ringing of the bells. Finally, Compline finished the day at around 7:00 p.m. At these hours, the monks gathered and prayed in prose, verse, and song.[56] Chart 2 provides a very general overview of the Divine Office.

---

56. For an in-depth overview of the services that accompanied the Divine Office, see Vincent Corrigan, "Music and the Pilgrimage," in Maryjane Dunn and Linda Davidson, *The Pilgrimage to Compostela in the Middle Ages* (New York: Routledge, 1996), 43–67; and *The Mass of St. James,* ed. Paul Helmer (Ottawa: Institute of Medieval Music, 1988) in which Helmer gives a Latin transcription and English translation of Book I, chapter 31. Elisardo Termperán Villaverde, "El libro primero del *Códice Calixtino* de la Catedral de Santiago de Compostela: ¿Un propio de la iglesia Compostelana en el siglo XII?" *Compostellanum* 37.1–2 (1992): 63–150 focuses on the theological

Chart 2 – Divine Office		
Possible Divisions	In CC	Comments
Matins	Yes	About 3:00 a.m.; known also as Vigil; may contain Nocturns
Lauds	Yes	About 5:00 a.m.
Prime	Yes	About 6:00 a.m.
Terce	Yes	About 9:00 a.m.
Sext	Yes	About Noon
None	Yes	About 3:00 p.m.
Vespers	Yes	About 6:00 p.m.
Compline	Yes	About 7:00 p.m.

The Liturgical Year

The Liturgical Year was a complex fabric of movement. The overarching seasons begin with Advent commemorating the wait for the coming of Christ at Christmas. It consists of four Sundays and is scheduled so the last Sunday coincided with the Sunday before Christmas. The Christmas Season followed, which ended with the Season of Epiphany. Epiphany was shortened or lengthened to accommodate the three "-gesimal" Sundays before Lent, which falls immediately before Easter. The Easter season lasted until Pentecost Sunday, seven weeks after Easter, thus the name from the Greek Πεντηκοστή *(pentekoste)* or "fifty" days, if one counts the day itself. From that point until the beginning of Advent, a varying number of Sundays occurred, from twenty-three to twenty-eight, depending on the date of Easter. The Last Sunday of Pentecost immediately preceded the first Sunday of Advent. Ember Days — days of fast and abstinence — occurred on the Wednesday, Friday, and Saturday before each season. Holy Days, such as Christmas, Ascension, and All Saints — could fall on various days of the week and varied over time and by region. There were also feast days for individual saints

---

aspects of the liturgy including the importance of the Trinity, the Eucharist, and the intercession of Saint James.

INTRODUCTION

that could be celebrated on every day of the year, although there were also "ferial" weekdays when, within certain bounds, no particular saint would be commemorated. Saints were catalogued by day as we find in the Martyrology of Usuard.[57] As mentioned, in the LSJ, Saint James had not one feast but three.[58] In addition to the feasts themselves, there were the Octaves (from the Latin *octo* or "eight"), a term that could refer either to the eighth day after the feast or all eight days following the feast (counting, as is the custom in some languages, the feast day itself). The largest compendium of the saints organized by feast day and including voluminous writings about each, was assembled by the Bollandists into the *Acta sanctorum*.[59] In addition to these calendar feasts, the liturgy includes Masses for special events, like weddings and funerals, although they might not be required or performed.

Book I of the *Liber Sancti Jacobi*

Book I of the LSJ consists of two sections. The first contains sermons and readings. These include six sermons directly attributed to Pope Calixtus (chapters 2, 6, 7, 12, 17, and 19) and a series of blessings (chapter 3). "Calixtus" also gives an introduction to the Passion readings contained in chapters 4, 5, and 9. "Calixtus" has a style that is ornate, vibrant, but also very conversational and flowing. There is one sermon by "Pope Leo" (chapter 15), who writes in a similar, if not the same, style as Calixtus. Both Calixtus and Leo are, in fact, likely pseudonyms for the author of the entire compendium. There are also seven other writers included in this book. Two sermons are from Bede (1 and 8); three are from Jerome (10, 11, and 13); two are from Pope Gregory I (14 and 18); and one (16) is a combination of texts from Saint Jerome and Saint John Chrysostom. The final chapter (20) engages in a sort of colloquium between Calixtus

---

57. Usuardus, *Martyrologium*, PL 123:599–987.
58. His Passion (July 25), his Calling and *Translation* (December 31), and the little-known feast of his Miracles (October 3).
59. Beginning with January, the first volumes of were published in 1643; the last volume, for December, was published in 1940.

and three other authors (Jerome, Gregory, and Augustine), where he has arranged the material in a subtle point-counterpoint with these authors. The texts of these older authors are quite precisely faithful to the originals. The chapters are arranged according to the chronological celebration of the successive feast days pertaining to Saint James. Chapters 1 and 2 are for July 24, the vigil of St. James, while chapters 4, 5, 6, 7, and 8 are for the feast day itself (July 25). Chapter 9 is designated for either the feast day itself (July 25) or the following day (July 26). Chapters 10 through 14 are for the successive days within the octave of Saint James. Chapters 15 and 16 are for the vigil of the octave as well as the octave, which was complicated by a conflict with another major feast, Saint Peter in Chains.[60] Chapter 17 is the longest chapter in this Book and is known as the *Veneranda dies* sermon, which focuses on the pilgrimage, with reasons to undertake the journey, the proper way of carrying it out, and the impediments along the route. Chapters 17, 18, and 19 are for the Feast of the *Translation* of the saint to Galicia, which was celebrated on December 30. Finally, the colloquium sermon of chapter 20 is intended for the Octave of the Feast of the *Translation,* which is celebrated on January 5. The author appears to have tried to bolster his case for Saint James with texts from older and well-respected writers: Bede, Jerome, Gregory, John Chrysostom, and Augustine, as outlined in Chart 3.

---

60. Book III, chapter 3 offers a detailed account of the complications of these overlapping feasts, along with descriptions of the purposes and history of all of the feast days related to Saint James. See Coffey and Dunn, *Miracles,* 88–95.

INTRODUCTION

Chap.	Roman Date	Date	Occasion	Reading	Sermon Author
1	9 Cal Aug	Jul 24	Vigil	James 1:1	Bede
2	9 Cal Aug	Jul 24	Vigil	Mk 3:13ff	Calixtus
3	Varied	Varied	Varied	Blessings	Calixtus
4	8 Cal Aug	Jul 25	Feast	Short Passion	Calixtus & Eusebius
5	8 Cal Aug	Jul 25	Feast	Great Passion; Various Sources	Calixtus
6	8 Cal Aug	Jul 25	Feast	Passion: Various Sources	Calixtus
7	8 Cal Aug	Jul 25	Feast	Acts 11 & 12	Calixtus
8	8 Cal Aug	Jul 25	Feast	Mt 20:20ff	Bede
9	8 Cal Aug	Jul 25	Feast	Various Sources	Calixtus & *Pasionario Hispánico*
10	7 Cal Aug	Jul 26	2 Octave	Mt 10:1ff	Jerome
11	6 Cal Aug	Jul 27	3 Octave	Mt 17:1ff	Jerome
12	5 Cal Aug	Jul 28	4 Octave	Lk 9:51ff	Calixtus
13	4 Cal Aug	Jul 29	5 Octave	Mt 26:37ff	Jerome
14	3 Cal Aug	Jul 30	6 Octave	Mk 10:35ff	Gregory
15	2 Pridie Aug	Jul 31	7 Octave	Varied	Leo
16	2 Pridie Aug	Jul 31	7 Octave	Mt 20:20ff	Jerome & John Chrysostom
17	3 Cal Jan	Dec 30	Feast	Varied	Calixtus
18	3 Cal Jan	Dec 30	Feast	Mt 4:18ff	Gregory
19	3 Cal Jan	Dec 30	Feast	Ecclus/Sir 44:16ff	Calixtus
20	None Jan	Jan 5	Octave	Mt 4:21ff	Jerome, Augustine, Gregory & Calixtus

SERMONS AND LITURGY OF SAINT JAMES

The second major section of Book I contains a mix of liturgical materials for use in the Divine Office and the Mass. However, it is not in any sense a modern-style Missal with the full ceremony of the Mass nor is it a Breviary with the full service of the Divine Office. It presents items of a Proper of the Mass unique to Saint James as well as sections of the Ordinary of the Mass. Large portions of this material are set to music with a fair amount of that music displayed on full staves, although in a few instances it appears *in campo aperto*, i.e. without a staff. The musical pieces of Book I are contained primarily between folios 101v and 139v; these are monodic in form and have garnered attention for being the most complete collection of musical materials dedicated to a single saint in the twelfth century. This music includes antiphons, responsorials, tropes, and processionals, with both older and original melodies.[61] The work is arranged overall by feasts, proceeding from the vigil of the Feast of the Passion of Saint James (July 24) through the Feast of the *Translation* and Calling (December 30). An overview of the Divine office is found in Chart 4.

---

61. The study of the musical pieces and their provenance is vast. The first modern notation of the music was published by Peter Wagner in *Die Gesänge der Jakobusliturgie zu Santiago de Compostela aus dem sog. Codex Calixtinus* (Fribourg: Universitäts-Buchhandlung, 1931). A musical transcription by Germán Prado was also published as volume II of Whitehill's edition, *Música Codex Calixtinus* (Santiago de Compostela: Seminario de Estudios Gallegos, 1944). Michel Huglo discusses the notational style and its geographic variations and includes multiple figures (photos) from the CC in "Les Pièces notées du *Codex Calixtinus*," in Williams and Stones, *The* Codex Calixtinus, 105–24. More modern research suggesting connections with earlier pieces found in other earlier antiphonaries include Justo Pérez de Urbel, "El Antifonario de León y el culto de Santiago el Mayor en la liturgia mozárabe," *Revista de la Universidad de Madrid* 3.9 (1954): 5–24; Ricardo López Pacho, "El Culto a Santiago en el antifonario visigótico-mozárabe de la Catedral de León," *Tierras de León* 38.107–8 (1999): 27–50; and Santiago Ruiz Torres, "New Evidence concerning the Origin of the Monophonic Chants in the *Codex Calixtinus*," *Plainsong and Medieval Music* 26.2 (2017): 79–94, https://doi.org/10.1017/S0961137117000031.

INTRODUCTION

	Chart 4 – Book I Liturgical Material				
Chap.	Roman Date	Modern Date	Occasion	Contents	Authorship
21	9 Cal Aug	Jul 24 Jul 25	Vigil of Feast Feast of Passion	Parts of Office Parts of Office	•Biblical •(Calixtus)
22	9 Cal Aug	Jul 24 Jul 25 Dec 30	Vigil of Feast But used other days as well	Parts of Office Responsorial Psalms Hymns Prayers	•Biblical •Calixtus •Fulbert of Chartres •William of Jerusalem •Gregory •Eusebius
23	-	-	Various	Responsorial Psalms Hymns Two Statements of Calixtus	•Biblical •Jerome •Gregory •Passions •William of Jerusalem •Bishop Pilgrim •Eusebius
24	9 Cal Aug	Jul 24	Vigil of Feast	Parts of Mass & Office	•Biblical •Calixtus •Gregory
25	(8 Cal Aug) (3 Cal Jan)	Jul 25 Dec 30	Feast of Passion Feast of *Translation*	Hymn / Conductum	•Calixtus
26	8 Cal Aug	Jul 25	Feast of Passion	Parts of Mass & Office Multilingual Sequence	•Biblical •Calixtus •Eusebius •Gregory
27	Open 7 Cal	Open Jul 26	Pilgrim Mass 2 Octave	Parts of Mass Parts of Mass Poem	•Calixtus •Biblical •Eusebius •William of Jerusalem
28	6 Cal Aug 5 Cal Aug 4 Cal Aug 3 Cal Aug 2 Cal Aug Cal Aug 5 None Oct	Jul 27 Jul 28 Jul 29 Jul 30 Jul 31 Aug 1 Oct 3	3 Octave 4 Octave 5 Octave 6 Octave 7 Octave Octave Feast of Miracles	Parts of Mass Parts of Mass Parts of Mass Parts of Mass Parts of Mass & Office Parts of Mass & Office Statement of Calixtus Parts of Mass	•Biblical •Eusebius •Calixtus

29	3 Cal Jan	Dec 30	Feast of Translation	Statement of Calixtus Parts of Office	•Biblical •Calixtus
30	3 Cal Jan None Jan	Dec 30 Jan 5	Feast of Translation Octave of Translation	Mass Letter of Calixtus *Benedicamus* Conducta	•Biblical •Anselm •Bishop of Benevento •Fulbert of Chartres •Cardinal Robert •Venantius Fortunatus
31	-	-	"Both" Feasts	Hymns Responsorial Psalms *Kyrie Gloria Sanctus Agnus Dei Benedicamus*	•Biblical •Fulbert of Chartres •Eusebius •A Galician Teacher

THE ADDENDA MATERIAL OF THE
CODEX CALIXTINUS

The addenda material of the CC (ff.185r–196v) served apparently as a catch-all for material that was relevant to Saint James but had not made it into the main body of the work. In some cases, if not all cases, this may be due to having appeared after the production of the main body of the five books in the LSJ. The exception may be the first folios (ff.185r–190v), which contain liturgical music with notation on staves in a hand similar to that of the main manuscript. Two of these pieces also appear in Book I. The hymn "Saint James, [Your Feast at Its Recurring Time]" *(Iacobe Sancte, [tuum repetito tempore festum]*, f.186v) is also found in Book I, section 30.4, and the next piece "Let There Be a Canticle of Happiness" *(Regi perhennis glorie)* appears in section 31.7. The versicle (attributed to Ato) "You Who Help Those in Peril" *(Qui subvenis periclitantibus ad te)* is attributed to an unnamed bishop in Miracle 8 of Book III. These musical pieces have received great attention as some of the earliest polyphonic music in Western Europe.[62]

62. See above, n. 61. The debate about the earliest known polyphonic music is laid out concisely by Hendrik van der Werf, "The Polyphonic Music," in

INTRODUCTION

The next folio (f.191) is missing according to the later Arabic numbering of the folios. The contents of this missing folio would be the last nine verses of the Hymn by Aymeric Picaud, "To the Honor of the Highest King" *(Ad honorem Regis summi)*. In the current volume, these nine verses have been supplied from the transcription by Whitehill who took them from the British Museum Additional MS 12213 (c.1325), where they had been incorporated prior to the folio's removal from the CC. The remaining folios (192r–196v) represent a random collection of material relevant to Saint James. In fact, folio 192 begins in mid-text with a post-communion from a Mass in honor of Saint James and is followed by a letter of Pope Innocent II that is intended to bestow legitimacy on the entire work. The hand of this folio is markedly different from that of the initial folios of the addenda material and from other texts that follow. In fact, the remaining texts give every appearance of having been disparate except for their relationship to Saint James. An overview of the addenda material is found in Chart 5.

The Codex Calixtinus *and the Shrine of St. James,* ed. John Williams and Alison Stones (Tübingen: Gunter Narr Verlag, 1992), 125–36. Theodore Karp interprets the polyphonic pieces of the St. Martial repertory (Paris Bibl. Nat. MSS lat. 1139, 3549, and 3719) and those of the CC in his *The Polyphony of Saint Martial and Santiago de Compostela,* 2 vols. (Berkeley: University of California Press, 1992). José López Calo, who first transcribed these polyphonic pieces into modern notation in his *La Música medieval en Galicia* (La Coruña: Fundación Pedro Barrie de la Maza, 1982) gives an updated and wide-ranging interpretation about all the musical pieces within the CC in "Dónde y cuándo nació el *Códice Calixtino:* Aportaciones musicales a la solución de un viejo problema," in *El* Codex Calixtinus *en la Europa del Siglo XII: Música, arte, codicolgía y liturgia* (Madrid: Gobierno de España, Ministerio de Cultura, Instituto Nacional de las Artes Escénicas y de la Música, 2011), 71–107. There are multiple interesting articles within this last work, which were presented at the symposium of the same name, July 15–17, 2010 in León, Spain.

SERMONS AND LITURGY OF SAINT JAMES

Chart 5 – Addenda Material of the Codex Calixtinus				
Item	Description	Identifier – Latin	Identifier / English Translation	Author
1	Hymn	*Nostra phalanx*	Happy phalanx	Ato of Trier
2	Hymn	*Congaudeant catholici*	Let Catholics rejoice	Albert of Paris
3	Hymn	*Gratulantes celebremus*	We give thanks as we celebrate	Jocelin of Soissons
4	Hymn	*Ad superni Regis decus*	To the honor of the highest King	Albetricus of Bourges
5	Hymn	*Annua gaudia*	The yearly celebrations of joy	Airardus of Vézelay
6	Hymn	*Iacobe Sancte*	Saint James [your feast]	Ancient Bishop of Benevento
7	Hymn	*Regi perhennis glorie*	To the King of eternal glory	Gauterius of Château Renard
8	Hymn	*Vox nostra resonet*	Let our voices resound	John Legalis
9.1 – 9.5	Various	Various & *Portum in ultimo*	Various & A port for the last [judgment]	Ato of Trier
10	Kyrie & Response	*Rex immense ... Misit...*	Immense King... Herod sent...	Fulbert of Chartres
11	Response	*Vocavit Ihesus...*	Jesus called...	Jocelin of Soissons
12.1 – 12.2	Kyrie & Benedicamus	*Cunctipotens Genitor & Benedicamus*	Almighty Father & Benedicamus	Gauterius of Château Renard
13.1 – 13.2	Benedicamus (2)	*Benedicamus*	Benedicamus	Droardus of Troyes
14	Hymn	*Ad honorem Regis summi*	To the honor of the Highest King	Aymeric Picaud
15	Fragment	[*Missa Sancti Iacobi*]	[Mass of St. James]	Anonymous
16	Letter	*Epistola*	Letter	Pope Innocent II
17	Miracle	*Subcinericium panem*	Ash-cake bread	Alberic of Vézelay

INTRODUCTION

18	Alleluia in Greek	*Efonisen ho Iacobon*	Greek Transliteration of *Jesus vocavit...*	Anonymous
19	Hymn	*Dum Pater Familias*	When the Father of the family	Anonymous
20	Poem	*Signa sunt nobis sacra*	We have sacred signs	Anonymous
21.1	Miracle	*De puero suscitato*	About the resuscitated boy	Anonymous
21.2	Miracle	*De facie torta*	About the twisted face	Anonymous
21.3	Miracle	*De fuga Sarracenorum a Portugalia*	About the flight of the Saracens from Portugal	Anonymous
22	Prayer	*Adonay Rex regum*	Adonai, King of kings	Master G.
23	Readings	*De Translatione*	Concerning the Translation	Pope Leo / Master Parucham
24	Miracle	*Que tua iusiticia...reformat...*	Your justice transforms	Anonymous
25	Fragments	*Karole magne*	[Historical personages]	Anonymous
26	Miracle	*De contracto erecto*	About the cripple who stood up	Anonymous
27	Miracle	*Petrus ad vitam resuscitatus*	Peter the resuscitated boy	Anonymous
28	Miracle	*Visio cuiusdam Fucconis*	The vision of a certain Foulques	Anonymous
29	Prayer	*Iacobe Sancte Pater*	James, Saint and Father	Anonymous
30	Poem	*Signa sunt nobis sacra*	We have sacred signs	Anonymous

Twentieth-Century Editions and Translations of the *Liber Sancti Jacobi*

In the early 1920s, an American historian and medievalist, Walter Muir Whitehill, spent several summers transcribing the Compostela manuscript. The publication of the transcription was a monumental

XLV

aid to scholars of the medieval pilgrimage and of the stories surrounding it. Its transcription process was fraught with problems, and the Spanish Civil War interrupted the work in the time leading up to its printing.[63] Despite its errors, some quite serious, it was the only printed version of the entire Latin manuscript until the 1998 publication of *Liber Sancti Jacobi: Codex Calixtinus*, an edition by Klaus Herbers and Manuel Santos-Noya.[64] A Spanish translation by Moralejo, Torres, and Feo,[65] based primarily on the Whitehill transcription, has been consulted by many scholars. It was revised and corrected in 2004, and revised again in 2014.[66] Another important boon to scholarly work on the LSJ came in 1993 when, to celebrate the Holy Year, a facsimile edition of the *Codex Calixtinus* appeared.[67] With its publication, scholars everywhere could consult and work with the text of this twelfth-century manuscript in a useful and faithfully reproduced format. More recently, in 2011, another facsimile, this time of the University of Salamanca manuscript 2631, was published under the technical and artistic direction of Juan José García Gil and Pablo Molinero Hernando.[68] While the

---

63. Díaz y Díaz, "El *Códice Calixtino:* Volviendo" recounts the story and some of the problems of Whitehill's work (126–28), as does Adalbert Hämel, *Überlieferung und Bedeutung des* Liber Sancti Jacobi *und des Pseudo-Turpin* (Munich: Bayerische Akademie der Wissenschaften, 1950), 8–9.
64. Santiago de Compostela: Xunta de Galicia, 1998.
65. *Liber Sancti Jacobi: Codex Calixtinus,* trans. Abelardo Moralejo, Casimiro Torres, and Julio Feo (Santiago: Consejo Superior de Investigaciones Científicas, Instituto Padre Sarmiento de Estudios Gallegos, 1951).
66. Rev. ed., Juan José Moralejo and María José García Blanco, 2004; rev. ed., María José García Blanco (Santiago de Compostela: Xunta de Galicia, 2014). According to their introduction, only for the difficult passages or obvious errors did they try to consult the CC and use it as a basis (xv). They apparently try to indicate this in their footnotes, but it is not always clear where they have relied on other sources. Their translation was also the first time that scholars attempted to identify citations and sources, but there are enough errors to require a double check of the supplemental information.
67. Madrid: Kaydeda Editorial, 1993.
68. *Codex Calixtinus de la Universidad de Salamanca,* ed. Juan José García Gil and Pablo Molinero Hernando (Burgos: Siloé, arte y bibliofilia, 2011).

INTRODUCTION

only complete editions of the entire manuscript are Whitehill's and Herbers's, and the only complete translation is Moralejo's, with the publication of this volume, the entire codex will be available in English translation.[69]

Notes on the Translation

The *Codex Calixtinus* (CC) served as the base text for this translation. In addition, the CC text was compared word for word with University of Salamanca MS 2631 (S), which revealed an apparent dependency of MS S on MS CC in almost all cases, although there were superior readings at times in Salamanca. Minor variations fall into a category of easily identified scribal errors. In addition, a passage of some twenty words that was marginal on folio 152v of the CC was copied into the main text of S. While not proof that S was a copy of CC, in conjunction with the corrections and the overall superiority of the readings of the CC, it is a good indication. Generally, the CC was used here as the authoritative text, and it was given preference in the translation where a distinction was required. The folio numbers, provided in brackets within the translation refer to the CC.

There are relatively few peculiarities in the language of the CC or of S apart from a rather capricious use of *h,* both adding it to words that do not have it, as with *hopus* for *opus* and dropping it from words that have it, as with *exalavit* for *exhalavit.* In addition, the CC serves as a repository of special vocabulary that was likely in flux at the time of the manuscript, in some cases retrofitting a word into a Latin mold. Names for clothing, precious stones, medications, and other words unknown to the Classical period are forced into the relatively highly inflected Latin language. The text of Chapter 17 (the *Veneranda dies*) contains a large number of words that were probably in flux: the names for the weights, monies, medicinal herbs, mineral dyes, and other cultural items vary somewhat from traditional Latin words. The author had a wide-ranging knowledge

---

69. See above n. 1 for details of each book.

of people, places, moneys, and daily objects connected with Saint James's pilgrimage. While a few items have been impossible to identify, and some items were difficult to identify to our complete satisfaction, the notes attempt to explain who, what, and where the author was writing about. Comparisons to other popular saints and important persons and mentions of certain specific geographical locations abound in the LSJ. For these, we have attempted specific identification in the notes and have tried to use modern equivalents where those are helpful.

The material throughout Book I is composed in a straightforward but animated style. Sermons supplied from earlier authors retain the style from their original composition; we have respected those differences in both style and vocabulary.

Neither the CC nor S manuscripts contain any indication of paragraph breaks; the chapters of both were written as one long and uninterrupted text, as was the case in the *Miracles* (Book II) and the *Translatio* (Book III). Each chapter begins with an illuminated capital and a rubricated heading but then continues unbroken until the end of the chapter. We have used modern punctuation and modern paragraphing to divide the text. Capitalization likewise reflects modern usage. Roman numbers are generally written to reflect modern usage (for example "iv" instead of the text's "iiii"). The historic present is found often in the Latin but could be used only rarely in the translation. For clarity, nouns were often used in English where pronouns were found in Latin. Commas or "and" or "but" and other transition words were used and modified as necessary for clarity rather than preserving their exact usage in Latin. Longer sentences were broken into smaller segments to improve readability. Overall, in the present translation, we have endeavored to render the twelfth-century Latin text into clear, readable, modern English. Within the *Sermons and Liturgy* and *Addenda* we have placed references to direct Biblical citations in square brackets within the text. Throughout, the Psalms are cited both with the numbering of the Vulgate and the King James translation with a slash dividing them.

INTRODUCTION

In general, the footnotes fall into five categories: 1) to note manuscript "errors" and peculiarities; 2) to identify Latin words not found in standard dictionaries; 3) to identify sources for quotations, allusions, and materials; 4) to identify specific saints and place names; and 5) to note significant variations between the CC and the Salamanca manuscript. In all instances, the guiding principle has been to increase readability and understanding for the general reader and scholar alike.

THE SERMONS
AND
LITURGY
OF
SAINT JAMES

BOOK ONE
OF THE
LIBER SANCTI JACOBI

—

THE SERMONS

"Dum Pater Familias." Codex Calixtinus, Santiago de Compostela, Cathedral Archive, s.n., f.193r.

[f.1r] From the Material It Is Titled:
This Book Is Called "James"[1]

May Glory Be to the One Writing It
and to the One Reading It

Here Begins the Letter of Pope Saint Calixtus[2]

Calixtus,[3] bishop and servant of the servants of God, to the most holy monastery of the basilica of Cluny[4] that is the site of his

1. From the Latin here, it would appear that the title given to the work, to the extent that works had what we consider a title, was simply "James." Over time this has morphed to the *Liber Sancti Iacobi* (often with the J variant rather than the more classical "I" variant). Throughout we use LSJ when referring to the work as a whole and not to a specific manuscript containing the work. For a concise discussion of the naming of this work, see Manuel Díaz y Díaz, "El texto y la tradición textual del Calixtino," in *Pistoia e il Cammino di Santiago: Una dimensione europea nella Toscana medioevale,* ed. Lucia Gai (Perugia: Edizione Scientifiche Italiane, 1984), 23–55.

2. Pope Calixtus II, (c.1065–1124) was born Guy of Burgundy and named archbishop of Vienne in 1088 and pope in 1119. His works are contained in PL 163:1073–1414, where there is a discussion of him relative to the LSJ at columns 1365–68. Among his many letters, there are several sent to Cluny and several to Diego Gelmírez, bishop and later archbishop of Compostela; the present letter is not among them. It is implicit that the editors of the *Patrologia Latina* considered the present letter to be spurious at best. For a detailed discussion of this letter's importance to the LSJ, see Coffey, Davidson, and Dunn, *Miracles of Saint James,* xxvi, xxxix–xl. The letter also appears there (3–7). It has been re-translated and re-annotated for this edition. See also introduction, n. 44.

3. The introductory headers do not appear in S. The initial letter, likely the illuminated letter *C,* is missing, having been pilfered at some point. A study of the remaining letters surrounding the resulting lacuna points to the entire header not having been copied. Thus, the word *–ixtus,* all that remains of the presumed *Calixtus,* marks the beginning of the manuscript and the start of (f.1r) in S.

4. Cluny, the powerful seat of a reform movement within the Benedictine order, is located near Mâcon in southern France. Here Calixtus was elected pope in February 1119.

1

apostolic election and to the most famous champions, William, patriarch of Jerusalem,[5] and Diego, archbishop of Compostela,[6] and to all orthodox people: Greetings and apostolic benediction in Christ.

Since in all of the regions of the world, more excellent champions than you cannot be found in dignity and in honor, I[7] have sent this book on Saint James to your paternal care. To the extent that you can find in it anything to be corrected, you, on your authority may emend it with care out of love for the apostle. I, in fact, have truly suffered immense troubles for this book. For when I was a young scholar who had loved the apostle from childhood, I walked through barbarian lands and provinces for a period of fourteen years and wrote down diligently whatever I found, even on a few vile and ragged sheets of parchment,[8] so that I might be able to compile them into a single volume,[9] so that those who are devotees

---

5. This could refer to either of two patriarchs named William, the first serving as patriarch from 1128–30 and the second, William of Messina, from 1130–45 (d.1185). Neither suggestion is completely satisfactory, and this is one indication of the spurious nature of this letter. See Intro., n. 43.

6. Diego Gelmírez, (c.1096–c.1139), bishop of Compostela from 1100 and archbishop from 1121 until his death. Under his leadership the Santiago Cathedral was raised to archdiocesan status in 1121 and subsequently to metropolitan status by Pope Calixtus II. There are several pieces of correspondence between the Diego and Pope Calixtus in PL 163. For a detailed biography of Gelmírez, see Richard Fletcher, *St. James's Catapult: The Life and Times of Diego Gelmírez of Santiago de Compostela* (Oxford: Clarendon, 1984); and Anselm Gordon Biggs, *Diego Gelmírez, First Archbishop of Compostela* (Washington, DC: Catholic University of America, 1949).

7. The use of the first person singular by a pope is unusual and is another indication that this letter is, in fact, counterfeit.

8. The Latin *schedulis* is clearly chosen for its disparaging connotation, such as the paper that one might use for making a schedule and then throw out when its function was served. This idea is reinforced by the word *hirsutis* to indicate the "hairy" side of parchment, the idea being "ragged."

9. This passage implies that the author saw other manuscripts concerning Saint James. Later in this prologue, the author stresses that the material of Bk. I came from authoritative holy writers, while the other books are based on known historical events as well as on oral reporting. In the miracles of Bk. II, for example, the author suggests that both written and oral sources

of Saint James might very aptly find all together the things that are necessary for reading on feast days.¹⁰ Oh wondrous fortune! I fell among thieves, and although all my possessions were taken away, I still retained the book. I was confined to workhouses, and although all my possessions were lost, I still retained the book. I fell multiple times into the water of the seas and was near death, and when I escaped, the book escaped with me undamaged. The house in which I was staying burned and all my things were consumed, but the book escaped with me unburned.¹¹ Because [f.1v] of these events, I began to ponder whether this book, which I was still trying to finish with my own hands, might be acceptable to God.

As I reflected on these things with greatest zeal, I was taken up at night in a kind of ecstasy. In a shining majestic room, I saw a Young Man adorned with inestimable beauty, surrounded by a splendid light, dressed wondrously in majestic attire, crowned with a royal crown. He entered the east door of this room, and He walked with several consorts, one of whom spoke, saying: "Behold the Son of the King." And immediately the One sitting on the finest chair, said to me sitting at His feet: "Offer Me the gloves that you have on your hands." I willingly offered them to Him. When He had accepted them from my hands and entered the inner room, one of His consorts, who was something like His seneschal said to me about Him: "For He is the Son of the Highest King." Then he

---

were consulted and included. For other early source materials about Saint James, see Thomas Coffey and Maryjane Dunn, *The Miracles and* Translatio *of Saint James* (New York: Italica Press, 2019).

10. The focus on the importance of Saint James's feast days is set out early in the codex. Later it becomes clear that the author is referring to the material of Books I and II. Bk. III, ch. 3 of the *Translatio*, discusses the dating and importance of the feasts of March 25, July 25, October 3, and December 30. See Coffey and Dunn, *Miracles,* 88–95.

11. Surviving after a fire as a sign of divine blessing is also found in the life of Saint Martin of Tours. Gregory of Tours tells that a book containing the Life *(Vita)* of St. Martin was involved in a fire in a monastery at Marmoutier in France in which everything was destroyed except the book. See Gregory of Tours, *De miraculis s. Martini libri quatuor,* Bk 3, ch. 42 (PL 71:983–84).

added: "Just as He took the gloves from your hands, so also will He take the apostolic book peacefully and willingly once you have completed it."

Another time, as I was thinking about the *Veneranda dies* sermon concerning the apostolic *translation*,[12] and while holding a written quaternion,[13] He appeared together with Saint James in my ecstasy,[14] saying: "Do not put off writing these teachings that are to be observed by all and that are pleasing to us. Write what you have begun, to reproach the evils of the depraved innkeepers dwelling on the route of My apostle."

Therefore, let no one think that I have written anything of my own opinion in it, but rather things from authoritative books, namely from both Testaments, and from the holy doctors Jerome,[15] Ambrose,[16] Augustine,[17] Gregory,[18] Bede,[19] Maximus,[20] Leo,[21] and of other Catholic writers.[22] Thus one should understand that it is

---

12. The technical ecclesiastical use of *translatio* "translation" in reference to the transfer of relics has not spread much beyond the domain of the church. To avoid the confusion with the more common meaning of translation as moving from one language to another, we use the word *translation* (in italics) to refer to the general relocation of a saint's remains.

13. The *Veneranda dies* sermon (fols 74r–93v in CC, and fols 44r–55r in S), does not technically form a quaternion (eight folios or sixteen pages) in either manuscript. This could indicate that the *Veneranda dies* existed in a separate document before being incorporated into the final compendium.

14. "Ecstasy" *(extasi)* is used here in its less common meaning of being in a trance-like state.

15. Saint Jerome (347–420).

16. Saint Ambrose, bishop of Milan, d.397.

17. Saint Augustine, bishop of Hippo, d.430.

18. Saint Gregory I, the Great, c.540–604, pope, 590–604.

19. Saint Bede the Venerable, English monk, d.735.

20. Saint Maximus, bishop of Turin, d.408 or 423.

21. Saint Leo I, the Great, c.400–461, pope, 440–61.

22. At least one sermon from each of these authorities is included in Bk. I. This reference to authorities is a near copy of the prologue of the *Homilary* of Paul the Deacon (aka Paul Warnefrid, c.720–c.799).

obvious that I have excerpted the things that are contained in the first book. However, the other things that are found in the following books are written in an historical way and are things that I either saw with my own eyes or found written down or learned from truthful reporting, and that I wrote down among the other things.[23]

Therefore, let no one look down on this book if one finds something written down in plain style,[24] for, in fact, we have written our[25] sermons in a plain style within it, so that these things might be accessible to the unlearned as well as the learned. Many look down on what they do not understand. The French look down on the Germans, and the Romans look down on the Greeks, because they do not understand their language. If I hear a Greek or a German preaching daily and I do not understand, what use is it for me?[26] For this reason, the saints for ages[27] have offered explanations on the four Gospels and on the Prophets, since they were not being understood. If you should give me unsliced bread at the table, I will

---

23. Concern for veracity is a recurring theme for this author. In Bk. II *(Miracles)* the author, ostensibly Calixtus, says he has written down "only those [things] that I have judged to be true, based on the truest assertions of the most truthful people" (Coffey and Dunn, *Miracles*, 2). Each miracle is attributed to an "authority": Calixtus himself (18 miracles), Anselm (2), Hubert (1), and Bede (1). In Calixtus's prologue to Bk. III *(Translatio)* the compiler specifically says he has copied from the letter of Pope Leo (Coffey and Dunn, *Miracles*, 70). Finally, Bk. V *(Pilgrim's Guide)* says that the reader will find the truth in the work because there are people still living who are witnesses to what it says (Melczer, *Pilgrim's Guide*, 84).

24. A reference to the three standard tiers of rhetorical style: the plain, middle, and grand.

25. This is the first use of the first-person plural by the author, although it is virtually the rule for popes to use it at all times. The first-person singular is found in a number of places in this manuscript alternating with the plural form.

26. This could be a hint of French authorship, since a French monk might well understand French and Latin, but not German or Greek.

27. The Church Fathers.

accept it happily; if it is sliced, I will accept it more happily.[28] [f.2r] The crust is of little value until the center[29] of the bread appears. A clear drink shows what is contained[30] in it. An unclouded and open eye sees more fully than a covered or closed one. A bright candle that sheds light to all those standing around is more useful than one that offers light to some people and denies it to others. Thus, therefore, this work is made open to all, so that it might be profitable for those who are skilled in the art of grammar as well as for those not understanding lofty things.

As to which part of it might be recommended by us to be read in the church, whatever is written in the first two books up to the sign that is similar to this sign:[31]

which stands for Jesus Christ, may be sung or read in churches, according to ordinance, for matins and for masses, for it is authentic and expressed with great authority. Whatever is written in the material following the sign may be read in refectories at meals,[32] for it is of great authority, but what is contained in the first two books is quite sufficient for reading at matins. And if all the sermons and miracles of Saint James contained in this book cannot be read on his feast days because of their length, they may be read afterward at least throughout each week in the refectory and certainly on such a day as was once his feast. No one should hesitate to sing the responses and the canticles

---

28. The meaning is that the more easily accessible the bread, the more readily it is appreciated.
29. The Latin *mica* means "crumb," although one can find *mica* used for "white bread" in DuCange and "small bread" in Maigne d'Arnis. However, the context here calls for the French: the "white" or "center of the bread." This offers another clue to French provenance.
30. Latin *latet* literally "hidden."
31. The sign, a crismon, is reproduced here. This sign also appears after Bk. II (f.155v), thus dividing the material of Books I and II from that of Books III, IIII and V.
32. Most monastic refectories had an elevated podium where a lector would stand and read to the monks during meals.

of the masses that we edited from the Gospels and that we wrote in this book.³³

There are some who say that the responses of the *Passion of Saint James*, that is, *James, the apostle of Christ...walking through the synagogues*,³⁴ are apocryphal, because not all the writings that are contained here on the passions of the apostles are received on great authority by all people. Some sing them, others do not sing them.³⁵ Nonetheless, in the city in which they were promulgated, they are not sung in full. Other responses, edited by a certain bishop of León, are sung in a disorganized way.³⁶ Some sing the response of a martyr or a confessor for Saint James: *O Saint James, apostle of Christ, hear the servants calling on you.* Others sing the response of John the Baptist: *Oh special honor.* Others sing the response of Saint Nicholas,³⁷ almost as if there were no responses proper

---

33. That is, one must use the correct Proper of the Mass for the saint whose feast is being celebrated. The story about the canon who uses the wrong prayer to celebrate his own pilfering (below p. 8) shows to what extremes one may stray if one does not pay attention to official instructions about appropriate prayers.

34. Juan Carlos Asensio ("Tropos y prosas del Calixtino: Aspectos musicales" in *El* Codex Calixtinus *en la Europa del siglo XII* [Madrid: Instituto Nacional de las Artes Escénicas y de la Música, 2011], 157–70) offers that this is one of the most complete sources of medieval religious offices dedicated to one specific saint (157). The liturgy, standardized during the Carolingian era, becomes more diverse through the addition of musical embellishments (tropes) and the inclusion of readings beyond the scriptures (159). The opening reading of the *Passion of James* (ch. 9, pp. 153–54) is an example of this inventiveness. Calixtus is justifying a sermon that is not based on this reading and that is not an authentic biblical passage but based rather on a later writing.

35. For details on the variation and inclusion of these tropes, see Asensio, "Tropos," 161–62.

36. Probably a reference to an antiphonary composed in Evora in the mid-tenth century, later copied by Totimundo or Teodemundo of León in the eleventh century. For its antecedents and transmission, see Justo Pérez de Urbel, "El antifonario de León y el culto de Santiago el Mayor en la liturgia mozárabe," *Revista de la Universidad de Madrid*, 3.9 (1954): 5–24.

37. Nicholas of Bari, bishop of Myra, d. 342.

to Saint James. A certain canon of Saint James, a cantor of this basilica[38] by the name of John Rudriz,[39] when it was his turn to work one week, commemorated himself as he was filling his purse from the offerings of the altar, which he did by singing a certain response of Saint Nicholas:[40] *He knew how to offer fitting gifts to his servants.* [f.2v] For this reason he used to sing this response in the choir of Saint James on his own feast but removing the name of the confessor [Saint Nicholas], and saying rather: *Saint James, having already obtained triumph, knows how to offer his servants fitting gifts.* Therefore, just as ecclesiastical custom holds that one should not sing something for an apostle, for a confessor, or for a martyr, this same usage also holds that something for a confessor or martyr or Saint John the Baptist or whatever type of saint should not be sung for an apostle. Some sing the introit: *Let us all rejoice in the Lord*[41] at the mass of Saint James, which the Church is accustomed to sing properly only for holy virgins, such as Agatha,[42] the Virgin Mary, and Mary Magdalene. Others sing the introit: *Let all be gladdened in the Lord,*[43] others: *Exceedingly however for me;*[44] yet others, as I

---

38. Probably the basilica of Santiago de Compostela.
39. Antonio López Ferreiro says that Johannis Rodrici was archdeacon from the end of the eleventh century until the first years of the twelfth century. See his *Historia de la Santa Apostólica Metropolitana Iglesia de Santiago de Compostela*, 11 vols. (Santiago: Seminario, 1898–1909), 1:413, n.1.
40. The full response for St. Nicholas is *"Beatus Nicolaus, iam triumpho potitus, / novit suis famulis praebere caelestia commoda, / qui toto corde poscunt eius petitiones; / illi nimirum tota nos devotione oportet committere."* (Saint Nicholas, having already obtained triumph, knows how to offer fitting heavenly things. To one who seeks with all one's heart requests of him, it is necessary to commit ourselves to him with all devotion beyond measure.) Cf. *Gregorian Repetory,* Académie de chant grégorien: https://gregorien.info/chant/id/952/0/en. Accessed 5/5/2020.
41. The introit for the feast of All Saints, November 1.
42. Saint Agatha, d.c.251, a virgin martyr of Sicily.
43. Cantus Manuscript Database: http://cantus.uwaterloo.ca/chant/444746, accessed 12/9/2020.
44. Ps 138:17 / 139:17.

might say, sing their own strophes according to the fancies of their own minds. For this reason we order that no one should any longer presume to sing any responses according to their own fancy, unless they be authentic Gospel responses that this book contains: *The Savior went forth a little*,[45] or *Behold I send you*.[46] Similarly no one should any longer sing any introit at James's mass, except for: *Jesus called James of Zebedee*,[47] with its canticles that follow, or *Exceedingly however for me*.[48] In fact, whatever is sung for Saint James must be of great authority. It is of special importance that this be observed for his servants, so that the devotion of the clergy may honor the matins of James. Let there be a third reading with responses. Nor should the hours be left out. Let the pilgrim people[49] hear these things. We order that these be done by the clergy of Saint James in his basilica, on all days except the day of the Birth of the Lord and Holy Thursday and Good Friday and Holy Saturday and Easter and Pentecost.[50] Similarly at the first mass, the Proper[51] of Saint James should be sung for the pilgrims on all days, except those mentioned above. Then, after the first prayer of the mass, this oration should consistently follow: *May the ears of your mercy be opened, we beseech, O Lord, to the prayers of the supplicant pilgrims of Saint James, so that...to those entreating....* One may seek the rest in

---

45. This is the *Salvator progressus pusillum*. See ch. 23.1.
46. The *Ecce ego mitto vos* is a standard responsorial and verse based on Mt 10:16, but it is not found among those in Bk. I, although mentioned in the "Statement" of Pope Calixtus in ch. 23.28.
47. This is the *Jesus vocavit* text. See ch. 21.2, n. 11.
48. See ch. 27.2
49. This is the first reference to pilgrims at services dedicated to St. James. What follows here clearly deals with pilgrims to the basilica in Compostela.
50. This appears to be special permission to celebrate Saint James on days other than his feasts, with the caveat that such celebrations not take precedence over the major feasts explicitly set out here.
51. The special prayers "proper" to the feast of Saint James, such as the introit, gradual, offertory, secret, communion, post communion, etc.

the first book.⁵² Therefore may whoever shall presume to go against or spurn or render invalid the things that this book contains with inane arguments or empty disputations be anathema with Arius⁵³ and Sabellius.⁵⁴

Be well, all, in the Lord.
Published at the Lateran on the Ides of January.⁵⁵

---

52. See ch. 27.1, where *Pateant aures* is found as a suggested prayer.
53. Arius (c.250–336) preached the Arian heresy, which challenged the doctrine of the Trinity. He was condemned by several councils with the approbation of Pope Sylvester I (pope 314–35) among others.
54. Sabellius, a theologian of the third century, was excommunicated by Pope Calixtus I for his interpretation of the Trinity.
55. The Lateran Palace served for many years as a papal residence. The Ides of January is January 13.

Here begin the chapters of this book[1]

Chapter I	Sermon of Saint Bede the Priest: *Since the vigils of Saint James*[2]... [f.3r] f. iv[3]
Chapter II	Explanation of Pope Saint Calixtus: The vigils of the most holy night... f. vi
Chapter III	Benedictions of this Same Pope Calixtus for the Readings: May the grace of God be present... f. xviii
Chapter IV	A Short Passion of Saint James: With Gaius for four years... f. xviii
Chapter V	A Sermon of Pope Saint Calixtus: Of the most holy celebration... f. xix
Chapter VI	A Second Sermon of this Same Pope Calixtus: Therefore with spiritual delight... f. xxiiii
Chapter VII	Explanation of this Same Pope Calixtus: There is present for us, most beloved brothers... f. xxxi
Chapter VIII	Homily of Saint Bede the Priest: Our Lord Creator and Redeemer... f. xliv
Chapter IX	The Great Passion of Saint James: After the Ascension of the Lord into heaven, the apostle of our Lord Jesus Christ... f. xlviii

1. The index in S is more a synopsis than a copy of the index in the CC. We have not indicated the variations here.
2. As is customary in medieval sermons, each is introduced and described by its opening phrase. In fact, the opening titular wording provided here may be several lines into the work: for example, after a biblical citation that is the real incipit. In addition, the Latin word order will cause an apparent divergence from the translation of incipit sentences and index entries.
3. The folio numbers here were inserted in a later hand. This is also true of various chapter numbers throughout the manuscript, as well as the pagination. We have supplied the actual folio numbers in square brackets throughout this translation.

Chapter X	Explanation of Saint Jerome: Apostolic and venerable solemnities... f. liii
Chapter XI	Explanation of this same Saint Jerome: Why Peter and James... f. lv
Chapter XII	Explanation of Pope Saint Calixtus: Distinguished solemnities... f. lvii
Chapter XIII	Explanation of Saint Jerome: In the present chapter it is shown... f. lxiv
Chapter XIV	Homily of Pope Saint Gregory: Since the death of Saint James the Apostle and Martyr... f. lxv
Chapter XV	Sermon of Saint Maximus the Bishop: Let us exult in the Lord, most beloved ones, and with fitting honors... f. lxvii
Chapter XVI	Explanation of Saints Jerome and Maximus: Today's solemnity... f. lxxii
Chapter XVII	Sermon of Pope Saint Calixtus: A venerable day... f. lxxiv
Chapter XVIII	Homily of Pope Saint Gregory: You have heard, dearest brothers, that... f. xciv [f.3v]
Chapter XIX	Explanation of Pope Saint Calixtus: The present sacred solemnities... f. xcviii
Chapter XX	Explanation of Saints Jerome, Augustine, Gregory, and Calixtus: *The feast of the Calling and* Translation... f. xcviii
Chapter XXI	The Chapters of Pope Calixtus on the Vigil of Saint James and on the Day of His Passion: *James, Servant of God and of our Lord Jesus Christ*... f. ci

LIST OF CHAPTERS

Chapter XXII	Responses of Pope Calixtus with his Antiphons and Hymns for the Vigil of Saint James: *The Redeemer imposed...*[4] f. ci
Chapter XXIII	Gospel Responses of this Same Pope Calixtus with His Antiphons and Hymns for Singing on Feast Days, Namely of the Passion and *Translation* of Saint James: The Savior went forth a little... f. cvii
Chapter XXIV	Mass of Pope Calixtus for Singing on the Vigil of Saint James with its Parts: James and John... f. cxiv
Chapter XXV	Verses of Pope Calixtus for Singing at a Procession of Saint James for Both of His Solemnities: Greetings feast day of James... f. cxvi
Chapter XXVI	Mass of this Same Pope Calixtus to be Said on the Feast Day of the Passion of Saint James Together with its Parts: Jesus called James... f. cxviii
Chapter XXVII	Mass of this Same Pope Calixtus for Pilgrims of Saint James, to be Sung Assiduously... f. cxxii
Chapter XXVIII	Seven Masses of this Same Pope Calixtus for singing Individually and on Individual Days of the Week of Saint James... f. cxxiv
Chapter XXIX	Chapters of this Same Pope Calixtus to be Said on the *Translation* of Saint James: James pleased God... f. cxxix
Chapter XXX	Mass of Pope Calixtus for Singing on the Feast Day of the *Translation* of Saint James... f. cxxix
Chapter XXXI	Filler for the Mass of Saint James, with the *Conducta* and *Benedicamus*... f. cxxxii[5]

4. This is not actually the incipit of this chapter. These words appear well into the material.

5. Another hand has added at the bottom of this folio: Lib. II. f. ccl; Lib. III. f. cclvi; Lib. iiiius f. clxiii; Epistola Innocentii f. cxcii.

[F.4R] [CHAPTER 1][1]

IX Calends of August[2]
Vigil of Saint James

A Reading of the Letter of Saint James the Apostle:[3]

"James, servant of God and of our Lord Jesus Christ, to the twelve tribes that are in dispersion: greetings," and so forth. [James 1:1ff.][4]

A Sermon of Venerable Saint Bede the Priest[5]

Since we already celebrate the vigils of Saint James, most beloved brothers, with desired rites and appropriate fasts, it is fitting that, for His honor, the praises of Christ from our tongues should not be silent commendations. James asserts that he is the servant of our Lord Jesus Christ in the very beginning of his epistle and he promises salvation for the faithful, so that he might indicate that whoever has persevered up to the end in the service of God will, without doubt, be saved in perpetuity.[6]

---

1. Chapter numbers that correspond with the table of contents have been added in another hand throughout the CC. They are not indicated in this way in S, making it likely that they were not originally in the CC.
2. July 24. To the left of this rubric in the CC is the famous miniature of Saint James holding his hand up in blessing. The miniature at the beginning of the S has been cut out.
3. Here and elsewhere there is confusion about the authorship of the Epistle of James and at times about the difference between St. James the Greater and St. James the Lesser.
4. In this case and in many others, the "and so forth" refers to the rest of the reading, which might include an entire chapter but more often a certain number of lines for the chapter indicated.
5. This sermon is part of Bede's Commentary on the Epistle of James I, an exegesis of James 1:1–14. The full commentary continues through the entire epistle to 5:20. See Bede, *The Commentary on the Seven Catholic Epistles of Bede the Venerable,* trans. David Hurst (Kalamazoo, MI: Cistercian Publications, 1985), 7–67. For clarity, this sermon has been divided into paragraphs based on each verse of the Epistle with its subsequent exegesis.
6. Bede actually begins with the quotation of Paul that follows.

CHAPTER ONE

The Apostle Paul said this about this James: "James, Cephas, and John, who were seen to be pillars, gave to me and to Barnabas the right hands of fellowship, so that we might be mindful of the poor among the Gentiles,[7] while they would be mindful among the circumcised." [Gal 2:9–10][8] Since, therefore, this apostle was ordained among the circumcised, he took care of those who were among the circumcised, and as he taught[9] those present by speaking to them, and consoled, instructed, reproved, and corrected those who were away in his epistle when he says: "To the twelve tribes that are in dispersion."[10] [James 1:1] We read that, with Saint Stephen killed by the Jews, "there happened in that day a great persecution against the Church that was at Jerusalem, and they were all dispersed to the regions of Judea and Samaria except for the apostles." [Acts 8:1] Saint James sent his epistle to those dispersed, who suffered persecution for the sake of justice, and not only to these, but also to those who had taken up the faith of Christ and who were not striving to be perfect in their works. Just as the following passages from the present epistle testify, it was also for those who remained deprived of faith and who even tried to pursue [f.4v] and disrupt it as much as they could in those who believed. Thus, all of those who were in dispersion were fugitives from their country for various calamities and were beset with countless slaughters and with deaths

---

7. The Latin *gens* means "people," "nation," or "Gentile," or those who were not Jewish or, at times, even those who were not Christians but rather pagans or heathens. We have translated it as "peoples" unless the context is clearly used as the contrastive sense, such as Jew and Gentile.
8. Biblical references are to the Latin Vulgate. In some cases, the Latin of the LSJ differs from the standard text of the Vulgate, therefore, we have retranslated all Latin citations, As a result, the translations here will not necessarily agree, word for word, with standard English translations.
9. Bede uses the verb "to teach," while both the CC and S use "to speak"; we have emended the LSJ text to follow Bede.
10. Isidore of Seville follows early writings about Saint James's post-Pentecost work describing how alongside Peter he preached to the dispersed Twelve Tribes of Israel and supporting the belief that Saint James the Greater wrote the Epistle of James. See Coffey and Dunn, *Miracles,* xxvi and xxx.

and hardships everywhere by their enemies, as the *Ecclesiastical History*[11] explains adequately. However, in the Acts of the Apostles we read that at the time of the Passion of our Lord, they were already dispersed far and wide, with Luke saying: "There were, however, living in Jerusalem Jewish people from every nation under the sky." [Acts 2:5] Of these nations several are explicitly expressed when he adds: "Parthians and Medes and Elamites and those who inhabit Mesopotamia and so forth." [Acts 2:9] And thus Saint James exhorts the just, lest through temptation, they fall from the faith. He castigates those sinning and admonishes them to refrain from sins and to advance in virtues, lest they be rendered fruitless for themselves, and indeed even damnable, because they had partaken in the sacraments of the faith. He admonishes the unbelievers that they do penance for the death of the Savior and for the other crimes in which they were implicated, before the wrath of heaven — either visibly or invisibly — rises up to attack.

He says: "Consider all the joy, my brethren, when you happen upon various temptations." [James 1:2] The discourse starts from the more perfect, so that it might come in turn to those whom he sees to be imperfect and to be corrected and to be raised to the height of perfection. And it should be noted that he does not simply say "rejoice or consider the joy"; he says: "Consider all the joy when you happen upon various temptations," as if he were saying: "Consider yourself worthy of all joy, if it should happen that you withstand temptations because of the faith of Christ." It is a grace, if, because of a sense of God, someone patiently sustains injustice, for as the apostle says: "The sufferings of this time are nothing like the coming glory that will be revealed in us." [Rom 8:18] And all the

---

11. Eusebius, bishop of Caesarea (260 or 265–339 or 340). For an accessible translation of the *Historia Ecclesiastica*, see the translation by Arthur Cushman McGiffert, *Eusebius: Church History* (Buffalo, NY: Christian Literature Publishing Co., 1890). The reference here is broad and could refer to Bede's own work of the same name (*Historia ecclesiastica*, PL 96: 9–412) or even to church history in general.

apostles "went out joyful from the sight of the council, since they were worthy to suffer reproach for the name of Jesus." [Acts 5:41]

Therefore, we must not be saddened if we are tempted, but only if we should be overcome by temptation, "knowing that the testing of your faith brings patience." [James 1:3] Therefore, he said, you are tempted by adversities so that you may learn the virtue of patience, and through this you can test and show what a firm faith in future recompense you bear in your heart. Nor must the opposite of this position be thought, but rather it must be understood as consonant with what Paul says: "Knowing that tribulation brings about patience. Patience, however, brings about trial." [Rom 5:3–4] For patience brings about [f.5r] trial, since whoever's patience cannot be overcome is judged to be perfect.

This is also taught here and subsequently when he says: "Patience, however, may have a perfect result," [James 1:4] and again: "A testing of faith brings about patience." [James 1:3] For that system makes the faithful keep busy through patience, so that through this their faith may be tested as to how perfect it may be.

"If one of you, however, needs wisdom, let that person seek it from God, Who gives to all abundantly and Who does not reproach, and it will be given to that person." [James 1:5] Certainly any wisdom of salvation is to be asked from the Lord, since as the wise man says: "All wisdom is from the Lord God, and it was always with Him."[12] [Ecclus (Sir) 1:1] Neither is anyone, through free will, without the help of divine grace, able to understand and know, although the Pelagians dispute this very much.[13] But here especially

---

12. This is "Ecclesiasticus" in the Vulgate translation of the Bible and generally in modern translations based on that source. It is known as "Sirach" in the Protestant (such as KJV) Bibles. It is referred to generally in the CC as *Sapientia* or "Wisdom," although the reference to it can be somewhat oblique: "a certain wise man says." We have used "Ecclus (Sir)" for ease of access to varied audiences.

13. Pelagians, followers of the British monk Pelagius (354–420 or 440), believed that original sin did not stain human nature and therefore human beings could choose to follow a sinless life and thus earn salvation through their own works.

one appears to speak of that wisdom that one needs to use with temptations. If one of you, he said, cannot understand the usefulness of temptations that come to the faithful for the purpose of testing, let him ask God that the understanding be given to him by which he may be able to discern with what piety the father punishes his sons, endeavoring to make them worthy of eternal inheritance. And he says deliberately, "Who gives to all abundantly," [James 1:5] lest someone, for example, conscious of his fragility, despair of being able to receive what he is asking, but rather each should recall that: "The Lord has heard the desire of the poor," [Ps 9:38 / 10:17] and as this same person said in another place: "The Lord blessed all those fearing Him, the small along with the great."[14]

It is true that many people ask many things from the Lord that in the end they do not deserve to receive, and Saint James adds how they should ask, if they desire to obtain a request: "One must ask, however, in faith and not hesitating." [James 1:6] That is, by living well he shows himself to be worthy to be heard when he asks. For whoever is aware of not having submitted to the precepts of the Lord, despairs of the Lord being attentive to his prayers by dint of merit.

For it is written: "Whoever hardens his ear so as not to hear the law, his prayer will be detestable." [Prov 28:9] "In fact, someone who hesitates is like the wave of the sea that is moved and carried about by the wind." [James 1:6] Whoever, with a knowledge of sin biting at him, hesitates about receiving heavenly rewards from a thrust of temptation, easily forsakes the state of faith in which he had appeared to serve God in tranquility at the whim of the invisible enemy, as if, at the blowing of the wind, he is carried away through the various errors of vices.

"A two-faced person is inconstant on all paths." [James 1:8] He says: "on all paths" — on favorable and unfavorable ones. The two-faced person has the mind of one who genuflects on praying to the Lord, who utters the words of the petitions, [f.5v] and yet distrusts his ability to obtain his request with his conscience

---

14. Perhaps an amalgam of various wordings from the Psalms.

bothering him inside. The two-faced person has the mind of one who wants to rejoice with the world here and to prevail with God there. The two-faced person also has the mind of one who does not seek recompense internally for the good things that he does, but seeks favor externally. About this, it is said well by a certain wise person: "Woe to the sinner walking the earth on two roads!" [Ecclus (Sir) 2:14] The sinner, of course, walks on two roads: God's, when he displays this with deeds, and the world's when he seeks these things through thought. All of them, however, are inconstant on all their roads, for if they are very easily deterred by the adversities of the world and are snared by its advantages, they deviate from the road of truth.

"Let the humble brother, however, be glorified in his exultation." [James 1:9] And so, Saint James said it is necessary for you to consider all joy when you should happen on various temptations, for anyone who suffers adversities humbly for the Lord will receive the rewards from Him of the heavenly kingdom. "The rich person will also [be glorified] in his humility." [James 1:10] Here the "be glorified" from the previous verse is understood, and it is agreed that this was said through the mockery that in Greek is called *irony*.[15] Thus, he said, he will remember his glory that will come to an end in which he took pride in his vices and with which he looks down on and oppresses the poor, so that he might perish and be humiliated for eternity with the purple-clad rich man who looked down on poor Lazarus.[16] "For he will pass away like the floret[17] of the grass."[18] [James 1:10] The floret of the grass pleases both with its scent and its sight, but it very quickly loses the charm of its beauty and sweetness. And so, the present happiness of the impious is very aptly comparable to this, which in no way can be long lasting.

15. The Latin *glorietur* ("boast, glory in") is a deponent verb that is generally active in meaning and passive in form; however, here the context requires the passive meaning to maintain the irony.
16. Cf. Lk 16:19–31.
17. The Latin *holus* refers to the edible part of the plant.
18. The Latin is *foeni;* it should probably have been *feni* from *fenum* or "grass, hay."

"For the sun rose with heat, dried the grass, and made its floret fall off." [James 1:11] He says that the heat of the sun is the sentence of the severe judge by which the temporary seemliness of the false one is consumed in the end. For the chosen flourish, but not like grass. "For the just man will flourish like the palm." [Ps 91:13 / 92:12] The unjust flourish temporarily, "since like grass they dry out quickly," [Ps 36:2 / 37:2] and like the florets of the grass they fall quickly. The just flourish like trees, since their flower, which is certain hope, awaits their eternal fruit. Their root, which is their charity, also endures fixed and immobile. Concerning this, the wise man says: "I have borne fruit like a vine, and my flowers are the fruits of honor and character." [Ecclus (Sir) 24:23] Then Naboth, the just man, preferred to die, rather than convert the vineyard of his forefathers into a vegetable garden.[19] In fact, to convert the vineyard of his forefathers into a vegetable garden is to convert the strong works of virtues, which we have received from the teaching of the fathers, into broken pastimes of vices. The just, however, prefer to place the soul above, rather than to choose earthly goods over heavenly goods. Whence it is sung well about them: "Since they will be [f.6r] like a tree planted near the flow of waters that will give its fruit in its own time," etc. [Ps 1:3]

And what about the unjust? "And the beauty of its form will perish, and so the rich man will wither on his roads." [James 1:11][20] He does not say every rich man, but the one who relies on the uncertainty of riches. For on the one hand, whoever sets a rich man against a humble father,[21] shows that he is talking about that rich man who is not humble. For Abraham was also rich in the world, nevertheless, he took a poor man after his death to his breast and left the rich man in pain. But he did not leave the rich person there

---

19. Cf. 1 Kgs (1 Sam) 21:1–16.
20. Calixtus uses the future "will perish" here for effect; when he gives this verse later (ch. 24.3), he uses the past tense, as does the Vulgate.
21. Bede gives *fratri* or "brother" rather than the *patri* or "father" of CC or the *pauperi* or "poor person" of S; while "brother" was intended by Bede, we have followed the CC here.

CHAPTER ONE

because he was rich — which he himself had been — but because he looked down on being merciful and humble, which he also had been.[22] On the other hand, he did not take up Lazarus because he was poor — which he had not been — but because he cared about being humble and innocent. Such a rich man, therefore, who is proud and impious and places earthly joys ahead of heavenly ones will "wither on his journeys," that is, he will perish in his iniquitous acts, for he has neglected to walk the right path of the Lord. While he falls like grass before the heat of the sun, the just man, by contrast, like the fruitful tree, suffers intact the heat of this same sun, that is, the severity of judgment, and, moreover, he delivers the fruits of good works for which he will be rewarded unto eternity.

Whence it is fittingly added: "Blessed is the man who suffers temptation, since when one has been tested, one will receive the crown of life, which God promised to those who love Him." [James 1:12] This is similar to the passage in Revelations: "Be faithful unto death, and I will give you the crown of life." [Rev 2:10] James says: "that He promised to those who love Him," [James 1:12] clearly recalling that it is fitting to rejoice all the more in temptations, as it is certain that God gives them to those whom He loves. And often a greater weight of temptations is clearly imposed so that those perfected in faith may be tested through the exercise of temptation. When, however, they have been truly tested to be faithful, that is perfect, whole, and in no way deficient, they may rightfully receive the promised crown of eternal life.

"Let no one, when he is tempted, say that he is tempted by God." [James 1:13] Thus far, he has discussed the temptations that, for the sake of testing, God allows us to endure outwardly. Now he begins to deal with those temptations that we tolerate inwardly, from the instigation of the devil[23] or even from the inducing fragility of our

---

22. Cf. Lk 16:22–25.
23. Latin *diabolo*, ablative of *diabolus*. Various terms are used for devils and demons in the CC; they are not capitalized by us. There are also references by various names to the principle devil — Satan, the Demon *(Demon / Demonium)*, the Devil *(Diabolus)*, Lucifer *(Lucifer)*, the Prince of Darkness,

nature. Here at first he tears down the error of those who, since they think it is certain that good thoughts are inspired in us by God, also think that bad thoughts are generated in our mind at His instigation. "Let no one, therefore, when he is tempted, say that he is tempted by God," [James 1:13] as, for example, in that temptation in which the rich man withers and falls on his roads. That means that no one, when he has committed pillage, theft, false witness, murder, debauchery, or other things of this type, [f.6v] may say that he necessarily had to perform them with God forcing him, and so he would not have been able to avoid carrying them out. "For God is not a tempter of evils," [James 1:13] which is understood as "of trials." He, in fact, tempts no one with any temptation that deceives poor wretches so that they might sin. For there are two kinds of temptation: one that deceives and another that tests. In respect to the one that deceives, God tempts no one. In respect to that which tests, God tempted Abraham. Concerning him the prophet says: "Test me, Lord, and tempt me." [Ps 25:2 / 26:2] "Each one, however, is tempted, drawn, and enticed by his concupiscence," [James 1:14] as one is drawn from the right road and enticed to the bad one.[24]

From this temptation and from concupiscence, by the merits and intercessions of Saint James, may Jesus Christ deign to take us away, Who, together with the Father and the Holy Spirit, lives and reigns as God. World without end.[25] Amen.

---

the Angel of Darkness (*Angelus Tenebrarum*), Prince of Hell *(Inferni Princeps)* which are capitalized. We have consistently translated this terminology, remaining as faithful to the Latin as possible. The adjective *demoniacus* or "demonic" or "demoniacal" is also used as a substantive for someone possessed.

24. Bede continues with his commentary for the rest of the Epistle of James. The LSJ stops, adding this short closing prayer.

25. A very common ending for a Latin prayer was *per omnia saecula saeculorum*, literally "through all the ages of ages." This admits several alternatives in general and in the LSJ: a simpler form *in saecula saeculorum*, "for ages of ages" and a more intensive form, *in infinita saecula saeculorum*, "for infinite ages of ages." We have translated these, in all but a few cases (where it is woven into the text or otherwise used in an intentional way) as "world without end." Additionally, this may be indicated by the acronym EUOUAE. We have followed the same translation protocol with this as well.

[CHAPTER 2]

IX Calends of August[1]
Vigil of Saint James of Zebedee,
Apostle of Galicia,
Which Is Worthily Celebrated
With the Devotion of Fasting and the
Appropriate Divine Office

A Reading of the Holy Gospel according to Mark:

"At that time, Jesus the Lord went up the mountain and called to Himself those whom He wished, and they went to Him. And He made it so that there would be twelve with Him and that He would send them to preach," and so forth. [Mk 3:13–14ff.]

A Sermon of Pope Saint Calixtus on this Same Reading

The vigils of the night of the most holy solemnity of Saint James of Zebedee, the apostle of Galicia,[2] have arrived, my most beloved brethren. In these vigils, it is up to us to cease from evils, to persist in good works, and to rejoice in the profound affection of divine love. Without doubt, it is fitting that we take pains to anticipate this feast with fasting and vigil-keeping,[3] and to the extent we can, that we cleanse the stains of our sins with lamentations, tears, and alms; that we be attentive to harmony and love; that we disdain the passing delights of the world; and that we love the true joys of the heavenly country with all eagerness of mind. And so that our debts may be forgiven by the Just Judge, for the love of Whom we should forgive the debts of our debtors, so that we may be worthy to be found to be such great men on such a great feast. It is for this

---

1. This is July 24.
2. This is the first reference in Bk. I to Saint James's special relationship with Galicia.
3. Reference to the immediacy of this message.

reason that the ecclesiastical religion has ordered that before the feasts of the great saints one should abstain from forbidden things, fast, and keep watch on the preceding day, so that on that day, the flesh might be diminished somewhat through this restraint and purified from the filth of sin. And while [f.7r] it is fitting to pray and abstain on all days, on this day it is even more necessary to attend to fasts, alms, and prayers. Lest you be sluggish toward those things which we exhort, dearest brethren, take an example for yourselves from everyday life.[4] Indeed, if you should receive some servant of a powerful worldly person, you would strive to make your house clean for the reception with loving care. Therefore, if you have put such efforts into receiving the powerful but mortal servant of an earthly king, why are you negligent in receiving the soldier of the eternal King? If the physical house is cleaned for the man about to enter, why is the house of the soul not especially prepared with the greatest diligence of cleanliness for God who is to come? For it should be known that whoever worthily and purely receives the soldier of the eternal King with solemn ceremony, also receives this very eternal King in receiving the soldier, with the Gospel as a witness, which says: "Whatever you have done for one of the least of Mine, you have done for Me." [Mt 25:40] If, therefore, what is done for one of the least of Christ's people is done for Him, then it follows that those things that are done for one of the saints are done for Him.

In this regard, finally, we are encouraged by the apostolic voice when it says: "It is already the hour for us to arise from sleep." [Rom 13:11] We are, in fact, asleep when we are stupefied in the pleasure of the flesh and when we remain in the habit of sinning. For just as the body is weighed down through sleep, so also is the soul weighed down through the pleasure of the flesh and the habit of sinning. And about that, it has been written in this way: "O you just ones, watch and do not sin." [1 Cor 15:34] Therefore we arise from a dream of this kind when we have set aside the pleasure of the flesh and have left behind the habit of sinning, and we are made to be disposed to the love of and service to God. However,

---

4. *Secularibus*, literally "worldly matters."

CHAPTER TWO

it is especially time now that we should arise from this sleep, as we are about to celebrate the venerable solemnity of the great James tomorrow, whose vigils, without doubt, we are already celebrating.

The Lord thus also exhorts us through Isaiah, saying: "Wash yourselves and be clean." [Is 1:16] And so it is necessary to wash from ourselves through confession, penance, weeping, and suffering the evils that we have taken up and to remain in that cleanliness, lest we be again soiled by these forbidden things. For just as one is washed [after touching] a dead man[5] and then touching him again is made unclean, so also the one who repeats an offense is held to be completely defiled. Whence the Psalmist says: "Turn away from evil and do good." [Ps 36:27 / 37:2] From this it is also clear that it is not sufficient for one to abstain from evil without doing what is good. This is shown when it is said again by Isaiah: "Abstain from doing evil; learn to do good." [Is 1:16–17] For just as we are separated from God by acting perversely, we are joined to Him by doing good. Know, dearest brethren, that just as it is dishonorable for a man about to eat at the table [f.7v] of an earthly king to approach with filthy clothing, so also is it unseemly for the soul of a Christian to come with any blemishes in celebration of such a great apostle. And as it is loathsome for the earthly king if he should see something filthy or reprehensible in one sitting at his table, so it is dishonorable in the divine sight of God if by chance there were something horrendous or reprehensible in a Christian celebrating at the feast of Saint James.

Therefore, it is also necessary that we should not only guard against a lapse into vices on his days, but we should also abstain long before then. Let us not approach the feasts of such a great apostle defiled by a serious offense, but rather adorned with the flowers of good works. Let it not be said to us what is said by the Lord to one having entered the wedding devoid of good works: "'Friend, how did you enter here, not having your wedding garment?' And he

---

5. The Latin is *lavatur a mortuo,* a case of the extreme economy of wording in Latin. The sense is clear from the sentence as a whole, but the minimalist "is washed of the dead man" is not sufficient to give the picture in English.

was silent. Then the king said: 'Put him out into the darkness with hands and feet tied, where there is weeping and gnashing of teeth.'" [Mt 22:12–13] Therefore pay attention dearest brethren, for just as he was thrown out of the community of the guests because he was without a wedding garment, so I fear someone may be made a stranger from the community of the saints if he has approached the celebration of the feasts of the saints devoid of good works. What then will happen to the one who approaches the feasts with bad works and without penance if the one who approaches the feasts being celebrated without good works is removed from their community? I fear they may suffer from similar punishment. However, it should be understood that whoever has justly and worthily celebrated the feasts of Saint James will, without doubt, participate in the eternal feast of the holy angels with James whose victorious day he honors. If, in fact, we honor his feasts in the world, the angels honor his feasts even more profoundly in heaven.

Oh, how fitting and glorious it is, dearest brethren, to honor the feasts of the saints with the angels whose realm we are to share together with them in the heavens! Consequently whoever has lapsed into fornication or murder or adultery or other vices should have recourse to the remedies of penance, so that he might be made suitable for celebrating the solemnities of the apostle of Christ; so that, after having celebrated his solemnity worthily, he may deserve to have a share in the eternal celebration. If, in fact, someone who has perchance lapsed into an offence should be at the sacred solemnities of Saint James, or should go to them with a sin committed previously or after being remiss in a good work or after being preoccupied with worldly affairs, unless he should have returned to his senses, he will celebrate vain feasts, since he will have offered vacuous[6] praises before God. Because of these reasons, the Lord, through the Prophet, has ordered abstaining not only from perverse acts but also from bad thoughts, saying to us: "Remove the evil of your thoughts from my eyes." [Is 1:16] For also celebrating

---

6. The CC has *suas* or "his"; this is omitted in S, and the context comports with S.

CHAPTER TWO

the feasts of the saints is showing [f.8r] perpetual rest of the heavens.[7] For when we find rest on those days from earthly business, we then show that just as the one whose earthly feast we honor is in eternal rest, so also we together with him will be in the eternal rest of paradise — if God grants this — if we cease from evil affairs and embrace the good. And when we fast on their vigils, then we show that just as we abstain from earthly food, so we should abstain from harmful affairs. For as long as he abstained from forbidden and corrupt food, Adam remained in paradise. However, as soon as he ate, he was immediately expelled. From this it is given to be understood that whoever has sanctified the vigils of the saints with fasts, prayers, and alms in the present, will be a partaker of them in the future. However, someone who has not fasted, or has been remiss in good deeds, as we have said, or has done illicit ones, will be a stranger from the perfect company of the saints.

And whoever fasts on other days and is free from evils and acts well, will have the crown. However, whoever does not fast on that day and does not act well and does not cease from evils, will endure punishment. However, what is worse, the inimical devil, who is the instructor of vices, who tempted Adam in paradise, and who never ceases to turn the holy away from good works, is accustomed to tempt those intent on keeping the solemnities of the saints more than on other days with his cunning incentives. There are also some, which is worse, who are accustomed to do worse things on feast days more so than on other days, rather than to improve. Certainly someone who is caught up in envy or in slander or in drunkenness or in fornication or in engagement in worldly things or in homicide or in hunting birds or beasts or in a game of dice or chess or in a siege or in revenge or in battle with an enemy or in the oppression of brethren or in some other serious offense on holy days is not celebrating the feasts of the saints. However, someone who has learned and practiced dispensing to the poor or hospitality or chastity or visiting the sick or holy reading or prayer or speaking of peace to those in disagreement or some other good

---

7. The Latin is *polorum* or polar stars, a synecdoche for the "heavens."

work is celebrating the feasts of the saints. This is shown in the deed of Moses and the Israelite people, when Moses stayed with the Lord on Mount Sinai, and the perfidious people honored the cast calf. Why is it that Moses stands with the Lord in divine contemplation, and the people adore the calf, except that religious people who desire to celebrate the feasts of the saints properly and to persist in contemplation, abstain from vices for a long time beforehand, and the perverse, on the contrary, who have abstained for many days, now commit sins and cease from good works? For this reason, Scripture says: "One celebrates the Sabbath [f.8v] badly, if one is free from good works."[8] And the Psalmist says: "They have changed his glory into the likeness of a calf eating hay. They have forgotten the God who saved them." [Ps 105:20–21 / 106:20–21] The perverse people change His Glory into the likeness of a calf. They honor the apostolic solemnities in a beast-like manner, and they attend to them continuing in their vices, or they go to celebrate them with their sins and without penance. And he speaks well: "They have forgotten the God who saved them," [Ps 105:21 / 106:21] for those who do not long to celebrate the sacred solemnities of His saints with good deeds but rather with drunkenness, sinful wantonness, or idleness, ignore God. The Hebrew people, however, perpetrated few sins in Egypt, but later in the desert fell into sin with the adored calf. Why do we read that the people sinned little in Egypt but that later they offended God in the desert through the calf, unless because there are some who abstain from vices before the feasts of this holy apostle of the Lord and now are captured by the snares of the devil by acting badly. Brethren, may God prevent this from happening to you! Behold, dearest ones, how we can celebrate the apostolic solemnity worthily! Behold in what manner we should tend to His people and his honorable assembly and prepare ourselves

---

8. Although the connection between faith and good works is found in various New Testament passages, (e.g., James 2:14–26), this particular aphorism was not found in the Bible. Prosper of Aquitaine attributes this proverb to St. Augustine (*Liber sententiarum ex Augustino delibatarum,* PL 51:442 and *Epigrammatum ex sententiis s. Augustini liber unus,* PL 51:524).

CHAPTER TWO

with the greatest cleanliness! We should consider, of course, in the meantime, making ourselves as clean as we can through abstinence, so that on the most celebrated day of his solemn feast we may be worthy to assist at his offices to the extent that when one comes on the last day with the twelvefold apostolic throng to judge the twelvefold Israelite throng, we may be worthy with his protections to avoid a judgment of vengeance and prevail with him in the celestial kingdoms without end.

The ecclesiastical custom that celebrates the vigils of the saints in the churches at night with confessions, lamps, and candles took its origin from the ancient fathers of the Old Law. Therefore, it is necessary on the day before the vigils to dust and clean the basilica with brooms, to decorate it with tapestries, coverings, curtains, and rushes [for the floor], so that the clergy and the people might more suitably be able to be at leisure for prayers. That it would be necessary for the faithful people to receive penance from the priests in the church on the day before the vigil, the book of Exodus shows, when it says: "And when the people washed their clothes, Moses said to them: 'Be prepared until the third day, and do not approach your wives.'" [Ex19:14–15] Therefore, just as the Hebrew people, when about to receive the law, wash their clothing and abstain from their own wives, so also the Christian people, when about to celebrate the apostolic solemnities, must not only wash their clothing on the day before the vigils, but also wash their hearts and bodies through the penance accepted from the priests and abstain from their own wives up until the eighth day. [f.9r] And certainly if one is to abstain from one's legitimate wife, how much more so from illicit defilements?

Thus, it would be necessary for the people to pray all night in church before the altar, to hold burning candles in their hands, to stand and not sit, to remain awake and not sleep,[9] the Lord testifies when he says: "Let your loins be girded, and let burning lights be in your hands." [Lk 12:35] He orders that their loins be girded

---

9. Four miracles in Bk. II (ch. 6, 18, 19, 21) describe the cathedral altar as being lit up and open for vigils at night.

to show that the wantonness in the loins should be repressed. He orders, of course, the lamp to be held in one's hands, so this may represent that good works are to be done. Paul testifies that those who keep watch should stand on their feet and not sit, except for a moment when he says: "Therefore stand with your loins girded in truth." [Eph 6:14] The Lord says to the prophet: "Stand on your feet." [Ez 2:1] Many have burned their faces at a time of drowsiness with burning candles lest they fall asleep. They preferred, in fact, to burn their beards and hair rather than stain their mind with filthy thoughts before the altar of God. The Israelite people give witness that each person's candle should burn from evening until the end of the first mass to give evidence that the Israelite people deserved to receive light from a column of fire that appeared at night as a cloud above them as they walked through the desert. It lasted, in fact, from the beginning of the night up until the appearance of the "light-bearer,"[10] which is the morning star. However, we should realize, among other things, that the candle, which the person keeping watch held in his hands, indicates the faith of the Trinity. In the wax God the Father is indicated, in the wick His Only-Begotten, in the flame the Holy Spirit Who proceeds from both.[11] The one who holds the candle at night must hold this faith firmly in his heart.

The curtains, silks, tapestries, and other ornaments hung on these days in the church introduce faith, hope, and charity, and the other virtues with which we must adorn the chambers of our heart, where we are worthy to receive the Highest Guest, namely the eternal King Jesus Christ. The reed that, along with other grasses, is trampled under our feet designates the pride that we must trample along with the other vices with our successive steps by doing good works.[12]

---

10. *Luciferum,* from which the diabolical name of Lucifer is derived, as testimony to his original high-ranking position among the angels.
11. This novel use of a candle as an analogy for describing the Trinity (wax, wick, flame) is also used much later in *Piers Plowman,* Passus XVII (c.1370–90).
12. The Latin is *bene operando.*

CHAPTER TWO

The paschal people[13] who wished to flee the sorrow of Egypt and enter the Promised Land demonstrate vigils of this kind. They gird their loins, keep vigils at night, put on footwear, are supported by staffs, and consecrate the door of their house with lamb's blood. If, therefore, the paschal people celebrate their passage from Egypt to the Promised Land with times of fasting and vigils at night, how much more must we celebrate by keeping vigil for the feast day of Saint James, on which he passed from a time of fasting to the paradisiacal abodes?[14] In fact, with his approval, we believe that we will pass from the exile [f.9v] of this flesh to paradise. If indeed these people ate the earthly — although figurative — lamb[15] with their families in their houses at night, how much more must we sacrifice and share the true immaculate Lamb Who takes away the sins of the world throughout churches at the break of dawn with the darkness of sins driven away on the feast of our James? If those who desired to be freed from their enemies by the hand of Moses kept watch at night, how much more must we who wish to be saved from vices and from demonic enemies by his help, keep watch on the night of the holy apostle? If moreover, they — that is, the first fathers — put on footwear, how much more must we secure our steps and tell of their deeds with the preaching and examples of the dead animals?[16] If they who hastened to undertake their journey were supported by staffs, how much more must we earnestly request of the saints that they help us on our journey to the heavenly kingdom? If they stained the doorposts of their houses with lamb's blood, how much more must we secure the abode of

---

13. The Hebrew slaves of Exodus 12 who experienced the miracle of the Passover prior to their flight from Egypt.
14. A reference to the date of Saint James's beheading during the time of Passover (Acts 12:1–3).
15. The Latin *figurativum* or "figurative" is used in the sense of "prefiguring" or pointing toward Christ.
16. He is comparing the footwear made from animal hides to the forefathers, with the implication that they have walked the path before us. In addition, the animal imagery of the sacrificial lamb had just been mentioned above.

our own hearts through a watchful eye against demonic trials with the standard of the Lord's cross? If indeed the Hebrew people who wanted to enter the Promised Land girded their loins, the Christian people, therefore, who wish to enter the heavenly land promised to them by God, must gird their loins as they keep watch to curb wantonness so they may be more refined in keeping vigil over James.

In the manner of those who watch over a dead body, we watch over the saints when we carry out their funeral services in the churches with prayers. Some, in fact, lament the death of their loved one, others rejoice in having received his honors or spoils, others approach with prayers, singing from psalters. Therefore, as the body watched over is attended to in the midst of those keeping watch, so truly Saint James dwells among those watching and carries their prayers up before God. Many, in fact, testify that they have seen him in an apostolic likeness while they were keeping watch on the vigil of his feast.[17] Therefore, on his vigil we must now lament our sins through the remorse of our heart and the confession of our mouth, and moreover also rejoice, since if we have observed it well, we will receive the honors and spoils of eternal life.

There should be rejoicing especially for the Galicians who have received his spoils, that is, his venerable body. If they receive his spoils daily — that is the gifts offered by the pilgrims — they should rejoice and lament daily: lamenting when they distribute them badly and rejoicing when they disperse them well, like Laurence.[18] There is a song about this that goes: "He has dispensed, he has given to the poor" [Ps 11:9 / 112:9] not to the rich. Likewise, as is the custom [f.10r] in the rites of the dead that the clerics sing

---

17. Saint James appears in 16 of the 22 miracles of Bk. II, but only once within the cathedral proper (ch. 19).

18. Saint Lawrence of Rome (226–58), one of the seven deacons of Rome under Pope Sixtus II, was martyred by the Roman Emperor Valerian. According to Saint Ambrose, when Valerian demanded the wealth of the Church, Lawrence delayed for three days, while he distributed the treasury to indigents in Rome. He then brought them to the prefect and announced that they were the Church's treasure; this so angered the prefect that he ordered Lawrence's death.

CHAPTER TWO

psalms, so there should also be singing of psalms with the heart and with the mouth by all those keeping watch on the vigil of Saint James. The Psalmist says: "Let us seize on the face of the Lord in acknowledgement, and let us shout out to Him in joy in the psalms." [Ps 94:2 / 95:2] The apostle also says: "I will sing with the spirit, I will sing also with the mind." [1 Cor 14:15] Many, in fact, were once ignorant of the psalms, and they gave great rewards on that night to those reading the psalters. Paralipomenon[19] testifies that they should observe the solemnities of Saint James — or the greater saints — for eight days, and it speaks of the Temple of Solomon, saying: "Solomon, therefore, carried out the solemnity at that time for seven days, and all of Israel with him, in a very big church." [2 Chr 7:8] And he made an offering on the eighth day, namely in the temple. Therefore, we should have praying and watch-keeping on that night, lest we fall into perverse temptations. Of course, it was written: "Watch and pray, lest you enter into temptation." [Mk 14:38] And again: "Watch, since you do not know in what hour your Lord is to come." [Mt 24:42] And elsewhere: "Watch and pray, work in all things." [2 Tim 4:5] And elsewhere: "Blessed is he who watches at my gates." [Prov 8:34]

The gates of wisdom are figurative for the apostles through whom the faithful enter the kingdom of heaven. Therefore, one who keeps watch on the vigils of the apostles watches at the gates of the kingdom of heaven. Truly, however, if someone has kept watch well on this night, he ought to hope to receive that reward that the prudent virgins received who held their lamps in their hands and persevered with good works up to the arrival of their True Spouse. When, in fact, the clamor of the arriving Spouse occurred at midnight, the prudent ones entered with Him to the perpetual celestial nuptials, and to the foolish ones sleeping in sins, the gate of the celestial abode was closed, and the response was given: "Amen I say to you, I do not know you." [Mt 25:12] Whoever, in fact,

---

19. From the Greek *Paraleipomenōn*, referring to 1 and 2 Chronicles.

does not know God from sins will not be known at the gates of the heavenly kingdom.[20]

Gideon warned his fighters that they should hide their burning lamps in pots, make gestures with their hands, and upon approaching their enemies, break the pots. And thus, it was done. The pots were broken, and out of astonishment from such brightness from the lamps, the thunderstruck enemy fled.[21] By these pots are meant figuratively our bodies, by the lamps are meant the hidden parts of our heart wishing goodness, by the enemies are meant demons and vices. We hide the lamps in the pots when we think about the heavenly goodness in our hearts. We break the pots when during these days we afflict our bodies through abstinence. We show the burning lamps when we give to all an example of good works. The enemies flee from the appearance of the lamps, since when the demons see us always intent on good works [f.10v] they, as well as vices, withdraw far away from us. And certainly, just as the Lord looked back upon the camps of the Egyptians in the morning vigil by means of the column of fire and the cloud, He killed their army and freed His people. Thus, if we have diligently celebrated the vigils and solemnities of Saint James with the lights of the heart and body, when the morning mass is celebrated, we believe that we will be liberated from vices and the demonic enemies by his apostolic merits.

Therefore, this night is similar to the night of the solemnity of Easter in many ways.[22] For just as that night represents salvation for many people — namely the believers — and damnation for many people — namely the non-believers — so also is this night salvation for some and damnation for others. Those, in fact, who have engaged in filth or vanities or idle words or quarrels or debauchery or adulteries or thefts or drunkenness or revelry,

---

20. Mt 25:1–13.
21. Judges 7:16–21.
22. James's Passion is compared to Jesus's, and also occurred during Passover. For a discussion of why James's saint's day was moved to July 25, see Bk. III, ch. 3 in Coffey and Dunn, *Miracles,* 88–93.

or have carried out or watched various joking players or have sung or listened to deceptive songs, unless they have returned to their senses, shall be certainly damned. Those, however, who have become penitent and held candles in their hands, as we have mentioned, and have persevered in divine prayers and speech up to that day, without doubt will be rewarded with eternal life by the Lord through the merits of the apostle. This night loves the chaste and hates the lustful, drives off the iniquitous and loves the pious, chides the somnolent and rewards the watchful, glorifies those praising and hates those sinning, loves the sober and refutes the drunken, augments the generous and condemns the miserly, raises up the hospitable and pays no attention to the cruel, blesses the rejoicing and restrains the irascible, condemns the malevolent and protects the loving, placates the peaceful and restrains the quarreling, gratifies the poor, helps the sick, delivers the penitent, and supports the true mourners.

Therefore, the sanctification of this night drives out evils, washes away faults, restores innocence to those fallen away, restores happiness to the sad, drives out hatred, provides harmony, and makes empires yield. This night is one that, throughout the whole world, restores to grace and unites to holiness those believing in Christ, namely those solemnly declaring[23] themselves as separated from the vices of the world. This is the night on which it is fitting to say: "And night is my illumination in my delights." [Ps 138:11 / 139:11] It will not be obscured by darkness, but, just as the day is lit by real light, it will be certainly be lit in the hearts of those truly celebrating it. Oh, truly blessed night that may cleanse the Egyptians from sins — namely those doing penance — and enriches the Hebrews — namely those believing — moving from the earthly things to the heavenly things! Oh, truly blessed night, whose day was worthy to know the time and the hour in which,

---

23. The Latin *sollempnizantes* is found with this general meaning in Du-Cange, and interestingly, his sole example is from a Cluniac document of 1243. One can see its meaning in the modern "solemnize" in English.

He is the first apostle who is deprived of fragile life,
And to him the first crown is given for his merits.[24]

These are miraculous things[25] [f.11r] that were carried out with divine vengeance on those not celebrating the feast of Saint James, and they should be remembered.

Among the Spaniards near Tui[26] on the feast day of Saint James, a certain peasant was thrashing wheat on the ground on the feast of Saint James. With day becoming evening, however, he entered the bath that was near that very castle that all agree was built through wondrous and old Saracen work.[27] And when he sat in it, with all looking on, immediately the skin of his back adhered to the walls of the bath from his upper body to his waist. Because of his transgression of such a feast, he gave up his spirit. This was done by the Lord, and it is miraculous in our eyes.[28]

Among the Basques near Albineto,[29] the people who daily reject honoring the day of Saint James were working. However, with

---

24. These verses are from the *Salve festa dies* found below in ch. 25 as part of a longer work with musical notation written by Calixtus for the procession on both of James's Passion and *Translation* feast days.

25. An unexpected rubricized "H" here introduces a series of exempla of vengeance miraculously wrought upon Galicians who failed to celebrate the feast of Saint James. These miracles do not appear in Bk. II.

26. The Latin is *Tudelionum* in CC and Videionum in S, which is likely a scribal error. There is some debate as to what town this refers to: Tui in the Province of Galicia or Tudela in the province of Navarre. Moralejo suggests Tudején, also in Navarra.

27. Commonly referred to as Mozarabic architecture, it incorporates features of Arabic architecture of the eighth to eleventh centuries, such as the horseshoe arch and the absence of exterior decoration.

28. This is the standard formulaic ending for declaring the validity of all the miracles in Bk. II, except for ch. 2 (attributed to Bede), 16, 17, and 18 (attributed to Anselm).

29. The Latin is *Wascones*. Like its alternative form *Vascones*, it is used for the modern "Basques." A likely candidate would be Aubiet on the Arrats river, mentioned in an anonymous article, "Notre Dame de Pitié," in *The Catholic World* 23, 1876, giving its Latin name as *Albinetum* (123). Aubiet is located in the old province of Gascony, about 25 km. east of Auch.

CHAPTER TWO

divine vengeance being carried out, the entire castle of these people was consumed by fire on the following night. And there was no one who knew from what house the fire proceeded, but it is said to have come from the sky. This was done by the Lord, and it is miraculous in our eyes.

In the diocese of Besançon,[30] on the day of Saint James, Bernard of Morre[31] transported bundles of wheat with his cart all day while his neighbors were speaking against it. With day becoming evening and with him working in this way, a powerful and fitting fire came from the sky and reduced the cart and the bundles and the cattle to ash, but several astonished women who were also there with this Bernard were carried off by the other forces to a nearby spring in such a way that they were able to avoid the heat of the fire. They barely escaped. This was done by the Lord, and it is miraculous in our eyes.

Also Arduin, a soldier of this same town, on the same day was driving his wagon with bundles of wheat all day, but divine vengeance blinded the eyes of his oxen late in the day. This was done by the Lord, and it is miraculous in our eyes.

Among the Goths in the province of Montpellier,[32] at the order of a certain soldier from Mirepoix,[33] a certain peasant woman in the

---

30. Besançon lies about 380 kilometers southeast of Paris. Guy of Burgundy (Pope Calixtus II) was born there. In Bk. II, the miracle of ch. 4 is related by Humbert, archbishop of Besançon.

31. *Maiorra* in CC and *Maiora* in S probably refer to Morre about 4 kilometers east of Besançon.

32. Bk. V (the Guide) mentions the city of Montpellier on the Saint-Gilles route. (Melzer, *Pilgrim's Guide*, 85).

33. *Micoriensis* in CC and *Murorensis* in S. Graesse gives *Mirapensis* and *Mirapicae* or *Mirapicum* for Mirepoix, which is southeast of Toulouse about 200 kilometers from Montpellier. One other possibility is Mirecourt. Graesse gives *Mercurii curtis, Mirecurtium, Mirecuriae,* and *Miracuria* as Latin variants for Mirecourt. Since this is a case of someone from another area, it is difficult to apply any logical arguments in deciding the location. Moralejo says: "Seguramente como mirgorense, melgoriense, melgorés, o sea, de Mergueil o Melgueil (sur de Francia), aplicados con frecuencia a la moneda de esta localidad, corriente en el condado de Montpellier." (29, n.24)

SERMONS OF SAINT JAMES

town of Saint Damian[34] made and baked bread on coals[35] on the day of Saint James. When it was brought to the table and broken in front of all lying around,[36] it appeared to be full of blood. And when it was further broken, it cast off more and more blood. This was done by the Lord, and it is miraculous in our eyes.

Therefore let us cease from works of the flesh, and let us do good works on this day of sacred solemnity.[37] Whoever, in fact, as we said, has ceased doing illicit acts and has persevered up to the end with good acts, must hope to ascend to the true mountain about which in today's reading Mark says: "The Lord Jesus went up the mountain and called to Himself those He wished, and they went to Him. And He made it so that there would be twelve with Him and that He would send them to preach." [Mk 3:13–14] The mountain in this sacred speech sometimes indicates the Church, sometimes the heavenly kingdom, sometimes the humble, sometimes the higher precepts, [f.11v] sometimes power,[38] sometimes saints, and sometime Jews. It indicates the Church, as when Truth says: "A city placed on a mountain cannot be hidden." [Mt 5:14] It indicates the heavenly kingdom, as when the Psalmist says: "Lord, who will live in Your tabernacle, or who will rest on Your holy mountain?" [Ps 14:1 / 15:1] And the Holy Spirit answered, saying: "Who goes in

---

34. Possibly a reference to Saint-Côme d'Olt near Espalion on the Le Puy pilgrim route. The town still boasts of its connections to Saint James and had a hospice for pilgrims dedicated to Saints Cosmas and Damian. However, this is quite a distance from Montpellier.

35. Latin *subcinericium panem* refers to a low-quality bread, baked in ashes rather than an oven as evidenced by the base *cinericius* or "ash-like." A miracle mentioning this same type of bread occurs in the additional material at the end of the CC on f.192v. See Coffey and Dunn, *Miracles,* 64–65.

36. The Latin *discumbentibus* carries the connotations of the lying position in which the Romans consumed their meals. Here it could also refer to pilgrims lying in a hospital setting who were being tended to.

37. Latin *in his sacris sollemnis,* literally "in these holy rites of the solemnity."

38. The Latin here and below in the example uses *virtutes;* while the example clearly uses this in the context of "power," one cannot divest the word of its other meaning of "virtue," especially in this context.

CHAPTER TWO

without stain and works justice, who speaks the truth in his heart, who has not done deceit with his tongue and has not done evil to his neighbor." [Ps 14:3 / 15:3] It indicates the humble, as when this same Psalmist says: "Let the mountains take up peace for the people, and the hills justice." [Ps 71:3 / 72:3] It indicates higher precepts, as when it is written in the Gospel: "Jesus seeing the crowds, ascended to the mountain." [Mt 5:1] It shows virtues, as when the Psalmist says: "The mountain of power of the beloved, of the beloved, and of beauty."[39] [Ps 67:13 / 68:13] It signifies saints, as when the same Psalmist says: "Why are you suspicious of curdled mountains?"[40] [Ps 67:17 / 68:16] It expresses the Jews, as when David says: "Mountains of Gilboa, may neither dew nor rains come over us." [2 Kgs (2 Sam) 1:21] However, over all these mountains, there is one mountain of God, namely the Only-Begotten, who has been raised above all the angels. This mountain is higher than all the heavens, deeper than all the abysses, wider than all the lands, higher than all the heights. Speaking to himself about this mountain, Job says to a certain person: "He is higher than heaven, and what will you do? Deeper than hell, and whence do you know Him? His size is wider than the earth and wider than the sea." [Job 11:8–9] In fact, just as voice and hand fail in telling the height of the sky and the extent of the earth and the depth of the abyss and the days of the world and the drops of the rain, so also the human mind fails in comprehending through thought the sublimity of the sacred power and will; however, there is still an increase in believing. What, in fact, a man cannot understand by human reason can be understood directly from God through perfect faith.

---

39. The Latin reads *Mons* or "mountain" rather than the *Rex* or "King" of the psalm; the CC drops the "c" from the first of the two occurrences of *dilecti;* S then drops the first *dileti,* probably in an attempt to correct the text.
40. *Coagulatos* both "coagulated" and "curdled" in Latin, when applied to a mountain would appear to mean rough as opposed to smooth. The word is clearly accusative case indicating that the mountains would have been the object of the verb and not the vocative.

God, Who cannot be understood by human reason, can be truly understood through faith. His sublimity as well as His immense depth is therefore to be believed, just as it was in the beginning and is now and forever. He is, therefore, the Mountain, of whom the prophet said: "Come, let us go up to the mountain of the Lord." [Mic 4:2; Is 2:3] This Mountain "called to Himself those whom He wished," [Mk 3:13] "Who wishes that all men become saved and come to a knowledge of the truth." [1 Tim 2:4] "And He made it so that there would be twelve with Him and that He would send them to preach, and He gave them the power to cure sickness and to cast out demons." [Mk 3:14–15] He offered to the apostles, whom the Lord sent out to preach, the power of performing miracles, so that they might confirm their preaching with succeeding signs. It was, in fact, fitting that those who should preach new things should do new things: "and he bestowed on Simon the name 'Peter'." Mark names Simon as "Peter" as a differentiation from the other Simon who is called "Cananaean."[41] However, it should be known that long before that, in another Gospel, it is read that [f.12r] the name "Cephas" was given to Simon by the Lord, namely, when he was called to Him together with his brother Andrew, and He looked at him and said: "You are the son of Jonah who will be called 'Cephas,' which means 'Peter'." [Jn 1:42] "Cephas" there is called "Peter" here, so that his name would be known among Chaldeans, Greeks, and Latins. For one says "Cephas" in Syrian or Chaldean for "Petrus" in either Greek or Latin, because the name in both languages is derived from *petra,* for that certainly is what Paul states: "Christ was a rock."[42] [1 Cor 10:4]

It should be noted that in the manner of this imposition of a name, the priest imposes names on children in baptism, and the bishop later confirms the most suitable names when he reconciles

---

41. Mk 3:18. Simon the Cananaean (or Canaanite in the King James Version) is commonly listed as Simon the Zealot in other translations.

42. Peter (*petra* in Latin) is "stone." The Aramaic for stone is *cephas,* while one word for stone in Greek is πέτρος *(petros).* The words "Syrian" or "Chaldean" are used here for what is actually Aramaic.

CHAPTER TWO

the sinner: "And he called James of Zebedee and John the brother of James and gave them the name "Boanerges," which means 'Sons of Thunder'."[43] Mark calls James "of Zebedee" to differentiate from the other James who is called "of Alphaeus."[44] The Lord called the two brothers, namely James and John, "Sons of Thunder" since, just as a good father instructs his son about his own business, so also He taught them to thunder as when the Father thundered to those listening on Mount Tabor in the Transfiguration, when He said: "This is My Beloved Son in Whom I have been well pleased." [Mt 3:17] Nor is it a wonder that they learned beforehand of thunder; and afterward they thundered. John thundered wondrously to the seven churches in Asia,[45] saying: "In the beginning was the Word, and the Word was with God, and God was the Word." [Jn 1:1] James, however, thundered at the Lord's command in all of Judea and Samaria and up to the farthest limit of the land of Galicia. Thunder makes frightful sounds, it irrigates the earth with rains, and it sends out lightening. Similarly, these two brothers sent out frightful sounds when "their sound went out into the whole world, even their words unto the limits of the orb of the earth." [Rom 10:18] They irrigated the earth with rains when with their preaching, they made known to the minds of believers the rain of divine grace. They sent out lightning bolts when they gleamed with signs and miracles.

And He called "Andrew and Philip, and Bartholomew and Matthew, and Thomas and James of Alphaeus, and Thaddeus and Simon the Canaanite, and Judas Iscariot who also betrayed Him." [Mk 3:18–19] The twelve apostles were named by their proper names by the Lord, and they are written by the Evangelists, lest pseudo-apostles might presume to have themselves glorified within the number of the chosen. The number of the apostles is not devoid

---

43. This is the *Jesus vocavit* text. See ch. 21.2, n. 11.
44. James, son of Alphaeus, identified with James the Lesser (or Younger), is named only four times in the Bible. Cf. Mk 15:40.
45. The Seven Churches of Asia (or of Revelations or the Apocalypse) are: Ephesus, Smyrna, Pergamon, Thayaira, Sardis, Philadelphia, and Laodicea. (Rev 2:1–29, 3:1–22)

of great mystery, for twelve is composed of the third and fourth, and so it shows them about to preach the faith of the Holy Trinity to the four regions of the world. It should be known that these heroes, as Paul says, were predestined before the arrangement of the world for the salvation of the human race. These men[46] are fishers of God, who draw the souls of sinners from the dangerous sea of the world. [f.12v] In this way, in fact, it was promised beforehand to the world by the Lord. The Lord, in fact, says through the prophet: "Behold, I will send to them many fishermen, and they will fish them…and my hunters, and they will hunt them." [Jer 16:16] Concerning these men, the Lord says again through Isaiah: "Who are these who fly like clouds and almost like doves to their windows?" [Is 60:8] "They are whiter than snow, more refined than milk, more ruddy than ancient ivory."[47] [Lam 4:7] The apostles are called clouds, since, just as clouds carrying rain move from place to place and irrigate the earth, so also the apostles went from city to city with the beneficial rains of the word of God as they irrigated the dried earthly hearts of men. Therefore, as the clouds disperse water over the earth, so also the Son of God is revealed to the world through these preachers. The prophet said: "Send down dew from above, O heavens, and let the clouds rain on the just one; let the earth open up and put forth a Savior." [Is 45:8] The heavens sent dew from above when the prophets from their celestial seats predicted that Christ was to come to the world, and the angels from the celestial Father similarly

---

46. The Latin *barones* has come to mean "men." Compare the Spanish "varones" for the English "men" or "males." It carries none of the etymological baggage of the Latin *baro* or "dunce," or the Germanic "baro" for "freeman."
47. The Latin *ebore antiquo* errs from the biblical citation "more ruddy than coral." This is perhaps a jump of the eye to the later metaphor of the elephant. José María Anguita Jaén, "Más rubicundos que un elefante viejo fueron los apóstoles" (*Ad Limina* 2.2 (2011):15–28), discusses the difficulty of this passage as it appears in Lamentations, with interpretations varying through its translations (Hebrew, Greek, and Latin) in which the word here translated as "ivory" may refer to bones, coral, a precious stone, ivory, or rock. According to Anguita Jaén, only the LSJ's exegesis of this image translates (confuses) the Latin *ebur* as an "old elephant."

CHAPTER TWO

announced He would come, and these very heavens sent Him. The clouds rained on the just when the Apostles preached Him to the world. The earth opened when the Virgin Mary received Him. The earth put forth a Savior when the Virgin Mother brought forth Christ who saved the world from the destruction of sin. This same Psalmist testifies that Saint Mary, the mother of God, is figuratively the earth when he says: "Truth has arisen from the earth." [Ps 84:12 / 85:11] The same Psalmist says that water is figuratively the Lord when in His person he says: "I have been poured forth like water, and my bones have been spread out." [Ps 21:15 / 22:14] The poured water was the Only-Begotten of God, since, just as water washes away filth and irrigates the earth, so He washed our sins with His blood, and He watered the hearts of people with His spirit and faith. The bones[48] figuratively are the apostles, since just as bones are firm in the body, so the apostles strengthen and join together in faith and work with the Son of God. The bones have been spread out, since the apostles were sent by the Lord throughout the world. These descend like doves from the highest windows to the lowest earthly regions[49] when in preaching they move down from the divinity of Christ to his humanity or from contemplation to action. They return from the lowest earthly regions to the highest windows, when in speaking they ascend from the humanity of Christ to his divinity or from action to contemplation. Snow is naturally white and cold and it hardens vegetables and waters the ground when the sun warms it. The apostles were, therefore, whiter than snow, since undoubtedly they made those who had been forced away by the heat of vices, cold and white through preaching and through their confession of faith. As the snow hardened the vegetables of the lands, so the apostles chastised the worldly tyrants with their preaching and completely destroyed the vices of the world. The

---

48. See above n. 47. Bones are mentioned in the next verse of Lamentations (4:8), although the next verse has not been presented here. This may be another instance of including by assumption, i.e., that subsequent verses are known and are to be included when a quote is given.
49. Latin *terras*.

sun warms the snow, since Christ filled the apostles with the Holy Spirit. The snow irrigates the lands, since the apostles delivered the Holy Spirit, [f.13r] Whom they had received from the Lord, by preaching to the believers. The milk is refined[50] in its whiteness and sweet in its fat. The apostles were more refined than milk, since they gleamed to the world with miracles. They were sweeter indeed than milk, since they nourished the childish world with their very sweet exhortations.

Since the elephant[51] is a pure animal, it performs mating only once, cannot bend its knees to the ground, has a pelt and bones, and has ruddy hair when it grows old. The apostles were ruddier than old ivory,[52] namely because they shed blood, as in the end they gave their bodies in diverse kinds of martyrdoms for Christ. John says: "For they washed their gowns," [Rev 7:14] that is, their bodies, through a shedding of blood, and they made them whiter in the blood of the true and innocent Lamb through the whiteness of faith. The pachyderm, that is, the elephant, is said to be a chaste animal, and that it is unable to bend its knees to the earth. Likewise, the apostles are said to have been chaste through restraint, and they assert that after their conversion they were not turned toward worldly affairs. The elephant has a pelt and white bones, and the apostles were truly made white inside through an acknowledgment of faith and outside by good work. The Lord again says through the prophet about these things: "How beautiful are the feet of those preaching peace and good things." [Rom 10:15] Before the Lord's coming there was discord and war between the world and God, but these men, bearing peace, strengthened eternal friendship between them. These are considered the salt of the earth,[53]

---

50. The Latin *nitidus* literally "glittering," "shining," "healthy-looking," or "polished."
51. Latin *ebur* means either "elephant" or "ivory". See also n. 47 above.
52. See n. 47 above. Since *ebur* in Latin means both ivory and elephant, it is not clear to which the author is referring.
53. Cf. Mt 5:13.

CHAPTER TWO

the light of the world,[54] towers of God's strength,[55] witnesses of truth, true rays of the sun, soldiers of heaven,[56] messengers of the Highest King,[57] shining windows of true light, doors of heaven, keys of the kingdom,[58] highest mountains, Olympic trumpets, heralds of Christ, serpentine sages,[59] simple doves, young lambs, true rams of Nebaioth,[60] announcers of the glory of heaven, true fathers, judges of the world, basins for washing souls, divine gold and silver, treasuries of divine writing, treasure chamber[61] of the New and Old Testament, even hands of the Lord, feet of Christ, eyes of God, givers of milk[62] to the Church![63]

It is, however, said by the Psalmist concerning these things: "The heavens tell the glory of God." [Ps 18:2 / 19:1] These are the heavens in which Christ lives and resides, in which He resounds and thunders with words, shines with miracles, and sprinkles with grace. These are the twelve hours of the true day and the twelve hours of the worldly night and the twelve rays of the true sun. They are depicted with great mysteries, with many figures and representations, even before they were born into the world. They are, in fact, shown through the twelve sons of Jacob, through the twelve princes of the twelve tribes of Israel,[64] through the twelve springs of

---

54. Cf. Jn 8:12, Christ speaking about himself.
55. Cf. Prov 18:10.
56. Cf. 2 Tim 2:3–4.
57. Cf. Dan 4:17.
58. Cf. Mt 16:19, Christ speaking to Peter.
59. The Latin adjective *prudentes* is used as a noun here.
60. Cf. Gen 25:12–16. Nebaioth is listed as the firstborn of Ishmael (Abraham's son through Hagar).
61. The Latin is *corbana* in both CC and S rather than the expected *corbona*.
62. The Latin is *mamme* and could be "breasts" or "mothers" for the Church.
63. A lengthy example of the rhetorical device of *accumlatio*, which he repeats again below.
64. Cf. Gen 49. The twelve tribes of Israel are based on and named for the twelve sons of Jacob.

Elim[65] — namely in the desert — through the twelve stones of the breastplate of Aaron,[66] through the twelve loaves of proposition,[67] [f.13v] through the twelve scouts sent by Moses into the Promised Land,[68] through the twelve stones from which the altar was made,[69] through the twelve stones lifted up from the Jordan,[70] through the twelve oxen who held up the bronze sea,[71] and through the twelve stars that are placed on the crown of any spouse,[72] through the twelve signs of the sky,[73] through the twelve months of the year, through the twelve Roman senators,[74] and through the twelve wise men.[75] They are also represented in the New Testament through the twelve baskets of fragments[76] and through the twelve names that John, in the Apocalypse, saw written above the door of heavenly Jerusalem,[77] and through the twelve foundations of that same city.[78] It should truly be noted that the Lord chose the apostles according to the number of the twelve patriarchs — namely the sons of Israel — and according to the number of the twelve prophets. And, just as there were three patriarchs — namely Abraham, Isaac, and Jacob — above the twelve sons of Israel, He also chose from among the twelve apostles three men as leaders, namely Peter, James, and John,

---

65. Cf. Ex 16:1.
66. Ex 28:15–22.
67. Cf. Ex 35:13, Mk 2:26.
68. Cf. Num 13:1–16.
69. Cf. 1 Kgs (1 Sam) 18:31.
70. Cf. Josh 4:1–11.
71. Cf. Jer 52:20.
72. Cf. Rev 12:1.
73. The Zodiac.
74. A possible reference to the two consuls elected during the Roman Republic (509–27BCE), each serving alternating months for a total of twelve per year.
75. See ch. 17, n. 127.
76. Cf. Mt 14:20.
77. Cf. Rev 21:12.
78. Cf. Rev 21:14.

CHAPTER TWO

above the others. He chose these three illustrious men in the same way on the Sea of Galilee.[79] He brought them with him without the other disciples to see the miracle when he raised the daughter at the house of the high priest.[80] He disclosed His secrets more fully to them than to the others. He showed His Transfiguration to them on Mount Tabor.[81] At His Passion, He suffered greatly with them, as a beloved person with beloved people, and He showed them the sorrow of His flesh, saying: "Sad is my soul, even unto death." [Mt 26:38] In likeness to these heroes, in fact, the Holy Spirit now places bishops in the Church over the priests.

It is, however, to be observed that the twelve apostles that the Lord sent out to preach, to whom He also gave the power of curing diseases and of casting out demons, stand for priests to whom He entrusted the function[82] of preaching and the power of curing diseases of the soul through the office of absolution and the power of casting out demons through the mystery of baptism. And it should be believed that what happened corporally then in the bodies through the hands of the apostles, happens spiritually now in souls through the hands of the priests, and even though they may not be strong, it happens through the working of the Holy Spirit. In fact, just as the Lord gave the power of curing diseases of bodies and souls to the apostles, so also he gave the power to priests, through divine providence, of curing souls and bodies.

What the names of the apostles signify by way of interpretation, the priests must practice in their work. For it is also fitting that they seek to resemble in practice the designations of those whose offices they hold.[83] Simon is interpreted as "obedient," Peter as "knowing,"

---

79. Cf. Mt 4:18–22.
80. Cf. Mk 5:21–43, Mt 9:18–26.
81. Cf. Mt 17:1–8, Mk 9:2–8.
82. The Latin here is *verbum* but is likely in this context to be the function of Jesus who was the Word or λόγος. Cf. Jn 1:1.
83. The list of the twelve disciples is found in Mt 10:2: "The first, Simon, who is called Peter, and Andrew his brother; and James of Zebedee, and John his brother; Philip and Bartholomew; Thomas and Matthew the tax

Bar Jonah as "son of a dove," Cephas as "head," and John as "grace of God."[84] He [as Simon] was obedient, since he obeyed the Lord unto death on the cross He had taken up.[85] He [as Peter] was knowing, [f.14r] since he confessed Christ as God and Man earlier than the others, saying: "You are Christ the Son of the Living God." [Mt 16:16, Jn 11:27] He [as Bar Jonah] was son of the dove, because he was filled with the Holy Spirit. He [as Cephas] is well said to be the head, since his church was held as the head of all churches. Peter [as Bar Jonah] is said to be the grace of God, since by his preaching, merits, and prayers, heavenly grace is given to the faithful. Thus, priests must obey God in all things and even undergo the death of the cross for Him, if that should be, perchance, inflicted upon them by their persecutors for the sake of justice. They must also know the secrets of the Scriptures, so that they might better announce to the minds of people the will of God through their preaching. They must also be sons of the Holy Spirit in faith and in work. They are, besides that, held to be the head of all, by whose sacrosanct mysteries all the faithful to be saved are sanctified.

---

collector; James the son of Alphaeus, and Thaddeus; Simon the Zealot, and Judas Iscariot, the one who betrayed Him." The author changes their order, putting Peter, James, and John at the beginning.

84. A somewhat random etymological explanation concerning Saint Peter. In fact, "Simon" comes from the Hebrew for "to hear" and thus "to pay attention to" and so "to obey"; "Peter" from "stone" or "rock" in Greek and Latin, while the word for "rock" in Aramaic is "Cephas." "Bar Jonah" means "son of a dove" in Aramaic and refers here to Peter's father, as in "Simon bar Jonah"; "John" comes from the Hebrew for "mercy of God" or "grace of God." The author appears to be giving an alternative of "John" for "Jonah" as Peter's father's name. Ascribing the idea of "knowing" to Peter is probably due to some confusion between the Aramaic word for rock, "Cephas," and the Greek word for "head": κεφάλι (cephali).

85. There are at least three possibilities here: the cross taken up eventually by Peter for his own crucifixion, the cross taken up by Christ that would be later taken up by Peter, or a confusion between Simon the Apostle and Simon the Cyrene who took up Jesus's cross when He was unable to carry it. Cf. Mt 24:32, Mk 15:21, Lk 23:26. Tradition held that St. Peter was crucified upside down.

CHAPTER TWO

James is interpreted as the "supplanter," since he supplanted in the hearts of the Gentiles their idolatry and perfidy through his preaching, and he curtailed their vices. Thus, priests must supplant the vices of people through examples of good works and through preaching the scriptures.

John is interpreted as "the grace of God," since he was worthy to have the privilege of the love of Christ by maintaining virginity. Thus, he imparted to the priests an example that they should live in the churches with chaste body and mind.

Andrew is interpreted as "manly"[86] or "valorous": manly through his suffering on the cross[87] and valorous through his acknowledgement from the heart. Concerning him, the people confessed in this way to Aegeas,[88] saying:

Grant to us the just man,

Restore to us the holy man,

Do not kill the man dear to God,

He is just and mild and pious.[89]

Thus, priests must be manly in enduring adversities and valorous through an acknowledgement of mind and mouth in confessing sins: "There is belief in the heart for justice, but the confession is made with the mouth for salvation." [Rom 10:10]

---

86. "Andrew" comes from the Greek word for "man": specifically ἀνδρός, *(andros)* that is paralleled in Latin with the word *vir* or "man/male." Both words emphasize the masculine traits and roles and have connotations of "virile" or "powerful." The Latin *vir* is also the stem of *virtus* meaning both "power" and "virtue."

87. The *Acts of Andrew* describe how Andrew was bound and crucified on a cross. Later, the cross was described as an X-shaped cross rather than the cross-bar type used for Christ.

88. According to the *Acts of Andrew*, the proconsul of the time at Patras was Aegeas or Aegeates; this is likely a reference to him. See Montague Rhodes James, *The Apocryphal New Testament* (Oxford: Clarendon Press, 1924), 348.

89. This is a standard antiphon from the middle ages associated with St. Andrew's feast day. The authorship remains unknown. See the Cantus Database: http://cantus.uwaterloo.ca/chant/231215. Accessed 5/15/2020.

Philip is interpreted as "mouth of the lamp,"[90] since what he felt with a faithful heart from God, he acknowledged by preaching with an open mouth. A lamp has oil in its narrow body and a wick in the oil and a fire on the wick, and it has a large mouth that is always open through which it sends out its light on those around it and expels the darkness. By the oil, the Son is represented; by the fire, the faith of the Holy Trinity; and by the mouth, those preaching this faith. The priests must have this faith in their hearts and must confess through preaching to all with their mouth, and they must cause the darkened minds of their listeners to be illuminated.

Bartholomew is interpreted as "son of one holding up the waters,"[91] which clearly signifies the Son of God Who raises and holds up the minds of those preaching toward the contemplation of heavenly things, as those preaching saturate the hearts of the earthly people with the droplets of their truly spoken words, and as these hearts then deeply desire the things above. [f.14v] That the waters signify the people is witnessed by the scripture that says: "Many waters, however, many people."[92] Therefore, as Bartholomew was the son of God through adoption and holds up the waters, that is, the people, to heaven through preaching, so priests must be sons of God through obedience and hold up the people of the water — namely those baptized in water — to the citadel of the heavens through their assiduous preaching.

Matthew[93] is interpreted as "given" or "received as a present," since he was given by the grace of God, and he was received from the mass of the lost when the Lord received him unto Himself

---

90. Cf. Jn 1:43–44 for the calling of Philip. In fact, Philip is from the Greek for "lover of horses": Φίλιππος *(philoppos)*.

91. Also called Nathaniel, cf. Jn 1:43–51. Bartholomew means "son of the furrows"; while one can think of fields supporting and/or holding the drops of rain, it is not clear that this was the intent of the author.

92. Cf. Rev 17:15; Herbers (22) suggests Isaiah 8:7. Neither text is entirely satisfactory. The expression was found in sources subsequent to the CC but not before it in the *Corpus corporum* (http://www.mlat.uzh.ch/MLS/). Accessed 5/9/2020.

93. Greek transliteration of the Hebrew for "gift of God."

CHAPTER TWO

from the custom house;[94] thus priests must, through restraint, be strangers to the lost doing bad works and given over to the grace of God through good work.

Thomas[95] is interpreted as "twin" or "abyss." Twin, because he was double in faith: while he did not want to believe the Lord at the Resurrection until he would see the nail prints, he also saw and believed.[96] He was an abyss, since afterwards he recognized and perceived the depth of the faithful sacraments of Christ and adhered to them when he accepted martyrdom of the sword for Him in India. Thomas is called Didymus,[97] that is, similar to Christ, since he was similar to the Lord with a regal stature. In a similar way, preachers must be the abyss, that is recognize the depth[98] or profundity of God's ministries and divine scriptures, so that they may understand with all the saints, what are the breadth, length, height, and depth.[99]

James was given the surname Alphaeus by Mark to differentiate him from James of Zebedee.[100] This James, like the other, is

---

94. The Latin *theloneo* (from *teloneum*) can mean either "custom house" or "toll booth"; here the emphasis is on the place where he was found. He is usually described by profession as a tax collector (cf. Mt 9:9–13).

95. The name is a Greek transliteration of the Hebrew word for "twin." The idea of it meaning "abyss" is found in some literature concerning this apostle, but its origin is unclear.

96. Jn 20:24–29.

97. Greek for "twin."

98. Latin *altitudo* is used for both "height" and "depth."

99. S corrects *profundum* (accusative and adjectival) to the more analogous *profunditas* (nominative and nominal), with the same meaning.

100. James, son of Alphaeus, is one of the most problematic of the Apostles. Within the Gospels he only appears four times, each in a list of names of the Apostles [Mk 3:16–19, Mt 10:2–3, Lk 6:11–16, Acts 1:13). In Mark 2:14 and Luke 5:27, the tax collector Levi is also called the son of Alphaeus. The author of the Epistle of James is often thought to be the same James as the apostle, but this James is also described as the brother of the Lord and is also called the first bishop of Jerusalem. Our author is aware of all of these portrayals. This section tries to clarify the relationship of the many "Jameses" named in the New Testament.

interpreted as supplanter, because he supplanted vices with a worthy life and with admonition for people, and this is quite suitable for preachers, since they must supplant vices with diverse sufferings and with numerous admonitions brought to bear. Concerning this James, it is written: "He did not drink wine or other intoxicating drink, nor ride an animal, nor eat meat, nor mount iron on his head, nor was he anointed with oil, nor did he use baths. He alone was permitted to enter the holy of holies."[101] Concerning this James, some wish to say that he should be known as the brother of the Lord on account of the fact that James is read to be the brother of the Lord both in the Gospels and in the Epistle to the Galatians.[102] Others say this about the other James, still others about both of them together. Indeed, others assert that there were three sisters, namely Mary the mother of the Lord, and Mary the mother of James of Alphaeus, and Mary the mother of the sons of Zebedee. At the time of the apostles, the descendent of a man and a blood relative were called brothers. However, since opinion differs on these diverse words, it should thus be reasonably defined that whichever of them has a blood relationship in the flesh, might be a brother of the Lord. Nevertheless, anyone while living by the will of God, may become His brother by sticking to this as the Lord affirmed when He said: "Whoever [f.15r] should do the will of My Father Who is in heaven is My brother." [Mt 12:50] It is greater to be a brother of the Lord spiritually than carnally. Therefore, whoever calls either James of Zebedee or James of Alphaeus the brother of the Lord speaks the truth. Alphaeus, the father of James, is interpreted as "learned," and this is in harmony with these very preachers who must be learned not only in both Testaments but also firmly in the divinity and humanity of God.

Thaddeus[103] is the one to whom Luke gave the name "Judah [brother] of James"[104] in his Gospel and in the Acts of the Apostles.

---

101. Eusebius, *Ecclesiastical History*, Bk. 2, ch. 23, sect. 5.
102. Cf. Mk 6:3, Mt 13:55–56, and Gal 1:19.
103. Cf. Mk 3:18 and Mt 10:3.
104. Lk 6:16 and Acts 1:13.

He was, in fact, the brother of James, the brother of the Lord, as he writes in his own Epistle,[105] whence he is also called a brother of the Lord with his fellow citizens who were amazed and who testified concerning his powers, when they said: "Is He not a carpenter and Son of Mary, Brother of James and Joseph and Jude and Simon?" [Mk 6:3] He, that is, Thaddeus, is called by some Letheus.[106] Thaddeus is interpreted as "little heart,"[107] as if it were a cultivating heart, since he cultivated through preaching with his mouth and brought to completion through labor with his hands the good desires inspired by God in his heart. In a similar manner, preachers must cultivate such desires by admonishing with their mouth, and they must fulfill them with their work.

Simon is presented as the "Canaanite" by Mark to differentiate him from Simon Peter, and Luke had presented him though interpretation as Simon the Zealot. Simon is interpreted as "obedient." Canaanite is interpreted as "zealot," that is, "zealous imitator," since he obeyed God in all things even unto death. He took the epithet "Canaanite" from Cana, a town in Galilee, and he was zealous in preaching to the peoples in spiritual imitation of God. "Emulation,"[108] when it is used in a good sense, expresses the "Holy Spirit," as when the apostle speaks and says: "For I emulate you zealously with the zealous emulation of God." [2 Cor 11:2] In a similar manner, those preaching must obey the commands of the Lord and must rouse their listeners with a special zealous imitation, so that they may be able to say, together with the apostle:

---

105. Jude 1:1.
106. The Latin is *Letheus*, probably related to the Lebbaeus found in the KJV, although not in the Vulgate. See, for example Mt 10:3 (KJV): "Lebbaeus, whose surname was Thaddeus."
107. The diminutive of *cor* "heart" would be *corculum* in the neuter, but here it has a masculine ending *(corculus)* presumably to match the masculine *Thaddeus*.
108. The Latin *aemulor* indicates "zealous imitation." It carries both good and bad connotations. The author is clearly aware of its ambiguity.

"For I emulate you zealously with the zealous emulation of God." [2 Cor 11:2]

Judas is presented by Mark as the one who betrayed the Lord in differentiation from Jude of James, as he took "Iscariot" either from the town in which he was born or from the tribe of Issachar as a foreboding word for his damnation. Issachar, of course, which is said to be "a fee," alludes to the price of damnation. However, Iscariot, which is interpreted as a "recollection of death," shows that he was not suddenly induced, but long reflected on carrying out the shameful deed of the betrayal of the Lord. But why did the Lord choose this nefarious one, when He knew that he would betray Him? For the apostle testified about him in this way, saying: "One of you[109] is a devil." [Jn 6:71] Why, therefore, did He prefer to choose a devil for the ranks of the apostolate? It was for this reason: He Who is perfect could have a nefarious servant and not fear this wretched servant, so that He might teach [f.15v] us to endure the bad among us and not to cast anyone out unless convicted of crime. It is also so that He might show that the apostolate and ecclesiastical ranks are not a reward but rather a service, since miracles and the divine sacraments could be performed as well through this impious one as through Peter. Saint Matthias, who is one of the seventy-two disciples, is asserted to have been elected by lot in his place.[110] Matthias in Hebrew is interpreted in Latin as "Given,"[111] since he was given by God to the ranks of the apostolate in place of Judas. He is an example of priests whom the Lord chose for apostolic succession by the lot of the Holy Spirit and gave to guide the faithful people of His Church.

Judas,[112] which is interpreted as "confessor" when it is used in its good sense, indicates priests who must confess to all with

---

109. The CC reads *unus ex vestrum* for *unus ex* (or *e*) *vobis;* S corrects this to *unus vestrum*.
110. Cf. Lk 10:1.
111. In Latin, the word used is *donatus*.
112. While Judas comes from the Hebrew word for "praised," the name has become inextricably linked to the notion of "traitor" as a result of the betrayal of Jesus.

CHAPTER TWO

their mouth the acknowledgement of faith that they have in their hearts and who must continually relate the Lord's Passion in their preaching. When, however, "Judas" is used in the bad sense, it stands for bad and iniquitous bishops, priests, abbots, monks, and prelates of the Holy Church, who like Judas sell the Lord when they accept money either for holy orders or for ordaining bishops or for granting ecclesiastical things or for a nuptial blessing or for burials of the dead or for the dedications of basilicas or for placing priests justly in churches — or even unjustly placed — or for funeral services of the dead or for baptizing children or for penances given to sinners or for excommunicating those permitted in the Church or for masses or for matins. Just like the merchant and scoundrel who makes in the meat-market three or six or twelve or thirty coins' worth[113] off of the meat set aside, the bad priests and monks follow

---

113. The Latin reads *nummatas* or "coins' worth." This is the first mention of the complex issue of money and currency in the text. The Latin *pecunia* is the most general word for "money." It is possible to deduce that the most valuable coin in the text was the *solidus* or "gold coin." A coin of lesser value is the *nummus*, which is used as a generic "coin"; at times it is clear that this is used in a contrastive sense with the larger coin, and we there translate it as "small coin" or "smaller coin." In one instance we find *obolus* or "very small coin." In addition, one finds the term *nummatus* to mean "a small coin's worth" and *solidatus* to mean "a gold coin's worth." Others include the *marca* or "mark," related etymologically to the "Deutschmark"; and the *talentum* or "talent" and the *minutum* or "mite" of biblical origin. There are also frequent mentions of *aurum* or "gold" and *argentum* or "silver," along with the adjective *argenteus*. These metals are directly related to money, since unnoticed, gold or silver could be shaved off for a profit. "Gold" and "silver" are also used as "money" or "valuable entity." *Deauratus* (gold-plated) and *deargentatus* (silver-plated) are used to indicate profit-making by passing off as solid coins what are only plated ones. The word *passut* is used for money deceptively gained, or possibly even produced. The words *falsus* and *contra-factus* are used for "counterfeit"; this is counterbalanced with the adjective *examinatus* for "tested" or formally examined and certified. The word *pretium* is used for "price," "cost," or "value." *Pacca* — related to the modern verbs *pagar* in Spanish, *payer* in French and "pay" in English — is used pejoratively for money, perhaps related to "pay-off." The word *acum* also seems to refer to a kind of coin; while the Latin *acus/acum* literally means "needle," the context suggests some relationship to currency. Although it is tempting to

the heresy of simony, selling ecclesiastical offices and making three or seven or thirteen or thirty coins worth off the Lord, even though singing without recompense masses and vigils and services for the dead, they seek seven or fifteen or thirty smaller coins or five gold coins for thirty masses. Let them know that they are to be damned unto perpetuity with that vengence with which Judas the destroyer is damned unto eternity. Just as Judas, who handed over the body of Christ and took the price of thirty coins, is damned, so also is the one punished who sings thirty — or more or fewer — masses and asks a fee of thirty coins — or more or fewer.

Some of these merchants, in fact, are called Judaites, others Simoniacs, and others Gehazites.[114] For just as Judas, who first accepted money and handed over a body for it, is damned, [f.16r] so also are bishops and priests, archpriests and deacons and archdeacons damned, who first take money and give ecclesiastical things for it. And just as Simon Magus, who offered money to Saint Peter the Apostle so that from him he would receive the Holy Spirit through Whom he might perform miracles, is damned[115] and deserved to hear from Peter: "May you and your money with you be unto perdition," [Acts 8:20] so also bishops and priests and clerics and monks who offer money to those greater so that they may obtain ecclesiastical ranks are damned. And just as Gehazi, the servant of Elisha the prophet, who asked for money from Naaman the Syrian after his purification from leprosy and who received, with his master

---

relate *acus/acum* to the French *écu,* this coin is generally believed to derive from the Latin word *scutum* "shield" which became *escut* and finally *écu* in French (and *escudo* in Portuguese), and this this coin was first struck some two centuries later.

114. The Latin is *Judaite, Simoniaci,* and *Giezite.* The author is apparently showing the words that can be derived from biblical individuals who have accepted money improperly: *Judaite* referring to the thirty coins accepted by Judas for betraying Jesus (cf. Lk 22, Mt 26–27, Mk 14, Jn 13); the *Simoniaci* referring to Simon Magus who took money in exchange for church offices (cf. Acts 8:9–24); and *Giezite* from Gehazi who took two talents improperly (Cf. 2 Kgs (2 Sam) 5).

115. Cf. Acts 8:9–24.

so judging, the leprosy that the prince had lost, is damned,[116] so also those who seek profit after giving spiritual gifts and blessings, will be filled with the leprosy of all the sins of those whose money they take and will be damned through divine revenge. Therefore, let us flee, brethren, the deeds of these people, lest we be damned with them in eternal pain. Let us learn to give freely what we have received freely from God: "You received freely, distribute freely to all." [Mt 10:8] The Lord did not seek from us a fee when He gave us a spiritual gift. Let us not seek earthly profit from those to whom we give one. One should realize that in receiving there is no sin, but rather in seeking. If, in fact, we seek money for an ecclesiastical office that is given, we sin. If the giver, of his own accord — that is, not compelled by any pressure — gives without our asking and we accept, we do not sin. Again, clerics and monks who sell land for a dead person for purposes of burial are damned. He is a strange merchant who does business with a dead man. He does a barbarous business who sells land to a dead person.[117] It is true what a certain melody says, in verse,[118] about Simoniacs:

> All equity has departed,
>
> Never does goodness appear,
>
> Iniquity and the vanity of
>
> Vanities fill all.[119]
>
> With a desire for coins
>
> The celebration of masses
>
> And all religious dedications
>
> Are reduced to a price.

---

116. 2 Kgs (2 Sam) 5.

117. The Latin *mortuo* can be translated "for a dead person" or "to a dead person." The author plays off that ambiguity.

118. The authorship is unknown, and this is possibly the first surviving text of this poem.

119. The verbs here are in the singular, as Latin permits agreement of the verb with only the last of several subjects, using the singular, where English would join these subjects into a conceptual plural.

> But all this destruction
> And this polluting
> Proceed from the beginning
> From the vice of priests.
> Many now hardly clerics at all,
> Are lovers of the world;
> They are now not disciples of Christ
>> But servants of Mammon.

Bad prelates who break a truce or commit greater sins or who accept money — for example, five or twenty gold coins, or one silver mark, or less or more — will be no less damned. Thus, in fact, a prelate said to a defendant standing and facing him: "Woe to you who have broken the truce or have done so many evils. Make it right with me, correct the truce, give me sureties for this correction." He does not say that he should satisfy God against Whom he sinned, but he says that he should make it right with him whom he had not offended. Moreover, this defendant, after giving sureties to the prelate, [f.16v] will give money in return according to this added provision, or the prelate will condemn him by a sentence of strict judgment or by excommunication. Oh! Oh! Excessively sad affair! He does not wish to impose a penance on the sinner for the sin, nor does he care about the salvation of his soul, but he places deceitful money in his purse, an anathema that is beyond what one is allowed to believe, and he shuts up his soul in hell. Woe! Woe for such deeds! This prelate is among those of whom the Lord speaks and laments through His prophet: "They feed on the sins of my people, and they raise their hands to their iniquities." [Hos 4:8] Those who take money from those subject to them in the way we said above consume the sins of the people of God. The evil judges and prelates consume the sins of the people of God when they subvert proper judgments through money or when they take money from those whom they must vindicate. The prelates and evil judges, who truly rejoice when they find someone subject to them before them as a defendant or other party whom they might accuse and extort money from, raise their hands to the iniquities of the people of God. Similarly, when any Church leader takes away a church from some priest or some honor from the holder on some bald pretext and gives it to another person after accepting money is damned. Just as the leader doing these things does not at all wish to be deposed from his position, he must not remove another on some trivial pretext, as the Lord says in the Gospel: "What you would not want for yourself, do not do to others." [Lk 6:31] This perverse practice arose from Gaul, and it was not established by the original holy fathers nor by the present ones, and therefore it is to be abolished and wiped out by all Catholics.

Certain false, demoniacal hypocrites have arisen, either clerics or lay people dressed in a religious habit, who, on the Vézelay or Santiago or Saint-Giles roads[120] or on the Roman Way, give false penances to pilgrims or others whom they find off guard in remote places. They walk, in fact, for a while with them and offer excellent words at first and tell everyone about all sorts of vices, one after another. They speak to each of them separately and ask them individually in secret places about their consciences and the individual sins they have committed. As soon as they have confessed, they impose on one thirty masses and on another thirteen for some sin. They say, "Have thirty masses celebrated for thirty coins by such and such priests who never [f.17r] have done debauchery, nor eaten meat, nor had their own things." However, the one who does not know how he might find such priests gives the thirty coins or the value of them to the one who says that he will find them. The person accepting does not care about the salvation of the sinner but puts the money in his purse and spends it wantonly, and he shuts up his cursed soul in hell. Many priests in the church do something of this type, as they, in the form of the twelve apostles, ask out of their own avarice for either the thirty coins with which Christ was sold or thirty small coins or fifteen gold coins for thirty masses and vigils from some dead or living person. Just as Judas sold the Lord for thirty coins, they also sell the body of Christ for thirty coins. Oh, what an evil business! What horrible profit! They

---

120. These refer to routes to Compostela described in Bk. V, the Guide.

are destroyers of truth, imposing false penances, selling the body of Christ, which is to be given freely to sinners. They are witnesses of falsehood, sending the souls of sinners into Orcus,[121] renewing the simoniac heresy — the blind leading the blind! These people are not only to be destroyed by the prelates of the Church but also ravaged by the secular powers.

The lustful priest who, when a woman comes to him for the sake of penance, incites her to sin with him through his lustful suggestions or ridiculous assurances is no less to be condemned. That woman is like someone who seeks water at the well, then slips into it and dies. She is similar to someone in the desert who is seeking the right road and finds a bear that devours her in a hidden place. This priest is similar to someone who boundlessly extends nets for catching a bird. When he sings sweetly, the gentlest bird comes and falls into the net and is captured.

I have seen on the road of Saint James a certain person hanged, who, before he was hanged, had been accustomed to call to pilgrims to get them underway before dawn at the entry of whatever village. In fact, he was calling in the usual pilgrimage manner in a loud voice: "God and Saint James, help!" And so, as a certain pilgrim was walking out with him to get underway, they went for a short while together until he came into a hidden area where his companions were waiting, and with them he immediately pillaged and killed the pilgrim. Clearly a priest who deceives with some lustful words a woman coming to him for the sake of penance is similar to him. He is the well drinking the one sliding into it, the bear devouring the lamb, the lion swallowing the sheep, the thief [f.17v] killing the traveler, the blind man leading the blind woman. Thus, it is to be carefully considered by bishops, so that they give the power of giving penances to such, if you will, chaste priests, who may

---

121. The Latin here is *Orco* from *Orcus*, which is the nominative form that has passed into English. We have followed as closely as possible the terms used by the author for Hell: Gehenna *(Gehenna)*, Hell *(Infernus/Infernalis)*, Orcus *(Orcus)*, Pit of Hell *(Puteo Infernali)*, Regions of Hell, *(inferna)*, Tartarus *(Tartarus)*, and Underworld *(Inferi)*.

CHAPTER TWO

impose the burdens of penance legitimately on sinners, not through avarice or hatred or love or ignorance or impurity, but according to the authority of the canons and the ability of the penitent. In fact, a penance for one and the same sin is to be given differently to the sick, the healthy, the cleric, the lay, the soldier, the religious, the one making a journey, the one staying in the same place, the adolescent, the old, or a woman. Therefore, let us lay aside the acts of evil ones, lest we perish with them in eternal pain. Let each person see to it that he not offer fraudulent penances for the sake of avarice, nor seek the price of his own damnation from masses that were to be sung for free. No sinner is to be advised by a priest to have a mass sung, but the priest is to be humbly asked by the sinner to sing it. A priest must perform the Eucharist whether willingly or unwillingly; however, the unwilling sinner must not be forced to offer his goods for a mass for the sins of the living or the dead. Therefore, let us hasten to the fellowship of the apostles whom we have commemorated, by living well and by preaching, so that, as we perform on earth in their place and are helped by their merits and intercessions, we may deserve to arise and rejoice with them in heaven.

Concerning these apostles and how each of them in each of the cities where they preached and were at first buried, are to arise on the day of judgment, Saint Fortunatus, the bishop of Poitiers[122] and a brilliant poet, once sang in a book of his praises, saying in this way:

The star-like nobles assembling for royal prayers

Eagerly come in, collecting for a chorus.

With the accompanying flight of Paul, skilled in law,

Peter, the prince, runs from the Roman arch.

They whose ashes the city, which is head of the world,[123] holds,

---

122. Venantius Fortunatus (c.530–600 or 609) was bishop of Poitiers from about 590 until his death. This poem is introduced in the CC text with a double sized, red, capital 'S': *Siderei*. It is from Bk. 8, ch. 6 of his collected works. See *Miscellanea*, PL 88:269–70.
123. Rome.

Come together at the same time bearing gifts for feasts.
The apostolic summit is glittering with radiant light.
Noble Achaia sends its Andrew;
Ephesus, to be venerated for its merits, sends the distinguished John;
Jerusalem offers James of Alphaeus.
That James, born of Zebedee, whom people repeatedly seek
The land of Galicia sends to the heavenly stars.
Fortunate and fruitful Hierapolis[124] with its prayers sends Philip;
Edessa brings forth its pious tribute, Thomas;
India brings triumphant [f.18r] Bartholomew from there.
High Naddaver[125] sends the extraordinary man Matthew.
Persia sends twin lights, Simon and Jude,[126] from there
From its expansive valley to the expansive stars.
On all sides, collected from the different parts of the world,
With the moving multitudes brought together,
A regal procession draws them.
They enter the gates, shining with starry radiance.
The opened city of the heavens receives these nobles.

In these verses, one should understand that the holy apostles — or really their bodies — are finally transferred from their former tombs on the Last Day together with the citizens of the cities in which they preached, and they are to be resurrected and crowned on starry seats. Therefore, let us pray brethren, that Jesus Christ our Lord may deign to lead us to their fellowship.

Who lives and reigns with the Father and the Holy Spirit. World without end. Amen.

---

124. City in ancient Phrygia; its ruins are near Pamukkale, Turkey.
125. Naddaver (Naddayer), Ethiopia. Tradition places Matthew's preaching and martyrdom here.
126. Simon and Jude, said to be sent to Persia after Pentecost, share a feast day, October 28.

[CHAPTER 3]

BLESSINGS OF POPE CALIXTUS FOR THE READINGS OF SAINT JAMES

May the grace of God, with which James is filled, be present with us.

May the One Who gave the crown of life to James deign to bring us a good life.

May the One Whom James served on the earth lead us to the celestial kingdoms.

May the One Who conveyed to James the eternal kingdom give us eternal joy.

May the One Who gave the gift of life to James protect us with His kindness.

May the One Who led James into the house of heaven create in us a love for celestial things.

May the desire of the mother of James be a strength and consolation for us.

May James lead us to heaven with the joys of this day.

May Christ grant to us in the kingdom the right-hand side that James sought from God.

May we be cleansed from all sins by the merits of the most beloved James.

May James, the light of the heavenly court, cleanse us from us all our vices.

May the One Who offered the reward of life to James grant us great kindness.

[CHAPTER 4]

Here Begins the Prologue of Pope Saint Calixtus On the Short Passion of the Apostle James of Zebedee of Galicia Which Is Celebrated on the VII Calends of August[1]

I have written down in this volume a short Passion of the apostle James of Zebedee, patron of Galicia, as well as of the wretched death of Herod who was justly stricken down by an angel because of the death of the apostle and with the same letters and words with which it is written in the *Ecclesiastical History*[2] in order that those who do not wish to read the [f.18v] long Passion of this apostle because of its size, may read this one, which is considered of great authority. Just as a pure stream proceeds from the purest spring, the long Passion is made prominent by the short one.[3] Each Passion is considered pure, as a pure stream and spring. Each Passion is separated from falsehoods, as the stream and the spring are cleaned from impurities. Therefore, as it pleases many people to drink from the greater water of the spring more than from the stream, so also it pleases many readers to read one Passion more than the other.[4]

Here ends the Prologue.

---

1. July 26.
2. This chapter is essentially the text of Eusebius, *Ecclesiastical History*, Bk. 2, ch. 8–10. For Eusebius, see ch. 1, n. 11.
3. The idea here seems to be that once one has read the *Short Passion* one may return to the longer one, as one follows a stream to its source.
4. Calixtus seems to indicate that the shorter Passion preceded the longer one and was closer to the spring. He may also be indicating that, like spring water, which is closer to the source and thus unadulterated with extraneous material, some may prefer the shorter one.

CHAPTER FOUR

Here begins the Passion.

After Gaius had served out his reign at Rome for not quite four full years, Claudius succeeded him as emperor.[5] However at that time a quite horrible famine possessed the whole orb of the world. Our prophets, however, had predicted this future event long before. As it is reported in the Acts of the Apostles,[6] a certain prophet, Agabus, had declared that a great famine would occur under the emperor Claudius. Truly Luke, who reports on Agabus, also adds this: that via the brothers Paul and Barnabas, who were at Antioch, they would send aid,[7] each according to his abilities, to the holy inhabitants at Jerusalem.[8]

And after, he[9] adds to this saying: "However, at that time" — without doubt designating the time under the reign of Claudius — "when there was a famine, King Herod sent his force to afflict some from the Church, and he killed James the brother of John with a sword." [Acts 12:1–2] Concerning this James, however, Clement of Alexandria, in the seventh *Book of Dispositions*[10] also writes a story worthy of memory, which had been conveyed to him from the teaching of his ancestors. He said:

> "For certainly, the one who had taken him" — that is, James — "to the judge for martyrdom was moved by penance, and confessed that he was also a Christian." He said: "They were both led together to a punishment of death. And while they were being led on the road, he asked James

---

5. Gaius Julius Caesar Augustus Germanicus (12–41CE), known as Caligula, was Roman emperor from 37–41; Tiberius Claudius Caesar Augustus Germanicus (10BCE–54CE) was Roman emperor from 41–54.
6. Cf. Acts 11:27–30.
7. Latin *sumptum* meaning "expenses," but perhaps here "whatever they collected" or "aid."
8. Eusebius's text (Bk. 2, ch.8) ends here.
9. Likely referring to Luke, as author of the Acts of the Apostles.
10. Clement of Alexandria (c.150–c.215). This work is sometimes referred to by its Greek name *Hypotyposes* ("Ὑποτύπωσες") or by the English *Outlines*. Only fragments such as those written down by Eusebius survive.

to grant him forgiveness. And James deliberated a short while and said, 'Peace be with you,' and he kissed him. And thus both were beheaded together."[11]

But then, just as divine scripture says,[12] Herod saw that the death of James was pleasing to the Jews, so he went further and cast Peter into prison, wishing, without doubt, to punish him. But divine help arrived, when an angel assisted him in the night, freed him miraculously from the bonds of the chains, and [f.19r] ordered him to go free to his ministry of preaching. And these things certainly happened to Peter.[13]

However, the king's sin committed against the apostles did not allow any delay of vengeance, but the divine right hand was immediately present, as the story written in the Acts of the Apostles teaches us. It says that when Herod went down to Caesarea, on a solemn day, dressed in bright regal clothing, he sat before the tribunal and spoke sublimely to the people, the people shouted to him: "The sounds of God and not of man!" It continues: "Immediately an angel of the Lord struck him, because he had not given glory to God, and he died, swarming with worms.[14]

It is worthy of a miracle for such consistency to be discovered between the divine scriptures and the historiographer of that people. For Josephus himself relates these things in the ninth *Book*

---

[11]. The Latin is *capite plexi sunt*; in this case we know that the use of capital or "head" punishment was literal, by beheading with the sword; the literal translation here would be "they suffered punishment with the head," although the usual Latin for the death penalty was *capitis poena*. This passage is from Eusebius, *Ecclesiastical History*, Bk. 2, ch. 2, beginning with "Concerning this James...." The actual words of Clement, begin with "Whereas a certain person...." Clement's words appear to end with "beheaded together."

[12]. The Latin has an added *inquit* ("he said") here, indicating either Calixtus or the Latin text he was using treated this paragraph as that of Clement. This *inquit* is not in the Greek text of Eusebius.

[13]. This marks the end of Bk. 2, ch. 9 of Eusebius.

[14]. Cf. Acts 12:1–10, 19–23.

of Antiquities,¹⁵ and he tells these things with the very words that are written below:

> He had completed the third year of the rule of all of Judea, when he came by chance to Caesarea, which previously was called Strato's Tower.¹⁶ There, when Herod set up spectacles for the citizens, on a day devoted to the prosperity of Caesar, and when the men possessed of honor and means had convened from the whole province, Herod went forth to the theater, early on the next day of the spectacles, dressed in gleaming garb that was marvelously woven with gold and silver. Then, when the front of his garment caught the first rays of the sun, it spread them out with reflected splendor, as the flash from the glimmering metal doubled the light for the spectators, so that the terrible power of the sight would stun the gaze of those looking on, and thereby this contriver would pretend to have more to him than is found in human nature. All around, the voices of the fawning people resounded, crying out honor and conveying destruction. And from here and there, from the shouting benches, a god might be moved, and as it would happen, he was submissively favorable to the people saying: 'Up until now we have nodded to you as a man, but from this we confess that you are of a super-human nature.' But the king did not curb this acclamation against divine law, nor did he dread the impiety of glorious adulation until after he looked and saw a threatening angel standing at his head, and Herod discerned him immediately as

---

15. Titus Flavius Josephus (37BCE–c.10CE). Josephus's work, *Antiquities of the Jews,* briefly references Jesus and the origins of Christianity. See Josephus, *Jewish Antiquities,* trans. Louis H. Feldman, Loeb Classical Library (Cambridge, MA: Harvard University Press, 1930–1965), 19.8.2, 343–61. An online version is available at: https://www.gutenberg.org/files/2848/2848-h/2848-h.htm#link192H_4_000. Accessed 5/15/2020. The text presented here, however, is quoted through Eusebius.
16. The Latin in the text is *Pyrgo Stratonis;* the original Greek was Στράτωνος πύργος.

the agent of his ruin, whom he had first known as the provider of good things. And behold! Suddenly he was tormented by an incredible pain in the stomach, and it attacked with swelling. And looking back at his friends, he said: 'Behold, I, your god, am driven out forthwith, and I am deprived of life. For certainly [f.19v] divine power declares that the cries conferred on me are false. And I, who a short while ago was called immortal by you, am already snatched headlong into death. But the judgment that God has set forth is to be accepted. For we have also lived or, speaking contemptuously, at least have completed a long life that one can consider to be happy.' And when he had said these things, being more violently tormented by the power of the pain, he was carried back to the palace. And when it was announced that he was to die not far off from that day, a large crowd of every age and sex convened. In the custom of their country, prostrate and wearing girdles,[17] they begged almighty God for their king's safety. However, every royal house was filled with wailing and lamenting. While the king, in the meantime, was lying on the highest terrace, he looked below and surveyed all those bent and prostrate with their weeping, and not even he restrained himself from tears. He suffered truly for five continuous days with pains in his stomach, and his life was cut off in the fifty-fourth year of his age and the seventh year of his reign, because he had killed Saint James. Herod had, in fact, reigned for four years under Gaius Caesar and three years under Claudius Caesar, and he had held the tetrarchy of Philip for three years,[18] annexing this for himself in his fourth year.[19]

17. A girdle or base garment, that is, minimal clothing sometimes worn in house investigations, to avoid accusations of planting objects at the scene of the investigation.
18. Philip the Tetrarch, sometimes called Herod Philip II by modern writers (b.c.19BCE, ruled from 4BCE until his death in 34CE).
19. The text of Josephus ends here, but Eusebius continues and in a short commentary concludes his chapter 10 by expressing his surprise at the

CHAPTER FOUR

With our Lord Jesus Christ reigning, who lives and reigns as God with the Father and the Holy Spirit. World without end. Amen.

---

consistency between Josephus and Scripture and his realization that the exact dates and names may have strayed from total accuracy because of the ravages of time. Calixtus, however, omits this commentary and adds one of his typical formulaic endings for this chapter.

[CHAPTER 5]

A Sermon of Pope Saint Calixtus On the Passion of Saint James the Apostle That Is Celebrated on the VIII Calends of August[1]

Brethren, a holy day for celebrating the most sacred solemnity of Saint James the Apostle has shone on us this day when it is fitting for us to offer a sacrifice of praise with prayers and hymns, so that the pious Favorer may offer us kindness as He offered the reward of life to His apostle.

This James, in fact, was born of Zebedee and was brother of John the Evangelist as the Gospel testifies. He was the glory of the Spanish, the advocate of the Galicians, blessed in life, distinguished in virtue, fervid in love, graceful in work, and splendid in speech. Divine providence not only consecrated him in his mother's bosom, but also chose him before the ordering of the world so that through him it might show the light of truth to this world and might give a shepherd of piety to the Spanish people. This [f.20r] James is to be very much honored since he held primacy in the honorable association of the apostles: he was the first of them to earn being crowned with martyrdom, to ascend to the heavens, and to possess the crown of glory and a seat in the heavens.[2] Luke, in fact, in the Acts of the Apostles does not say that any of them died before Saint James, but rather even after he tells of his passion, we read that the other apostles lived on. Because of this, it is clear that in the apostolic choir he remains the first crowned with martyrdom. For Christ the Lord, who divides His gifts among individuals and Who granted martyrdom to Saint Stephen to hold the preeminence of protomartyr[3] in heaven and Who set up Saint Peter as the prince of

---

1. July 25.
2. This is the *Hic Iacobus valde venerandus* text. See ch. 23.8, n. 16.
3. Cf. Acts 7:54–60.

CHAPTER FIVE

the apostles on the earth because of the merit of his faith, granted to His beloved Saint James preeminence among the apostles in the heavens through this first triumph of martyrdom. And so, he is closer to Him by far and honored before all in glory, as he was His imitator before the other apostles in his passion.

We order that the sacrosanct solemnities of his passion be celebrated on the eighth day of the Calends of August[4] with a vigil and fasting and octaves in the churches, not only in Galicia but also far and wide and generally in the whole world. We also order that his calling[5] and *translation* be celebrated on the third day of the Calends of January,[6] marking when he was chosen by the Lord on the Sea of Galilee and when he was transferred from Jerusalem to Galicia, and also that a feast of his miracles be celebrated on the fifth day of the None of October,[7] celebrating how he raised a man who had killed himself and performed other miracles.[8] We also order that these things be announced by all bishops in synods and by priests in churches in a loud voice and that all the people assemble at church with the entire clergy and that they cease from earthly works and spend those days in praise of Christ and that these sacred solemnities be honored in a festive manner with ringing bells and with tapestries, banners,[9] and fine altar cloths[10] unfurled

---

4. July 25.
5. The word "calling" (*electio* in Latin) refers to Jesus's selection of James to become an apostle (cf. Mt 4:21–22).
6. December 30.
7. October 3.
8. This clause "celebrating ... miracles" appears in the margin of CC with its insertion point indicated by a red cross; it is included within the text of S. This refers to the miracle of the castrated pilgrim in Bk. II, ch. 17 (Coffey and Dunn, *Miracles*, 45–51).
9. Latin *cortinis*, "curtains."
10. Latin *palleis*. In the *Translatio* (Coffey and Dunn, *Miracles*, 94) the author refers to the *cappa pallee*, in this case the pallium reserved for highest ranking clerics of the Church. Here, without the *"cappa," palleis* likely refers to the altar cloth.

in basilicas, and with extra songs.[11] And if some basilica somewhere should be under interdict, the interdict is loosened on the part of the Lord and the apostle for those days to the extent that the divine office with matins and appropriate hours may be celebrated solemnly and with great joy for all those entering and listening. In this way, rewards come to those honoring these solemnities and torments to those rejecting them. Therefore, those who honor his solemnities and await his favors do so beneficially just like those who honor the distinguished solemnities of the apostles Peter and Paul. Therefore, may the court of heaven exult in the Lord with hymns of praise! May the earth revel with celestial joys on these sacred solemnities of James, the lofty apostle of Christ! May the Church of the Faithful, adorned with his virtues, rejoice! And may the human mind, illuminated by his protections, resound in delightful praise to God! It certainly behooves us on earth to convey with all devotion praise on earth to him to whom the angels display this bestowing of honor [f.20v] in the heavens.

If, in fact, all of my body's joints were turned into tongues and resounded with a human voice, I would still not sufficiently praise the great James in Christ! Therefore, what praises shall I declare for the one who, as soon as he heard the voice of the Lord along the Sea of Galilee, left all and followed the Redeemer? Who is more blessed than the one who, because of Christ, with Herod overcome, was constant in faith and handed over his body to the torments of his passion? Who could worthily perform[12] commendations of praise for the person who was worthy of seeing the One born of God transfigured in the light of the Father? The Lord said, "Blessed are the eyes that see the things that you see!" [Mt 13:16, Lk 10:23] Or what praises could the throng of the faithful on earth devote to the one to whom the Lord granted preeminence among the apostles in heaven? For, just as someone who has walked into a field

---

11. The Latin *multiplicatis* probably refers to additional songs one might sing at a high feast.
12. The Latin is unclear and could be either *parare* "to prepare" or *patrare* "to perform."

CHAPTER FIVE

abounding in various flowers and contemplates the great variety of flowers has his gaze drawn here and there and truly does not know which of them he should take and which he should leave, so now I, who have walked into the meadow of the virtues and miracles of the great apostle James, am wavering as to what I should say first. Certainly, I want to pick all the flowers of his deeds, but since they appear as immense as an ocean, they are not quickly grasped by us. For when I see the noble things that he did with the others at the Lord's direction before the Lord's Ascension, and the extraordinary love that the Lord had for him, I am astonished. And when I look at the great things that he worked through divine grace after the coming of the Holy Spirit and Paraclete[13] before he suffered, I begin to fear. When, however, I recall again in the depths of my heart the indescribable and incomprehensible miracles that he performed with God's help from the day that he suffered until today, not only in Galicia but also among all the peoples who invoke his name — and indeed that I have seen with my own eyes — I am utterly stunned. But since the authority of the Evangelists compels me to mention first those things that are contained in the Gospels about him, I shall explain by narrating these.

We all revere in the Lord James of Zebedee, the patron of Galicia, who was worthy to be revered by our Lord and Savior Jesus Christ before all among the apostles, for he holds the third place in choosing and calling. According to Matthew, he is third as to calling, since when our Savior passed by the Sea of Galilee, He first called Peter and Andrew, and then he went on a little and "saw two other brothers, James and John of Zebedee, with Zebedee their father, repairing their nets, and he called to them saying: 'Come, follow [f.21r] me and I will make you fishers of men.'"[14] Oh wondrous mercy of the Redeemer! From the unlearned, he has

---

13. Paraclete, from the Greek παράκλητος, entered Latin with the meaning of "helper" or "advocate." It is used as an alternative English name for the Holy Spirit.
14. Cf. Mt 4:18–21, Mk 1:17. Calixtus seems to have conflated the stories of his calling.

made doctors; from the perverse, good; from the foolish, expert; from fishers, brilliant preachers. Oh, great mystery of the Savior! Oh, admirable reward by which the fishers of fish were worthy to be made fishers of souls! For as Saint James and John had been fished by Jesus, we are in turn fished in the net of faith by his preaching. These apostles who were fished by the Savior have fished and taken us from the salty waters where the dragon heads[15] are. In fact, the Restorer of the human race, before the incarnation of His Son, promised these fishermen to the peoples endangered on the sea of this world through the prophet Jeremiah who said: "Behold I shall send many fishers to you." [Jer 16:16] Born through merit, He also called to Himself and sent out fishing for souls those whom the Father had chosen. They were the fortunate apostles who followed the Master alone. They were the fortunate ones who could shine with the sun present. They were the fortunate ones to whom it was said: "Follow me," and who immediately set aside father and net and ship, and followed the Savior. They follow the Lord, not only with their footsteps, but with the imitation of good works. Therefore, those who follow the Lord with the footsteps and with an imitation of good works follow the Lord rightly.

True faith does not know the love of worldly things, does not know blood relationships, is unacquainted with the nature of father and mother, and denies any reason for refusal. In fact, it is written in the Old Law: "Who said to his father and his mother, I know you not; and to his brothers, I am unacquainted with you, these will guard my speech and will keep my covenant, says the Lord." [Dt 33:9] These brothers, whom we distinguish for the gracious Christ, declare to father, affirm to mother, and say to brothers, sisters, and children, to friends and to every acquaintance: "We do not know you. Do you want us to know you? Believe in Our Father, and we begin to have you as brothers of the Father. We do not know father; we do not know mother. There is, in fact, one Father who has begotten us. We know the Father. Do you wish

---

15. The term, however, can also refer to the devil. Cf. Ps 73:13–14 / 74:13–14 for the specific mention of dragon heads.

that we also know you? Then know the true Father also, so that we may all be brothers."

Therefore, the apostles are fortunate — and their fortune is to the benefit of the world! In fact, if James and John had not valued their parents so lightly, their name would not be so honored as it is today. If they had not valued them so lightly, so many churches would not resound with them today in the world. Unless they had valued so lightly their father, I would not know them as teachers. Unless James and John had left their father, I would not be worthy to have them as brothers. Therefore, they set aside lesser things and found [f.21v] greater things. They left their earthly father and found a heavenly One in Whom the fathers of all believers are made manifest. They valued little the power of an earthly father, but they accepted the power of binding and releasing. They valued little earthly inheritance, but they were made heirs of the heavens. They left their home in a small town, but they became princes of churches in the whole world. They valued little acquaintances and in-laws, but they produced acquaintances and brothers throughout the world. They left all earthly things, and they found all heavenly things. If, therefore, they left all and kept nothing for themselves, what will happen to us who have left little and possess all things? Indeed, we possess mentally those things that we do not have as well as what we do have. James and John, in fact, unless they had valued little the things of the flesh, would not have the spiritual things. Thus, we also will not have heavenly things at all, unless we leave behind the things of the flesh. They left all things and found all beneficial things. They did not lack even temporally, for they had the Dispenser of all good things with them. Thus, those who have left behind all things will certainly lack nothing if they have God with them. He testifies to this when His disciples asked Him and He said: "'When I sent you without a wallet and satchel and shoes, what did you lack?' And they said: 'Nothing.'" [Lk 22:35–36] And He said elsewhere: "Seek first the kingdom of God, and all these things will added unto you." [Mt 6:33; Lk 12:31] The Lord, in fact, has done all things. The world is His; He created all things. Whoever has Him, has His things. Whoever has such a great treasure will never lack anything. "Hope in the Lord," says the Psalm writer, "and do good and inhabit the earth and feed on his divine foods." [Ps 36:3 / 37:3] And elsewhere: "Cast your thought unto the Lord, and He will feed you." [Ps 54:23 / 55:22] Therefore, let nothing disturb the Christian. Let him not think of the next day. "The evil of the day is, in fact, sufficient for that day." [Mt 6:34] Therefore, let us praise the Lord our Savior Who has chosen the brothers James and John from the world and causes them to delight in His kingdom.

This is true brotherhood that could not be disrupted among worldly vicissitudes but that quickly follows the felicitous footsteps of the Redeemer after all these earthly things have been abandoned. In valuing little the earthly things, they came to heavenly things. They were brothers on earth, and they are found as brothers in the heavens.[16] They were brothers in their earthly father, and they are found as brothers in their celestial Father. They are truly brothers, whom the Lord chose "in unfeigned love." [2 Cor 6:6] And He offered them the heavenly kingdoms with whose teachings the Church shines like the sun and moon. It shines like the sun among the contemplative, while the moon shines [f.22r] among the active.[17] The lights of the celestial room are paired, and facing the Lord are two shining candelabra whose light never ends for eternity. One is truly purple-colored for martyrdom. The other is white, however, for acknowledgement. "For those that the Lord has called He has also justified; and those whom He has justified, He has also glorified." [Rom 8:30] He has truly glorified those in the heavenly places for: "O God, Your friends are exceedingly honored." [Ps 138:17 / 139:17][18] "While the Redeemer was on the mountain, He gave most fitting names to the disciples," as Mark narrates, "He

---

16. The words "and they are found as brothers in the heavens" are in the margin of CC, with a red cross designating their place in the text. They are in the body of the text in S.
17. The reference is to the active and contemplative life that has its roots in the story of Martha and Mary in the Gospel of Luke 10:38–42.
18. This verse differs considerably between the Vulgate and post-Reformation texts.

CHAPTER FIVE

called them 'Boanerges,' that is, 'Sons of Thunder'."[19] For just as the sounds of thunder echo on earth and cause it to tremble, so also the whole world resounded and trembled with their voices, when they "preached everywhere with the Lord working with them and confirming their word with accompanying signs." [Mt 16:20] However the Lord gave so much grace to this James on Mount Tabor that He showed him His venerable body transfigured in the glory of the Father.[20]

For James, the beloved of the Lord, with Peter and John standing by as witnesses with him, gazed upon the face of the Lord shining like the sun and upon His clothing glittering like snow, and he heard the Father speaking with Him and saying: "'This is My beloved Son in Whom I have been well pleased. Listen to Him.'" [Mt 17:5, 2 Pet 1:17] And he saw two prophets speaking with Him, namely Moses and Elias, one of whom had died many ages before and the other had been carried off to heaven. Oh, wondrous thing! Those who were counted already among the dead appeared living. The Transfiguration of our Savior shows figuratively a sign of future resurrection and a likeness of eternal life. For the face of the Lord, which shone like Titan,[21] shows the incomparable glory of the saints and the inestimable joy that we are to receive on the last day. Scripture says: "The just will shine like the sun in the kingdom of their Father." [Mt 13:43] His clothing, which glittered like snow, shows the immortality of our body that we will receive in the resurrection. Paul says: "It is necessary that this corruptible thing puts on incorruption, and this mortal thing immortality." [1 Cor 15:53] The Old Law is designated by Moses, and prophecy is shown by Elias, and by the three disciples is shown the law of new

---

19. This is a form of the *Dum esset Salvator* responsorial and versicle, though "Savior" is replaced by "Redeemer" here. See ch. 21, n.11.
20. Cf. Mt 17:1–8, Mk 9:2–9, Lk 9:28–36.
21. Here used in reference to Titan's embodiment as the sun-god from Greco-Roman mythology. In the Miracles, ch. 19, James's clothing and military bearing are claimed to shine brighter than Titan. (Coffey and Dunn, *Miracles,* 56)

grace, which is held through faith in the Trinity. Therefore, our most gentle Redeemer wished to appear transfigured between the two teachers and the three disciples [f.22v] so that the Old Law and prophecy and the gospel might afford testimony in the world of His true divinity and assumed humanity, and so that "in the mouth of two or three witnesses would stand the whole Word," [2 Cor 13:1] namely the One "that was made flesh and has dwelled among us." [Jn 1:14] "To Him also all prophets afford witness." [Acts 10:43] Tabor is interpreted as "coming light"[22] to which the Lord led His disciples from the valley of the hills. He makes known that this Only-Begotten of God is the eternal light to come at the time of judgment, Who will lead out His elect from corruption to incorruption, from mortality to immortality, from the lower places to the height of the heavens, and in the future resurrection His face will be glad with light as Saint James saw it figuratively on that very mountain. Oh, how fortunate the eyes that, of all the saints, saw the Redeemer transfigured in the splendor of the Father! Oh, sublime reward of the three to whom it happened that these things were seen in the world that are not believed to be for the world! Oh, prophecy of Isaiah that "the eyes of those seeing the Lord will not be clouded!" [Is 32:3]

It should, furthermore, be known that on that mountain, namely in the place where the Lord was transfigured, as the Christian religion grew, the faithful people built a basilica of wondrous work in the name of the Holy Savior in memory of that Transfiguration and placed in it priests of a monastic rule. The inhabitants of that mountain also report that such splendor gleamed on the day of the Transfiguration on that mountain that a stone that was previously black, on that day appeared to be white like alabaster and is so until

---

22. There is no support for this etymology of the name, if that is what the author is expressing here. In the extended metaphor, however, the equation of "Tabor" and "light" seems based on the sun hitting the peaks of a mountain first and also on the brightness (radiance) of the appearance of Moses and Elias. It may be, just as with Judas becoming synonymous with "traitor," the Transfiguration took on the meaning of light.

CHAPTER FIVE

today. From that stone the inhabitants of that place even now make small crosses with iron files, and pilgrims traveling to and visiting those sacrosanct places receive the crosses from the inhabitants, and in testimony of the Lord's Transfiguration, they wear them carefully suspended from their necks when they return to their own places. And however much the stone is cut for this work, it is asserted that same amount to be added back by the beginning of the year.[23] From the genuine wine in which the cross of this very stone is boiled many colon diseases[24] are cured.

Most worthy James, exceedingly fortunate and pleasing to God and also most worthy of all praise to whom the Father of the heavens wished to show the Savior of the world, up to this point mortal, transformed to the divinity of the Father, which neither prophet nor patriarch ever once saw! Happy is he who was worthy to see the promised Christ! Because of this he among the others, through the grace of a special love, was very honored by the Lord. For when [f.23r] the Eternal Friend, the Most Pious Redeemer, and our Savior raised the daughter of the chief priest, He did not permit anyone to follow Him into the building, according to Mark, to see the miracle, except for James together with two followers,[25] since He Who knows how to lead the good with Him into eternal rest and to hold back the unacceptable from Him, deigned to show to His most beloved James that miracle. Oh, unutterable grace of the Savior! Oh, His honorable work! Through this, the Maker of the world shows to Saint James the restored vessel before it was shattered by a double death.

Then this same James, together with his brother John, astonishingly sought that most excellent gift from the Lord, that none of the other disciples or prophets before or after dared to seek. As Matthew says, the mother of the sons of Zebedee approached

---

23. This miracle of the regenerating stone on the Mount of the Transfiguration has not been found elsewhere.
24. The Latin *coliniti* is not found in the usual dictionaries, the meaning is clear from the context.
25. The raising of Jairus's daughter from the dead, Mk 5:21–43.

Jesus, entreated and asked from Him, with her sons James and John, that they might be able to sit one at His right hand and one at His left hand in His glory.[26] It should, however, be known that the sons of Zebedee received the dignity of the seats of Christ, but not in that separation that the mother sought, such that one should sit on His left in His kingdom and the other on His right. For no one in the heavenly kingdom is said to be seated at the left, as all the elect may be read to be coming to the right hand of Christ at the Final Judgment. It appears impossible, in fact, that anyone might sit between the Father and the Son, when the same Son sits at the right hand of the Father, and the Father abides at the left hand of the Son. Thus, Saint Luke[27] in the book of the Acts of the Apostles also testifies, saying: "Certainly the Lord Jesus, after He spoke to His disciples, was assumed into heaven and sits at the right hand of God." [Mk 16:19] And Saint Stephen testifies to this same thing, saying: "Behold I see the heavens opened, and Jesus standing to the right of God." [Acts 7:55] But if one wants the left and right of Christ to be understood in the mystical sense, it is certain that some have sat on seats to His right and left, but in this place by the seat on the left is understood the present life and by the seat on His right is mystically understood eternal life. Thus, in fact, it has been written: "The length of the days is at her right hand and at her left hand are riches and glory." [Prov 3:16] On the seat to the left of Christ sits whoever strives to guide the faithful people worthily in the present life. On the seat to His right sits whoever holds the place of quiet in eternal life. Therefore James and John, the sons of Zebedee, have both sat in a temporal sense at the left of Christ while they have presided over and have guided faithful peoples in the present life in apostolic rule, namely in that kingdom of the nourishing Church [f.23v] of which Truth says: "The kingdom of God is within you." [Lk 17:21] In fact, by kingdom is understood the Church of God, just as elsewhere it is said by this same Son of

---

26. Cf. Mt 20:20–28. The mother's request occurs in Mk 10:35–45.
27. Mk 16:19, not Luke or Acts of the Apostles.

CHAPTER FIVE

God: "The Son of man will send his angels, and they will collect from His kingdom all scandals." [Mt 13:41]

Therefore, at the right hand of Christ — that is in the eternal happiness — James and John are declared to sit with the other apostles seeing the desired face of God, from where they are said to be coming with Him as judges of all the generations on the Last Day. But since we said how they may sit at the left and right hand of Christ, let us see what this mother or what these sons or what this Zebedee will signify. Mystically, this venerable mother depicts the present Church, which with the bath of holy rebirth for her two sons — that is, of the two peoples, namely the Jews and the Gentiles — becomes their mother, for whom she went to the Lord and prayed with the Psalm, saying, "From the ends of the earth I have called unto you: while my heart was made anxious, you have exalted me on a stone." [Ps 60:3 / 61:2] The church of the Jewish people is a mother, since many from that group once came to Christ, among them was Paul, who holds the seat on the left of Christ for guiding the past, present, and future faithful peoples with the teachings of his *Epistles*. The mother of the people of the Gentiles is the Church; for many from that group were once converted to the faith of the Lord through baptism. Among them were Cornelius and many others.[28] Therefore with these children, the nourishing mother — the Church — procured from Christ the seat on the Lord's left. When from among them He set the bishops and priests to guide the faithful people in the present life for Him, He obtained from God the seat, in fact, on the Lord's right for them, since He has the children whom He regenerated through the grace of baptism, now seated, through the perseverance of faith and good work, in heavenly happiness. The spouse of this mother is Zebedee, who is interpreted as "sacrifice" or "abandoning the fleeing devil,"[29] but designating in this place that Spouse of the Church Who offered Himself as a living Victim to God the Father on the altar of the cross for our sins and Who also left behind the fleeing and proud devil

---

28. Cf. Acts 10.
29. Zebedee really means "gift of God."

when He separated him from the assembly of the good angels and appeared in the flesh and cast him from the world, saying: "Now the prince of this world will be cast outside." [Jn 12:31] However, this Zebedee, when the name is used in a bad sense, is interpreted as "the fugitive devil leaving," but when it is used in a good sense, as in this place, then with the changed sense Zebedee is interpreted as "abandoning the fleeing devil."

The son of this spouse is John, whose name is interpreted as "grace of God," and this figuratively designates those [f.24r] who have received the grace of baptism and keep it until the end of their lives with good acts. In these persons, the grace of God abounds so much that not only do they raise themselves up to the heavenly things, but they also rouse others by advising them and by performing good works. The great James is also the son of this spouse, whose name is interpreted as "supplanter" and "consoler." For Jacob is said to be "supplanter." There is an addition of *"-us"* as *"Job"* is written *"-hus,"* and it is interpreted as "consoler."[30] Therefore James is beautifully said to be "supplanter" and "consoler," since he confirmed with the consolation of the Holy Spirit by the imposition of his hands in the faith of Christ, those whom he once supplanted away from vices with preaching. Now, however, through prayers and protections before God, he is accustomed to supplant from evil those calling on him. And those he supplanted from vices, he strengthens in sacred virtues through the same consolation of the Holy Spirit. And just as the farmer or the gardener eradicates extra vegetation from his garden by planting good vegetables, so also

---

30. It is not certain what this etymology indicates or how it is based on the Hebrew. Jacob means "holder of the heel" in the sense of "supplanter" in the inheritance of his Father. The name Job means "hated" or "persecuted." The addition of *–us* was to match a Latin declension. There is also a variant of "Uz" and "Hus" in the Bible (cf. Job 1:1), but its meaning here is not apparent. This passage seems an example of fourfold exegesis: the literal (what happened / mother requesting), the moral (this part / how to act, supported by a bad etymological argument), the allegorical (the Mother is the Church) and the anagogical (who sits where in heaven / good versus evil and eschatological sense).

CHAPTER FIVE

Saint James as a worshipper of Christ, once cut off the thorns and brambles from the field of the Holy Church by his preaching, in inserting the roses and lilies of virtues, and this shows figuratively those who supplant the delights of the flesh with repenting and doing good works.

But it should be noted that for all those desiring the kingdom of God, it is necessary to have these two sons of Zebedee. For, unless each one of us should have these two brothers with us, we will not at all possess the kingdom of the heavens. Unless we have the grace of God and supplant our vices, we will not at all have eternal life. We have John by retaining the grace of God in us, and we have James by supplanting the vice of the flesh. However, in these two brothers are represented all the saints who have existed from the beginning of the world until today. They all have had the grace of God. They all have supplanted the delights of their flesh. However, it should be observed that it is advantageous for us to have James first and then John. For unless we have first supplanted the vices from us, we will not at all have the grace of God, as Solomon says: "For the Holy Spirit of discipline will flee the feigned." [Wis 1:5] We must first therefore supplant the offences of the flesh, so that we may be worthy to possess the grace of God. For James first cleanses the temples of the heart with his supplantation; then John adorns it with divine grace. May James now clean, we pray, the temple of our hearts so that the grace of God may dwell in them.

Because John is said to have been more beloved by the Lord among the others and [f.24v] is known to be a stranger to the pollution of the flesh and from the persecution of the sword, he signifies that the contemplative life is beloved by the Lord and is calm among adversities and is a stranger to the corruption of the flesh. Because it is read that James was a supplanter of vices and was crowned with martyrdom, he signifies that the active life must supplant vices by diverting vices from oneself and tolerating adversities of the present life, until one may be crowned with harmonious contemplation. For truly the active life is spent sometimes in tranquility and sometimes in adversity. However, the contemplative life is found in tranquility more than in the active life.

That is what the Lord testifies to when he speaks to the ministering Martha in designating the active life, saying: "Martha, Martha, you are anxious, and you are disturbed about many things." [Jn 10:41] And after a few words he said, concerning the contemplative life: "Mary has chosen the best part for herself, which will not be taken away from her." [Jn 10:42] In this part, namely the chosen and wished for, may we therefore also deserve to enjoy fully until we are able, together with Saint James, whose votive solemnities we celebrate, to rejoice in the heavenly kingdoms with our Lord Jesus Christ standing by, Who lives and reigns with the Father and the Holy Spirit. World without end. Amen.

[CHAPTER 6]

Sermon of Pope Saint Calixtus On the Passion of Saint James the Apostle That Is Celebrated on the VIII Calends of August[1]

With spiritual joy, therefore, we rejoice in the Lord, most beloved brethren, on this sacred day of the most distinguished apostle, James of Zebedee, patron of Galicia, with whom Christ suffered greatly in his passion, as beloved with beloved, showing grief for his flesh and saying to him: "My soul is sad up unto death." [Mt 26:38, Mk 14:34] The Lord was not, however, sad "in death" but "up unto death," for He did not say: "My soul is sad unto death," but "up unto death." He was sad [f.25r] "up unto death," for He, Who had taken on the human body, had to undergo those things that are of the body, such that He would hunger and thirst, suffer pain, and be saddened. His divinity, however, is incapable of being altered by these bodily feelings. In death He was not sad, but He put on flesh from the bosom of the Father and came so that He could redeem the human race, and He went up on the wood of the cross willingly for us. On this Isaiah said, "He was offered up, since He willed it" [Is 54:7] and "He bore our sorrows." [Is 53:4] But it should also be noted that the last meal the Lord is said to have had was at the Sea of Tiberius[2] with Saint James, because of the superabundant love with which He esteemed him, and with Peter and Thomas, Nathaniel and John, and two others.[3] Oh, truly fortunate man! Beloved to God! To him the venerable Savior deigned to confer such grace that He would eat and have conversation with him! Why is it then that the Lord would celebrate the last meal with seven followers except that He is declaring that they who are

---

1. July 25.
2. Also known as the Sea of Galilee (cf. Jn 6:1).
3. This refers to the third post-Resurrection appearance of Jesus, described in Jn 21:1–14.

filled with the spirit of sevenfold grace are to be with Him at the eternal banquet! Let each one of us, therefore, cease from evil and let each do good, so that each may be able to have the grace of the Holy Spirit and may be able to be restored at the eternal banquet with the Lord! For, "if someone does not have the Spirit of God, he is not of Him." [Rom 8:9] Then, after the coming of the Holy Spirit, James, the apostle of Christ, preached the word of God and gave witness to the Resurrection of our Lord Jesus in Judea and gave many signs and performed many miracles, and he converted countless cohorts of peoples to the faith. And so, he went and evangelized the word of salvation to all peoples. There is no one who can establish how many of the Gentiles were converted at that time to Christ. However, he also restored sight to the blind, walking to the lame, hearing to the deaf, speech to the mute, and life to the dead. He also cured people from all kinds of diseases for the praise and glory of Christ. He kindled the dry hearts of the Gentiles from within with the fervor of the divine word, following the counsels of his Teacher who said: "Cure the sick, raise the dead, and cast out demons." [Mt 10:8] And elsewhere He said: "'Whoever believes in Me, will do the works that I do and will do greater than these.'" [Jn 14:12] It is not, in fact, with any medicines, electuaries, confections, syrups, various plasters, potions, solutions, emetics,[1] or the other antidotes of physicians, but rather by the accustomed grace of God, obtained from God for himself, that the most gentle apostle restored the weak to full health: namely, the lepers, the mad, those with [f.25v] kidney problems,[2] the crazed, the mangy, the paralytics, the arthritic, the dim-sighted, the phlegmatic, the jaundiced, those possessed by the devil, the confused,[3] those with tremors,[4] those with headaches, migraines, gout, strangury, dysuria,

---

1. The Latin is *vomitibus* "by vomiting(s)"; but the probable meaning is what causes the vomiting.
2. The Latin is *nephriticos* meaning clearly a "kidney problem," perhaps a kidney stone. The word was not found as such in the standard sources.
3. The Latin is *devios* from *devius* and indicates "off the mark."
4. The Latin is *tremulosos* and may refer to shivering, shaking, or tremors.

fevers; suffering heat; having liver complaints, fistulas, phthisis; those with dysentery or wounded by snakes; the hysterical or epileptics; those with stomach issues or with catarrh; the frantic; those with epiphora or white spots; and those pained by many diseases. He did not apply the strongest tincture, whether the Alexandrine compound, the Saracen compound, the great compound,[5] the purging tincture,[6] the reddish tincture,[7] the Pauline tincture, or *apostolicon,* or *gera logodion,* or Hadrian medicine, or any potion to them, but he infused them with the grace given above. In fact, melancholy, red bile, black bile, phlegm, or blood in no way prevails in doing harm where His most potent power is present.[8] He helps humankind with the salutary applications of divine medicine better than Hippocrates, Dioscorides, Galen, Macer, Vindicianus, Serenus, Tullius,[9] or the other physicians involved with the physical

---

5. Latin *triferam,* a compound medicine with many various recipes.
6. The Latin is *geram pigram.* Nathan Bailey, *An Universal Etymological English Dictionary* (London: Printed for E. Bell, 1724) defines "hiera picra" as "a purging electuary made of aloes, lignum aloes, spikenard, saffron, mastic, honey, etc." *Medieval Medicine: A Reader,* ed. Faith Wallis (Toronto: University of Toronto Press, 2010), 546, describes *gera* as "a generic and honorific title for certain noteworthy compound medicines. The most widely known was *hiera* (or *gera*) *pigra,* 'holy bitters,' a cathartic of which the principal ingredient was tincture of aloes. *Hierologodion* was used to treat melancholy."
7. Latin *geram rufinam,* assuming it derives from *rufus* (red) with a diminutive ending, it could refer to a reddish herb.
8. A reference to the four humors (blood, phlegm, black bile, yellow bile), in turn related to the four elements (air, water, earth, fire); the four personality types (sanguine, phlegmatic, melancholic, choleric); and symbolic of the world (four seasons, four directions).
9. Hippocrates, Greek physician, 450–370BCE; Pedanius Dioscorides, Greek physician, d.90CE; Aelius or Claudius Galen of Pergamon, Greek physician, 129–210CE; either Aemelius Macer (d.c.16BCE), a poet who wrote on birds, serpents, and natural phenomena or Macer Floridus, a French physician named Ode de Meung-sur-Loire (first half of 11th C), author of *De Viribus herbarum* under the name Macer Floridus; Helvius Vindicianus, Roman physician, 340–400CE; Quintus Serenus Sammonicus, Roman medical writer, d.212CE; perhaps Marcus Tullius Cicero, 106–43BCE for *De natura deorum* or *De senectute et de amicitia.*

arts. Hippocrates, in fact, and his followers were useful only to the human body. James, however, has power from heaven for the body and soul. It is not worth the pain of describing how many powers and signs and wonders Christ showed to people through him. He lived for a short time after the Passion of Christ, but he gained a great number of people. He was, in fact, very handsome in form, decorous in appearance, tall in stature, chaste in body, devout in mind, amiable in demeanor, gifted in prudence, bright in temperance, firm in internal strength, assiduous in forbearance, robust in patience, mild in humility, thoroughly moved in love, patient in hope, sensible in vigils, assiduous in prayer, kind in teaching, most truthful in word, cautious in speech, most prudent in counsel, chained to the world with no shackle, prolix in liberality to the needy, ready for allegiance to the servants of God, very strong like mustard in adversities,[10] cautious in temptation, most cheerful in hospitality, fearless amid abusive situations, generous amid animosities. The enemy of the human race could not, in fact, find within him anything that would deceive by fraud or anything that would obscure by deceit.

What more should I dwell in saying? In his every conversation, he shone [f.26r] like Venus among the stars and gleamed like a great torch. For Christ, the King of kings, had chosen him as a soldier, as one whom He would direct like the gentlest lamb against the most monstrous legions of beasts. He said, "'Behold! I send you like lambs among wolves.'" [Lk 10:3] And so, the man of God, vigorous with the Holy Spirit, the strongest warrior, the proper soldier, the extraordinary standard bearer, protected by a shield of faith, dressed in the laurel of justice, powerfully girded with the sword of the word of God, covered with the helmet of salvation, furnished with shoes in preparation for the Gospel of peace,[11] went

---

10. A probable reference to the story of the mustard seed in the Bible, referring to the plant's quick growth and large size in contrast to its seed. Cf. Mt 13:31, 17:19; Mk 4:31; Lk 13:19, 17:6. Given the previous passage about medicines, it might also be a reminder of mustard's medicinal qualities

11. Cf. Eph 6:10–18; James is described as wearing the full armor of God.

CHAPTER SIX

forth into public battle against the ancient enemy. He ground down all the vilest weapons, he subdued the lofty powers, and with the strength of Christ, he plucked the men created by God from the hand of death, and the Church of Christ obtained many spoils from the enemy that he conquered. One should be as anxious about the enemy of the human race as about what is necessary for the human race, in as much as he sought not only his own salvation but also that of many. Therefore, it is fitting that the one who was the redeemer of so many through Christ should be praised by the mouth of many in Christ. It is not only being told which miracles he performed, as much as recognizing the power of the miracles,[12] which in his days acquired a great number of people for the kingdom of heaven. Oh, what a venerable apostle of Christ! Oh, what a marvelous man, overflowing with piety, abounding with mercy, flourishing with charity! He is, in fact, the true cultivator of God, who has planted the Church with his blood, adorned it with great humility, cultivated it with true charity, increased it with preaching, and watered it with the celestial dew of perpetual salvation. From there, divine mercy, through his watering, yielded many increases of faith among the peoples. He, however, not only gleamed brightly in the regions around Jerusalem through the light of his preaching and works of piety, but he also, like the morning star, hastened as a herald of the light of day and scattered the nocturnal shadows on the even surfaces of the fields of the oceans. Thus, his fame lit the outer nations and regions with the grace of miracles as he moved here and there, so that in the whole globe his glory would fight on up until today.

---

12. The words "recognize the power of the mira-" are found in the margin of CC with a red cross designating their insertion point in the text; they are in the body of the text in S. Bk. II specifically describes 22 miracles, but there are numerous others included in these sermons and in Bk. V, the *Pilgrim's Guide*.

Concerning his virtues and exhortations, Saint Fortunatus, the extraordinary versifier, confessor, and bishop sang in this way, saying:[13]

1. The sound of the cultivator of the Lord goes out in the world
2. There is no place where the towering glory is denied.
3. The noble one, coming from the ancient seed of the fathers
4. But much more noble in the service of Christ;
5. Honored summit, nourishing grace, most favorable light
6. In whose praises all grace does service.
7. Spring of his family, protector of his country, reproach [f.26v] of the people,
8. River of eloquence, spring of good taste, wave of loquaciousness,
9. Preserving with modesty his members unstained for God
10. Because faith conveyed him toward the stars for his merits.
11. Patience rules as victor under his chest;
12. Thought was an anchor in so many waves.
13. Lacking in bitterness, placid in mind, fed on sweetness,
14. The ire of animosity cannot bring on retaliation.
15. Sweet in eloquence, peaceful in sacred moderation,
16. In his thought, ire has lost its place.
17. The agitation of the one overcomes in his enduring chest,
18. While shallowness has vexed him, he has born it with gravitas.

---

13. This poem is not set apart in either CC or S. In order to clarify its sources, we have numbered each line. This poem is a collection of verses from Venantius Fortunatus's *Miscellanea* (PL 88) with two verses (27–28) from Calixtus (verses 7–8 of his *Salve Festa dies,* found below, ch.25, p. 369). The breakdown for each verse of this poem to Fortunatus's book, chapter and verse follows: verses 1–2 are 1:9:1–2; 3–4 are 4:11–12; 5 is 5:9:1; 6–9 are 3:8:16–18; 9 is 4:6:7; 10 is 4:6:6; 11–14 are 4:6:9–12; 15–18 are 4:1:11–14; 19–20 are 4:6:13–14; 21–22 are 2:11:7–8; 23 is 10:7:45; 24 is 3:22:14; 25–26 are 2:11:13–14; 29–42 are 5:2:29–42; and 43–56 are 5:2:45–58. Some variations occur in word order and word choice: for example, *Offensi nescit* for *Nescit offensi* in verse 14 and *Fons* "Spring" for *Flos* "Flower" in verse 7.

CHAPTER SIX

19. As cultivator of the temples, he restores the citizens with melody.
20. He was a faithful remedy for the wounds of the country,
21. Choosing to break the chains of the bodily prison
22. So that man might join together more fully with the Lord.
23. He who furnishes many miracles for the earthly lands,
24. Whence a more singular love arises for the people
25. Showing with words, adding miracles to the deeds,
26. So that works might accompany what words had presented.
27. He teaches the Gentiles, he rebukes the Jews,
28. He plants faith on the earth and is fruitful to God.
29. He affixes to the branches of heresy the pious seeds of faith,
30. And what was a wild olive tree, flourishes as a strong olive tree.
31. That which stood thin and devoid of leaves
32. Is ready to bear food and flourishes with new honor.
33. Without hope, the sad fig tree is about to be set on the hearth:
34. One prepares a vessel for the fruit from cultivated dung.
35. The swelling grape of the vine branch, about to be lacerated by the plundering of birds,
36. Because of this good guard, it will not to perish until [it is] in the vat.
37. The vine dresser beforehand has directed with apostolic tools,
38. Moving with a hoe through the field, pressing with a knife on the shoot.
39. From the field of the Lord, he cuts out the sluggish wild grape
40. And what was before brush, presents itself as a cluster of grapes.
41. From the sowing of God, he plucks the bitter cockles,
42. And the equally gladdened wheat arises.
43. By the effort of the shepherd coming back around his enclosed places
44. He preserves, out of love, his flocks, lest the wolf enter among the sheep.
45. He supports them with his hand and leads them to the nourishment of Christ

46. Lest, straying to the mountain, beasts destroy the tottering sheep.
47. His voice flows to the people from the salubrious spring
48. So that they may drink the faith with their ears; he offers salt from his mouth.[14]
49. He has certainly prepared damage for the enemies and pious prayers for the Lord.
50. He brings back doubled the talents entrusted to him.
51. This nourishing laborer looks toward the divine voice
52. So that it may be said to him: "Young and good servant, hasten!
53. Since you were faithful to Me over small things,
54. You will be set over many things beyond measure.
55. Behold now the joys of your Lord and enter more gladly,
56. And for this short work, great things are prepared for you."

Wisdom describes his great goodness and says among other things: "He will appear in the midst of great men and in the sight of the ruler, and he will pass over in the land of foreign peoples [f.27r] for he will handle good things and bad things in all." [Ecclus (Sir) 39:4–5] Saint James ministered "in the midst of the great men," since he afforded with his preaching the salubrious rations of eternal life to the hearts of kings and princes. He appeared "in the sight of the ruler," since he preached undauntedly the word of the Lord before King Herod. He passed over "in the land of the foreign peoples," since he spread the name of the Lord from Jerusalem to Galicia. He "handled good and evil in all things," since he introduced the Gospel teaching to the Jewish and Gentile people, and he cut away heretical depravity. In fact, the Lord ordered him to do this through the prophet Isaiah, saying, "I place you as a light for the peoples, so that you may be for salvation up to the end of the earth." [Acts 13:47, Is 49:6] The holy apostle is placed "as a light for

---

14. The comparison carries through obliquely in English, but essentially one must flavor the words to make them more appetizing to the ear.

the peoples," since he cast out the darkness of sins and brought the light of the true faith to the peoples with his preaching. He was "for salvation up to the end of the earth," since He Who is the salvation of all people made him known to the farthest islands of the seas.

Thus, in fact, the Lord once promised through the prophet Joel to all peoples, as he said: "Exult, daughters of Zion and rejoice in the Lord your God, since He gave you a teacher of justice, and he will make morning rain and evening rain come down to you in the beginning." [Joel 2:23] "The daughters of Zion exult in the Lord" when the souls of the baptized — which are the daughters of Zion, that is, of the Holy Church — rejoice in Christ through doing good work and through divine contemplation. Saint James was the "teacher of justice" given to the daughters of Zion, since with his divine word he made it obvious to the daughters of the Church by what route of just faith they should go to the kingdom of the heavens. He made an agreeable "morning rain come down to them," since by the grace of God the Spirit came down to the voice of his preaching, so that it might rouse the listeners. The prophet calls the Holy Spirit the "morning rain," since, just as the morning rain renders the earth wet so that the sun does not excessively damage the seeds, so also the nourishing Spirit fortifies the minds of the listeners with the word of God, lest the temptation of the devil and warm and depraved fickleness destroy it. The prophet calls the Spirit of the Lord the "evening rain" since, just as the evening dew moistens the cultivated and uncultivated ground but makes only the cultivated germinate, so the nourishing Spirit, although it breathes on all, abides and bears fruit only among the good. In fact, the Lord Himself says elsewhere through the prophet: "Over whom does my spirit rest other than above the humble and the quiet dreading my words?"[15] The prophet calls God the Father the Beginning, since all things have taken their beginning and will finally [f.27v] take their end through Him. He said: "I am 'the beginning who also speaks to

---

15. This is not found in the Bible, although it was a quote found among writers. It is unclear if it resulted from readings of a biblical text or through some other route.

you.'" [Jn 8:25] Therefore Saint James made "the rain come down" to the daughters of Zion in the beginning, since he shows the Holy Spirit to be in the Father and in the Son in his preaching to the daughters of the Church. This fulfills what Isaiah said: "The Lord has made my mouth like a sharpened sword." [Is 49:2] The apostle is a sharpened sword, for just as the two-sided sword cuts quickly to the right and left, so those He has judged to be good and saved are to come to the right of the future judge and those judged to be bad and damned are to come to the left.

Again Isaiah says: "And he made me like a chosen arrow." [Is 49:2] Certainly the chosen arrow is the one that, once sent, kills its enemy. And as three things exist in the arrow — namely, the iron that penetrates, the wood that keeps it straight, and the feather that directs it — the arrow shows the trinity and unity of the Lord. And so, Saint James was the chosen arrow, since as the quick arrow of the one shooting it kills the enemy, so he also destroys the enemy of the human race and has destroyed the heaps of vices by preaching the unity and trinity of the Lord. Again, the prophet says: "In his quiver He hides me." [Is 49:2] The quiver is figuratively the womb of the inviolate Blessed Virgin Mary, in which the chosen arrow — that is, the Son of God, the one and triune God — lay hidden. The arrow is hidden in the quiver, since the divinity is lodged in His humanity. For in it "lived bodily the fullness of His divinity." [Col 2:9] Therefore, the Lord hides Saint James in His quiver, since He imbued him in the abode of his humanity with propitious teachings. And He said to him again through the prophet: "'Make your cords long and make your nails firm. You will penetrate, in fact, to the left and the right; and your seed shall inherit the peoples.'" [Is 54:2–3] By cords, of course, are meant those things by means of which two different things of whatever type are usually joined together, and they designate the precepts of the Lord, by which God and man, through the maintenance of good works, join together. Disunion once happened between God and man through the sin of the first man, but now there is union through the practice of the Lord's precepts. Therefore, he [James] made his apostles into long cords, since he extended the Gospel teachings from Judea to

CHAPTER SIX

the Mediterranean or Western Sea. He made his nails firm, since he fastened the counsels of the Catholic Faith to the hearts of men. He penetrated to the right and left, since [f.28r] he foretold of the heavenly reward for the good works for the chosen and the terror of the last judgment for the condemned. And his seed inherited the peoples, since through the seed of his preaching he made faithful peoples heirs of the heavenly kingdom.

Just as the sun of the day lights the day and the moon lights the darknesses of night, so also he shone in the Holy Church with doctrines. Just as the rainbow shines with various colors among the clouds in the sky, so he shone fervently with divine virtues among the adversities of the savage Gentiles and Jews. Like a rose blooming among thorns and the lily flowering near the waters, so he flourished with divine examples among the peoples. Just as incense and frankincense emit a scent with fire, so also he arose as the scent of eternal life for the salvation of all the peoples so that he might call all to the kingdom of eternal happiness. For divine virtue shone in him in life, in manners, in preaching the word, in gentleness and mildness of spirit, in proofs and signs, and also in all mortification of the flesh, in fasts and in divine prayers. He went around estates, fortresses, small villages, and through the synagogues of the Jews, preaching the word of God, insisting in an unbridled and opportune way, that the one light and law of perpetual life might become clear to all people ignorant of God, and together all would rise again to life who had descended to death.

Indeed, being fortified with the zeal of faith, he did not cease to preach the name of Christ within the sight and hearing of the savage Jews and Gentiles either because of threats of princes or the words of the unjust until the hour of his death. Truly, like a follower sent by a great emperor to great crowds of peoples, he did not fear to send out the light of truth, so that where many were gathered, many would be instructed by his example or teaching. For just as a fisherman extends his nets where he knows a great number of fish gather, and just as the most skilled birdcatcher or hunter extends his snares where he knows a great number of birds or land animals are brought together so that when many are gathered there a great portion of them may be caught, so Saint James, the fisher of men and hunter of wild creatures, did not cease to extend the nets of his preaching to the multitudes of the peoples, so that, as many were gathered near the hold of this device, many would be caught by the great snare of his preaching. And just as the faithful steward is set over his family by the Lord so that he might give them food at the required time, so also he hastened to refresh the barbarous peoples with all sorts [f.28v] of foods: teaching mercifully, instructing very well, and striving with all his strength to bring all back from the errors of idols. Oh, that abundant vessel of the Holy Spirit that serves in abundance the people the fullness of the grain of Christ and the happiness of the oil and the sober intoxication of the wine! He was an eye for the blind and a foot for the lame, a father of the poor and wretched, and a comforter of orphans and widows. He was like a sailor who led the ship of the Church, filled with the riches of people, through the sea of this undulating world and put down the anchor of faith at the port of salvation. He was like the keeper of vineyards who planted the ecclesiastic vineyard with great labor, eradicating the thistles of vices, cutting back the thorns of perverse acts, establishing good branches, tending the fence of Gospel teachings around it against the barbarous beasts, driving out far from it the heretical foxes whose custom it is to destroy the vines, building the structure[16] for a new altar and a tower of faith in the vineyard. He first skillfully ploughed the uncultivated land, like the modern ploughman with the ploughshare of his new preaching and the plough of faith, so that also those coming later could more quickly plough with preaching, and so that the ground cleansed from the brambles of vices might take the seed and more abundantly bear fruit — one a hundredfold, another sixty-fold.[17]

---

16. The Latin *torcularem* means both a "press" and a "cellar," referring generally to the structures needed for the vineyard, and thus the translation of "structure."

17. In Latin, "sixes" were often used where we would use tens or hundreds. This is likely akin to our use of "dozens."

CHAPTER SIX

And just as someone knowing the difficulties of this science lays out a path in woody places toward some city, so the blessed apostle, bearer of the new law, a most appropriate traveller, built a road of faith toward heaven: leveling the rough road, pushing back hard rocks, straightening the crooked path, driving the impediments of the divine commands into the thickets next to it; and so that those following might be able to go more clearly, he made the narrow path into a wide road for the journey of those coming after him. Behold, the path is, in fact, crooked along the way![18] The path of the Old Testament was narrow and crooked, through which few walked to heaven at that time, but now the road of the New Testament is wide and straight, through which many walk. And so, as the fame of the great James grew far and wide throughout the world, many Jews came to him, and Gentiles, and worshipers of idols, and they were baptized, and the idols were destroyed by those who had made them. For this reason the ancient enemy suffered, seeing himself losing the peoples that Christ was acquiring through his servant, and he turned all the devices of his trade to attacking the Church of God, and he inflamed Herod, the king of the Jews, and moved him to such a rage of indignation [f.29r] that he would take the apostle and kill him. And thus Herod, roused by the dart of envy, "sent his band of men so that it might afflict some from the Church, and he killed James, the brother of John, with the sword." [Acts 12:1] Woe! Woe! Exceedingly treacherous business! He killed the one whom the angel of the Lord had once released from prison in Jerusalem. He killed the one whom the Lord had chosen from the world and consecrated and whom He made worthy and dear to Him. He murdered the one through whom the Lord had worked signs and miracles in the world. But after James the Great, apostle and champion of Christ the invincible martyr, endured willingly out of love for Christ the sword of Herod, and his nourishing soul, freed from bodily chains and liberated from

---

18. "Behold the path...along the way" is written in the margin in CC, with a red cross designating the insertion point in the text; it is in the body of the text in S.

earthly pressures, finally mounted toward the applauding angels and returned joyfully to its Creator, the body returned to the soil, the spirit returned to the seats of paradise, where it was brought together with the assembly of angels and reigns and exults in the greatness of its merits. Propitious, therefore, the pain of the wound by which he acquired the palm of eternal life, as he conquered death with death, grasped the golden crown, and possessed the kingdoms of paradise. Having shed his blood, he became a victim for God. And so with Herod killing James, the phalanx of angels rejoiced because it had received a comrade. The flock of the faithful on the earth was saddened because it had lost its shepherd. The crowd of idolaters was gladdened, because it saw its prosecutor dead. Concerning the most glorious death of Saint James, Fortunatus, the bishop of Poitiers, confessor of Christ, and splendid versifier,[19] sang in this way in pentameters, saying:[20]

1. James sent his soul from the lands to Olympus.
2. O happy one, by whose violent death, death is suppressed.
3. Before the sepulchers of the pious, at times, the gifts of salvation are given
4. And his mutilated body assists many bodies.
5. Say where, hostile death, do you lie? Where, vanquished death, do you rest?
6. When do you see prayers delivered badly at the funeral rites of a saint?
7. What well-being did you believe by death to have finished off?
8. He gives life to many, and he keeps his own.

---

19. See ch. 2, n. 122.
20. As with the previous poem in this chapter (pp. 90–92), this poem is not set apart as such in either CC or S. We have again numbered each line. It also is a collection of verses from Venantius Fortunatus (PL 88, various columns). The following gives the book: chapter: verse of Fortunatus's *Miscellanea* work for each verse of this poem: verses 1–2 are 2:12:17–18; 3–18 are 2:11:37–52; 19–20 are 4:4:31–32; and 21–22 are 4:2:11–12. There are some variations in the wording. Notably James is not present in Fortunatus; the word *Iacobus*, appears as *Hac ope* or "with this strength" in line 1.

9. You lie here, captive one, who thought you ruled yourself;
10. By assailing you die, by raging you destroy yourself.
11. Your pain bears down on you; your chains also twist you.
12. Those sighs you wish to utter, you moan from carrying them;
13. The exulting martyr retains the heavens, you are sad and livid.
14. Death, you inhabit the black and hostile inferior regions for yourself.
15. The blessed one now stays without end on a flowery seat
16. Among the fragrant bands of heaven with glowing incense.
17. With the judge appeased, he has not feared any situations.
18. The victorious soldier seeks to have rewards
19. Out of merit: thus, James is carried [f.29v] to the heavens,
20. The urn of the grave does not press him down, but the arm of God holds him up.
21. If you seek merit, the miracles of his deeds stand out,
22. Through him, kind salvation is procured for the weak.[21]

But it should be considered that Herod, the beheader of James, signifies figuratively the devil reigning in the world pursuing the Lord through his followers as is said: "A skin for a skin and let a man give all that he has for his soul." [Job 2:4] And elsewhere: "The enemy said, 'I will pursue and seize, I will divide the spoils, and my soul will be filled.'" [Ex 15:9] For just as our adversary the devil wanted to upset the Passion of Christ — that is our salvation — through the dreaming wife of Pilate, saying: "it is nothing for you and for this just man," [Mt 27:19] thus Herod, with the devil's coaxing, wished to upset the apostolic preaching destined by God for the peoples by killing James. Herod is interpreted as "made of skins" or the "glory of skin."[22] This interpretation is fitting for him,

---

21. CC here reads *dabilis* or "for the possible" while Venantius and S have *debilibus* or "for the weak."
22. An invented etymology. Herod actually derives from the Greek ἥρως (heros) meaning "hero," or "warrior," and ᾠδή (oides) meaning "ode" or "song."

since he did not think of heavenly glory but of the glory of the skin and flesh. Such are those "whose God is the stomach, and purpose is death, and glory is in their blushing, and who savor earthly things." [Phil 3:19] And so Herod killed the apostle of the Lord, for he thought he would lose his kingdom though him. He feared losing the earthly kingdom more than the eternal one. But since the Lord wanted to avenge the death of his apostle, he permitted Herod to suffer death in the way that the book of the Acts of the Apostles[23] says: "Herod, seeing that the death of James seemed to be pleasing to the Jews…and took Peter the apostle and cast him into prison." [Acts 12:3–4] But Peter, with an angel of the Lord leading him, escaped at night unharmed. When, however, day had broken, and Peter was not found,[24] the sorrowful Herod

> went down from Judea to Caesarea; and he stayed there. He was, however, angered with the Tyrians and the Sidonians. They, however, all decided to come to Herod, as Blastus who was the king's chamberlain had persuaded them to do, and they sought peace, because their regions were maintained by him. On the appointed day, Herod, dressed in regal garb, sat before the tribunal, and spoke sublimely to them. The people, in fact, exclaimed: "The sounds of God, and not of man!" However, an angel of the Lord immediately struck him, and he died, consumed by worms, because he had not given honor to God [Acts 12:19–22]

and because he had shed the blood of Saint James unjustly. And so, Herod killed James, and the angel of the Lord killed him. An innocent man was murdered by an impious man, and the impious man was killed by the angel. Rarely do we read that any one of the persecutors of the apostles was killed by the Lord through an angel, except for this Herod who beheaded James. From this it is understood that this James was loved by the Lord because of the great honor [f.30r] of his preference ahead of the others. Therefore, he was loved greatly by the Lord both on earth and in heaven. O Herod, impious king, cruel enemy of the Lord, why did you kill

23. Acts 12.
24. Cf. Acts 12:5–18.

such a great man? Did you not know that you would be killed by the Lord? You killed the armor bearer, and you were killed by a soldier. You killed a servant, and you were killed by his Lord. O nourishing apostle of God, why did you endure so many things? You certainly endured so many things, since you were worthy to suffer reproaches in the name of Jesus. You knew, in fact, that "the sufferings of this time are not worthy of comparison to the future glory." [Rom 8:18] O pious God, why did you allow the apostle to be killed? So that you might kill the king later? Therefore, assuredly, as you would prepare a crown for the apostle, you would also prepare a death for the wicked king. Then both received the pay due for their merits. You gave to each according to his merit, since you bestowed on the apostle the crown of the kingdom and on the king, the Gehenna[25] of fire. And so what is read in the Book of Wisdom, is fulfilled with this deed:

> The just dead man, however, condemns the impious who are living, and the youth killed quickly condemns the long life of the unjust man, for they shall see then the end of the wise man and will not understand what God was considering with him and why the Lord would protect him, for they will see him such that they despise him, but the Lord will laugh at them. After this, they will fall without honor, and they will be in reproach among the dead forever. [Wis 4:16–19]

Therefore, the apostle of Christ rejoices in that perpetual happiness where happiness is without pain, life is without death, and joy is unspeakable. He fought for the faith of God on earth. Therefore he is crowned in glory, revered by the angels, honored by all the saints, whiter than snow, brighter than the sun, more brilliant than a star, more refined than milk, and redder than ancient ivory.[26] Now he sees face to face the One Whom he saw in the apparition on Mount Tabor. Now he sees eternally, then it was temporally. Now it is with love, then it was with fear. Now he is restored at the divine feasts with the Lord eternally, while he celebrated the final banquet after the Resurrection at the Sea of Galilee temporally. Now

---

25. This is the first use in this text of Gehenna as a variant for hell.
26. See ch. 2, n. 47.

he possesses that most excellent gift in the heavens that he sought from the Lord when he was on earth. He knowingly possesses the seat with the chosen on the Lord's right that he unknowingly sought from Him. His solemnities are not called funereal but natal, since he then began to live when he left this world. And as was written [f.30v] about a certain perfect man: "He was removed from living among sinners," [Wis 4:10] "since his soul was pleasing to God." [Wis 4:14] Concerning such things it is indeed said by Solomon: "The just man is freed from distress." [Prov 11:8] Concerning men of this kind the Lord says through Malachi: "He walked in peace and equity with me, and he turned many from iniquity." [Mal 2:6] On this, the Lord speaks through Isaiah saying: "I have called him and blessed him, and his way is made straight." [Is 48:15] On this also He says in the Book of Ecclesiasticus: "To the one fearing God it will be well at the end, and on the day of death, he will be blessed." [Ecclus (Sir) 1:13] On this the Book of Wisdom says: "The fruit of his good labors is glorious," [Wis 3:15] "and he triumphs crowned forever." [Wis 4:2] Thence the Psalmist says: "The just man shall be in eternal memory; he shall not fear bad news." [Ps 111:7 / 112:6–7] Truly the one whom the Lord exalted with the grace of preaching and miracles is worthily kept in the memory of angels and men. "He will not fear bad news" when the Lord says: "Depart from me, accursed ones." [Mt 25:41]

This James is truly not only read about in the New Testament, but he is also pointed out in the Old Testament: he is fashioned on Jacob; he is demonstrated in Israel. And since the name "James" comes from the prophet Jacob, and he is interpreted as a supplanter like him, he is known to have been of his race, and he is like him in many aspects. It should be noted, however, that Jacob, the son of Isaac, symbolizes the Gentile people; Esau, the Jewish people; Isaac, God the Father; and Rebecca, the Holy Spirit. The grace of blessing was once fitting for the Jewish people, but since they hesitated to come to the faith almost out of venery, the Gentile people received it. The disciples spoke to the Jews in this manner: "It was certainly necessary to speak the word of God first to you, but since you have rejected it and have judged yourselves unworthy of eternal life, we

CHAPTER SIX

are turned to the Gentiles." [Acts 13:46] Just as Jacob, in fact, obeyed the counsels of his mother, whence he acquired the blessing of his father, so also our James obeyed the nourishing Spirit, whence he acquired the grace of the Father. Jacob, in giving beans, bought the first-born rights of his brother, and our Jacob in leaving his earthly things behind purchased the heavenly things. Jacob observed the angelic throng on Mount Bethel, while our James also beheld not angels but the Son of God Himself transformed in the glory of the Father on Mount Tabor. Jacob the patriarch, in supplanting his brother, obtained his father's blessing, while James, in supplanting the vices of the flesh, obtained association with the Lord. Jacob begot twelve sons, while James brought forth many children in faith. He is figuratively one of the twelve sons of Israel from which he created peoples of the faithful Church. He is figuratively one of the twelve [f.31r] springs of Elim that the Hebrew people found, along with sixty palms while walking through the deserts. From these, up until today, the Church is watered. He is figuratively one of the twelve princes set up by Moses to guide the Hebrew people. From these princes the nourishing Church takes guidance to some extent. He is figuratively one of the twelve precious stones portrayed on the garment of Aaron, from which the Church stands, "on the right of God in gilded clothing, surrounded by the variety of the merits of the saints." [Ps 44:10 / 45:9] He is one of the twelve loaves of proposition,[27] always warm, offered on the table of the Lord, from which the whole world is fed. He is figuratively one of the twelve scouts sent out by Moses to the Promised Land, who, on coming back, carried between two of them a palm hanging on a pole with a grape cluster and also carrying pomegranates and figs. Understand the grape cluster between the two to be Christ between the two Testaments, the pomegranates as the martyrs, the figs as the doctrines of the Church, and the scouts as the twelve apostles who up until today do not cease to announce the delights of the heavenly kingdom to the Church of God. He is one of the twelve stones of the Jordan that are carried by the chosen men of the twelve tribes into the places of the forts in testimony of the miracles of God, in

---

27. Cf. Ex 35:13.

which every building of a church is constructed. He is figuratively one of the twelve stones that Joshua placed in the midst of the channel of the Jordan, where the feet of the priests bearing the Ark of the Covenant stood,[28] and they remain unmoved up until today and show the way to the faithful in the baptism of Christ.

By his prayers may we deserve to be helped by our Lord Jesus Christ, Who with the Father and the Holy Spirit lives and reigns as God. World without end. Amen.

---

28. The Ark of the Covenant was brought into the Holy Land when Joshua crossed the Jordan with the Twelve Tribes. See Joshua 3–5.

[CHAPTER 7]

VIII CALENDS OF AUGUST[1]
PASSION OF SAINT JAMES OF GALICIA

A READING FROM THE ACTS OF THE APOSTLES:

"In those days, prophets came to Antioch from Jerusalem, and one of them by the name of Agabus rose up and indicated through the Spirit that a great famine was to come over the whole world, and it occurred under Claudius," and so forth. [Acts 11:27–28ff.]

A SERMON OF POPE SAINT CALIXTUS ON THIS SAME READING: [F.31V]

Dearest brethren, the most illustrious feast day of the most glorious and distinguished James of Zebedee is at hand for us. On this day, the holy apostle and patron of Galicia, with the bonds of the flesh broken, transcended the heavens and bonded with the angelic throngs.[2]

Today James, the champion of Christ, earned the glory of the heavens in which he reigns happily with the Lord and is joined with the bands of angels. Today is that day on which the ancient enemy is overcome, God is exalted, and the Christian people are made illustrious. The Christian people are made illustrious on this day, for whenever a martyr suffers for the faith of Christ, an example of suffering is left for the world, and the devil is confounded.

Let Spain rejoice, since it is led by his merits to the palaces of heaven! Let Galicia be glad, since it is made famous by his presence! Let the whole Church exult throughout the world, since it is enriched through his examples! Let the court of the heavens delight, since it is increased in glory through his fellowship! Let all the islands throughout the seas be glad, since they have obtained a defender in their distress! Let all the world be glad, since today

---

1. July 25.
2. The Latin plays off the words *nexibus* "bonds" and *annexus* "bonded."

its enemy, the devil, has been conquered with the grace of God at work through James! Let the throng of the faithful exult, since today James subdues the enemy of the human race! Let the faithful chorus rejoice as one, since today the apostle, girded with the arms of faith, has triumphed over Herod!

Today the soldier of Christ, with the enemy conquered and with Herod overthrown, has ascended to the palace of the eternal King, so that he may sit with the princes of the heavens and possess a throne of glory. He has run the race of martyrdom successfully, whence he has deserved to receive the reward of victory of the heavenly kingdom eternally. Therefore, since today he lawfully triumphed over the evil king, he has acquired the kingdom of the heavens as a victor. For as often as martyrs suffer for Christ, their recompense is that much increased with God, but the punishment of those pursuing them is not diminished.

Today the conqueror climbs to the heavens, since he has overcome the impious Herod. Therefore, his passion is celebrated in the world, so that, in the manner of his strength, our weakness may be lifted up in God. He, in fact, who died for the faith of Christ on earth, shows us an example of holding fast to the faith and suffering in practice and life; and when we celebrate the day of the one who died with a solemn service, [f.32r] we show that he may truly live with God and may be resurrected happily on the last day, and we may receive the crown of perpetual glory together with him. And so today, the head of the ancient serpent is destroyed, and the power of faith is increased, and an example of victory is handed to the faithful, confusion is given to the unfaithful, and the banners of virtues are raised just as the large assembly of this present day testifies. For when the Church celebrates the solemn feasts of the martyrs, it not only honors their victory, but also the confused barbarity of the unfaithful is set aside.[3] Once, in fact, the heretics and many unfaithful persons used to chatter nonsense about the

---

3. The Latin is *deliratur*, presumably from *delirare* meaning "to deviate"; apparently here it is used in a passive sense of "is made to deviate" or "is set aside."

CHAPTER SEVEN

holy martyrs when they saw them endure diverse punishments for the faith of Christ, but now, with things turned round, they rave whenever a feast of the martyrs is celebrated.

Today the Passion of Saint James is venerated, since he is crowned happily in glory. Today the proven irreverence of Herod is set aside and detested, since he was stricken by an angel of the Lord, consumed by worms, and died. Today the devil was overcome in his follower[4] Herod, and Christ triumphed in his follower James. James was compelling Herod to turn away from idols and enter the faith by stealth, but Herod threatened him if he would not attend to the gods. However, James was indifferent, and in fact, rejoiced in having that Helper Whose glory, majesty, voice, and power he had once seen on Mount Tabor. He trusted in Him Whom he had observed resurrected from the dead after breaking the chains of death and triumphing over the Prince of Hell and Whom he knew to reign with the Father. He was, without doubt, filled with His Spirit. He had his hope in the One Who had called him to Himself on the Sea of Galilee for the love of Whom he left all things, and Whose steps he imitated unto the heavens through the suffering of the body. Today that day has shone brightly on the world, on which the holy apostle of the Lord drank the cup and obtained possession of a seat of glory in heaven. Thus, in fact, he was promised before by his Teacher Who said: "You will certainly drink My cup." [Mt 20:23; cf. Mk 10:39]

Today he drank the cup of martyrdom and was made a friend of God, as the present solemnity makes clear. Today he, who is already rejoicing in heavenly glory, was killed by Herod. He took off the mortal tunic and put on the immortal stole. However, in what order or at what time or under which people the blessed apostle wanted to drink the cup, should be considered by us. The lawful man James, of course, wanted [f.32v] to have as witnesses known people — kings and emperors and prophets — namely Agabus the prophet, Claudius emperor of Rome, and Herod, king of the

---

4. The Latin is *membro* or "member"; the sense in English requires "follower."

Jerusalemites. In this way he would show that not only prophets of the Old Law, but also kings and emperors of the Gentiles and all the great men of the world must by right first enter the faith of Christ. Since under them he freely endured his passion for the faith of Christ, he showed that not only the great men of the world, but also those placed below them, must accept the same faith of Christ. Thus, in fact, Saint Luke the Evangelist says in this reading: "Prophets came to Antioch from Jerusalem; and one of them by the name of Agabus rose up and indicated through the Spirit that a great famine was to come over the whole world, and it occurred under Claudius." [Acts 11:27–28] And since Saint James not only wanted to have prophets and emperors but also kings as witnesses of his passion, the Evangelist says a little afterward: "At that same time, however, King Herod sent a force to afflict some from the Church. And he killed James, the brother of John, with a sword." [Acts 12:1–2]

However, one should first seek out what this famine that occurred under Claudius meant, so that through this matter we may come to a contemplation of heaven. Saint Luke the Evangelist also testifies that Saint James drank the cup of martyrdom at the time when the dire famine was at hand, which was proclaimed by Agabus the prophet in Antioch while Claudius was reigning as emperor over the whole world. The brothers who were at Antioch sent aid — according to what each had — through the hands of Saul and Barnabas to the holy inhabitants of Jerusalem, lest they perish from the famine.[5] Famine in sacred speech usually means a famine of the soul desiring the spiritual food of divine scriptures. For just as the body dies unless it should have bodily food, so also the soul is worn away unless it should have the spiritual food of the divine scriptures. The Lord spoke about this famine through the prophet: "I will send famine over the earth, not a hunger[6] for bread nor a thirst for water, but for hearing the word of God." [Amos 8:11] The

---

5. Cf. Acts 11:28–30.
6. The Latin *fames* can be both "hunger" and "famine"; it is rendered here as one or the other according to context.

sacred words of the scriptures are food for the soul. They supply the unfailing Bread of eternal life to those speaking and working. It is that Bread that speaks of Itself: "I am the Bread of life Who has come down from heaven." [Jn 6:41; 6:51] The time of the famine in which the blessed apostle was killed was the time from Adam up until the coming of the Lord, the designated One that the whole human race and all the prophets wanted to see, almost like someone dying from hunger. The prophets, in fact, knew [f.33r] that kings could not be satiated or altogether saved, unless He should come Who would obliterate the sins of the world and take way the yoke of eternal death and offer the human race a remedy and open the entry of the kingdom of the heavens through His coming. On this, Truth speaks to the disciples: "Many prophets and kings wanted to see the things that you have seen and have not seen them and to hear the things that you have heard and have not heard them." [Lk 10:24] On this, Moses, almost famished[7] and desiring to be satiated with this Bread of life, says to God: "I pray, Lord, send the One You are to send." [Ex 4:13] He wanted this Bread who said: "Come, Lord, and do not delay, forgive the sins of Your people."[8] Isaiah said this same thing: "If only You would break asunder the heavens and come down, the mountains would disappear from Your face." [Is 64:1] He suffered great hunger who said: "Where is the word of the Lord? Let it come." [Jer 17:15] Of course, that is the "Word that was made flesh and dwelled among us." [Jn 1:14] This Word — that is the Son of God — was pointed out by the one who said: "Iron passed through his soul until his word came." [Ps 104:18–19 / 105:18–19] And again: "My heart uttered a good word," [Ps 44:2 / 45.1] as if he were saying: "Secretly the heart of the divinity of God uttered a good word," that is, "sent His Son into the womb of the Virgin." The Psalmist wanted to be satiated with

---

7. S gives the better reading, *famelicus* rather than the *familicus* of CC.
8. This antiphon has been recorded, but its source is not well identified. It is not in G.M. Dreves and C. Blume, *Analecta hymnica* (Leipzig: Altenburg, 1907, henceforth "AH"), although it has served as material for Mendelssohn and other composers.

His presence when he said: "I will be satiated when Your glory has appeared." [Ps 16:4 / 17:4] Solomon testifies that this glory is the Son of God when he says: "The glory of the Father is the knowing Son." [Cf. Prov 13:1] And in the Old Law it is written: "And the glory of the Lord appeared over Sinai." [Ex 24:16] Jeremiah testifies that the whole human race would desire this Bread, when he says: "Every people was weeping and seeking bread." [Lam 1:11] And elsewhere: "The little ones sought bread, and there was no one who would break it for them." [Lam 4:4] By little ones seeking bread, the prophets of the Old Law were principally indicated, those who desired, as we said, the true Bread, but there was no one who would break it for them, as the time had not yet come in which the Son would be sent by God and would come into being through the Virgin. But when the fullness of time came, in which "God sent His Son born from a woman, done under the law, so that He might redeem those who were under the law," [Gal 4:4–5] then the true Bread that is always complete, endures, is broken and made visible, and is shown to men what His taste is and what His power is. He remains complete in His unchangeable divinity, while He is broken by His Passion in His humanity. How wonderful! He feeds not only angels but also men, and He remains complete. He imparts to all, and He is found complete. But when this food — that is, the Son of God Who will feed the heavenly [f.33v] beings with His continual satiation in heaven — is made a man for the salvation of the world, then man has eaten the Bread of angels, and hunger is extinguished, and the human race is satiated by Him, and then this prodigal Son, in likeness to that father, after returning to Himself, said to Himself: "Here I am dying of hunger, I will arise and go to My Father." [Lk 15:17–18]

Agabus, who with the other prophets arrived from Jerusalem at Antioch and predicted a great famine in the world, signifies the first man of his race, who, when he disregarded the commandments of the Lord and was disobedient to Him, announced a hunger for the divine word to occur in the world. For, just like earth not bearing fruit because of its sterility announces a hunger for bread to its planters, so also the human race, through the offense of disobedience, foretold a hunger for the word of God. And just as the planter of the lands, after the seed is sowed on the earth, lets the land still not bearing fruit go for a time, and it starts to sprout thorns and bramble-bushes instead of grain, so also God permitted the human race to become wrapped in the thorns of vices, since it did not wish to enter under His commands.[9] Thus, in fact, it was promised by the Lord after the committed offense: "When you have worked the earth, it will not give its fruits, but it will sprout thorns and thistles for you."[10] It is as if he were saying: "Therefore, because you have not worked the earth well — that is, you yourself, by transgressing my commandments — you will not receive fruits of worthy repayment in the future, but it will sprout thorns and thistles for you."[11] By thorns that prick when touching them, the sins of the human race are represented, with which one is pricked when one is afflicted by the infernal torturers in Gehenna. Whence the prophet says: "This people surrounded me with the thorns of their sins."[12] By bramble-bushes, which is the hard and rough food of asses, the hard and rough precepts of the Old Law are signified, with which the human race was fed from the beginning up until the coming of the Lord because of its iniquity, as an ass is fed with rough and unrefined foods. And then it was the rule to take from someone a tooth for a tooth, an eye for an eye, a hand for a hand, and a foot for a foot. Whence it is said by the prophet Job: "Let a thistle grow for me instead of grain and a thorn instead of barley." [Job 31:40] And it is well said, for the prophets arrived at Antioch from Jerusalem so that there they might announce the coming famine to

---

9. The Latin is *subintrare* or "enter secretly": the context here seems closer to the etymological root of the word "to enter under"; DuCange gives the notion of "take possession of"; however, the general sense is "to obey."
10. Cf. Gen 3:17–18; the first clause is a paraphrase, the second a direct quote from Genesis.
11. "It is as if…for you" appears in the margin of CC, with a red cross designating its insertion point; it is in the body of the text of S.
12. This quote is found in Isidore of Seville, *De fide catholica contra Iudaeos*, Bk. 1, ch. 31, sect. 2 (PL 83:482). Isidore attributes it to Jeremiah, though it does not appear in modern versions of this prophet's work.

the world, for the human race was expelled from paradise, the land regarded as one of eternal peace, and thus Agabus might announce the coming hunger for the word of God to all the prophets and patriarchs on this exile of pilgrimage caused by their disobedience.

Claudius, under whom the famine occurred and to whom the world was subject, represents the law of the Old Testament, the laws to which the human race was subject. The *Ecclesiastical History* reports about this Claudius and [f.34r] this famine with these words: "When Gaius had served not quite four years in his reign, Claudius succeeded him as emperor. However, as to a rather dire famine taking hold of the whole world, our prophets had long before predicted such an event."[13] In the time, therefore, of Claudius the emperor a famine occurred in the world since the human race, through the precepts of the Old Law, before the Lord's Incarnation, could not be justified, fulfilled, or satisfied until He came Who would give the grace of redemption to all. The apostle, therefore, shows that man may not be saved by the law but through grace when he says: "We know that the law has led no one to be perfect."[14] And elsewhere: "By grace you are made saved through faith." [Eph 2:8] Elisha the Prophet showed this clearly when he brought a dead man back to life, not by sending a staff nor by a messenger, but by himself. For Elisha stands as the figure of the Lord, the staff as a figure of the harshness of the law, the messenger as a figure of Moses, and the dead man as a figure of the human race. Therefore, Elisha sent the staff via a slave to be laid over the dead boy, and he did not come to life again. Elisha came himself, joined and fit himself to the body, and it came back to life. Since clearly our Lord sent the law through Moses, and it did not profit the dead human race in its sins, He came Himself and descended

---

13. Eusebius, *Ecclesiastical History*, Bk. 2, ch. 8, sect. 1. See ch. 1, n. 11.
14. Cf. Hebrews 7:19. This paraphrased wording may be from a biblical commentary.

with grace, humbled Himself, took on our mortality, and man the sinner — that is, the human race — came back to heavenly life.[15]

Acts goes on: "The disciples, however, proposed that, to the extent that they were individually able, they would send aid to the brethren living in Judea." [Acts 11:29] Therefore, aid is sent by the disciples to the brethren in Judea, since the sterile land was abandoned through the famine. In fact, the dire famine is a customary happening in the world because of the land's sterility. Sterility of the land often happens, either when the accepted seed is overwhelmed by ryegrass[16] or when the seed is not given to it by the sower. The accepted seed is said to be overwhelmed by ryegrass, since a seed in the ground with ryegrass overcoming it cannot grow. Thus, also the seed of the divine word is not able to bear fruit in the human race with sins or varied and foreign teachings overcoming it. Therefore, just as the sower does not give seed to the earth because he lacks it, so also the preacher often does not give the seed of the word of God to the human race, because he loses his eloquence with the divine word because of the iniquitous acts of the people or because of his own perverse works. And so the grace of the Holy Spirit is taken away from the preacher because of the iniquity of the people, as the Lord says through the prophet: "I shall make your tongue adhere to your palate, and you will be mute, not like a rebuking [f.34v] man, because the house is exasperating." [Ez 3:26] And elsewhere the Lord says through the prophet: "I shall order that the clouds not send down rain upon you." [Is 5:6] The Lord Who hates all iniquity in all things orders the clouds of heaven not to send down rain on the human race since He takes away the rain of His grace from that preacher because of the iniquity of the subjects. Solomon, in testifying to this, says: "The holy spirit of doctrine will flee the feigned, since wisdom will not enter into the malevolent soul, nor will it live in a body subjected to sins." [Wis 1:4–5] Again

---

15. This analogy is based on the story of Elisha reviving the Shunnamite's son in 2 Kgs (2 Sam) 4:18–37.

16. The Latin *lolio* refers to unwanted, fast-growing vegetation, such as ryegrass, sometimes translated as "darnel" or "cockle."

the preacher loses the grace of the word of God because of his own perverse works, as is said to him by the Lord through the Psalmist:

> The Lord, however, said to the sinner: "Why do you speak my justices and claim my covenant with your mouth? On the contrary, you have hated my teaching and cast my words back. If you saw a thief, you ran with him, and you invested your share with adulterers. Your mouth abounded with malice, and your tongue brought forth deceptions. While sitting you spoke against your brother, and you placed a stumbling block against the son of your mother. You did this, and I was silent. Consider, O unjust one, if I were like you! Certainly, I will show you and set things against your face. Understand these things" — O you shepherds of the churches — "who forget God, so that someone" — the devil — "may not at some point take you" — from the world — "and there not be someone else who might take you away" — from His hand! [Ps 49:16–22 / 50:16–22][17]

And elsewhere it is written: "Why do you teach not to steal and then you steal?" [Rom 2:21] And Solomon said: "Because of the cold, the sluggish one could not plough," [Prov 20:4] as if he were openly saying: "A shepherd of the Church does not wish to plough the land of those placed under him, that is, to care for them, since he is made sluggish by living badly through the cold of his vices." And since in these ways the grace of the word of God is taken away, therefore the seed is not given by Him to the earth — that is, to the human race — but it is considered as if sterile and useless land. And just as the tiller of the land cannot sow seeds on a field unless he has it ready, so the preacher cannot distribute the seeds of the divine word, unless it be given to him by God. This is shown when he says: "The disciples, however, proposed that, to the extent that they were individually able, they would send aid to the brethren living in Judea." [Acts 11:29]

---

17. The author inserts "shepherds of the churches," "the devil," "from the world," and "from His hand" to ensure the point is not missed and to make it directly applicable to his argument.

CHAPTER SEVEN

They were not sending what they were lacking, but what they had. Because of this, whoever wishes to preach the word of God, unless he should lose the grace of the Holy Spirit because of his sins, should see to it that he lives lawfully in Christ, so that he may disburse the word of God quite fully to all. Similarly, the people should see to it, lest they lose on account of their unjust works the grace of the divine word that is owed to them by the preacher, that they persist in good deeds, so that the temple of the grace of God may be there [f.35r] perpetually. For if the earth and the sower are both good, the land will no longer be sterile but fruitful and will produce fruit, one a hundredfold and another sixty-fold.

The *Ecclesiastical History* reports that through the brothers Paul and Barnabas, who were at Antioch, aid was sent to the holy inhabitants of Jerusalem, each according to his ability.[18] Jerusalem, of course, is interpreted as a "vision of peace." However, by the disciples who sent aid to the holy inhabitants of Jerusalem, are understood, evidently, the teachers, prophets, patriarchs, and kings of the Old Law. They gave to those preaching the aid — that is, the testimonies of their law to the teachers of the New Law of grace — and a vision of true peace, which is Christ. With these testimonies they would affirm our Redeemer and Son of the eternal God, born of the inviolate Virgin Mary, and would strengthen the Gospel teaching. It should be known, however, that the law of new grace is known through the law of the Old Testament, where the Birth, Passion, Resurrection, and Ascension are declared with testimonies of this same thing in the Gospel. For it is written: "The old things have passed, and behold, new things have been made." [2 Cor 5:17] He says beautifully that the old things have passed on, since the precepts of the Old Law have been transformed into the grace of the New Law, and behold, new things have been made by the regeneration of baptism. The commands of the Old Testament have passed on to the grace of the New Law, and they are recreated by faith. They did not pass on so that they would not exist, but they passed on from an age of harshness, so that they might be new graces

---

18. Eusebius, *Ecclesiastical History,* Bk. 2, ch. 8, sect. 22.

in sweetness. This is the broken wheel that Ezekiel the Prophet once saw in the middle of the wheel.[19] This is the water converted to wine at the wedding in Cana of Galilee.[20] This is the change to the right hand of the Most High. This is the transfer of which Jeremiah foretold, saying: "All Judea is transplanted in a complete removal." [Jer 13:19] And therefore, so that the Lord would show Himself as a bearer of the New Law and not show Himself to be a destroyer of the Old Law, He said: "I did not come to dissolve the law but to fulfill it." [Mt 5:17] The law is fulfilled through the fullness of love, as the apostle says: "Therefore, the fullness of the law is love." [Rom 13:10] Whoever, therefore, desires to be a preacher of the New Law, must accept the New Testament so that he does not cast away the Old Testament, but he should bring forth new and old things from the divine treasury. Thus, in fact, Paul the Apostle says: "Do not extinguish the spirit. Do not scorn the prophecies." [1 Thes 5:19–20] By spirit is signified the grace of the New Law, and by prophecy, which is a part of the Old Testament, consequently the entire Old Law is understood.

But what should we see in this verse where Luke says: "The disciples, however, [f.35v] proposed that, to the extent that they were individually able, they would send aid to the brethren living in Judea." [Acts 11:29] But what did they have, or what did they propose? In reality, they had that with which a dire famine could be annihilated and the human race could be satisfied. The prophets and patriarchs in the Old Law truly proposed the Birth, Passion, Resurrection, and Ascension of Christ in writing their books, and they assiduously supplied the hands of the Evangelists and apostles and other teachers of the New Law. They had, in fact, at hand the birth of the Son of God, in which He is born of the Father, as one of them, Isaiah, certainly said: "Who shall explain His begetting?" [Is 53:8][21] They also had in the safe-box of their heart His second birth by which He would be born from a virgin,

19. Cf. Ez 1:15–19.
20. Cf. Jn 2:1–11.
21. Cf. Acts 8:33.

as Isaiah himself says: "And He is a man, and who will recognize Him?"[22] And elsewhere he said: "Behold a virgin will conceive and will bear a Son, and His name will be Emmanuel, and this is interpreted as 'God with us.'" [Is 7:14][23] And again, he said: "And there will come out a branch from the root of Jesse, and a flower will arise from its root." [Is 11:1] Jeremiah also had in the safe-box of his heart the coming of Christ when he said: "Like a tiller you will have come into the land and like a traveler turning away from staying." [Jer 14:8] The Lord came like a tiller to the earth, since He cultivated with the sweetness of His new grace the human race that had been in the bitterness of the first parent. He came like a traveler on the earth, as He made obvious to believers by the blood of His Passion the way through which they would go to the heavenly mansion. The Lord came while turning away from staying. When He might have been with the Father above, He lay down in the womb of the Virgin in order to save the human race, so that through His unutterable love He might live in those who pay heed to His will and remember to keep His commandments. He confirms this Himself when He says: "If someone loves Me, let him keep My Word, and My Father will love him, and We will come to him and will make a dwelling with him." [Jn 14:23] And elsewhere the Lord says: "And I will go in them and dwell." [2 Cor 6:16] The holy prophets had at hand, in addition, the triumphant Passion of Christ by which He would redeem the world, as one of them said: "They have pierced my hands and my feet. They have counted out all my bones." [Is 21:17–18] And another says to an impious throng of Jews: "You will see your life hanging before you, and you will not trust in your life." [Dt 28:66] Also another said:

---

22. This is not found in the Bible, but *Et homo est et quis cognoscet Illum,* is found in Bede, "De hominibus et partibus eius," Bk. 6, ch. 1 of *De rerum naturis:* "Et homo est et quis cognoscet eum?" Chapter 7 contains a number of citations that were not located where they were indicated to be. It may be that this sermon was given but not polished for publication.

23. Cf. Mt 1:23.

"Impious men said, 'Let us oppress the just man unjustly.'"[24] They also had His glorious Resurrection, of which one of them speaks in this way: [f.36r] "'Because of the misery of the destitute and the sorrow of the poor, I will now arise,' says the Lord." [Ps 11:6 / 12:5] Again another says: "He will revive us after two days. On the third day, He will raise us up." [Hos 6:3] They also had in the poor box[25] of their heart His miraculous Ascension that one of them pulled from the treasury of his heart and sent to his brethren in Jerusalem, saying: "God ascended in jubilation; the Lord in the sound of the trumpet." [Ps 46:6 / 47:5] Another also says: "I beheld in a vision of the night, and behold, the Son of man came and arrived even to the Ancient of the days." [Dan 7:13] The Ancient of the days is said to be God the Father, Who remains eternal in the Trinity before all times. It is read that His Son ascended to Him. They had also in the treasuries of their knowledge the coming of the Holy Spirit and Paraclete upon the disciples, as one of them says in the person of God: "I will pour out of My Spirit above every flesh, and your sons and daughters will prophesy." [Acts 2:17] And again: "'When I have been sanctified in you, I will bring you together from all the lands, and I will pour over you pure water, and you will be cleansed from all your filths, and I will give you my Spirit,' says the Lord."[26] They had, moreover, the Day of Judgment at hand, as one of them testifies, saying: "God will plainly come. Our God will also not be silent. A fire shall blaze in His sight." [Ps 49:3 / 50:3] And another says: "The dead shall arise, and those who are in sepulchers will rise up."[27] And another said: "That day, a day of wrath, a day of calamity and misery, great and exceedingly bitter.

---

24. The exact quote is not found in the Bible, but as the *Responsorium* in the Gregorian Repertory: https://gregorien.info/chant/id/8720/0/en (Accessed on 5/17/2020).

25. The Latin is *gazofilacio;* DuCange gives the meaning of a place used to store funds for distributing to the poor; clearly a place for keeping valuables; *tesauro* for "treasury" is used as a synonym in the next clause.

26. Cf. Ez 36:23–25, 37:14.

27. Cf. Jn 5:28, Is 26:9.

[Zeph 1:15–16][28] These are, dearest brethren, their treasures; these are their foods. These are their storehouses of grain from which the disciples — that is, the prophets of God — have received the glorious grains and the aid for eternal life, and they sent these to the holy inhabitants at Jerusalem. In these treasuries, however, is not found disappearing bread, but the food of heavenly life. That Bread, however, not only feeds men but also nourishes the angels, in fact, makes them steadfast. This very Bread, however, speaks of Himself: "Whoever eats this bread will live for eternity." [Jn 6:59] This is the bread without which the hunger of the human race is not extinguished but is extended. This is the bread that is sent as an aid by the disciples to the brethren living in Judea, so that the hunger of death no longer may be in the world, but rather the food of heavenly life, as He Himself says: "The bread that I have given is My flesh for the life of the world." [Jn 6:52]

But why is it that Luke says that "they proposed...individually... that they would send aid to the brethren living in Judea," [Acts 11:29] when the *Ecclesiastical History* says that they sent the aid to the holy inhabitants at Jerusalem,[29] if not to show that the preaching of the Gospel by the Lord Himself would first be revealed in Jerusalem [f.36v] and then in all of Judea? Just as Luke himself asserts that the Lord had said this, saying: "And you will be witnesses for Me in Jerusalem and in all Judea and Samaria and up to the end of the earth." [Acts 1:8] And since Jerusalem is interpreted as "vision of peace" and Judea as "confession," the aid for life is properly sent to those dwelling in them, so as to show openly that heavenly grace is given by God to those who believe in Christ through a confession of faith and to those who gird themselves in heart and deed for the vision of peace of the eternal homeland. And since the Lord dwells in those who love peace, it is properly said by the prophet: "Over whom does my Spirit rest, if not over the

---

28. This is from the *Libera me* or the Office of the Dead and resembles the *Dies irae* sequence, sung at the requiem mass.
29. Eusebius's text gives Judea in harmony with Acts, however, the copy available to Calixtus must have had "Jerusalem" as a variant for "Judea."

humble and the quiet and the one fearing My words?"[30] And the Psalmist says: "Great Peace" — that is, Christ — "to those loving Your law and for whom it is not a stumbling block." [Ps 118:165 / 119:165] And since through a confession of true faith, the Holy Spirit, Who is the aid for eternal life, desires to dwell in men, He appropriately reminds us through the Psalmist to anticipate His face in confession, saying: "Let us win over His face in confession." [Ps 94:2 / 95:2][31] "And they did this, and sent aid to the elders by the hand of Barnabas and Saul." [Acts 11:30] The aid is not read in this lesson as being sent by the brethren, but to the brethren living in Judea, while it says that there is a famine present in the whole world. Why is it, therefore, that the Holy Spirit, Who is upon the disciples and Who also does not take sides with people, is read to have sent aid only to the brothers in Judea and not everywhere, while a famine is read to have occurred in the whole world? But it is understood more easily, if it is understood spiritually. The aid for life is certainly read as being sent to the brethren in Judea, so that it may signify that all those who desire to persevere through good works in confession of the nourishing and undivided Trinity are made brothers in Christ and are filled with the grace of God. The Lord Himself says in the Gospel: "Whosoever should do the will of My Father Who is in heaven is My brother." [Mt 12:50] And elsewhere: "You are all brothers." [Mt 23:8] Barnabas and Saul, through whom the aid is sent by the disciples to the brethren in Judea, are figuratively two bands of preachers, namely of apostles and teachers, by whose exhortations the Lord sent His aid, that is, the grace of His word by means of a confession of His name, to the famished peoples, when "their sound went out to every land

---

30. Cf. Is 62:2. This is close to the Hebrew but far removed from the Latin Vulgate verse. One finds similar wording if one combines Is 11:2 and Is 66:2. It was evidently the wording in circulation since it is found in Augustine's *Expositio ad Galatas,* ch. 45 (PL 35:2138) and Jerome's *Epistola* 39 (PL 22:468–69).

31. This is the text of the Vulgate. The Reformation Bibles (e.g., KJV) do not include this wording.

CHAPTER SEVEN

and their words" went forth "to the ends of the earth." [Ps 18:5 / 19:4].[32] Just as, in fact, the bodily aid is sent by the disciples through Saul and Barnabas to the brethren in Judea, so also is the spiritual food of the faith sent by these two bands of preachers to the world. There were those who lived before the Passion of Christ to whom the Lord entrusted the aid [f.37r] that is the word of life: "He sent them two by two before His face... to the place to which He was to go." [Lk 10:1] From the other band, however, there were those who appeared after His Passion to whom He entrusted the same aid, and He sent the aid through these preachers to the world when He said to them: "Go unto the whole world and preach the Gospel to every creature. Whoever believes and is baptized will be saved and whoever does not believe will be condemned." [Mk 16:15–16] Therefore, from the time when the Lord sent them out two by two up until today, all those who have faithfully announced to peoples' hearts the words of eternal life or who have left writings for the coming generations in their books, have brought the aid of restoration to the brothers of Antioch to Judea just like Barnabas and Saul. However, since this aid was very desirable, precious, and necessary, many gave the precious things they possessed, so that they might have it.

What then is that precious thing that a man gave so he might have this aid?[33] Certainly nothing is more precious to a person than oneself. Therefore, Saint Peter gave himself for this aid when he placed his body on the cross, so that he might have this aid. For this aid Paul gave himself when he handed over his body for beheading. Andrew gave himself for this aid when he extended his joints on the cross with eager heart. For this aid Saint Stephen, the first martyr, gave himself when he consented to be stoned for Christ. Saint Bartholomew gave up everything precious for this aid when he

---

32. The author adds "went forth" *(processerunt)* to the passage to make the meaning clearer. It is only implicit in the Psalm.
33. The use of the word "aid" has moved from the original monetary collection for those in hunger to "whatever it takes to gain entry to heaven" with this sometimes requiring martyrdom.

consented to be stripped of his skin. The holy men gave such acts worthy of reward and such gifts for the aid to possessing eternal life, as Jeremiah affirms when he says: "They gave everything precious for food to revivify the soul." [Lam 1:11] The people gave up their precious things[34] for they lacked food, and they handed themselves over to various tribulations for the life of the soul. However much they gave their bodies over to suffering or abandoned their flesh to tears or prayers or daily fasting or various afflictions or crimes or desires, to that extent they gave up whatever precious things they had so that they might receive this aid. They knew, in fact, that nothing precious could be equal to or compare with this gift but would be vile in comparison with it. The one who sought good pearls is a witness to this point. After finding one that was precious, he gave all his things and purchased it.[35] That the aid for the heavenly kingdom can be compared to this pearl is testified to by the one who sought the kingdom of the heavens and purchased it. And we, dearest brethren, must not become foreign to this aid to life, but if we cannot give [f.37v] our bodies to the martyrdom of an outpouring of blood, as our ancestors did, nonetheless we can offer what we have for this aid to life. If, in fact, we bless those who hold us in hatred, if we tolerate patiently the injuries inflicted on us by our neighbors, if we offer to all the needy, to the extent that it is in our power, both types of salutary food, if we love our neighbors as ourselves, if we submit our limbs in free service to God by keeping vigil, praying, fasting, hating vices, laying aside sins that have been committed, fleeing unlawful things, rejecting the praise of the world, without doubt we will receive the aid to eternal life. Nor did the most glorious apostle James hesitate to give his most precious things for this incomparable aid, namely when he handed over for Christ the most precious sum[36] of his body of his

---

34. The precious things refer to that "of greatest worth" or "of greatest value" in the sense of importance rather than, or at least in addition to, endearment.
35. Cf. Mt 13:45–46.
36. The Latin *talentum* originally referring to the coin, is also used to mean "a sum" or "amount."

CHAPTER SEVEN

own free will to the torments of his passion at the hands of cruel Herod, as the present solemnity makes clear, when today's reading says: "At that time, however, King Herod sent a force to afflict some from the Church, and he killed James, the brother of John, with a sword." [Acts 12:1]

Why is it, brethren, that at the very time when a famine was occurring in the whole world, Saint James handed his body over to the punishment of death for Christ, except in order to show openly that those who are oppressed by hunger for the word of God and who desire the kingdom of the heavens with all their heart must divest themselves of the vices of the flesh and dress themselves with the virtues of the soul? The blessed apostle set aside the body of original sin and put on the virtue of patience and love of God while he sustained patiently the torments of his passion for Christ. By this example, we also, dearest brethren, must destroy the enticements of our flesh if we wish to possess the eternal kingdom. Through Saint James, of course, who at the time of the famine dies in body for the love of Christ, are signified figuratively the bodies of the saints who, because of a desire for the kingdom of the heavens, assent to dying to the world and living for God. They die to vices and live for divine virtues, as Saint Paul the Apostle affirms when he says: "Now, however, I do not live, but Christ lives in me." [Gal 2:20] Now he was not living through a desire of the flesh, as he had destroyed the vices of his flesh in himself, but Christ was living in him, since he was now gleaming with virtues. And so, man dies to the world when he, out of love for the divine, renounces his perverse acts with which he was accustomed to lead his vain life. He lives [f.38r] for God when he has already begun to improve his life with good works. He dies to the world when he stops being a pagan, and he lives for God when he begins to be a Christian. He dies to the world when he stops being a Jew, and he lives for God when he has begun to be a Christian. He dies to the world when he stops being a heretic, and he lives for God when he begins to be faithful in all things. He dies to the world when he stops being a thief, an adulterer, a fornicator, a jealous, miserly, and corrupt man. And he lives for God when he begins to repent for all these.

This is that true mortification and divine vivification that Paul suggests we exhibit when he says: "Let us always carry around in our body the mortification of Jesus, so that the life of Jesus may be in us." [2 Cor 4:10]

And it is asserted that James, whose name is interpreted as "supplanter" and who is brother of John whose name is said to be "grace of God," was killed by the sword in a time of famine. They are thus properly designated by Paul since they overthrow vices from themselves for good virtues and they are made brothers of the grace of God with their good works, since they, out of a desire for the heavenly kingdom, take up freely with the ear of their heart the sword of the spirit — that is the word of God — and with this sword they may clearly be able to die to vices and live for good works. Clement of Alexandria writes a story worthy of memory about this James in his *Seventh Book of Depositions:*[37]

> When he, however, had come to death, the one who had led him away to the judge for martyrdom, seeing him condemned to death, was led by penance and confessed that he was a Christian. Both, moreover, were led together to the ridge of the mountain.[38] While they were being thus led, he fell down on the road at James's feet and asked James to give him pardon. James deliberated a short while then said, "Peace be with you," and he kissed him, and thus both were beheaded together.

The one who first led the apostle away to the judge for martyrdom and finally was led by penitence, who showed himself

---

37. This work is often referred to by its Greek name *Hypotyposes* (ὑποτύπωσες) or *Outlines*. Only fragments such as those written down by Eusebius survive. Cf. Eusebius, *Ecclesiastical History,* Bk. 2, ch. 9 (PG 20:157–58). For a translation of this work relative to James, see Coffey and Dunn, *Miracles,* xxv.

38. The Latin is *ad supercilium montis* ("to the ridge of the mountain"), but this is likely a scribal error with *montis* ("mountain") for *mortis* ("death"), yielding something like "to the threshhold of death"; it is *montis* in S as well, though with a superscript line for the "n." Calixtus here appears to be working with a different copy of Eusebius than what he had used for the text as presented in ch. 4, pp. 65–66.

to be a Christian, and who accepted the crown of martyrdom together with the apostle, figuratively designates the perverse and unfaithful person who first pursues Christ, either by living badly or by afflicting the saints, and who finally, through a confession of penitence and affliction of the body and faith of the heart and perseverance in good work, is converted to God. Saint Paul is one of these, as he pursued Stephen the Levite and the Church of Christ and was finally converted to the faith of Christ and accepted his passion for Christ.[39] In fact, however, the name by which the one who took away the apostle to the judge is known, as is shown rather clearly in the *Acts of His Passion* when it says: "Then [f.38v] the scribe of the Pharisees, by the name of Josias, who placed the rope on his neck...dragged him forth...threw himself at his feet," and so forth.[40] And Josias is beautifully interpreted as the "Lord's salvation," since he obtained the salvation of Christ after the delivery of the apostle. This shows to all the perverse people that, even after their perpetrated wrongs, the desired salvation of the Lord for their souls can be obtained if they want to cease from evil things and devote themselves to good things. This is that salvation of which Truth says: "'I am the salvation of the people,' says the Lord."[41] And the prophet says: "All, in fact, who call on the name of the Lord will be saved." [Joel 2:32][42] The heretics who say that a man after falling into guilt cannot regain mercy through a confession of penance are included in this sentence, but it remains to be seen

---

39. Cf. Acts 7:54–8:2.
40. Found in the "Pseudo-Abdias" within which one finds the "Passio Iacobi." See Johann Albert Fabricius and Hermas, "De historia ac rebus gestis Jacobi majoris Apostoli," *Codex apocryphus Novi Testamenti*, 2nd ed. (Hamburg: Benjam. Schilleri & Joh. Christoph. Kisneri, 1719), 2:516–31. For a translation, see Coffey and Dunn, *Miracles*, 97–105.
41. Cf. Ps 34:3 / 35:3, where David speaks to the Lord asking for Him to "say unto my soul, I am thy salvation." This phrase has come to be used in introits and offertory prayers.
42. Cf. Rom 10:13, Acts 2:21. The Latin *omnis* means "every," "all," and "whole"; the author here plays off this multiple meaning, and we have translated using these various meanings, as necessary.

by us how all who call upon the name of the Lord may be saved. For many who are not saved call on the name of the Lord, such as the Jews, Gentiles, heretics, and the many unfaithful who are certainly damned. And the prophet placed "all" at the beginning of this sentence effectively in order to show that "every person" — and not that half that loves God and observes His commandments — may become perfect and may be without doubt saved if this person calls on the name of the Lord, that is, Jesus Christ with all his heart and with good works. Solomon testifies to this when he says: "Fear God and observe His commandments; this is the whole person." [Ecclus (Sir) 12:13][43] Every person who fears God with love and who observes His commandments is a whole person and not a half person. He certainly observes the precepts of the Lord who perseveres in good works at the end, and the Psalmist assuredly shows how close the Lord may be to a person's call when he says: "The Lord is near to all those calling on Him, to all those calling on Him in truth. He will do the will of those fearful and will hear clearly their plea, and He will make them saved." [Ps 144:18–19 / 145:18–19] The Lord is near for all those calling on Him in truth. Whoever, in fact, calls on Him in the truth of faith and good work will be saved without doubt. The Lord is near for all those calling on Him in truth,[44] since He had pity on the human race in His Son Who is the way and the truth and the life, and He deigned to send Him into the world through a virgin for its salvation.

It goes on: "And Herod went down from Judea to Caesarea and stayed there." [Acts 12:19] Do not wonder, O wise reader,[45] if in this reading a little before this verse, the jailing of Saint Peter is omitted, since the ecclesiastical order may read, out of blameless habit, the things pertaining to the present solemnity that one celebrates and

---

43. The text connotes "this is all there is to being a person." Different translations of the Bible have approached the passage with a variety of circumlocutions.
44. Cf. Jn 14:6.
45. This rhetorical apostrophe or appeal to the "reader" appears in a chapter labeled a "sermon," which one would normally associate with oral delivery.

CHAPTER SEVEN

may leave out other things either because they are not to be read [f.39r] or because they are wearisome to be read. Thus, in fact, in the reading of Saint Stephen that begins in this way: "Stephen, full of grace and strength," [Acts 6:8] many things are left out before the verse that says: "Hearing, however, these things, they were cut to the heart and gnashed their teeth at him." [Acts 7:54] But those things that are left out are inserted elsewhere in the Acts of the Apostles. An occurrence of this type is observed again on the day of the Birth of the Lord in the reading that is read in many places at the mass, and that begins in this way: "The people of the nations who walk in the darkness saw a great light," [Is 9:2] before it says: "A little boy was born to us." [Is 9:6] It leaves out many things that are in the sequence of the book of the prophet Isaiah. Again, an occurrence of this type is observed in the reading at the mass for one confessor:[46] "Behold the great priest who in his days pleased the Lord."[47] And in several places in the book of readings for masses this same thing is found. Thence it is correct that today the reading about Saint Peter that speaks of his imprisonment should not be read at the mass but should be recited rather on his solemnity.[48]

But let us see what this Peter, who is held in a prison, signifies. Peter, to be sure, is the one who, after James has died, is put back in prison by Herod, bound with chains, taken away from there by an angel, and led up to the iron gate that leads to the city. He signifies the human race, since the Son of God comes in the flesh, and He is the angel of great wisdom Who frees from the chains of one's sins

---

46. This refers to the proper of the mass "common" for classes of saints, such as one martyr, several martyrs, a virgin, etc. In addition, some saints had very particular introits, graduals, and the like that could be used for them. The common filled in for the group, where such particulars were lacking.

47. This is the opening line of a hymn still used today in services. The point seems to be that this hymn contains words from here and there in the scriptures, such as from Ecclus (Sir) 50:1, 48:25, and other places.

48. A solemnity is the highest-ranking liturgical celebration of the Catholic Church, outranking celebrations of lesser importance, which would affect the way that it would supersede these celebrations. It also required the recitation of certain prayers.

with which the devil has bound it by evilly tempting it and Who leads it up to the gate of faith that leads with His grace to the city of the kingdom of the heavens. The gate is said to be iron because of its strength, since it is not opened to the unclean or contaminated, but to the pious and mild. "For the kingdom of the heavens, in fact, suffer violence, and the violent take it away." [Mt 11:12] And since we have heard something briefly about the seizing of Saint Peter, let us look now at the foul death of the unjust king Herod who perpetrated so many bad deeds against the Lord's apostles.

In fact, the miserable death of this Herod must be recited in today's reading, so that it is openly shown that he was killed by the angel for this reason: because he had killed the apostle of the Lord with a sword. Afterward, however, he inflicted on the apostles so much villainy that it is said in today's reading:

> He went down from Judea to Caesarea, and he stayed there. He was, however, angered with the Tyrians and the Sidonians. They, however, all came to him, as Blastus who was the king's chamberlain had persuaded them to do, and they sought peace because their regions were maintained by him. On the appointed day, Herod, dressed in regal garb, sat before the tribunal and spoke sublimely to them. [f.39v] The people, in fact, exclaimed: "Sounds of God and not of man!" However, an angel of the Lord immediately struck him, and he died, consumed by worms, because he had not given honor to God. [Acts 12:19–22]

Moreover, it is worthy of a miracle that one can observe so much agreement of divine scriptures with the historiographer of that people. Truly Josephus himself reports about this Herod in his nineteenth *Book of Antiquities*[49] that:

> After he was pursued by an angel, he had incredible pain and swelling in the stomach,[50] and being more violently

---

49. Josephus, *Antiquities,* 19.8.2; this text, however, appears to be cited through Eusebius.
50. The wording, "After he was pursued by an angel" is not in Josephus, and the rest of this clause is an abbreviated presentation of the Josephus text, after which the text follows Josephus as cited by Eusebius almost exactly.

tormented by the power of the pain, he was carried immediately from the assembly area[51] to the palace. And when it was announced that he was to die not far off from that day, a great throng of every age and sex convened. In the custom of their country, being prostrate wearing only girdles,[52] they begged almighty God for the their king's safety. However, every royal house was filled with wailing and lamenting. While the king, in the meantime, was lying on the highest terrace, he looked below and surveyed all those bent and prostrate with their weeping, and not even he restrained himself from tears. He suffered truly for five continuous days with pains in his stomach, and his life was cut off in the fifty-fourth year of his age and the seventh year of his reign. Herod had, in fact, reigned for four years under Gaius Caesar and three years under Claudius Caesar, and he had held the tetrarchy of Philip for three years,[53] annexing this for himself in his fourth year.[54]

But we should discover what this unjust Herod signifies. Herod, moreover, who with his unjust domination carried out a persecution against the apostles when he killed James and cast Peter into prison, appears as the demon who, with his inimical domination, miserably subjected the whole human race to himself before the Lord's Incarnation through the sin of the first created persons.[55] He is properly read to have descended from Judea, which is interpreted as "acknowledgement"[56] to Caesarea that in this place signifies "world,"

---

51. The wording "from the assembly area" is added subsequent to Josephus and Eusebius.
52. See ch. 4, n. 17.
53. See ch. 4, n. 18.
54. The text of Josephus ends here. See ch. 4, n. 19.
55. Latin *prot<h>oplasti;* this is masculine singular in Latin and might indicate Adam, though, given the story in Genesis 2–3, it would probably refer to both Adam and Eve. We have thus made it plural in accordance with this story.
56. The Latin *confessio* ("confession" or "acknowledgement") can only with difficulty be brought into harmony with the etymology for Judea, which comes from the Hebrew for "praise" or "thanksgiving."

since it is as if the demon went down from an acknowledgement of God into the world when he fell into hell through the envy that he had from the contemplation of God. "He was, however, angered with the Tyrians and the Sidonians." [Acts 12:20] Herod, however, who was angered with the Tyrians and the Sidonians, shows himself to be the demon who was angered with the human race when out of envy he shrewdly tempted it in paradise. The demon was angered since he had lost his seat in the heavens. He was angered because he thought the human race was to sit on the seat from which he had fallen. And he was more angered when he lost the crowd that he held captive with him in hell when the Lord [f.40r] liberated them. The demon was also enraged when he saw the good persevere in perfect work, was enraged when he saw sinners return to penance, and when he lost those whom he held bound through vices. "They, however, all decided to come to him, as Blastus, who was the king's chamberlain, had persuaded them to do, and they sought peace because their regions were maintained by him." [Acts 12:20] The fortunate peoples of Tyre and Sidon, who unanimously came to Herod seeking peace, signify the prophets and patriarchs and kings of the Old Law, who came to the demon in hell as captives because of the guilt of the first man. For this reason, they sought the peace of God and man, desiring the coming of the Lord. What, therefore, were they, who were held captives through the debts of guilt of the first parent, seeking other than true peace between God and man, which is Christ, who is true peace? Assuredly the one wanted true peace who said: "And peace will be on our earth when He will come." [Mic 5:5] And the one who said: "Justice will arise in our days and an abundance of peace." [Ps 71:7 / 72:7]

However, in the days of the coming of Christ, justice arises, since it is because of this that the Son of God is born: to show the world about sin and justice and judgment. And an abundance of peace was born with Him, since He came into the world and strengthened the eternal peace between God and humanity. Thence it is that the choir of angels sang at the Lord's Birth, saying: "Glory to God in the highest, and peace on earth" — which is Christ — "to men of good will." [Lk 2:14] In the days of the Lord, however, there was so

CHAPTER SEVEN

much peace on earth that no man dared to bear warlike arms against a man. The prophet affirms this when he says: "And they will melt their swords into ploughshares and their lances into sickles. People will not raise a sword against a people, nor will they exercise any more for battle." [Is 2:4] Thence it is that the Psalmist says: "Come and see the works of the Lord, what wonders He has placed on the earth, taking away wars up to the end of the earth. He destroys the bow and shatters arms and burns the shields with fire. Take time and see that I am God." [Ps 45:9–10 / 46:8–10]

"On the appointed day, Herod, dressed in regal garb, sat before the tribunal and spoke sublimely to them." [Acts 12:21] The magnificent regal dress with which Herod was clothed signifies the pretense of arrogance of the demon with which he is accustomed to deceive the good, since, while he may be the Angel of Darkness, he transfigures himself into an Angel of Light so that he might more subtly deceive them. That Herod was making a speech to the people shows the devil's suggestions and temptations, with which he does not cease to offer to mankind evil vices, namely, lust, wantonness, avarice, hatred, murder, adultery, fornication, theft, idle talk, slander, disobedience, and others [f.40v] similar to these. But after the demon has inflicted or perpetrated all these things on humankind, as the soul is leaving a person's body, he asks for his works, and he reads off the evil things that he persuaded the person to do, so that he may drag this companion soul to torments. One must resist him through good works, as Paul says:[57] "Be cautious and watch, for your adversary, the devil, is going around like a roaring lion seeking someone that he may devour. Resist him strongly in faith." [1 Pet 5:8–9] The people, in fact, exclaimed: "The sounds of God and not of man!" [Acts 12:22] since they believed that the eternal peace of a god could be more profitable to them than that of man. The people who exclaimed "the words of a god and not of man" point to the prophets and kings of the Old Law, who wished

---

57. This is corrected to Peter in the margin of CC by another hand. It remains *Paulus* in S; the correction was probably made after the Salamanca text was copied.

for true peace, that is, the Son of God Who would come in the flesh, as we said above. Of these, one is Saint Simeon, who received an answer from the Holy Spirit that "he would not see death if he had not first seen Christ the Lord." [Lk 2:26] And just as the people could not have peace while Herod was living unless the angel who would kill Herod came from the sky, so also the human race could not have the eternal peace of God unless the Son of God — Who is the angel of great wisdom — should come, Who would destroy Herod — that is, the devil — through the blood of His Passion and by His divinity and Who would also strengthen true peace between God and humanity.[58] This is that peace that the Son of God Himself, after He destroyed the demon in hell and arose from the dead, gave to His disciples, saying: "My peace I give you, My peace I leave you." [Jn 14:27]

"However, an angel of the Lord immediately struck Herod, and he died, consumed by worms, because he had not given honor to God." [Acts 12:23] The angel of the Lord who struck Herod shows the Son of God Who, as we said, is the angel of great wisdom, Who came in the flesh, and Who destroyed the devil. Job the Prophet, desiring his apprehension and defeat, said to the Lord: "Can you not catch the leviathan with a hook?"[59] For a leviathan is a sea serpent.[60] Like all serpents — even those surpassing the magnificent towers of the earth with their size — it lives in foreign waters, which signifies all the rivers of the lands, by which the peoples denote it, as Job himself describes it, as absorbing but insatiable, until it flows into the mouth of the Jordan, by which Christians are signified.[61] What is worse, this leviathan up until this point absorbs some Christians through diverse vices. It swallows up one through covetousness,

---

58. The word *ho-i-e-* for *hominem* for "humanity" is added and surrounded with a rubric line in the margin. The word *hominem (ho-iem)* is within the text of S.
59. Cf. Job 40:20ff. and 41:1ff.
60. The Latin is *aquosus* or "abounding in water"; the "sea" expresses the thought better in English.
61. Cf. Job 40:23.

CHAPTER SEVEN

another through avarice, another through hatred, another through extravagance, another through fraud, another through various sins. Certainly, the demon is understood by "leviathan" and by the hook outwardly is shown the flesh of some worms for the fish to eat [f.41r] and inwardly is hidden the point for catching the fish. This represents the Son of God, in Whom God the Father shows the suffering flesh to the devil and hides the divinity by which He destroys this demon by this very Son's flesh that suffered on the cross. When the Lord went down to the underworld for the sake of freeing His own, the demon thought that he would hold Him with his tormentors, and like the fish, he would swallow the flesh from the hook; but the hook — that is, the Son of God —had covered its point with flesh and had hidden it until then and now showed the point of its divinity to him. With this, He destroyed the demon mightily, and He shattered his iron bars. The worms that ate Herod's unjust flesh signify the infernal worms that torment the evil ones in the abyss. Of these the Lord in the Gospel calls out fearfully: "Where the worms are that do not die and the fire is not extinguished." [Mk 9:43, 45, 47; Is 66:24] Understand that these worms are sharp, rapacious, devourers of animals, barbarous, fiercer than all animals, and never die. Just as souls cannot die, so also these cannot die. In hell is the fire that does not die but is found to always burn. Certainly, this fire does not burn wood or stone or any flesh,[62] but it burns and consumes the souls of sinners.[63] Its sparks are the adverse spirits of sins. Therefore, let those tremble with fear who do not offer honor to God and who act badly, since unless they have a taste for pursuing good deeds, they will be seized by these torments. Thus, in fact, Herod is punished by worms because he did not give honor to God. Like those who do not honor God by doing good works, he will be punished in hell with these infernal worms. Certainly, in Orcus there is said to be so much heat that if anyone should touch a little of it, he would no longer live. Such cold

---

62. Latin *pinguedinem* or "fat" but apparently contrasted here with the soul that can burn in hell.
63. This is the first reference to the fires of hell.

is also thought to be there that no one can live who feels it. Blessed Job testifies, however, that the souls of sinners may be tormented in the heat and cold, when he says: "They will pass from excessive infernal heat to the cold waters of the snows."[64] The souls burn and are tormented in the excessive infernal heat, as they die shamefully in the heat of their vices. Their souls are tormented in the cold infernal waters. They are made cold by their perverse work, and they are held to be devoid of the warmth of the Holy Spirit. Because of this, it has been said beautifully in poetry by some wise man:[65]

> To the decree of truth,
> Give heed, you who go astray;
> The road leading to eternity
> In hell is to be avoided.
> This is the road of a dire fate
> Under the eternal yoke of death,
> Where there are always tormentors
> Fiercer than all others.
> If one should ever feel them
> And afterward come back to life,
> One would prefer to be burned by fire here
> Than to be tormented by them.
> Let us avoid that place
> Where we know there is a fire; [f.41v]
> Its pains do not decrease,

---

64. Cf. Job 24:18–20.
65. These are versicles from the Latin Office of the Dead. It was edited by Rudolf Pörtner as "'Ad consultum veritatis attendite': Ein moralisch-paränetischer Rhythmus in der Handschrift Leiden BPL 130 (um 1100)," in *Arbor amoena momis: 25 Jahre Mittelalterliches Seminar in Bonn, 1965–1990* (Stuttgart: Steiner, 1990), 151–54. The poem in his edition, with select lines translated, contains 100 lines. The lines are sometimes presented as having mid-rhyme, reducing the overall number of verses by half, and at times as here showing end rhyme. It has the same meter as the famed *Dies irae,* although in couplets rather than tercets.

CHAPTER SEVEN

> Its flames do not cool off.
> Christian, beware, beware,
> You who are carried on the ship of the world!
> It may not be believed by a faithful person
> That there may be any honor other than that of heaven
> Where there is always light and day,
> Eternal peace, rest from the yoke,
> Brightness, I say, lacking clouds,
> Is that day that is always illuminating.

Thus, in fact, no earthly good can be compared to the celestial goods, and no earthly evil can be compared to the evils of Gehenna.

Therefore, brethren, let us be wary of the pains of the eternal abyss, and let us pass over from vices to virtues! Let us flee the glory of the world lest we be damned with wicked King Herod to perpetual punishments, but may we be glorified with the beneficent apostle in eternal joys! Herod, who is interpreted as "made of skins" or "glory of the skin," designates those who love the glory of the world more than of God. "Their God is their stomach, and their end is death, and their glory is in disorder who savor earthly things." [Phil 3:19] Without doubt, this Herod was among those about whom the Lord says in the Gospel: "They have sought the glory of men rather than of God." [Jn 12:43] It has, in fact, been written about Herod: "And he saw that thus far it seemed to be pleasing to the Jews, and so he went further and took Peter." [Acts 12:3] He wanted to please the Jews with the death of the apostles rather than God in defending the nourishing Church, and so he was killed by the angel, since those who please men are confounded, since God has scorned them. Woe! Woe! Cruel king and wicked tyrant, is it not sufficient for you to have killed James without putting Peter in jail? You carried this out for the increase of your ruin, since the one that you once killed now is joyful in heavenly glory, as your soul assuredly is tormented in the pit of hell. What, therefore, wicked king, is to be said at the Final Judgment when you will see the apostles whom you killed and held in prison sitting on thrones and judging not only you but also the twelve tribes of Israel? What are you to do, or what are you to say before God, when you have as judges those whom you killed with your own sword? What, O wretch, are you to say before the illustrious King Whose lawful student you killed? You will truly be silent, accused one, when you see the apostle that you butchered rejoicing in glory, while you suffer in eternal hell. James, the herald of Christ, the expressive trumpet, will remind you of faith. You, however, inflicted death on him. He invited you to eternal life. You on the contrary truly resisted and inflicted on him temporal death. You have slipped into the misfortunes of which the prophet says: "Is evil to be returned for good?" [Jer 18:20] You have given back evil for good, so that the prediction found in the Book of Wisdom might be fulfilled: "The justice of the righteous liberated him, and the unjust are taken up [f.42r] with snares." [Prov 11:6] "The just man has been liberated from distress, and the impious man will be handed over in his place." [Prov 11:8] And a little later it says: "The city shall exult in the good things of the just, and there will be praise in the ruin of the wicked." [Prov 11:10] Then the justice of the righteous — that is, of God — freed Saint James not only from the bodily chains but also from the original and infernal obligations.[66] Since Christ dies on the cross for James's redemption, James also dies by the sword for Christ's honor. Thus, the blessed apostle gives back exchange for exchange in fulfilling that prophetic saying: "You sat at the great table, remember what things are prepared for you, since it is necessary that you prepare the same."[67] James of Zebedee sat at the great table when at the Supper he took from the Lord's hands the perpetual food of heavenly life — that is, the body and blood of the Savior. Then he remembers the things that are set for him when after the Lord's Resurrection he believed in the One Who placed His body on the cross to die for the salvation of the faithful, and he endured the torments of his passion out of love for Him. Such an illustrious man! James prepared for the Lord, since, as was said,

---

66. A reference to original sin.
67. Cf. Ecclus (Sir) 31:12, 14, 19.

CHAPTER SEVEN

he gave back to Him a death for a death. This is what the Psalmist says: "What shall I give back to the Lord for all the things that he has given to me? I shall accept the cup of salvation." [Ps 115:12–13 / 116:12–13] The illustrious apostle accepted the chalice of salvation, since he chose martyrdom for Christ, as He had undertaken it for him, just as He once promised him, saying: "You will certainly drink My cup." [Mt 20:23] And so it is consistent that "the justice of the righteous liberated him, and the unjust are taken up," [Prov 11:6] since those who vanquish the saints in this present life will be damned to eternal death in the infernal destruction. "The just man has been liberated from distress," [Prov 11:8] since Saint James was freed from carnal chains and received into heaven by angels. "And the impious man will be handed over in his place," [Prov 11:8] since for Saint James's death the body of the unjust king Herod was stricken by an angel of the Lord and handed over to violent worms, and his spirit is held in a bitter land. It has been written about the unjust, in fact, in this way: "to destroy them with a double grinding, O Lord our God." [Jer 17:18] The Psalmist says the same: "Place iniquity upon iniquity." [Ps 68:28 / 69:27] Iniquity is placed on iniquity when the impious are provided for the present with temporal pain and in the future condemned to eternal death. "The city shall exult in the good things of the just." [Prov 11:10] The good things of the just are his miracles, protections, and prayer offerings, and the city is figuratively the Church of the faithful. Therefore, "the city shall exult in the good things of the city," because as the news of the miracles of Saint James and the belief in his strengths spread throughout the world, the Church is rendered illustrious and is increased. [f.42v] "And there will be praise in the ruin of the wicked, [Prov 11:10] since after the day of the Final Judgment, the saints will see themselves rise up to the heavens[68] and receive eternal happiness and the wicked, who beat them, cast down into hell. The joyful will praise the Lord Who conducted them to the joys of the heavens and Who permitted

---

68. "And the wicked who beat them cast down into hell" is written in the margin of CC with a red cross designating its insertion point; it is within the body of the text of S.

the wicked to go to their death. Then the illustrious apostle James will see himself gladdened in perpetual rejoicing and will see the wicked Herod who killed him fallen into the Gehenna of fire, and he will praise God and will say with the Psalmist: "Behold the man who did not place God as his helper but hoped in the multitude of his riches and had power in his vanity: I, however, like the fruitful olive tree have hoped in the mercy of my God for eternity and for the world without end."[69] [Ps 51:9–10 / 52:7–8] And so, in James is shown the reward of good things and in Herod the destruction of evil things. Just as, in fact, it is for the good to tolerate patiently the persecutions inflicted by their neighbors, so it is for God to reward them in celestial glory. And since the bad inflict evils on the good, God punishes them with eternal death: "For the wages of sin are death." [Rom 6:23] Neither will good be unrewarded nor evil unpunished. Because of this the apostle says: "Do not defend yourselves, brethren, but give place to wrath. Revenge[70] is mine. I will repay, says the Lord." [Rom 12:19] The Lord will pay back the vengeance against the enemies of the saints, since it should be "given back to each according to his works."[71]

But why is it that the blessed apostle, before he suffered and while he was living, could not convert all those he wanted to the faith of Christ, and now after his passage to the heavens, so many people come in multitudes to his basilica in Galicia? It is because if he had not accepted his passion for the faith of Christ, he would not have converted many to Christ. It has been certainly written: "Unless the grain of wheat falls on the earth and dies, it remains alone." [Jn 12:24–25] For "grain of wheat" is understood as either Christ or any martyr, for unless each should fall and die in suffering,

---

69. The Latin is *in seculum seculi* or "the century of the century"; a unique variant on the *saecula saeculorum* or "century of centuries" that we have translated here as elsewhere as "world without end." See ch.1, n.25.
70. The author uses the accusative *vindictam* (revenge); the Vulgate uses the nominative as translated here, since this verse is so well known.
71. This phrase "to each according to his works" is found in numerous places in the Bible. Cf. Mt 16:27, Rom 2:6, Rev 22:12, etc.

CHAPTER SEVEN

each would remain without converts to the faith, but if each should die, each would bring forward the fruit of good things. However, just as the grain of wheat remains alone, unless it should first die upon the earth, so also the blessed apostle, unless he first died for the faith of Christ, would remain as if alone without the multitude of converts. And just as the grain of wheat, after it had died, brought forward fruit on the earth, so also James, the man of Christ, after the triumph of his passion, brings forth, with his God-sanctioned patronage and with Christ granting it, multitudes of peoples coming to him in Galicia, as he brings forth, as it were, well-ripened and fragrant fruit in glory. Thus, as plants of leeks and vegetables in gardens are uprooted and transplanted elsewhere so that they may grow better, Saint James in his bodily presence is uprooted from Jerusalem [f.43r] and is transplanted among the Galicians so that he might increase in glory through all the peoples coming to him. The peoples of all the climes of the world come together, in fact, now at his basilica in Galicia, telling the glories of the Lord and His powers and the miracles that He did through this apostle in them. He is the fruit of God, the fruit of the penitent of the Church, the fruit of apostolic acquisition, to whom the Lord once promised, saying: "And may your fruit remain," [Jn 15:16] as if he were saying: "May the fruit of your acquisition remain in the heavens." Therefore, the fruit of Saint James will long remain, since it will last with God in eternity. And so, many are his fruits from the far climes of the world! They accomplish the journey with tired bodies and with excessive labors, kissing the sacred thresholds[72] of his basilica and requesting his favors. His fruit will last unto eternity, since a diverse multitude of peoples has heard his name, sees or hears with daily report his innumerable miracles, accepts penance for their sins through his love, and flows to his basilica in Galicia for the sake of prayers. And he converts those with a pure heart and good works

---

72. The word *limina*, "threshold," is a recurring synecdoche for the basilica of St. James at Compostela. Here it is used as well for the shrines of other saints.

to God the Savior, and this multitude will without doubt remain eternally with him as an odoriferous fruit in the heavenly places.

Thus, in fact, the Lord once promised to him, saying: "Come follow me. I will make you fishers of men." [Mt 4:19, Mk 1:17] Where was the Lord to go, such that the disciples would go after him? The Psalmist shows where He came from and where He was going, when he says: "His departure is from the highest point of heaven, and his destination[73] is to up to its highest point." [Ps 18:7 / 19:6] The highest point of heaven is God the Father, whose immense majesty is above all the heavens. Therefore, the departure from the highest point of heaven occurs when He came from the bosom of His Father into the womb of the Virgin. His excursion to the highest point of heaven was when He returned from the womb of the Virgin to the Passion, from the Passion to hell, from hell to the Resurrection and from the Resurrection up to the highest point of heaven, that is to God the Father above all the heavens. And so the apostle of the Lord came with these steps after Christ, since he truly believed in Him Who is the true Son of God and the true man born of the chaste Virgin, Who suffered on the cross for the salvation of all, Who was revived on the third day and was raised above the heavens, and James acted like Him through the passion of his body up to the heavens. Along this road, therefore, he came after Christ, since like Christ and for Him, he handed over his body to the torment of his passion. For this reason, he imitated Him in glory, as He testifies Who says: "And where I am there will My minister also be." [Jn 12:26] And He fittingly calls him at first to come after Him [f.43v] and not until after He promises to make him a fisher, so that he might show that first it is necessary for him to follow the examples of His Passion and then become a fisher of men. And so, it is consistent according to the Lord's promise that he follow Christ through his passion, and now he is made a fisher of souls. He is made a fisher of men as often, in fact, as people are converted through his exhortation from the idols of the Gentiles

---

73. The Latin is *occursus* or "meeting"; here the sense is something more of a metonymy.

CHAPTER SEVEN

and from the synagogue of the Jews to the faith or are drawn out from their difficulties through his intercession or are strengthened in good works through seeing his miracles; or are truly wrested from deep earthly whirlpools by him and are caught by the net of faith and led to the gate of salvation. And he leads away to the soil of paradise from the worldly Sea of Galilee as many as travel around and direct their course toward him in the country of Galicia with clear desire. Again the Lord once promised him, saying: "And you will be witnesses for me in Jerusalem and in all of Judea and Samaria and up to the end of the earth." [Acts 1:8] In Jerusalem, Saint James was a witness of the faith of Christ, since in its regions he is said, according to Luke, to have preached Christ and to have accepted his suffering from Herod, king of the Jerusalemites for the faith of God. In all of Judea and Samaria, he was a witness to the truth, since according to the story of his deeds, he dispersed Gospel preaching especially from Jerusalem up into Judea and Samaria. He proved a true witness to Christ up to the farthest point of the earth, since he is said to be buried with great honor in Galicia where one finds the border of the earth and sea[74] and where his basilica is built, and where there is evidence that he is adorned with frequent, divinely sanctioned miracles and with patronages not only in the regions of Galicia and Spain but also within the confines of the whole world. And as many of his miracles as there are and wherever they might be sought from him, or as many as are the peoples from foreign regions traveling to his basilica in Galicia, he gives that many testimonies to the faith of Christ in the Church. In the end, however, he is a witness to Christ alone, since he who dies for the faith of God by the sword offers an example to those coming to him in Galicia that they should die to vices and live for perpetual virtues. For this reason, it was written by Luke in this reading: "The word of the Lord, however, grew and was multiplied exceedingly." [Acts 6:7]

---

74. The Latin is *ultimum terre* or "farthest point of the earth" in the first instance here and *finis terre* in the second. The *ultimum* places the emphasis on the place at the extreme, while the word *finis* emphasizes the border, here between the earth and the sea.

Before the passion of the apostle and the death of Herod, the word of God is not said to have increased, but afterward it is read that it was extended, since if Saint James had not suffered for the faith of Christ, and if Herod, who was opposed to the word of God, had not been killed by the angel, the Word of God — namely the Word that was made flesh or the Son of God — could not be known openly in the world, nor could the Christian people, that were to believe through hearing [f.44r] his word, be increased. Since, just as the children of Israel in Egypt are read to multiply more before than after Joseph died, so also are the Christians said to be multiplied more before than after the Lord died. And just as the faithful are read to have increased after the Lord's death, so also after the death of Saint James the faithful people coming from all the climes of the world to Galicia are said to be increased more than before for the praise of the Lord.

And certainly, the gathering of many people, which he caused before his death, is worthy of praise, but the immense gathering of all the peoples that he now performs must be praised much more. For it is written thus: "Do not praise a man in his life, but praise him after its finish."[75] Just as, in fact, each one of the apostles immediately after the persecution of Saint James proceeded immediately to the place ordered beforehand by God and summoned the people to be saved to the faith of Christ, as the illustrious apostle James, freed from the flesh, is said to have been transferred from Jerusalem to Galicia, and he is believed, after his arrival, to have summoned to the veneration of God the once impious and unbelieving people of that land with his miracles demonstrated everywhere and with the grace of Christ at work. What he did not accomplish, in fact, while alive, he then fulfilled when dead. If, in fact, while alive he converted with his preaching and wonder a vast people, he now, freed from the flesh, has attracted with his miracles and powers an even more vast people to God with the mercy of the Holy Spirit at work. He is, in fact, in favorable times and in tribulation a helper to

---

75. Cf. Ecclus (Sir) 11:30.

CHAPTER SEVEN

those who clearly have[76] trust in him. It has been granted to him by the Lord that he is a hope to his own to all the ends of the earth and widely over the sea. Many, in fact, attest that they felt his protections in the difficulties and on the seas and when captured, and even to have seen him bodily in his finest form freeing them. In fact, he helps those afflicted by dangers, on land he relieves the oppressed, and he restores those shipwrecked in the deep whirlpools of the sea.

Oh, how admirable and praiseworthy is God in his saints! He has chosen such servants who, even when dead, have converted and helped the living! The Psalmist said: "Blessed is the one whom You have chosen and taken up, O Lord, he will dwell in Your courts." [Ps 64:5 / 65:4] As if he were saying: "Blessed is the one whom You chose, O Lord, and whom You took from the world upon the Sea of Galilee, for he lives with You in the temple of the heavens." "Therefore, praise the Lord in His holy places; praise Him in the firmament of His powers." [Ps 150:1] For God is glorious in His holy places, is wonderful in majesty, does wonders, is wonderful and praiseworthy, and [f.44v] performs miracles. "Therefore, praise the Lord of heaven and exult. O Earth, call out true mountains in joy," for through James[77] "the Lord has consoled His people and has had mercy on His poor." [Is 49:13] He, however, with His grace converted the predicted famine of the human race to a most healthy restoration and abundance, and He has crowned today His venerable and illustrious apostle through the monstrous torments of passion with the unfading laurel of eternal life.

May Jesus Christ our Lord deign to help us and lead us in the heavens, Who reigns with the Father and the Holy Spirit as God. World without end. Amen.

---

76. Here the reading of S is better: *habent* or "they have" rather than *habentur* or "they are held."
77. The author inserts "through James" in a tmesis to the text of Isaiah.

[CHAPTER 8]

VIII CALENDS OF AUGUST[1]
PASSION OF SAINT JAMES OF ZEBEDEE
THE APOSTLE OF GALICIA

ACCORDING TO MATTHEW:

"At that time, the mother of the sons of Zebedee came to the Lord Jesus with her sons, James and John, adored Him, and asked something from Him. He said to her: 'What do you wish?' She said to Him: 'Say that these two sons of mine may sit, one at Your right hand and the other at Your left hand, in Your kingdom.' And Jesus answered and said: 'You do not know what you are asking,'" and so forth. [Matthew 20:20–21ff.]

HOMILY OF THE PRIEST SAINT BEDE THE VENERABLE:[2]

Our Lord, Creator and Redeemer, wanted to cure the wounds of our pride, and when He was in the form of God and accepted the form of man, He humbled Himself and was made obedient up unto death; and He advises us also, if we wish to rise to the height of true loftiness, to take for ourselves the road of humility. If we wish to see true life, He orders us to bear the adversities of the present world as well as death. While He promised the gifts of glory, He set down beforehand the strife of battle. He promised this when He said: "Your reward will be great, and you will be sons of the Most High." [Lk 6:35] But He said beforehand and ordered: "Love your enemies and do good things and give to each other and hope for nothing in return." [Lk 6:35] Therefore He promised recompense to the chosen, so that He might show suitable rewards for this recompense. Thus, He gives eternal life as He also marks off the narrow gate and the confined road for arriving at it. On this He

---

1. July 25.
2. Bede, *Homiliae genuinae 18*, "In Natale Sancti Jacobi Apostoli" (PL 94:228–33).

CHAPTER EIGHT

says: "Strive to enter through the narrow gate." [Lk 13:24] Truly no small amount of striving is necessary if one wishes to rise to the heights. For as we ascend the peak of the mountains with a great deal of sweat, a great deal of toil is necessary [f.45r] so that we may deserve to have a place to rest on the holy mountain of the Lord in the heavens about which the Psalmist sings.[3]

Whence also in today's reading of the holy Gospel, when the sons of Zebedee sought seats in heaven from Him, He immediately recalls drinking His cup, that is, imitating the agony of His Passion, so that they might be mindful that that they must seek the heights of the heavenly only through the lowly and troublesome things of the worldly. It says: "At that time, the mother of the sons of Zebedee came to Him with her sons, adored Him, and asked something from Him. He said to her: 'What do you wish?' She said to Him: 'Say that these two sons of mine may sit, one at Your right hand and the other at Your left hand in Your kingdom.'" [Mt 20:20–22] Certainly no one, however, should judge their mother to have sought for her sons without their consent and their wish, but rather one should understand that their intention was determined with a single mind for all; that through their mother — whom they knew was beloved to the Lord[4] — the disciples would make known to Him their desire. For this reason, when Mark the Evangelist brings this up, he is silent on the intervention of their mother but makes mention only of the disciples, whose heart's desire he knew, as he says: "And James and John, the sons of Zebedee, approached the Lord and said: 'Master, we wish you to grant us what we are asking You to do for us.' But He said to them: 'What do you wish Me to do for you?' And they said 'Grant us that we may sit, one at Your right hand and the other at Your left hand, in Your glory.'" [Mk 10:35–37] He therefore asserts that only they went to the Lord and asked Him, and he looks on their desire for asking as more important, but he

---

3. Cf. Ps 14:1 / 15:1.
4. Possibly a reference to the supposed relationship of Maria Salome, the mother of James, with Mary, the mother of Jesus.

recognizes that their[5] mother had encouraged their asking with her exhortation. It is, however, to be believed that this is especially the cause, either as the womanly tendency of a mother or because she had spurred the minds of the disciples to ask these things, since they recalled the word of the Lord, Who said: "When the Son of man will sit on the seat of His majesty, you also will sit on twelve seats judging the twelve tribes of Israel." [Mt 19:28]

And the disciples would know among themselves, and especially with Peter, that they were made aware of hidden things that the others would not know, as the repeated text of the holy Gospel indicates. It is from this, in fact, that the name was also imposed on them, in the same manner as with Peter, so that, just as he was called "Simon" before, he merited the the name of "Peter" because of the strength and stability of his unconquerable faith. Thus they were called "Boanerges," that is, "Sons of Thunder,"[6] since they, of course, alone along with Peter, would hear the voice of the Father above the Lord made bright[7] on Mount Tabor,[8] and they learned several other secrets of the mysteries before the other disciples. And because especially it pertained to this matter, they felt themselves [f.45v] adhering with their full heart to the Lord, and they felt Him embrace them with the greatest love. And so they did not believe it could happen that they could sit more closely around Him in the kingdom, especially when they saw John, who, for singular purity of mind and body, was held in such great love that he would recline against His bosom at the Last Supper. But let us listen to what the Knower of merits and the Distributor of seats answered to those seeking the dignity of the seats: "Jesus answered and said 'You do not know what you are asking.'" [Mt 20:22] Truly they

---

5. The words "desire for asking as more important and…their" are in the margin in CC, with a red cross designating their insertion point in the text; they are in the body of the text in S.
6. Cf. Mk 3:17.
7. The Latin *clarificatum* would normally be used figuratively as "made famous" but seems to be used literally here.
8. Cf. the story of the Transfiguration, Mt 17:1–8, Mk 9:2–9, Lk 9:28–36.

did not know what they were asking. They thought that anyone could be seated at the left side of Christ in the kingdom of the heavenly country, when, at that decision of the Final Judgment, it is read that all the chosen are to come to the right hand of the highest King and Judge. That life has, of course, no left[9] side. Eternal happiness has nothing false. Eternal peace retains nothing frail. However, the left side of Christ, when it is taken in the good sense, is understood as the present life of the Holy Church. About this, it has been written: "The length of the days is on her right hand, and on her left hand riches and glory." [Prov 3:16] The length of days on the right hand is, of course, the wisdom of our Redeemer, since perpetual light is given in that country of the celestial dwelling to the chosen angels and men. Its glory and riches are on the right hand, since we are restored through this exile of pilgrimage by the riches of virtues and the glory of the faith until we arrive unto the eternal. The apostle speaks clearly of this glory: "And we glory in the hope of the glory of the sons of God. Not just that, however, we also glory in tribulations." [Rom 5:2–3] Concerning these riches he says: "For in all things you are made rich in Him, in every word and every knowledge." [1 Cor 1:5] They did not know what they were seeking, since they believed they could be chosen through human will, on which seats each would be in the future and by what recompense this would be conferred, and above all they are asking the Lord that they should manifest the trust and glory of the hope that they had by behaving well to the true end. And they knew that whatever good they might do, He would repay it with a lasting reward. And certainly their pious simplicity is worthy of praise, as they request with the trust of a devout mind to sit near the Lord in the kingdom, but His prudent humility is even more to be praised, who, knowing His own fragility said: "I have chosen to be abject in the house of My God rather than to live in the tents of sinners." [Ps 83:11 / 84:10] They did not know what they were

---

9. The Latin *sinistram* carries the connotations of awkward, wrong, perverse, etc. The following explanation of lack of negatives in heaven emphasizes this.

seeking, as they [f.46r] sought the loftiness of the rewards from the Lord rather than the perfection of works. However, the heavenly Teacher introduces them to what is to be sought. He calls them back to the path of labor by which they might reach the reward of recompense. He said: "Can you drink the cup that I am to drink?" [Mt 20:22] Certainly He is speaking of His cup as the bitterness of His Passion that is offered frequently to the just from the bitterness of the unfaithful. For whoever takes this up humbly, patiently, and joyfully for Christ will reign with Him by merit. However, since the sons of Zebedee wished to sit with Him, He warns them first to follow the examples of His Passion and thus finally to strive for the height of their wished-for majesty. The apostle teaches which condition of living is to be followed by all the faithful, when he says: "If, in fact, we have been planted in the likeness of His death, we shall also be in the likeness of His Resurrection." [Rom 6:5] "They said to Him 'We can.'" [Mt 20:22] They straightforwardly lay open their minds and devotion, as it was at that time when they testified that they would drink from the cup. Afterward they showed clearly how much weakness there was in this when the time came in which the Lord would drink this very cup as they fled with His other disciples and abandoned Him. However, this fear of drinking from the cup did not press long on their hearts. Rather, those who fled the Lord Who was about to suffer, returned quickly to Him when He arose. And what they feared in the whirlwind of the Passion, they quickly set right in the glowing triumph of His Resurrection. As for the rest, after having taken the grace of the Holy Spirit, they held an enduring disposition for drinking from the cup of the Lord, since they began to be invincible in suffering, dying for Him in fulfillment of His promise in which He told them that they would drink from His cup. For this follows: "He said to them, 'You will certainly drink My cup.'" [Mt 20:23]

And then this follows: "However, to sit at My right hand and left hand is not Mine to grant to you, but it is for those for whom it was prepared by My Father." [Mt 20:23] The one who rejoices in lofty happiness in direct sight of Him sits at the right hand of the Savior. The one who presides over the priestly guidance of His holy

CHAPTER EIGHT

Church on this pilgrimage sits on the left. However, one should look closely and critically at how the true Teacher spoke to those asking Him: "This is not for Me to give to you, but it is for those for whom it was prepared by My Father," [Mt 20:23] when He may have said elsewhere: "All things have been handed over to Me by My Father." [Mt 11:27, Lk 10:22] And so this is consistent with the fact that whatever the Father had given or prepared as gifts for the faithful, the Son prepares or gives [f.46v] together with Him. For the Lord says again about the Father: "Whatever, in fact, He has done, the Son also likewise does."[10] [Jn 5:19] How does the Son say: "It is not Mine to give you, but it is for those for whom it was prepared by My Father," [Mt 20:23] unless it is because this Son is both God and man? And so, through His Gospel, He sometimes speaks with the voice of divine majesty, which is equal to the Father, and sometimes from the voice of the assumed humanity, which is made equal to us. However, in this reading, He was to demonstrate a form of humility, and He says everything from His assumed human nature. For in the beginning, as the mother came to Him to ask together with her sons, He inquired as to what she wanted, asking like a man, as if unaware of the hidden things or unknowledgeable about future events, while He, in the eternal nature of divine power, knows all things before they occur. And since she brought forward these things in a request to His humanity rather than for a reckoning from His divinity — because she asked for a seat for her sons at His left or right side — which He certainly had in His bodily state, while in His divine majesty He is formed with no assembly of limbs. Consequently, He, with the glory of His Deity remaining quiet, revealed an account of the Passion that He was about to accept in His humanity, and He proposed that this would be imitated by his disciples when he confirmed their agreement with His attestation, as He said: "You will certainly drink My cup." [Mt 20:23, Mk 10:39] Then he suitably added to this, saying: "However, to sit at My right

---

10. The words "Whatever, in fact, He has done, the Son also likewise does" are in the margin in CC, with a red cross designating their insertion point; they are in the body of the text in S.

hand or My left hand is not Mine to give to you, but it is for those for whom it was prepared by My Father." [Mt 20:23, Mk 10:40] It was as if He were openly saying: "You will certainly follow in the suffering of the Passion that I will undergo according to the flesh, but it is not Mine according to the flesh, in which I bear the essence of human frailty, to give you the rewards of heavenly gifts. The things prepared by the Father for those worthy to receive them, as I likewise in that same divinity prepared and gave them, for all that He has done, I also have likewise done Myself through the unity of the divine power." However, since the sons of Zebedee had their mind ready to drink from the cup of the Lord, it is consistent that they seek, together with the other apostles, the dignity of the seats that they sought to receive, not so much through the distinction by which they were seeking — that one would be on His right side in His kingdom and the other would be on His left side — but in harmony with what we expressed above. Both would first for a time be on His left side and soon both would deserve to sit on His right side forever. [f.47r] Of course, they were sitting on the left side of Christ, as they presided in guiding with apostolic right the peoples of the faithful in this life. Certainly in that kingdom about which He said: "The kingdom of God is within you," [Lk 17:21] they sit now in that life that knows no death at His right side as judges of the world with Him, because each of these seats was prepared for them by the Son together with the Father. And the granting of gifts cannot be separated in Them, in whom the unity of nature is forever inseparable, as this very Son testifies when He says: "I and the Father are One." [Jn 10:30]

One should also not pass over without consideration the way in which the Lord said, indifferently, that the sons of Zebedee would drink from His cup. For we know that one of these, namely James, was to finish his life with an outpouring of blood, while the other, that is, John, would come to rest in the peace of the Church. For Luke openly testifies about the martyrdom of James that: "King Herod sent a force to afflict some from the Church, and he killed James, the brother of John, with a sword." [Acts 12:1] The *Ecclesiastical History* also reports an event worthy of memory concerning his passion. It says: "Since certainly the one who had taken him" — that is, James — "to the judge for martyrdom was moved by penance and confessed that he was also a Christian." He said, "They were both led together to a punishment of death. And while they were being led on the road, he asked James to give him forgiveness. And James deliberated a short while and then said 'Peace be with you,' and he kissed him, and thus both together were beheaded."[11] Afterwards, trustworthy stories tell about John. When he knew within himself that the day of his departure was arriving, he called together his disciples in Ephesus, expressed many proofs of signs of Christ, went down to the place dug for his tomb, said a prayer, and was committed to his fathers. He is found to be a stranger to the pain of death and to the corruption of the flesh. How then, is he said to have drunk the cup of the Lord, since it is agreed in his case that he did not at all leave his body through a death of suffering, unless it is because this cup is drunk in two ways? In one way, death brought about by a persecutor is accepted patiently. In another way, the mind is kept ready for the suffering when life is conducted as worthy for martyrdom. For John himself taught how ready he was to drink the cup of death for the Lord, when, with the other apostles, as we read in their Acts, [f.47v] he tolerated prison and lashes with a joyful mind, when he was consigned[12] to the island of Patmos because of the word of God and because of his testimony for Jesus. When, as the *Ecclesiastical History* narrates, he was hurled into a vat of boiling oil by the ruler Domitian, he came out unharmed and clean, as much by the gracious Lord as by his life and mind that were most chaste.[13] Thus, as his exile was upon him, in which he appeared to be more forsaken by human solace, he deserved all the more to be consoled by the multitude of heavenly citizens. For this reason, he is also truly understood to

---

11. See ch. 4 for the full account.
12. Both CC and S have *religatus* or "fastened," but the sense is that of *relegatus* or "consigned."
13. This story is not found in the *Ecclesiastical History*, but comes from Tertullian, *De Praescriptionibus adversus Haereticos*, ch. 36 (PL 2:49).

have drunk from the cup of the Lord with his brother James, who was killed by the sword, because he sustained so many things for the sake of truth and he showed that he was ready to receive death itself if it were offered to him.

Dearest brethren, even if we do not suffer anything similar, and if we tolerate neither chains, nor whips, nor prisons, nor such punishments to the body, nor any persecution by men for the sake of justice, we also may still receive the cup of salvation and the palm of martyrdom. If we take care to chastise our body and to submit to service, if we become accustomed to beseech the Lord in a spirit of humility and with a contrite soul, if we busy ourselves with accepting with a placid mind the abuses inflicted by our neighbor, if we rejoice in loving those who hold us in hate and bring injury to us and do good for them and reconcile with them for the sake of their life and safety, if we strive to be adorned by the virtue of patience and the fruits of good works, then in this way we preserve ourselves, and we deliver our bodies according to the apostle as a living and holy and pleasing sacrifice to God, then heavenly honor will be given, and we will be rewarded with a glory that is common to those who have given their limbs unto death for the Lord. For our life may be precious in the sight of the Lord, just as is theirs, and we may be worthy, with the chains of the flesh broken asunder, to enter the atria of the highest city to offer, among the choruses of the blessed martyrs, prayers of thanks to our Redemptor.

May Jesus Christ our Lord deign to be present, Who gave His cup to His disciples James and John to drink and to possess the eternal kingdom, and Who lives and reigns with the Father and the Holy Spirit. World without end. Amen.[14]

---

14. Bede's sermon is essentially presented in its entirety with the final paragraph only slightly altered to the formulaic endings of the sermons in this collection.

[CHAPTER 9]

Here Begins the Prologue of Pope Saint [f.48r] Calixtus, Which Is Celebrated before the Great Passion of Saint James on the VIII Calends of August,[1] Which Also Can Be Read for Saint Josias the Martyr On the VII Calends of August[2]

It is evident that those who say that the Passion of Saint James is apocryphal are entirely mistaken. They do not know it agrees with the modest-sized Passion that we have taken from the *Ecclesiastical History*,[3] which is held to be of very great authority. In fact, it is found in both passions[4] that a servant of Herod by the name of Josias at the instigation[5] of the Jews brought the apostle before Herod's tribunal, that he was moved by penance when he saw the miracle of the sick man,[6] that he admitted he was a Christian, that he was reborn by the grace of baptism, and that he was crowned together with this same apostle with the triumph of martyrdom. This passion indeed is in sound agreement with Luke when he says: "King Herod sent a force to afflict some from the Church, and he killed James, the brother of John, with a sword." [Acts 12:1–2] I have found nothing to be reproached in it, except for the name of the father of Herod, which I have corrected according to the truth of the Acts of the Apostles, saying: "King Herod, however, ordered him to be decapitated." No one must reject the illustrious dispute with

---

1. July 25.
2. July 26.
3. A reference to Eusebius's *Ecclesiastical History*, see above ch. 4.
4. This refers to the short passion of Eusebius (ch. 4) and this longer passion.
5. The CC has the reading *in tinctu* "in dyeing" or "in coloring," while S has *instinctu* or "at the instigation," which is clearly the better reading.
6. Reference to the paralytic cured by St. James, as Josias was leading James to his beheading. See below p. 162.

Hermogenes and the laudable conversion contained in it. On the contrary, one must embrace and read it out of love for the apostle. One has in it the prophetic testimonies of the Lord's Incarnation, Birth, Passion, Resurrection, and Ascension, and therefore it is to be especially valued. I have translated the apostolic prayer found at the end of the Passion from the books of the Greeks into Latin. I have set forth the death of Herod inflicted on him by an angel for the sake of the apostle from a book of the Acts of the Apostles. For this reason, this entire Passion may be safely read in churches and refectories.

Here Ends the Prologue.

Here Begins the Passion.

[f.48v] After the Ascension of the Lord to the heavens,[7] James, the apostle of our Lord Jesus Christ and brother of John the Apostle and Evangelist, visited all of Judea and Samaria, went through the synagogues, and showed all the things predicted according to the Holy Scriptures that were completed in our Lord Jesus Christ. It happened, however, that a certain magician named Hermogenes sent his disciple named Philetus to James. When Philetus came to James with some Pharisees, he tried to assert that Jesus Christ the Nazarene was not the true Son of God, as the apostle claimed Him to be. [PH 2] James, however, acted confidently in the Holy Spirit, overcame all his assertions, and showed from the Holy Scriptures that He was the true Son of God. Philetus returned to Hermogenes and said to him:

> Know that you cannot overcome James, who claims to be the servant of the Nazarene God and His apostle. For

---

7. Calixtus borrows the text of the *Pasionario Hispánico* (PH) on Saint James, beginning here with sect. 2 of that work. Section 1 is simply a sentence-header for the rest of the sections and is not included in the borrowing. Section 17 drifts off toward the end into what may be a Calixtus work for the last segments of this chapter, and sect. 18 states simply, "To Him is honor and glory. World without End. Amen."

CHAPTER NINE

I have seen him casting out demons in His name from the bodies of the possessed, illuminating the blind, and cleansing the lepers. They also assert, my dearest friends, that they have seen him raising the dead. But why dwell on these many details? He holds all the Holy Scriptures in his memory, from which he shows that no one else is the Son of God, except the One Whom the Jews crucified. May my advice therefore be pleasing to you: Come to him and ask forgiveness from him for yourself. If you do not do this, know that your magic art will be useful in no way at all. Know, however, that I am going to him and asking that I might be worthy to be his disciple. [PH 3]

However, when Hermogenes heard this, he was filled with jealousy, and he encircled Philetus's body with fetters so that he could not move and said to him: "Let us see if your James may free you from these fetters." Then Philetus quickly sent his servant to James. When he had arrived and told this to James, James immediately sent his handkerchief to him, saying: "Let him accept this and say: 'The Lord Jesus Christ lifts those who are shattered, and He releases those who are shackled!'" Then, as soon as the one who had brought it had touched him with the handkerchief, he was freed from the fetters of the magician, and he ran to James, reviling [f.49r] the evil deeds of the magician. Hermogenes the Magician, however, distressed that Philetus would insult him, summoned demons with his art, and sent them to James, saying: "Go immediately and bring this James here to me, together with my disciple Philetus, so that I may vindicate myself lest my other disciples dare to insult me in this way." [PH 4] The demons, however, came to where Saint James was praying and began to make howling sounds in the air and said: "James, apostle of God, have mercy on us, since we are already burning before the time of our burning has come." Saint James said to them: "For what reason do you come to me?" The demons said to him: "Hermogenes sent us, so that we might bring you and Philetus to him. As soon as we entered, an angel of God bound us with fiery chains, and we are tormented." James the Apostle said to them: "In the name of the Father and the Son and the Holy Spirit, may the angel of God release you, so that you may return to Hermogenes, and without hurting him, bring him fettered here to me." [PH 5] They headed off, and they tied his hands behind his back with ropes and thus led him, saying: "You sent us where we were burned and tormented and were intolerably destroyed."

Meanwhile, when Hermogenes had been led to Saint James, the apostle of God said to him: "Stupidest of men, you who believe you can converse with the enemy of the human race! Why do you not consider whom you have asked to send his angels to you to injure me and whose fury I have not allowed them to show to you up until now?" The demons also called out saying: "Give us power over him so that we may vindicate your harm and our burning." James the Apostle said to them: "Behold, Philetus stands before you. Why do you not take him?" The demons said to him: "We cannot touch even an ant that is in your room." Then Saint James said to Philetus: "So that you know that this is the sect of our Lord Jesus Christ and so that men may learn to give back good things for evil things: he bound you, and you are to release him. He tried to bring you bound by the demons to him, and you are to permit him who is held by the demons to go free." [PH 6] When Philetus freed him, Hermogenes began to stand — confused, humbled, and dejected. Saint James said to him: "Go freely wherever you might wish. It is not our teaching that anyone be converted unwillingly." Hermogenes said to him: "I know the wrath of the demons. Unless you give me something that I may have with me, [f.49v] they will seize me and kill me with diverse pains." Then Saint James said to him: "Take this staff of my journey, and go securely with it wherever you might wish." And he took the scepter of the apostle and went off to his own house, and he placed it over the nape of his neck and over the napes of the necks of his disciples.[8] And he brought sacks full of books to the apostle of God, and he began to burn them in fires. Saint James said to him: "Lest perchance the stench of their burning damage those unaware, put a stone along with lead inside

---

8. This is likely symbolic of bearing the yoke as oxen might bear their burden.

CHAPTER NINE

the sacks and make them sink in the sea. When Hermogenes had done this, he returned and began to grasp the feet of the apostle and asked him, saying: "Liberator of souls, accept the penitent one whom you have until now tolerated while he was envious and disparaging." Responding, Saint James said: "If you have offered true penance to God, you will also receive His true forgiveness." Hermogenes said to him: "I offer to God true penance to the extent that I have thrown away all my books in which there was illicit presumption, and I have at the same time renounced all the arts of the enemy." [PH 7] The apostle said to him: "Now go through the houses of those whom you have subverted, so that you may call back to their Lord those you have taken and teach that what you said was false is true and what you said was true is false. Shatter the idol that you used to adore as well as the predictions that you thought within yourself were answered by it! Spend the money that you acquired through bad work on good works, so that you who were a son of the devil by imitating the devil are made son of God by imitating God Who daily offers benefits to the ungrateful and provides food to those blaspheming Him! If, in fact, when you were bad toward God, the Lord was good toward you, how much more favorable will he be if you cease being bad and begin to be pleasing with good works?" [PH 8] Saint James said these things and things similar to these, and Hermogenes submitted in all things, and he began to be perfect out of fear of God, so that many miraculous things were done by the Lord through him. Therefore, the Jews saw that James had converted this magician whom they thought was insuperable, such that even all his disciples and friends who used to come together at the synagogue believed in Jesus Christ because of James. They brought money to two centurions who were ruling in Jerusalem, Lysias[9] [f.50r] and Theocritus, and they seized James and sent him into custody. [PH 9]

---

9. Claudius Lysias appears in Acts 21–24. He was a commander of the Roman garrison in Jerusalem. In Acts 24:6b–8b he insists that Paul be tried as a Roman, rather than by Jewish law.

When there was civil discord among the people, it was said that he must be brought forth and heard according to the law. Then the Pharisees said to him: "For what reason do you preach that Jesus is man and God, Whom we all know was crucified between thieves?" Then James, filled with the Holy Spirit, said:

> Listen, brethren and all you who know that you are sons of Abraham. God promised to our father Abraham that all peoples would inherit through his seed. His seed, however, is not with Ishmael but with Israel. For Ishmael, in fact, was cast out with his mother Hagar and has been excluded from his share in the seed. It was said to Abraham by God: "In Isaac will your seed be called." [Gen 21:12] Abraham was, however, called a friend of God[10] before he accepted circumcision, before he observed the Sabbath, and before he knew any law of divine ordination. He became a friend of God, not by circumcising himself, but by believing in God, since all the peoples would inherit through his seed. If, in fact, Abraham became a friend of God by believing, it follows that one becomes an enemy of God if one does not believe in God. [PH 10]

The Jews, therefore, said: "And who is it who does not believe in God?" James answered:

> Whoever does not believe that all peoples shall inherit through his seed and whoever does not believe in Moses when he says: "The Lord will raise up with you a great prophet. You will hear him as you hear me, by all things that he will teach you." [Acts 3:22, Dt 18:15] Isaiah, however, predicted by what course this promise would happen. He said, in fact: "Behold a virgin will conceive and bear a Son, and His name will be called Emmanuel," [Is 7:14] "which is to be interpreted as 'God with us.'" [Mt 1:23] Jeremiah, however, said: "Behold your Redeemer will come, Jerusalem, and this will be His sign: He will open the eyes of the blind, He will restore hearing to the deaf, and with His voice He will raise the dead." [Is 35:4–5]

---

10. Cf. James 2:23.

CHAPTER NINE

And Ezekiel points it out saying: "Your King will come, O Zion, so that He may restore you."[11] Daniel, however, says: "The Son of man will come just like a river, and He will obtain rule and power." [Dan 7:13] David, however, says with the voice of the Son of God speaking: "The Lord said to Me, 'You are My Son. I have begot You today.'" [Ps 2:7] And elsewhere: "He will call out to Me, 'You are My Father.'" [Ps 88:27 / 89:27] And the voice of the Father says about the Son: "And I shall place the Firstborn One on high above the kings of the earth." [Ps 88:28 / 89:28] However, the word of God speaks to this very David, saying: "Of the fruit of your womb I will place upon My [f.50v] seat." [Ps 131:11 / 132:11] [PH 11] Concerning His Passion, however, Isaiah says: "He was led like a lamb to the slaughter." [Is 53:7] And David says about His humanity: "They have pierced My hands and My feet. They have numbered all My bones. They have looked on Me and inspected Me; they have divided among themselves My garments and have cast lots for My cloak." [Ps 21:17–19 / 22:16–18] And elsewhere this same David says: "They gave Me bile as food, and in My thirst, they have given Me vinegar to drink." [Ps 68:22 / 69:21] Concerning His death, however, He says: "My flesh will rest in hope, for You will not leave My soul in hell, nor will You give Your holy One to see corruption." [Ps 15:9–10 / 16:9–10] The voice, however, of the Son said to the Father: "I shall rise, and I am still with You."[12] And again: "'Because of the misery of destitution and the sighs of the poor, now I shall rise up,' says the Lord." [Ps 11:6 / 12:5] Concerning His Ascension, however, he says: "He ascended on high and brought the captive to captivity."[13] And again: "He ascended above the cherubim and flew off." [Ps 17:11 / 18:10] And again: "The Lord ascended in jubilation." [Ps 46:6 / 47:5] Also, Hannah, the mother of

---

11. Cf. Zech 9:9, Ez 36:11.
12. Cf. Ps 138:18 / 139:18.
13. Cf. Eph 4:8.

holy[14] Samuel, says: "The Lord ascends into the heavens and has thundered."[15] And many other witnesses are found in the law about His Ascension. For, as to His sitting at the right hand of the Father, David says: "The Lord said to my Lord: 'Sit at My right hand.'" [Ps 109:1 / 110:1] And, as to His coming to judge the world by fire, the prophet says: "God shall surely come, and our God will not be silent. In His gaze, a fire will burn and surrounding Him will be a strong storm." [Ps 49:3 / 50:3] [PH 12] All these things that were performed were fulfilled in our Lord Jesus Christ, and those that have yet to be done will be fulfilled just as they were prophesied. For Isaiah said: "The dead who are in the tombs shall rise and rise again."[16] If you should ask: "What will it be like when they have risen?" David says that he heard the Lord speaking about what it will be like. But so that you might judge what it might be, listen to what he says: "Once God spoke, I heard these two things: that God is power, and mercy is Yours, O Lord, for You give back to all according to one's works." [Ps 61:12–13 / 62:11–12] Whence, my brethren, let each of you do penance so as not to receive "according to one's works," as each knows that he is a participant with those who fixed Him to the cross Who freed the whole world from sufferings. For with His spit, He opened the eyes of the one born blind[17] so that He might be proven to be the One who had formed Adam from the slime of the earth. He made mud with His saliva and placed it upon the places of the eyes that sickness had not blinded [f.51r] but that were defective by nature. For we asked our Lord Jesus Christ, saying: "Who sinned — he or his parents — such that he should be born blind?" And He answered us, saying: "Neither he sinned nor his did his

---

14. The Latin is *sancti*, although Samuel is considered a prophet and not counted among the saints in the Roman Church. He does enjoy sainthood in some Lutheran and Orthodox churches.
15. Cf. 1 Kgs (1 Sam) 2:10.
16. Cf. Is 26:19.
17. Cf. Jn 9:1–12.

CHAPTER NINE

parents, but it was so that the works of God would be manifest in him." [Jn 9:1–3] That is so that the Maker Who had made him would be made evident when He would do what had been not quite done in him. [PH 13] For also the fact that He would receive bad things for us was predicted for His human person by David when he said: "They paid Me back with bad things for good." [Ps 34:12 / 35:12] And elsewhere: "They gave Me back bad things for good and hatred for My love." [Ps 108:5 / 109:5] Then, after He cured the crippled, cleansed the leprous, illuminated the blind, cast out demons, and raised the dead, they all called out with a single voice: "He is guilty of death." [Mt 26:66] And that He was to be handed over by His disciple is foretold in this order by David: "The one who was eating My bread has increased hypocritical deceit against Me." [Ps 40:10 / 41:10]

Brethren, sons of Abraham, the prophets predicted these things with the Holy Spirit speaking through their mouths. If we do not believe these things, why would we be able to avoid the punishment of perpetual fire? Or why are we not to be punished deservedly, when even the Gentiles believe in the words of the prophets, and we do not believe in the words of the patriarchs and prophets? Such crimes are shameful and to be punished in so many acts and wicked deeds, and we should lament them with tearful voices so that the pious Forgiver might accept our penance, so that those things might not happen to us that happened to the hateful people of whom the Psalmist says: "The earth opened up and swallowed Dathan and covered the synagogue of Abiram. Fire burned in their synagogues, and a flame consumed the sinners." [Ps 105:17–18 / 106:17–18] [PH 14]

When Saint James said these and similar things, the Lord conferred so much grace through His apostle that all called out with a single voice: "We have sinned! We have acted unjustly! Give us a remedy that we might do, holy apostle of God!" Saint James said to them: "Brethren, do not despair. Just believe and be baptized, so that all your sins may be erased." After they heard these things, they were baptized in the name of the Lord. However, after a few days, when Abiathar, the priest for that year,[18] saw that so many people believed in the Lord that he was filled with jealousy, he aroused very great civil discord with money and then ordered the apostle of the Lord to be beaten. And thus, one of the scribes of the Pharisees put a rope on Saint James's neck and then led him to the palace of King Herod. King Herod, however, [f.51v] ordered him to be decapitated. [PH 15] While he was being led to the beheading, he saw a paralytic lying prostrate and calling to him: "Saint James, apostle of Jesus Christ, free me from the pains that all my limbs are suffering." And James said to him: "In the name of my crucified Lord Jesus Christ, for Whose faith I am being led to beheading, arise healthy, and bless your Savior." And he immediately arose and began to rejoice and to run and to bless the name of the Lord Jesus Christ. Then this scribe of the Pharisees, named Josias, who had put the rope on his neck, released James, threw himself at his feet, and began to say: "I beg you to give me forgiveness and make me a partaker in His holy name." At this, James understood that his heart had been visited by the Lord and said to him: "Do you believe that my Lord Jesus Christ, Whom the Jews crucified, is the true Son of the living God?" And Josias said: "I believe, and it is my belief from this hour that He is the Son of the living God." [PH 16] Then Abiathar the priest had him seized and said to him: "If you do not depart from James and curse the name of Jesus Christ, you will be decapitated with James." Josias said to him: "May you be cursed, and may all your gods be cursed. The name of Jesus Christ of Whom James preaches is blessed unto the centuries." Then Abiathar ordered

---

18. The author possibly takes the name Abiathar from Mk 2:25–27, "And he said to them, 'Have you never read what David did when he and his companions were hungry and in need of food? He entered the house of God, when Abiathar was high priest, and ate the bread of the Presence, which it is not lawful for any but the priests to eat, and he gave some to his companions.'" Mark's reference is incorrect; the priest's name was Ahimelech as originally narrated in 1 Kgs (1 Sam) 21:1–9, and his son was Abiathar. The other synoptic Gospels leave out this reference. The name is anachronistic here.

CHAPTER NINE

his face to be struck with blows and sent a report to Herod about him and asked that he be decapitated together with James. Having come, then, to the place where they were to be decapitated, James said to the executioner: "Before you behead us, have some water given to us." And a vessel filled with water was brought to him. Then he ordered Josias to be uncovered.[19] He took the vessel and said to him: "Josias, do you believe in God the Father Almighty, the Creator of heaven and earth?" And he said: "I believe." Then the apostle said: "Do you believe in Jesus Christ His only Son and our Lord, Who was born and died and was raised and is seated at the right hand of the Father?" And he said: "I believe." Then the apostle said: "Do you believe in the Holy Spirit, the Holy Catholic Church, the communion of saints, the forgiveness of sin, the resurrection of the flesh, and life after death?" And he said: "I believe." Then the apostle poured the water on him three times in the name of the threefold Deity and said to him: "Give me, my son, the kiss of peace." And when he had kissed him, he placed his hand upon his head and blessed him and made the sign of the cross of Christ on his forehead [PH 17][20] and said to him: "Let us pray, brother, to the Lord that the One Who made our souls may deign [f.52r] to receive them." And then Saint James asked the executioner for a space for prayer, and he prayed to the Lord with the gaze of his heart raised toward heaven, with his hands extended, and looking upward. He then said in Hebrew:

> Lord Jesus Christ, Who reigns eternally with the Father and the Holy Spirit, Who formed Adam wondrously from the earth of paradise, Whom the malicious enemy deceived and brought with him to Tartarus, Who redeemed not with gold or silver but with Your own blood, Who, although being God became a man because of man, Who was born from a pure virgin, Who suffered on the cross,

---

19. The Latin is *expoliari* in the sense of the verb *spolio*, "to be uncovered," referring likely to removing headgear for the baptism.
20. The phrase "on his forehead" marks the end of the borrowing from the *Pasionario Hispánico* text.

Who descended to regions of hell, and Who brought this Adam back to paradise from whence he had fallen, and Who arose from the dead on the third day. You, O Lord, chose twelve men from all who were in the world, so that they might be witnesses of Your works in the world. Among their number you deigned to include me, not by my merits but by Your unutterable grace. You called me while I was on the Sea of Galilee, and I left my father and all my things, and I followed You together with my brother John. For You deigned to show us the secrets of Your wonders as You raised the daughter of the chief priest in his home.[21] You let no one else enter except Peter and my brother John and me. And when You were on Mount Tabor and were transfigured by the will of the Father, You permitted none of the apostles to see this, except me, Peter, and my brother John.[22] You appeared to me truly with the other apostles after Your Resurrection in many representations, and You ate and drank with us with proper love. On the day of Your Ascension, when You would return to Your Father, You would send Your apostles, once filled with the Holy Spirit, throughout the world, so they would reveal Your Gospel to all peoples and baptize them in Your name. I have truly revealed Your name not only in Judea but also in all of Samaria, and I was a witness of Your wonders all the way to the western peoples[23] among whom I have suffered many things for You: reproaches, blasphemies, mockeries, and strife. Now, O Lord, like the servant who returns to his lord by whom he was sent, so I return to You Who sent me. May You may take me as Your disciple and open for me the gate of eternal life and lead me to the heavens, so that I may be worthy to await and see my brother apostles who are to come after me. Therefore, grant, I beg, to those who have heard me and who have believed through me and who will believe in

---

21. Cf. Mk 5:21–43, Mt 9:18–26, Lk 8:40–56.
22. Cf. Mt 17:2, Mk 9:2–3, Lk 9:28–36.
23. This inclusion of the western peoples is noteworthy.

CHAPTER NINE

You, salvation in Your kingdom, since You are Christ my Teacher [f.52v] Whom I have esteemed, Whom I have loved, in Whom I have believed, and Whom I have followed up to this hour in which I am to die for You Who reign without end in the eternal ages.

When he had finished this prayer, Saint James removed his garments and gave them to his persecutors. Then he bent his knees to the ground, extended his hands, and raised them toward heaven, then extended his neck to his persecutor and said: "May earth take my earthly body in the hope of rising again! May heaven take my heavenly spirit!" And when he had said this, the persecutor unsheathed his sword and raised it on high and struck twice on his neck and cut off his most holy head, and immediately precious blood flowed out. And his head did not fall to the ground but the holy apostle, by the power of God, held it fully in his arms that were raised to heaven. And thus he remained, on bended knees, holding his head in his arms until night came when his disciples took his body. Meanwhile, some who had been sent by Herod tried to take his head, but they could not, For their hands grew stiff above the most precious body of Saint James. The persecutor beheaded Saint Josias right away as a martyr of Christ and a disciple of Saint James. Soon there occurred an enormous earthquake, and heaven opened, and the sea shook, and unbearable thunder occurred, and the earth opened and swallowed up a very large part of the unjust, and a great light flashed in that region, and an angelic throng was heard by many in the air, bearing their souls to the celestial seats where they may rejoice without end.[24]

Oh, what a bitter and wicked day was that for the perverse ones! What a splendid and glorious day for the just in which the saints travel to heaven and the evil to hell! For the death of saints is splendid in the sight of the Lord, and the death of sinners is wicked, and "those who have hated the just do wrong." [Ps 33:22 / 34:21] All who were there were frightened and struck with terror, and they

---

24. The author has brought in details from Christ's Passion, in addition to the miracle of James holding his own head after death.

began to cry out saying: "That is the true God Whom he preached and Whom the Jews crucified." Others however said: "Truly he was a man of God, and justly will the Lord destroy this place and this city because of his death, for he was unjustly beheaded." However, when that day was done, in the following night, his apostles came to him and found him, as we have said, on bended knees and holding his head in his arms, and they placed his body and head in a bag of deerskin with precious spices, and they transferred it from Jerusalem to Galicia with an angel of the Lord accompanying them on the sea. There they buried his body where it is venerated [f.53r] to this very day.

As to Herod, who was guilty of the death of Saint James, the book of the Acts of the Apostles tells of the most ugly death to which he was condemned in this way: and seeing that it was pleasing to the Jews, he took Peter the Apostle and placed him in prison, but he escaped unharmed with an angel of the Lord leading him out at night.[25] When day dawned and Peter was not to be found, a sorrowful Herod[26] went down from Judea to Caesarea and stayed there. He was, however, angered with the Tyrians and the Sidonians. They, however, all decided to come to him, as Blastus, who was the king's chamberlain had persuaded them to do, and they sought peace because their regions were maintained by him. On the appointed day, Herod, dressed in regal garb, sat before the tribunal and spoke sublimely to them. The people, in fact, exclaimed: "The sounds of God and not of man!" However, an angel of the Lord immediately struck him, and he died, consumed by worms, because he had not given honor to God and he had shed the blood of Saint James unjustly. The word of the Lord, however, increased and grew greatly.[27]

---

25. Cf. Acts 12:3–10.
26. The following begins with a summary of Acts 12:3–7.
27. Cf. Acts 12:19–24, with some variations and the addition of "and he had shed the blood of Saint James unjustly."

CHAPTER NINE

After a short time, however, Jerusalem was destroyed by the emperors Titus and Vespasian,[28] as a faithful history tells, such that not a stone remained on a stone, because it had shed the precious blood of the martyrs unjustly, namely that of the Savior, of Stephen the proto-martyr,[29] and of both Saint James the Greater and James the Lesser.

With our Lord Jesus Christ reigning over all things, Whose reign and rule remain without end. World without end. Amen.

---

28. Vespasian (9 CE–79 CE, reign 69–79) subjugated Judaea during the Jewish rebellion of 66 CE. Titus (13 CE–81 CE, reign 79–81), Vespasian's son, was in charge of ending the Jewish rebellion. He besieged and captured Jerusalem and destroyed the city and the Second Temple (70 CE).

29. Stephen (5 CE–34 CE) is considered the first martyr of the Christian faith; Saul (Paul) witnessed his stoning. See Acts 6 and 7.

[CHAPTER 10]

VII Calends of August[1]
II Day within the Octaves of Saint James[2]
The Office of the Solemnity of Saint Josias the Martyr and Saint James Is Celebrated at the Same Time and this Gospel Is Read

A Reading of the Holy Gospel According to Matthew:

"At that time, the Lord Jesus called His twelve disciples, gave them the power over unclean spirits so that they could cast them out and cure every disease and weakness. The names of the twelve apostles, however, are these: first Simon, who is called Peter, and Andrew his brother, James of Zebedee and John his brother, Philip and Bartholomew, [f.53v] Thomas and Matthew the publican, James the son of Alphaeus and Thaddeus, Simon the Canaanite and Judas Iscariot, who also betrayed Him," and so forth. [Mt 10:1–4ff.]

A Sermon of Saint Jerome the Doctor on This Reading:[3]

We have much to do to make known the apostolic solemnities to be venerated, dearest brethren, and to examine this Gospel reading with an explanation for your hearts. The kind and gentle Lord and Teacher did not deny His powers to His servants but just as He had cured every weakness and every sickness, so He also granted to His apostles the power to cure every weakness and sickness. However, there is a big difference between "to have" and "to grant" and between "to give" and "to receive." Whatever He did, He did with the power of the Lord; if they do something, they confess both

---

1. July 26.
2. July 27. The Octaves were celebrated from VIII Calends (July 25) through Calends Augusti (August 1st). The end of the octave was also the first day of the octave of Saint Peter in Chains; Bk. III *(Translatio)*, ch. 3 discusses how these feast days aligned. See Coffey and Dunn, *Miracles*, 88–95.
3. Saint Jerome, *Commentariorum in Evangelium s. Matthaei liber I* (PL 26:60–64).

CHAPTER TEN

their weakness and the power of the Lord, saying: "In the name of Jesus, arise and walk." [Acts 3:6]

It should, however, be noted that the power of signs is given to the apostles in a relationship of twelve: "The names of the twelve apostles are these." [Mt 10:2] The enumeration of the apostles is given so that future pseudo-apostles might be separated from them: "First Simon, who is called Peter, and Andrew his brother." [Mt 10:2] It was up to Him Who understands the secrets of the heart to apportion to them rank and reward. Simon, with the epithet of Peter, is written down first in differentiation from the other Simon, who is called the Zealot, from the town of Cana[4] in Galilee, where the Lord turned water into wine. He also called James "of Zebedee," because there also was the follower James of Alphaeus. He also associates them in joint pairs. He joins Peter with Andrew his brother, not so much in the flesh as in the spirit, and James and John, since they left their bodily father and followed the true Father. He joins Philip and Bartholomew; and also, Thomas and Matthew the Publican. The other Evangelists, in connecting the names, place Matthew first and then Thomas, and they do not ascribe the name of "Publican," so as not to appear to insult the Evangelist by being mindful of the Old Law. [f.54r] Matthew, however, as we said above, also placed himself after Thomas and calls himself a publican, as in "where sin abounds, grace abounds even more." [Rom 5:20] Simon of Cana is the one who is called the Zealot in the other Gospel;[5] Cana is interpreted, of course, as "zealot."[6] The *Ecclesiastical History*[7] reports that Thaddeus the Apostle was sent to Edessa to King Abagar of Osroene,[8] and he is called Judas of James

---

4. The Latin appears to be *Ohana* in CC and *Thina* in S, but it is clearly Cana from the context.
5. Lk 6:15.
6. The word "Cana" in Hebrew indicates "reeds"; the basis for this etymology is unclear.
7. Eusebius, *Ecclesiastical History*, Bk. 6, ch. 13.
8. The Latin is *Hosroec,* but the context indicates King Abagar V, who ruled over Osroene, in modern Turkey.

by Luke the Evangelist,[9] and elsewhere he is called Lebtheus,[10] which is interpreted as "little heart." It should be considered that he had a triple name just like Simon Peter. The sons of Zebedee were also called "Sons of Thunder" for their firmness and the greatness of their faith. Judas Iscariot, however, took his name from either the place in which he was born or from the tribe of Issachar, as if he were born with a prophecy of his condemnation. Issachar, in fact, is interpreted as "hire,"[11] as if it might signify the "price" of a traitor.

"Do not turn aside onto the road of the Gentiles, and do not enter the city of the Samaritans, but rather go to the sheep that are lost from the house of Israel." [Mt 10:5–6] This text is not contrary to the one that afterward says: "Go, teach all peoples, and baptize them in the name of the Father and of the Son and of the Holy Spirit," [Mt 28:19] because the latter was commanded before the Resurrection and the former after the Resurrection. And it was necessary first to announce the coming of Christ to the Jews, lest they have a just excuse by saying thereby that the Lord had rejected them since He would have sent apostles to the Gentiles and the Samaritans. It is perceived by us, however, who are known by the name of Christian, in a metaphorical way, lest we walk on the road of the Gentiles and in the error of the heretics. "Go, rather, and preach and say, 'The kingdom of heaven is at hand.' Cure the sick, raise the dead, cleanse the lepers, and cast out demons. You received freely, give freely." [Mt 10:7–8] Lest no one should believe rustic people who are without the elegance of eloquence and are unlearned and illiterate but who promise the kingdom of heaven, He gives the power to cure the sick, to cleanse the lepers, and to cast out demons, so that the greatness of the signs might show the greatness of the things promised. And since spiritual gifts always,

---

9. Cf. Acts 1:13. Judas is called the brother of James in this verse.
10. Some versions of the Bible use Lebbaeus for Judas in Mt 10:3, yet in others, Judas appears as Jude, and there are occurrences of Lebbaeus and Thaddeus used together.
11. The name concerns "hire" or "person hired" or the "wage" paid. The idea is to make a connection with thirty silver coins. Cf. Mt 26:15.

CHAPTER TEN

if a price is present, become rather vile, a condemnation of avarice is added on: "You received freely, give freely," [Mt 10:8] that is: "I, the Teacher and Lord have granted this to you without a price, and you are to give without a price, lest the grace of the Gospel be corrupted." [f.54v]

"Do not possess gold or silver or money in your purses, or a wallet for the road, or two coats, or shoes, or a staff in your hand. For the workman is, in fact, worthy of his food." [Mt 10:9–10] Consequently, He orders these things to the evangelizers of the truth, to whom He had said earlier: "You received freely, give freely." If, in fact, they preach in such a way that they do not accept any money, the possession of gold, silver, and coins is superfluous. For if they had gold and silver, they would appear to preach not for the sake of the salvation of people but for the sake of profit. "Or copper in your bags" [Mt 10:9]:[12] Whoever cuts off riches likewise also diminishes the necessities of life. As the apostles were being formed as teachers of the true religion with great prudence, this would show that they could govern themselves and not think of the next day. "Or a wallet for the road" [Mt 10:10]: From this injunction, he attempts to expose the philosophers who are called by the people Cynics,[13] because they were despisers of the world and considered all things as worth nothing, yet carried provisions with them. "Or two coats" [Mt 10:10]: With the two tunics, of course, the garment appears to me to mean "double faced." It is not that in the numbing locales of Scythia[14] with glacial snow one should be content with a single tunic, but rather we should understand by this tunic that we are dressed in one and keep another one for ourselves out of the fear of things to come. "Or shoes" [Mt 10:10]: Plato also ordered that the two peaks of the body should not be covered up, nor should one become accustomed to softness for the

---

12. The text here uses a biblical variant *es* for *aes* ("copper") rather than *pecunia* ("money").
13. The Latin is *bactroperite,* a term used to describe those with a purse, and it was specifically applied to the Cynics.
14. An area of Central Eurasia north of the Black Sea.

head and feet.[15] For when these have firmness, the other parts are more robust. "Or a staff" [Mt 10:10]: Why would we, who have the Lord's help, seek the aid of a staff? And since He had, in a way, sent the apostles unclothed and without baggage for preaching, and the condition of the teachers seemed to be harsh, He tempered the severity of the command with the following thought, saying: "The workman, in fact, is worthy of his food." [Mt 10:10] He is saying: "Take as much in food and clothing as is necessary for you." Whence the apostle replies, "Having food and clothing, let us be content with these." [1 Tim 6:8] And in another place: "Let the one who is being instructed in the Word share in every good thing with the one who is instructing him." [Gal 6:6] As the disciples lay out their spiritual things for these people, let these people make them their partners in the bodily things and not out of avarice but out of necessity. We have said these things historically. In another way, according to the mystical, it is not permitted for teachers to own the gold and silver and money that is in their belts. We often read silver to be "meaning," gold to be "word," and copper to be "utterance." It is not permitted for us to accept these things from others, but to own them as given by the Lord. It is also not [f.55r] permitted to accept the doctrines of the heretics and the philosophers of evil teachings, nor to be burdened by the weight of the world, nor to be of a duplicitous mind, nor to have our feet tied by lethal chains. We should enter the holy land with bare feet, not having a staff that may turn into a snake, not relying on any aid of meat, since a staff and stick of this kind are but a reed that is broken if you press on it a little and that pierces the hand of the one seeking support.

"In whatever city or town you enter, ask who is worthy in it, and stay there until you depart." [Mt 10:11] Concerning the ordination of a bishop and deacon, Paul says: "It is necessary, however, that they have good testimony from those who are on the outside." [1 Tim

---

15. *Dialogues of Plato*, trans. B. Jowett (New York: Charles Scribner's Sons, 1897), 135: "And care should be taken not to destroy the natural covering and use of the head and feet by wearing shoes and caps; for the head is the lord of the body, and the feet are the best of servants."

CHAPTER TEN

3:7] The apostles who entered a new city could not know who was of what quality, therefore the host is to be chosen from the report of the people and by the judgment of the neighbors, so that the worth of the preaching is not disfigured by the infamy of the one taking them in. While they must preach to all the people, a single host is chosen, and the one who is to stay at his residence does not do any favor for the host but just accepts this. In fact, it is said: "Who is worthy in it," [Mt 10:11] as he would know how to accept rather than give a kindness. "Go, moreover, into the house and greet it... and if the house is worthy, your peace will come over it, but if it is not worthy, your peace will be returned to you." [Mt 10:12–13] In a hidden way, it expresses the greeting of the Hebrew and Syrian languages: what is said in Greek as *"Chaire"* and in Latin as *"Ave,"* is said in the Hebrew and Syrian as *"Solom lach"* and *"Salam alac,"* that is, *"Pax tecum."*[16] What He is ordering is this: When you go into a house, call down peace on the host and set aside whatever your wars of discord may be. If, however, an objection should arise, you will have the reward of an offered peace, and they will have the war that they have wanted to have. "And if someone does not receive you or listen to your words, leave the house or the city and shake off the dust from your feet." [Mt 10:11] The dust is shaken from the feet in testimony of His work, because they entered the city and the apostolic preaching would come to them, but rather the dust is shaken off, so that the disciples receive nothing from those who have rejected the Gospel, not even the needed food. [f.55v] "Amen I say to you, it will be more tolerable for the lands of Sodom and Gomorrah." [Mt 10:15] If it will be more tolerable for the lands of Sodom and Gomorrah than for this city that would not accept the Gospel, this is because there was no preaching to Sodom and Gomorrah, but there would be preaching to this one,

---

16. The Latin *Ave* and the Greek Χαῖρε *(chaire)* mean "Be well," while the Hebrew and Syrian indicate "Peace be with you." This etymological digression may explain the Christian "Peace be with you" as a greeting and as a part of the liturgy.

except they had not welcomed the Gospel. Therefore, there are various entreaties even among sinners.[17]

To these requests and from all adversities may Jesus Christ, our Lord, in His overwhelming mercy, not turn away. Who reigns as God with the Father and the Holy Spirit. World without end. Amen.

---

17. The Jerome text ends here. The final sentence was added, presumably by the author of the LSJ.

[CHAPTER 11]

VI Calends of August[1]
III Day within the Octave of Saint James[2]

A Reading from the Gospel According to Matthew:

"At that time, after six days, Jesus took Peter and James and his brother John and led them up to a high mountain, and He was transfigured before them," and so forth. [Mt 17:1–2ff.]

A Sermon of Saint Jerome the Doctor[3] on This Same Reading:

We have frequently spoken about why Peter and James and John would be separated out in some places in the Gospels from the others, or why they might have privilege beyond the other apostles. Now one should seek out how after six days he would take them and lead them up to the very high mountain, when Luke the Evangelist places the number at eight.[4] However the easy answer is that they are placed as middle days, with the first day added as well as the last day.[5] It is, in fact, not said that Jesus took Peter and James and John after eight days, but on the eighth day, and led them up on the very high mountain. To lead the disciples to mountainous places is a function of the kingdom. They are brought up, since "many are called, but few are chosen." [Mt 20:16] And He was transfigured before them. The future appeared to the apostles such as it would be at the time of the Judgment. For Matthew says: "He was transfigured before them." [Mt 17:2] No one should think that He lost His original form and face [f.56r] or that He lost His real body and

---

1. July 27.
2. See ch. 10, n. 2.
3. Jerome, *Commentariorum in Evangelium s. Matthaei liber I* (PL 26:121–23).
4. Cf. Lk 9:28.
5. The full six days plus a partial day at the beginning and the end for "eight."

assumed a body that was either spiritual or ethereal. The Evangelist, however, shows the manner in which He was transfigured when he says: "And His face shone like the sun, and His clothing became as white as snow." [Mt 17:2] Here the brightness of His face is shown, and the whiteness of His clothing is described, and the physical is not taken away but transformed through glory. "His face shone like the sun." [Mt 17:2] Certainly the Lord was transformed into that glory with which He is to come and afterward be in His kingdom. The transformation added splendor but did not take away His face. As to whether His was a spiritual body and whether His clothing was changed, another Evangelist said how white they had become: "They were such that no fuller on earth could make them." [Mk 9:2–3] It is corporeal and subject to touch and is not spiritual or ethereal. This description appeals to the eyes, and a sense of feeling may be distinguished in the apparition.

"And behold! Moses and Elias appeared to them and talked with Him." [Mt 17:3] He did not want to give signs from heaven to agitate the Pharisees and Scribes seeking them, but He refuted the perverse request with a prudent response.[6] However He gives the sign from heaven so that He might increase the faith of the apostles: Elias descended from heaven to which he had ascended, and Moses rose from the lower places, just as Ahaz was commanded by Isaiah, to ask for a sign either from on high or from below for himself.[7] For this was said: "Moses and Elias appeared and talked with Him." This is also reported in another Gospel[8] that informed them that He was to suffer in Jerusalem. And the law of the prophet is shown: They would announce with frequent words the Passion of the Lord and the Resurrection.

"And Peter answered and said to Jesus: 'Lord, it is good for us to be here.'" [Mt 17:4] Since he had gone up to the mountainous places, he does not want to go down to the earthly places but rather to continue being forever in the sublime regions. "If you wish, let

6. Cf. Mt 12:38–42.
7. Cf. Is 7:11–12.
8. Cf. Mk 9:2–8, Lk 9:30–31.

us make three tabernacles: one for You, one for Moses, and one for Elias." [Mt 17:4] You are wrong, Peter, as the other Evangelist testifies: "You do not know what you are saying."[9] Do not seek three tabernacles when there is one tabernacle of the Gospel in which the law of the prophets is summed up. If, moreover, you seek three tabernacles, you will never unite the servants with the Lord. Do not build three tabernacles but rather one — for the Father and the Son and the Holy Spirit — so that just as Their divinity is one, there may be one tabernacle in your breast.

"While he was still speaking, behold a bright cloud overshadowed them. And a voice from the cloud said: 'This is My beloved Son [f.56v] in Whom I am pleased. Listen to Him.'" [Mt 17:5] As he had asked foolishly, there was, therefore, no need for an answer from the Lord, but the Father answered for the Son so that the word of the Lord would be fulfilled: "I speak this witness not for Myself, but the Father Who sent Me will Himself speak the witness for Me." [Jn 5:36–37, 8:18] The cloud, however, appears as brightness and overshadows them as those who seek a carnal tabernacle from the foliage or from the tents would be covered by the shade of the bright cloud. The voice of the Father speaking from heaven is also heard, which grants witness to the Son, and Peter is removed from error so that he may teach the truth — and indeed through the other apostles as well. "This is My beloved Son." [Mt 17:5] For Him the tabernacle is to be made. To Him it is to be submitted for He is My beloved Son. Moses and Elias serve Him. They must also be with you in the depths of your heart to prepare the tabernacle for the Lord.

"And when the disciples heard this, they fell on their faces, and they feared greatly." [Mt 17:6] They were terrified with fear for a threefold reason: because they realized they had erred, because the bright cloud had covered them, and because they had heard the voice of God the Father speaking. For human weakness cannot endure bearing the sight of very great glory and is consumed completely in mind and body and falls to the earth. In as much as one has sought

---

9. Cf. Lk 9:33, Mk 10:38.

greater things, all the more fully one falls to the lower things if one has not recognized one's limits.

"And Jesus came and touched them," [Mt 17:7] since they were lying and could not get up. He mercifully went and touched them so that by the touch He would dispel the fear and their weakened limbs would be firmed up. "And He said to them: 'Arise and do not be afraid.'" [Mt 17:7] He cured with His hand. He cures with His power. "Do not fear." First the fear is expelled, and then the teaching is conferred.

"And lifting their eyes, they saw no one except Jesus alone." [Mt 17:8] They saw only Jesus after they had arisen and with reason. If Moses and Elias had remained with the Lord, the voice of the Father would be viewed as uncertain as to Whom the voice gave a most powerful witness. Therefore, they saw Jesus standing. The cloud was gone, and Moses and Elias had disappeared. For after the cover of the law of the prophets that had cloaked the apostles with a veil went away, both of these things would be found in the Gospel.

"And when they were coming down from the mountain, Jesus ordered them, saying 'Tell no one about this vision until the Son of man has risen from the dead.'" [Mt 17:9] The prediction of the future kingdom and the glory of the triumphal one had been shown on the mountain. He did not however want this to be preached to the peoples, lest they [f.57r] be incredulous about the greatness of this event, and because the cross that was to follow would cause scandal to uncultured minds after such great glory.[10]

May the One Who showed the glory of His Transfiguration to His venerable disciples, Peter, James, and John, make us safe in the glory of His coming Resurrection, as Jesus Christ our Lord, Who together with the Father and the Holy Spirit lives and reigns as God. World without end. Amen.

---

10. This ends the Jerome text. The final sentence was added, presumably by the author of the LSJ.

[CHAPTER 12]

V Calends of August[1]
On the Fourth Day
Within the Octaves of Saint James

A Reading from the Holy Gospel According to Luke:

"At that time, the Lord Jesus set his sight firmly on going to Jerusalem. And he sent his messengers James and John before His gaze, etc." [Luke 9:51–52ff.][2]

A Sermon of Pope Saint Calixtus on This Reading:

Today's remarkable feast of the apostle Saint James of Zebedee, the patron of Galicia, suggests to us, dearest brethren, that in these days, our tongue should not refrain from godly words nor our hand from alms. Therefore, the countenance of the Lord, Who was going to Jerusalem, signifies the grace of the Holy Spirit, by which God mercifully illuminates His saints who are going to Jerusalem with heavenly faith and deed. In fact, just as a person turns his countenance on what he admires, so also God sets His gaze on those to whom He has given His grace. The godly prophet wished to see this gracious face of the Lord when he said: "Show us, O Lord, Your face, and we shall be saved." [Ps 79:4, 8, 20 / 80:3, 7, 19] The Lord showed us His countenance when He demonstrated to all the human flesh, which He took on for us in the Virgin. After these things, He was seen on the earth when He also lived among men. And just as the Lord fortified His countenance for going to Jerusalem, we must strengthen all of our attention for going to Jerusalem with godly faith and work.

However, some may wish to understand figuratively what was on the face of the Savior, namely the mouth, the nose, and the eyes.

---

1. July 28.
2. The names "James and John" are interpolated into the Vulgate text here.

The preachers of the Church are understood by the mouth in which the tongue speaks, and through these the Holy Spirit speaks just as He desires. For this reason, Truth itself says to His disciples [f.57v] in the Gospel: "You are not, in fact, the ones who are talking, but it is the Holy Spirit Who speaks through you." [Mt 10:20] And it is said by the Psalmist: "Open your mouth, and I shall fill it." [Ps 80:11 / 81:10] And elsewhere: "I shall hear what the Lord God may say through me." [Ps 84:9 / 85:8]

Perseverance in good works is insinuated by the nose. Perseverance in good works is beautifully understood by the nose, for just as any very pleasant scent enters through it into the human body, so also the faithful of Christ are accepted in the heavenly places like a pleasant scent, and they are united to the Lord's body, and whoever shall persevere until the end will be saved. Concerning these things, almost as if speaking about good scent, Paul says: "We are the good scent for God in every place." [2 Cor 2:15] And the prophet says: "The Lord smelled an odor of sweetness, and He blessed them."[3] Heretics, however, whom the Lord has vomited like phlegm out of the communion of His body and His Church, are figuratively understood by the phlegm that exits the body through the nose. For this reason, the Lord says through John to any infidel: "Since you are lukewarm, I will begin to vomit you from My mouth." [Rev 3:16] Concerning these, the apostolic voice says: "They went out from us, but they were not of us." [1 Jn 2:19]

By the two eyes of the Savior, the two precepts on love, namely of God and of neighbor, are pointed out to be exercised. And since the eye contains seven membranes and three humors[4] within it, the seven spiritual gifts,[5] and the three nourishing Persons of the Trinity are fittingly implied by it. With these the Lord fills the hearts of

---

3. Cf. Gen 8:21. It actually says that God would not curse them.
4. For medieval concepts of the eye, see Edward Grant, ed., *A Source Book in Medieval Science*, (Cambridge, MA: Harvard University Press, 1974), especially the work of John Pecham (c.1230–92), 399.
5. Wisdom, understanding, counsel, fortitude, knowledge, piety, and fear of the Lord. Cf. Is 11:1–2.

CHAPTER TWELVE

those serving Him. By the pupil of the eye, the apostles and the true preachers are particularly shown about whom the Lord Himself says: "Whoever touches you, touches the pupil of My eye." [Zech 2:8] And the Psalmist says: "Watch over me, Lord, like the pupil of my eye." [Ps 16:8 / 17:8]. Saint John testifies in his Apocalypse that the eyes of the Lord indicate the seven gifts of the Holy Spirit with which He fills His faithful when he says: "I saw the lamb as if slain, having seven horns and seven eyes, and these are the seven spirits of God sent throughout the world." [Rev 5:6] These seven spiritual gifts are compared fittingly to horns, since, just as a young bullock or a ram pierces and runs through and flings away wild opposing animals with its horns, these seven gifts prod the hearts of the just toward penitence and repel sins from them. These are the horns with which the Church of the faithful sings perfectly on the feasts of the apostles as the Psalmist says: [f.58r] "The horns of the just shall be exalted." [Ps 74:11 / 75:10] The horns of the just are said to be exalted since the apostles of the Lord are just and filled with the seven gifts, and they are adorned with divine miracles on the earth, and they are exalted above all in the heavenly kingdoms as the Psalmist testifies elsewhere when he says: "Your friends, O God, have been exceedingly honored." [Ps 138:17 / 139:17] These spiritual gifts are similarly compared to the eyes, since just as the eyes illuminate the body and lead it on the right path, so also these gifts illuminate the soul and lead it up to the kingdom of heaven. These are exactly the eyes about which the Psalmist says: "The eyes of the Lord are upon the just." [Ps 33:16 / 34:15] The eyes of the Lord are said to be upon the just, since the Lord watches them mercifully and enriches and renews them with these seven gifts. Daniel says that he saw these seven eyes in a single stone, namely in Christ: "I saw in one stone seven eyes."[6]

Again, concerning these gifts, the prophet Isaiah says: "Seven women took hold of one man on that day." [Is 4:1] Seven women took hold of one man, since the seven spiritual gifts filled the Son of God the Father. These gifts are clearly and fittingly compared

---

6. Cf. Zech 3:9.

to women, since just as a woman nourishes the child sweetly with her breasts, so also these gifts attentively nourish the body and the soul of the just. These are, in fact, the sweetest breasts that Mother Church had on the chest of its single body from which the milk of the divine word flows to us all. Concerning these breasts of the Church, a wise person has said: "Your breasts are better than wine, smelling of the best ointments."[7] Again concerning these gifts, the same wise person says in another place: "Wisdom built a house for herself, cut out seven pillars, slew her victims, mixed in wine and set her table, and sent her handmaids so that they might call to her stronghold and to the walls of the city." [Prov 9:1–3] Wisdom built herself a house and set up seven columns in it, since the Son of God, Who is the wisdom of the Father, built a church for Himself which he adorned fittingly with seven gifts. These gifts are compared very well to the columns, since the palace of a king is held up by columns just as the just person is guided among the favorable and unfavorable things of this world with these heavenly gifts. Wisdom slays its victims as the Son of God suspended His body [f.58v] on the cross for us as the saving victim. Wisdom also mixed in wine, since the Son of God shed His own blood with which He washed away our offenses. Wisdom set its table, since the Only-Begotten of God set up His holy altar throughout the churches, whence the throng of the faithful would be accustomed to receive His body and blood for the remission of their sins. Wisdom sent her handmaids so that they might call to the stronghold and to the walls of the city, since the Son of God sent His apostles and teachers into the world, so that they would call back the people not only to the stronghold of the heavens but also to the walls of the city, that is to the heavenly virtues of the soul, namely to faith, hope, charity, humility, obedience, and perseverance.

Again, concerning these gifts, Isaiah says: "The light of the sun will be sevenfold just like the light of seven days." [Is 30:26] The light of the sun was sevenfold like the light of seven days, since Christ the Lord, Who is the true light of God the Father, shone

---

7. Canticle of Canticles / Song of Solomon 1:1; and cf. 4:10.

with a sevenfold form in the world. And just as the sun lights the world with its seven rays, so also the Only-Begotten of God enlightens just people with these seven gifts. And the seven gifts of the Holy Spirit are fittingly compared to the seven days, since just as the world cycles itself around seven days, so also the just person, filled with these heavenly gifts, wanders toward the height of the heavens from one virtue to the next. It is in this seventh year in which the Old Law commands the Hebrew slave to be liberated saying: "If you buy a Hebrew slave, he may serve you for six years, and in the seventh he may go free without payment." [Ex 21:2] A slave is ordered to serve for six years, since the human race, from the beginning up until Christ, has served demons by adoring idols, but in the seventh year — that is, in Christ — it is set free by believing. And the Son of God is fittingly understood by the seventh year, since just as the seventh year is fulfilled by the number of seven years, so also is Christ the Lord fulfilled by the number seven of spiritual rewards. Again, Isaiah describes these seven spiritual gifts more evidently when he says: "And the Spirit of the Lord, the spirit of wisdom and understanding, the spirit of counsel and strength, the spirit of knowledge and piety, and the spirit of the fear of the Lord will rest upon Him." [Is 11:2] That is, they are upon Christ. The seven properties of this Spirit are appropriately called gifts and not assets, since they are not the rewards of earthly money but are imparted to the just through divine grace. Thus, in fact, [f.59r] concerning these gifts the Lord said to His disciples: "You received freely, give freely to all." [Mt 10:8][8]

The Holy Spirit is fittingly said to repose, and not to work, in Christ, since this same Holy Spirit worked within sinners so as to call them back to the path of truth. He reposed more exactly in Christ, Whom He found without stain of sin. Therefore, He reposed in Him, since He found no one except Him without the contamination of offense. And since the Holy Spirit is said to work in perverse people, Isaiah spoke rightly about Him: "My soul hated your calends and your festivals; they have become troubling to me;

---

8. The wording "to all" is an interpolation into the Vulgate text.

I have taken pains to endure them." [Is 1:14] And the Psalmist says: "The sinner has afflicted the Lord." [Ps 9:25 / 10:4] And this same Spirit testifies that He rests in the good when He says through the Wise One: "I have sought rest in all, and I shall dwell in the inheritance of the Lord." [Ecclus (Sir) 24:11] That the Only-Begotten of God is part of the inheritance of the Father is testified to by the Psalmist who says: "The Lord is part of my inheritance." [Ps 15:5 / 16:5] And thus Wisdom may say in the Person of the Holy Spirit: "For in all things I have sought rest and not found it, thus in the inheritance of the Lord" — that is, in Christ — "I have taken quiet delay."[9] Of this the Lord Himself says through the prophet: "On whom does My spirit rest, except on the humble and the quiet and the one fearing My words?" [Is 11:2; 66:2] Therefore, when Isaiah says that the Spirit of the Lord rests on Him, he is indicating openly the Trinity and Unity. When he says "on" Him, he is indicating the person of Christ. When he says "Spirit," he is intimating the person of this same Holy Spirit. When, however, he says "of the Lord," he is indicating the person of the Father. When, moreover, he says that he rests on Him — that is, on the Son of God — he is indicating that the unity of persons of the Spirit and of the Lord is completed in Christ. He, in fact, is the Christ of Whom Paul says: "In Him the fullness of all divinity has dwelled bodily." [Col 2:9] In this passage, there is the question of why, if there is one Spirit of the Lord, Isaiah says "the Spirit" five times? In fact, he says it in this way: the "Spirit of the Lord, the Spirit of wisdom, the Spirit of counsel, the Spirit of knowledge," and "the Spirit of fear." On that account, the prophet repeats Spirit not because they are multiple, but because this can be one and the same Spirit Who has multiple functions. For as the apostolic authority preaches, there is one Spirit and one Faith and one baptism. For this one Spirit has the power of all wisdom in Him, has the power of all divine understanding as well as of all good counsel, has the power of strength of all fortitude, [f.59v] and of all wisdom and piety and fear. Again, there is a question of whether the Only-

---

9. Cf. Ecclus (Sir) 24:11.

CHAPTER TWELVE

Begotten of God received this Spirit when It appeared above Him in the Jordan River in the form of a dove and the voice of the Father was heard, or whether He had It before then. It is answered in this way: This Son of God Who is always with the Father and Holy Spirit is one God and is never without the Holy Spirit Who is the very same Spirit. Nor did He accept Him first, rather the Holy Spirit showed Himself in the form of a dove, so that when the people had seen and heard Him above the Son, they would believe in the Son, as the Father testified when He said: "This is My beloved Son in Whom I am well pleased. Listen to Him." [Mt 17:5] However, the human body of Christ received the Holy Spirit at that moment when the Son of God, Who had been inexplicably begotten by the Father before all the ages, namely true God from true God, Light from Light, of one being with the Father, accepted it from the Virgin as the same angel foretold to the Virgin, saying: "The Holy Spirit will come unto you, and the power of the Most High will overshadow you." [Lk 1:35] And in the Jordan, the Holy Spirit, Who had never departed from the Father and Son, descended over Christ and also reposed in Him in the Virgin. Therefore, the Spirit of wisdom rested perfectly in the Son of God when this same Son, together with the Father and the Holy Spirit, with ineffable wisdom, miraculously founded the heavens and the angels for serving Him as the Psalmist says: "You have done all things in wisdom." [Ps 103:24 / 104:24] The Spirit of intellect reposed in Him when, in restoring the seat of the fallen angels, He made man with His unfathomable intellect. In fact, He understood all future and hidden things as well as those past and present. The Spirit of counsel reposed in Him when He, Who is the Messenger of great counsel, took on human flesh in the Virgin in order to call back fallen man to the kingdoms of the heavens. He is also the Counselor of all good things. The spirit of strength reposed in Him when this Only-Begotten of God, like a strong lion from the tribe of Judah and the root of David, subdued the devil through the strength of His holy cross with His unbending strength and cast him from the world, saying: "Now the prince of this world will be cast outside." [Jn 12:31] Concerning His strength, the Psalmist says: "The Lord has dressed Himself with strength and has girded Himself with virtue." [Ps 92:1 / 93:1] And elsewhere: "Who is this King of glory?" [Ps 23:8, 10 / 24:8, 10] And the Holy Spirit answered him saying: "The strong and mighty Lord, the mighty [f.60r] Lord in battle." [Ps 23:8 / 24:8] The Spirit of strength also reposed in Him when He plundered hell and arose from the dead as Victor. The Spirit of knowledge reposed in Him when He knowingly ascended to the heavens from which He had descended as He speaks to the Father through the prophet, saying: "I have arisen and still am with You." [Ps 138:18 / 139:18] "Your knowledge has become wonderful for Me. It has comforted Me." [Ps 138:6 / 139:6] Of this the prophet says: "Let old things depart from your mouth for the Lord is the God of knowledge." [1 Kgs (1 Sam) 2:3] The Lord was the God of knowledge when He filled His apostles with all knowledge of scriptures and all manner of languages. Again, the Spirit of all knowledge is said to repose in Him, since He is held to be the teacher, not only of the seven arts, but also of the Old and New Law and indeed of all earthly and heavenly things, as He demonstrated when He appeared in the Synagogue and began to read the Book of Isaiah, saying: "The Spirit of the Lord is upon Me, because He has anointed Me." [Is 61:1, Lk 4:18] And the Jews wondered and said: "How does He know the letters when He had not learned them?" [Jn 7:7] And the Psalmist speaks of His person in this way: "I have understood Myself above all the teachers." [Ps 118:99 / 119:99] And Wisdom wonders at His knowledge and says: "Oh, the depth of riches of the wisdom and the knowledge of God! Oh, how incomprehensible are His judgments and how unsearchable are His ways! Who has known the meaning of God or who has been His counselor? [Rom 11:33–34] The Spirit of piety reposed in Him, since He filled His apostles with His unutterable sweetness, love, mercy, clemency, patience, and holiness on the day of Pentecost. Again, He was the spirit of piety when He said: "Whoever comes to Me will not be cast out." [Jn 6:37] And this one: "Whoever has believed and has been baptized will be saved." [Mk 16:16] And this one to Peter: "I say to you Peter, not seven times but up to seventy times seven." [Mt 18:22] Our most clement Savior shows

CHAPTER TWELVE

us great and indescribable clemency when He concedes to return us to a restoration of salvation through the lamentations of penance after the fall into sin.[10] The spirit of fear will fill Him, since, on the day of the Last Judgment, the Lord will appear gentle for the just and terrible for the unjust. At His coming, not only the impious but also the angels and archangels will tremble. On this the Psalmist says: "Let the whole world fear Him." [Ps 32:8 / 33:8] Let no one hesitate to accept these gifts from God in baptism. [f.60v] The apostle speaks in this way: "Grace has been given to each one of us according to the measure of giving from the Lord. Because of this, He ascended on high, held captivity captive, and gave gifts to men." [Eph 4:7–8] Those rewards of the Lord are, in fact, venerable, sacrosanct, higher than other rewards, great, and inexplicable. With these rewards, the Lord enriched the prophets and apostles and all the chosen who have lived from the beginning of the world until now. With these gifts, if we are found enriched by good works, kept away from vices, adorned with all virtue, and estranged from demons, we shall be crowned with the brightest of crowns in the heavenly kingdom. Therefore, whoever believes that heavens and angels and men were created by God and that the Son of God was born, suffered, arose, and ascended to the heavens, has in himself, without doubt, these spiritual gifts if he perseveres in good works.

But there are also seven vices opposed to these seven spiritual gifts, and they hinder humankind. Therefore, there is a good and bad wisdom, a good and bad understanding, a good and bad counsel, a good and bad strength, a good and bad knowledge, a good and bad piety, and a good and bad fear. Concerning good wisdom, Wisdom says: "All wisdom is from the Lord God." [Ecclus (Sir) 1:1] And concerning bad wisdom the apostle says: "The wisdom of this world is foolishness before God." [1 Cor 3:19] And the prophet says: "They are wise such that they may do evil, but they do not know how to do good." [Jer 4:22] Again the Lord says through the prophet: "I shall destroy the wisdom of the wise, and I shall reject the prudence of the prudent." [1 Cor 1:19] Therefore, whoever contemplates

---

10. Reference to the fall from paradise.

sensibly the celestial secrets with his full heart and thinks of how he may please God in all things, without doubt, has true wisdom within him. Who, however, thinks of what should not be pondered, namely so that he might commit evil, has bad wisdom in him.[11] Again concerning good understanding, the Psalmist says: "Blessed is the one who understands about the needy and the poor." [Ps 40:2 / 41:1] Elsewhere this Psalmist also speaks about bad [f.61r] understanding: "The unjust man refused to understand so that he might act well; he meditated on iniquity in his bed, he was present on every path that was not good, but he did not hate evil." [Ps 35:4–5 / 36:4–5] Therefore, when someone understands good things with his heart and carries them out in deed, without doubt, he has in him good understanding, but whoever understands bad things with his heart and carries them out in deed incurs the perdition of bad understanding. Again, concerning good counsel, this Psalmist says: "In the counsel of the just and in the congregation, the works of the Lord are great." [Ps 110:1–2 / 111:1–2] And concerning bad counsel, this same Psalmist says: "Blessed is the man who has not gone off in the counsel of the impious." [Ps 1:1] And elsewhere: "The Lord destroys the counsels of the nations." [Ps 32:10 / 33:10] Whoever, therefore, devotes himself to good works and advises his neighbors so that they may be recovered from bad works and so that they may apply themselves to good works, without doubt, has in him the spirit of good counsel. And whoever counsels either his neighbor or himself on how to carry out perverse works will incur the spirit of wicked counsel. Again, concerning good strength, Wisdom says: "Love is as strong as death." [Cant 8:6] For just as death separates the soul from the body, so also does the love of God remove a person from mundane vices and join that person to God. Again, the prophet Job says concerning strength: "His force is in his loins, and his strength is in the navel of his belly." [Job 40:11] Whoever, therefore, remains strong against the vices of the flesh and patient against all adversities is certainly filled with the spirit of

---

11. This sentence is written in the margin in CC: a red cross designates its insertion point in the body of the text in S.

CHAPTER TWELVE

good strength. And whoever is strong in perverse speech, in greed, theft, drunkenness, perverse judgment, murder, or other perverse works is filled with the spirit of bad strength. Again, concerning bad knowledge, the apostle says that it is necessary to serve God: "in knowledge, patience, pleasantness, and the Holy Spirit." [2 Cor 6:6] And concerning bad knowledge, they were filled with it, as is written in Job: "Who said to the Lord God 'Depart from us, as we do not want the knowledge of your ways.'" [Job 21:14] Whoever, therefore, knows the mandates of the Lord and engages in good works, without doubt, has in him the spirit of good knowledge. However, whoever knows these mandates and refuses to do them has filled his heart with perverse knowledge. As scripture says: "For if someone knows the law and does not follow it, it is a sin for him." [James 4:17] And if a slave knows the will of his lord and does not do it, he will be flogged. And it is better not to know the way of truth than to depart from it after knowing it. Saint Paul had the spirit of good knowledge when he mercifully said out of compassion for his neighbor: "Who is weakened and I am not also weakened?" [2 Cor 11:29] Eli was once overcome by a spirit of false piety [f.61v] when he did not wish to strike his offending sons with the rod of justice. Because of this, he struck himself along with his sons with cruel condemnation before the severe judge. For the sons of Eli, Hophni and Phinehas, were taking by force the raw meat of the sacrifice and eating it and were sleeping with the women who were watching at the door of the Tabernacle. Because of this sin, they were killed in battle by the Philistines, and the Ark of the Lord was taken. When Eli heard this, he fell back from the seat where he was sitting, broke his neck, and died.[12] Therefore, whoever helps his neighbors in all needs, to the extent he is able, is filled with the spirit of good piety. And a prelate of the Church or a judge who does not wish to strike his offending subjects with the rod of justice because he is overcome by love or money is driven by the spirit of false piety. Concerning good fear, Wisdom says: "Whoever fears God will do good things." [Ecclus (Sir) 15:1] And concerning bad

---

12. Cf. 1 Kgs (1 Sam) 2:12–17, 22–25; 4:4–11, 17–18.

fear, the apostle says: "Do not, however, be afraid of their fear,... but sanctify Christ the Lord in your hearts." [1 Pet 3:14–15] And the Lord says in the Gospel: "Do not fear those who kill the body and cannot kill the soul." [Mt 10:28] Therefore, whoever fears God such that he perseveres in good works is filled with the spirit of good fear and will be saved in the future as Wisdom says: "To the one fearing God, it will be well in the end, and on the day of his death, he will be blessed." [Ecclus (Sir) 1:13] And whoever fears the impious, such that he ceases to have faith or do good work, is uselessly overcome by the spirit of inane fear.

The just are accustomed to singing seven special psalms against the seven criminal vices — equal in number to them — for the sake of penitence. These spiritual gifts are compared with the seven petitions of the Lord's Prayer. In fact, the Lord speaks in the Gospel of Matthew in this way: "Our Father Who art in heaven, hallowed be Thy name." [Mt 6:9] To this first petition the spirit of wisdom is perfectly compared. For whoever recognizes that he has God the Father in heaven and prays in the name that he accepted in baptism may be hallowed in Him by good works and is filled with the spirit of the wisdom of God in a wondrous way.

"Thy kingdom come." [Mt 6:10] To this second petition, the spirit of understanding is fittingly compared. For whoever believes and hopes to prevail after the resurrection in the eternal [f. 62r] kingdom of God is filled with the spirit of divine understanding.

"Thy will be done on earth as it is in heaven." [Mt 6:10] To this third petition, the spirit of counsel is perfectly compared. Nothing, in fact, stands between the will of God and His counsel. And whoever seeks that the will of the Lord, as it is done in heaven among the angels, be done in this way also among humankind on earth is filled with the spirit of counsel in a wondrous manner.

"Give us this day our daily bread." [Mt 6:11] To this fourth petition, the spirit of divine strength is perfectly compared. For just as bodily bread strengthens the body, so the bread of the Holy Spirit strengthens a person engaging in good works with its powerful and unfailing virtue and offers him power against the vices of the flesh.

CHAPTER TWELVE

And whoever is strong against the vices of the flesh is furnished with the heavenly bread of eternal life.

"And forgive us our debts, as we forgive our debtors." [Mt 6:12] To this fifth petition, namely the remission of sins, the spirit of knowledge is most fittingly compared. For by the same knowledge with which we forgive those sinning against us, we believe we will be forgiven by God. One acts knowingly who forgives those sinning against him just as he will be forgiven by God.

"And lead us not into temptation." [Mt 6:13] To this sixth petition, the spirit of piety is most justly compared, for the Lord looks mercifully with His eyes of piety on the one whom He guards from the temptations of the flesh and the demons. For this reason, we must pray to God that He may free us with His indescribable mercy from every temptation and that we may serve Him forever, happily, and without impediment.

"But deliver us from evil." [Mt 6:13] To this seventh petition the spirit of fear is perfectly compared. For the fear of God and the freedom of penance are two very similar companions. With these a person is lead most justly to the heavenly kingdoms. For the spirit of fear leads a person to the freedom of penance, as that same freedom keeps him within the civil kingdoms. And so, a person who is goaded by fear of the Lord represses his vices and ends up being liberated from all evils. And therefore, God is to be petitioned so that He might fill us with the aforesaid seven heavenly gifts and free us through them from all evil.

In a similar way it follows: "And the Lord sent His messengers James and John ahead of Him."[13] Both messengers, whom the Lord sent, introduce the double [f. 62v] charity that we must practice, namely of God and of neighbor; they also show clearly the throngs of preachers that the Lord sent to the Jews, namely the apostles and prophets. Of these Saint Paul says: "And the Lord Himself certainly gave some apostles and in other cases some prophets." [Eph 4:11] But with all of these, the Jews were not converted just as both the Old Law and the apostle affirm by saying: "'For, in other tongues

---

13. Cf. Lk 9:52.

and on other lips, I will speak to this people, and even in this way, they will not hear Me,' says the Lord." [1 Cor 14:21] For thus the Lord speaks through Isaiah, who says: "He will speak to this people in another tongue." [Is 28:11] And after a few more words, he says that "they did not want to hear." [1 Cor 14:12] "And they will have the word of the Lord: 'Command, command again, command, command again, expect, expect again, expect, expect again, a little here, a little there, so that they go and fall back, are worn down and snared and taken.'" [Is 28:13] That he says four times "command" and repeats the same number of times "expect" and repeats "a little" twice indicates the four kinds of messengers, namely: Moses, the bearer of the law; the prophets; the Son of God Himself; and the apostles. The Lord sent them so that they would abandon their errors and submit to the faith. He sent them to the Jews in both ages, namely of both laws as is represented by the doubling of "little," but they have not been converted in all these ways. That he says "so that they go and fall back, are worn down and snared and taken" proclaims their coming reproach. If, in fact, they should remain in the rigor of their infidelity, they would surely not only be snared by their impieties but also taken in the burning fires of Gehenna. Again, that he says twice "a little there"[14] is permitted to be understood morally as the space of two ages, namely youth and old age, in which if a very wretched person has refused to withdraw from sins, it is beyond doubt "a little" that he has remained in this wretched life, but it is exceedingly "long" that he is to be ensnared and enchained in the unending torments of Tartarus.

"And they went and entered a city of the Samaritans to prepare things there. And they did not welcome Him, because His focus was on going to Jerusalem." [Lk 9:52–53] The Samaritans, who are interpreted as "guards," who did not want to receive the apostles, signify the Jews to whom the Lord gave the law for them to observe. However, they did not want [f.63r] either to observe the law or

---

14. The Latin is literally "a little there, a little there" although English uses the contrasting "a little here, a little there." Thus, in Latin this is exactly a double, while in English, it is not.

CHAPTER TWELVE

accept the grace of baptism. For this reason, the apostles said to them: "First it was necessary to speak the word of God to you, but since you rejected it and have shown yourselves unworthy of eternal life, behold, we are turning to the Gentiles." [Acts 13:46] And this is what is said in the last verse: "And they went away to another town." [Lk 9:56] The other town in which the disciples are received introduces the people of the Gentiles, who received the word for the resisting Jews. Therefore, they received the grace that the Jews resisted since this was once predestined by the Lord. The Hebrew people will not be saved until the Gentile people are saved, and apostolic authority affirms this, saying: "When the fullness of the Gentiles will come in, then all Israel will be saved." [Rom 11:25–26] There is, however, a command to preach the Gospel to the Jews, so that they might have no excuse for guilt if they should not believe in Him. "However, when His disciples James and John had seen this, they said 'Lord, do you wish us to command that fire descend from heaven and consume them, as Elias did?'"[15] [Lk 9:54] This expression "as Elias did" is not found in many books, but in those in which it is written it is better than in those in which it is absent because Luke wrote it in his Gospel and Theophilus, bishop of Antioch,[16] copied it very early into his four gospels in one volume. Therefore, in the volume of Kings, it is written that in the time of Elias the Prophet: "Ochozias,[17] the king of Israel, fell on the lattices in his upper room in Samaria and grew ill. And he sent his messengers and said to them: 'Go and consult Beelzebub, the god of Accaron,[18] as to whether I can live from this sickness.'" [4 Kgs (2 Kgs) 1:2][19] Immediately Elias was sent by the Lord and resisted them, saying: "Go back because the king will die."

---

15. On "as Elias did," See ch. 23.4, n. 5.
16. Theophilus of Antioch, d.c.184. PG 6.
17. Ochozias is known as Ahaziah in other Bible translations.
18. Modern Ekron.
19. Catholic bibles label Kings as 1, 2, 3, and 4 Kings, while in Protestant bibles, these books are named 1 and 2 Samuel and 1 and 2 Kings. We have given the Protestant book in parenthesis.

[4 Kgs (2 Kgs) 1:6] And Elias went up on the mountain. As soon as the king heard that Elias was on the mountain, "He sent to him a captain of fifty men and the fifty men who were under him." [4 Kgs (2 Kgs) 1:9] And they said to Elias with a proud voice: "Man of God, the king orders that you come down." [4 Kgs (2 Kgs) 1:9] And he said: "If I am a man of God, let fire come from heaven and consume you." [4 Kgs (2 Kgs) 1:10] And they were immediately consumed by fire. Again, another fifty were sent in the same way, and they were consumed. Again, another fifty were sent, and with a humble voice and bended knees, they asked him to come with them, and they led him to the king. And Elias said to the king: "The Lord says these things: 'Since you sent messengers to consult Beelzebub, the god of Accaron, as if there were not a God or a prophet [f.63v] in Israel from whom you could ask for a response, therefore you will not get out of the bed upon which you have climbed but will die from death.' The king consequently died according to the word of the Lord and of Elias." [4 Kgs (2 Kgs) 1:16–17] And this is what the disciples were saying to the Lord: that the Samaritans should be burned with fire, just as Elias burned the messengers of the aforementioned king on a worldly pyre. If someone wished to understand this allegorically, the Antichrist is to be understood by the king who in his punishment is killed together with his fifty people at the word of God and Elias. At the coming of the Lord and Elias at the end of the world, the Antichrist together with his followers is to be destroyed by the spirit of the Lord as the prophet says: "And by the breath of His lips He will kill the impious one." [Is 11:4] And the apostle asserts it in this way, saying: "And the Lord will destroy him with the brightness of His coming." [2 Th 2:8] Therefore, that the apostles ask the Lord that fire descend from heaven and burn the Samaritans signifies those unwise preachers who unjustly excommunicate and curse those not wanting to accept them. For the earth is not able to bring forth fruit unless the dew should be provided for it, which lessens[20] the dryness and the hardness. For this reason, one should ask the most

---

20. Latin *dulcescat*, literally "sweetens."

CHAPTER TWELVE

excellent Dispenser of grace, not that He consume with the fire of wrath those rejecting the word of God but that He pour the grace of remorse into them. It is shown to be thus in the following words where he says: "And Jesus turned and reproached them, saying 'Do you know of what spirit you are?'" [Lk 9:55]

The rebuke of the Lord, by which the apostolic ignorance is restrained, indicated the austerity of divine scripture with which the teachers and the doctors of the Holy Church must at times correct the stupid, who speak badly and act iniquitously and who do not know whether they are of a malign spirit or a good one: "For the Son of man did not come to destroy souls but to save them." [Lk 9:56] The Only-Begotten of God is called the Son of man, not because He was created by the seed of man, but because He took on human flesh in the Virgin, who certainly came from human seed. He did not come to destroy souls but to save them, for He wants, as the apostle says, "All men to be saved and to come to the recognition of truth." [1 Tim 2:4] He wants no one to perish, and He said He preferred the life, rather than the death, of a sinner.[21] "And the disciples went away to another town." [Lk 9:56] That the disciples withdrew to another town when they were not [f.64r] received by the Samaritans indicates that preachers of the Church, who, if by chance in the place where they strive to preach are not taken up by these people, need to go elsewhere.

Therefore, this apostle of the Lord, James, whose solemnity we celebrate in these days, is deemed worthy to prevail upon the majesty of the Lord both for our salvation and for that of all people, such that our Lord Jesus Christ, Who fixed His most beautiful and venerable countenance on going to Jerusalem, Who diligently rebuked the rigidity of His disciples James and John, Who imbued them with His divine commandments, Who told them that He had come to save souls and not to destroy them, Who strengthens us with good works, Who takes away the rigor of our sins from us, and

---

21. The source of this is unknown, but it appears in Bk. IV, the Pseudo-Turpin as "qui dixisti te malle vitam peccatoris *quam* mortem," where the word *mortem* is used for *laetum*, both meaning "death."

Who fills us with heavenly teachings, may save our souls, so that we may be salubriously worthy in the heavenly Jerusalem with James leading us to see the beloved countenance of Him Who together with the Father and the Holy Spirit lives and reigns as God. World without end. Amen.

[CHAPTER 13]

IIII Calends of August[1]
Fifth Day within the Octaves of Saint James

A Reading from the Holy Gospel According to Matthew:

"At that time, after the Lord Jesus took Peter and the two sons of Zebedee, James and John, and He began to grow sorrowful and to be sad," and so forth. [Mt 26:37ff.]

A Sermon of Saint Jerome the Doctor on This Reading:[2]

In this chapter it is shown that the Lord would test the reality of assumed humanity and would become truly and certainly saddened; however, so that the suffering would not rule his mind, he would begin to grow sorrowful. It is one thing, in fact, to grow sorrowful and another to begin to grow sorrowful. He grew sorrowful, however, not out of fear of suffering, as He had come so that He would suffer, but it was because of the most miserable Judas, the cowardice of Peter — which he had predicted — and the scandal of all the apostles, and the rejection of the Jewish people and the destruction of unfortunate Jerusalem. Jonas, on the withering of a gourd or of ivy, grew sad, not wanting to lose his former tent.[3] If, however, the heretics interpret this as a sadness of the mind and not as a feeling of the Savior toward those about to perish, then let them answer how they explain what is said in the person of God through Ezekiel: "And [f.64v] you saddened me in all these things."[4]

"Then He says to them: 'My soul is sad, even unto death. Stay here and keep watch with Me.'" [Mt 26:38] What is saddened is the soul, and it is not sorrowful because of death but unto death, until He frees the apostles with His Passion. As to what He orders,

1. July 29.
2. Jerome's *Commentariorum in Evangelium s. Matthaei liber I* (PL 2b:197–99).
3. Cf. Jon 4:6–10.
4. Cf. Ez 16:43.

"Stay here and keep watch with Me," He does not prohibit with imminent distinction those whose time was not at hand from sleep, but from the sleep of infidelity and from a sluggishness of mind. Therefore, those who suspect that an unreasonable Jesus has taken up a soul may say this as to how He might be saddened and might know the time of sadness, although, in fact, even stupid animals may be saddened although they may not know either the reasons or how long they should be saddened.

"And He went forth a short way and fell on his face and He prayed and said, 'My Father, if it is possible, let this cup pass from me, but not as I wish, but as You wish.'" [Mt 26:39] After He gave the apostles a command to stay and keep watch with their Lord, He went forth, fell on His face, and showed humility of mind in the appearance of His flesh and says courteously: "My Father," and He asks if it is possible that the cup of suffering pass from Him, about which we spoke above. He does not, however, ask out of fear of suffering but out of mercy for His former people so that He might not drink the cup prepared by them. For this reason, He expressly did not say, "Let the cup pass from Me," but "this cup" — that is, of the Jewish people — who cannot have any excuse for ignorance if they should kill Me while having the law and the prophets who daily foretell of Me. And returning to Himself, since from His human persona He distances Himself anxiously while confirming with the persona of the Son of God: "but not as I wish, but as You wish." He did not say, "let it be done, because I am speaking from a human perspective, but because I descended to earth by Your will."

"And he came to His disciples and found them sleeping, and He spoke to Peter in this way: 'Could you not keep watch with me for one hour?'" [Mt 26:40] He Who had earlier said: "Even if everyone should be scandalized about You, I will never be scandalized about You," [Mt 26:33] now could not overcome sleep because of the extent of his sadness.

"Watch and pray so that you may not enter into temptation." [Mt 26:41] It is impossible that the human soul not be tempted. For this reason, we say in the Lord's Prayer "and lead us not into temptation" that we cannot bear, not that we oppose inwardly

CHAPTER THIRTEEN

bearing the temptation [f.65r] we cannot bear, but rather we ask for the power of withstanding the temptation. Therefore, even in this case, He does not say: "Watch and pray so that you not be tempted" but "so that you may not enter into temptation." That is, may temptation not overcome you and conquer you and hold you within its errors. For example, a martyr who sheds blood for acknowledging the Lord is certainly tempted but not tied up by the snares of temptations. Whoever denies, however, runs into the traps of temptation. "The spirit certainly is willing, but the flesh is weak." [Mt 26:41] He says this against the rash people who think that they can do whatever they would believe. And so, we are as confident in the eagerness of the mind as we fear the weakness of the flesh. However, according to the apostle, works are destroyed by the spirit of the flesh.[5]

"And He went away again, a second time. He went back and prayed, saying: 'My Father, if it is not possible that this cup pass away unless I drink it, may Your will be done.'" [Mt 26:42] This second time He prays that if Nineveh cannot be saved in any other way than the gourd being dried up,[6] let the will of the Father be done, which is not contrary to the will of the Son, as He said through the prophet: "My God, I wanted to do Your will." [Ps 38:9 / 39:9]

"And He came again and found them sleeping, for their eyes were heavy." [Mt 26:43] He prays alone for all, just as He suffers alone for everyone. They become listless, however, and the eyes of the apostles are pressed together by a similar denial. "Then He came to His disciples and said to them: 'Now sleep and rest. Behold the hour has arrived.'" [Mt 26:45] After He had prayed a third time, so that every word would remain in the mouth of two or three witnesses, and He had sought to have fear of the apostles corrected with the following penance, and certain of His Passion, He went to those pursuing Him and offered Himself moreover to be killed. And He said to His disciples: "Arise! Let us go. Behold the one who is to betray Me has approached." [Mt 26:46] Let them not find us as if

---

5. Cf. 1 Pet 3:18.
6. Cf. Jon 4:1–11.

we were fearful and reluctant, but let us go moreover toward death, so that they may see the confidence and joy of one about to suffer.[7]

Therefore, may the One of whom we speak, Jesus Christ our Lord, deign to lead us confidently to the everlasting joy of the heavenly kingdom. He suffered in His Passion for His beloved James and his brother John, as the beloved for his beloved, showing His grief to them and saying "My soul is sad, even unto death." [Mt 26:38] He lives and reigns with the Father and the Holy Spirit. World without end. Amen. [f.65v]

---

7. This ends the text of Jerome. The closing is apparently by the author of the LSJ.

[CHAPTER 14]

III Calends of August[1]
VI Day within the Octaves of Saint James

A Reading from the Gospel According to Mark:

"At that time, James and John, the sons of Zebedee, approached the Lord Jesus and said: 'Master, we wish You to grant us what we are asking You to do for us.' And He said to them: 'What do you wish Me to do for you?' And they said: 'Grant us that we may sit, one at Your right hand and one at Your left hand in Your Glory' and so on." [Mk 10:35–37ff.]

A Homily of Pope Saint Gregory[2] on this Reading:

Since we celebrate the birth of Saint James the Apostle and Martyr on this very day, my brothers, we must never consider ourselves distant from the power of his patience. For if we, with the help of the Lord, strive to preserve the virtue of suffering,[3] and if we live in the peace of the Church, we may still attain the palm of martyrdom. There are, in fact, two types of martyrdom: one of the mind and another in both mind and deed. And so, we can be martyrs, even if we are not cruelly slain by those striking with any iron. To die, of course, by a persecutor is martyrdom openly displayed, but to sustain abuses or to love the person who hates is a hidden martyrdom of thought. For since there are two kinds of martyrdom, one of hidden thought and the other of public display, Truth testifies as to what He is asking from the sons of Zebedee when He says:

---

1. July 30.
2. Gregory I, the Great, *Homiliarum in Evangelia liber II, Homilia 35* (PL 76:1263–64).
3. The word *patientia* in Latin covers a vast territory that includes "patience," "submission" and "suffering."

"Can you drink the cup which I am to drink?"[4] and when they immediately answered Him: "We can," and when the Lord immediately responded to this and said: "You will certainly drink My cup." [Mk 10:39] What, in fact, do we accept by the cup other than the pain of the Passion? He speaks about this elsewhere: "Father, if it can be done, let this cup pass from Me." [Mt 26:39] And the sons of Zebedee, that is James and John, did not both die through martyrdom, and still both heard that each would drink the cup. John, in fact, did not at all finish his life through martyrdom, but he was still a martyr since he observed the passion in mind, that he had not accepted in body. And we, therefore, by this example can be martyrs without the sword if we truly keep suffering in our mind. [f.66r]

I do not think, dearest brethren, that it is off topic if, for your edification, I speak of one example of maintaining suffering. In our days, there was a certain man named Stephen, a priest in a monastery built near the walls of the city of Rieti. He was a very holy man and unparalleled in the virtue of suffering. And there are still many who knew him and tell of his life or death.[5] He was of rustic speech but of learned life. For love of the heavenly kingdom, he looked down on all things, avoided possessing anything in this world, and fled from the tumult of people. He was intent on frequent and lengthy prayers, and the virtue of patience grew increasingly and vehemently in him so that he thought that a person was his friend who would inflict him with some distress. He gave back thanks for abuse. If something harmful were given to him in his indigence, he considered it a great advantage. He considered all his adversaries as nothing other than helpers. When the day of death pressed him to leave his body, many people came together so that they might commend their souls to a person with such a holy soul that was leaving the world. And when all of those who had come together were standing around his bed, some saw with their bodily eyes

---

4. The wording is analogous to Mark, whose text is the subject of this sermon, but is literally here the periphrastic wording of Matthew 20:22.
5. St. Stephen of Rieti, abbot, d.590. His feast is February 13.

CHAPTER FOURTEEN

angels coming in, but they could say nothing in any way. Others saw nothing at all, but such a vehement fear endured in all who were there that no one could remain standing close by as that holy soul was leaving. And those, moreover, who had seen something, as well as those who had seen nothing, were all stricken with fear and fled terrified. And no one there could attend to the dying man.

Think, therefore, brethren, how almighty God may terrify when He comes as a severe judge if He could terrify those standing around when He came as one pleasing and rewarding. Or think how He can be feared when He will be able to be seen when He overwhelms the minds of those present even when He cannot be seen. Behold, dearest brethren, the peak of reward to which He raised this man [Stephen of Rieti] when he maintained his suffering in ecclesiastical peace. What did his Creator give to him deep within, with which He made known to us such glory on the day of his exit and entry? With whom may we believe he was united if not with the holy martyrs, when it is agreed that he was also taken up by blessed spirits before the bodily eyes of those standing around. He did not die from being struck by any sword and still, on his departure, he received the crown of suffering that he held [f.66v] in his mind.

We test daily that truth that has been said before us: that the Holy Church, filled with the flowers of the chosen ones, has lilies in peace and roses in war. Moreover, one should know that the virtue of suffering is usually carried out in three ways. Some, in fact, we sustain from God, others from the ancient foe, and yet others from neighbors. For we tolerate persecutions, injuries, and abuses from our neighbor, temptations from the ancient foe, and scourges from God. But in all three types, the mind must, with a vigilant eye, look around itself lest one be led astray toward retribution with evil in the face of our neighbor's evils or lest one be seduced toward a delight or consent to pleasure in the face of our foe's temptations or lest one rush toward an excess of murmuring in the face of our Maker's scourges. For the foe is conquered perfectly when our mind is kept from delight and consent amid its temptations and when it is guarded from hatred amid our neighbor's abuses and when it is restrained from murmuring amid God's scourges. Let us not seek good things in the present by doing these things in retribution for ourselves since, for the toil of suffering, the good things of the life to come are to be hoped for as the reward for our work begins when all our toil completely stops. Whence the Psalmist says: "The poor shall not be consigned to oblivion in the end, the suffering of the poor shall not perish in the end." [Ps 9:19 / 9:18] In fact, the suffering of the poor is perceived to have vanished since nothing is paid back to the humble for it in this life. But the suffering of the poor does not perish in the end, since it is received in His glory when all laborious things are ended once and for all.

Therefore, brethren, keep suffering in mind and exercise it when in your work the matter calls for it. Let their abusive words move none of you to hatred of your neighbor. Let no injuries by things that will perish cause disturbance. For if you fear with a fixed mind the enduring injuries, you will not consider as serious the injuries of transient things. If you desire the glory of eternal reward, you will not lament a temporal injury. Therefore, tolerate your foes, but love the brothers whom you tolerate. Seek eternal rewards for earthly abuses. Let none of you be confident of being able to fulfill this with your own powers, but hold fast with prayers that He who reigns may offer them. [f.67r] And we know that He will gladly hear those entreating when something is sought that He approves of bestowing. When this is driven continually in prayer, there is quick help in temptation through Jesus Christ our Lord, Who lives with Him as ruler and reigns as God in the unity of the Holy Spirit. World without end. Amen.

[CHAPTER 15]

II Calends of August[1]
Day VII within the Octaves of Saint James

A Sermon of Pope Saint Leo on Saint James:[2]

Let us rejoice in the Lord, most beloved, and celebrate the feast of Saint James with fitting honors. Through the care of divine grace, a patron has been given to us whom the whole world venerates in common. Who is, then, such a steadfast despiser in the world who would not avidly desire to be protected by the patronage of Saint James? For to him, in fact, from throughout the world — through the rugged caverns of mountains, through the ambushes of thieves, through the uncertainties of robbers, through the countless frauds of innkeepers — there is a frequent flocking of pilgrims to Galicia.[3] And it is certainly fitting that all should venerate on earth him whom God has raised to heaven and who glitters with virtues. He is the chancellor of Christ, Who had received on the mountain a foretaste of the sweetness of the coming Resurrection.[4] He is carried into battle in the manner of a good standard bearer. The obstinate blindness of the Jews does not turn him away from the faith, and the known cruelty of Herod does not slow him from good work. He is, in fact, one of the three columns of the Holy Church that Paul the Apostle mentions in Galatians, and not an inferior column.[5] In fact, just as according to the number of sons of Jacob the Lord chose twelve disciples whom He also called apostles, so also does it accord to the number of holy patriarchs, namely, Abraham, Isaac,

---

1. July 31.
2. While the sermon has been attributed to Pope Leo, it is known only from this collection.
3. These references foreshadow not only the *Veneranda dies* sermon, but also situations described in Bk. II (Miracles) and Bk. V (Guidebook).
4. The Transfiguration of Christ; cf. Mt 17:1–13.
5. Cf. Gal 2:9.

and Jacob, that He established, as princes and columns for the others, three apostles, namely Saint Peter, Saint James, and John his brother through a certain preference for love and virtue. [f.67v] He confirmed, in fact, from the mouth of the most wise Solomon, that a slender rope tripled is not easily broken.[6] In fact, He established them as teachers and instructors like a cord joined by the glue of love with which the others are tied and protected. He revealed to them His secrets more fully than to the others. Before the Resurrection, He showed them in the Transfiguration the glory of the future resurrection. He also brought in only them when He was to cure the daughter of the archpriest.[7] When His Passion was approaching and when He wanted to show them the humanity of the flesh that He had taken on and that He had taken on for us so that people, on sensing the weakness of His flesh, would not despair, He took them so that they would pray with Him in the Valley of Gethsemane as He was about to commend His time of agony to His Father.[8] If, in fact, He revealed His secrets to all, either His Passion could be prevented or the chosen ones could be scandalized upon seeing His Passion. For this reason, the apostles were ordered to be silent about Christ,[9] and those cured by His healing were prohibited to boast of it, and demons were commanded to be silent about the Son of God.[10] The apostle says: "We speak of the wisdom of God as hidden in ministry[11]...about which none of the princes of this world knew." [1 Cor 2:7–8] If, in fact, they had known, they would never have crucified the Lord of glory. That is, they would never have had the Lord redeem me by His death.

Therefore, He revealed His secrets to these whom He knew, according merits, recognizing those who were firm and constant in their love for Him and who, He knew, would be active at the right

6. Cf. Eccles 4:12.
7. Cf. Mt 9:18–26, Mk 5:21–43.
8. Cf. Mt 26:36–56, Mk 14:32–42.
9. Cf. Mk 8:27.
10. Cf. Mk 1:34, Mk 3:12, Lk 4:35.
11. The biblical text reads "mystery" rather than "ministry."

CHAPTER FIFTEEN

time in instructing their neighbors. This can be weighed carefully in their calling. For Peter was called on the Sea of Galilee along with his brother and John with his brother. They alone must be considered worthy of the office of preaching who are connected with their neighbor by fraternal love and who hasten, not out of earthly opportunity, but out of love alone, to deliver the words to the others. Upon the calling of the Lord, Peter left his little boat with his nets and that was all that he had. However, Saint James not only left his boat with his nets, as Peter had done, but also his father, whom the law orders one to love and honor, and at the word of the Lord, he did not look back. What shall I say about their mother? Certainly, a mother — in part as a benefit of a long time of upbringing and in part because it is more the role of the mother than of men to lead sons by coaxing them — was usually dearer to sons than a father was. However, Saint James also left her without a farewell. He was a fortunate transgressor of the law who did not propose the law to the bearer of the law in the Jewish manner. [f.68r] James did not consider natural affections, for the Creator of nature was the cause for this action. He knew, in fact, that a father was to be honored and a mother was to be loved, but he knew that God was to be placed before them. He had the fondness of a pious son, but obedience to the Creator was of greater importance. A father, in fact, is to be honored, and parents are to be honored. A good neighbor is also to be honored, but God the Creator is to be honored and revered above all others. Therefore, Saint Peter is to be praised since he left his possessions at the call of the Lord. Saint James is to be raised up more, as he not only did not give heed to the law alone, but also for the sake of God was not mindful of paternal and maternal fondness. For it is necessary that human matters be placed after the divine ones. For if the duty of piety toward parents is to be shown, how much more is it to be toward the Creator of the parents to Whom thanks are owed even for the parents?

In this point, it appears reasonable that an intricate sophistry is pushing us. Why, in fact, did God, the most equitable paymaster, set as prince of the apostles Peter, who left few things and had almost no comparison to Saint James and his brother John when Saint James and his brother John — who were relatives of the Savior according to the flesh[12] —left behind much more than Peter for the sake of the Lord? What verbal difficulty some are trying to unravel in this way! They are asserting that Peter, in fact, had loved the Lord more than the others.[13] If they tested this through Gospel attestation, we would judge that they would agree that he was without rival. Why is it so astonishing, in fact, if God conferred preeminence over the others on him who had loved Him above the others through a prior choice of love?[14] However, unless this can be confirmed by Gospel affirmation, we consider it to be a rash judgment about the love of the apostles. When, in fact, the Lord questioned Peter saying: "Simon, son of John, do you love Me more than these?" [Jn 21:15] Simon, who had already been instructed not to make assumptions, answered: "Lord, You know that I love You." [Jn 21:15] It was as if he were saying: "I know that I love You with my whole heart, as You know very well, but I do not know how much the others love You." If Peter does not know, then who is wiser than the prince of the apostles who might try to affirm that Peter loved the Lord more among the apostles? So then, leaving aside these obscurities, let us say, along with Saint Jerome, that, because of his age, the Lord set Peter over them.[15] In fact, Saint James was young, and John his brother was hardly more than a boy, while Peter was older and of advanced age. Therefore, the good Teacher Who might bring an occasion [f.68v] for strife had said to them: "My peace I give you, My peace I leave you." [Jn 14:27] He would appear to be furnishing a cause for ill-will if He placed young men above a man already advanced in years. The most prudent Lord also wanted to offer us an example so that we would not presume to raise anyone except with the bar

---

12. It is suggested that James's and John's mother was [Mary] Salome, the sister of Mary, mother of Jesus. Cf. Mt 27:56, Mk 15:40, and Jn 19:25.
13. The ambiguity of this construction could mean either Jesus loved Peter or Peter loved Jesus.
14. The may be a reference to Peter's being chosen first, before the others. Cf. Mt 4:1–22.
15. Jerome, *Adversus Iovinianum,* Bk. 1, ch. 26 (PL 23:258).

CHAPTER FIFTEEN

of advanced age to the leadership of the Holy Church. Young men, in fact, are generally accustomed to feign religion so that they may be quickly raised to undue honor. Often, even though they may be good, since they have not been tested, they may fall into a worse state because of the honor. It is not within our power to say how many calamities have occurred in the Holy Church from negligence of this kind. For this reason, Joseph did not receive rule over Egypt before thirty years of age,[16] nor did John the Baptist, compared to whom "no one greater had arisen among those born of women," [Mt 11:11] start his work of preaching before thirty years of age. Nor was Ezekiel entitled to the ministry of prophesying until that time, and the Lord himself instituted these customs with Himself as He did not declare the beginning of His salubrious preaching until thirty years old. We can also say that the prudent Lord, for that reason, did not want to give preeminence over the others to his relatives, although they were good, lest it should appear that He had done it not for their holiness but rather because of their blood relationship. In fact, He already wanted at that point to avoid the depravity of some who give ecclesiastical honors and even money owed through the spirit to the poor, not to the Church,[17] but to blood relations. Besides, James and John his brother had, up until then, acquaintance with earthly things exerting a preference over others. They had pushed their mother, whom they knew very well had influence with the Lord — both from closeness of family and a sense of honor — to ask for preeminence. Thus, the Lord understood within Himself how many, either by themselves or by the powers of this world, would force themselves into ecclesiastical honors without right, and wanted to give advice to the Church so that it would not take up those who pushed themselves forward and would not admit them to the primacy. After the Ascension, as previously instructed, they did not seek primacy but unanimously

---

16. Cf. Gen 40:1–23, 41:1–41.
17. The Latin *religioni*, literally "religion" or "something sacred" theoretically embodied in the Church.

made James the Just[18] bishop over them because of the prominence of his holiness with which he shone among the people. They taught that the one who should be moved to govern the Church should be such a one who might gain the favor of the people through his sanctity. For this reason, Clement of Alexandria, the distinguished doctor, in his sixth *Book of Outlines*[19] said: "After the Ascension of the Savior, Peter and James [f.69r] and John, although they were, as I might say, given preference by Him in all things, nevertheless still did not claim the glory of the primacy for themselves. However, they made James, who is called "the Just," bishop of the apostles." He was, in fact, holy from his mother's womb, did not drink wine or any spirits, did not raise iron over his head, was not anointed with oil, and did not make use of baths.

For these reasons, we believe it was obvious that the Lord preferred Peter to James and his brother John. It is also a very exalted mystery that these three were set as columns for the others. In fact, the main virtues are represented by them, namely, faith, hope, and charity. One understands by Peter the faith with which we begin, by James the hope by which we are raised up, and by John the charity by which we are consumed. Therefore, Peter justly holds preeminence since without faith it is impossible to please God. However, since faith is useless unless the wantonness of the flesh is constrained and the devil is banished from the temple of the heart, James, who is interpreted as 'the supplanter,' follows.[20] However, when we have done this, we must not ascribe it to our own powers but to divine grace, and for this reason, John follows, who is called

---

18. James the Just (d.62 or 69CE) is sometimes called "the Lord's brother" and may be the same as, or confused with, the apostle James, son of Alphaeus, also known as James the Lesser. Some believe he was a biological child of Mary, while others suggest he was a step-brother of Jesus from a previous marriage of Joseph. He is sometimes identified as the James who wrote the Epistle of James.
19. See ch. 4, n. 10.
20. See ch. 5, n. 30.

CHAPTER FIFTEEN

"the grace of God."[21] Nor should one pass over in silence the fact that the Lord gave names to these three alone. Simon, in fact, because of his soundness of faith, which he admitted when the Lord asked, was called Peter.[22] However, James and his brother John, because they were connected through true brotherhood, did not get separate names, but both were called "Boanerges," that is, "Sons of Thunder," from the steadfastness and greatness of their faith.[23] What is then, this thunder of which Saint James and John are made sons? It is surely the One Who thundered from the cloud above Christ: "This is My beloved Son with Whom I am very pleased."[24] Oh, astonishing and wonderful benevolence of the Savior Who gave what He had as His own from nature to Saint James and John to hold through grace! For, since they had left behind their father in the flesh for Him, He gave James and John the heavenly Father to hold with them. Oh, happy recompense! But this is not foreign to the Lord, whose remuneration is always overflowing.[25]

Now, brethren, let us contemplate the efficacy of the thunder so that we may know what it is to be a "son of thunder." It is not something small or trifling that was given by the Lord, Who is abundant in repaying to the sons leaving their fathers, which was beyond the others. In short, thunder strikes the clouds, emits lightning, makes the earth tremble, and irrigates with rains. Therefore, the Lord confers this figuratively on Saint James and on John. And since Saint James was [f.69v] greater in age, order demanded that he should thunder first. Therefore, after the Ascension of the Lord, the most blessed James, filled with the Holy Spirit, struck the Jewish clouds with his preaching. For he disclosed

---

21. Again, the author plays off the Hebrew origin and meaning of the name for John or "God is gracious."
22. Here the author plays on the word *Peter* or "rock" with the implication of soundness or firmness.
23. Cf. Mk 3:17.
24. Cf. Mt 3:17, 17:5; Lk 3:22; 2 Pet 1:17.
25. This is an indirect reference to Lk 6:38, where repayment is heaped up, pressed down, and overflowing.

their malice, upbraided their harshness, confounded their envy. There was malice since, while they should feel ashamed of their sins, they were not only failing to correct themselves, but they were also persecuting with incurable hatred those reproaching them. There was hardness too, since they, almost through innate stupidity, were not grasping the promises of the Lord or the clear witness of the prophets. On the contrary, to their own foolishness, they altered these things with some incredible narratives. Then there was envy, since if they saw any people filled by divine grace, not only did they not want to hear them, but they also afflicted them with slander and hatred and frequently with torments as if they were criminals. Above all, James exposed them to Jesus Christ when he showed the promise from the law and from the prophets. He reminded them of the favors He had procured, and he made known to them the eternal torments — if they were ungrateful for these great favors — unless they should do penance. Thus, the most blessed James thundered with threats by dissipating the thickness of their sins. He also flashed with miracles in illuminating the hearts of the simple. He poured out salubrious rain in reviving and comforting the minds of the young. He revealed the pronouncements of the prophets, he revealed the mysteries of scriptures, and he disclosed Christ through all things. The scribes and the Pharisees were confounded and were destroying the law with foolish explanations rather than making it intelligible. The Sadducees were confounded and were denying the Resurrection with incredible narratives.[26] Those who crucified Christ were confounded above all the others as they were refuted with unbreakable reasoning, and they did not know what to do or where to turn. They were overcome by his reasoning, they were ashamed by his reputation, and they were confounded by the power of his miracles.

There was at that time a certain magician by the name of Hermogenes, who was led astray by the science of the enemy and

---

26. There were multiple cultural and religious differences between the Pharisees and Sadducees; the author sets them apart by their legalism (Pharisees) and their disbelief in Resurrection (Sadducees). Cf. Acts 23:6.

did not cease leading others astray. This magician was so familiar with the enemy of the human race that he appeared to rule more than the one who ruled him. The Jews, therefore, implored the help of this magician against Saint James so that they might, though the magician's sorcery, at least not be overcome by his reasoning, which they were unable to refute. And since the magician was endowed with worldly knowledge and propped up by the falsehood of his miracles, the Jews contrived to subdue with human knowledge the thunder of Saint James, and they hoped to obscure his miracles through the magician's miracles [f.70r]. Saint James, however, not only destroyed the assertions of the magician, but also annihilated the miracles that Hermogenes was performing through demons' art, and he converted this very magician along with his disciple to the Lord.[27] O Jews, who are foolish at heart, why do you toil with vain labor against the son of thunder? With what barrier are you preparing to obstruct the mouth of the one who always grows above the obstacle? He is not stopped by threats. He is not seduced by deceit. If you want to end his noise, remove the density of your sins. Certainly his sound would not be so frightening if there were not the uproar of the dense clouds. Discharge the clouds from your hearts, and the terror of the thunder will lose its powers. Therefore, when the magician had been overcome and converted, the Jews were in despair and could not tolerate the thunder of Saint James, and they, to their great wickedness, drew in Herod the King with money and without much difficulty, and they provoked the death of Saint James.

Who this Herod was and from what parentage he was born appear to be accepted but opinion about him varies because of a lack of information from even expert writers of history. Many, in fact, believe Herod the Tetrarch was the son, if you will, of the great Herod who beheaded John the Baptist, and they are surely mistaken through a misunderstanding of history. For Herod the Tetrarch, as the *Ecclesiastical History*[28] reports, based on the testimony of

---

27. See ch. 9, pp. 154–57 and ch. 17, n. 223.
28. Eusebius, *Ecclesiastical history*, Bk. I, ch.6.

Josephus,[29] was condemned to perpetual exile after he had been tortured in many ways by Gaius Caesar.[30] The Herod, however, who killed Saint James, as we will mention in its proper place, ended his life in his own kingdom. There are some who imagine that he was the son of Archelaus,[31] but their opinion is easily refuted by the fact that no history recounts that Archelaus had a son whom he would leave after him as an heir. Having set aside these opinions, we will follow the true histories. The histories, in fact, tell that Herod the Great,[32] who killed the innocents in place of Christ, had two sons from Marianne,[33] who was of royal lineage, namely Aristobol and Alexander,[34] whom he killed as adults because he suspected them of parricide. But Aristobol left after him a surviving son by the name of Agrippa[35] to whom Gaius Caesar handed over dominion of the Jews. Luke the Evangelist, either because of the dignity of the kingdom or more likely because of a cruelty similar to Herod's, called him Herod so that he would establish him not only as the heir of the kingdom, but also because of the wickedness of Herod. Just as the earlier Herod wanted to kill Christ through killing those boys, this Herod, in like manner, was incited by the money of the Jews and by his own wickedness, and he tried to crush Him through crushing the apostles. Therefore, he killed Saint James with a sword, for he was eagerly and strenuously [f.70v] preaching Christ to others and was refuting the Jews with his testimony on the law and the prophets.

Saint James was the first of the apostles to be crowned with martyrdom, however, with the Paschal feast at hand, in about the eleventh year after the Passion of the Lord, in the third year of the

29. See ch. 4, n. 15.
30. See ch. 4, n. 5.
31. Herod Archelaus (23BCE–18CE), son of Herod the Great and half-brother of Herod II.
32. Herod the Great (73–4BCE) had multiple wives over time.
33. Also known as Mariamne or Miriam (d.29CE).
34. Both died 7BCE.
35. Marcus Julius Agrippa, 11BCE–4CE.

CHAPTER FIFTEEN

empire of Claudius, as Bede remarks on in his Acts of the Apostles.[36] Herod, however, saw that the Jews were greatly pleased with the death of James, and so he went further and took Peter,[37] since Peter seemed to be distressing the Jews as well. But the Lord knew within Himself the excessive future desolation for His Church, if His two greatest pillars should succumb at the same time, and He, in his kindness, freed Peter from the hands of Herod and from the expectations of the Jews. However, God did not forsake Saint James for long but avenged him without delay and terribly. For as Saint Luke says in the Acts of the Apostles:

> Herod went down to Caesarea and on a solemn day, when he was dressed in splendid clothing and sat before the tribunal and spoke loftily to the people, and the people called out to him: "Words of God and not of man!" Immediately an angel of the Lord struck him because he had not given glory to God. Then, swarming with worms, he died in the fifty-fourth year of his age and the seventh year of his reign.[38]

From this, brethren, it is evident how true the knowledge of the most learned Solomon is, when he says: "The wicked man, when he has come into the depth of sins, is disdainful." [Prov 18:3] Herod, in fact, since he did not extinguish the fire of evil desire, thus did not fear accepting the money of the Jews for the death of a just man. However, from that he was raised to such pride that he usurped even divine honors offered to him by flatterers. Therefore, he perished, justly stricken by the angel, since neither care for his well-being nor reverence for Saint James nor divine nobility called him back from iniquity.

---

36. Cf. Bede, *Super Acta Apostolorum*, ch. 12 (PL 92:971–73). While the information here is clearly not dependent on Bede, it likely refers to Bede's extended discussion of the dating of Claudius and the famine (PL 92:971–72).
37. Cf. Acts 12:3, but the wording is paraphrased.
38. Cf. Acts 12; however, this wording is from Eusebius (*Ecclesiastical History*, Bk. 2, ch. 8–10).

Now, most beloved brethren, we gaze on the mighty works of Saint James. This was done in a fitting and appropriate order so that the one who was first in dignity would be first in passion. And the one who was first in teaching would be made a teacher in martyrdom. He was certainly vehement in his claim on the kingdom and was more vehement in its acquisition. He was first seized by the Lord and strove after this kingdom without effort, and now he deserves to be praised since he has obtained the kingdom through his virtues. It was fitting, moreover, for the son of thunder to walk the earth, to enter heaven, and to offer an example to others. For the more one knows the secrets of the Lord, the more ardently one should imitate Him [f.71r] rather than others. But the prayers of his mother with which she sought a seat in the kingdom for her sons were not rendered void, for as a wise man in hymns of praise asserts:[39]

For Asia on the right fell to John
And to Saint James fell Spain
On the left…

as the regions were placed in the division of the provinces. Thus, as it is believed, Saint James, at his suggestion, after his passion was conveyed by his disciples to Spain and is buried honorably in the farthest point of Galicia, now called Compostela, so that he might not only guide the Spanish with his patronage, which happened to fall by fortune to them, but might also comfort them with the treasure of his body.

Rejoice, therefore, great and illustrious Spain, with splendor, with dance, and with the error of superstition cast off! Rejoice because through the arrival of such a guest you put aside bestial ferocity and have placed under the yoke of the humble Christ your previously untamed neck! The humility of Saint James has brought

---

39. This is a probable reference to "O Word of God Revealed By the Mouth of the Father," *(O Dei Verbum)* verse 5. See Coffey and Dunn, *Miracles,* 107–9. The wording differs slightly, but there is an unmistakable similarity with the same meter (12/12/6) here.

CHAPTER FIFTEEN

you more, in fact, than the monstrousness of all your kings. It truly has lifted you toward heaven, while they weighed you down into the abyss. They contaminated you with sacrificing to idols; this has cleansed you by handing over the reverence of the true God. Spain, you are fortunate with an abundance of many things, but you are more fortunate with the presence of Saint James. You are fortunate because you are similar to paradise in temperature, but you are more fortunate because you are given to the bridegroom of heaven. You had certainly once been glorious with the renown of vain thought for the Columns of Hercules,[40] but now you are more fortunately supported by the very steadfast column of Saint James. Those things entangled you to the devil through pernicious superstition. This, with pious intercession, has joined you to your Creator. Those stone entities increased your faithlessness, this spiritual entity has procured for you salubrious grace. We, therefore, most beloved brethren, return thanks to the Dispenser of all good things in Whose fragrant mercy we are enriched with such a great treasure.

Let us celebrate the solemnities of Saint James, however, with devout minds, and let us solicit his patronage with the incense of our pious prayers to be present for us.

If one wishes to honor his solemnities,

One must subdue desires of the flesh.

No pollution of sensual desire may stain one,

And no haughtiness of self-pride may inflate one.

One should not be excited by the flame of wrath,

One should not be twisted with the malice of envy.

Since, in fact, the one who is holy is praised,

The one who venerates must be pure.

For one's glories are sullied

If one constructs frauds in the heart.

---

40. A reference to the Straits of Gibraltar. This rock imagery is bolder when one considers the earlier metaphor of the three columns and the rock image for the primacy of Peter.

Let us therefore cleanse our hearts
So that our commendations [f.71v] may be accepted.
Let us strive to be similar to him,
If we wish our praises to be accepted.

For this reason, John of Golden Mouth, the extraordinary doctor, says: "Whoever discusses the glories of the just with frequent praise, should imitate holy ways and justice."[41] Either one must imitate if one praises, or one must not praise if one refuses to imitate. For if we love the saints and the faithful because of these things, because in them we accept justice and faith, we can also be what they are if we do what they have done.

Let us imitate, therefore, Saint James, and with our imitation of him and with help from him, let us become sons of thunder! Let us break asunder the clouds of our sins with our preaching! Let us not pamper ourselves with the flattery of adulation! Let earthly things not take hold of us, but let us quake with our roused strength! Let us water the hearts of the simple with the salubrious rain of preaching, and let us offer the seeds of virtue with our admonitions! If we have truly acted in this way, we will be sons of thunder. Certainly, the violence of the Jews did not frighten Saint James, and the arrogance of the Pharisees did not subdue him, and the boundless insanity of Herod did not hold him back from preaching the word of God.

Brethren, let the pride of the rich not move us! Let the advantages of the flesh not allure us! Let the torments of the wicked princes not discourage us such that we may carry out our duties of preaching! Let us imitate the piety of Saint James with which he cured the

---

41. John Chrysostom, c.349–407. Although we have not located this in Chrysostom's work, others have made this attribution. See, for example, the *Abecedario Real e regia instrucçam de principes lusitanos,* ed. Joam dos Prazeres (Lisbon: Gaume, 1692), at entry 6 under X, where it is attributed to his "Serm. De Conf." It is also found in the *Ecclesiastico provveduto ovvero esortazioni famigliari per tutte le domeniche, e feste principali dell'anno,* ed. Casimiro di Firenzi (Venice, 1878), 4:182, where it is attributed to his "Ser. de Confess."

CHAPTER FIFTEEN

paralytic!⁴² Let us also imitate his love so that we show kindness even to our enemies! Assuredly Josias had placed the rope on his neck and was dragging him to the cruelest judge, but after he saw the paralytic cured by Saint James, he soon repented of his sins. And when he threw himself at Saint James's feet, he obtained with his prayers the forgiveness that he sought.⁴³ Oh, what a true disciple of Christ, who was prepared to be forgiving! He did not offer retribution to Josias because he first had set impious hands on him, but in a wonderful way he made him, whom he had perceived as a persecutor, worthy to be a partner in his passion. This is truly an exchange with the right hand of the Most High. And so, we, brethren, should have love for one another. We should harm no one. And we should tolerate calmly someone attacking us. Thus, truly, will we be made imitators of Saint James! Thus will we deserve to have him as our patron! Thus will he carry our prayers to the font of mercy! And thus will he make our prayers efficacious with his prayers. With Christ our Lord helping, to Whom is honor and glory. World without end. Amen. [f.72r]

---

42. This sentence is in the margin of CC with a cross to indicate its position but is missing in S. This is one of the few instances where the scribe of S has failed to incorporate a marginal addition into the text.
43. See ch. 9, n. 162.

[CHAPTER 16]

II Calends of August[1]
Day VII within the Octaves of Saint James

A Reading of the Holy Gospel According to Matthew:

"At that time the mother of the sons of Zebedee came to the Lord Jesus with her sons, James and John, adored Him, and asked something from Him. He said to her: 'What do you wish?' She said to Him: 'Say that these two sons of mine may sit, one at Your right hand, the other at Your left hand in Your kingdom,'" and so forth. [Mt 20:20–21ff.]

A Sermon of Saint Jerome the Doctor and of John the Bishop on This Reading for the Birth[2] of Saint James, Who is the Brother of Saint John and Who Rests in the Territory of Galicia.[3]

We celebrate most devoutly, dearest brethren, today's solemnity of our most glorious and pious patron, Saint James the Apostle. This solemnity is worthy of respect throughout the whole world. Let us go over this reading of the Gospel with an explanation, so that your mind may understand how it should desire the kingdom of God.

The mother of the sons of Zebedee, in fact, said to the Lord, "Say that these two sons of mine may sit, one at Your right hand and

---

1. July 31.
2. The Latin *natale* or "birth" is used here, with the meaning of birth unto everlasting life, that is, of course, the "death" or "passion" of one's earthly existence.
3. This is a mix of quotations from Jerome, *Commentariorum in Evangelium s. Matthaei liber I*, Bk. 1, ch. 20 (PL 26:142–45) and from St. John Chrysostom, *Homilia 35* as found in Joannis Chrysostomi, *Archieepiscopi Constantinopolitani Opera Omnia que exstant*, ed. Bernard de Montfaucon (Paris, 1835), vol. 6. For the remainder of this chapter, we give merely Jerome, *On Matthew* or John Chrysostom, *Homily 35* with the PL column(s) or Montfaucon page respectively. Presumably some of the unidentified wording is that of the compiler of the CC.

CHAPTER SIXTEEN

the other at Your left hand in Your kingdom." [Mt 20:20] Based on this, the mother of the sons of Zebedee holds an expectation of the kingdom, as when the Lord said: "The Son of man will be handed over to the chief priests and the scribes, and they will condemn Him to death and will hand Him to the Gentiles to be mocked and beaten and crucified." [Mt 20:18–19] As He had announced the ignominy of His Passion to the fearful disciples, she seeks the glory of one in triumph. I believe that it is for this reason: [f.72v] that the Lord had said after all these things, "on the third day He will rise again," [Mt 20:19] and the woman thought that He would reign immediately after the Resurrection and that what is promised, for the Second Coming was to be completed during the first coming, and with feminine eagerness, she wanted the present things and was unmindful of future things.[4]

"He said to her: 'What do you wish?'" [Mt 20:21] He does not ask as someone who does not know so He would hear what she wanted, but by explaining this, He would make their irrational request obvious, since they were certainly seeking as devout people and lovers of heavenly grace and not as people having the skill of harmful or profit-seeking people. For the Lord frequently allows His disciples to say, do, or think something incorrectly so that He might find opportunities from their mistake to teach and explain the rule of piety. He knew that, with Him there as a teacher, their error would do no damage and that His teaching would instruct all, not only at the present time, but also in the future.[5]

She said: "Say that these two sons of mine may sit, one at Your right hand and the other at Your left hand in Your kingdom." [Mt 20:21] The mother of the sons of Zebedee is asking, however, through womanly error and a feeling of piety, not knowing what she was seeking. It is not astonishing that she was making her case unskillfully, as this may be said also about Peter, when he wanted to make three tabernacles and did not knowing what he was saying.[6]

---

4. This paragraph is from Jerome, *On Matthew* (PL 26: 142).
5. This paragraph is from John Chrysostom, *Homily 35*, 889.
6. Cf. Mt 17:4. This paragraph is from Jerome, *On Matthew* (PL 26:143).

Matthew writes that this mother of the sons of Zebedee had asked the Lord on behalf of her sons, but Mark wants to reveal to the reader the sons' desire and plan while making no mention of their mother's intervention, and he says rather that they asked since he knew that their mother had asked at their request.[7]

And then the Lord, according to both of the Evangelists, answered them and not their mother: "You do not know what you are asking." [Mt 20:22] The desire was certainly good, but the request was not thought out. Thus, even if the bluntness of their request had to be ineffective, there was no need to confound them, since it had its origin in the love of the Lord. For this reason He did not reprove either their will or their request, but He only found fault with their lack of knowledge when He said: "You do not know what you are asking."[8]

They did not know what they were asking since they sought the seat of glory that they did not yet deserve from the Lord. The height of honor, in fact, already allured them, but first there remained a road of labor for them to travel. They desired to rule loftily with Christ, but first there remained humble suffering for Christ. Therefore, we must also not ask of God [f.73r] what we judge to be good, but let us pray and place ourselves in the power of God so that He might grant to us what He knows to be advantageous for us.

This follows: "Can you drink the cup that I am to drink?" [Mt 20:22] In fact, with the word "cup," He pointed out the passion of martyrdom, which it behooved Him and them to consume. As when taking on for Himself his own Passion, "He prayed saying, 'Father if You will, take this cup from Me.'" [Lk 22:42] And how could the Lord not know that they could imitate His Passion? He spoke in this way so that, with the Lord asking and them responding, we might all hear this, since no one can rule with Christ without imitating the Passion of Christ. "They said to Him: 'We can.'" [Mt 20:22] They answered not so much through confidence in their hearts as through ignorance of the trial. To those not knowing it,

7. Compare Mt 20:20–23 and Mk 10:35–40.
8. This paragraph is from John Chrysostom, *Homily 35*, 890.

CHAPTER SIXTEEN

war is desirable. Just as war is desirable to those not knowing it, so also to those without experience, the trial of passion and death appears easy. If, in fact, the Lord, when He came to the trial of His Passion, said: "Father, if it can be done, let this cup pass from Me,"[9] how much more would they not be saying "we can," if they knew what the trial of death would be. Passion holds great fear, but death holds a greater one.

"He said to them 'You will certainly drink My cup.'" [Mt 20:23] One might ask how the sons of Zebedee, James and John, would drink this cup, when scripture tells that only James, the most pious apostle, had his head cut off by Herod, while John the Evangelist finished his life with a natural death. However, if we read the ecclesiastical histories in which it is reported that, in something close to martyrdom, John was put in a vat of boiling oil and thus proceeded to receive the crown as a champion of Christ, and he was immediately sent[10] to the island of Patmos.[11] We will see that John does not fall short of martyrdom in mind,[12] and he drank the cup of acknowledgment, as three boys drank it in the fiery furnace,[13] although the persecutor did not shed his blood.[14]

He also added this: "However, to sit at My right hand and left hand is not Mine to give you, but for those for whom it was prepared by My Father." [Mt 20:23] Thus it is to be understood that the kingdom of heaven is not so much for the one giving but for the one receiving. It is not granted to persons by God, but whoever has shown oneself worthy of the kingdom of heaven will receive

---

9. Cf. Mt 26:39.
10. The Latin here is *ligatus* or "tied," probably for *legatus*, "sent," while Jerome uses *relegates* for "relegated."
11. This may refer to ecclesiastical histories in general, but only Eusebius mentions his exile to Patmos (Bk. 3, ch. 18).
12. See ch. 14, pp. 201–2 above, where Gregory makes a distinction between martyrdom "in mind" and "in deed."
13. Reference to the story of Shadrach, Meshach, and Abednego in Dan 3:8–30.
14. This paragraph is from Jerome, *On Matthew* (PL 26:143).

what has been prepared, not for the person but for the life lived. Therefore, in fact, the names of those to be seated in the [f.73v] kingdom of heaven are not pronounced lest, with only a few named, others would think they were excluded. If then, you are such that you should attain the kingdom of heaven that, "My Father has prepared" [Jn 14:2] for the triumphant and the victorious, you will receive it.[15]

Also, "it is not Mine to give you, but for those for whom it was prepared." [Mt 20:23] It is as if He were saying: "It is not Mine to give to the domineering, but for those for whom it was prepared by My Father." Hitherto, they were, in fact, just this. However, if you want to receive the kingdom, do not be what you now are. It is prepared for others, so be these others, and it is prepared for you. What is "be these others"? First, humble yourselves, you who want to be exalted.

"When the ten heard this, they grew indignant with the two brothers." [Mt 20:24] The ten apostles did not become indignant with the mother of the sons of Zebedee, and they did not blame the womanly boldness for the request, but rather the sons because they did not know their proper measure for ordinary desire and were angered. To them the Lord had said: "You do not know what you are asking."[16] [Mt 20:22]

Just as they sought from Him in the flesh, so also were they saddened in the flesh. In fact, just as, if they had understood spiritually, they would not have been about to ask to be above all others, so also, if they understood spiritually, they would not be about to be saddened because others were before them, for to want to be above everyone is certainly blameworthy. However, to hold another person above oneself is exceedingly glorious.[17]

"But Jesus called them to Him and said: 'You know that the princes of the peoples dominate them, as those who are greater exercise power over them.'" [Mt 20:25] The mild and humble

---

15. This paragraph is from Jerome, *On Matthew* (PL 26:144).
16. This paragraph is from Jerome, *On Matthew* (PL 26:144).
17. This paragraph is from John Chrysostom, *Homily 35,* 891

CHAPTER SIXTEEN

Teacher does not blame the two asking out of unbridled desire, and He does not chide the other ten for disdain and envy. However, He sets out an example by which He may teach: One becomes greater who would be lesser, and one becomes master who is servant to all. Therefore, either they sought in vain excess things, or they lament over their longing for the greater since they would come to the height of virtues not by power but by humility. Thus, from these words of the Lord, we understand that one comes to the kingdom through humility, and one enters heaven through simplicity.[18]

Whoever desires to attain the summit of the divine should pursue the depths of humility. Whoever wants to come to rule over his brother should first surpass him in submitting. Finally, in case words were of little importance, so that they would blush at deeds, He gave an example by saying: "Just as the Son of man has not come to be served but to serve and to give His soul for the redemption of many." [Mt 20:28] [f.74r] Note that we have frequently said that the One who might minister was called the Son of man. He placed here "soul" for "body," as He called His body a soul in His Passion, as He said: "My soul is saddened even unto death." [Mt 26:38][19] And elsewhere: "I have the power of laying down My soul and taking it up again." [Jn 10:18] The Lord gave His body in the Passion and received it back in the Resurrection. He gave His soul when He accepted the form of a servant so that He might shed blood for the world. He gave His soul as the redemption of many when He sent redemption to His people and delivered it up as His eternal witness, and He deigned to lay down His soul for His sheep and to die for His flock. And He did not say to give His soul for the redemption of all but for many, that is, for all who would want to believe.[20]

Jesus Christ our Lord, therefore, paid no less a price for us wretches than Himself, so that He might allow us to rejoice together,

---

18. This paragraph is from Jerome, *On Matthew* (PL 26:144).
19. Cf. also Mk 14:34.
20. This paragraph follows fairly closely the text of Jerome, *On Matthew* (PL 144–45).

and His reign and His rule remain without end. World without end. Amen.

[CHAPTER 17]

A Sermon of Pope Saint Calixtus for the Solemn Feast of the Calling and *Translation* of Saint James the Apostle, Which Is Celebrated on the Third Calends of January[1]

A day to be honored, brethren, is the solemn feast of Saint James the Apostle,[2] and it has dawned today on the world. Let us exult and rejoice in it. This is a day more celebrated than many, more renowned than many, more illustrious than many, more worthy than the rest, and more holy than the others. On this day the great apostle James, patron of Galicia, joyously adorned the heavens with his spiritual arrival, hallowed the Spanish and the Galician peoples with his bodily arrival, and enriched people everywhere with his widespread miracles. He, who faithfully enhanced the lands, perpetually enriched the heavens on this day. For this the court of angels delights in heaven, and for this Mother Church rejoices here on earth.

A double solemn feast[3] is celebrated by the faithful today: namely, the calling of this very Saint James, or how he was chosen by the Lord into the apostolic order along with John, Peter, and Andrew near the shores of Galilee, as well as his *translation*, [f.74v] that is to say, how his most precious body was moved from Jerusalem to the city of Compostela. These are, in fact, solemn, sacrosanct, apostolic feasts to be honored, celebrated, and cultivated by all peoples. These

---

1. December 30.
2. This sermon is often referred to as the *Veneranda dies* ("A day to be honored") in keeping with the traditional practice of referring to sermons by their opening words. An earlier translation of this sermon was included in Coffey, Davidson, and Dunn, *Miracles of Saint James*, 8–56; it has been retranslated for this edition.
3. A double feast because it is celebrating two events in the life of Saint James: his *electio* or "calling" to be an apostle and his *translatio* or transfer of his body to the tomb. See Introduction, pp. xxx–xxxvii.

are the feasts on which heavenly rewards are divinely given to the just and eternal salvation is promised to sinners.

The books of the Evangelists expound on how the venerable Apostle James was chosen. Of these Evangelists, Matthew, among the others, says: "Jesus, went forth from there" — namely near the Sea of Galilee — "and saw two brothers, James of Zebedee and John, his brother, in a boat mending their nets with their father Zebedee; and He called them. And they immediately left their nets and their father and followed Him." [Mt 4:21–22] Saint Paul also mentions this calling, saying, "What stupid things of the world God has chosen so that He may confound the wise; and God has chosen the weak things of the world so that He may confound the strong; and God has chosen the ignoble and contemptible things of the world and things that do not exist so that He may destroy those that exist lest any flesh be glorified in His sight."[4] [1 Cor 1:27–29]

The splendid poet Sedulius, reflecting on the venerable calling of Blessed James, also sang the praise of Christ with a faithful pen, saying:

> Furthermore, from fishermen He made men suitable
> For fishing human souls, which, rashly following the slippery
> Delights of the world like the azure waves of the Black Sea,
> Pass over the blindness and uncertainty of the deep.
> These He orders to be His disciples, and such as these He
>   brings to
> Eternal life, whom a proud blood nourishes, not with a puffed-up
> Glory of speaking nor with a haughty nobility,
> But, being quiet with renown, shining with a humble
> Mind, that the brightness in heaven might make neighbors of
>   the people.

---

4. This passage does not refer to Christ's calling of James. However, this sermon writer uses it to support and amplify the idea of a lowly fisherman being raised to the rank of apostle and expands it to a figurative and moral commentary.

CHAPTER SEVENTEEN

For God, the powerful One, has chosen the foolish and lowly things
Of the world, breaking the strong and destroying the wise.[5]

How the *translation* of this apostle occurred is declared from the mouths of many faithful people who say that after he was killed by Herod,[6] his entire body was carried across the sea from Jerusalem to Galicia with an angel of the Lord accompanying it in a boat with his disciples as sailors and with various miracles experienced along the way. Galicia and Spain are regenerated by the grace of baptism, through his *translation,* and the preaching of the apostolic disciples, and the kingdom of heaven is enriched. It is right to speak of this venerable *translation* as it was once written by a wise man: "He was pleasing and beloved by God and was removed from living among sinners." [Wis 4:10] On this day honoring the apostle, [f.75r] the joyful Church of the faithful is accustomed to sing this verse three times:[7] "James pleased God and was transported to paradise so that he might give repentance to the peoples."[8] But we should consider what there might be for us to understand in his *translation* and in his calling. In his calling, then, the setting aside of sins and perseverance in good works are figuratively insinuated, and in his *translation* eternal rest is represented.

Thus, in fact, the blessed apostle, on the day when he was chosen, not only set aside his boat, his father and mother, and his own work, but also the faulty accumulation of the old culture because of divine love, and from then on he persevered in good works. In this same way, we must eradicate our whole collection of faults and persevere in good works. For this reason, in fact, the Lord ordered people to set aside all possessions, because He does not want those serving Him preoccupied with earthly things but focused only on

---

5. Sedulius (first half 5th c.), *Carmen Paschale* 2:220–30 (PL 19:621–22).
6. Herod Agrippa I, 10BCE–44CE; ruled 41–44CE.
7. CC contains an interlinear notation *iii-* for "three times."
8. Cf. Ecclus (Sir) 44:16. The name of *Enoch* has been replaced by *James*. This verse opens the ch.19 sermon (p. 296) and also the verse of a vespers reading in ch.29 (p. 403).

the heavenly. As the apostle says, "No one serving under God's banner may implicate himself in worldly affairs, so that he may be pleasing only to Him to Whom he has proven himself." [2 Tim 2:4][9]

By the boat, which Blessed James abandoned on the sea's waves when the Lord called him, it is right to understand figuratively the Synagogue of the Jews, which was tossing about on dangerous laws like a ship on the sea's waves. After hearing the evangelic word, the human race abandoned the ancient law, just as James abandoned the little boat, and then subjected itself to the Catholic Church. By the nets, it is right to understand the ancient law of circumcision and sacrifice in which the Jewish people were caught and held captive like a multitude of fish in a net. After accepting the Church through the grace of the new baptism, they thus cast off this ancient law, just as James did his nets. By Zebedee, the father of Saint James, one can infer the devil. For, as James abandoned his father like a fugitive, the devil himself left God and fled to Orcus. After accepting the precepts of Christ, the human race renounced the devil just as James renounced his father, and James ascended to the seat from which the devil had fallen. By the *translation* of Blessed James, therefore, eternal rest is represented, since as the apostle's venerable body was delivered from the place of his martyrdom to the place of his tomb, and as his soul was carried to eternal rest by the angels, we are also to be raised justly from the harshness of our good life[10] to the eternal rest of paradise through perseverance in good works. The Lord makes it manifest that no one can move on to eternal rest except through the labor of this present harsh life when He says: "Come to me, all who labor and are burdened…and you will find rest for your souls." [Mt 11:28–29] In the Book of Wisdom [f.75v] it is written: "God will return the price of the labors of His

---

9. The verse concerns soldiers of Christ. Saint James identifies himself as a soldier in Bk. II, miracle 19. See Coffey and Dunn, *Miracles*, 54–57. He is also portrayed as a soldier above in ch. 6 (p. 88) and ch. 7 (pp. 105–6).
10. Here "good life" is used as opposed to an "evil" or a "sinful" life. Harshness refers to the suffering related to the human condition.

holy ones."[11] The apostle also says: "It is necessary for us to enter into the kingdom of God through many tribulations." [Acts 14:21]

Thus, the blessed apostle was chosen on this day so that he might tear the world from the devil's jaws by his preaching. He was translated so that he might strengthen with his patronage, bestow with his benefits, shine with his countless miracles, and prepare seats in the heavenly realm for those loving him with all their hearts — not only for the Galicians but also for those visiting his holy tomb.

At the time when ice is hard like crystal, and snow is sowed over the world like flour, and everyone is crushed by the oppression of the cold, the *translation* of Saint James is celebrated.[12] At the time when the fruit of the earth is collected and the storehouses are being replenished with healthful grains, his passion in honored.[13] This is the meaning: it is a fitting time to honor the passion of Saint James when the fruit of the earth is being collected, just as the present age is a fitting time for doing good works. The time when his calling and his *translation* are honored and every kind of mortal creature is crushed by the oppression of the cold indicates a future age in which no one will be allowed to work.[14] Therefore, anyone who has performed no good works for their souls in this world will be the especially[15] needy in the future.

However, there should be no silence about apocryphal things. On the contrary, these things, which many irrational people, who are shamefully sliding toward heresy, are accustomed to say about James and his *translation* should be announced so as to be corrected. What is worse, they dare to write about these things with the pen of falsehood. Some, for instance, think he is a son of the Lord's mother, because they have heard James called "brother of the Lord," both in the Gospel and in the Epistle to the Galatians, but

---

11. Cf. Wis 10:17.
12. December 30.
13. July 25.
14. The reference is to the time when people will be in heaven.
15. The Latin of CC is *peculialiter* for *peculiariter;* S has it as *peculiariter.*

this is not so.[16] Others say that he came from Jerusalem to Galicia over the waves of the sea without a boat, sitting on a large stone[17] with the Lord instructing him and that a certain part of this large stone has remained behind in Joppa.[18] Others say that this very stone arrived on the boat together with his lifeless body. However, I declare both stories to be false.[19] Truly, when I once saw the great stone, I knew it was a stone originally from Galicia. There are, however, two reasons why the great stone of Saint James is to be worthily venerated: first, because as it is reported, the apostle's body at the time of its *translation* was placed upon it at the port of Iria Flavia; [f.76r] and second — and the greater reason — because the Eucharist was assiduously celebrated on it.[20]

Some also say that the apostle of Galicia cursed the soil so that it would not bring forth any more wine, because a certain lady by the name of Compostela,[21] as they say, drunk on wine and weighted down by sleep, did not disclose to him the Lord visiting the basilica when she was slumped over in her sleep. In fact, as they say, the apostle had told her to tell him when the Lord would arrive. Others, however, say that the Lord appeared to her, stripped

---

16. Passages open to such interpretation can be found in Mt 13:55, Mk 6:3, and Gal 1:19. The Latin *quod absit*, probably does not mean, "which may not be there" (the literal translation), but "it is not so," in the sense that such an interpretation may not be found there.

17. The Latin *petronus* is found only with the meaning *pile of rock* (cf. Maigne d'Arnis and DuCange). Here the context would point to a contamination with the vulgar usage of the *on* suffix/infix to indicate "large stone."

18. Today called Jaffa in English. It is the oldest section of the port city of Tel Aviv, Israel.

19. Note the change from the "we" discourse to "I."

20. The relationship between Saint James and the megalithic and Roman heritage of the Galician region is complex. See Harold Peake, "Santiago: The Evolution of a Patron Saint," *Folk-Lore* 30.3 (1919): 208–26; and José Suárez Otero, "Iria, Padrón, Santiago: Geografía mítica y realidad arqueológica," in *Padrón, Iria y las tradiciones Jacobeas* (Santiago de Compostela: Xunta de Galicia, 2004).

21. It is not certain if the woman's name was "Compostela" or if this figured as part of her name in the sense of "from Compostela."

CHAPTER SEVENTEEN

the bark[22] from a stick in His hands and promised her that she would be cleansed just as that stick was stripped of its bark, and thus would people praying and seeking His threshold be cleansed of their sins. This is determined to be an error in this way: if the sinner is cleansed like the stick, he is thus not well purified, since the stick cannot be purified on the inside but only on the outside, and it would be necessary that the sinner be cleansed on the inside and the outside, namely in body and soul. Some say that angels have spoken openly in James's basilica and that they once sang in front of everyone. Others dream that angels carried his body through the air from Jerusalem to Galicia without human help. Similarly, others babble that this same body was carried from Jerusalem to Galicia in a certain glass boat over the waves of the sea with men as sailors. We[23] judge dreams and tales of all these types and others similar to them to be apocryphal. We reject them completely, and we repudiate them entirely, even declaring them anathema, so that no one may any longer dare to write anything about the saint except the authentic things that this codex called "James"[24] contains. This codex,[25] in fact, relates those things that are necessary for reading or singing on the feast days of this very Saint James, and they are extracted from authentic codices as are indicated in it. However, we grant permission to write down, for the edification of the faithful, those miracles that he has yet to perform as long as they

---

22. There is no Latin word *scortice*. In all likelihood this is a prothetic *s-* attached to *cortice*. In the context of the story of a "woman who deserves punishment," it is difficult to avoid mentioning possible confusion with, and thus the influence of such words as *scortum*, "harlot," and *scortari*, "to whore."
23. The author resumes the "we" discourse. The sermon moves between "I" and "we" several more times.
24. See the Introduction, pp. xiii–xiv and the Letter of Calixtus, p. 1, on the title of the LSJ.
25. This is supposed to be a sermon, but the author is focused on the codex in which it is contained.

have been testified to by two or three witnesses.[26] With us rejecting the aforementioned errors and asserting universally the truthful testimony about him and contemplating his most excellent deeds, there should be rejoicing on earth over him about whom the angels give thanks in the celestial domain.

The hearts of others resound with human praise, but let me have some time to commemorate things that are just.[27] The work of the victor, in fact, is one of piety, and it spurs the inclination to compose books. [f.76v] There are two reasons for this. One reason is that it is fitting to relate great things about those who are great, for whoever conceals good things is the author of a crime. The other reason is to inspire, for the one who has read his deeds is inflamed by love and desires better things.

"Praise the Lord," says the Psalmist, "in His holy places." [Ps 150:1] If we are ordered to praise the Lord in His holy places, then we are ordered all the more to do so with Saint James, who looked upon the Son of God in human form transfigured by the will of the Father on Mount Tabor.[28] Neither Moses on Mount Sinai[29] nor Abraham at the root of Mamre,[30] nor Jacob on Mount Bethel,[31] nor the other saints were ever able to see Him fully. We must praise and

---

26. This invitation may be manifest in the Addenda. There one miracle is recounted in the same style as Bk. II as well as three in poetic form. The permission allows for James's new miracles after the completion of the CC. In fact, the miracle format of Bk. II would have been set prior to this codex. See Coffey and Dunn, *Miracles,* liii and 64–65.
27. Throughout this sermon, the author varies between "I" and "we"; here, there is an even more personal, oral aspect as the author interjects "let me" into the text, giving one the sense that this is really a sermon that was performed, not just composed. See the Introduction, pp. xxiv–xxviii.
28. Cf. Mt 17:1–8, Mk 9:1–7, and Lk 9:28–36. Although the name of the mountain is not given in the Gospels, in the Middle Ages, it was believed to be Mount Tabor.
29. Cf. Ex 19:20.
30. Cf. Gen 18:1.
31. Cf. Gen 28:19.

CHAPTER SEVENTEEN

commemorate him[32] with worthy veneration. He is, in fact, that "just one" who is kept alive in the eternal memory of angels and men, as the Psalmist testifies, when he says: "The just one shall live in eternal remembrance." [Ps 111:7 / 112:7] Eternal remembrance of the heavenly kingdom is said to be blessedness in which the just one who does good work is praised by the angels without limit. Therefore, Saint James is rightly and worthily kept alive in the memory of angels and men since he has passed to the joy of the heavens and since he has settled in body alone in this earthly pilgrimage as he dwells in thought and desire in the eternal land. Freed from the bonds of the flesh, he returned to the highest King double the talents given to him by the Lord.[33] To him the Lord will say most fittingly on the day of retribution: "Well done, good and faithful servant, since you have been faithful over a few things, I shall set you over many. Enter into the joy of your Lord." [Mt 25:23]

Thus, concerning the praise of Saint James, it proper to understand what was said by a certain wise man: "The just one will sprout up like the lily" [Hos 14:6] and will flower for eternity before the Lord.[34] The lily's leaves die in winter, and then the lily brings forth the finest white flowers with an aromatic shoot in the summer. By the lily, which dies in winter and sends forth white flowers with an aromatic shoot in the summer, Saint James is represented. He is crushed as if it were wintertime by the affliction of his passion in this world, and in the summer richness, that is, in the pleasantness of paradise, he flourishes eternally in the presence of God through the merits of his good works. The aromatic shoot brings forth the lily. Saint James was, as Paul says, the good perfume of Christ in every place:[35] preaching, praying, doing good works, together

---

32. The Latin is ambiguous. A close reading leads us to believe that the passage refers to St. James.
33. Cf. Mt 25:14–30. This reference is to the parable of the talents.
34. Here *Israel* has been replaced by *Iustus* the "Just One." The second clause, of unknown origin, appears regularly as a response to this verse of Hosea in various breviaries and offices.
35. Cf. 2 Cor 2:14–15. Paul is not referring specifically to St. James.

with giving all kinds of good example to all. The lily's leaves die, but there is life in its roots, just as [f.77r] Saint James mortified his external person with many labors while he quickened and grew the virtues within him. Dioscorides, a teacher of medicine, describes the powers of the lily, saying:

> The lily is known to physicians, and its powers can soften the hardness of sinews: its leaves are beneficial when cooked and applied to burned areas, and they cure the damage of serpents. Its sap, when cooked and mixed with honey in a new vessel, mends old wounds. Its root, when roasted and rubbed with oil, is also suitable for burns from fire, and it even softens the womb and brings on a menstrual purging. Its seed, in fact, when given as a drink, induces menstruation, brings on labor, and works for the bite of a serpent. The flowers of the lily are useful for any hardening of the womb.[36]

The powers of the lily are said to soften the hardness of bodily sinews, just as Saint James, filled with the strength of the Holy Spirit, is allowed to release sins from souls and the hard bonds of vices through the power of absolution. The leaves of the lily when cooked are beneficial to burned areas, just as the good works and divinely inspired eloquence of Saint James, tested by the fire of the Holy Spirit, are beneficial to humankind, burned up until now with flames of corruption. The leaves of the lily treat the damage of serpents to people's bodies, just as Saint James has treated the suggestions of the devil in the souls of sinners with his preaching and absolution. In fact, just as a serpent punctures the flesh of a person with the venom of its fang, the devil injures one's mind with his depraved suggestion. The sap of the lily mends old wounds, just as James mends the errors of the Old Law and the putrid wounds of sins through his mellifluous preaching and divine absolution. The root of the lily, when roasted and rubbed with oil, is fitting for burns

---

36. Dioscorides, *Herbal,* 3:116. Dioscorides's first-century Greek herbal was popular throughout the Middle Ages. Cf. Pedanius Dioscorides, *The Greek Herbal of Dioscorides,* ed. Robert T. Gunther (New York: Hafner, 1959), Bk. 3, sect. 116.

CHAPTER SEVENTEEN

from fire and brings on menstrual purging, just as the apostolic faith, when mixed with the oil of piety and mercy and infused in the mind by the fire of the Holy Spirit through divinely inspired preaching, produced a remedy for the flames of corruption to the burned human race and brought on a purging of its sins through the washing of baptism. That the seed of the lily, when given as a drink, provokes menstruation and treats the bite of a serpent implies the same thing as the root and even the flower. That it brings on labor shows that the virginal chastity of Blessed Mary ever virgin is to be believed by the faithful. A certain sage sang [f.77v] most splendidly about this in praise of this Virgin, saying:

The lily of chastity has flowered,

As the Son of God has appeared.[37]

Saint James was, therefore, a lily and an honor to the world, since by living well, preaching, working divine miracles, and patiently tolerating various kinds of suffering, he sprouted up on the earth, and crowned for divine service, has flowered for all eternity before the Lord.

Again, it is right to understand concerning him what the divine poet once sang: "The just shall flower like the palm and be multiplied like the cedars of Lebanon." [Ps 91:13 / 92:12] The palm is a very good tree: it has a tough root in the earth, it expands greatly at the top, and it bears at its peak a round object like cheese, which is sweet when eaten and from which palms and spikes arise.[38] Pilgrims returning from Jerusalem appropriately carry these palms in their hands, showing themselves to be victors over pagan vices and

---

37. The source of this quote is unknown. It is, however, found in a number of breviaries. The hymn is reproduced in the AH 20:223, which attributes it to Pierre de Corbeil (d.1222). This CC manuscript, however, antedates Peter's work.

38. The author is grappling with an explanation of the palm tree with which he was only vaguely familiar, using *palma* or "palm" for the tree as well as the more elliptic *arbor palmarum* or "tree of palms." He describes the fruit as "like a ball of cheese" attempting to explain these seeds, some of which were edible.

demons.[39] The palm tree with its tough root in the earth signifies Saint James who, while he was on earth, led a harsh life beset by many labors. That it rises from the earth expanding greatly at the top indicates the one who has risen from "virtue to virtue," [Ps 83:8 / 84:7] that is to say, from faith to certain hope, from hope to two-fold charity, from charity to perseverance in good works, from perseverance to the heights of paradise. That it bears sweet food at its peak from which the palms arise implies the hope of future heavenly rewards. For this hope, Saint James, after overcoming the enemies of the faith, delivered his venerable body to the various pains of martyrdom, and with the palm of victory, he has not only passed through the heights of the air but has also penetrated the heights of the heavens, trusting in the blades and spikes of heavenly virtues. Just as an army returning from the field of battle after conquering its enemies used to carry palms through the city praising the Creator who gave it victory, the assembly of saints, either through the shedding of blood or the demonstration of good works, after overcoming vices and the enemies of the faith, was accustomed to go toward the heavenly court with the palm of victory. With Herod conquered, Saint James has arisen for these people and has penetrated heaven with the palm of victory.[40] The Hebrew children came to Jerusalem with palms to meet the Lord, just as the saints have passed from vices to heavenly virtues by living well and have met the Lord in heavenly Jerusalem after this present life.

This great James, therefore, now happily delights in perpetual glory. [f.78r] With the great virtue of James, not only Spain but

---

39. See Dante's *La vita nuova*, ch. 40: "If they [pilgrims] cross the sea, they are called 'palmers,' because they frequently bring back palm leaves. Those who go to the church in Galicia are called 'pilgrims,' for James's tomb is farther from his native land than that of any other apostle." (Translated by David M. Gitlitz.)

40. The palm is often a symbol for martyrdom. This is a reference to James's martyrdom on order of Herod Agrippa, while Herod serves also a metaphor for the non-believers.

also Galicia[41] now shine like the moon with the sun.[42] He rejoices in heaven as its churches flourish in the world. He not only preached to Judea and Samaria but also graced Spain and Galicia and built that once impious people into the Church with the aid of Christ. In fact, the apostle's holy power, translated from the regions around Jerusalem to the country of Galicia, shines anew with divine miracles.[43] For at his basilica, divine miracles are very often performed by the Lord through him.[44] The sick come and are cured, the blind are given sight, the lame are lifted up, the mute speak, the demoniacs are set free, consolation is given to those mourning, and what is greater, the prayers of the faithful are heard, and there the heavy burdens of transgressions are set aside, and the bonds of sins are loosed. Oh, with what holiness and grace Saint James gleams in heaven, who by the power of God works such miracles on the earth! Just as the height of heaven or the depth of the seas cannot be examined or measured by anyone, the magnitude of his miracles and his powers cannot be counted by anyone. There, in fact, the choirs of angels frequently come down, accept the vows of the humble, and carry them back to the ears of the highest King in the heavens.[45]

---

41. Note the distinction between Spain *(Yspania)* and Galicia *(Gallecia)*. Through the time of the CC, Galicia was a separate kingdom with fluid borders, sometimes linked with Asturias, at other times with Leon. Colin Smith suggests that references to "Yspania" are fluid throughout the CC, (at least in Bk. IV, the Pseudo-Turpin): "When the designations are paired, 'Yspania' means 'Muslim Spain' and 'Gallaecia,' 'Christian Spain.'" See his "The Geography and History of Iberia in the *Liber Sancti Jacobi*," in *The Pilgrimage to Compostela in the Middle Ages*, ed. Maryjane Dunn and Linda Kay Davidson (New York: Routledge, 1996), 23–41 at 32.
42. S gives *sol et luna* for "the sun and the moon."
43. For an introduction to James's early Eastern hagiographic tradition, see Coffey and Dunn, *Miracles,* xxiii–xxvi.
44. Only six of the twenty-two miracles in Bk. II occur within the city of Santiago, and only four in the basilica. This is the first of this sermon's several lists of the saint's miracles.
45. Previously (see p. 233 above) the author has declared that the singing of angels in the basilica is false.

At this place the barbarous and civilized peoples of all the regions of the world[46] arrive: namely, French, Normans, Scots, Irish, Welsh, Germans, Iberians, Gascons,[47] Bavarians[48] impious Navarrese,[49] Basques, Goths, Provençals, Garasqui,[50] Lotharingians, Gauti,[51] English, Bretons,[52] Cornwallians, Flemings, Frisians, Allobroges,[53] Italians, Apulians, Poitevins, Aquitainians, Greeks,

46. Ch. 7 also refers specifically to large numbers of people rushing to the saint's tomb in Galicia. See Carlo Pulsoni, "Notes on Some of the Ethonyms in the *Veneranda dies,*" *Ad Limina* 1.1 (2010): 151–59 for a discussion of the organization of these places and peoples.
47. The Latin *Vasconi* would normally indicate the Basques; however, they are mentioned below as *Bascli.* This may refer to the Gascons living to the north of the Pyrenees.
48. The Latin is *Baioari,* possibly "Bavarians."
49. The Navarrese are the only people to be singled out with an adjective. The author of this sermon had an opinion about the Navarrese similar to that of the author of Bk. V, the *Guide,* who describes them as liars and thieves (Melczer, *Pilgrim's Guide,* 88–89).
50. An unidentified group, perhaps from the area of the Garonne.
51. While this could be any number of groups, it may refer to the Swedes under the modern name *Geats* with an earlier form *Gautar.*
52. It is not certain if the author intends Angles or English, Bretons or British.
53. The Latin *Allobroges* represents roughly the modern areas of Savoy and Dauphiné, the area between the Rhône and Isère Rivers, in the province of Vienne, the province where Calixtus had been archbishop. This area is mentioned again in Bk. II, Miracle 13.

CHAPTER SEVENTEEN

Armenians, Danes,[54] Norwegians,[55] Russians, Ioranti,[56] Nubians[57] Parthians, Romans, Galatians, Ephesians, Medes, Tuscans, Calabrians, Saxons, Sicilians, Asians, Pontics,[58] Bithynians,[59] Indians, Cretans, Jerusalemites, Antiochians, Galileans, Sardians,[60] Cyprians, Hungarians, Bulgarians, Slovenians,[61] Africans, Persians, Alexandrians, Egyptians, Syrians, Arabs, Colossians, Mauritanians,[62]

---

54. Dacia was originally the Roman province north of the Danube River, presently Romania. According to Aryeh Grabois, *Illustrated Encyclopedia of Medieval Civilization* (New York: Mayflower, 1980), 253, this name was "erroneously used during the Middle Ages to designate Denmark and other Scandinavian provinces." Erroneous or not, Pulsoni ("Notes") makes the case that through proximity to the reference to Norwegians, *Daci* refers to the Danes. Dacia is referred to once again in the last paragraph of this sermon about the various routes to the saint's tomb, as well as in Bk. IV, the Pseudo-Turpin. See Kevin Poole, ed., *Chronicle of Pseudo Turpin*, (New York: Italica Press, 2014), 52, 108.

55. This is one possibility for *Noroequi*, although another is the Noricans, who lived between the Alps and the Danube.

56. The Latin is *Ioranti;* possibly from the noun *Hierapolis* or the modern Königsberg or Kaliningrad. It could also be Hieropolis in Turkey.

57. "Greeks...Nubians," is inserted in the margin of CC in a similar, if not the same, hand, with a red cross designating its insertion point above "Aquitanians." It is in the body of S.

58. Those from *Pontus,* at the south of the Black Sea, settled by Greeks, now located in Turkey.

59. Bithynia is a region to the west of and later linked to *Pontus*. Once part of the Byzantine Empire, it is now part of Turkey.

60. From Sardis, the ancient capital of Lydia. Its ruins are located in Turkey.

61. Latin *Esclavoni*. Because of the specificity of this list, "Slovenians" from the area of modern Croatia and Slovenia seems more likely than the more generic "Slavs." The place is also used in Bk. II, Miracle 22, where one finds *Iazeram in Esclavonia,* which seems to be Zadar in modern Croatia (Coffey and Dunn, *Miracles,* 61, n.170).

62. The Latin *Mauri* could indicate Mauritanians, sometimes used as synecdoche for Africans, or less likely in this context, Moors, depending on the author's intentions.

Ethiopians, Philippians, Cappadocians, Corinthians, Elamites,[63] Mesopotamians, Libyans, Cyrenes, Pamphylians,[64] Cilicians, Jews, and the other countless peoples. All languages, tribes, and nations go to him in bands and throngs, fulfilling their vows to God with thanksgiving and bearing tributes of praise. Whoever sees these choruses of pilgrims keeping vigil around the venerable altar of Blessed James marvels with extreme delight. Germans remain in [f.78v] one area, French in another, Italians in another, in separate bands, holding burning candles in their hands, which light up the whole church like the sun or like the brightest of days. Each person sagaciously carries out his vigils by himself with his countrymen. Some sing with lutes, some with lyres, some with drums, some with flutes, some with pipes, some with trumpets, some with harps, some with violas, some with British or Gallic zithers, some with psalters.[65] Some keep vigil by singing to the various kinds of music; some lament their sins; some read psalms; and some give alms to the blind. Various languages are heard there: various barbarian calls, the words and songs of Germans, English, Greeks, and the other tribes and various peoples of all the regions of the world. "There is no speech and no language with which their voices do not resound." [Ps 18:4 / 19:3] Assiduous[66] vigils of this type are held there; some come, some leave, and various people offer up various gifts. Thus, someone approaches sad and leaves happy. Some solemn feast is always and constantly being celebrated there, some feast is being zealously performed, and day and night some great gathering is being tended to. Praise and jubilation, joy and exultation are

---

63. Probably those from the region of southwest Persia, on the northeast end of the Persian Gulf. It is located in modern Iran.
64. Pamphylia was a small region bordering on the Mediterranean Sea between Lycia and Sicilia in what is now Turkey.
65. The point here is probably to show diversity. These instruments are not exact equivalents of modern instruments, and thus the translation is more suggestive than exact.
66. The Latin of the manuscript is *assidue*. It could be used to mean either "assiduous vigils" or "heard assiduously."

CHAPTER SEVENTEEN

proclaimed together in song. All days and nights are honored in an almost continuous solemn feast for the honor of the Lord and the apostle. The doors of this basilica are never closed day or night, and it is never dark at night within, since it gleams like noon from the splendid light of the tapers and candles.

To this place go the poor, the happy, the fierce, the knights, the infantrymen, the satraps, the blind, the crippled, the aristocrats, the nobles, the heroes, the princes, the bishops, and the abbots. Some go with bare feet, some without their own goods, some bound in irons for the purpose of penitence. Some bear the emblem of the cross in their hands like the Greeks, some give their things[67] to the poor, some bring iron or lead in their hands for work on the apostle's basilica. Some, doing penance and bewailing their transgressions, bear on their arms iron bars and manacles from workhouses for the wicked from which they are liberated by the apostle. This is a chosen race, a holy people, a people of God, the favored of peoples, the fruit of apostolic acquisition, of a new grace, of the penitents of the nourishing Church, the fruit offered by the apostle to God in His heavenly seat. That this fruit of the Lord's apostle may remain in the heavenly kingdom is shown by the Lord, Who once promised when He said to him: "And your fruit may remain," [Jn 15:16] as if He were saying to the apostles: [f.79r] "The fruit of your acquisition may remain in heaven." It is believed, in fact, that whoever goes to the venerable altar of Blessed James in Galicia for the sake of pure and worthy prayer, if truly penitent, will obtain absolution from the apostle and pardon from the Lord for his transgressions. For the Lord did not take away from him after death that gift and power that He had given him before his passion.[68] It was, in fact, granted to him by the Lord that the sins would be completely forgiven for those whom he has forgiven. The Lord, in fact, says to him and to the other apostles: "Whose sins you shall have forgiven,

---

67. The word *sua*, "their things," is added interlineally. It is in the main text in S.
68. The text here must refer to the "passion" of St. James rather than of Jesus Christ. Cf. John 20:23, where the power for forgiving sins was granted after the Resurrection.

they shall be forgiven them." [Jn 20:23] It is therefore certain that those whose transgressions the renowned apostle shall forgive, will have them forgiven by the Lord.

Oh, how blessed are those who have such an intercessor and such a pardoner! Why then, devotee of Saint James,[69] do you delay to go to his place where not only all the tribes and languages but also the angelic hosts convene and where the sins of humankind are forgiven? There is, in fact, no one who can tell how many benefits the Blessed Apostle has bestowed on those beseeching him with a sincere heart. Indeed, many poor people have gone there who afterwards were made happy through God's grace, many weak afterwards healthy, many dissenters afterwards agreeable, many perverse afterwards pious, many lustful afterwards chaste, many worldly afterwards monks, many misers afterwards generous, many usurers afterwards giving their goods bountifully, many haughty afterwards gentle, many deceitful later truthful, many plunderers of the belongings of others afterwards giving their own clothes to the poor, many perjurers afterwards becoming law abiders, many declaring falsehood afterwards asserting truth, many sterile afterwards bearing children, and many dishonest afterwards becoming just. Behold that the city of Compostela, through the support of Saint James, has been made sacred and a salvation for the faithful and a help for those coming to it! Oh, with what reverence is that sacred place to be honored and revered in which many thousands of miracles are reported to have been performed and in which the most sacred limbs of the apostle, which touched God when present in the flesh, are buried!

The great James gleams with divine miracles in Galicia, and he gleams in other places if the faith of petitioners requires it. Indeed, he also performs great and unutterable signs throughout the whole earth not only privately but publicly. For he gives back former health to the sick, liberation to the bound, fecundity [f.79v] to those barren of offspring, delivery to those bearing children, a port of safety to those at risk on the sea, safe return to the homeland

---

69. *Iacobi* is added interlineally. It is in the text proper in S.

CHAPTER SEVENTEEN

for pilgrims, and food to the needy. He often accords life to those placed in agony and solace to all the poor. He breaks bonds quickly. He opens prisons rapidly. He represses an overabundance of rain. He brings serenity to the air. He repels the winds of storms. He suppresses the conflagrations of evil fires with the prayers of men.[70] He restrains thieves, robbers, as well as mischievous and treacherous people so that they may not harm the peoples of the faithful however much they may desire to do so. He placates wrath and malice, and he grants tranquility. To everyone beseeching him, he shows the desired help with the support of God, even to the pagan if he should faithfully call upon him.[71]

By right, therefore, this James, who has been accustomed to give great rewards to everyone everywhere, is called "Great." From this the question arises: Why does he perform miracles in places where he does not lie bodily, as he does in Galicia? However, if one looks into this with a sense of discernment, it is quite quickly apparent: he is, in fact, always and everywhere at hand to help without[72] delay those at risk and those in tribulation calling to him whether on sea or on land. Concerning the presence of the holy martyrs, we can read the following:

> There is no doubt that where the holy martyrs lie bodily, they can show many signs and they do so. They also manifest true miracles to those petitioning with a pure mind. However, since it is possible for weak minds to doubt whether the martyrs are present to hear them, in places where a weak mind might doubt their presence, and where it is agreed they are not present in body, it is necessary that these holy

---

70. Such a miracle is not described in Bk. II. Fire is used to punish those not aiding pilgrims in Poitiers (Melczer, *Pilgrims Guide*, 133). Fire is also found as punishment in one of the miracles of the CC Addenda and in two miracles that befall persons who did not observe the saint's feast day. See ch. 2, pp. 36–37.

71. This situation is common to most of the Bk. II miracles, although there is no instance of a pagan being saved.

72. The word *sine*, "without," is added interlineally, but in the body of the text in S.

martyrs show even greater signs. However, those whose minds are fixed on God have so much greater merit of faith in that they know the martyrs are bodily far off and yet are not out of range of hearing. From this, Truth[73] also speaks about Himself to increase the faith in the disciples: "If, in fact, I have not gone away, the Paraclete will not come to you." [Jn 16:7] Since, in fact, it is agreed that the Paraclete, the Holy Spirit, proceeds eternally from the Father and the Son, why does the Son say that He will go away so that the One who never retreats from the Son might come? But indeed, since the disciples viewing the Lord were thirsting to see Him physically with their eyes, it is rightly said to them: "Unless I have gone away, the Paraclete will not come," as if He were saying: "If I do not take away My body, I will not show what the love [f.80r] of the Spirit is. And if you have not stopped viewing Me bodily, you will never learn to love spiritually."[74]

Therefore, Saint James, who gladdens the eastern people through divine miracles, lies in corporeal presence among the western people.[75]

Who[76] like the high lighthouse sends out[77] light toward the Indians,

Whom Spaniard and Moor, Persian and Briton love.

The Orient has him, the Occident has him; Africa and the North have him

---

73. The Latin *Veritas* is used for the Bible, God, or, as here, Christ.
74. Gregory I, the Great, *Dialogarum liber II*, cited in St. Benedict, *Prolegomena*, Bk. II, ch. 38 (PL 66:204).
75. The inclusion of the eastern peoples is somewhat ironic following a paragraph in which there is reference to the Holy Spirit proceeding from the Father *et Filio*, "and the Son." Although normally *Filioque*, "and from the Son," the notion of the Holy Spirit proceeding from both the Father and the Son was one of the causes of the East-West schism.
76. Venantius Fortunatus, *Miscellanea*, 10:7:7–12 (PL 88:332).
77. Venantius's verb *pertendit* has been changed to *protendit*, but without significant change in meaning.

CHAPTER SEVENTEEN

Whom the world celebrates and whom every rain honors[78]
And who also passes over waves of the ocean's boundary,
And so, virtue proceeds, on which foot, no one is certain.[79]

Therefore, Saint James is to be honored by all, as he helps without delay everyone everywhere calling on him. However, since we have dealt above with the various peoples traveling to him and with the remuneration given them by the Lord, it remains for us now to treat the pilgrim route of these people.

The pilgrim route is certainly very good but very narrow. The road that leads a person to life is, in fact, narrow, and the road that leads to death is wide and spacious. The pilgrim route is for the righteous: lack of vices, mortification of the body, restoration[80] of virtues, remission of sins, penitence of the penitent, journey of the just, love of the saints, faith in the resurrection and remuneration of the blessed, distancing of the infernal, and appeasing of the heavens. The pilgrimage road reduces rich foods, checks gluttony of the stomach, tames lust, suppresses carnal desires that militate against the soul, purifies the spirit, motivates a person toward contemplation, humbles the lofty, blesses the humble, loves poverty, hates the inventory of goods[81] that greed keeps, loves the one who dispenses bountiful things to the needy, rewards those abstaining and doing good works, but does not absolve those who are greedy and sinning against it.

Not without reason do those heading for the thresholds of the saints accept the staff and the blessed purse in the church. When,

---

78. Line 10 in Venantius reads, "It is the honor of Martin by which the world holds these places."
79. Line 12 of Venantius reads, "That he may be a surety for all, he has canvassed the route of the world."
80. The standard meaning of the Latin *relevatio* is "relief" or "lightening," here has the sense of "restitution" or "restoration" as found in DuCange and Maigne d'Arnis.
81. The word *census* originally was an official list of assets, but it could be used as collateral in times of need. We have rendered it "inventory of goods" or "goods" as the context requires.

in fact, we send pilgrims to the strongholds of the saints for the sake of penance, we give them the blessed purse with ecclesiastical ceremony, saying,

> In the name of our Lord Jesus Christ, accept the purse, this symbol of your pilgrimage, that you may be worthy to arrive chastened and cleansed at the threshold of Saint James to whom you wish to go, and when your journey has been completed, may you return safely and joyfully, with the help of Him Who lives and reigns as God. World without end. Amen.

Likewise, when we give the staff to someone, we say the following:
> Accept this staff as a support for the journey and for the labor [f.80v] on the route of your pilgrimage, so that you may be able to overcome all the bands of the enemy and arrive secure at the threshold of Saint James, and after your journey has been completed, may you return to us joyfully with the agreement of Him Who lives and reigns as God. World without end.[82]

By the purse[83] — which the Italians call *scarsella*, the Provençals call *sporta*, and the French call *ysquirpa*[84] — generosity of alms and mortification of the flesh is signified. A purse is a narrow little bag

---

82. The blessing for the staff and purse is common to medieval Catholic liturgy. For examples and analyses, see James A. Brundage, "*Cruce signari:* The Rite for Taking the Sign of the Cross in England," *Traditio* 22 (1966): 289–310. Also M. Cecilia Gaposchkin, "From Pilgrimage to Crusade: The Liturgy of Departure, 1095–1300," *Speculum* 88.1 (January 2013): 44–91; and Pedro Romano Rocha, *L'Office divin au moyen âge dans l'église de Braga: Originalité et dépendances d'une liturgie particulière au moyen âge* (Paris: Gulbenkian, 1980). For the text of the blessing and the pilgrimage mass in English, see A. Harford Pearson, trans., *The* Sarum Missal *Done into English* (London: The Church Printing Company, 1884), 547–50, 595–96.

83. The Latin is *peram*.

84. The author offers vernacular words showing the diversity of pilgrims. For a detailed study of some of the rare words found in the LSJ and in particular in the *Veneranda dies,* see José María Anguita Jaén, "Ensayo de interpretación de algunos términos inexplicados del *Liber Sancti Iacobi (Codex Calixtinus):* '*cinnatores*', '*trebuchetum*', '*marsicias*' etc.," in *Iacobus: Revista de Estudios Jac-*

CHAPTER SEVENTEEN

made from the hide of a dead animal with its mouth always open and not bound with ties.[85] That the purse is a narrow sack signifies that the pilgrim, trusting in the Lord, must carry along with him a small and moderate provision. That it is made from the skin of a dead animal signifies that the pilgrim himself must mortify his flesh with its vice and concupiscence — through hunger and thirst, many fasts, cold and exposure, and many insults and hardships. That it is not bound with ties but that the mouth is always open signifies that one must expend one's own things on the needy. Furthermore, one must be prepared to receive and to give.

By the staff, which the pilgrim prayerfully[86] accepts almost as a third foot for his support, is implied faith in the Holy Trinity in which one must persevere. The staff is the defense for a person against wolf and dog. The nature of the dog is to bark at people and of the wolf to devour sheep. By the dog and wolf is signified that waylayer of the human race, the devil. The demon barks at a person when he stirs the mind toward sinning by the bark of his suggestions. He bites like a wolf when he draws one's limbs toward sinning and through a habit of sin swallows the soul in his greedy jaws. For that reason, we must admonish the pilgrim when we give him the staff so that he might wash away his sin through confession and so that he might closely protect his breast and limbs with the banner of the Holy Trinity against diabolical deceits and apparitions.[87]

Similarly, it is not without reason that pilgrims prayerfully coming back from Jerusalem carry palms and that those returning from the threshold of Saint James bear small shells.[88]

---

obeos y Medievales 1 (June 1996): 15–29 and 2 (December 1996): 11–23. He treats the terms *ysquirpa, sporta,* and *scarsella.*

85. In spite of (or perhaps because of) the multiple names for this item, the author gives a very specific description of how and of what a pilgrim's purse should be constructed.

86. The Latin is *orator* or "the one praying."

87. The staff is reminiscent of the "Pauline armor" of Eph 6:13–17.

88. The Latin *crusilla*, likely for *cruisille* of Old French. It is the same word used in the Guide (Bk. V, ch. 9) and in the Miracles (Bk. II, ch. 12) to describe

Notwithstanding, the palm signifies triumph, and the small shell signifies good works. For just as victors returning from the battle once used to carry palms in their hands showing that they had been triumphant, so also the pilgrims returning from Jerusalem carry palms showing that they have subdued[89] [f.81r] all vices. Therefore, drunks, fornicators, misers, coveters, quarrelers, usurers, the wanton, adulterers, or other corrupt people who are still at war with vices must not carry the palm but only those who have completely overcome their vices and who have adhered to virtues.

There are, then, some fish in the sea of Saint James that the people call *veras*,[90] having two shields, one on either side, between which the fish is concealed, for example, as between two shells like an oyster. These shells that are chiseled like the fingers of a hand are what the Provençals call *nidulas*[91] and the French call *crusilles*. The pilgrims returning from the threshold of Saint James sew them on their capes and wear them back to their own country with great exultation in honor of the apostle and in his memory and as a sign of this great journey. The two shields with which the fish is protected on either side represent the two commandments of charity with which the bearer must truly protect his life: that is, to love God above all things and to love one's neighbor as oneself.[92] A person who loves God is one who keeps His commandments. A person who loves one's neighbor as oneself is one who does not do to anyone what he does not want done to himself and who does

---

Santiago pilgrim mementos. See Christopher Hohler, "The Badge of Saint James," in *The Scallop: Studies of a Shell and Its Influences on Humankind*, ed. Ian Cox (London: Shell Transport and Trading Co., 1957), 49–70, on the scallop shell as pilgrimage symbol.

89. The Latin *mortificasse* has the sense of "put an end to" or "subdue." The modern "mortify" has morphed fully away from this original meaning towards "humiliate."

90. The modern Galician is *vieiras*. See Melczer, *Pilgrim's Guide*, 57–58 for a discussion of this type of mollusk.

91. The CC uses *nidulas* here, while S reads *indillas*. For more information on these words, see Anguita Jaén, "Ensayo."

92. Cf. Mt 22:37–39, Mk 12:29–31, and Lk 10:27.

CHAPTER SEVENTEEN

to others what he would justly want done for himself. The shields, however, which are modified in the shape of fingers, signify good works in which the bearer of this sign must persevere. And good works are beautifully signified by fingers, since[93] we work through them when we do something. Therefore, just as the pilgrim bears the shell[94] as long as he is on the journey of this present life, he must also bear the yoke of the Lord, that is, submit to His commandments. And it is truly right and just that someone who has sought such a great apostle and such a great man in such a remote region through toil and hardship should persevere in good works so that he may receive, along with Saint James, a crown in the heavenly land. If he has been a robber or thief, let him become a dispenser of alms. If he has been a spendthrift, let him become temperate. If he has been a miser, let him become generous. If he has been a fornicator or adulterer, let him become chaste. If he has been a drunkard, let him become sober. Similarly let him restrain from now on from every sin by which he was previously gripped.

O pilgrim of Saint James, do not lie with that mouth with which you have[95] kissed his altar! Do not go toward depraved works with the feet with which you have taken so many steps for him! Do not work evil with the hands with which you have touched his venerable altar! If you have commended your whole body to him for [f.81v] safekeeping, then preserve all your limbs for him. If, as a faithful sheep, you have entrusted yourself to him, do not be a stray in the thorns of vices. Do not give to the wolf what you have given to him! Do not serve the devil, when by right you must serve God and His apostle! If you wish to have a powerful patron, you have for yourself in Saint James a protector, helper, and devotee.

---

93. Three dots under the *q* of *quia* ("since") in CC indicates it should be removed, although it is necessary here; S has *qz,* a standard abbreviation for *quia.*
94. Latin *veram.* See above n. 90 and 91.
95. The word *es,* "you have," is added interlineally in CC. It is in the text in S.

Many, in fact, give witness that they have experienced his help in many adversities.

We must explain how the pilgrim road has its origins among the ancient fathers and how it should be walked. In fact, it takes its beginning from Adam, and it also stems from Abraham and Jacob and the sons of Israel up to Christ, and through Christ and the apostles it has increased up to today. Adam is considered the first pilgrim, since he was sent from paradise into the exile of this world because of his transgression against God's commandment, and he was saved by Christ's blood and His grace. Similarly, a pilgrim is sent by his priest on a pilgrimage into a type of exile from his own region because of his transgressions, and if he has confessed properly and completed his life, after accepting proper penitence for himself, he is saved through the grace of Christ. Abraham the Patriarch was a pilgrim, since he went forth from his country to another as he was told by the Lord: "Go out from your land and your people…and come into the land that I will show to you, and I will make you grow into a great people." [Gen 12:1] And that is how it happened. He went out from his own land, and his holy offspring were increased in a foreign land. In a similar fashion, if the pilgrim should go out from his own land, meaning his earthly business and his depraved habits, and his own people, that is, away from the notoriety of his guilt, and should he persevere in good works, the Lord will without doubt cause him to grow into a great angelic people[96] in blessed glory. Jacob the patriarch was also a pilgrim, since, after he went out from his country, he traveled to Egypt and stayed.[97] Just as Jacob stayed in Egypt, which is interpreted as mourning and darkness, so also the pilgrim, after he has gone out from his own country and requested the support of the saints, must remain in grief of mind and eye and in the darkness of penance because of

---

96. CC has *gente* ("within a people"), while S has *gentem* ("into a great people"). Both manuscripts would indicate the *gente* reading, although it does not parallel the cited scripture: *gentem magnam* ("into a great people"). The confusion apparently arises from the missing *m* in the CC.

97. Cf. Gen 25–35.

CHAPTER SEVENTEEN

the recollection of his sins. The sons of Israel were also pilgrims while they traveled from Egypt into the Promised Land through their diverse experiences of hardships and vicious wars. Just as they entered the Promised Land through many hardships, so pilgrims also travel through the innumerable deceits of innkeepers, the ascents of mountains, descents into valleys, fears about plunderers, and worries about various hardships while requesting the support of the saints so that they might enter the heavenly [f.82r] country promised to the faithful.

Our Lord Jesus Christ Himself, returning from Jerusalem after He had risen from the dead, appeared first as a pilgrim, as the disciples meeting Him said: "You alone are a pilgrim in Jerusalem." [Lk 24:18] About these disciples it was later written that they recognized the Lord in the breaking of the bread. On the road the Lord is not recognized, but when someone is fed, He is recognized. Likewise, when the happy pilgrim feeds the poor, he is recognized by the Lord. For the Lord recognizes whoever feeds the poor, and He allows Himself to be recognized by him and makes him blessed, as the Psalmist says: "Blessed is the one who understands about the needy and the poor. On the evil day, the Lord liberated him." [Ps 40:2 / 41: 1–2] He will be liberated "on the evil day," [Eph 6:13] because he will be liberated on Judgment Day from the diabolical grasp, and he will be saved.

The apostles whom the Lord sent from there without money or footwear were also pilgrims. Because of this, it is not at all allowed for pilgrims to bring money, unless they spend this money on the needy. If He sent the apostles without money, what will become of those who now travel with gold and silver, eat and drink to fulfillment, and give nothing to the poor? They are certainly not true pilgrims but thieves and bandits of God. Those who take along their goods and give away nothing to the needy pilgrims are truly alienated from the apostolic company, and they appear to travel on a different route. They may expect what the Lord Himself might say to His pilgrims on route: "Do not possess gold or silver or money in your purses, or a wallet for the road or two coats or shoes or a staff." [Mt 10:9–10, Lk 9:3] In sending the apostles out in this way, it is to be understood that it would not be permissible for a pilgrim to bring along his own things unless he strives to give them to the needy. Either he should not bring along goods, or if he brings them, he should strive to dispense them to the poor. If he does otherwise, he may expect what the Lord Himself says to a certain man questioning Him: "If you wish to be perfect, go and sell all that you have and give it to the poor…follow me." [Mt 19:21] Therefore, it is not those who sell their goods and spend the money on their pilgrimage who follow the Lord, but those who sell their goods and are generous to the needy. Just as the multitude of believers once had one heart and one soul and no one called anything his own, but all held everything in common, so must all things be held in common by all pilgrims [f.82v] with one heart and one soul. It is, in fact, very disgraceful and a great dishonor and a most grave sin when one of the pilgrims is thirsty and another is drunk.[98] Every good brought forth for the common good shines more brightly. I also fear that the pilgrim who carries expensive goods on the journey beyond what is necessary for him and does not set them out for the needy but brings them back to his own home may be damned together with Ananias and Sapphira. For these two held back on the price of a field they sold, received a curse from Saint Peter the Apostle, and suddenly fell dead.[99]

If the Lord rode to Jerusalem not on a horse or a mule but on an ass, what will become of those who go there with large and plump horses and mules with saddlebags[100] of keepsakes?[101] If Saint Peter went to Rome without footwear or money and finally went to the Lord after being crucified, why do many pilgrims who go to Him ride with great sums of money and a second set of clothes,[102] eat

---

98. Implying that the one pilgrim drank excessively while others lacked drink.
99. Acts 5:1–11.
100. Maigne d'Arnis gives *trosellus* as a synonym for *fasciculus* or "small bundle." For travel on horseback, this would be the equivalent of a saddlebag.
101. The Latin is *felicitatum*, "of happinesses."
102. Latin *vestimentis duplicibus* refers to Christ's injunction about a second tunic. Cf. Mt 10:9–10.

CHAPTER SEVENTEEN

delicious foods, drink very strong wine, and share nothing with their needy brethren?[103] If Saint James went through the world as a pilgrim without money and footwear and then finally went to paradise after his beheading, why do pilgrims go to him oversupplied with diverse riches and paying out nothing to the needy? If Peter and James walked through the world without money and prayed without interruption, what will become of those who go to their thresholds with money acquired from robbery or other harm or from usury or with corrupt extravagance, false tales, idle words contemptuous speech, drunkenness, or chatter?[104] If Saint Giles[105] or Saint William[106] or the extraordinary Leonard,[107] as confessors of Christ, had contempt for worldly happiness, sought secluded and deserted places where they were removed from their relatives and friends, were sustained on raw herbs and water, lived on their own,[108] led a celibate life, and were intent upon frequent vigils

---

103. This is the first reference in Bk. I to Rome as a pilgrimage center vying in importance with Compostela.

104. The reference to James and Peter traveling and preaching together is part of the Eastern hagiographic tradition. Cf. S.C. Malan, trans., *The Conflicts of the Holy Apostles, an Apocryphal Book of the Early Eastern Church, Translated from an Ethiopic MS* (London: D. Nutt, 1871), 172–78; and Agnes Smith Lewis, *The Mythological Acts of the Apostles, Translated from an Arabic MS in the Convent of Deyr-es-Suriani, Egypt, and from MSS in the Convent of St. Catherine on Mount Sinai and in the Vatican Library* (London: C.J. Clay and Sons, 1904), 30–34.

105. Saint Giles (Aegidius, d.721 or 725) is mentioned six times in this sermon. His tomb in Saint-Gilles-du-Gard is the most important pilgrimage center on the southern route (Via Tolosana) to Compostela. See Melczer, *Pilgrim's Guide*, 98–102.

106. Saint William (d.812) is mentioned once in this sermon. The *Pilgrim's Guide* mentions his remains in Toulouse as meriting a visit. See Melczer, 102–103.

107. Saint Leonard (d.559) is mentioned once more in this sermon. His tomb is in Saint-Léonard-de-Noblat on the Vézelay route. See Melczer, *Pilgrim's Guide*, 105–7.

108. The Latin is *sine proprio* or literally "without one's own," in the sense of "without anything of one's own."

and fasting, what will become of those who travel to them with a great inventory of goods, pay out nothing to the needy, and eat and drink to fulfillment? Again, one group appears to have taken a different route than the other has taken. For, in the former group, they disburse their goods to the poor and are made happy; in the latter group, they do not distribute theirs at all and are certainly destitute of heavenly gifts. The former group will have abundance forever; the latter will beg for eternity. What will become of those who keep watch and beg for their goods — without doubt not their own but someone else's — and then die dishonorably on the route itself with that money? [f.83r] The pilgrim who dies with money on the route of the saints is certainly separated from the kingdom of true pilgrims. Certainly, the one who gives sustenance to all those asking and who is made poor if his goods have been relinquished for the sake of heavenly love uses[109] his possessions well on the route of the saints. The pilgrim who does not dispose of alms or resources received on the route from another pilgrim who has died in the manner the dead person ordered, but who keeps and spends them on himself, is damned.

What does it profit someone, most beloved brethren, for someone to take up[110] the pilgrimage route, unless one has gone on it legitimately?[111] Someone goes legitimately to Saint James's threshold if he forgives those who have injured him before he begins his journey, if he makes appeasement — when it is right for this to occur — for all prior matters of which he is accused either by others or by his own conscience, if he receives lawful leave from his priests, his subjects, his wife, or any others to whom he is bound, if he gives back — when possible — what he has held

---

109. The Latin is *portat*, "carries," "conveys."
110. The Latin is *adripere*, literally to "seize upon."
111. Many of the legal issues concerning pilgrims were codified in the 13th century in Title 24 of the First Partida of the Spanish legal codex, *Las siete partidas,* patronized by Alfonso X el Sabio (1221–84), king of Castilla and León. See http://www.pensamientopenal.com.ar/system/files/2014/12/legislacion33312.pdf, 26–27. Accessed 11/21/2020.

CHAPTER SEVENTEEN

unjustly, if he transforms dissent against his power into tranquility, accepts penance[112] from all, sets his house in good order, arranges for his own things to be given away, including[113] alms, in the event of his death according to the advice of his associates and priests, if — as we have already said — he gives the necessities of body and soul — as far as is possible — to poor pilgrims as if to his brothers after beginning the journey, if he speaks not idle words but saintly stories, flees drunkenness, strife and lust, hears the divine office at least on Sundays and feast days — if not every day — if he prays without interruption, tolerates all adversities patiently, and if he abstains from the illicit things and perseveres in good works after returning to his own region until he dies, then he may sing with the Psalmist: "Your justifications were songs to me, O Lord, in the place of my pilgrimage." [Ps 118:54 / 119:54] If someone misses masses and matins because of the pilgrim route, then he loses the better of two goods. If someone is truly poor and patiently endures both adversity and prosperity, he may request the necessary things for himself from those having them, and he should pray for the well-being of his benefactors and of all people.

On the route, pilgrims should be cautious that there is not any split or strife among them. For, in fact, in the venerable basilica of Saint Giles the most pious confessor, I once saw on a certain night some people keeping vigil and arguing over the chair of the saint. The French were sitting on the seat near the arch, and the Gascons, who wanted to sit on it, were fighting them. [f.83v] During this time the fighting and hitting with sticks, stones, and fists became so great among them that one of them was pierced through with a serious wound, fell to the ground, and died. Another who was struck on the head went down the road to Périgueux[114] toward

---

112. Latin *penitentiam,* meaning either "penitence" or "repentance" and later "penance."
113. The Latin is *ceu* or "like" or "just like," but the sense here seems to be that one set up one's legacy plans including alms.
114. The Latin *Petragoricensi* could refer to the town of Périgueux or to the Perigord region as a whole, neither of them directly on any route toward Compostela from Saint-Gilles.

Châteauneuf and died there.[115] Because of situations like this, strife is to be completely avoided by pilgrims — and drunkenness as well. In fact, these are two vices that all the saints and all the scriptures abhor. A certain sage wrote concerning strife: "The greatest strife sometimes grows from the smallest words." And again: "Do not refer back to the harsh words of past strife."[116]

Concerning this, Saint Paul says: "While intensity and contention may be among you, are you not carnal...are you not men?" [1 Cor 3:3–4] This is what the Psalmist says: "Grow angry and do not sin." [Ps 4:5 / 4:4] The wise man must patiently mitigate his wrath, lest he sin. Again Saint Paul says: "Let the sun not set on your rage. Do not give a place to the devil." [Eph 4:26–27] For whoever sins through wrath, without doubt gives a place to the devil. Contention once increased so much that it extended its foothold not only to the sons of Israel but also to the Lord's disciples. For dissension arose between Paul and Barnabas such that they parted from each other.[117] Contention also occurred among the disciples of Jesus as to which of them appeared[118] to be greater. The Lord presented to them, with modest reason, the form of humility, which they might follow: "Whoever might want to be first among you should be the servant of all." [Mk 10:44; cf. Mk 9:34 and Mt 20:26][119] And lest the mind of any leader be captivated by elation with power, it is justly said by a sage: "They will ordain you as

---

115. Although there are over a dozen places called Châteauneuf with various spellings, none is sufficiently close to Saint-Gilles to warrant being a reference point. One is tempted to interpret *castellum novum* as a common noun or "the new castle" as did Whitehill (158). Périgueux is also quite distant from the named site.

116. Dionysius Cato (c. 4th c.), *Catonis Disticha,* introduction by Erasmus of Rotterdam (Augsburg: Michael Manger, 1581), folios 14v–15r).

117. Cf. Acts 15.

118. The CC has *videtur* ("appears") while S has the better *videretur* or "appeared" / "would appear."

119. Ironically, it is to James and his brother John, the sons of Zebedee, that these verses refer.

CHAPTER SEVENTEEN

leader. Do not be extolled but be among them as one of them."[120] One must be careful that a functionary's teaching or judgment not be too rigid or lax.

Therefore, just as contention is tempered by humility, the vice of drunkenness should also be held in check by a modest drinking of watered wine, as it is best said by a certain sage: "Drunkenness is a firebrand; drinking watered wine is peace."[121] The drunk provokes his comrade to combat, loves strife, hates peace, sows discord, breaks the heads of his comrades, even strikes his father and mother, offends God, loses his senses, serves lust, loses his force, and says shameful words. What more can one say?[122] "The poor drunk takes on horns."[123] For this reason the wise once used to drink watered wine, for watered wine taken moderately renders a person healthy, happy, [f.84r] productive, sober, strong, and loquacious. Wine imbibed immoderately, as we have said, renders a man drunk, oblivious, raging, idiotic, silly, insane, lustful, and given over to sleep. Concerning drunkenness it has been written: "Where wine rules, one keeps no secret."[124] Noah first planted the vine, and drunk from its wine, exposed his private parts.[125] Of this Isaiah says: "Woe to you who are powerful in drinking wine and

---

120. Cf. Ecclus (Sir) 32:1.
121. This is ascribed to an author known as Walther. It is mentioned in, among others, *Proverbia sententiaeque latinitatis medii aevi*, ed. Hans Walther (Göttingen: Vandenhoeck & Ruprecht, 1963). The full text of the seven-line poem is found in *Magistri Salernitani*, ed. Piero Giacosa (Milan: Fratelli Bocca, 1901), 374.
122. The rhetorical question *Quid plura?* is used several times in both the Miracles and the *Translatio* as well as in Bk. I.
123. Compare with Ovid, *Art of Love* (Loeb Classical Library, 28–29) Bk. 1, part 7, line 11: *Tunc pauper cornua sumit*, the notion being "the poor man takes on the horns" of Bacchus, the god of wine and partying in general.
124. Cf. Prov 31:4.
125. Cf. Gen 9:20–27. The CC has *verenda suam*, which was copied into S and corrected to *verenda sua* or "private parts." This copying of a mistake, later corrected, indicates that S depended on CC, either directly or indirectly.

to you men who are strong in mixing in drunkenness." [Is 5:22] And again, he says:

> "Woe to those who arise in the morning seeking drunkenness and drink until evening so that they glow with wine. The lute and lyre, drum and flutes, and wines are at your feasts, and you do not look on the work of the Lord, nor do you consider the works of His hands. Because of these things my people have been led captive, since they had no knowledge, says the Lord." [Is 5:11–12]

Concerning the vice of drunkenness, Joel the Prophet says: "Arise, you who are drunk, and weep and cry out all you who drink wine in sweetness, since your soul has departed through your mouth." [Joel 1:5] And since wine provokes venery in the drinker's body, the wise one says properly: "Wine and women cause wise men to become apostates." [Ecclus (Sir) 19:2] Of this Saint Paul says: "Do not become drunk on wine, in which is found dissipation." [Eph 5:18] Dissipation does not come out of the wine, but lust is born from the one drinking the wine. Therefore, it is not the wine's fault but the drinker's fault. Wine is a good and splendid thing, created, of course, by God, but since it serves up venery in drunks guzzling it without discretion, it should not be permitted for anyone to become drunk from it. Again, Proverbs justly says that it should not be allowed for anyone to become drunk: "You should not admire wine when it has yellowed in the glass and when its color has brightened, for it begins blandly, but in the end it will bite like a snake, and it will spread its poisons like a basilisk." [Prov 23:31–32] The snake is accustomed to bite a sleeping person, and the basilisk not only bites but also diffuses deadly poisons in the wound. The snake, that has bitten a sleeping perso, symbolically portrays the devil, who excites and pierces with the fire of lust the one whom he finds sluggish from the vice of drunkenness. The basilisk, which diffuses poisons in the flesh of man, similarly represents the very enemy of the human race who provides many vices to the hearts of the drunk, such as contention, envy, wrath, strife, dissension, jealously, hatred, fraud, venery, and an apostate mind. These are clearly the vices born [f.84v] of drunkenness that Saint Paul exhorts the followers of the Lord to avoid.[126] In pentameter verses in the *Book of the Twelve Wise Men,* Basilius proclaims that these two vices, namely venery and drunkenness, should be prohibited to all Christians:[127]

> You should be held by love of neither venery nor wine,
> > For wine and venery injure in a single manner.
> As Venus weakens one's forces, so also does an abundance of Bacchus,
> > Each tempts one's steps and weakens one's feet.
> Blind love forces many to confess secrets,
> > Wild drunkenness uncovers mystery.
> Untamed Cupid often causes deadly war,
> > Bacchus himself often calls hands to arms.
> Wanton Venus wasted Troy with horrendous war,
> > And you, Iacchus,[128] destroy the Lapitae,[129] in harsh combat.
> In short, since both madden the minds of men,
> > And modesty and probity and fear are all absent,
> Restrain Venus with foot irons and Lyaeus[130] with chains,
> > Lest both injure you with their works.
> Let wines soothe thirst, let nourishing Venus serve those
> > To be created in birth: to have crossed these borders is injurious.

---

126. Cf. Rom 13:13.
127. This is found in the *Carmina duodecim sapientum de diuersis causis* (*Poetae Latini minores,* vol. 4), where Vitalis is named as one author and Basilius another. It has also been erroneously ascribed to Virgil and Basil the Great. See Alexander Riese, Franz Buecheler, Ernst Lommatzsch, eds., *Anthologia latina: Sive poesis latinae supplementum* (Leipzig: B.G. Teubner, 1894): 59–95 for the complete text. Vitalis and Basilius were two of the twelve; the others were Palladius, Asclepiadius, Eusthenius, Pompilianus, Maximus, Asmenius, Vomanius, Euphorbius, Julianus, and Hilasius.
128. A god associated with, if not another name for, Dionysus or Bacchus.
129. A mythological people from the mountains of Thessaly.
130. Bacchus's surname.

But what shall I say about evil innkeepers who deceive pilgrims with so many frauds? Just as Judas received punishment for his guilt from the Lord Jesus Christ in His Passion, and just as the thief received his reward for his confession, the evil innkeepers will also receive punishments in Orcus for their iniquities on the route of Saint James, and truthful pilgrims will receive the rewards of their good works and their hardships in heaven. Therefore, the evil innkeepers on the route of Saint James are damned for injuring pilgrims with countless frauds. Some, in fact, go out to meet them at the gateways of the villages, kissing them as if they were their relatives coming from faraway regions. What more do they do? They lead them into their homes, promise them all sorts of good things, and do evil things. Whom shall I say they are like except the traitor Judas, who betrayed the Lord by kissing Him? For ahead of time they show them the best wine to sample and sell them inferior wine if they can. Some sell cider[131] for wine and spoiled wine for good. Some sell fish or cooked meat that is two or three days old[132] from which the pilgrims grow sick. Some show them a large measuring device, but sell, if they can, with a small one. They have deceptive measures for wine and oats, very large on the outside but narrow, scant, and not fully hollowed out on the inside, which the people call *marsicias*.[133] Isaiah makes reference to such a truly [f.85r] depraved innkeeper when he complains by saying: "They are the worst vessels of the deceitful person. For this person cultivated thoughts for destroying the mild with the speech of falsehood." [Is 32:7][134] Another, when he draws

---

131. *Sicera* is Latin for both alcoholic cider and liquor in general. If the term is used as "cider" here, it shows acquaintance with an Iberian connotation of the word.

132. *Biduanam* is not found in standard Latin, while *triduanam* is standard Latin for "three days." While DuCange and Maigne d'Arnis both define it as "a fast of two days," the sense must be "two-days-old."

133. The term *marsicias* is problematic but clearly refers to a fraudulent type of container or barrel with thicker than normal walls. See Anguita Jaén, "Ensayo de interpretación," *Iacobus* I, 25–29.

134. The biblical verse refers to the deceitful person in general and not innkeepers specifically.

wine from the barrel, fraudulently adds water to the vessel if he can. Others promise the best beds and give them bad ones. Some, when other guests come along, throw the first guests out after already taking their payment.[135] The evil innkeeper does not give a good bed to his pilgrim guests unless they have bought a meal or given him an extra coin. If the pilgrim's coin should be worth two coins of the village where he seeks to eat, the evil innkeeper does not accept it except on a one-to-one par. If it is worth only one coin, he does not take it except as a coin of very small value. The evil innkeeper offers his guests the best wine so that he may inebriate them, and while they sleep, steals their sack or bag[136] or something else. The evil innkeeper kills them with his deadly potions so that he can have their goods. Those who have in one and the same barrel a middle area and place inside it two wines each set apart from the other and first offer the better of these for tasting and then later, on a second draw,[137] offer the inferior wine for the meal, will go to a harsh punishment. Some sell them a measure of barley or oats, which the Spanish call *cafhit*[138] or *aroa*,[139] for at least ten or twelve coins, when it could justly be had in that village's market for perhaps six coins. If, in fact, it is sold there for twelve coins, they take twenty coins or two gold coins from them. Similarly, if a pint[140] of wine in that village might be bought for twelve coins in a customary sale in that country, then they take from them either

---

135. The Latin is *pacca*. For more information on money, see ch. 2, n. 113.
136. The text word *gurlum* has not been located. The translation is hypothesized from the context. Moralejo (215) suggests this translation.
137. *Ductileus* is found in DuCange as an adjective. It is based on the Latin *ducere* meaning, among other things "to draw." Here the context makes clear that it means "on the second draw."
138. The word *cafhit* is not found, but Maigne d'Arnis gives the forms *caffium, caficium,* and *cafisa* as measures. Both CC and S agree on these readings.
139. The manuscript has *aroam;* it is surely a rendering of the Spanish measure *arroba* (from Arabic *arrúb*) and a term for a dry weight measure of about twenty-five pounds.
140. The Latin is *sextarius* can be rendered as "pint" for liquid. Again, these are not exact measurements.

twenty coins or two gold coins for it. And what shall I say about the wicked servant who at the order of her mistress pours out the water of the house when it is late so that thirsty pilgrims will buy the innkeeper's wine when they find no water at night to drink? And what shall I say about the person who steals oats or barley at night from the mangers with the consent of her innkeeper? She is utterly anathema. The innkeepers' servants on the route of Saint James who, for the sake of debauching and obtaining money, are accustomed to go to any pilgrim's bed of at night at the instigation of the devil, are utterly damned. The whores who for this reason are accustomed to come to the wooded areas to meet the pilgrims between the Minean Bridge[141] and Palas del Rey[142] are not only to be excommunicated [f.85v] but also are to be held in shame by all and to have their noses cut off.[143] Usually a single one appears to a solitary traveler. I cannot write down, brethren, in how many ways the demon can open his depraved nets and the cave of perdition to the pilgrims of Saint James.

Again, what shall I say about wicked innkeepers who, out of cupidity, keep for themselves the goods of the pilgrim who has died in their house and from which alms should be given to the clerics and the poor? Certainly, they are damned. Wicked innkeepers of the city of Saint James give the first meal to guests without any charge only to sell tapers or wax to them. Oh, violable charity! Oh, false piety! Oh, generosity filled with every fraud! If the pilgrims are caught up in a deal to buy twelve candles, the harsh innkeeper

---

141. At Portomarín, in Lugo, Galicia, there was a Roman bridge crossing the river Miño. The bridge was both destroyed rebuilt in the early twelfth century. The town was flooded during the construction of the Belesar dam between 1956 and 1962. It is mentioned in the *Pilgrim's Guide* (Melczer, 88, 89, 142).

142. Palas del Rey, in Lugo, Galicia, is mentioned in the *Pilgrim's Guide* (Melczer, 86, 87).

143. The Latin *ab omnibus depredande nasibusque verecundande* literally means "to be plundered by all and to be shamed with their noses." The punishment (or threat thereof) of nasal disfigurement or amputation is common throughout history. Cf. Ez 23:25.

CHAPTER SEVENTEEN

offers them as a meal a first course of meats or fish, which can be had for a fair price of eight small coins in the market of the city, and he later sells them for six gold coins the twelve tapers that he gets in the city market for four gold coins or for four small coins each, or he plainly and fraudulently sells each one to them for six small coins. Similarly, he sells them with this plate trick[144] four small coins worth of wax for six small coins, and likewise the same number[145] of gold coins' worth for six gold coins. What more can I say? He gives them eight small coins worth of meat or fish to feast on, but he sells this fraudulently at a price of two gold coins. Oh, what an abominable marketplace and detestable profit! Some even boil ram or goat fat or scraped or boiled broad beans[146] with the wax from which they make candles. Some tell those false or abominable tales, which we previously mentioned to pilgrims, asking about the true and venerable acts of Blessed James.

Another from the city of Saint James sent his ally as a traveling[147] conspirator all the way to the Minean Bridge[148] to meet the pilgrims there, and he spoke to them in this way: "My brothers and friends, I am a citizen of the city of Saint James, and I have not come here for the sake of visiting, but because I am watching the sick mule of a certain lord of mine in this village. Go therefore to his house and report to him, I beg you, that his mule will soon be cured, and take up lodging there, since he will do all sorts of good things for you

---

144. Literally "with a tricky platter"; in other words he uses the free meal as an inducement to buy the overpriced candles.
145. The same number would be "four"; in other words, the innkeeper pulls the same trick with both small and large coins in this case. The author uses the *nummi* ("small coins") and *solidi* ("gold coins") to show relative values and to describe how deceitful innkeeper, making a 50% profit, cheats the pilgrim. See ch. 2, n. 113.
146. "Or peeled or boiled broad beans" is interlinear in a different hand in CC, while it is in the text of S.
147. The Latin is *perendinator*, which has its root in the verb *perendinare*, "to put off to the next day." It has also been used as a circumlocution for *go* or *travel*, according to DuCange.
148. See n. 141 above.

who are reporting these things out of love for me." And when they go there, they find all sorts of bad things. Another goes to meet them at Barbadelo or Triacastela,[149] and when he has found and greeted them and has deceitfully talked to them about other matters, he then says to them: "My brothers who seek Saint James, I am a fortunate citizen of his city, [f.86r] and I have not come here for the sake of visiting, but so that I might speak with a certain brother of mine who is staying in this village, and if you wish to have good lodging in Saint James's city, stay as a guest in my house and tell my wife and my family that they should provide well for you out of love for me, and I will give you a token that you can show to them." And so, with such words he will give his knife as a token to one group, a belt to another, a key to another, a bootlace to another, a ring to another, a headband to another, and a glove to another, and he will send them to his house. And when the pilgrims have traveled to his house and are lodged in it, and when they have been given the first course at the table of that inn, the lady sells them a taper worth four small coins for eight or ten small coins. Thus the pilgrims of Saint James are deceived by the innkeepers. And if any pilgrim should have a silver mark to sell that might be worth thirty gold coins, his wicked innkeeper will lead him to a moneychanger, an accomplice of his, and the crafty innkeeper will give him deceitful advice that he should give the moneychanger that mark for twenty gold coins so long as that wicked innkeeper receives his cut[150] from the seller, or twelve *passut*[151] coins more or less. They call *passut* deceitfully obtained coins, and *reva* is interpreted as "unjust goods." Similarly, if the pilgrim should have anything that might be of great value to

---

149. Barbadelo, approximately four days' walk from Compostela, and Triacastela to its east, are both in the province of Lugo between Sarria and Portomarín. Both of these towns are mentioned in the *Pilgrim's Guide* (Melczer, 86, 87).
150. Maigne d'Arnis defines *reva* as "toll." Here it obviously means "commission" or "cut."
151. The *passut* is used here as a fraudulently obtained or produced coin. For more on coins, see ch. 2, n. 113.

sell, the innkeeper might suggest to him that he give it to him for a low price so that the wicked innkeeper might get from the same buyer or from another one a large commission. And if he should have coins to be exchanged, the same innkeeper suggests to him, for the sake of the commission that he wishes to receive, that he give twenty of his coins for twelve of the land that he is passing through, while sixteen of them perhaps might be more their value. And thus, the evil innkeepers deceive the pilgrims and are damned.

The guards who watch the altars of the basilicas[152] along the route to Saint James, namely Giles, Leonard, Martin of Tours,[153] Saint Mary of Le Puy, and Peter the Apostle at Rome, are accomplices in fraud with the evil innkeepers when they lead the pilgrims to all the altars for the sake of cupidity and indicate to them that they should make offerings on them so that the innkeepers might get a commission from them and the guard might also fraudulently get a portion. But what shall I say of the guard? After he has stolen offerings from the top of the altar, he wishes to get his share of the remaining money from the masters of that altar and that church.

Pilgrims should be wary of the thieves, [f.86v] called by the people *cinnatores*,[154] who beset them on the road. Some, in fact, give them counterfeit money in an exchange. Others, when they are making an exchange, steal coins. Others sell a bootlace, girdle, belt, glove, candle, or anything else, pretending that they are offering them at a low price, and while one of them shows these things to the pilgrim, and the pilgrim gives him the coins, the thief places this pilgrim's good coins in his sack and gives the pilgrim counterfeit

---

152. The Latin *basilicum,* rather than the expected *basilicarum,* occurs in both CC and S.

153. This is the first mention of Martin of Tours (316–97). The LSJ Guide author describes the saint's miracles and his tomb, not bothering with a *vita* (Melczer, *Pilgrim's Guide,* 108–9). St. Martin is also mentioned in Bk. II, Miracle 3 (Coffey and Dunn, *Miracles,* 16–17), when discussing a saint's power to raise someone from the dead.

154. The etymology of this word is unknown. However, the definition "cogger," indicating a deceptive, cheating person, is found in the *Dictionarium etymologicum latinum,* ed. Francis Holyoke (London: Felix Kingston, 1639).

coins. Now and then one of them throws copper ore on the road as the pilgrims pass by, and then, as if finding it, he bends over and picks it up from the ground while the pilgrims watch. Then, since these pilgrims are more or less finders of the ounce of ore along with him, they want to have their share just like him. But this wicked thief presents himself to them as poor and sells them his share dearly either for four or five gold coins, as if it were the finest gold, when it may be worth only as much as a needle.[155] Whom do they resemble other than Dathan and Abiram whom the earth swallowed up?[156] Pilgrims should also be very wary of certain evil innkeepers who fraudulently place their ring or silver cup[157] in the purses or bags of their guests at night while they are sleeping, follow them for about a mile beyond the village when they are leave the inn, and then on this bald pretense plunder them. The Italians are especially damned,[158] as they allow thieves to kill pilgrims in secret places. If perchance the thieves should be captured, the Italians take the money from them and let these thieves go unharmed.[159] Therefore they are damned along with the thieves, since those perpetrating a deed and those conspiring in it are punished with equal pain in Orcus.

And what shall I say of false pardoners?[160] There are some deceitful hypocrites, either clerics or lay persons, who are filled with demons and dressed in religious habit, who appear as mild as sheep on the outside but are rapacious wolves on the inside, and who find either pilgrims or others traveling in remote areas on the

---

155. The Latin is *acum*. The use of needle here is problematic. See ch. 2, n. 113.
156. Cf. Num 16:1–33 and Dt 11:6.
157. Both CC and S consistently read *cyphum* for s*cyphum*.
158. Only the Italians and the Navarrese are singled out as evil or bad people.
159. The Guide (Bk. V) does not mention a route beginning in Italy, but this clearly refers to thieves and crimes that took place in territory controlled by Italy.
160. This passage repeats a portion of the sermon for 24 July. See ch. 2, pp. 59–60.

CHAPTER SEVENTEEN

route to Vézelay or Santiago or Saint-Gilles or Jerusalem and give them false penances. Sometimes, in fact, they walk with them, offer well-chosen words at first, and tell everyone all of the vices in order.[161] Then they speak to each of them separately in secret and ask the individuals about their consciences and the sins they have committed. As soon as the pilgrims have confessed to them, they impose thirty masses on one and thirteen on another [f.87r] for whatever sin. They tell the pilgrim: "As a sign of the thirty coins with which the Lord was sold, have thirty masses celebrated with thirty of your very good coins by priests who would never have anything to do with women, who would not eat meat, and who would not possess property." However, this individual, who does not know how he might find such priests, offers the thirty coins to this person who says he will find one. This vulture[162] does not care about the well-being of the sinner but places the money in a sack, spends it lavishly, places his soul under anathema, and opens himself up to hell. One should be very wary of these, who are like hungry wolves.

I am not sure what I should say about certain hypocrites who, although they are healthy, feign the appearance of illness, sit along the route of Saint James or some other saint, and show themselves to the passersby. Some, in fact, out of cupidity, show the passersby their legs and arms, which have been dipped in rabbit blood or ash or whipped with animal hides, and tremble in a most miserable manner so that they might extort alms from these passersby. Others stain their lips or cheeks with dark coloring. Others have Jerusalem-type palms and capes, and they paint their faces and hands with woodland bulbs,[163] which the French call *lotuessas*,[164] so that they might

---

161. These vices, enumerated in order, are most likely the seven deadly sins of sloth, pride, flattery, anger, avarice, gluttony, and lust.
162. The Latin is *acceptor*, which DuCange defines as a bird of prey, such as a falcon. In this context, however, "vulture" describes someone on the lookout for an easy target.
163. The Latin is *buleiis* probably for *bulbis*, "bulbs."
164. This could be a kind of lotus, although modern French has *lotus* or *lotos*, and the Old French variant is simply *lote*. See Frédéric Godefroy, *Lexique de l'ancien français* (Paris: Champion, 1971).

have a sickly appearance. Similarly, others pretend that they are mute or deaf, although they are not. Others similarly stain their arm or foot, once cut off for robbery, with bovine blood, as if they had lost it from some other illness, and show this to the passersby. Others who were blinded for thievery sit near the road and show themselves as if they had lost their eyes through some other illness. Others show their foot or hand as if it were twisted or dried up or rigid, although it is not. Others show themselves to the passersby puffed up like a skin bag or a cow's stomach for the sake of gaining money. Some of them, who are bandy-legged and who certainly could walk upright with their staffs, set aside the staffs, get on bended knees, and hold on to stools with their hands as if they were crippled,[165] crawl on the ground, and beg for alms in the deserted places of the roads. They are so filled with pride that they do not want to accept bread or modest alms but take coins or cloth or wax.[166] However, whoever gives them alms out of love of God and of the apostle will without doubt receive a reward. These beggars are not to be refused alms or repudiated but are to be recalled from their perverse cupidity with the food of the divine word. Saint Isidore says: "Do not choose on whom you should have mercy. Give to everyone seeking. You do not know in what way you may please God more."[167] Therefore, while you are going to the threshold of Saint James or whatever saint, do not judge those to whom you should give alms [f.87v] but correct them diligently when you return. For, as Saint James says: "Whoever has caused a sinner to be converted from the error of his way will save his soul from death and will cover up a multitude of his own sins." [James 5:20]

---

165. The Latin in CC is *contincti,* while S offers the better reading of *contracti,* or "crippled."

166. This sentence is inserted at the bottom margin of CC in a similar, if not the same hand, with a red cross designating its insertion point. It is in the body of the text of S.

167. Cf. Ambrose of Milan, *Epistola [ad Florianum]* (PL 17:750–51). This passage was not found in Isidore.

CHAPTER SEVENTEEN

And what shall I say of the women who make tapers to sell, but who put so little wick into the tapers and candles that they cannot burn long enough for a mass or for readings? And what shall I say about those who far and wide sell bread, wine, oats, fruit, cheese, meat, and fowl too expensively to the multitudes of arriving pilgrims? All iniquity and all fraud abound on the routes of the saints. And what shall I say about the false moneychangers whom the people call *cambiatores*?[168] If twelve coins of the pilgrim are worth sixteen of the coins of the moneychanger who wants to have them, the moneychanger, at the urging of this pilgrim's perverse innkeeper, will not even give thirteen or fourteen of his coins for them. If they are worth twenty coins, the moneychanger will give only sixteen or less, if possible. If twelve coins of the moneychanger are worth sixteen of the pilgrim's, he will not give them to him for less than twenty. If they should be worth thirteen, he will take sixteen from the pilgrim. If a pure silver mark is worth thirty gold coins, the moneychanger will only give him twenty for them. The wicked moneychanger has various weights, large and small. He buys silver with the heavy and larger weight by the pound,[169] and he sells them with the lighter and smaller one. He praises his gold and his silver and his keepsakes and disparages those of others. He sells dearly, he buys cheaply. If he can, he deceives the other person and guards himself from this. He suspends the coins separately on a weight, which they call a trebuchet,[170] and he sells the one that is heavier to others, or he melts it in fire in a furnace with other silver. He corruptly cuts and shaves larger coins with pincers. Woe to him and again woe to whoever commits so many frauds! Again, what does that crafty one do? If he can, he sells to the ignorant a

---

168. The Latin *nummularii* as "moneychangers" is used interchangeably with *cambiatores* within this passage. *Cambiatores* is clearly an early form of modern Spanish "cambiadores," from "cambiar" meaning "to change."
169. The Latin *marca* can mean either "mark" as a type of coin or "pound" as a type of weight; presumably this could be a partial pound as well.
170. *Trebuchetum* means "trebuchet," a type of sling-catapult and is used here as a term for scales, which can resemble a catapult.

silver-plated ring or cup or candelabra or some bronze object as pure silver. Similarly, if the work is gold-plated, he sells it corruptly for pure gold. He sells his silver mark and gold talent[171] dearly, if he can, for tested silver and gold although they have not been tested,[172] and he buys cheaply the tested item of another person as if untested, although [f.88r] it may have been tested. If a pilgrim's mark or talent is valued at four coins less than the true weight, he buys it for twelve less. If, however, it is the gold or silver of this same moneychanger in a ring or cup or candelabra or bit or in some other work, he sells it as pure although it may not be pure, and he also resells the work even more dearly. And if the pilgrim wants to sell him the very same thing in the same type of work, he will buy it only as untested gold and silver. Similarly, he sells to the ignorant non-precious[173] stones that resemble precious stones and that people call "counterfeit" as very precious ones. He does these and similar things such that the trap of hell comes to him who is unaware of it, and the deception that he hides catches him, and he falls in that very trap. Give heed,[174] therefore, false moneychangers, to what the Psalmist says concerning you when he says: "The deceitful sons of men with their scales, from concern for vain things, are captured with that very thing.[175] You are ensnared by your works, for your works are leading you to the underworld. "With that same measure with which you have measured, it will be measured back to you." [Mt 7:2, Lk 6:38] Measure upon measure, mark upon mark, pound upon pound are at your table. Therefore, consider what a certain wise man says to you: "Weight and weight, measure and measure,

---

171. The talent was another of the coins in use at the time. See ch. 2, n. 113.
172. The Latin *examinato / examinatum* may be something like "certified" by an appropriate authority.
173. *Non* is interlinear in CC but in the body of S.
174. The Latin is *avertite* or "turn away" while the context calls for *advertite* or "give heed."
175. Cf. Ps 61:10 / 62:10. The author changes the *decipiant* of the Psalm to *decipiantur*. Instead of catching others with their deceit *(decipiant)*, they are caught up by it *(decipiantur)*.

CHAPTER SEVENTEEN

both are abominable to God." [Prov 20:10] For the Lord once turned your tables in the Temple upside down, as it is written in the Gospel: "The Lord overturned the tables of the moneychangers and the chairs of those selling doves." [Mt 21:12, Mk 11:15]

But what should I say about the crafty spice merchants? For some keep types of plants up to the point where they putrefy and sell the putrefied as good. Others sell adulterated types as the most costly. Others, so that pepper might weigh more on the scale, sprinkle water on it. Others mix in roasted ginger[176] grains or dark sand similar to it. Others add a foreign mineral[177] similar to alum, while undoubtedly removing any softness from it. Some add the resin of pine or some others tree sap to the frankincense. Others, when selling colors for painting, put in other elements[178] similar to them. Others sell to the unwitting *viride terrestre* for the Greek

---

176. The Latin for ginger was *gingiber* according to Maigne d'Arnis, while this text has *genebrii*, probably a variant. During the Middle Ages the price of pepper was much higher than many other spices, including ginger: "In the latter centuries of the medieval world...a pound of pepper represented the equivalent of two to three weeks' wages for an agricultural laborer" (Reay Tannahil, *Food in History* [New York: Stein and Day, 1973], 189).

177. The manuscript reads *gliscem,* likely a form of *glis* or "clay." In conjunction with *barbaram,* it is likely more general, and so "mineral" or even "substance." Maigne d'Arnis gives *glis* as "clay," possibly connected to the Latin *glissomarga.*

178. The Latin is *terram* or "earth," meaning of "earth element" or "mineral" or "substance."

color.[179] Others sell *minium*[180] for vermilion. Others mix *minium* in with the vermilion. Others sprinkle water on the azure[181] so that it might weigh more on the scales. Similarly, they adulterate other colors and spices with various foreign substances, which are similar to them. [f.88v] Physicians do the same thing. They are not afraid to adulterate wickedly their electuaries and confections and syrups[182] and other antidotes with foreign substances. They add bad things to good things and sell adulterated wares for precious ones.

And what should I say about crafty merchants? Some buy cloth with a large measuring stick and sell it with a small one. Others keep

---

179. For the classification of pigments and the fabrication of dyes, see Daniel Thompson, *Materials and Techniques of Medieval Painting* (New York: Dover, 1956), 162–63: "there is some reason to believe that *viride terrestre,* 'earth green,' is not the same as terre verte, 'green earth,' and the medieval references to it may at least sometimes signify malachite and not terre verte.... The name *terre verte* is applied to several different minerals, but the sort which seems to have been most important in medieval painting is the light, cold green of celadonite, found chiefly in small deposits in rock in the neighbourhood of Verona in Northern Italy. The chief deposits of glauconite, which yields the yellowish and olive sorts, are found in Czechoslovakia." In modern English the *terre verte* color is sometimes called "Verona green." The author is noting the fraud of selling a cheaper mineral in place of the more expensive "Greek color," verdigris, as suggest by Thompson (168).

180. *Minium* made from red lead was apparently less costly than vermillion made from cinnabar. In the first instance, the red-lead color was being sold outright for vermillion, and in the second, that vermilion was being adulterated with the red lead. See Thompson, *Materials,* 102–7, for a discussion on the production of various red compounds. *Minium,* which was used primarily in manuscript production, gives us the word "miniatures," which were colored using the red-lead compound.

181. Maigne d'Arnis gives *azurus* as "blue or sky-colored." Thompson (*Materials,* 130–33) posits that the Latin *lazurium* (later *azurium*) was borrowed from the Persian *lajoard,* which originally referred to lapis lazuli and came later to apply to blue in general. He provides a description of its production and use.

182. Albert Blaise (*Lexicon latinitatis mediae aevi* [Turnholt: Brepols, 1977]) gives this meaning for *syropus,* while Maigne d'Arnis gives *syroporius* as one who prepares *syropos,* without an entry for "syrop" itself. The word, introduced from Arabic, is not found in classical Latin.

CHAPTER SEVENTEEN

cloth so long that it rots and then sell from it as if it were good. Others sell bootlaces or skins from the forest animals or a girdle or gloves or whatever they have to sell more dearly to pilgrims than to their neighbors. Others frequently make false oaths for the least thing. For this they are damned. Others unjustly and malevolently stretch out in their hands the new cloth that they have for sale so that it might be made longer and wider. To those unaware, others fraudulently sell sheep or pig or horse skin for deerskin either as girdles or purses or breeches[183] or pig and sheep sheaths for those made of deerskin. Oh, cunning cupidity! Those who endeavor to make teachers of fraud out of their boys, send them to Le Puy, Saint-Gilles, Tours, Piacenza, Lucca, Rome, Bari, or Barletta! For in these cities, above all, is a school of all manner of fraud.[184] O deceptive innkeepers and crafty moneychangers and wicked merchants, convert to the Lord your God! Set aside your wickedness! Give up your cupidity! Sweep away your sinful frauds! What will you say on the Day of Judgment when you see all those whom you have defrauded accusing you before God? Know that God has looked down upon you with your uncountable iniquities! Truly, unless you shall be converted from your innumerable deceits, you will have the very saints, namely James and Peter, Giles, Leonard, the very mother of God, Mary of Le Puy,[185] Mary Magdalene,[186] Martin of Tours, John the Baptist of Angély,[187]

---

183. The Latin *bragarios* is etymologically related to "breeches" and originally of Celtic origin. Maigne d'Arnis gives *braca* and *bracae* for "breeches." While the manuscript indicates *bracarius* or "maker of breeches," the context indicates "breeches."
184. The passage "Oh, cunning cupidity…of all manner of fraud" is in the margin of CC with a red cross designating its insertion point; it is in the body of the text of S.
185. This is the second occasion that the writer links the Virgin Mary with two apostles and three popular French saints.
186. Mary Magdalene was especially honored at Vézelay.
187. Many believed that John the Baptist's head was in Saint-Jean-d'Angély, on the Paris-Tours Road to Compostela, although several churches in France claim it. See Melczer, *Pilgrim's Guide*, 179, n. 257.

Michael on the Sea,[188] Bartholomew of Benevento,[189] and Nicholas of Bari,[190] as accusers before God, whose pilgrims you have defrauded. To convince God, they will say about those of you coming to judgment: "These, O Lord, are the ones who deceived our pilgrims with so many and such great frauds and perpetrated[191] so many iniquities on them." "Give unto them according to the works of their hands, give them their retribution, for they have not understood the works of the Lord, and so according to the works of their hands, you will destroy them and shall not build them up." [Ps 27:4–5 / 28: 4–5] "May death come over them and may they descend alive to hell, for there are iniquities in their dwellings and in their midst." [Ps 54:16 / 55:15] What will become of you? Where [f.89r] will you be able to flee? Whose help will you seek, since on the Day of Judgment you will have the greatest saints as accusers whom you should have as supporters? You will have as accusers those whom the whole world wants to have as supporters, whom all the world venerates, to whose basilicas all people travel, whose tombs all embrace with pious love, whose dust and ashes are kept diligently in a vessel as if they were select gold or precious stones, and by whose power and merit and prayer transgressions are forgiven for sinners, the sick are cured, the blind are made to see, the lame are straightened up, the desolate are consoled, and the bound are set free.

The prayers of the pious venerate the relics of these saints.

They stand before God and pray night and day

So that sinners might merit forgiveness for themselves.

No one knows better intercessors than these!

---

188. The Latin *Michaelem marinum* may refer to the pilgrimage site of Mont-Saint-Michel on the coast of Normandy or to the sanctuary of San Michele Arcangelo on Monte Gargano on the east coast of Italy.

189. According to the Synoptic Gospels, Bartholomew was an apostle, although other sources name him Nathaniel. The basilica of St. Bartholomew in Benevento, Italy claims to house his relics.

190. St. Nicholas of Bari (d.345 or 352) is often called St. Nicholas of Myra. His relics are housed in the basilica of St. Nicholas in Bari, Italy.

191. CC reads a meaningless *ingecerunt;* S corrects it to *iniecerunt* or "to cast." The sense is clear from context.

CHAPTER SEVENTEEN

> God granted to those[192] chosen and to those carried above the heavens
> That all the things they desire to have done for themselves are soon done.
> And with the people praying, the things sought through the saints from God
> Are all granted without limit with God's consent.

Those who are helping others will accuse you. And unless you have come to your senses in this world, not only these saints but also your iniquities will take the kingdom of God away from you in the future. Those whom you have defrauded will rejoice in heaven, but you will go to Tartarus in the fires of Gehenna. They shall delight in heaven. You shall weep with Satan in Orcus. They will be crowned in heaven. You will be planted in hell on the eternal funeral pyre, as the Lord says through Isaiah:

> Because I have called, and you have not answered, I have spoken, and you have not listened, and you were doing evil in My eyes, and you have done what I have not wanted, because of this, the Lord God says these things: "Behold My servants shall eat, and you shall hunger. Behold My servants shall drink, and you shall thirst. Behold My servants shall rejoice, and you shall be confounded. Behold My servants shall praise Me from exultation of heart, and you shall call out from pain of heart and from sorrow, you shall make your breath howl, and you will give up your name." [Is 65:12–15]

Behold that you will give up in the future not only the riches that you have wickedly amassed with innumerable frauds, but also your soul and your own name, and you will delight like the one who is captured by the enemy and is wounded, plundered, closed up in a work house, afflicted with torture, and is truly tormented with hunger and cold and tedium to the ultimate degree. You will no

---

192. The Latin *Quis Deus* is in both CC and S. Since *quis* is not possible in this context, this must be shorthand for *quibus* or "[to] those."

longer say: "I am the one who used to be a happy guest," but rather: "I am a wretch in pain." Whoever loses himself [f.89v] makes a poor profit and loses everything. Give heed to what the Book of Wisdom says to you: "Hired servants are brothers in reward with whoever has shed blood and committed fraud." [Ecclus (Sir) 34:27] Know that your profits, with which you fill your purses by injuring pilgrims, are not profit but damnation. For a profit that keeps its master from the kingdom of God and sends him to Orcus is not a profit but a damnation. Your arts and your very sharp talents, by which you deceive the pilgrims, keep you entirely away from the kingdom of God and bring you into the depths of Tartarus. What does it profit you to amass money by wicked frauds and to lose your souls in hell? "What does it profit a man if he should gain the whole world but lose himself and fashion his own defeat?" [Lk 9:25, Mt 15:26, Mk 8:36] You amass monstrous and illicit profits because of your cupidity whence you practice innumerable harmful vices. Of this Paul says, "Cupidity is the root of all evil. Some who are eager with it have wandered from the faith and have brought unto themselves many pains." [1 Tim 6:10] Just as all good things are born of charity, all vices arise from cupidity. Through cupidity a man sets aside faith, lies, becomes a miser and is held a simoniac. Christ is sold, God is offended, love of neighbor is abandoned, the poor person is forgotten, all charity is left behind, the kingdom of heaven is forgotten, human judgments are overthrown in the court of heroes, fornication and adultery are committed, robbery and sacrilege and false oaths are perpetrated, all kinds of evils and vices are carried out deep within, and — what is worse — the clerical ranks are made vile, riches are amassed by which the true poverty, which Christ orders the religious to respect, is violated, and every level of vice is discharged. If you did not have cupidity, you would not hoard property. If you did not have riches, you would not practice vices. If you sometimes wanted to whore, to feast on splendid things, to be dressed in precious clothes, to build palaces, and to be honored by all, you would lack the wealth with which these things could be performed. Of this Isaiah says:

CHAPTER SEVENTEEN

Woe to you who join house to house and who couple field to field.... Woe to you who draw...sin like the chain of the plough.... Woe to you who call evil good and good evil, who consider darkness light and light darkness, [f.90r] and who consider the bitter sweet and the sweet bitter. Woe to you who are powerful at drinking wine and who are men strong in mixing in drunkenness. Woe to you who are wise in your own eyes and who justify wickedness for tributes and take away the justice of the just man from him. [Is 5:18–23]

Your insatiable cupidity, by definition, would injure all if it had that power. When you cannot injure someone, then you are excessively grieved. You always have the will, but you often lack the power, whence guile is always at hand for you. For that reason, things endure, because you lack power. If demons are damned because they wanted what God did not want to give them, then you who want what God does not want you to have are also damned by divine judgment. Your avarice is like an insatiable person with dropsy. When someone with dropsy drinks, that person wants to drink more. Similarly, when you acquire more riches from fraud, you work to acquire even more. Your avarice is similar to the bottomless abyss and to the deep well and to the sea. Just as your cupidity is without measure, your pains in the fires of Gehenna will also be without limit. Give heed to what Isaiah says: "Because of these things, hell has widened its soul and has opened its mouth without end. And its strong ones and its people and its high and glorious ones shall go down into it." [Is 5:14] Oh, monstrous grief! The glorious and mighty of the world descend into the lower regions. Remaining in your vices, you sometimes yearn for the kingdom of God, but your thought is frustrated. Thus, in fact, Isaiah speaks to you, saying: "While he dreams, the hungry person also eats...and the thirsty person also drinks...when, however, he has awakened, his soul is still empty...thus there will be a multitude of evil ones." [Is 29:8] Hence it is said openly by the people that "whoever acts badly and hopes greatly, works in vain."¹⁹³ While some people take respite on feast days from the works of the flesh, many of you do not fear to injure your brothers through your business in your markets and shops. Because of this, your transgressions surpass the infractions of others. The Lord scorns such manner of solemn feasts, as He says through the prophet: "My soul hated your calends and your festivals; they have become troubling to Me; I have taken pains to put up with them. And when you extend our hands, I will turn My eyes from you. And when you have increased your prayer, I will [f.90v] not listen to you. For your hands are full of blood." [Is 1:14–15] And elsewhere the Lord says: "Why do you call to Me? Your grief is incurable." [Jer 30:15]

Therefore, whoever has not injured those traveling, whether in a market or a shop, a changing house or an inn, or in any of the previously mentioned frauds, but who has conducted himself most properly toward them, will without doubt have a reward here and in the future from the Lord. And whoever has injured them or taken anything from them by theft or plundering or by any fraud will have his share without doubt with Dathan and Abiram¹⁹⁴ and the devil.

And what shall I say of those who charge the pilgrims of Saint James tolls? The toll collectors at the gates of Ostabat or Saint-Jean or Saint-Michel at the foot of the Pass of Cize¹⁹⁵ who take unjust tolls from them are utterly damned. No tongue, in fact, can narrate how many evils they inflict on pilgrims. Hardly anyone passes through there and is not robbed by them. By the authority of God the omnipotent, Father and Son and Holy Spirit, and by all the saints, they are excommunicated a hundred times, and they are anathematized, and they are sequestered from the threshold of paradise through the mouths of the many holy bishops and priests and monks who are so frequently robbed there. For this reason,

---

193. Cf. Fulcher of Chartres (c.1059–1128), *Historia Hierosolymitana*, Bk. 2, ch. 26 (PL 155:882): *Qui male facit, et bene sperat, ipse siquidem delirat.*
194. See ch.9, p. 161 and ch. 17 n. 156.
195. See Melczer, *Pilgrim's Guide*, 85.

CHAPTER SEVENTEEN

it is better to be silent than to talk about them.[196] And for this reason the aforementioned scoundrels, namely the innkeepers, the moneychangers, the merchants, and the toll collectors, are to be admonished by all qualified people so that they may recover their senses. If someone would scorn me for speaking and writing down the previously mentioned vices of these perverse people, let him listen to the greatest doctor and instructor of all, directing me in the following way: "Raise your voice and announce to my people their wickedness." [Is 58:1] For if I should not announce to the wicked his wickedness, the Lord will be questioning me about the blood of his death on my hand since I, by not correcting him, have become the murderer of his soul.

Therefore, let those who have treated his pilgrims properly on his route in all their business dealings rejoice in the sacred solemn feasts of the lofty apostle James! Let the pilgrims exult who are seeking his threshold and who are about to receive the crown of glory for their labors with his approval! Let us celebrate his venerable feasts happily in our lands, most beloved brethren, until we may deserve to delight in heaven in that solemn apostolic feast which is without limit! Above all, let you, the people of Galicia who have been rewarded by receiving such a great leader and shepherd, take delight! Let the Western peoples exult and all the islands of the seas that are illwminated [f.91r] by such a patron! Let Samaria, imbued with his example, rejoice! Let Jerusalem, reddened by his blood, be gladdened! Let all those who celebrate his feasts and bear proclamations of praise in their heart and mouth and work give thanks to the Lord!

O favored people of Spain and Galicia, who are honored by the virtue of such a prince, you are not exalted by the praise of your goodness but elevated by the merits of the glorious apostle. He has enhanced you, adorned you, blessed you, honored you! Your

---

196. The Latin is *Quapropter de illis melius est silere quam loqui.* The author seems to have mixed up the placement of *silere* and *loqui,* placing them on the wrong sides of *quam.* The correct meaning would then be "it is better to talk about them than to be silent."

night, which had no day, has turned into the light of the true faith whose splendor cannot be explained with speech. To you, who were once without grace,[197] great grace is given. You, who once did not know your Creator, now recognize your Maker through the apostle. You, who were once stranded in error, now have been called to the apostolic faith. You, who once were consigned to deceptive laws, now have been furnished with the foundations of the freeborn.[198] You have renounced what you were and have begun to be what you were not. You were the partisan of unclean spirits, but now have become the patron of the true God. You, who once lay on the dung heap of infidelity, now shine in the apostolic faith. You, who were once like a widow, now have been joined to the celestial Husband. You, who were once sterile, now bear children. You, who were once forsaken, now are reconciled to the Creator. You, who once strayed like sheep without a shepherd, now are joined to the heavenly patron. You, who were once stupid without an instructor, now have been joined to a faithful teacher. In fact, just as the sun spreads its light and dispels the darkness, this ray of the true Sun has banished the darkness from you and has led you to the true Light. And although some regions of the world may temporarily lose the rays of the sun, the ray of the true Sun never ceases to shine for you with the splendors of its virtues.[199] Although Titan[200] may not always shine on the world, the apostolic ray of the true Sun, present in the divine miracles and support, shines on you always. Just as the mountains are illuminated first by the gleaming sun and then the valleys, so also have you, once a dark valley, begun to shine with the

---

197. The word *ingratiosa* was not found; the meaning, however, is clearly "not filled with grace."
198. The overarching idea of the Latin *rudimentis liberalibus* is "a new foundation, being freeborn," a probable reference to being born again through baptism.
199. Here James is compared to a ray and God to the sun.
200. Titan is the sun-god from Greco-Roman mythology; this reference to his brightness in comparison to Saint James is also found in Bk. II, Miracle 19, where James's clothing shines brighter than the sun. (Coffey and Dunn, *Miracles,* 56).

CHAPTER SEVENTEEN

apostolic light. First the mountains are illuminated and then the valleys. First the apostles are illuminated and then the peoples. And like lightening that comes out from the East and gleams all the way to the West, the apostolic ray shines through divine miracles not only in your province but also through the whole world where his churches are built. There arose in the [f.91v] darkness an astonishing light, and your darkness shines like midday, for in the region of the shadow of death light has appeared for the inhabitants. It is no wonder if you once lay in the darkness of infidelity, for you did not have the light of doctrine. If, in fact, you did not see the ray of the sun, you would not know the sun. Accordingly, you have known the sun of justice, since you have looked on its[201] ray and on the very sun that illuminates everyone coming into this world and the very sun of which the Psalmist says: "He has placed his tabernacle in the sun." [Ps 18:6 / 19:4] Of this the prophet says: "On you who fear the Lord, the sun of justice will shine,"[202] and elsewhere: "The sun has risen and the moon has stood in its place."[203] Then the sun set, when Christ died on the cross. Then it rose when Christ arose from the dead. Then the sun sent out its rays when Christ sent His apostles, filled with the Holy Spirit, throughout the world.

Therefore, live lawfully, people of Spain, for you have accepted one of these rays. Keep the ray of the true Sun with good practices, so that it may always deign to shine on you with its virtues. Guard the treasure. Preserve the living rock chosen by the Lord on the Sea of Galilee, distinguished among the apostolic rocks, and built in the sanctuary of the Lord. Favored soil of Galicia, you who have deserved to hold such a treasure, you have found a celestial pearl, you have found a yearned-for treasure — a pearl shining with divine miracles, a continual treasure of divine favors. The yearned-for treasure rests on your shores. Whoever has this treasure lacks nothing. For what can be lacking to the one who possesses the virtue of such a treasure? But why is it that you, an uncivilized people,

---

201. The word *eius* is added interlineally in CC, and is in the text of S.
202. Cf. Mal 4:2.
203. Cf. Hab 3:11.

should have such a treasure? It appears that the proverb spoken by the people has been fulfilled in you: "To a fool on the street, a fortune is given." So, tell me: Who has endowed you? Perhaps you will tell me that: "The Orient has visited us from on high." You speak the truth, for "the Orient visited you from on high" [Lk 1:78] when it deigned to give you the virtue of its apostle. For while you were exiled to the ends of the earth, and if I may say so, situated at the most remote parts of the world, nevertheless the ray of the true Sun arises for you that it may shine "on those who are in darkness and sit in the shadow of death to direct the feet" [Lk 1:79] of the many seeking the apostle of the Lord in your country. In fact, all the foreign peoples from all the regions of the world rush to you in throngs, [f.92r] bearing with happiness offerings of praise for the apostle of the Lord. For it is right to understand about you what the Lord once said through Isaiah:

> Behold in My hands I have described you; your walls are forever before My eyes.... I live, says the Lord, that you may be vested with all peoples as with an ornament, and you shall surround yourself with these peoples as if a bride. For your wastelands and your solitary places and the lands of your ruin will be narrow before the inhabitants, and those who were absorbing you will be far put to flight. Up to this time the children of your sterility shall speak in your ears: "The place is narrow for me, make space for me so that I may live." And you shall say in your heart: "Who has begotten these for me? I was sterile and not bearing, exiled and captured, and who has nourished them? And I was destitute and alone, and where were these children?" The Lord God says these things: "Behold, I raise My hand to My people, and I shall raise My sign up to the peoples, and they shall bring your sons in their arms, and they will bring your daughters on their shoulders. And kings will be their providers, and queens shall be their nurses. With faces turned down toward the earth, they will honor you and will lick your dust. And you will know that I am Lord about Whom they who await Him will not be confounded.... I shall judge those who have judged you, and I shall save your children. And I shall feed your

CHAPTER SEVENTEEN

enemies with their own flesh, and they will be inebriated with their own blood as if with wine. And all flesh will know that I am the Lord Who saves you." [Is 49:16–26]

To whom shall I compare you except to a man who finds a treasure hidden in a field, who, out of his joy, sells all his things and buys that field?[204] Again I will compare you to a merchant, a man who seeks good pearls, who, finding a precious one, gives up all of his things and purchases that one.[205] What then have you given, and what have you received? Certainly, you gave yourself by believing, and you have received the pearl already shining in heaven. You have given yourself by annihilating the idols and building the church, and you have accepted the apostolic virtue in giving heed to these things.[206] Your acquisition is better than any business with silver or the best and purest gold. The fruit of your acquisition is more precious than all opulence, and all the things that are yearned for cannot be compared to it. His routes are beautiful routes, and all his paths are peaceful. Concerning his most beneficial coming, Saint Fortunatus,[207] [f.92v] that splendid poet, confessor, and leader, once, in the book of his divine praises, advised you to take delight saying:

Strike up, people of Galicia,[208] new songs for Christ,[209]

At the coming of James[210] give prayers to God.

Behold, the hope of the flock has come, father of the people and the patron of the city,

Let the sheep be made happy by the service of the shepherd.

---

204. Cf. Mt 13:44.
205. Cf. Mt 13:45.
206. An inferred reference to James's *translation* and Queen Lupa's conversion and subsequent destruction of idols and her support in constructing his tomb and church. (Coffey and Dunn, *Miracles,* 83.)
207. Venantius Fortunatus, *Miscellanea,* 5:3:1–2, 5–6, 17–34, 43–44 (PL 88:184–85). See ch. 2, n. 122 and ch. 6, n. 13. Fortunatus's text was addressed to the people of Tours and concerned their bishop, Gregory.
208. Venantius's text reads "happy" rather than "Galicia."
209. Venantius's text reads "hold prayers" rather than "songs for Christ."
210. Venantius's text reads "of the bishop" rather "of James."

With his support, the flocks are guided to holy pastures,
>And they gather gifts from the seed of paradise.

The one who keeps clean the sheepfolds of Christ the benevolent
>Lest they be exposed to swift wolves to be torn apart,

He governs[211] the stable with watchful vigilance and without fail
>Lest any plundering disturb the entrusted flock.

May he fortify the enclosed lambs with their precious pelts,
>And may this watchman protect those sleeping.[212]

May the flowering[213] vine with divine care grow fertile
>So that its grape may also be beautiful when it is mature,

So that the storehouse of heaven may be filled up with endless fruits,
>Thus, souls may drink at the live flowing fountain.

So that the thirst would not cause torment, a rich person tried to soothe it
>With a moistened finger as he sought relief.[214]

But rather may they flourish, made to lie in the bosom of Abraham,
>And may the shepherd lead the sheep toward the stars in the peaceful bosom.

Thus, with the talent committed to him well doubled,
>May he enter into the true delights of his Lord,

---

211. Venantius's text reads "May he govern" rather than "He governs."

212. Venantius's text reads "those saved," for "those sleeping," although the latter is a variant reading.

213. Venantius's text reads "florid" rather than flowering.

214. There appears to be a corruption in the Venantius text for lines 29 and 30 (this and the previous line). The PL gives two alternate readings for the text "that a rich ... relief"; one of them: "...Lazarus, to soothe with that moistened finger, sought to bring relief from the burning"; and the other: "...Lazarus with a moistened finger in order to soothe it, then sought to relieve the burning."

CHAPTER SEVENTEEN

And crowned with the worthy reward of his labors, may he[215]
    Obtain as a soldier of the king a place in the arch of the heavens.

Therefore, pray earnestly with us, people of Galicia, to the Lord's apostle and venerable teacher, so that he may intercede and assiduously implore Christ the King seated in heaven on account of our continuous failings, so that we may be able to reject worldly things and love heavenly things, so that we may have him as a supporter who on the last day is to be seated over the twelfth throne and whom we believe is to judge over twelve tribes of Israel, and so that we may be worthy to be placed together with him with God's help.

O great Saint James,[216] beloved of Christ, loving offspring of Zebedee, brother of John the Evangelist, who with the Lord reigns happily in the citadel of heaven, whose immense dwelling stands in Galicia and confers well-being on those seeking him, grant that those who seek you there or anywhere may receive all manner of useful things and that they may experience you always as intercessor in all their needs before God in heaven to the extent that they seek you and confide in you. Be a guardian of our souls on the day of our death, O advocate of the pilgrims.

Saint James, most loving of all, who left not only what you possessed but also all that you could have possessed because of the Lord's calling you near the bank of the Sea of Galilee, [f.93r] grant us by your bountiful merit, we beg, that all the things that might displease God may be forgiven and that those that please Him may be accomplished in all their vigor and that together with you we may be worthy to be made participants in perpetual glory. You, who have exercised great powers before God by giving sight to the blind, correcting those straying, and raising the dead, by your merits clear the fog over our hearts and sever the bonds of our depravity. For God exhibited such great respect for you that, when He raised

---

215. Venantius's text reads "they may."
216. The sermon ends with this prayer addressed to James.

the daughter of the archpriest,[217] He respectfully allowed you to enter the house when He did not permit others to go in so that He might show you clearly the venerable miracle. And so we run to the liberating power of your holiness so that you might raise us from the death of the soul with your most glorious interventions and so that you might obtain for us from God a spirit good for resisting vice and concupiscence to the extent that the Dispenser of forgiveness may agree to dull with weeping the transgressions we committed so that we return to them no more. You were worthy to climb with the Lord to Mount Tabor to see His Transfiguration[218] and to hear the wondrous voice of God the Father and to perceive the immense brilliance of His divinity, which no one had ever been allowed to see. Because of these things, O renowned apostle, we implore your blessedness that you may allow us by your prayers to climb from the valley of vices to the mountain of virtues, so that we may be worthy to enjoy perpetual brightness together with you in the resurrection that you beheld on Mount Tabor. You who arrived by the sword of Herod[219] at the starry inner chamber and who are the consort of holy angels, obtain for us solace in tribulation and strength in every time of temptation so that we may be worthy to overcome the adversary. You, who are the honor of the Spanish, the refuge of the poor, the strength of the weak, the consoler of those in tribulation, the deliverance of pilgrims, the fisher of souls, the eye for the blind, the foot for the lame, the hand for the destitute, the protector of those sailing and calling on you, the intercessor of peoples, the father of all, the destroyer of vice, and the builder of virtue, we beg you with humble heart that with your pious intercession you extinguish the fires of our vices and you kindle in us the fervor of chastity and love and the other virtues.[220] We

---

217. Cf. Lk 8:49–56.
218. Cf. Mt 17:1–9, Mk 9:2–10, Lk 9:28–36.
219. A reference to Saint James's beheading at the hands of Herod, Acts 12:1–2.
220. The writer concludes with one last reference to the miraculous powers of Saint James, all of which have been mentioned at least once before.

CHAPTER SEVENTEEN

all believe that from whatever necessity we have called on you, we are helped by your prayers. We know, in fact, that whatever you petition from God is most easily obtained. For God has offered a gift to you toward which all the foreign peoples [f.93v] of all the regions of the world run with offerings and sing the praise of the Lord. Indeed, the route from Dacia and Ethiopia to Galicia[221] turns worthily into a route of penitence and deliverance from sin because of you. For thus the prophet once prophesied by descriptively saying: "Nations from afar shall come to you and shall bear offerings and shall adore the Lord in you and shall hold your land in holiness. They shall invoke a great name in you." [Tob 13:11] And shortly after he says: "You, however, shall rejoice in your children, for all shall be blessed and gathered to you. Blessed are all who love you and delight in your peace." [Tob 13:14–15] For the Lord speaks thus through Isaiah: "The work of Egypt and the business of Ethiopia and of Sabaim[222] and high men shall pass over to you and will be yours. They shall walk after you, they shall go bound in manacles, and they shall adore the Lord in you and beseech you. God is so much in you." [Is 45:14]

Precious James, brother of the virginal John,

Who piously called Hermogenes,[223]

Who was ferocious of heart, back from the vices of the world

To the honor of the Omnipotent,

Pray for us all with continual prayer.

James, hope and relief for your servants,

---

221. Dacia, Ethiopia, and of course, Galicia are also mentioned in the *Miracles*. For Dacia, see above, n. 54. Ethiopia referred both to the modern region as well as to Africa in general. Dacia is mentioned by Calixtus in the introductory letter of the *Miracles* (Coffey and Dunn, 1) and Ethiopia is mentioned in Miracle 22 (Coffey and Dunn, 60–63).
222. Those from Sheba.
223. Hermogenes is named as one of James's disciples and as bishop over them in the prologue of the *Translatio* (Coffey and Dunn, *Miracles*, 70–71). See above, ch. 9.

Mercifully accept the pious prayers of your servants.[224]
To your people, restore life, desired for so long a time,
So that we may be worthy to be joined above in the dwellings among the stars.[225]

Be mindful, therefore, most magnificent father, of your children throughout the ages, for it is[226] your practice to pray for the pilgrims asking this of you so that we may be pulled out of all difficulties and so that we may all be worthy to possess together with you the everlasting kingdom of heaven.

May Jesus Christ our Lord deign to guarantee this Who lives with the Father and Son and reigns as God. World without end. Amen.

---

224. The Latin *servorum* has a broader extent than in English, meaning both "slaves" and "servants." Here the first instance is probably "slaves" and the second "servants."

225. The Latin *ut superum castris iungi mereamur in astris*. The Latin uses *astris* ("among the stars"), rather than *stellis,* failing to incorporate the folk etymology for Compostella as being the "field of stars."

226. The word *est* is interlinear in CC but is in the text of S.

[CHAPTER 18]

III Calends of January[1]
Translation of Saint James of Zebedee from Jerusalem to Galicia and His Calling and How in the Rank of the Apostolate He Was Chosen on the Sea of Galilee Is Celebrated

A Reading of the Holy Gospel According to Matthew:

"At that time, Jesus was walking along the Sea of Galilee and saw two brothers, Simon, who is called Peter, and Andrew his brother, who were casting their nets into the sea, for they were fishermen. And He said to them: 'Come follow me, and I will make you fishers of men.' [f.94r] And they immediately left their nets and followed Him," and so forth. [Mt 4:18–20ff.]

A Homily of Pope Saint Gregory[2] on This Reading:

You have heard, dearest brethren, that at the sound of a single command, Peter and Andrew left their nets and followed the Redeemer. They had not, however, yet seen Him perform any miracles, and they had not heard anything from Him about repayment with eternal reward. And yet, at a single command of the Lord, they forget what they seemed to own. How many miracles do we see and with how many lashes do we yield and with what harshness of threat are we worn down, and still we defy the One calling us to follow? He is seated already in heaven Who warns us about conversion. He has already submitted the necks of the people to the yoke of the faith. He has already leveled the glory of the world. He already announces the nearness of His Final Judgment as He increases His destruction,

---

1. December 30.
2. Gregory I, the Great, *XL Homiliarum in Evangelia liber I, Homilia 5* (PL 76:1092–95). The preface to the sermon states that it was delivered on James's feast day in the basilica of Saint Andrew, probably Sant'Andrea in Vaticano. See *The Marvels of Rome*, trans. Francis Morgan Nichols, ed. Eileen Gardiner (New York: Italica Press, 1986), 78, 88.

and still our proud mind does not wish to forsake willingly what it loses daily unwillingly. Therefore, dearest brethren, what are we to say during His judgment, when, because of a love of the present world, we do not bend to commands and are not corrected by scourges?

But might someone perhaps say in one's quiet thoughts: "At the voice of the Lord each of these fishermen forsook what he had, when he had hardly anything"? But in this matter, dearest brethren, we must think of the outcome[3] rather than the amount of property. One who has retained nothing for oneself gives up a great deal.[4] One who even has given up everything, however small it may be, has given up a great deal. Certainly, we also possess our belongings with great love and seek things that we do not have out of desire. Thus, Peter and Andrew gave up much when they both left behind the things they wanted to have. One who has renounced all one's longings together with what one has possessed has given up much. Thus, as many things were given up by the followers as could be longed for by those not following. Therefore let no one, even when seeing some people giving up many things, say to oneself: "I want to imitate those disdainful of this world, but I have nothing to give up." You give up many things, brethren, if you renounce worldly longings. Our outward things, in fact, are sufficient to the Lord, no matter how small. For He weighs the heart and not the substance, nor has He weighed [f.94v] the size of the sacrifice but the amount of care with which it is offered. For if we consider the outward substance, behold how our holy merchants have bought the eternal life of the angels by giving up the nets and the ship. A person does not, of course, have any real estimated price, but the kingdom of such a great God is nevertheless worth as much as one has. And for Zacchaeus,[5] the value was giving half of his property, since he had kept back another half to use for quadruple restitution for what he had unjustly taken. For Peter and Andrew, the value was

---

3. Here CC and S have *effectum* or "outcome," while Gregory had *affectum* or "outlook."
4. This sentence is in the margin of CC with a red cross designating its insertion point; it is in the body of the text in S.
5. Cf. Lk 19:1–10.

CHAPTER EIGHTEEN

giving up their nets and ship. For a widow the value was two small coins.⁶ The value was a cup of cold water for another.⁷ And so the kingdom of God, as we said, is worth as much as one has.

Therefore, think brethren, about what is bought more cheaply and what is more expensive when owned. But perhaps neither is a cup of cold water that is offered to the poor person sufficient, but even so, the divine Word promises us a guarantee. At the birth of the Redeemer,⁸ the citizens of heaven revealed themselves and cried out: "Glory to God in the highest, and on earth peace to men of good will." [Lk 2:14] In fact, before the eyes of God, the hand is never devoid of a gift if the chamber of the heart is filled with good will. About this, in fact, the Psalmist says: "In me, God, are Your prayers, which I will relinquish to You as praise." [Ps 55:12/ 56:12] It is as if he were plainly saying: "Even though I do not have gifts to be offered outwardly, I find within myself what I place on the altar for Your praise. For You are not maintained by our gift, You are pleased more by the offering of the heart." Nothing is offered more richly to God than with good will. Good will is when we fear for the adversities of others as we fear for our own, when we rejoice in the good fortune of others as we rejoice in our own success, when we hold the harm of others as our own, when we consider the advantages of others to be our own, when we love a friend not because of the world but because of God, when we tolerate even an enemy with love. It is when you do not make anyone suffer what you do not want to suffer, when you refuse to deny anyone what you might justly want yourself, and when you hasten to help with your neighbor's needs according to your abilities, and when you want to be useful even beyond your powers. What is, therefore, more opulent than this offering, when the soul elevates and offers itself to God on the altar of the heart?

---

6. Cf. Mk 12:41–44 and Lk 21:1–4.
7. Cf. Mt 10:42.
8. Here S offers the appropriate spelling of *Redemptore* while CC has *Redemptori*.

However, this sacrifice of good will is never fully discharged unless the desire of this world is fully relinquished. For whatever we long for in it, we will without doubt envy in our neighbors. It appears, [f.95r] in fact, that we are missing what another gains. And since envy is always inconsistent with good will, as soon as envy has seized the mind, good will vanishes. For this reason, the holy preachers also tried to love their neighbors as perfectly as they might be able in this world and to love nothing in this world and to long for nothing ever and to possess nothing out of desire. Isaiah brings attention well to these when he says: "Who are these who fly like clouds and like doves at their windows?" [Is 60:8] Certainly he sees them as disdaining earthly things, approaching heavenly things with the mind, raining down words, and glittering with miracles. And holy preaching and a sublime life had kept them from earthly contamination, and he declares them to be like flying clouds. The window, however, is our eyes, since the soul looks through them at what it desires on the outside. The dove, in fact, is a simple animal, and it differs from the evil of the cat. Doves that desire nothing in this world and simply behold all things and who are not dragged by the longing of greediness are therefore at their windows. Whereas, unlike a dove, a hawk that pants with a desire for plunder at anything it sees with its eyes being at their windows would be the opposite. Therefore, dearest brethren, as we celebrate the solemnities of Saint James the Apostle, we must imitate what we cherish. Let the solemnity reveal the offering of the unwavering devotion of our mind. Let us hold in disdain the things that are worldly! Let us purchase the eternal things by relinquishing the temporal! If, however, we cannot yet give up our own things, at least let us not long for the things of others! If our mind is still not ignited by the flame of charity, let it at least have the restraint of fear on its ambition, so that the mind is carried forward on its steps and enlivened yet constrained from the longing for the things of others as it is brought to disdain possessions. May He deign to be present, Whose kingdom and rule remains without end. World without end. Amen.

[CHAPTER 19]

III Day of the Calends of January[1]
The Feast of the Calling and *Translation* of Saint James of Zebedee Is Celebrated

A Reading from the Book of Wisdom:

"James[2] pleased God and was transported to paradise so that he might give repentance to the peoples," etc.[3] [Ecclus (Sir) 44:16ff.]

A Sermon of Pope Saint Calixtus on the same reading:

[f.95v] Most beloved brethren, on this very day, in considering the present holy solemnities, namely of the Calling and *Translation* of Saint James of Zebedee, the apostle of Galicia and brother of Saint John the Evangelist, we must pick flowery words in sweet and worthy ornamentation to explain this most beautiful reading for the glory of our Lord Jesus Christ. The divine reading, in fact, says "James pleased God and was transported to paradise." In that regard, he was carried to the land of the living since he pleased God in the land of the dying. However, in the first part of this short verse, namely, where James is written, one sees Enoch in the story of the Book of Wisdom. Since what is written about this Enoch may be understood figuratively and could just as well be about Christ or about any just person, still the matter requires that this be shown about Saint James. Thus, one should, first of all, examine why Enoch might be transported to paradise. In that account, Enoch, while living in his own body, "was transported to paradise," because he is to come in the end to battle the Antichrist with Elijah the Prophet whom the Lord once similarly took by a whirlwind to heaven. But

---

1. December 30.
2. Here and below, in the biblical text, this is Enoch rather than James.
3. We have translated literally here, although it is customary to supply context such as "an example of penance" or "an inspiration for penance." The Latin text does not give this clarification.

on what do Elijah and Enoch live and with what are they dressed, since they are placed beyond this world yet are considered carnal beings? Since He once fed the children of Israel in the desert with manna, this benevolent Lord feeds them just as He wishes. And why will the Lord send men to battle the Antichrist and not the angels or archangels? Because just as God once sent a man, namely His Son, and not an angel, to battle the devil and free humankind, so He has determined to send men and not angels to overcome the Antichrist. Accordingly, why will He send men of the Old Law and not the apostles who are closer to Christ and of the household of God more than they are? It is because if he sent the apostles or any saints of the New Law, there would be no witnesses of the Old Law. In fact, there are three ages: one before the law, another under the law, and another under the grace of baptism. From these, the Son of God wished to have witnesses of truth against the Antichrist: namely Enoch from the people who were before the law, Elijah from under the law, and the apostles from under [f.96r] the grace of baptism. He had the apostles as witnesses in His first coming. He is to have Elijah and Enoch for the Second Coming. And why has He saved men who are still to die in human flesh for this work? Could He not resurrect some of His disciples or apostles or people holier[4] than those men at the end of the present world are? Certainly, He could if He wished to. But if He called back to life at that time people already dead, they would certainly not fight well, when they knew that they would die again, since they would fear dying again. The shadow of death is, in fact, of such bitterness that anyone who has once tasted it fears tasting it again. Therefore Enoch, whose name is interpreted as "dedication," signifies Christ Who consecrated[5] His Church with His blood. That Enoch pleased God with words and examples and good works indicates, in fact, the Only-Begotten of God, Who pleased God in all things

---

4. The CC has *sanciores* while S has *santiores*, for what must be *sanctiores* ("holier").
5. The wordplay of the Latin — *dedicatio* "dedication" vs *dedicavit* "consecrated" — is not possible in English.

CHAPTER NINETEEN

and through all things, as the Father Himself testifies on Mount Tabor with Saint James listening,[6] as well as over the Jordan, when the Father says about Him: "This is My beloved Son in Whom I am well pleased." [Mt 3:17, 17:5] That Enoch, while living, was transported in body to paradise, shows the Son of God Himself resuscitated in His own body from the dead and Whom God the Father after triumphing over the prince of hell, raised not only to paradise but also over all the angelic hosts and above the highest peaks of the heavens. That Enoch is to come in the end and is to give repentance to the peoples and triumph over the Antichrist, shows Christ, Who is triumphant over the world and Who has cast out the prince of this world — that is, the devil — and Who says: "Now the prince of this world is cast out." [Jn 12:31] He gave [an example of] repentance to all those coming to Him, as the Gospel says: "Do penance, for the kingdom of heaven is at hand." [Mt 4:17] And just as Enoch "pleased God and was transported to paradise," so also Saint James pleased the Lord in faith and deed, in Whom there is great pleasure over those fearing Him and over those who hope in His mercy, and James was transported to the heavenly seat of paradise.[7] He above all preached penitence, as is written in the Epistle of James:[8] "Do penance and be converted so that your sins may be forgiven." [Acts 3:19]

"He was found perfect and just and became a conciliator in a time of wrath. The covenants of the world were placed with him so that [f.96v] not all flesh would be destroyed." [Ecclus (Sir) 44:17, 44:19] These two small verses are written about Noah, whose name is interpreted as "rest" and who is found to be perfect and just, and

---

6. The Transfiguration. Cf. Mt 17:2, Mk 9:2–3, Lk 9:28–36.
7. The Latin *paradisiaca sede politica* is ambiguous. The standard meaning for *politica*, from Greek noun πόλις *(polis)*, is "civil"; however the LSJ also constructs an adjective meaning "heavenly" from the Latin noun *polus*, a cognate with and possibly derived from the Greek πόλος *(polos)* for "pole" or "sky" through its use with the polar star.
8. This is another confusion about which James was meant. See the Introduction, p. xvi and ch. 2, n. 100. The reading is not from the Epistle of James but from Acts.

they indicate the Son of God, Who is more just than all the just and is more perfect than all the perfect and in Whom are found eternal rest, unending peace, and unrelenting tranquility. In Him the souls of the saints rest as He said to His disciple: "And you shall find rest for your souls." [Mt 11:29] Thus, in a time of wrath — namely of the flood — Noah reconciled the world through the wood of the ark, which he built, and the water on which he sailed, and he signifies Christ Who reconciled the lost world to God the Father through His cross and through the water of His baptism, as Saint Paul says: "Christ through the blood of His Passion reconciled the world to God." [Rom 5:10] And another scripture says it in this way: "The lamb redeems the sheep. The innocent Christ has reconciled the sinners."[9] And just as in the time of Noah, He became as a witness for the world so that all flesh would not be destroyed, thus the Son of God was given as a witness before God the Father so that all flesh might not be destroyed in the time of perdition. The Father, in fact, says of His Son through the prophet: "Behold I have given Him as a witness to the peoples, as a leader and teacher for the peoples." [Is 55:4] And Blessed Job says: "My witness is in heaven, and my confidant is on high." [Job 16:20] As we have said: by Noah, Christ is implied; by the ark, the Church is implied; by the water, the baptism of Christ is implied; by those dead in the water, our sins wiped out by baptism are implied, and by those saved in the ark, the faithful saved in the Church are implied. Those who are outside the Church — namely the heretics, the Jews, the Gentiles, and those who are anathema — incur the perdition of the flood. And just as Noah made a window on the side of the Ark so also our most kind and benevolent Redeemer, Who consoles the wretched, offers on the cross His side to be opened by the soldier so that the most fitting rivers might flow from it, namely the blood of redemption and the water of baptism by which our sins are washed away. That Noah constructed the ark so that he might save the rest of the world, gives one to understand James, who, by

---

9. This second verse of the Sequence for Easter is not biblical scripture. Its authorship remains uncertain.

CHAPTER NINETEEN

his preaching and by shedding his own blood, built the Church so that he might call the world to the saving[10] faith. In fact, this same Church rejoices and sings for the praise of Christ together with the apostles saying: "These are the living in the flesh who planted the Church with [f.97r] their blood."[11]

"A great father of a multitude of peoples and no one is found similar to him in glory who would keep the law of the Most High." [Ecclus (Sir) 44:20] This little verse, with the four following verses, is written about Abraham. Abraham, whose name is interpreted as "distinguished father," is also said to be the father of a multitude of peoples. The Son of God is also understood to be the benevolent father of all believing in Him, and He is regarded as higher, not only for all peoples but also for the heavens and all the angels. Of Him the Psalmist testifies and says: "The Lord is the highest above all the peoples, and His glory is above the heavens." [Ps 112:4 / 113:4] He is, in fact, above all things and within all things, and whatever exists is in Him. Of Him, blessed Job, when talking to himself, says the following: "He is higher than heaven, and what will you do? He is deeper than hell, and whence do you know Him? He is greater in size than the earth and wider than the sea." [Job 11:8–9] In addition, He is such a great and distinguished Maker of all things, containing the world in His fist while enclosed within the safety of the womb of the Blessed Virgin Mary for the salvation of the world. In all things and through all things Abraham observed the law of the commandments of the Highest Father. For this reason there is found no one similar to him in the glory of the angels nor of men as the Psalmist says: "There is no one similar to You among the gods, O Lord, and there is no one close to You in regard to Your works." [Ps 85:8 / 86:8] And elsewhere: "God, who

---

10. The Latin *salvatricem* is not a standard adjective, but the meaning is evident.

11. This first line of a hymn *("Isti sunt qui viventes in")* is found in several manuscripts. See the Cantus Manuscript Database: http://cantus.uwaterloo.ca/chant/186831 (accessed 5/5/2020).

is similar to You?"[12] And just as Abraham was a father of many peoples, so also is Saint James the father and benevolent helper of many traveling to him in Galicia, and while he lived he diligently kept the law of the highest God in all things. But there is not found anyone similar to him in glory among the apostles. He was, in fact, worthy to follow Christ to heaven before the other apostles because of the sword of Herod, and he was worthy among the apostles to sit nearer to Christ on the most distinguished throne. And the Lord "was in covenant with him." [Ecclus (Sir) 44:20] Just as the Lord was in the covenant of circumcision and the progeny of Abraham, so God the Father and Holy Spirit with Christ were even more in the grace of baptism and in the new progeny of Catholics, and He was at hand for Saint James through the grace of divine preaching.

"In his flesh he made the covenant stand, and in temptation he was found faithful." [Ecclus (Sir) 44:21] Just as the Lord had the covenant of circumcision stand in the flesh of Abraham, so also in Christ and James and the other apostles, He made the covenant of the new grace of baptism remain. And [f.97v] in fact, the witness and founder of circumcision was Abraham, and the apostles are the witnesses of the new grace of baptism. And just as Abraham, in the temptation by the Lord, when he was told: "Take your son, Isaac, whom you love, and offer him as a sacrifice," [Gen 22:2] is found faithful, so our Lord Jesus Christ, when it is said to Him in the temptation by the devil: "I will give you all these things if you fall and adore me," [Mt 4:8] is found most faithful. Similarly, as long as he lived, Saint James was faithful in the temptations of the devil in both adverse and favorable times. In the same way, we must also act faithfully and enduringly, whether we are tested by the Lord or the devil. Concerning temptation by the Lord, it is written by the apostle: "In fact, God tempts you, so that He may know if you love Him."[13] Concerning the temptation by the devil, it is said to the Lord in the Lord's Prayer: "And lead us not into

---

12. The Psalmist provides several expressions of this: Ps 82:2, as well as 34:10 / 35:10, 70:19 / 71:19, 89:8 / 90:8, etc.

13. Cf. Dt 13:3, also James 1:13.

CHAPTER NINETEEN

temptation, but deliver us from evil." [Mt 6:13] For that reason, let any Spaniard — or whatever Christian if perchance he should be captured among the Moors — be faithful up to the obligation of death in all matters, so that one may receive the recompense that God promised when He said to the faithful: "Whoever has persevered, however, up to the end shall be saved." [Mt 24:13]

"Therefore, He gave an oath to him that his seed would grow in his people like the dust of the earth[14] and that his seed would rise up like the stars." [Ecclus (Sir) 44:22–23] The seed that the Lord gave by oath to the people of Abraham is, strictly speaking, the flesh of our Savior, which descended from the offspring of Abraham, which is compared to the best seed, since just as from one single grain of seed, many grains arise, so also from the blood of His flesh, the grace of baptism, thousands of people and nations are regenerated. For these increased like the dust of the earth, since the Lord, Who is the accumulator of all good things, accumulated prophets and patriarchs, apostles, martyrs, confessors, and all those chosen above the peaks of Olympus. "The seed of Abraham" is exalted "like the stars," [Ecclus (Sir) 44:23] since the flesh of the Redeemer was lifted above the angelic choirs. "And they would inherit from sea to sea and from the river to the ends of the earth." [Ecclus (Sir) 44:23] The heirs of Abraham inherit from sea to sea, since the faithful of Christ are multiplied everywhere through the provision of divine grace. And just as Abraham is held as "the father of many peoples," [Ecclus (Sir) 44:20] so also is Saint James confirmed as the pious father of diverse peoples and [f.97bis-r][15] nations who come to his venerable sepulcher in Galicia. And just as the seed of Abraham is "increased like the dust of the earth," and is exalted "like the stars,"

---

14. The Latin is *terre cumulum* or "accumulation of soil," usually rendered with the analogy to dust, as here and below; the intent is to show a large number.

15. In the earliest surviving numbering of the folios, two were numbered *Cvii* (97) with no folios added or lost. The mistake was resolved by adding "bis" ("again/repeated"). Thus, the sequence is 97r, 97v, 97bis-r, 97bis-v, 98r, 98v.

[Ecclus (Sir) 44:22–23] so also are the pilgrim people of Saint James increased daily on the earth and exalted above the stars of heaven together with James in the heavenly country.

"And he acknowledged him in his blessings and gave him an inheritance and divided his share into twelve tribes." [Ecclus (Sir) 44:26] This little verse, together with the following, is about Jacob. Therefore, because Jacob excessively esteemed blessings, the Lord approved of him and loved him as He said through the prophet: "I loved Jacob, and I held Esau in hatred." [Mal 1:2–3] Jacob covered his hands and the exposed parts of his neck with the pelts of young goats, denied that he was himself, changed his name and his speech, pretended to be in the likeness of his brother, asserted a lie for the truth, injured his brother, and defrauded his father so that he might obtain for himself a blessing from him.[16] He had himself locked up[17] all night on Mount Bethel with an angel so that he might be able to obtain a blessing from the Lord.[18] For this reason he saw the Lord at the top of a ladder, and the Lord acknowledged him.[19] Therefore, we must also cover, with repentance of mind and mortification of the flesh, our souls, which the wicked enemy has stripped of holy virtues and the delights of paradise through the misfortunes of vices so that we may be worthy to be blessed by God our Father. Again with that angel, who is an angel of great counsel, namely the Lord Jesus Christ, we must struggle, not with the arms of vain power but with assiduous prayers and frequent fasting and with alms and divine preaching until we are worthy to be blessed by the Lord — not on Mount Bethel but in heaven. The inheritance that the Lord offered to Jacob is figuratively the Christian people that God the Father presented to his Only Begotten. About this, Truth testifies and says: "A praiseworthy people whom the Lord of hosts has blessed, saying: 'You are the work of my hands and my

---

16. Cf. Gen 27:15–30.
17. The Latin is *claudus* ("lame"), probably a scribal error for *clausus* ("locked up" or "hidden").
18. Cf. Gen 28:10–22.
19. Cf. Gen 28:12–13.

legacy, Israel.'"[20] Concerning this inheritance the Psalmist says: "My inheritance is magnificent to me." [Ps 15:6 / 16:6] The heir of this inheritance is the Son of God, whom the Lord, as the apostle says, "appointed Heir of all things and through Whom He made the world." [Heb 1:2] This inheritance is said to be the Christian share that the Lord divided for His Son into twelve tribes, since the Lord separated this part for Himself from the heretics and Jews and unfaithful peoples and sent his twelve [f.97bis-v][21] apostles to preach. In fact, when one divides something up, one keeps a share and relinquishes a share. Thus, the Lord, here and on the day of Final Judgment, casts off the wicked part of the perverse and accepts the good part. About this it is written in an old volume: "I hoped to separate you from the other peoples so you might be mine." [Lev 20:26] And elsewhere: "If you separate the precious thing from the vile, you will be My mouth." [Jer 15:19]

"And he preserved for himself men of mercy who found grace in the eyes of all flesh." [Ecclus (Sir) 44:27] Jacob, for whom the Lord preserved men of mercy — that is, his twelve sons as the twelve patriarchs of the world — signifies the Only Begotten of God for Whom God the Father faithfully preserved men of mercy — that is, the twelve apostles here and in the future — just as this Son asked the Father for them, saying: "Holy Father, preserve in Your name those You have sent to Me." [Jn 17:11] And elsewhere He said to them: "Not even a hair on your head will perish." [Lk 21:18] And just as the twelve patriarchs found grace in the eyes of all flesh, so much more so did the twelve apostles find unfailing grace in the eyes of the true deity of Christ, the Son of God. Jacob, who looked on the Lord on Mount Bethel, signifies[22] James who saw the Lord transfigured in the deity of the Father on Mount Tabor. Jacob is interpreted as "supplanter," and our James is similarly call a supplanter, since he, who fraudulently accepted the blessing of his father, supplanted his brother, and this shows our James who

20. Cf. Is 19:25.
21. See above, n. 15.
22. The Latin is *innuit* meaning "gives a nod to" or "gives a sign to."

supplanted human vices through the mortification of his flesh, and at the same time, through preaching the divine word to others.

"He is beloved by God and men, and his memory is a blessing." [Ecclus (Sir) 45:1] This verse is a description of the person of Moses. Moses, whose name is interpreted as "watery," since he was found in the water, and who is beloved by God and men, signifies Christ the Son of God, Who was watery when He gave the kingdom of heaven to the faithful through the water of baptism and the blood of His Passion and Who is found in water when he bestows his grace through sweet rivers of tears for the repentant. Thus, in fact, He says through the prophet: "Seek the Lord while He may be found." [Is 55:6] In Him, in fact, is found the love of God the Father and of men. If Christ is loved by God and by men, then in Him a person is united to God through love and humanity is united with the heavenly.

Oh, how precious and glorious it is, brethren, to love our Savior, Whom [f.98r] God the Father loves! Just as the groom is joined to the bride by love in marriage, so is our love joined to the love of the Father in Christ. When, in fact, we love Christ with a worthy love, we are united with God. We were alienated from God through the sin of the first man, but we are united to Him through love in Christ. So long as our love is in Christ, and so long as God the Father is with us, we are also with Him. We must, therefore, "provide good things not only before God but also before men," [2 Cor 8:21][23] so that through a love of God and neighbor we may be worthy to be loved by God and men.

James is bountiful and is loved by God. Because of his merits, the Lord has worthily crowned on the seats of heaven the one whom He chose on this very day along the Sea of Galilee. He is also loved by the people in this world since from the four regions of the world he is loved, invoked, revered, and honored by all the faithful, and he is especially sought in Galicia. Therefore, this most pious apostle of Christ, James, the solemnities of whose calling and *translation* we are celebrating, deign to help with all our needs and lead us to the

---

23. Also cf. Rom 12:17.

CHAPTER NINETEEN

heavenly kingdom. With Jesus Christ our Lord present, Who lives and reigns as God together with the Father and the Holy Spirit. World without end. Amen.

[CHAPTER 20]

ON THE NONE OF JANUARY[1]
THE OCTAVES OF THE *TRANSLATION* OF SAINT JAMES ARE CELEBRATED

A READING OF THE HOLY GOSPEL ACCORDING TO MATTHEW:

"At that time, Jesus was walking along the Sea of Galilee and saw two brothers...James of Zebedee and John, his brother, in a boat with their father Zebedee, mending their nets, and he called them. And they immediately left their nets and their father and followed him," and so forth. [Mt 4:18, 21–22ff.]

A SERMON FROM SAINTS JEROME, AUGUSTINE, GREGORY, AND CALIXTUS ON THIS READING:[2]

[CAL] In reflecting on the Feast of the Calling and *Translation* of Saint James the Apostle, let us explain, brethren, the reading of the holy Gospel so that your love may learn how our nourishing patron James, the pastor and leader of the people of Spain and Galicia, who was called by the Lord and who left behind his earthly things and deserved to be associated with our Savior, so that by invoking him your life may acquire an [f.98v] example for its salvation. The Evangelist recounts, in fact, that our Savior, in going along the Sea of Galilee, saw two brothers, James of Zebedee and John, his brother, and He called them. He called James "of Zebedee" for the sake of distinguishing him from the other James "of Alphaeus."

---

1. January 5.
2. This is a compilation from the various authors named. Their works are interwoven and indicated to the extent that they can be identified. Some, but not all, are indicated in the margins of CC in a different ink, if not a different hand. Those identified appear within {curly brackets}; attributions not marked in the manuscript are included in [square brackets]: CAL for Calixtus, GREG for Gregory I, JER for Jerome; and AUG for Augustine. S does not identify the authors.

CHAPTER TWENTY

[JER] These two brothers — the sons of Zebedee, namely James and John — bear original names that are most apt to their merits. James, in fact, is interpreted as "supplanter" and John is said to be "in whom is grace" or "grace of the Lord." In fact, when the Lord called, James rejoiced in supplanting the care of the flesh, and when Herod murdered him, in disdaining that flesh. John, because of the grace of special love that he earned through his virginal glory, rested at the Last Supper on the chest of the Redeemer. These two brothers left their bodily father and followed that day our true Father and Savior. According to the Gospel of Mark they were called "Boanerges" or "Sons of Thunder" by the Lord, because "each sounds like the voice of thunder on the wheel of the world," [Ps 76:19 / 77:18] and thus their sound went to the ends of the entire earth, and their words went forth to the ends of the world.[3] And they are fittingly called "Sons of Thunder." One of them called out and from the heavens thundered the theological utterance that no one previously had known how to express: "In the beginning was the Word and the Word was with God and God was the Word." [Jn 1:1] He left this utterance, which is so deep and weighty so that if one ever wanted to thunder more, the world could not grasp it. But both were worthy to be led up to Mount Tabor by the Lord and to perceive the terrific sound from the cloud at one point: "This is My beloved Son. Listen to Him." [Lk 9:35]

[AUG] But one could ask how the Lord called both sets of fishermen brothers from their boats, first Peter and Andrew, and then after going a little farther, another two brothers, the sons of Zebedee, as Mathew and Luke recount.[4] When Luke says that both boats were filled with a large catch of fish, he is speaking of the companions of Peter — James and John, the sons of Zebedee — who were called to help when the full nets could not be drawn up. At the same time, as they were wondering at the great multitude of fish that was caught, He said to Peter only, as they followed Him to the land and left their boats: "Do not fear, from now on you will be a fisher of men." [Lk 5:10] From this it is to be understood that this first happened

---

3. Cf. Ps 18:5 / 19:4, Rom 10:18.
4. Cf. Mt 4:18–22, Lk 5:1–11.

as Luke [f.99r] implies: they were not then called by the Lord but only Peter was foretold that he would be "catching" people. This was not, however, said in such a way that no fish would be caught. For also after the Resurrection of the Lord, we read that they were fishermen. Therefore, it was said at that point that he was to catch people, and it was not said that he already was not to catch fish. From this a situation is given to be understood that they returned to catching fish out of habit so that these things would happen as Matthew and Mark recount, when he called both sets of brothers, and he ordered that they follow Him. The first two were Peter and Andrew, and then the other two were the sons of Zebedee, namely James and John. Then, in fact, they left the boats for the land with no intention of returning, but they just followed Him, as he called and ordered that they follow Him.[5]

This follows: "And they immediately left their nets and their father and followed Him." [Mt 4:22]

{CAL} Saints James and John, therefore, heard the bounteous word of the Lord on the Sea of Galilee and immediately left their nets and their father and followed the Redeemer of the world and left us an example for salvation. For just as they, at the sound of a single order, left behind earthly things and imitated our Savior, so it is fitting that we, who are also called by the admonishments and examples of the Lord, leave behind earthly things and adhere to good works for our Savior. If, in fact, as soon as they heard the voice of the Lord they followed the Savior, what, therefore, will we say, who have so many teachers, and who read so many miracles and examples in the scriptures, and still refuse to go after the Lord?

{GREG} For the Lord Himself calls us: the Lord calls us through the apostles, He calls us through the angels, He calls us through the prophets, He calls us very often through the miracles of the saints, and He calls us very often through scourges. Sometimes He calls us through the favors of this world, and sometimes through adversities,

---

5. Augustine of Hippo, *De Consensu Evangelistarum,* Bk. 2, ch. 17, sect. 41 (PL 34:1096–97); Whitehill correctly ascribed this paragraph (and the following sentence erroneously) to Augustine.

and still our proud mind does not wish to forsake willingly what it loses daily unwillingly. We do not bend to commands, and we are not corrected by scourges. However, might one perhaps say in one's quiet thoughts: "James and John, when they were fishers, at the voice of the Lord left whatever and as much as they had, but they had almost nothing? But in this matter, dearest brethren, we must think of the outlook rather than the amount of property. Those who have retained nothing for themselves have left behind a great deal. However little many have left behind, they have abandoned all. Certainly, we also possess our belongings with love; out of desire, we seek things that we do not have. [f.99v] Therefore, James and John left behind a great deal when they left behind the things they wanted to have. Thus, as many things were given up by the followers as could be desired by those not following. Therefore let no one, even when seeing some people leaving behind many things, say to himself: "I wish to imitate those who disdain this world, but I have nothing to give up." You leave behind many things, brethren, if you renounce all carnal desires.[6]

{CAL} But there are some who leave behind many things and retain carnal desires. Ananias and Sapphira are the very image of such people, as they retained the money from a field that was sold and received a curse of death from Saint Peter the Apostle.[7]

{GREG} Behold how our holy merchants, James and John, purchased the eternal life of the angels with the nets and the boat. You have no real estimate of price, of course. O man, the kingdom of heaven is worth as much you have! For Zacchaeus, the value was giving half of his property.[8] For the widow, the value was two small

---

6. The text "For the Lord...sometimes through adversities" is from *XL Homiliarum in Evangelia liber I, Homilia 36* (PL 75:1272). The rest of the paragraph is from *Homilia 5* (PL 76:1092–95); this text, cited also in ch. 18 above (p. 293), is a little more faithful to the original. A marginal note near the beginning of this paragraph is too faded to read.
7. Cf. Acts 5:1–11.
8. Cf. Lk 19:1–10.

coins.[9] The value was a cup of cold water for another.[10] And for James and John, it was worth the relinquishing nets and their father. So, it will be worth to you what you have given for the hope of the heavenly kingdom. It can, in fact, be asked why Peter and Andrew, James and John, who were fishermen before their conversion, [f.100r] went back to fishing after their conversion, when Truth says: "No one who places a hand on the plough and looks back is fit for the kingdom of God." [Lk 9:62] In fact, we read that they fished after their conversion, as was said. Why therefore did they seek out what they had given up? If, however, the power of discretion takes a look at this, it becomes more readily apparent. For without doubt, a profession that existed without sin before a conversion will even after the conversion be without guilt for those taking it back up. For above all we know that Peter was a fisherman and Matthew was a tax collector. After his conversion Peter went back to fishing. Matthew, however, did not go back to the taxing profession. For it is one thing to seek to earn one's living through fishing and another to increase one's money with the profits of tax collecting. There are several professions that cannot be exercised without sin either at all or hardly. It is necessary that one's mind not turn back after a conversion to those professions that implicate one in sin.[11]

{CAL} Behold, we have heard, brethren, how the earthly fishers are called by God and converted to Him, but let us see in what way they were made fishers of souls. In fact, after Peter and Andrew and James and John heard "Follow Me and I will make you fishers of men," [Mt 4:19][12] they wove for themselves from the New and Old Testaments a net of the Gospel teachings, and they placed it in the sea of this

---

9. Cf. Lk 21:1–4.
10. Mt 10:42.
11. Whitehill ascribes this paragraph to Gregory. This is at least true for the first section from "Behold how" to "cold water for another," a passage also found in ch. 18 (pp. 293–94). At the beginning of this paragraph in CC, a marginal notation, G-G- possibly indicates Gregory as the author. A note in the margin at the end of this paragraph reads *Nō*.
12. Cf. Mk 1:17.

CHAPTER TWENTY

world, and it still travels on the open waves today, catching from the salty and bitter waters whatever happens by in it, both good fish and bad fish — that is, both good men and bad men — since it is not a vulture[13] of persons. Oh, how wondrous is the call of Christ, and what a divine inspiration how the holy apostles were worthy enough to leave behind their earthly things and join the Savior! And those who were fishers of earthly fish were worthy to become fishers of souls. Today is fulfilled the prophecy of Jeremiah: "Behold, I will send to you many fishermen!" [Jer 16:16]

{GREG} In fact, these fishers of the Lord drew fish with the net of the faith to the firmness of the shore, since they showed with the voice of holy preaching the security of the eternal land to the faithful. They did this with words. They did it with letters. They do this daily with the signs of miracles. At their tombs, in fact, miracles very often occur. The sick come and are cured, the blind are illuminated, the lame are made upright, the demoniacs are freed, consolation is given to the sorrowful, and what is more, the prayers of the faithful are heard attentively, and the bonds of sin are broken. Whenever, therefore, we are converted by their preaching or miracles to the love of eternal peace, whenever we are separated from the tumults of earthly things, what else are we but dragged like fish sent into the net who are dragged to the shore?[14]

Then this follows: "And Jesus walked around all of Galilee teaching in their synagogues, preaching the gospel of the kingdom, and healing every sickness and every infirmity in the people." [Mt 4:23]

{CAL} The compassionate and merciful Lord, Who makes His sun rise on the good and the evil, Who rains on the just and the unjust, Who came in the assumed form of a slave to walk His route, and Who came to do the will of the Father, wanted to show this bodily form to

---

13. See ch. 17, n. 162.
14. Whitehill ascribes this paragraph to Gregory. This is true for "In fact, these fishers...with signs of miracles." (*XL Homiliarum in Evangelia liber I, Homilia 24,* 4 [PL 76:1185–86]) "At their tombs...are broken" has been added. "Whenever, therefore...to the shore" is from Gregory, but "by their preaching or miracles" has been inserted; in Gregory it is "by this." Whitehill also appends the opening biblical quote from Mt 4:23 to the Gregory text, which is not the case.

the good and the evil. Some were unable to come into His presence, and He would help these people through the unseen Deity and the goodness of humanity, as those who would see His works or would hear His preaching and would believe in Him through His demonstrated authority [f.100v] would be cured bodily and spiritually. However, such as these who did not want to believe would be doubly guilty in the judgment of God omnipotent.

"And His fame went out in all of Syria, and they brought all the sick people seized by various illnesses and torments and those who had demons and were lunatics and paralytics, and He cured them." [Mt 4:24]

[JER] They were not really lunatics but those thought to be lunatics because of a trick of the demons who observe the lunar phases[15] and who want to defame the creature so that they would abound in blasphemy against the Creator.[16]

{CAL} Matthew, after the calling of the disciples, whom the Lord ordered to fish as they followed Him, reports that He went around Galilee teaching in synagogues and preaching the gospel and curing every sickness. Then, gathering crowds to Himself, He went up on the mountain, and He then used an extended sermon. He therefore gave a reason to understand that what Mark reports after the calling of the disciples happened then: that He went around Galilee and taught in their synagogues. Then afterward he also recalled what he had left out about Peter's mother-in-law, mentioning later what he had left out although he would not recall all omissions.[17]

"And many crowds followed Him from Galilee and Decapolis[18] and Jerusalem and Judea and beyond the Jordan." [Mt 4:25]

---

15. This refers to the theory that "lunatics" are affected by the moon, particularly the full moon.
16. Jerome, *Commentariorum in Evangelium s. Matthaei liber I*, ch. 4 (PL 26:33).
17. The story of Peter's mother-in-law appears later in Matthew (8:14–15) than in Mark (1:29–31) or Luke (4:38–41); however, why he had concerns over this is not clear here.
18. The Decapolis was a group of ten cities on the eastern frontier of the Roman Empire. There is some variation in the group, but it includes towns in modern day Jordan and Syria.

CHAPTER TWENTY

[CAL] We know the fourfold crowd that followed the Lord in the Gospel. One group of them was the one that adhered by faith and heavenly love to the teaching, like the apostles and the other faithful who were called disciples. A second group, however, consisted of invalids and the sick who followed the Lord for the sake of the cures for their health, whom He helped both internally and externally. A third group consisted of those that only rumor and fame brought together, wishing to experience what the work of the Lord might be, so that, by seeing and hearing, they would know whether they should believe. The fourth group of the crowds consisted of those who were led by envy and who wanted to disparage the work of the Lord so that they might seize upon His speech and accuse Him before the princes and so that they might deliver Him to death. And they did this when He permitted it, not when they wanted to.

[CAL] Therefore, brethren, since we celebrate double solemnities, namely of the Calling and of the *Translation* of Saint James, on this very day, we must imitate what we celebrate. If Saint James left his father, mother, and nets and all his earthly [f.101r] things and followed the Lord up to a seat in the heavenly realm through the triumph of martyrdom, we must also leave behind temporal things until, in persevering in good works, we may follow the Lord up to the dominion of the stars where He is seated with Saint James helping.[19] May our Lord Jesus Christ deign to be present for us, Whose kingdom and rule remain without end World without end. Amen.[20]

---

19. The Latin is *disponente* or "arranging, ordering, setting in motion."
20. Whitehill ascribes the text from "The compassionate and merciful Lord" to the end of the sermon to Calixtus.

THE SERMONS
AND
LITURGY
OF
SAINT JAMES

BOOK ONE
OF THE
LIBER SANCTI JACOBI

—

THE LITURGY

ABBREVIATIONS

Ant.	Antiphon
Cant.	Cantor
Cants.	Cantors
Col.	Collect
Com.	Communion
Gosp.	Gospel
Inv.	Invitatory Prayer
Lect.	Lector
Off.	Offertory
Or.	Oration
Pref.	Preface
Ps.	Psalm
R.	Responsorial
Sec.	Secret
Seq.	Sequence
P.Com.	Post Communion
V.	Versicle

[CHAPTER 21]

Here Begins the Office of the Feast of Saint James[1] As Arranged by Pope Saint Calixtus
[21.1][2] For the Ninth Calends of August[3] The Vigil of Saint James

Chapter for Matins[4]

James, servant of God and of our Lord Jesus Christ, to the twelve tribes that are in dispersion: greetings. [James 1:1ff.][5]

Chapter for Terce

James[6] in his days did not fear a prince, and no one overcame him with power, and no word overcame him. [Ecclus (Sir) 48:13–14]

---

1. The text is presented in CC with musical notation, but in S, there is no notation, although there is a rudimentary staff in the form of a line.
2. We have added section numbering to facilitate cross-referencing.
3. July 24.
4. The labels for Chapter, Antiphon, Psalm, etc. are usually abbreviated in rubrics in the text; for example, Antiphon can be *An* or *Ant* or even just *A*. In S, these labels vary somewhat, but we followed CC. We have used left justified headers in a Luminari font to indicate these various entries. This font has also been used for the directions, like "see above," which were in small caps in the manuscript. We have reserved italics to indicate that musical notes accompany the text, with or without staff. Major divisions of the text are marked with a centered Luminari font. This translation concentrates on the text itself, and while making use of the visual cues such as physical placement of the Latin words and the illuminations on the folio, the ornamentation level of letters, and the use of rubrics, these are not footnoted except in salient cases. The headers are almost uniformly in rubrics, but we have used Luminari font here to indicate then. The illuminations and ornamentations are generally of specific letters; these are not able to be shown for two reasons: the illuminated or ornamented letter is often not the same letter as in the English translation, and the word order often places the highlighted letter or word in non-initial position, making it awkward and confusing to indicate.
5. The amount of material referenced is not limited to the words cited; the "ff." indicates that more verses were likely to be included during the service.
6. This is Elias in the biblical text.

Chapter For Sext

In his life he did wondrous things, and in death he worked miracles. [Ecclus (Sir) 48:15] He showed future things and hidden things before they would happen. [Ecclus (Sir) 48:28]

Chapter for None

In every mouth the memory of him becomes as sweet as honey and like music at a banquet of wine. [Ecclus (Sir) 49:2]

Chapter of Saint James for Vespers

"King Herod," he said, "sent his force to afflict some from the Church and he killed James, the brother of John, with a sword."[7]

[21.2] For the Eighth Calends of August[8]

Chapter for Matins

The one who had taken James to the judge for martyrdom was moved by penance and confessed that he was also a Christian.

For Terce

While they were being led on the road, Josias asked James to grant him forgiveness.

Chapter for Sext

And James deliberated a short while and said, "Peace be with you" and kissed Josias, and thus both together were beheaded.[9]

---

7. The "he said" likely refers to Luke, believed to be the author of the Acts.
8. July 25.
9. These four "Chapters" (Vespers of July 24, and Matins, Terce and Sext of July 25) are from Eusebius and convey and amplify the text of Acts 12:1–2. The Vespers text follows Eusebius (Bk 2, ch. 9, sect. 1) and is distinct from the similar text below (the first of the two chapters designated below as "Other"), which is taken directly from Acts of the Apostles, as indicated by the use of *inmisit* rather than *misit* for "sent" and the placement of *suas* ("his") before

CHAPTER TWENTY-ONE

Chapter for None

James[10] overcame crowds not by strength of body or by power of weapons, but rather he subdued the one who vexed him through words. [Wis 18:22]

Chapter for Vespers

Jesus called James of Zebedee and John, the brother of James, and imposed on them the name "Boanerges," which means "Sons of Thunder."[11]

"force," the insertion of *inquit* for "he said," and the use of an infinitive rather than a clause to express "to afflict." These elements consistently mark the Latin version of Eusebius's text of these two verses and are not exactly reflective of the original Greek. Likewise, the three following passages are from Eusebius: Matins (Bk. 2, ch. 9, sect. 2), Terce (Bk. 2, ch. 9, sect. 3), and Sext (Bk. 2, ch. 9, sect. 3). They follow the text of Eusebius exactly with one exception: Calixtus inserts the name Josias, which he has supplied from the Pseudo-Abdias texts on Saint James. Josias's encounter with Hermogenes, the conversion of Josias, and his relationship to Hermogenes are mentioned in the *Veneranda dies* (p. 289) and in the prologue to Bk. III's *Translatio*. See Coffey and Dunn, *Miracles,* xxiii–xxviii, 70–71, 97–105. Additionally, Eusebius attributes the text of the Matins, Terce, and Sext chapters to Clement of Alexandria.

10. The person is not named in the Biblical text, but it is construed to be Aaron.

11. This is the first instance of a text in the liturgy about bestowing on James and John the surname *Boanerges* ("Sons of Thunder," which is a Greek attempt to translate the dialectal Hebrew "Sons of Rage"). This text draws on material from Mk 3:13–17. There are three major variants of this text. The first variant of the text has Jesus ascending the mountain, calling James and John, and then givng them the surname *Boanerges*. It is based entirely on wording from Mk 3:13–17. Some word variation can occur, such as the omission of ascending the mountain. The text begins in Latin *Ascendens* ("Going up" or "He went up") or *Ihesus vocavit* or the inverted *Vocavit Ihesus* ("Jesus called"), and occasionally it appears to begin with the *imposuit* ("He gave") for giving the name *Boanerges*. The most complete rendering of this variant is in ch. 26.7. We designate this variant as the *Jesus vocavit* text. The second variant of the text has the bestowing of the surname *Boanerges* on James and John, but adds the bestowing on Simon the name of "Peter" (meaning "rock"). It is also based on wording from Mk 3:13–17. Minor word variation can

Another Chapter

James[12] was great in accordance with his name and greatest in saving God's chosen and in wiping out insurgent enemies so that he might obtain the inheritance of Israel. [Ecclus (Sir) 46:1–2][13]

Another Chapter

At that same time Herod sent a force to afflict [f.101v] some from the Church, and he killed James, the brother of John, with a sword. [Acts 12:1–2]

Chapter

However, an angel of the Lord immediately struck Herod, and he died, consumed by worms, because he had not given honor to God. [Acts 12:23]

---

occur. It begins with the word "Redeemer," or in one instance, "Jesus." The most complete rendering of this variant is found at 22.4. We designate this variant as the *Redemptor imposuit* text. The third variant of the text has Jesus already on the mountain, giving fitting names to the disciples, and bestowing on James and John the surname *Boanerges*. It has two verses: the first verse is based on Mk 3:13–17; the second is based on Ps 18:5 / 19:4, Ps 28:3 / 29:3, Ps 76:19 / 77:18, Mk 3:17, and Rm 10:18. Minor word variations may occur. The most complete rendering of this variant is found at ch. 23.2. We designate this variant as *Dum esset Salvator*. This Chapter for Vespers is the *Jesus vocavit* variant.

12. Jesus, son of Nave, in the biblical text.
13. "James" is added here. This refers also to the story of Jacob ("Supplanter") in which he takes the birthright of his older brother Esau and ultimately receives the name Israel ("He who contends with God") and becomes a patriarch of the Israelites. Cf. Gen 27–32.

[CHAPTER 22]

IX Calends of August[1]
Vigil of Saint James
[22.1] Responsorials of Saint James
Published by Pope Calixtus from the Gospels

Inv.   *Come, let us adore the Lord and King of kings on these sacred vigils of Saint James.*

Ps.   *Come, let us rejoice...* [Ps 94 / 95][2]

[22.2] Hymn of Saint James
Published by Lord Fulbert, Bishop of Chartres[3]

The heavenly chorus sings!
Let the people of faith rejoice
Let them now intone the eternal
Glory of the apostles.

In their chorus, James
Shines as the first apostle
For by the sword of Herod
He first took up a seat in heaven.

This James of Zebedee
Is called great and virtuous.
He performs in Galicia

---

1. July 24.
2. As with the sermons, we give both the Vulgate numbering of the Psalms, with the KJV numbering of the same Psalms where they differ.
3. Fulbert of Chartres, b.952–970, bishop from 1004–d.1028. Dreves, in the *Analecta hymnica* (AH), presents this and other hymns in a special section of his volume 17 (pp. 189–236), which contains the material that he presents as *Carmina Compostellana* from the CC. His notes on the various works are helpful but sporadic. This work is known as the *Psallat chorus* (AH 17:191).

Thousands of miracles.

To his splendid temple
From all the regions of the world
All peoples come
Proclaiming the praises of the Lord.

Armenians, Greeks, Apulians,
English, French, Dacians, Frisians[4] —
All peoples, languages, and tribes
Go there with offerings.

May zeal of the Father and the Son
And the Holy Paraclete,
Pierce our inner core
Through the intercession of James. Amen.

[22.3] Sung[5] in the First Tone[6]

Ant. *O venerable apostle of Christ, James, propagator of the pious teachers of God, flower of the teachers, lift up the prayers of your people and see fit to intercede for us with the Lord. World without end. Amen.*[7]

Ps. *Confess to the Lord and invoke...* [Ps 104 / 105]

Ps. *Confess...* (the second one) [Ps 105 / 106] [f.102r]

Ps. *Confess...* (the third one) [Ps 106 /107]

V. Pray for us, Saint James.

---

4. See ch. 17, p. 240.
5. The Latin is *Cantus* ("chant") and fits that description here. However, given its application to the various types of passages, we have translated it as "sung."
6. The tones or modes refer to musical settings based on intervals and scales. Each piece begins on the next higher note. For example, Ionian begins on C, Dorian on D, Phrygian on E, Lydian on F, Mixolydian on G, Aeolian on A, and Locrian on B.
7. See ch. 1, n. 25.

CHAPTER TWENTY-TWO

V. That we may be made worthy…[8]

[22.4] A Passage[9] from Mark Sung in the First Tone

R. *The Redeemer gave to Simon the name "Peter" and to James and John the name "Boanerges."*[10]

V. *When Jesus went up the mountain, He called to Himself James and John and gave them the name "Boanerges."*[11]

[22.5] A Passage from Mark Sung in the Second Tone

R. *Jesus called James and John "Boanerges," which means "Sons of Thunder."*[12]

V. *For just as the crash of thunder makes the earth tremble, so also the whole world trembles at their voices.*[13]

Which means…[14]

---

8. The wording of this responsorial and versicle became the final two lines of the prayer "Hail Holy Queen" that originated at Cluny in the 12th century and that was often recited at the end of a mass. Here the usual "Pray for us, O holy Mother of God," is altered to "Pray for us, St. James," to which is added "that we may be made worthy of the promises of Christ." It may be seen in full at ch. 22.15. This formula has its origins in the prayer of Gregory I, the Great, *Roman Orders* (PL 78:1258), where there are directions for the deacon to recite the verse: "Pray for us, Saint N., Alleluia"; to which all respond: "That we may be made worthy of the grace of God." This variant is found in ch. 22.40.

9. The Latin *sermo* has many possibilities, but here and elsewhere in Bk. I, it is used in the sense of "passage."

10. This is the *Redemptor imposuit* text. See ch. 21.2, n. 11.

11. This is the *Jesus vocavit* text. See ch. 21.2, n. 11.

12. This is a short version of the *Jesus vocavit* text. See ch. 21.2, n. 11.

13. This is the *Dum esset Salvator* text. See ch. 21.2, n. 11.

14. This indicates a repetition end of the responsorial: "which means 'Sons of Thunder.'"

[22.6] An Oration of Pope Calixtus
Sung in the Seventh Tone

R. *Most merciful God, Who had us arrive at the solemnities of Saint James, grant that we celebrate them, we beseech, with a clean heart and body.*

V. *Remove us from vices and bestow eternal virtues, so that we may be worthy* [f.102v] *to enjoy with him the solemnities of paradise.*
Grant that we...[15]
Glory be to the Father and the Son and the Holy Spirit...[16]
Grant that...[17]

V. *Jesus gave to James and John*
R. *the name "Boanerges."*[18]
Alleluia. Alleluia.

For Lauds
[22.7] A Passage from Mark
Sung in the First Tone

Ant. *Jesus gave to Simon the name "Peter" and to James and John the name "Boanerges."*[19]
Alleluia.
World without end. Amen.

Ps. *Have mercy on me, O God...*[20]

---

15. This indicates a repetition of the end of the first line of the responsorial: *"grant that...and body."*
16. This standard prayer is prompted but familiar enough that it was never given in full: "Glory be to the Father, and to the Son, and to the Holy Spirit. As it was in the beginning, is now, and ever shall be. World without end. Amen."
17. This indicates a second repetition of the end of the first line of the responsorial: *"grant that...and body."*
18. This is an abbreviated form of the *Jesus vocavit* text. See ch. 21.2, n. 11.
19. This is the *Redemptor imposuit* text. See ch. 21.2, n. 11.
20. No Psalm begins with these words, but Psalms 50 / 51, 55 / 56, and 56 / 57 have them as a second or third line.

CHAPTER TWENTY-TWO

[22.8] A Passage from Mark
Sung in the Second Tone

Ant. *Jesus called James and John "Boanerges," which means "Sons of Thunder."*[21]

Alleluia.

World without end. Amen.

Ps. O Lord, refuge... [Ps 89]

[22.9] A Passage from Pope Calixtus
Sung in the Third Tone

Ant. *For just as the crashes of thunder make the earth tremble, so also the whole world trembled at their voices.*[22]

World without end. Amen.

Ps. O God, my God, to You... [Ps 62]

[22.10] A Passage from Jerome
Sung in the Fourth Tone

Ant. *They are fittingly surnamed Sons of Thunder, as one of them, intoning sound from the heavens, uttered: "In the beginning was the Word."* [Jn 1:1][23]

World without end. Amen.

Ps. Hear, O heavens, what... [Dt 62:1ff.][24]

---

21. This is the *Jesus vocavit* text. See ch. 21.2, n. 11.
22. This is the second part of the *Dum esset Salvator* text. See ch. 21.2, n. 11.
23. This is the *Recte filii tonitrui* from the first quotation from Jerome in ch. 20, incorporating the passage from Jn 1:1.
24. This is the first, but not last, time that a "Psalm" is a text from other than the Psalms of David.

[22.11] A Passage from Jerome Sung in the Fifth Tone

Ant. *James and John heard* [f.103r] *the terrific thunder from the cloud on Mount Tabor: "This is My beloved Son. Hear Him."*[25]

World without end. Amen.

Ps. *Praise the Lord from the heavens...* [Ps 148]

Ch. *James [servant] of God and of our Lord,* **as above**.[26]

[22.12] A Hymn on Saint James Published by Lord Fulbert, Bishop of Chartres[27]

O most holy James,
A brother who is in the family
Of John the Evangelist,
Pray for us assiduously.

You, who are called the supplanter,
Remove us from our vices
So that by your holy prayers
We may be joined with the citizens of heaven.

[May] the zeal of the Father...[28]

V. *James was great*
In accordance with his name... [Ecclus (Sir) 46:1–2][29]
Alleluia.

---

25. This is the *Iacobus et Ioannes tonitrum* from the first quotation from Jerome in ch. 20, incorporating the passage from Luke 9:5.
26. James 1:1, as above in ch. 21.1, Chapter for Matins.
27. This work is known as the *Sanctissime O Iacobe* (AH 17:191); on Fulbert, see ch. 22.2, n. 3.
28. The final stanza of *Psallat chorus* in ch. 22.2.
29. Likely as in ch. 21.2, in the first occurrence of "Another Chapter."

CHAPTER TWENTY-TWO

[22.13] A Passage from Mark Sung in the Eighth Tone

Ant. *Jesus went up to the mountain, called to Himself James and John, and gave them the name "Boanerges."*[30]
Alleluia.
World without end. Amen.
Ps. *Blessed...*[31]
Or. [In the day following] the sacred vigils, **as above**.[32]

[22.14] For Prime

Ant. *Jesus gave...*[33]

[22.15] For Terce

Ant. *Jesus called...*[34]
Ch. James in his days... [Ecclus (Sir) 48:13–14][35]
R. *Pray for us, Saint James.*
Alleluia. Alleluia.
V. *That we may be made worthy of the promises of Christ.*[36]
Alleluia. Alleluia.
Glory be to the Father...

---

30. This is the *Jesus vocavit* text. See ch. 21.2, n. 11.
31. There are a dozen Psalms that begin with *Benedictus* or "Blessed."
32. This is the oration *Vigiliarum sacrarum* or "In the day following the holy vigils..." of Gregory I, the Great. Although the rubric says "as above," it is actually found below in ch. 24.2, where it is attributed to Gregory.
33. This is the *Jesus vocavit* text. See ch. 21.2, n. 11.
34. This is an abbreviated *Jesus vocavit* text. See ch. 21.2, n. 11.
35. See ch. 21.1, n. 6. Chapter for Terce.
36. See ch. 22.3, n. 8.

Pray for us…[37]
V. *Jesus gave…* **as above**.[38]

[22.16] For Sext

Ant. *For just as…*[39]
Ch. *In his life he did wondrous things…* **as above**.[40]
V. *Jesus gave to James and John…*
Alleluia. Alleluia.
V. *The name "Boanerges"*[41]
Alleluia. Alleluia.
Glory be to the Father…
R. *He gave…*[42]
V. *Herod, however, killed James.*
R. *The brother of John with a sword.* [Acts 12:1–2]
Alleluia.

[22.17] For None

Ant. *They are fittingly…Sons…*[43]
Ch. *In every mouth…as…honey,* **as above**.[44] [Ecclus (Sir) 49:2]
R. *However, Herod killed James* [f.103v]
Alleluia. Alleluia.

---

37. This likely indicates a repetition of the responsorial and verse.
38. This is an abbreviated *Jesus vocavit* text. See ch. 21.2, n. 11.
39. This is the second part of the *Dum esset Salvator* text. See ch. 21.2, n. 11.
40. This is likely a reference to the formulation of the Chapter for Sext in ch. 21.1, combining Ecclus (Sir) 48:15 and 48:28.
41. This is an abbreviated *Jesus vocavit* text. See ch. 21.2, n. 11.
42. This likely indicates the repetition of the responsorial and versicle above. The wording "He gave" is interlinear in CC, but in body of the text of S.
43. See ch. 22.10, n. 23.
44. Refers to the "Chapter for None" in ch. 21.1.

CHAPTER TWENTY-TWO

V. *The brother of John with a sword.* [Acts 12:1–2]
Alleluia. Alleluia.
Glory be to the Father...
However, [Herod] killed...[45]

V. *James was great...*
In accordance... [Ecclus (Sir) 46:1–2][46]

Gospel Responsorials on Saint James the Apostle Published by Pope Saint Calixtus with His Antiphons And Hymns for the Feast Days, Namely of the Passion and Translation of This Very Saint James, To Be Sung on the Eighth Calends of August,[47] The Passion of Saint James, and the Third Calends of January,[48] His Translation and Calling Is Celebrated

For Vespers
[22.18] Words of Calixtus
Sung in the First Tone

The sick come to the Tomb of Saint James and are cured, the blind are illuminated, the lame are made upright, the demoniacs are freed, consolation is given to the sorrowful, and, what is greater, the prayers of the faithful are heard assiduously. There barbarous peoples of all the regions of the world come in bands bearing gifts of praise to the Lord.
Alleluia.
World without end. Amen.

Ps. *Children, praise...* [Ps 112 / 113]

---

45. Likely indicates a repetition of the responsorial and versicle.
46. On this versicle, see ch. 21.2, nn. 12 and 13.
47. July 25.
48. December 30.

[22.19] Words of Calixtus Sung in the Second Tone

Ant. *Oh, with what sanctity and grace Saint James shines in the heavens! Through the power of God, he performs so many miracles on the earth. There is no one who can tell how many favors he has offered to those repenting with all their hearts.*
World without end. Amen.

Ps. *Praise the Lord, all you peoples...* [Ps 116 / 117]

[22.20] Words of Calixtus Sung in the Third Tone

Ant. *Let the Galician people [f.104r] rejoice who were worthy to receive such a leader and shepherd as the nourishing James! Let the western peoples and all the famous islands rejoice over such a patron! Let Samaria, imbued with his examples, be glad! Let Jerusalem, reddened by his blood, be glad! Let all those celebrating his feast say:*[49] *"Glory to you, O Lord."*[50]
World without end. Amen.

Ps. *Praise, O my soul...* [Ps 145 / 146]

[22.21] Words of Calixtus Sung in the Fourth Tone

Ant. *Most holy apostle James, assiduous in the welfare of all the people, intercede for us with Christ. You who help those at sea or on land calling to you in their peril, help us now and at the point of death.*[51]

---

49. Included in the *Veneranda dies*, see p. 282; the word "say" has been added here to incorporate the following song.
50. This is the *Gaudeat plebs Gallecianorum* text.
51. This text, known as the *Sanctissime Apostole Iacobe*, consists of two parts. The first part ends with "intercede for us with Christ." The remaining text (from "you who help" to the end) is the versicle of the *O adiutor omnium*, which is found with only one change — *clamantibus ad te* rather than *ad te*

CHAPTER TWENTY-TWO

World without end. Amen.

Ps. *Praise the Lord, since good...* [Ps 146 / 147]

[22.22] Words of Calixtus Sung in the Fifth Tone

Ant. *James, hope and relief for your servants...*
To your people restore life, desired for so long a time,
So that we may be worthy to be joined above in the dwellings among the stars.[52] [f.104v]

Ps. *Praise, O Jerusalem...* [Ps 147 / 147:12ff.]
Ch. *He said Herod sent...* **as above**[53]
R. *While the Savior was...*
V. *For just as...*[54]

[22.23] A Hymn on Saint James Published by Lord William, Patriarch of Jerusalem[55] To be Sung at Vespers and at Lauds

Let the happy people of God through all the churches
Devoutly give to Christ offerings of praise.
He has repressed the cunning of the demon
And has restored to us the alliances

---

clamantibus ("calling to you") — at the end of Miracle 8; on this, see Coffey and Dunn, *Miracles,* 31. See also ch. 23.12, n.33 on the *O adiutor omnium* text.

52. This text consists of the last three lines of the *Iacobe virginei frater* prayer, found in its most complete presentation at the end of the *Veneranda dies,* ch. 17, p. 290.

53. Eusebius, *Ecclesiastial History,* Bk. 1, ch. 9, sect. 1ff. See ch. 21.2, n. 9, Chapter for Sext.

54. This is the *Dum esset Salvator* text. See ch. 21.2, n. 11.

55. Dreves, (AH 17:193) identifies this William as born in Belgium, who was patriarch of Jerusalem from 1130 to 1145 or 1146, and who died in September 1185. This work is known as the *Felix per omnes.*

That lead us to heavenly graces.

Incited by the fire[56] of his love,
James, near the Sea of Galilee,
Spurned for Christ his father, boat, and nets,
Left all, and followed the greater good,
Spreading everywhere the seeds of life.[57]

Christ gave to him the name "Boanerges."
He was found worthy to see Jesus
Transfigured in the majesty with which He shone,
And he who preferred to sit at His right hand
Instructed both Jews and Gentiles.

James the Greater with the rod of the word of God
Destroyed the obstacles of the idols,
Confirmed the peoples in the rule of faith,
Gives various drinks of salvation to the suffering,
And raises the dead piously through the ages.

When he preached the King of all to all people
He fulfilled the ministry of the apostles.
He suffered the lethal sword under Herod,
And he was the first of them to suffer martyrdom,
For which he holds the privilege of the crown.

An angel, however, approaches Herod
And now his flesh is consumed by worms,
His spirit suffers things suitable to his deeds,
As James is elevated with suitable praises,

---

56. The Latin in both CC and S is *fraglancia,* clearly a mistake either for *fragrancia* "odor" or *flagrancia* "burning," given the word *accensus* "kindled" or "incited"; this is in harmony with expressions of "burning love."
57. The Latin *seminaria* is more like "nursery gardens" than "seeds."

CHAPTER TWENTY-TWO

And his body is sought out in Compostela. [f.105r]

Therefore, for the victory of such a soldier,
His church raises up melodies,
Glory be to the Father, to the Begotten, to the Spirit
And may we have the perseverance of this good man
By which we may enjoy the heavenly country. Amen.

V. *Pray for us, Saint James...*[58]

Ant. *With humble devotion, we celebrate the honorable feast of our distinguished patron of this day, James, the apostle of the Lord, so that through his nourishing prayers we may be worthy to be freed from all harmful things.*

Ps. *[My soul] magnifies...*[59]
World without end. Amen.

Or. O God, Who...this... **as below.**[60]

For Compline
[22.24] Words of Gregory
Sung in the Fifth Tone

Ant. *Alleluia, O most holy James!*
Alleluia, intercede for us!
Alleluia! Alleluia![61]

Ps. *When I called upon...* [Ps 4]
World without end. Amen.

---

58. Possibly a free-standing prayer or the formulaic *Ora pro nobis, Beate Iacobe.* See 22.3, n. 8.
59. This is the *Magnificat* prayer as recited by Mary at the Annunciation and drawn from Luke 1:46–55.
60. This is the *Deus qui presentem* of Gregory I, the Great. Oration for Vespers. See ch. 24.4 for complete text.
61. This is the *Alleluia Iacobe sanctissime,* attributed here to Gregory I, the Great.

Ꜧymn   The [heavenly] chorus sings, **as above.**[62]
Ch.   You however are in us, O Lord… [Jer 14:9]
V.   Keep us, O Lord…[63]

[22.25] Sung in the Sixth Tone

Ant.   *Nourishing glow of perpetual light, James the Apostle, illuminates the impure inner parts of your servants so that they may be able to conduct their time in the world in a way that they may capture the joys of life.*[64]

Ps.   *Now dismiss…*[65]
       World without end. Amen.

Or.   God who…this night, **as above.**[66] [f.105v]

Inv.   *Come all you Christians for adoring Christ the eternal King Who honored His apostle James miraculously.*[67]
       Come let us rejoice… [Ps 94]

[22.26] Ꜧymn on Saint James[68] Published by Lord William, Patriarch of Jerusalem,[69] To Be Sung after the "Venite"

Let one rejoice
And be happy.

---

62. This is the *Psallat chorus*. See ch. 22.2 for full text.
63. Cf. Ps 16:8. The wording *Custodi nos, Domine* is used as a response in breviaries and often tied to Psalm 16:8, where it reads "Keep me" rather than "Keep us."
64. This prayer, known as the *Alma perpetui luminis,* attributed here to Gregory I, the Great.
65. The *Nunc dimittis* (Lk 2:29–32) is also known as the *Canticle of Simeon.*
66. This is the prayer *Deus qui hanc noctem,* "O God who illuminates.…" See ch. 24.4, Oration for Compline.
67. This is known as the *Venite omnes Cristicole.*
68. This hymn is known as *Iocundetur et letetur.* AH 17:193–94.
69. See ch. 22.23, n. 55.

CHAPTER TWENTY-TWO

Let the assembly of the faithful
Be increased.
Let one celebrate with solemnities.
Let one celebrate with music.
Let one celebrate with instruments
In spiritual joy.

On this day
In which pious
Melodies
Give due praises,
Let the feast of James
Be celebrated,
Be chanted,
And be raised up.

Let the needy one sing
And the throng of heaven,
And the happy world,
And let our happy gathering clap its hands.
But let the devotion be pure
Of the one singing
And of the one listening
And of the one rejoicing.

Let one send out a song.
Let one bend down the heavens.
Let one touch the sinners[70]
With sonorous words.
Let the earth resound,

---

70. The Latin is *theos,* which is not viable here. AH 17:194 suggests *reos* meaning "defendant, guilty," which has been adapted as "sinners" here.

LITURGY OF SAINT JAMES

Let it give thanks,
Let heaven thunder
And reverberate with praises.

Let nothing sorrowful,
But rather honorable,
Throughout this feast
Be done in all things.
Let the victory of James
Be reveled in,
Be consecrated,
And be praised.

Let the whole world
About to rejoice
Be joyful,
Let the assembly announce this.
Let humanity be amazed
With the signs worthy
Of such a great
And distinguished man.

Oh, happy feast,
To be wondered at,
To be loved,
To be sung!
Oh, solemnity of James
To be amazed at,
To be cultivated,
To be observed!

To the Trinity,
To the Unity,

CHAPTER TWENTY-TWO

To the Deity
Be honor and glory,
To the Triumphing
To the Ruling
To the Reigning
In the heavenly country. Amen.

[22.27] A Passage from Matthew Sung in the First Tone

Ant. *Jesus the Lord saw two brothers, James of Zebedee and John, in a boat with their father Zebedee* [f.106r] *mending their nets, and He called them.* [Mt 4:21]

Ps. *The heavens tell...* [Ps 18 / 19]
World without end. Amen.

[22.28] A Passage from Matthew Sung in the Second Tone

Ant. *"Come follow me," said Jesus to James and John, "and I will make you fishers of men."* [Mt 4:19][71]

Ps. *I will bless the Lord...* [Ps 33 / 34]
World without end. Amen.

[22.29] A Passage from Matthew Sung in the Third Tone

Ant. *James and John immediately left their nets and their father and followed the Savior.* [Mt 4:22]
Alleluia.

Ps. *[My heart] uttered...* [Ps 44 / 45]
World without end. Amen.

---

71. This was actually said to Peter and Andrew, not James and John.

[22.30] A Passage from Mark Sung in the Fourth Tone

Ant. *Jesus called James and John his brother and gave them the name "Boanerges."*[72]
Let all the peoples... [Ps 46 / 47]
World without end. Amen.

[22.31] A Passage from Matthew Sung in the Fifth Tone

Ant. *Jesus led Saint James above to a high mountain and was transfigured before him.*[73]
Ps. *Hear, O God, the supplication...*[74]
World without end. Amen.

[22.32] A Passage from Mark Sung in the Sixth Tone

Ant. *James and John said to Jesus: "Grant that we may sit one at Your right hand and the other at Your left hand in Your* [f.106v] *glory."* [Mk 10:37]
Ps. *Hear, O God, the prayer...*[75]
World without end. Amen.

---

72. This is a variant of the *Jesus vocavit* text. See ch. 21.2, n. 11.
73. Cf. Mt 17:1–2.
74. This is likely Psalm 60 / 61, though several others (e.g., 38:13 / 38:12 and 64 / 65) have similar wording.
75. At least three psalms begin this way (53 / 54, 54 / 55, and 63 / 64) and several others include the general wording (e.g., 4 and 83 / 84).

CHAPTER TWENTY-TWO

[22.33] A Passage from Mark Sung in the Seventh Tone

Ant. *Jesus however said to James and John: "Can you drink this cup that I am to drink?" And they said to Him: "We can."* [Mk 10:38–39][76]

Ps. *Let us confess...* [Ps 74 / 75]
World without end. Amen.

[22.34] A Passage from Gregory Sung in the Eighth Tone

Ant. *The place on high already allures you, but first a road of labor occupies you.*[77]

Ps. *The Lord has reigned, let one exult...* [Ps 96 / 97]
World without end. Amen.

[22.35] A Passage from Luke Sung in the First Tone

Ant. *King Herod sent a band to afflict some from the Church. And he killed James, the brother of John, with a sword.* [Acts 12:1–2]

Ps. *The Lord has reigned, let them be angry...* [Ps 98 / 99]
World without end. Amen.

---

76. The direct "that I drink" of Mark is replaced by the periphrastic wording of Mt 20:22 "that I am to drink."

77. This is the second of two verses found in Gregory I, the Great, *Homilia 27*, 4 (PL 76:1206): *Iam locum celsitudinis quaerebant, ad viam illos Veritas revocat per quam ad celsitudinem venirent. Ac si dicatur: Iam vos locus delectat celsitudinis, sed prius via exerceat laboris* ["They were already seeking the place on high, but Truth calls them back to the road by which they might come to the high place. As if to say, "A place on high already allures you, but first a road of work occupies you."] The full text appears in ch. 23.5. We have designated it as *Iam locum celsitudinis*. It has a few variants (e.g., allures "us" or "you" or "them"). This verse is found, at least in part, in ch. 16, p. 222.

[22.36] A Passage from the Ecclesiastical History Sung in the Second Tone

Ant.   *Herod saw that the death of James was pleasing to the Jews, and he cast Peter into prison.*[78]
World without end. Amen.

[22.37] A Passage from the Ecclesiastical History Sung in the Third Tone

Ant.   *However, the king's sin committed against the apostle suffered no delay of vengeance, but the divine right hand* [f.107r] *was immediately present as an avenger.*[79]

[22.38] A Passage from the Ecclesiastical History Sung in the Fourth Tone

Ant.   *Immediately an angel of the Lord struck Herod because he had not given glory to God, and he had killed James and he died swarming with worms.*[80]
Alleluia.
World without end. Amen.

[22.39] A Passage from Pope Calixtus Sung in the Fifth Tone

Ant. ad canticum[81]

O great James, with the name "Supplanter," remove us from vices through your nourishing merits.[82]
World without end. Amen.

---

78. Eusebius, *Ecclesiastical History,* Bk. 2, ch. 9, sect. 4.
79. Eusebius, *Ecclesiastical History,* Bk. 2. ch. 10, sect. 1.
80. Eusebius, *Ecclesiastical History,* Bk 2. ch. 10, sect. 1.
81. The Latin *ad canticum* can indicate that this is to be intoned as a solo.
82. This antiphon is known as the *Iacobe magne supplantor.* The description of James as supplanter is found in various sermons of Calixtus, especially in

CHAPTER TWENTY-TWO

[22.40] Oration of Saint Gregory

V. Pray for us Saint James
That we may be made worthy of the grace of God.[83]

[22.41] From the Gospel of Mark

V. Jesus gave to James and John
The name "Boanerges."[84]

[22.42] From the Acts of the Apostles

V. However, Herod killed James,
The brother of John, with a sword. [Acts 12:1–2]
Alleluia. Alleluia.

[22.43] From the Book of Wisdom

V. James was great
In accordance with his name. [Ecclus (Sir) 46:1][85]
Alleluia. Alleluia.

[22.44] From the Book of Wisdom

V. He was divinely directed
For the penance of the people. [Ecclus (Sir) 49:3]
Alleluia. Alleluia.

Bk.1, ch. 2. It is also mentioned above in the hymn, *Sanctissime O Iacobe* of Fulbert of Chartres. See ch. 22.12.
83. See ch. 22.3, n. 8.
84. This is an abbreviated *Jesus vocavit* text. See ch. 21.2, n. 11.
85. See ch. 21.2, n. 12.

[22.45] From the Book of Wisdom

V. In his life he did wondrous things,
And in death he worked miracles. [Ecclus (Sir) 48:15]
Alleluia. Alleluia.

[CHAPTER 23]

Responsorials
[23.1] A Passage from Mark Sung in the First Tone

R. *The Savior went on a short way along the shore of Galilee and saw James of Zebedee and John his brother, who were mending their nets* [f.107v] *in a boat, and He called them.*

V. *And they left their father Zebedee on the boat with his hired workers and they followed Him.*[1]

And them...[2]

[23.2] A Passage from Mark and Jerome And the Psalmist Sung in the Second Tone

R. *While the Savior was on the mountain, He gave most fitting names to His disciples and He called James and John "Boanerges," which means "Sons of Thunder."*

V. *For just as the crash of thunder resounds on the wheel of the world, so the sound of the preaching of Saint James went out to all the earth.*[3]

Which means...[4]

---

1. This combination of responsorial and versicle is known as the *Salvator progressus pusillum*. It is based on Mk 1:16–20.
2. This indicates a repetition of the ending of the responsorial: "who were mending...followed Him." The Latin *et ipsos* (literally, "and them") refers to the "who were mending" of this passage.
3. This is the *Dum esset Salvator* text. See ch. 21.2, n. 11.
4. This indicates a repetition of the last words of the responsorial, "which means 'Sons of Thunder.'"

[23.3] A Passage from Mark Sung in the Third Tone

R. *James and John approached the Savior and said: "Master, grant that we may sit, one at* [f.108r] *Your right hand and the other at Your left hand in Your glory."*

V. *Jesus however said to them: "You do not know what you are asking. Can you drink the cup that I drink or be baptized by the baptism with which I am baptized?"*[5]

Grant us…[6]

Glory be to the Father and to the Son and to the Holy Spirit…

Grant us…[7]

[23.4] A Passage from Luke Sung in the Fourth Tone

R. *When James and John saw, however, that the Samaritans did not welcome them, they said to Jesus: "Lord, do you wish us to command that fire should descend from heaven and consume them, as Elias did?"*

V. *And Jesus turned and reproached* [f.108v] *them saying: "Do you know of what spirit you are? The Son of man did not come to destroy souls but to save them."*[8]

As Elias…[9]

---

5. Cf. Mk 10:35–38; this wording is the *Accedentes ad Salvatorem* text.

6. This indicates the repetition of the ending of the responsorial: "grant that we…in Your glory."

7. This indicates the repetition of the ending of the responsorial: "grant that we…in Your glory."

8. Cf. Lk 9:52–55. This wording is the *Cum vidissent autem* text. The last three words, "as Elias did," are not found in the Vulgate, though they are in the KJV and likely were in the version of the Bible used by Calixtus.

9. This indicates the repetition of the last three words of the responsorial: "as Elias did."

CHAPTER TWENTY-THREE

[23.5] A Passage from Gregory Sung in the Fifth Tone

R. *James and John already were seeking a place on high. Truth calls them back to the road by which they might come to the place.*

V. *Already the place on high allures us, but first a road of labor occupies us.*[10]

To the road...[11]

[23.6] A Passage from Luke Sung in the Sixth Tone

R. *However, an angel of the Lord immediately struck Herod, and he was consumed by worms and died because he had not given honor to God and he had killed James.*[12]

V. *On the appointed day, however, Herod, dressed in royal garb, [f.109r] sat before the tribunal, and spoke sublimely to the people.*[13]

And he was consumed...[14]

Glory be to the Father and to the Son and to the Holy Spirit...

Ps. *And he was consumed...*[15]

---

10. This is the *Iam locum celsitudinis*. See ch. 22.34, n. 77.
11. This indicates a repetition of the end of the responsorial "to the road...come to the place."
12. The words "and he had killed James" are not in the biblical text or in Eusebius.
13. Cf. Acts 21–23. This is the *Confestim autem percussit* text. The addition of "and he had killed James" is not found in Acts or Eusebius and appears to be a Calixtus insertion.
14. This indicates a repetition of the end of the responsorial: "and he was consumed...had killed James."
15. This indicates a repetition of the end of the responsorial: "and he was consumed...had killed James."

LITURGY OF SAINT JAMES

[23.7] A Passage Excerpted from the Gospels Sung in the Seventh Tone

R. *This is James, the beloved apostle of Christ, who was worthy to be honored by the Lord before all of the apostles. Among the apostles, he held third place in the calling and numbering and first place in being crowned with martyrdom.*

V. *Oh, how venerable is Saint James! On Mount Tabor, he was worthy to see our Savior, until then mortal, transformed into the Deity, which no prophet or patriarch was ever able to see.*[16]

Among the apostles...[17]

[23.8] A Passage from Luke[18] Sung in the Eighth Tone [f.109v]

R. *King Herod sent a force to afflict some in the Church. And he killed James, the brother of John, with a sword.*

V. *This James is to be honored greatly. He held primacy among the apostles. He was first among them to be crowned with martyrdom. He was worthy to be first to rise to heaven and to possess the scepter of victory, the crown, and a seat in heaven.*[19]

He killed...[20]

---

16. This is the *Hic est Iacobus dilectus,* based on an enumeration of accomplishments of St. James similar to that of the *Hic Iacobus valde venerandus* of ch. 23.9.
17. This indicates a repetition of the second part of the responsorial: "among the apostles...with martyrdom."
18. Luke, as the author of the Acts of the Apostles, a quote from which begins this passage.
19. This is one of several *Misit Herodes rex* texts. It consists of a passage from Acts 12:1–2 and the *Hic Iacobus valde venerandus* passage by Calixtus and is found in ch. 5, p. 70.
20. This indicates a repetition of the end of the responsorial: "he killed...with a sword."

CHAPTER TWENTY-THREE

[23.9] A Passage Excerpted from Matthew and Mark Sung in the First Tone

R. *The Lord suffered together with this James at the time of his passion, as a beloved for a beloved, showing the grief of His flesh and saying to him,*

V. *My soul is sad even unto death.*[21]

Showing...[22] [f.110r]

Glory be to the Father and to the Son and to the Holy Spirit...

Showing...[23]

[23.10] A Passage Excerpted from Both Passions Sung in the Eighth Tone

R. *When Saint James approached the place of his passion, bound with a rope by Josias, he looked and he saw a certain person lying and languishing, and he had mercy on the man and thereupon offered him health.*

V. *When he saw this miracle, Josias was filled with confidence and was baptized by the apostle. And immediately both were together decapitated at the order of Herod after having bent their necks for the name of Christ.*[24]

---

21. This is the *Huic Iacobo condoluit* based on the texts of Mt 26:38 and Mk 14:34. It is also found in CCA 9.2, where it is attributed to Ato of Trier. Some of this wording is found in the Sermon of Calixtus in Bk. 1, ch. 6.

22. This indicates a repetition of at least the ending of the responsorial "showing his grief and saying to him" and probably including the entire versicle as well.

23. This indicates a repetition of at least the ending of the responsorial "showing his grief and saying to him" and probably including the entire versicle as well.

24. This does not represent an exact quote from any of the passions but is drawn from the material found in Bk. 1, ch. 9 in the section based on the PH 16.

He saw a certain person...[25]
Glory be to the Father and to the Son and to the Holy Spirit...
He saw a certain person...[26]

[23.11] A Passage by Lord William, Patriarch Of Jerusalem, Excerpted from the Great Passion[27] Sung in the Eighth Tone

R. *Precious James, brother of the virginal John,*[28]
Who [f.110v] *piously called Hermogenes,*
Who was ferocious in heart, back from the vices of the world
To the honor of the Omnipotent.

V. *Pray for us all with continual prayer.*
Who piously...[29]
Glory be to the Father and to the nourishing Begotten and to the Holy Flame...[30]

---

25. This indicates the repetition of the the end of the responsorial: "he saw a certain...health."
26. This indicates the repetition of the the end of the responsorial: "he saw a certain...health."
27. What follows is not from any known passion, though it uses some passages from Eusebius.
28. This is the *Iacobe virginei frater* text, possibly by Calixtus (ch. 17, p. 290) or by Ato of Trier (CCA 9.3) or by William, as attributed here. Its most complete presentation is that of ch. 17, except for its unique "Glory be" ending found here and in CCA 9.3. In ch. 17, there is a prayer attached to be recited apparently after the work has been sung.
29. This indicates the repetition of Lines 2–4 above: "Who piously...the Omnipotent."
30. The author has varied the usual "Glory be" prayer here, probably to adapt it to the meter of a first line of a stanza. Ato of Trier gives this variation to accompany his work in CCA 9.4.

CHAPTER TWENTY-THREE

To the honor...[31]

Seq. Feasts worthily... **Look for it at the end of the book.**[32]

[23.12] A Certain Bishop Returning from Jerusalem, Snatched from the Dangers of the Seas by Saint James, Published This in the First Tone

R. *O helper of all ages,*
O honor of the apostles,
O bright light of the Galicians,
O advocate of the pilgrims,
James, supplanter of vices,
Release the chains of our sins
And lead us to the port of safety.[33]

V. *You, who help those at sea or on land calling out to* [f.111r] *you in their peril, help us now and in the trial of our death.*
And lead us...[34]

---

31. This indicates the repetition of line 4 above: "To the honor of the Omnipotent."

32. The words *Prosa: Festa digne* may have been inserted later, likely by the same scribe, as it extends well into the left margin and even the *"require in fine libri"* is interlinear. These words are copied into S. The words as written are problematic, consisting of *"festa"* which is either a plural noun ("feasts") or an adjective ("festive"), which is followed by the adverb *"digne"* ("worthily"). Vincent Corrigan, "Music and the Pilgrimage" (Dunn and Davidson, *Pilgrimage*, 55), observes: "Apparently a prosa, *Festa digne*, was to accompany *Iacobe virginei* but no trace of it remains, either in the monophonic section or in the polyphonic troper." It seems possible, however, that *Festa digne* is a mistake for *Salve festa dies*, a work which occupies all of ch. 25.

33. This is the *O adiutor omnium* text. It is included in the texts of Ato of Trier (CCA 9.4) and is also found in ch. 8 of Bk. II of the Miracles, where it is, as here, credited to a bishop returning from Jerusalem. See Coffey and Dunn, *Miracles*, 30–31.

34. This is a repetition of the line "And lead us to the port of safety." Manuscript S indicates this line with a "Ps" that is not found in CC; we know from Miracle 8 that this is a repetition of the last line of the responsorial.

Glory be to God the most excellent and nourishing Father and to His highest and pious Son, and to the Holy Spirit of Them both...

And lead...[35]

V.   *James was great...* [Ecclus (Sir) 46:1][36]

For Lauds
[23.13] A Passage from the Ecclesiastical History Sung in the First Tone

Ant.   *"King Herod," he said, "sent his force to afflict some from the Church, and he killed James, the brother of John, with a sword."*[37]

Alleluia.

Ps.   *The Lord reigned...* [Ps 92 / 93]

World without end. Amen.

[23.14] A Passage from the Ecclesiastical History Sung in the Second Tone

Ant.   *The one who had taken James to the judge for martyrdom was moved by penance and confessed that he was a Christian.*[38]

Alleluia.

Ps.   *Rejoice unto God...*[39]

World without end. Amen.

---

35. This indicates a repetition of the line: "And lead us to the port of safety."
36. See ch. 21.1, Matins, for the full text.
37. Eusebius, *Ecclesiastical History*, Bk. 2, ch. 9, sect. 1; Cf. Acts 12:1–2. For this and the other selections that follow here from Eusebius, see ch. 21.2, n. 9.
38. Eusebius, *Ecclesiastical History*, Bk. 2, ch. 9, sect. 2.
39. Psalm 97 and 99 (98 and 100) begin with these words, and three others have it toward the beginning: 46 / 47, 65 / 66, and 80 / 81.

CHAPTER TWENTY-THREE

[23.15] A Passage from the Ecclesiastical History Sung in the Third Tone

Ant. He said: "They were both led together to the punishment of death."[40]

Alleluia.

Ps. O God, my God...[41] [f.111v]

World without end. Amen.

[23.16] A Passage from the Ecclesiastical History Sung in the Fourth Tone

Ant. While they were being led on the road, Josias asked James to give him forgiveness.[42]

Alleluia.

Ps. Bless...[43]

World without end. Amen.

[23.17] A Passage from the Ecclesiastical History Sung in the Fifth Tone

Ant. And James deliberated a short while and said, "Peace be with you," and kissed him, and thus both together were beheaded.[44]

Alleluia.

Ps. Praise the Lord from the heavens... [Ps 148 /149]

World without end. Amen.

---

40. Eusebius, *Ecclesiastical History*, Bk. 2, ch. 9, sect. 3.
41. Three psalms begin with this: 21 / 22, 42 / 43, and 62 / 63.
42. Eusebius, *Ecclesiastical History*, Bk. 2, ch. 9, sect. 3. Josias is not named by Eusebius.
43. While no psalm begins with this, it is found within Psalms and also in a number of passages of Daniel.
44. Eusebius, *Ecclesiastical History*, Bk. 2, ch. 9, sect. 3.

Ch. The one who had taken…[45]
R. *Pray for us, Saint James.*
V. *That we may be made worthy of the promises of Christ.*
Glory be to the Father and to the Son and to the Holy Spirit…
Hymn Happy through all…[46]
V. He was divinely directed… [Ecclus (Sir) 49:3]

[23.18] Sung in the First Tone

Ant. *O James, apostle of Christ, invincible soldier of the eternal King, you who in the brilliant court of the apostles shines like the sun and glistens among the stars in glory, our throng beseeches you that, through your prayer, you may remove all our sins, and that, with you as our leader, we may be worthy to ascend to the realms of heaven.*[47]
Ps. Blessed…[48]
World without end. Amen.
Or. Most glorious solemnity, **as below.**[49]
R. *Pray for us, Saint James,*
V. *That we may be made worthy of the promises of Christ.*[50]
Glory be to the Father and to the Son and to the Holy Spirit…[51] [f.112r]

---

45. Eusebius, *Ecclesiastical History*, Bk. 2, ch. 9, sect. 2. This wording also forms the text of the antiphon in ch. 23.14.
46. This is the *Felix per omnes* hymn from ch. 22.23.
47. This is the *Apostole Christi Iacobe*.
48. A dozen psalms begin with *Benedictus* ("Blessed").
49. This is the *Gloriosissimam sollemnitatem* text. See ch. 26.1, Oration.
50. This is the *Ora pro nobis Beate Iacobe* text. See ch. 22.3, n. 8.
51. The responsorial, versicle, and "Glory be…" were added in a smaller but seemingly the same or a similar hand below the text. They do not appear in S, possibly indicating a later addition.

CHAPTER TWENTY-THREE

[23.19] For Prime

Ant. *He said: "He sent in..."*[52]

[23.20] For Terce

Ant. *The one who had taken...*[53]
Ch. *While they were being led*[54] *on the road...* **as above.**[55]
R. *Pray for us, Saint James.*
Alleluia. Alleluia.
V. *That we may be made worthy of the promises of Christ.*
Alleluia. Alleluia.
Glory be to the Father...
R. *Pray for us...*
V. *He gave...*[56]

[23.21] Another Responsorial

R. *O James, hope [of slaves] and relief for your servants.*[57]
Alleluia. Alleluia.
V. *Mercifully accept the pious prayers of your servants.*[58]
Alleluia.
Glory be to the Father and to the Son and to the Holy Spirit...

---

52. Eusebius, *Ecclesiastical History*, Bk. 2, ch. 9, sect. 1. Ch. 23.19 is omitted in S.
53. The passage is from Eusebius, *Ecclesiastical History*, Bk. 2, ch. 9, sect. 2. This likely contains the same wording as ch. 23.14 above. Section 23.20 is omitted in S.
54. The Latin should read *ducerentur* for "were lead" as is the case in CC, but S has a scribal error *induiterentur*.
55. Eusebius, *Ecclesiastical History*, Bk. 2, ch. 9, sect. 3. This likely refers to the wording of the antiphon of ch. 23.16.
56. This is an abbreviated *Jesus vocavit* text. See ch. 21.2, n. 11.
57. This is line 6 of *Iacobe virginei frater*. See ch. 23.11, n. 28 Responsorial.
58. This is line 7 of *Iacobe virginei frater*. See ch. 23.11, n. 28 Responsorial.

R.   *O James...*[59]
V.   *Jesus gave...*[60]

[23.22] For Sext

Ant.   He said: *"They were led..."*[61]
Ch.   And James deliberated a short while...[62]
R.   *Jesus gave to James and John*
       Alleluia. Alleluia.
V.   *The name "Boanerges."*[63]
       Alleluia. Alleluia.
       Glory be to the Father...
R.   *He gave...*[64]
V.   *Herod, however, killed...*[65]

[23.23] Another

R.   *James, invincible shepherd, lift up our prayers.*[66]
       Alleluia. Alleluia.
V.   *Stretch out your hand to the fallen, so that we may be able to rise.*
       Alleluia. Alleluia.
       Glory be to the Father and to the Son and to the Holy Spirit...

---

59. This likely indicates a repetition of the previous responsorial.
60. This is likely an abbreviated *Jesus vocavit* text. See ch. 21.2, n. 11.
61. Eusebius, *Ecclesiastical History*, Bk. 2, ch. 9, sect. 3.
62. Eusebius, *Ecclesiastical History*, Bk. 2, ch. 9, sect. 3.
63. This is an abbreviated *Jesus vocavit* text. See ch. 21.2, n. 11.
64. This indicates a repetition of the previous responsorial.
65. Eusebius, *Ecclesiastical History*, Bk. 2, ch. 9, sect. 1.
66. These five lines, together with the repetition of the last responsorial, constitute the *Iacobe pastor inclite* text.

R.	James...[67]
V.	He, however, killed James...[68]

[23.24] For None

Ant.	When they were led on the road....[69]
Ch.	James overcame crowds... **as above**.[70]
R.	Herod, however, killed James... [f.112v] Alleluia. Alleluia.
V.	The brother of John, with a sword.[71] Alleluia. Alleluia. Glory be to the Father and to the Son... He killed...[72]
V.	Jesus gave...[73]

[23.25] For Vespers

Ant.	He said: *"He sent... "*[74]
Ps.	The Lord said... [Ps 109]
Ant.	He who had taken...[75]
Ps.	Praise, you children... [Ps 112]
Ant.	They were led...[76]

---

67. This indicates a repetition of the responsorial: "James, invincible shepherd...."
68. Eusebius, *Ecclesiastical History*, Bk 2, ch. 9, sect. 1.
69. Eusebius, *Ecclesiastical History*, Bk 2, ch. 9, sect. 3.
70. Cf. Wis 18:22. See ch. 21.2, Chapter for Nones.
71. Eusebius, *Ecclesiastical History*, Bk 2, ch. 9, sect. 1.
72. This indicates a repetition of the responsorial: "Herod...sword."
73. This is an abbreviated *Jesus vocavit* text. See ch. 21.2, n. 11.
74. Eusebius, *Ecclesiastical History*, Bk 2, ch. 9, sect. 1.
75. Eusebius, *Ecclesiastical History*, Bk 2, ch. 9, sect. 2.
76. Eusebius, *Ecclesiastical History*, Bk 2, ch. 9, sect. 3.

Ps. I believed... [Ps 115 / 116:10ff.]
Ant. *While they were being led...*[77]
Ps. In converting...[78]
Ant. *And James [deliberated] a short while*[79]
Ps. Lord, you have tested me... [Ps 138 / 139]
Ch. Jesus called James...[80]
R. O helper of all...[81]
Hymn Let the happy people of God through all...[82]
V. He was [divinely] directed... [Ecclus (Sir) 49:3]

[23.26] Sung in the Third Tone

Ant. O light and honor of Spain, most holy James, who holds primacy among the apostles and was the first of them to be crowned with martyrdom! O singular help, who was worthy to see our Redeemer, until that time only as a mortal, transformed into the Deity, hear attentively the prayers of your servants and intercede for our salvation and that of all the peoples.[83]

[My soul] magnifies...[84]

World without end. Amen.

Or. God, Who this feast day... **as below.**[85]

---

77. Eusebius, *Ecclesiastical History*, Bk 2, ch. 9, sect. 3.
78. Two psalms (9 and 125 / 126) have this expression.
79. Eusebius, *Ecclesiastical History*, Bk 2, ch. 9, sect. 3.
80. This is the *Jesus vocavit* text. See ch. 21.2, n. 11.
81. This is the *O adiutor omnium* text. See ch. 23.12
82. This is the *Felix per omnes* hymn. See ch. 22.23. There are no notes above these words, but they are placed below the staff, surely indicating that they be sung as found above.
83. This is the *Lux et decus Hispanie* text.
84. This is the *Magnificat*. See ch. 22.23, n. 59.
85. This is the *Deus qui diem festum*. See ch. 26.9, Oration for Vespers, where it is ascribed to Gregory I, the Great.

CHAPTER TWENTY-THREE

[23.27] For Compline

Ant.	*Alleluia, O most holy James...*[86]
Ps.	When I called... [Ps 4]
Hymn	The [heavenly] chorus sings... **as above.**[87]
Ch.	You, however, are in us... [Jer 14:9]
V.	Keep us... [f.113r][88]
Ant.	Nourishing [glow] of perpetual light...[89]
Ps.	Now dismiss...[90]
Or.	O God, Who this night...[91]

[23.28] A Statement of Pope Calixtus On the Matins of Saint James

All nine psalms to be performed on the feast day of Saint James, or at least three of them, should be carefully read[92] at matins, as well as three readings from the preordained sermons throughout each day up to the end of the octaves. And all the hours should be sung just as they are on the feast day. And the same psalms, like "The Lord said," [Ps 109] should be read at vespers. However, on the second day after the feast of Saint James, matins should be read with nine readings because of the feast of Saint Josias the Martyr, which must be celebrated on that day. There should also be read-

---

86. This is the *Alleluia Iacobe sanctissime.* See ch.22.24, n. 61.
87. This is the *Psallat chorus.* See ch. 22.2 for full text. The Latin here is *psallet* or "let the chorus sing" (subjunctive) as opposed to above where the Latin is *psallat* or "the chorus sings" (indicative).
88. This is the *Custodi nos.* See ch. 22.24, n. 63.
89. This is the *Alma perpetui luminis.* See ch. 22.24, n. 64.
90. This is the *Nunc dimittis* or Canticle of Simeon. See ch. 22.25, n. 65.
91. This is the *Deus qui hanc noctem*, attributed to Gregory I, the Great. See ch. 24.4, Oration for Compline.
92. In this passage, the Latin verbs *dico* ("to say") and *decanto* ("to sing") are used in most cases to indicate the "reading" as opposed to the "singing" of the passage.

ings from the *Great Passion*,[93] in which the passion of Saint Josias is written. And the responsorial: "Behold I send you"[94] should be read. Since Josias received the crown of martyrdom with the apostle, the apostolic office must be fittingly celebrated in the manner of that kind of feast for Josias as well. However nine responsorials: "When he approached,"[95] and the Antiphons for the lauds, "He said, 'He sent,'"[96] and the hours should be sung similarly to the day of Saint James. The octaves of Saint James must be celebrated with nine readings, just as one should celebrate on the feast day itself, but on the second Calends[97] of August, because of the feast for Saint Peter in Chains,[98] which is celebrated on the eighth day of the feast of Saint James.

[23.29] Another Work of Pope Calixtus On Both the Masses and Matins of Saint James

If the vigil of Saint James should fall on a Sunday, it should be celebrated on the Saturday before with fasting and the proper of the mass and matins for him, or this should be celebrated on the Sunday itself without fasting. If, however, one wants it to be celebrated on the Sunday itself, only the six responsorials and the psalms of the first two nocturnes from the Sunday should be sung, and three psalms and three responsorials of the third nocturn from the vigil should be read, as well as nine readings from the exposition:

---

93. See above, ch. 9, pp. 153–67.
94. Cf. Mt 10:16, Lk 10:3, Jn 20:21; however, no such responsorial is found in Bk. 1.
95. See ch. 23.10.
96. Eusebius in *Ecclesiastical History*, Bk. 2, ch. 9, sect. 1.
97. July 31. The "second Calends" is usually the *pridie* ("the day before"), though both references are found in this manuscript.
98. See Acts 12:3–9. For more information about the complications of overlap of these two feasts, see Bk. III, *Translatio* (Coffey and Dunn, 90–92).

CHAPTER TWENTY-THREE

"The vigils of the most holy night"[99] and the greater mass[100] and lauds and the hours and all the other parts of the vigil should be read.[101] If, however, the feasts should occur on Sunday, the proper of the mass of Saint James and the matins proper to this apostle should be sung. For, in fact, the Sunday matins and masses can be sufficiently celebrated before and after. And if the Sunday should occur within the octaves or on the seventh day of the octaves, the proper of the mass of Saint James and nine of the readings of matins should likewise be sung. However, the octave of Saint James should be celebrated on the second Calends of August[102] with the proper matins and the proper of the mass, since they may not be celebrated on the eighth day because of the feast of Saint Peter in Chains that occurs at that point. On each and every day from his vigil until the eighth day of his feast, I have published the proper of the mass for the honor of the apostle, with the Holy Spirit dictating it.

In the chapters of the readings composed for the masses of Saint James, namely within the octaves and on the present vigil and for his *Translation,* I brought together readings, of course, that are drawn from the Book of Wisdom, and I have composed these with the name of "Saint James," that is "Jacob," in part because it is fitting and in part because the ecclesiastical usage established by Saint Jerome and Saint Gregory in the lectionary book pertains [f.113v] in this way: "Behold the great priest"[103] and "The Lord has led the just man through the straight roads" [Wis 10:10] and "The just man, if he should be preoccupied by death." [Wis 4:7] The beginnings of these readings are not found in the same

---

99. This is a reference to the sermon of Calixtus of ch. 2, pp. 23–62.

100. The Latin is *maior* and while literally "the greater," it could refer to the main or high mass.

101. The text "celebrated on the...should be read" is found in the margin of CC but in the text of S.

102. July 31.

103. The hymn *Ecce sacerdos magnus* is of uncertain origin. The term "great priest" appears in Ecclus (Sir) 50:1, without the "Behold," but with other words added.

manner in the reading as they are found in the Book of Wisdom from which they are drawn. For, in fact, one does not find in the Book of Wisdom "Behold the great priest," but something else is found for these. Similarly, where "the just one" (as object) or "the just one" (as subject) is written, something else is found for this in the Book of Wisdom. Likewise, in several places in the lectionary, this same thing happens. Therefore, let no one desiring the truth yet unaware of it dare to remove the name of Saint James, which we justly composed in the headings of the readings, nor should one prohibit them from being read. Similarly, no one should reject reading in the church that reading, which is composed for the mass of the sixth day within the octaves, in which there is also understood to be a reproach of evil innkeepers on the road of Saint James.[104] Although, in fact, that reading may be understood to be about the exit of Israel from Egypt, still something about it is fitting to be understood about the evil innkeepers of the road of Saint James. And whatever is written in the aforementioned readings, in the beginnings of which the name of Saint James is placed, although it may be read about other holy people, still it is completely acceptable to be understood to be about James.

No one should reject reciting the reading from the *Ecclesiastical History:* "He said, 'He sent...,'"[105] which we composed for the mass of the feast day of Saint James, since it is of great authority. In fact, the book of the *Ecclesiastical History* and the book of the Acts of the Apostles are held to be of equal authority, since both speak about the "acts of the apostles," not in spiritual or expository ways but historically.

On the vigil of Saint James with the lord archbishop of Compostela or with clerics of any church singing a litany in a procession with a cross and thurible and blessed paschal candle, one

---

104. See ch. 15 (pp. 205–19) but particularly ch. 17 (pp. 227–90), the *Veneranda dies.*
105. Eusebius, *Ecclesiastical History,* Bk. 2, ch. 9, sect. 1, citing Acts 12:1. Calixtus appears to be aware that the Latin *misit* ("sent") was used in Acts and *inmisit* ("sent" or "sent off") was used in Eusebius.

CHAPTER TWENTY-THREE

should go to bless the fonts and to baptize infants, if any should be present. Moreover, they can be blessed on that day with the same degree of authority with which the fonts are blessed within Pentecost season and at the feast of Saint Michael or at another time. If, in fact, the fonts are blessed and infants are baptized not only on the vigil of Easter and Pentecost but also on other days in the course of the year as an ordinary practice, then with how much greater justice must they be blessed on the vigils of the holy apostles whom the Lord established as ministers of this very baptism, [f.114r] when He said: "Go and teach all peoples and baptize them." [Mt 28:19] And if the fonts cannot be blessed on all the vigils of the apostles — either because of preoccupation with other matters or because no children are present for baptizing — they may at least be blessed on the vigil of Saint John the Baptist and of the holy apostles Peter and Paul and of Saint James of Zebedee. Thus, if there were no fonts in some church, or if there were either some monks or some religious present before the mass on the vigil of Saint James, they may sing a full litany, with *"Kyrie, eleison,"*[106] "Christ, hear us" and "God the Father of heaven, have mercy." The clerics may, however, read while going to the fonts, three or four saints from each order. And at the end of the litany, they should say three times, as is the custom, the *Agnus Dei*,[107] and the fonts should be blessed. Then an infant should be baptized, if one should be present. After the infant is baptized, the clerics should go back to the chorus reciting the litany: including *"Kyrie, eleison,"* "Christ, hear us," "Holy Trinity, one God, have mercy," "Holy Virgin of virgins,"[108] and three or four other saints from each order should be read. And before the *"Agnus Dei"* is said three times at the end of the litany and before the final *"Kyrie, eleison,"* the cantor should say on the third one "Light

---

106. This is the only Greek prayer left in the ordinary of the mass: "Lord, have mercy."
107. This is the Latin prayer beginning "Lamb of God...."
108. These are lines typical of litanies that were sung in a verse response manner. He is listing some of the lines that should not be omitted or should be included in the baptism.

up": a first time in the first voice, a second time in the second voice, and a third time in the third voice. And then the candles must be lit around the altar, which signifies the "Light up."

Here ends the statement.

[CHAPTER 24]

IX Calends of August[1]
[24.1] A Mass Published by Lord Pope Calixtus for the Vigil of Saint James of Zebedee That Is Sung About the Ninth Hour As on the Vigil of Pentecost

> Lord, have mercy.
> Christ, hear us.
> Father of Heaven… **should follow**[2]

And on this day the fonts must be blessed.

> James and John said to Jesus: "Grant that we may sit, one at Your right hand and the other at Your left hand, in Your glory." [Mk 10:37]

[24.2] Gregory

Ps.   *Already the place on high allures us,* [f.114v] *but first a road of labor occupies us.*[3]
       Glory be to the Father…
       Ages… Amen.[4]

Or.   In the day following the holy vigils of Your apostle James, which we carried out with devout fasts and with worthy offices, we ask, O Lord our God, that to the degree that his venerable celebration comes near we may move forward much more devotedly in celebrating fittingly his salubrious

---

1. July 24.
2. This indicates the start of a standard litany. Here it is likely the Litany of the Saints, which begins with several lines of the *Kyrie*, then an appeal to the triune Godhead, with a listing of appeals to saints following that. This last line is usually *Pater de caelis Deus* and it is followed with *miserere nobis* or "have mercy on us."
3. This is the *Iam locum celsitudinis*. See ch. 22.34, n. 77.
4. The text reads *seculorum Amen* ("of ages. Amen.") presumably for "World without end. Amen."

mystery, such that we may be worthy to have his fellowship in heaven. Through our Lord …[5]

A Reading from the Book of Wisdom:
"James, in his days, did not fear a prince, and no one overcame him with power, and no word overcame him. And his dead body prophesied. In his life he did wondrous things, and in death he performed miracles." [Ecclus (Sir) 48:13–15][6] "He showed future things and hidden things before they would happen." [Ecclus (Sir) 48:28] "The memory of him[7] has become like a compound of fragrance and the work of the unguent merchant. In every mouth, the memory of him will be as sweet as honey and like music at a banquet of wine. He was divinely directed for the repentance of the people." [Ecclus (Sir) 49:1–3] "He[8] raised up for us the walls that were knocked down and he made the gates and the locks hold and he raised up our houses." [Ecclus (Sir) 49:15] He[9] was the prince of his brethren, the support of the people, the ruler of his brethren, the stability of the people. "And his bones were visited, and after death they prophesied." [Ecclus (Sir) 49:17–18]

[24.3] Mark

Tract *Jesus called unto Himself James of Zebedee and John, the brother of James.*

V. *And He gave them the name "Boanerges," which means "Sons of Thunder."*[10]

The Lord be with you.

---

5. This is the *Vigiliarum sacrarum*. See ch. 22.13, n. 32.
6. See ch. 21.1, n. 6, Chapter for Terce.
7. The biblical "of Josias" has been replaced by "of him."
8. The biblical text is referring to Nehemias.
9. The biblical text is referring to Joseph the Patriarch.
10. This is the *Jesus vocavit* text. See ch. 21.2, n. 11.

CHAPTER TWENTY-FOUR

Be present, we beseech, almighty God, so that, as you order us to abstain from forbidden [f.115r] foods at this consecrated fast of the vigils of Saint James Your apostle, you may also grant us, though his pious intervention, to abstain from all vices, such that we may be able to celebrate worthily his feast with purified hearts, through our Lord...

A Reading of the Epistle of Saint James the Apostle:

James, servant of God and of our Lord Jesus Christ, to the twelve tribes that are in dispersion, [sends] greetings. Consider all the joy, my brethren, when you happen upon various temptations. Know that the testing of your faith produces patience. Patience, however, may have a perfect result, so that you may be complete and whole and lacking in nothing. If one of you, however, needs wisdom, let that person seek it from God, Who gives to all abundantly and Who does not reproach, and it will be given to that person. One must ask, however, in faith and not hesitating in any way. In fact, someone who hesitates is like the wave of the sea that is moved and carried about by the wind. That person, therefore, should not count on receiving anything from the Lord. A two-faced person is inconstant on all paths. Let the humble brother, however, be glorified in his exaltation. The rich person will also [be glorified] in his humility and will pass away[11] like the floret of the grass. For the sun rose with heat, dried the grass, and made its floret fall off, and the beauty of its form disappeared. Thus also, the rich person will waste away on the path. Blessed is the one who suffers temptation, since when one has been tested, one will receive the crown of life, which God promised to those who love Him. [James 1:1–12]

R. *Your friends are exceedingly honored, God, and their principality is exceedingly strengthened.*

V. *I will count them, and they will be multiplied more than the sand.* [f.115v] [Ps 138:17–18 / 139:17–18]

---

11. CC and S both read *transivit* ("passed away") for the biblical *transibit* or ("will pass away").

LITURGY OF SAINT JAMES

Tract *James[12] in his life did wondrous things and in death he worked miracles.* [Ecclus (Sir) 48:15]

V. *He[13] was divinely directed for the repentance of the people,* [Ecclus (Sir) 49:3] *and his[14] bones were visited.* [Ecclus (Sir) 49:18]

Continuation of the Holy Gospel according to Mark:

At that time, Jesus went up the mountain and called to Himself those whom He wished, and they came to Him. And He arranged that there would be twelve with Him and that He would send them to preach. And He gave them the power to cure sickness and to cast out demons. And He gave Simon the name "Peter." And He called James of Zebedee and John, the brother of James, and He gave them the name "Boanerges," which means "Sons of Thunder," and also Andrew and Philip and Bartholomew and Matthew and Thomas and James of Alpheus and Thaddeus and Simon the Canaanite and Judas Iscariot, who betrayed Him. [Mk 3:13–19]

[24.4] Gregory

Off. *Certainly, while the sons of Zebedee, through the intervention of their mother, sought to be allowed to sit one at the right of God and the other at* [f.116r] *the left, and heard, "Can you drink the chalice that I am to drink?"[15]*

Alleluia.

V. *James and John were already seeking a place of honor. Truth calls them back to the road by which they might come to the honor. And He says: "Can you drink?"[16]*

---

12. In the biblical text, this is said for Elias.
13. In the biblical text, this is said for Josias.
14. In the biblical text, this is said for Joseph the patriarch.
15. This is the *Certe dum filii* text. It is based on Gregory I, the Great, *Homilia 27*, 4 (PL 76:1206); cf. Mt 20:20–22.
16. This begins as a form of the *Iam locum celsitudinis* from Gregory I, the Great, *Homily 27*, 4 (PL 76:1206) and is amplified with words from Mt 20:22.

CHAPTER TWENTY-FOUR

Sec. Lord, we beseech You that You might deign to sanctify these gifts offered to You on these holy vigils of Saint James Your apostle, with Your gentle blessing, so that, through them, we may be joined in association with him in the heavens, whose birth we have already preceded on earth with fitting offerings, through...

Pref. Eternal God...[17]and to entreat Your majesty humbly that we, who have gone forth with fasts and devout offices at the solemn[18] feast of Your apostle Saint James, may be helped in Your sight by his merits and that we may be instructed by his examples, through Christ our Lord, through Whom...

Com. *I chose you from the world so that you would go and bring fruit, and so that your fruit would remain.*[19] [Jn 15:16]

P.Com. [f.116v] We accept Your desired sacraments, O Lord, as we venerate the vigils of your nourishing apostle James with desired compliance and worthy fasting. Be present, we beseech, that through these things You may cause us to be cleansed from our sins, to be devout in celebrating his coming feast, and to be inhabitants of the heavenly kingdom, through...

Oration for the Hours:

Most merciful God, Who had us come to the solemnities of Saint James Your apostle, grant, we beseech You, that we may celebrate them with a clean heart and body, so that we may be worthy to enjoy the solemnities of paradise, through...

Oration for Vespers:

God, Who illuminates this most holy night of Saint James Your apostle, grant, we beseech, that those who convene

---

17. After this opening, the elipsis indicates the insertion of wording from an appropriate preface to be followed by the wording provided here.

18. While the Latin is the nominative *sollempnis,* the ablative would seem to fit here.

19. Cf. Jn 15:16; however, the "from the world" is interpolated from Jn 15:19.

LITURGY OF SAINT JAMES

in churches for celebrating his feast may be rewarded with spiritual joys together with him in heaven, through…[20]

Oration for Compline:

God, Who brightens this solemn night of Saint James Your apostle, remove from us the darkness of vices and brighten our hearts with the light of virtues, through…[21]

In the Night for Matins:

God, Who wishes to lighten this serene night, or day, of your beloved apostle James with celebration, grant, we beseech, that our minds be cleansed from the darkness of sins and gleam with an abundance of virtues, through…

---

20. This is the *Deus qui presentem* text.
21. This is the *Deus qui hanc noctem* text.

[CHAPTER 25]

Verses of Pope Calixtus for Singing in the Procession Of Saint James on the Solemnity of His Passion[1] And of His Translation

1. Greetings, festive and venerable day for the victory of Saint James.
2. On this day he enters the heavens and is close to God.
    Greetings, festive...[2]
3. At the first sound of the Lord, James of Zebedee
4. Set aside father, net, and boat for the faith.
    Greetings... [f.117r]
5. Leaving all things, he served divine love,
6. For Whom he did not fear reproaches or whippings or dying.
    Greetings...
7. He teaches the Gentiles, and he rebukes the Jews.
8. He sows the faith on earth, and he is fruitful for God.
    Greetings...
9. He strives to submit the human race to Christ alone
10. And is indignant at abiding vain idols.
    Greetings...
11. In fighting heresies he needs no excuse.
12. He castigates the reprobates while helping the good.
    Greetings...
13. While he is so fruitful, he suffers the sword under Herod.
14. After life, he enjoys perpetual life.
    Greetings...

1. July 25.
2. In CC, this text is spaced as in this translation, stretching over three full folios, with each line separated and assigned its own staff. While this is the norm for modern works, it is unusual in a time when parchment was scarce and expensive. In addition, many of the lines have the empty staff for the music extended to the right margin, where "Greetings" is indicated. This work is found in the AH 17:194–95. Here the lines have been numbered to reflect their order in CC, whereas the order in S is: 1, 2, 3, 4, 5, 14, 6, 15, 7, 16, 8, 17, 9, 18, 10, 19, 11, 20, 12, 21, 13, 22, 23, 29, 24, 25, 30, 26, 31, 27, 32, 28, 33. This first line (or possibly lines 1 and 2) serves as the refrain throughout.

15. *He is the first apostle who is deprived of fragile life,* [f.117v]
16. *And to him the first crown is given for his merits.*
    Greetings…
17. *An angel kills Herod for the death of James*
18. *And presses him with the punishment due for such a horrible crime.*
    Greetings…
19. *His unfortunate spirit is held subject to a bitter end.*
20. *What was his flesh before became food for worms.*
    Greetings…
21. *With God avenging the punishments of an innocent friend,*
22. *Herod is stricken with a double punishment.*
    Greetings…
23. *And James, free from his carnal prison, rejoices.*
24. *The world celebrates him, and the rain respects him*
    Greetings…
25. *To him on Mount Tabor, He was evident in the light of divine appearance*
26. *Now, however, He is made evident to him in fullness.*
    Greetings… [f.118r]
27. *Asked by James for the left side and by John for the right side,*
28. *Now Christ offers the right side to both.*
    Greetings…
29. *He is the honor of the land that the most distant sea surrounds,*
30. *This is the land of Galicia, a land very close to the seas.*
    Greetings…
31. *This very place itself rejoices from all the peoples approaching it.*
32. *Because of the merits of the just man, it is to be cultivated.*
    Greetings…
33. *May the one who bestows solace in the face of disease and injuries from people,*
34. *Help us. Cantor, sing "Amen!"*
    Greetings…

[CHAPTER 26]

VIII Calends of August
[26.1] Mass of Saint James
Published by Lord Pope Calixtus

Jesus called James of Zebedee and John the brother of James, and He gave them the name "Boanerges," which means "Sons of Thunder."[1]

Ps. *The heavens tell...* [Ps 18 / 19]
Word without end. Amen. [f.118v]

Or. While considering the most glorious[2] solemnity of the sacred passion of Saint James of Zebedee, the patron of Galicia, we humbly implore You, O Lord, that as Your agreeable apostle was worthy to triumph through suffering over the ferocity of the pernicious Herod with You there for him, so may we be worthy to overcome the enticements of our flesh and the machinations of the ancient enemy to the extent that we can arrive at the heavenly kingdom with him leading the way, through Christ...[3]

A Reading from the Book of the Ecclesiastical History:

In those days, he said,[4] King Herod sent his force to afflict some from the Church, and he killed James, the brother of John, with a sword. Concerning this James, however, Clement of Alexandria, in the seventh book of his *Dispositions,*[5] writes a story worthy of memory, which had been handed down to him from his ancestors. Clement

---

1. This is the *Jesus vocavit* text. See ch. 21.2, n. 11.
2. The Latin *Gloriosissimam* is the first word of this passage and is one of the larger illuminated letters in the CC, stretching down the entire left margin.
3. This is the *Gloriosissimam sollemnitatem* text.
4. Likely referring to Luke and/or the Acts of the Apostles.
5. See ch. 4, n. 10.

said, "For certainly, the one[6] who had taken him," that is James,[7] "to the judge for martyrdom was moved by penance and confessed that he was also a Christian." He said, "They were both led together to a punishment of death. And while they were being led on the road, he asked James to grant him forgiveness. And James, deliberated a short while and said: 'Peace be with you,' and he kissed him. And thus, both together were beheaded."

But then, just as divine scripture says,[8] when Herod saw that the death of James was pleasing to the Jews, he went further and cast Peter into prison, wishing without doubt to punish him. But divine help arrived when an angel assisted him in the night, freed him miraculously from the bonds of the chains, and ordered him to go free to his ministry of preaching. And these these things may have certainly happened to Peter,

However, the king's sin, committed against the apostles, did not allow a delay of vengeance, but the divine right hand was immediately present as an avenger, as the story written in the Acts of the Apostles teaches us. It says that when Herod went down to Caesarea on a solemn [f.119r] day, dressed in bright regal clothing, he sat before the tribunal and spoke sublimely to the people, and then the people called out to him, "The sounds of God and not of man!" Immediately an angel of the Lord struck him because he had not given glory to God. And he died, swarming with worms.[9]

---

6. Traditionally in the *Passio Iacobi* (known also as the Pseudo-Abdias), as well as Bk. III (the *Translatio*) this man is known as Josias, a servant of Hermogenes. See Coffey and Dunn, *Miracles,* 85, 104–5.
7. This clarification is likely an interpolation subsequent to both Clement and Eusebius.
8. See ch. 4, n. 12.
9. Eusebius, *Ecclesiastical History,* Bk. 2, ch.9, sect. 1–4 and Bk. 2, ch.10, sect. 1; cf. Acts 12.

CHAPTER TWENTY-SIX

[26.2] Luke[10]

R. *King Herod sent bands that he might afflict some from the Church.*

V. *He killed, however, James, the brother of John, with a sword.* [Acts 12:1–2]

[26.3] Calixtus

Alleluia.

Most holy apostle James, intercede with Christ assiduously for the wellbeing of all the people.[11]

[26.4] Calixtus

Alleluia.

This James is to be honored greatly, [f.119v]. *He held primacy among the apostles. He was first among them to be crowned with martyrdom.*[12]

[26.5] Mark

Alleluia.

Jesus called James of Zebedee and his brother John and gave them the name "Boanerges," which means "Sons of Thunder."[13]

---

10. Luke, as author of the Acts of the Apostles.
11. This is the *Sanctissime Apostole Iacobe*. See ch. 22.21, n. 51.
12. This is the *Hic Iacobus valde venerandus*. See ch. 23.8, n. 19.
13. This is the *Jesus vocavit* text. See ch. 21.2, n. 11.

[26.6] A Sequence[14] of James with Latin, Greek, and Hebrew Words, and Shortened by Lord Pope Calixtus

Alleluia
Let us give thanks and rejoice
With greatest gladness,
Let joyful and agreeable[15]
Spain be glad
In the glittering victory[16]
Of the glorious and nurturing James,
Who rises[17] *to the heavens today*[18]
And is crowned[19] *with glory.*

This James of Zebedee,
Brother[20] *of blessed*[21] *John,*
On the Sea[22] *of Galilee,*
Is called[23] *by the Savior* [f.120r]

---

14. The Latin is "prosa" and usually is used for a straightforward piece unrestrained by poetic conventions, such as rhyme and meter. According to DuCange, "prosa" can be also used as a variant for the sequence, which was poetic in nature, the most famous of which may be the *Dies irae...* or "Day of wrath,..." which was used at requiem masses. Here and elsewhere in the LSJ, it is probably best translated as "Sequence." This sequence is known as the *Gratulemur et letemur*. Dreves (AH 17:196) gives the Hebrew words cited in the Hebrew alphabet.
15. The text reads *cemeha* with an interlinear Latin translation of *iocunda* for "agreeable."
16. The text reads *nizaha* (Hebrew) with an interlinear *victoria* ("victory").
17. The text reads *hole* with an interlinear *scandens* ("rises").
18. The text reads *haiom* with an interlinear *hodie* ("today").
19. The text reads *nichtar* with an interlinear *coronatur* ("is crowned").
20. The text reads *ahiu* with an interlinear *fratre* ("brother").
21. The text reads *movorah* with an interlinear *benedicti* ("blessed").
22. The text reads *iamah* with an interlinear *mare* ("sea").
23. The text reads *nicra* with an interlinear *vocatur* ("is called").

CHAPTER TWENTY-SIX

At Whose order, he spurned all things
    And the faith of the nourishing Trinity,
As a preacher[24] of truth,[25]
    He preached in Judea.[26]

James, strong[27] with grace,
    Gives testimony of the law
And spreads Christ through the ages
    In going to the regions[28] of the world.[29]
The incarnation of the Messiah
    And the suffering under Pilate
Is the holy Word[30]
    And the wondrous Resurrection
And the wondrous Ascension of Christ
    Is his lofty[31] preaching.

He speaks[32] of the great works of God
    And calls on the proclamations

---

24. The text reads *mezaper* with an interlinear *predicator* ("preacher").
25. The text reads *emuna* with an interlinear *veritatis* ("of truth").
26. The text reads *inbihuza* with an interlinear *Iudea* ("Judea").
27. The text reads *ysquirros* with an interlinear *fortis* ("strong").
28. The text reads *climata* with an interlinear *partes* ("regions").
29. The text reads *cosmi* with an interlinear *mundi* ("of the world").
30. The text reads *devar quezossa* with an interlinear *sermo* ("word") plus an interlinear *sancta* ("holy"). Here one would expect the masculine *sanctus;* this reference to the "holy word" or "holy Word" may be masculine under the influence of the *Word as God* as expressed in the Gospel of John, where one finds the use of the very complex word *logos* in the statement Καὶ θεὸς ἦν ὁ λόγος or "God was the Word," where it is masculine. This still does not explain the use of *sancta* in the feminine, as there are really no feminine words for "word" in Latin, and it is here clearly juxtaposed with the masculine *sermo*.
31. The text reads *rama* with an interlinear "alta" ("high" or "lofty").
32. The text reads *omer* with an interlinear *dicit* ("speaks").

Of the prophets as witness.
   And the predictions of David
Are in harmony with him,
   As he declares[33] *all these things openly.*

Then he performed great[34] *miracles*
   And showed remarkable signs.
The champion of Christ casts out evil demons[35]
   While gleaming[36] *with divine grace.*

He gave[37] *himself to martyrdom*
   Under the malignant rule of Herod [f.120v]
For the immortal[38] *Begotten of the highest King,*
   But now he rejoices in glory.

His body[39] *was transferred*
   From his homeland of Jerusalem
To fortunate Galicia in which
   He now performs miracles.

His sacred sarcophagus is sought
   By the sick who receive health.
All peoples, languages, and tribes go[40] *there,*

---

33. The text reads *magiz* with an interlinear *nunciat* ("declares").
34. The text reads *guezoloz* with an interlinear *magna* ("great").
35. The text reads *sezim rahim rozef* with the words *demonia mala eiciebat* ("cast out evil demons").
36. The text reads *zarhaque* with an interlinear *splendens* ("gleaming").
37. The text reads *nazan* with an interlinear *dedit* ("he gave").
38. The text reads *athanato* with an interlinear *inmortali* ("immortal").
39. While the usual meaning of *gleba* (classical Latin, *glaeba*) is "dirt," it can be used for "body."
40. The text reads *vunt* with an interlinear *vadunt* ("go"). *Vunt* is likely an Old French form of the modern French *vont*.

CHAPTER TWENTY-SIX

> *Crying out, "Rise up and go forth!"*[41]
> *And they sacrifice various offerings,*
> *Confessing properly their vices.*
>
> *You, who are proclaimed "Boanerges,"*
> *You are called "Son of Thunder."*
> *You, who are named "Supplanter,"*
> *Supplant the vices from within us!*
>
> *You, who saw on Mount Tabor*
> *The Begotten transformed in the Father,*
> *Make us able to see Jesus*
> *In the eternal*[42] *glory of heaven.*
>
> *O James, follower of Christ,*
> *Be the protector of your people,*[43]
> *So that we may rejoice with Christ,*
> *Together* [f.121r] *with you, unto the ages."*[44]
> Amen.

Continuation of the Holy Gospel according to Mark:

At that time, the sons of Zebedee, James and John, approached Jesus Christ the Lord and said: "Master, we wish You to grant us what we are asking You to do for us." And He said to them: "What do you want Me to do for you?" And they said: "Grant that we sit, one at Your right hand

---

41. The text is *suseia, ultreia* with an interlinear gloss *sursum perge, vade ante*. These words became a pilgrim greeting. The exact etymology is not clear, although the meaning is evident: "Get up and go forward." These words are also found in the chorus of *Dum Pater Familias: "E ultreia e suseia, Deus aia nos,"* which is found in the Addenda (CCA 19).
42. The text read *leholam* with an interlinear *eterna* ("eternal").
43. The text reads *amaha* with an interlinear *plebi tue* ("your people").
44. The Latin is *in secula* ("unto the ages"). While we usually translate these endings uniformly, this one seems to be poetically designed to be taken as written, rather than as a formulaic ending.

and the other at Your left hand in Your glory." Jesus, however, said to them: "You do not know what you are asking. Can you drink the cup that I drink or be baptized with the baptism with which I am baptized?" And they said to Him: "We can." And Jesus said to them: "You will certainly drink the cup that I drink and be baptized with the baptism with which I am baptized. However, to sit at My right hand or My left hand is not Mine to grant you, but it is for those for whom it was prepared." And when the ten heard this, they began to become indignant about James and John. Jesus, however, called them and said to them: "You know that those who appear to rule over the peoples dominate them, and their princes have power over them. However, it is not this way with you. On the contrary, whoever wishes to be the greater will be your servant, and whoever wishes to be first among you will be the servant of all. For the Son of man also did not come to be served, but rather to serve and to give His soul for the redemption of many." [Mk 10:35–45]

I believe in one…[45]

[26.7] Mark

Off.   *Jesus went up the mountain, called to Himself James of Zebedee and John, the brother of James, and gave them the name "Boanerges,"* [f. 121v] *which means "Sons of Thunder."*[46]
       Alleluia.

V.   *And Your arrows, O Lord, pierce as the voice of Your thunder in the world.* [Ps. 76:18–19]
       Which means…[47]

---

45. This is the beginning of the Creed that is read or sung at many masses. It is not indicated in any other section of the chapters on the liturgy.
46. This is the the most complete expression of the *Jesus vocavit* text. See ch. 21.2, n. 11.
47. This likely indicates the repetition of the final words of the offertory prayer: "which means 'Sons of Thunder.'"

CHAPTER TWENTY-SIX

Sec. Have mercy on us, most beautiful Father and most pious God, and yield to our prayers to You, and we beseech, deign to accept and consecrate these gifts that we offer You in honor of Saint James so that they may continually nourish in our minds the love of Your Son through Whom Your venerable apostle powerfully overcomes the insanity of the wicked Herod, through the same Lord…

Pref. It is truly fitting…eternal God,[48] that, on this famous celebration of Saint James Your apostle, we confess to You and present offerings of praise. As soon as he heard the voice of Your Son calling on the shore of Galilee, he left behind all and followed the Redeemer. To him You granted seeing the Transfiguration of Your Begotten on Mount Tabor and hearing Your wondrous voice and beholding the brightness at the table of Your divinity, which You had never granted to anyone. Then You accepted him in the heavenly palace, as a living offering that was pleasing to You after he had been beheaded by Herod, and You made him a consort of the angels. Oh, happy pain of such a wound! Oh, precious scar! Through this he engendered for himself a crown, he wore down death with death, and he ascended to the heavens. You were there as such a great Gift for him after these things, because of which all the peoples of all the regions of the world run to him in Galicia to ask for his help. To You, O Lord and highest King, we bear offerings of praise with joy, and we are consoled by all his sufferings. And so, with the angels and… [f.122r]

---

48. Here the illuminated letters *V* and *D* are written together for the Latin *Vere dignum* ("truly fitting"); it is part of a larger formula that varies slightly from one type of feast to another, but it picks up the last response of the first part of the preface, which ends *Dignum et iustum est* ("It is fitting and just)" and includes wording similar to "It is truly fitting and just, right and helpful to salvation for us always and everywhere…" before continuing on with the appropriate "preface" wording, as we have here. It ends with the *Sanctus*.

[26.8] Mark

Com. *Jesus says to James and John: "Can you drink the cup that I am to drink?" And they say to Him: "We can."*[49]

[26.9] Gregory

V. *If your mind seeks what is sweet, first drink what causes pain.*[50]
Can you drink…?[51]

P.Com. God, Whose Son invited the blessed sons of Zebedee, James and John, to drink His cup, grant us, we beseech, to sit on the right side of Your kingdom through the merits of both of those whom You wished to become participants of His chalice, through the same…

Oration for Terce:

Almighty and eternal God, Who granted us this very day of exultation[52] on the solemnity of Your apostle Saint James, be there, we beseech, that we may be associated in heaven with his blessed soul whose precious passion we celebrate on earth, through…

Daily Oration for Sext:[53]

Grant, we beseech, almighty God, that just as Saint James Your apostle, the honor of Galicia, received his inheritance through the sword of the impious Herod, we may thus be

---

49. This is the *Ait Jesus*, which consists of a blend of Mt 20:22 and Mk 10:39. While *ait* can be either present or past, the *dicunt* ("they say") would indicate it is present here.

50. This is the *Si mens vestra*, which consists of wording from Gregory I, the Great, *Sermon 27*, 4 (PL 76:1206).

51. This likely indicates a repetition of the portion of the communion prayer of ch. 26.8.

52. While *exultabilis* is not found in dictionaries, the meaning is clear as a derivative of *exulto*.

53. The word *cotidiana* or "daily" is added in the margin in CC and is placed before *oratio* ("prayer") in S, in both this and the following section.

worthy to have his association through the demonstration of good works, through...

Daily Oration for None:

Be there, almighty God, so that we, who celebrate the solemnities of Your apostle Saint James, may acquire forgiveness through his requests, through...

Oration for Vespers:

God, Who, among Your laudible acts, deigned to offer the feast day of our nourishing James, Your apostle, to us, we pleadingly implore Your mercy, so we may be joined in heaven through increases of good works to James, to whom we show veneration on earth, through...[54]

Oration for Compline:

God, Who caused us to go through the space of the day of Your apostle Saint James with joyful minds, [f.122v] grant us, we beseech, to pass through the course of this night with all impediment removed through his pious acquisition, through ...

---

54. This is the *Deus qui diem festum* text. See ch. 23.26, n. 85.

[CHAPTER 27]

[27.1] Mass for the Pilgrims of Saint James to Be Said Assiduously at All Masses and Published by Lord Pope Calixtus

Or. May the ears of Your mercy be opened, we beseech, O Lord, to the prayers of the supplicant pilgrims of Saint James so that You may concede to those seeking what is desired and grant the things that they seek that find favor with You, through…[1]

Another Prayer:
Almighty and eternal God, Who has deigned to lead barbarous nations of all the regions of the world to the sacred altar of Saint James, Your apostle, be there, we beseech, with him praying that they might obtain whatever good they ask and that we may obtain the joys of paradise together with them, through…

Sec. Through the most pious prayers of Saint James, Your apostle, and pleased with the gifts of our reconciliation, we beseech, O most beautiful Father, that You accept the prayers of those coming to his sacred basilica, fulfill just desires, cleanse all the faithful from all vices, illuminate them always with sacred virtues, and free them from all adversities, through…

P.Com. God, Who allows the venerable altar of Saint James, Your apostle, to be visited by foreign and domestic people, be there, we beseech, so that, aided by having received the sacraments, they may go back to their own places safely, and through perseverance in good works, they may be worthy to reign together with Saint James unendingly in the heavenly kingdoms, through…

---

1. Calixtus notes this prayer, the *Pateant aures,* in his letter, p. 9.

CHAPTER TWENTY-SEVEN

VII Calends of August[2]
[27.2] Second Day within the Octaves of Saint James
Mass of Saint Josias the Martyr
Together with Saint James

      Exceedingly however for me... [Ps 138:17 / 139:17][3]

Ps.   *You have tested me, O Lord...* [Ps 138 / 139]

Or.   Almighty and eternal God, Who joined Saint Josias the Martyr to James, Your apostle, in the passion, grant, we beseech, that we may be protected by the patronage of those whose feasts we celebrate against all adversities, through...

Reading from the Book of the Ecclesiastical History:

      In those days, he sent, he said... **as above**[4]

R.   You shall set them... [Ps 44:17 / 45:16]

V.   For your fathers... [Ps 44:17 / 45:16]

      Alleluia.

      Jesus called... **as above**[5]

[27.3] Sequence of Saint James to Be Sung Frequently, Published by Lord William, Patriarch of Jerusalem[6] [f.123r]

      Having mercy on the cries
          Of your servants,
                James, grant help.
      Flower of the apostles,
          Honor of the chosen,

---

2. July 26.
3. This line from Psalm 138 / 139 is mentioned by Calixtus in his letter, pp. 8–9.
4. Likely the reading from ch. 26.1, based on Eusebius, *Ecclesiastical History*, Bk. 2, ch. 9–10.
5. This is the *Jesus vocavit* text. See ch. 21.2, n. 11.
6. This is the *Clemens servulorum gemitus;* on William, see ch. 22.23, n. 55.

> James, grant help.
> Leader of the Galicians
> And of the Spaniards,
> James, grant help.
> The voices of all
> The ages call on you,
> James, grant help.
> You are solace of
> The desolate defendants,
> James, grant help.
> Medicinal compound for those sick,[7]
> Cathartic for those ill,[8]
> James, grant help.
> You, who break the bonds
> Of captives and wretches,
> James, grant help.
> Break the bonds
> Of our sins,
> James, grant help.
> Be the preserver
> Of your pilgrims,
> James, grant help.
> Grant the kingdom of heaven
> To us, O hope of the fallen,
> James, grant help.
> Therefore, let praise be to God
> From all of us,
> James, grant help. Amen.

---

7. The Latin *trifera* is explained in ch. 6, n. 5.
8. The Latin *gera* is explained in ch. 6, n. 6.

CHAPTER TWENTY-SEVEN

Continuation of the Holy Gospel according to Matthew:
At that time, Jesus called His twelve disciples together and gave them power over unclean spirits [f.123v] so they could cast them out and cure every disease and every weakness. The names of the twelve apostles, however, are these: first, Simon, who is called Peter, and Andrew his brother, James of Zebedee and John his brother, Philip and Bartholomew, Thomas and Matthew the Publican, James of Alpheus and Thaddeus, Simon the Canaanite and Judas Iscariot, who betrayed Him. Jesus sent these twelve and commanded them by saying: "Do not turn aside onto the road of the Gentiles and do not enter into the cities of the Samaritans, but rather go to the sheep that are lost from the house of Israel. Go rather and preach and say that the kingdom of heaven is at hand. Cure the sick, raise the dead, cleanse the lepers, and cast out the demons. You have received freely, give freely. Do not possess gold or silver or money in your purses, or a wallet for the road, or two tunics or shoes, or a staff for your hand.[9] The worker is worthy, in fact, of his food. In whatever city or town you enter, ask who in it might be worthy and stay there until you should leave. Go, moreover, into the house and greet it, saying, 'Peace be to this house.'[10] And if the house is truly worthy, your peace will come over it, but if it is not worthy, your peace will be returned to you. And if someone does not receive you or listen to your words, leave the house or the city and shake off the dust from your feet. Amen I say to you, it will be more tolerable on Judgment Day for the land of Sodom and Gomorrah than for that city." [Mt 10:1–15]

Off. You will set them... [Ps 44:17 / 45:16]

---

9. The words "for your hand" are not in the Vulgate text.
10. The text "saying, 'Peace to this house'" *(Dicentes: "Pax hic domui")* appears in the margin of CC with a red cross designating its insertion point; it is in the body of the text of S.

Sec. We beseech, almighty God, that this offering, infused[11] by Your desired blessing, may excite our intention to the higher things as You made this day of James Your apostle and Josias Your martyr to be most solemn and most sacred, through...

Jesus said... **as above**[12]

P.Com. Almighty and most merciful God, Who received Your apostle James together with Saint Josias the Martyr through the triumph of the passion, grant us, we beseech, that through these holy things that we have taken up, we may be worthy to have in heaven the companionship of those whose healing solemnity [f.124r] we have celebrated with devout minds on earth, through...

Or. God, Whose angel killed Herod for the death of James, be there, we beseech, so that we may be protected by the help of the one in whose[13] triumphs we rejoice, through...

Or. God, Who grants us to celebrate the solemnities of Your great James, grant us, we beseech, to rejoice in perpetual joy with him, through...

---

11. The Latin is *inspiratus*, literally like "breathed upon" or "inspired," which do not carry the image of being permeated by the breath.

12. This is the *Ait Jesus* text. See ch. 26.8 for the full text.

13. The antecedent is ambiguous in Latin; it may refer to either James or Josias.

[CHAPTER 28]

VI Calends of August[1]
[28.1] Mass of Saint James
Day III within the Octaves

Jesus called...[2]

Ps. *The heavens tell...* [Ps 18 / 19]

Col. God, You Who placed Saint James, Your great apostle and advocate for Galicia, on a seat in paradise through the triumph of the passion, and You Who deposed Herod, his adversary, from the royal seat by angelic striking, repel from us pride and give us the virtue of humility, through...

A Reading of the Book of Wisdom:

James was great in accordance with his name. He was greatest in saving God's chosen and in wiping out insurgent enemies, so that he might obtain the inheritance of Israel. What a glory he has acquired in raising his hands and hurling weapons against cities! Who could thus stand against him? For the Lord Himself delivered the enemies. And was the sun not stopped by His wrath? And did not one day become as if were two? He called on the highest Power in fighting enemies on all sides. And the great and holy God supplied him with very strong hail stones. He made a strike against the enemy, and in his descent he destroyed the adversaries so that the people might recognize his powers since it is not easy to fight against God. And he followed from behind the mighty One.[3] [Ecclus (Sir) 46:1–8]

R. Herod sent... [Acts 12:1]
V. He killed... [Acts 12:2] **as above**

---

1. July 27.
2. This is the *Jesus vocavit* text. See ch. 21.2, n. 11.
3. The text of CC and S read *potentes* or "mighty ones from behind," but the Vulgate has *potentis* for "behind the Mighty One." It is necessary to follow the Vulgate here to avoid contradicting the biblical meaning.

Alleluia.
Most holy apostle…[4]

Seq.   You, who are called "Boanerges"…[5]

According to Matthew:
At that time, after six days, the Lord Jesus took Peter and James and his brother John and led them high up upon the mountain and was transfigured before them. And His face shone like the sun, and His clothing became as white as snow. And behold Moses and Elias appeared speaking together with Him. In response, however, Peter said to Jesus: [f.124v] "Lord, it is good that we are here. If you wish, let us make here three tabernacles: one for You, one for Moses, and one for Elias." While he was still speaking, behold a bright cloud came over them. And behold a voice from the cloud said: "This is my beloved Son in Whom I am well pleased. Listen to Him." When the disciples heard this, they fell on their faces and feared greatly. And Jesus went up and touched them and said to them: "Arise, do not fear." Lifting their eyes, however, they saw no one except Jesus alone. And as they were coming down from the mountain, Jesus ordered them saying, "Tell no one about the vision until the Son of man has risen from the dead." [Mt 17:1–9]

Sec.   God, Who with Your wondrous provision, transformed the earthly things into heavenly ones, be there, we beseech, so that these gifts offered to You may be converted into the true body of Christ Your Son to the extent that He Who through the blood of His Passion redeemed us on the cross, through the prayers of Saint James, may free us from sins, Who together with You…

P.Com.   We have taken, O Lord, while venerating the birth of Saint James Your apostle, the salubrious sacrament of the body and blood of Your Son. Grant, we beseech, that we may

---

4.   This is the *Sanctissime Apostole Iacobe*. See ch. 22.21 for the full text.
5.   This is the *Boanerges qui nuncuparis* text, which is the antepenultimate stanza of the *Gratulemur et letemur* sequence of Calixtus, found in ch. 26.6. It may also indicate that the last two stanzas are to be used here.

CHAPTER TWENTY-EIGHT

        be worthy to be joined to him in heaven, by whose merit You have satiated us on earth, though the same...

Or.   God, Who granted us the feast of James, Your most pious apostle, to celebrate, be there, we beseech, so that we may always feel him intercede with You for our sins in whom we confide as the heir of Your angelic glory, through...

Or.   Bestow, we beseech, O Lord, that we, who have been worthy to perceive the solidity of faith in the teaching of Your apostle Saint James, may be able to overcome the subtlety of the ancient enemy, through...

V Calends of August[6]
[28.2] Mass of Saint James
Day IV within the Octaves

Jesus called...[7]

Ps.   *The heavens* tell... [Ps 18 / 19]

Or.   Be there, we beseech, almighty God, so that we who celebrate the most happy triumph of Your great apostle James on the earth with placid heart, may, through his help, be worthy to be brought into desirable association with him in heaven, through...

Reading from the Book of Wisdom:

    James overcame crowds not by strength of body or [f.125r] by power of weapons, but rather he subdued the one who vexed him through words, by calling to mind the oaths and covenant of the ancestors. When, in fact, the dead had fallen in groups on top of each other, he stood in the midst and curtailed the assault. And he cut off the road that led to the living, for on the priestly garment of great length that he wore was the whole world. And the great things of the ancestors were engraved in four groupings of stones. And the magnificence of God was written on the

---

6.   July 28.
7.   This is the *Jesus vocavit* text. See ch. 21.2, n. 11.

LITURGY OF SAINT JAMES

diadem on his head. The one destroying stopped with these things and feared these things, and the proof of wrath alone was sufficient. [Wis 18:22–25] For wrath without mercy overcame the impious up to the end. [Wis 19:1]

R. Herod sent... [Acts 12:1]
V. He, however, killed... [Acts 12:2]
Alleluia
This James... **Look for it above**[8]

Seq. Having mercy...of...servants...[9]

Continuation of the Holy Gospel according to Luke:

At that time, Jesus the Lord set His sight firmly on going to Jerusalem. And He sent His messengers James and John beyond His range of sight. And they went and entered the city of the Samaritans to prepare things there. And they did not welcome Him, since His focus was on going to Jerusalem. However, when His disciples James and John saw this, they said: "Lord, do you wish us to command that fire descend from heaven and consume them, as Elias did?"[10] And Jesus turned and reproached them, saying, "Do you not know of what spirit you are? The Son of man did not come to destroy souls but to save them." And they went away to another town. [Lk 9:51–56]

Off. Jesus went up...[11]

Sec. May this offering that we present to You, O Lord, we beseech, be made holy through the blessing of Your grace, so that it may also become the body and blood of Your Son, and through the pious intercession of Saint James, may it repel all adversities from us and bring us prosperity, through...

Com. Jesus said...[12]

---

8. This is the *Hic Iacobus valde venerandus* text. See ch. 23.8, n. 19.
9. This is the *Clemens servulorum gemitus* sequence. See ch. 27.3.
10. On "as Elias did," see ch. 23.4, n. 8.
11. This is the *Jesus vocavit* text. See ch. 21.2, n. 11.
12. This is the *Ait Jesus* text. See ch. 26.8 for the full text.

CHAPTER TWENTY-EIGHT

P.Com. God, for Whom it is even easy to create bread and wine from nothing, how much easier is it to transform them into the body and blood of Your Only Begotten! Be there, we beseech, for us who are confiding these things and enjoying the remission of sins and the society of Saint James in the heavens, through…

Or. God, indivisible Trinity, Who made these days of Your beloved apostle, the great James, to be solemn, we beseech, that through his merits You might grant [f.125v] indemnity from all adversities of the present and future life, through…

Another Oration:
God, in Whose love Saint James took on the bodily passion, we beseech, cleanse our minds of all the incentives toward vice and grant us perseverance in good works, through the Lord…

IIII Calends of August[13]
[28.3] Mass of Saint James
For Day V within the Octaves

Jesus called…[14]

Ps. *The heavens* tell… [Ps 18 / 19]

Col. Grant, we beseech O most pious God, that we may exult together with Saint James in the continued joy without any limit or end in heaven as we solemnly and devoutly celebrate the yearly feast of his passion on the earth, through…

Reading from the Book of Wisdom:
James,[15] the fierce conqueror, hastened to the midst of the land of destruction. A sharp sword carried Your undisguised commandment, O Lord, and he stood and filled all things

---

13. This is July 29.
14. This is the *Jesus vocavit* text. See ch. 21.2, n. 11.
15. "James" is inserted here; the biblical text reads "the almighty word."

LITURGY OF SAINT JAMES

with death, and he stood on the earth and he reached to heaven. Then suddenly visions of evil dreams disturbed them, and unexpected fears came over them, and another was thrown somewhere half alive, and because of this the cause of death was shown. The visions, in fact, that disturbed them were warning them of these things so that they would not perish unaware of why they were suffering these evils. This trial of death then touched the just, and a commotion with the multitude occurred in the wilderness. But Your wrath did not last long, O Lord. [Wis 18:15–20]

R. Herod sent... [Acts 12:1]
V. He, however, killed... [Acts 12:2]
Alleluia
Jesus called...[16]

Seq. "Boanerges"...[17]

Continuation of the Holy Gospel according to Mark:

At that time, Jesus the Lord took Peter and James and John with Him and began to fear and grow weary. And He said to them: "My soul is sorrowful even unto death. Stay here and keep watch." And when He had gone a short way, He fell down with His face on the ground and prayed that, if it were possible, this hour would pass from Him. And He said: "Abba, Father, all things are possible for You. Remove this cup from Me, but not what I wish, but what You wish." And He came and found them sleeping. And He said to Peter, "Simon, are you sleeping? Could you not remain awake for one hour? Keep watch and pray so that you might not enter into temptation. The spirit is certainly willing, but the flesh is weak." And He went away and prayed again, [f.126r] saying the same words. And when He came back, He found them sleeping again, for their eyes were heavy, and they did not know how to respond to Him. And He

---

16. This is the *Jesus vocavit* text. See ch. 21.2, n. 11.
17. This is the *Boanerges qui nuncuparis* text. See ch. 26.6, antepenultimate stanza, for the full text. It may also indicate the last two verses.

CHAPTER TWENTY-EIGHT

came a third time and said to them, "Sleep now and rest. It is enough. The hour has come. Behold the Son of man will be handed over to the hands of sinners." [Mk 14:33–41]

Off. Jesus went up...[18]

Sec. On these offerings, O Lord, we beseech, pour out the most welcome rain of Your blessing so that with the intervention of Saint James, they may purify us from sins and lead us to the eternal solemnities of the heavens, through...

Com. Jesus said...[19]

P.Com. God, Who in this consuming of the sacrament of the most reverent body of Your Son, You wished to retain the color and flavor of the bread and wine so that it might be more readily consumed, lest human weakness perhaps would be horrified if it should see the color of the flesh and blood and experience its taste. Be there, we beseech, so that we who believe these things that we are tasting to be really the true body and blood of Christ Your Son. Defend us from the fury of vices, guard us in the holiness of virtue, and may we be worthy with the help of Saint James to be led to the celestial kingdoms, through the same...

Another Oration for Terce:

Grant us, O Lord, we beseech, that in these holy solemnities of Saint James the Apostle, with vices subdued, we may receive an increase in virtues, through...

Or. God, Whose Only Begotten led Saint James the Apostle from the valley of the hills to Mount Tabor and made visible to him the most bright Transfiguration, grant us, we beseech, to rise from the valley of vices to the mountain of virtues, so that we may be worthy to enjoy with him the eternal brightness of the heavens, through the same...

---

18. This is the *Jesus vocavit* text. See ch. 21.2, n. 11.
19. This is the *Ait Jesus* text. See ch. 26.8 for the full text.

III Calends of August[20]
[28.4] Mass of Saint James
For Day VI within the Octaves

Jesus called...[21]

Ps. *The heavens tell...* [Ps 18]

Col. As we celebrate most devotedly the birth of Your beloved and great James the Apostle, we beg You most pleadingly, O Lord, that those who seek his help in tribulation may be freed from all adversities, through...

Reading from the Book of Wisdom:
The evil innkeepers[22] suffered justly according to their iniquities for they established [f.126v] a very inhospitable and detestable business. Certainly some would not take in unknown strangers. Others, however, took good guests into a sort of bondage. Beyond this, there will be, however, a certain leniency for the former innkeepers, for they took in the strangers, although unwillingly. However, the innkeepers who welcomed the strangers with joy, then profited off them with injustices and afflicted them with most savage pains, have been stricken with blindness just like those at the door of the righteous man, who were covered with sudden darkness as they sought passage through their own doors. [Wis 19:12–16][23]

R. Herod sent... [Acts 12:1]

V. He, however, killed... [Acts 12:2]

Alleluia.

O most holy...[24]

Seq. Having mercy [on the cries] of [your] servants...[25]

---

20. July 30.
21. This is the *Jesus vocavit* text. See ch. 21.2, n. 11.
22. Innkeepers replace the "sinners" of the biblical text.
23. Calixtus, in his "statement" in the second paragraph of ch. 23.29, mentions that this text was not originally written about innkeepers but was applicable to them.
24. This is the *Sanctissime Apostole Iacobe*. See ch. 22.21 for the full text.
25. This is the sequence *Clemens servulorum gemitus*. See ch. 27.3 for the full text.

CHAPTER TWENTY-EIGHT

Continuation of the Holy Gospel according to Mark:
At that time the sons of Zebedee approached Jesus... [Mk 10:35ff.]

Off. Jesus went up...[26]

Sec. Pour out Your abundant blessing on these offerings presented to You, O benign Lord, which may cleanse us outside and lead us to the company of Saint James in the heavens, through...

Com. Jesus said...[27]

P.Com. Be there, we beseech, omnipotent God, so that these holy sacraments, which we have consumed, through the intercession of Saint James, may be passed on to expedite us from worldly errors, through...

Or. God, You Who grant to us to attend to the solemnities of Saint James Your apostle, grant us, we beseech, through his merits to be defended in the present world from all adversities and after death to be admitted to the ethereal asylum of the heavenly court, through...

Or. As we commemorate most devotedly the celebration of Your nourishing apostle, the great James of Zebedee, we beseech, O Lord, Your clemency, so that we be rewarded, even with the multitude of our offenses, through his intervention and with Your approval, that we be ripped from it, through...

II Calends of August[28]
[28.5] Mass of Saint James
For Day VII within the Octaves

Jesus called...[29]

Ps. *The heavens tell...* [Ps 18]

---

26. This is the *Jesus vocavit* text. See ch. 21.2, n. 11.
27. This is the *Ait Jesus* text. See ch. 26.8 for the full text.
28. July 31.
29. This is the *Jesus vocavit* text. See ch. 21.2, n. 11.

LITURGY OF SAINT JAMES

Col. As we recall the solemn celebrations of Saint James Your apostle, we implore Your clemency, most beautiful Lord, so that we may experience the patronage in all our needs of the one whose victorious passion we commemorate, through...

Reading from the Acts of the Apostles:
[f.127r] In those days, prophets came from Jerusalem to Antioch, and one of them, by the name of Agabus, arose and indicated through the spirit that a great famine was to come throughout the whole world, and this happened under Claudius. The disciples, however, proposed that, to the extent that they were individually able, they would send aid to the brethren living in Judea. And they did this and sent it to the elders through the hands of Barnabas and Saul. [Acts 11:27–30] At the same time, Herod the king sent a force to afflict some from the Church, and he killed James, the brother of John, with a sword. [Acts 12:1–2] And Herod went down from Judea to Caesarea and stayed there. He was, however, angered with the Tyrians and Sidonians. And they all came to him, as Blastus, the king's chamberlain, had persuaded them to do, and they requested peace because their regions were maintained by him. On the appointed day, however, Herod, dressed in regal garments, sat in front of the tribunal, and spoke sublimely to them. The people, in fact, exclaimed: "Sounds of God and not of man!" Immediately, however, an angel of the Lord struck him, and he died, consumed by worms, because he had not given honor to God. The word of the Lord, however, increased and grew greatly. [Acts 12:19–24]

R. Herod sent... [Acts 12:1]
V. He however killed... [Acts 12:2]
Alleluia.
Jesus called...[30]
Seq. Let us give thanks and rejoice... **see above**[31]

30. This is the *Jesus vocavit* text. See ch. 21.2, n. 11.
31. This is *Gratulemur et letemur* text. See ch. 26.6 for the full text.

CHAPTER TWENTY-EIGHT

Continuation of the Holy Gospel according to Matthew:
At that time, the mother of the sons of Zebedee came to Jesus with her sons James and John and expressed reverence and asked something from Him. He said to her: "What do you wish?" She said to Him: "Say that these two sons of mine may sit one at Your right hand and the other at Your left hand in Your kingdom." Jesus, however, answered and said: "You do not know what you are asking. Can you drink the cup that I am to drink?" They said to Him: "We can." He said to them: "You will certainly drink My cup. However, to sit at My right hand and left hand is not Mine to give to you, but it is for those for whom it was prepared by My Father." When the ten heard this, they grew indignant with the two brothers. But Jesus called them to Him and said to them: "You know that the princes of the peoples dominate them and those who are greater exercise power over them. It will not be so among you. Rather whoever should wish to be greater among you, will be your servant. And whoever among you wishes to be first, will be your slave, just as the Son of man did not come [f.127v] to be served but to serve and to give His soul for the redemption of many." [Mt 20:20–28]

Off. Jesus went up…[32]

Sec. May the present sacrifices to Your Majesty, we beseech, O Lord, sanctify the offerings on this feast of Saint James Your apostle. Be there, so that we who are weighed down by the size of our iniquities may be liberated from all our sins and may serve You with a free mind, through…

Com. Jesus said…[33]

P.Com. Fulfill, O Lord, we beseech, the just desires of Your exultant Church, and grant to it to serve Your worthy[34] majesty always, as You have remade it with Your worthy sacraments on this celebration of Saint James, Your apostle, through…

---

32. This is the *Jesus vocavit* text. See ch. 21.2, n. 11.
33. This is the *Ait Jesus* text. See ch. 26.8 for the full text.
34. The Latin *digne* could be either "worthy" or "worthily," so instead of "worthy majesty" one could also read "serve always and worthily."

Oration for Terce:

O God, Who deigned to show Your Son transformed in the Deity to Saint James Your apostle, grant, we beseech, that he may entreat Your majesty always for us until we may be worthy to be led to that brightness in the future resurrection, which he was worthy to see on Mount Tabor in Jesus Christ our Lord and Your Son, Who with You...

Oration for Sext:

O Lord, we beseech, hear mercifully our cries, so that we, who celebrate the solemnities of Your great apostle James, may be able to avoid through his merits all dangers, through...

Oration for None:

Be there, we beseech, O Redeemer of the world, for freeing us from all evils through the prayers of Your great apostle James so that we who cannot be justified by our works may be worthy to be saved through his merits, through...

Oration for Vespers:

O God, Who allowed us to celebrate the repeated solemnity of Saint James Your apostle, grant, we beseech, that by his intercession, we may be worthy to arrive at the perennial joys of the heavens, through...

Calends of August[35]
[28.6] Mass for the Octave of Saint James to Be Sung In the Morning after Prime Because the Greater Mass Of the Day of Saint Peter in Chains Must by Regulation Be Celebrated on This Day after Terce

Jesus called...[36]

Ps.   *The heavens tell...* [Ps 18]

---

35. August 1.
36. This is the *Jesus vocavit* text. See ch. 21.2, n. 11.

CHAPTER TWENTY-EIGHT

Let Us Pray:
>As we commemorate the venerable solemnity of the octave of Saint James Your great apostle, O Lord, we ask Your indulgence, so that whenever we slip into sin, we may get up again through his prayers, through...

Reading from the Book of the Ecclesiastical History:
>[f.129r] He said, "Herod sent..."[37]

R. Herod sent... [Acts 12:1]
V. He, however, killed... [Acts 12:2]
>Alleluia.
>This James...[38]

Seq. Having mercy [on the cries] of [your] servants...[39]

Continuation of the Gospel according to Mark:
>At that time, the sons of Zebedee approached the Lord Jesus Christ... [Mk 10:35ff.]

Off. Jesus went up... **as above**[40]
Sec. Offer, we beseech, O Lord, Your most generous blessing on these offerings so that, with the help of the Holy Spirit and the prayer of Saint James, they may be converted into the true body and blood of Christ Your Son and may work in us for eternal salvation, Who with You...
Com. Jesus said...[41]
P.Com. Grant, we beseech, omnipotent God, that we who celebrate the feast of the octave of Saint James Your great apostle, through these holy things that we consume, may be worthy

---

37. Eusebius, *Ecclesiastical History*, Bk. 2, ch. 9. sect. 1. The length of the reading is not indicated.
38. This is the *Hic Iacobus valde venerandus* text. See ch. 23.8 for the full text.
39. This is the *Clemens servulorum gemitus* text. See ch. 27.3 for the full text.
40. This is the *Jesus vocavit* text. See ch. 21.2, n. 11.
41. This is the *Ait Jesus* text. See ch. 26.8 for the full text.

to arrive at the solemnities of the heavens that are without measure, through...

Oration for Vespers:
God, Who causes us to rejoice after the completion of the days of the solemnities of Saint James Your apostle, grant, we beseech, that with his help, we may be able to arrive with exultant minds at those feasts that are not annual but continuous, through... [f.128r][42]

[28.7] Pope Calixtus
On the Feast of the Miracles of Saint James
That Is Celebrated on
Day V of the None of October[43]

The feast of the Miracles of Saint James — as, for example, James, with the help of Mary the Mother of God,[44] raised a man who had killed himself at the persuasion of the devil, or he tore twenty men from the capture of the Moabites through the power of God,[45] or

---

42. Folio 128 is a half folio inserted between folios 127 and 129. The text of 128 (both recto and verso) is indicated for insertion about midpoint in folio 129r. The insertion is indicated by a Greek cross on both the text and at the insertion point on f.128. Additionally, f.129r is indicated as beginning at two different points: when it starts with the text continuing from f.127v and again after it resumes subsequent to the insertion of f.128 and after the referral cross. Evidently, the scribe left out the material contained on f.128 and noticed it probably well after completing f.129r. For a description of the physical aspects of the CC with regard to this inserted folio, see Díaz y Díaz, *El Códice Calixtino*, pp. 151–52. To see a photo of this half folio, see Elisardo Temperán Villaverde, *La Liturgia propia de Santiago en el Códice Calixtino* (Santiago de Compostela: Xunta de Galicia, 1997), p. 93, fig. 5.
43. October 3.
44. This opening refers to three miracles included in Bk. II. This miracle is one of two ascribed to Saint Anselm in Bk. II (ch. 17); a third (ch. 18) is also found in Anselm's *De miraculis* but is attributed to Calixtus in the LSJ. See Coffey and Dunn, *Miracles*, 41–54.
45. This is the miracle (Bk. II, ch.1) written down by Calixtus. See Coffey and Dunn, *Miracles*, 7–11.

he carried a dead man for burial from the Pass of Cize up to the city of Compostela, a twelve-day[46] journey, in one night, or other miracles he performed — was ordered by Saint Anselm, archbishop of Canterbury, to be celebrated on the fifth day of the None of October, and we corroborate that same thing.

Fifth Day of the None of October[47]
[28.8] Mass of the Miracles of Saint James

Jesus called...[48]

Ps. The heavens tell... [Ps 18 / 19] **as above**[49]

O God, Who made Saint James Your apostle, shine with innumerable miracles for the praise of Your name, grant to us who celebrate the feast of his miracles, through his intercession, to bloom with the flowers of virtue and to arrive unto the joys of paradise, through...

Reading from the Book of Wisdom:

James[50] in his days did not fear... **as above** [Ecclus (Sir) 48:13ff.]

R. Herod sent... [Acts 12:1]
V. He, however, killed... [Acts 12:2]

Alleluia.

Jesus called...[51]

Seq. Having mercy [on the cries] of [your] servants...[52]

---

46. The Latin *bissenas dietas* indicates "twice six" or twelve, however, in Bk. II, ch. 4, this journey is reported as taking fifteen days. See Coffey and Dunn, *Miracles,* 18–22.
47. October 3.
48. This is the *Jesus vocavit* text. See ch. 21.2, n. 11.
49. This direction probably indicates use of the musical notation from ch. 26.1.
50. On "James," see ch. 21.1, n. 6.
51. This is the *Jesus vocavit* text. See ch. 21.2, n. 11.
52. This is the *Clemens servulorum gemitus* text. See ch. 27.3 for the full text.

LITURGY OF SAINT JAMES

Gosp. Jesus called [His] twelve... [Mt 10:1ff.]

Off. Jesus went up...[53] [f.128v]

Sec. Pour out, O beneficent[54] Lord, the blessing of Your grace on these offerings presented to You. Be there, so that, through the intervention of Saint James Your apostle, they may take away from us all adversities and lead us to the heavenly kingdoms, through...

Com. Jesus said...[55]

P.Com. God, Who refreshed[56] us through Your worthy sacraments on this celebration of Saint James Your apostle, grant, we beseech, that we may arrive through his merits at the refreshment of eternal life in paradise, through...

Or. God, You Who granted to us to celebrate the solemnities of the miracles of Saint James Your apostle, grant us, we beseech, to exult together with him, through his merits, in the delight of paradise, through...

R. The Savior went forth...[57]

Selections from the Miracles of Saint James Should Be Sung or Read.[58] [f.129r]

---

53. This is the *Jesus vocavit* text. See ch. 21.2, n. 11.

54. The Latin is *benignus* where one would expect *benigne* for "beneficent"; this use of nominative for vocative case may be based on the model for words ending in *–eus*, or may be a simple scribal slip.

55. This is the *Ait Jesus* text. See ch. 26.8 for the full text.

56. This passage uses the verb *reficio* and its nominal form *refectio;* it means to grant food that will both strengthen and refresh. No single English verb carries the fullness of this idea.

57. This is the *Salvator progressus pusillum* text. This was written in rubrics by mistake. See ch. 23.1 for the full text.

58. The text from "Pope Calixtus on the feast of the miracles" through this line are on the inserted half-folio, 128r/v. The last lines of the chapter, from "R. The Savior went forth" to "sung or read," which are located on the inserted half folio, are in rubrics; only this last line should have been in rubrics as it gives instructions.

[CHAPTER 29][1]

Pope Calixtus on the Translation of Saint James

We order that the *translation* of Saint James — how he was transferred to the Galicians — and his calling — how he was selected by the Lord on the Sea of Galilee to the order of the apostolate — be celebrated on the Third Calends of January.[2] On this day, the responsorial from the Gospels, "The Savior went forth…"[3] with its antiphons and hymns, the "Let one rejoice…"[4] and the "[Let] the happy [people of God] through all …"[5] should be sung.

Chapter for the Vespers from the Book of Wisdom:
> James[6] pleased God and was transported to paradise so that he might give repentance to the peoples,[7] and he[8] was found perfect and just, and he became a conciliator in a time of wrath. [Ecclus (Sir) 44:16–17]

---

1. Though not marked, this appears to begin ch. 29. Neither the table of contents, nor the beginning words of the table, nor the wordings in the text match exactly. It would appear that ch. 29 should begin where the half-folio, (f.128r/v) was inserted, though the indication for the chapter is in the side margin toward the top of f.129v. In addition, the running indicator of books and chapters for that folio is "lib. i, Cap xxix y xxx," where the "y" is likely the Spanish for "and" rather than the Latin *et*.
2. December 30.
3. This is the *Salvator progressus pusillum* text. See ch. 23.1 for the full text.
4. This is the *Iocundetur et letetur* text. See ch. 22.26 for the full text.
5. This is the *Felix per omnes* text. See ch. 22.23 for the full text.
6. In the biblical text, this is Enoch.
7. See ch.19, n. 3 on this passage.
8. In the biblical text, this is Noah.

Chapter for Matins from the Book of Wisdom:
A great father[9] of a multitude of peoples, and no one is found similar to him in glory, who would keep the law of the Most High. [Ecclus (Sir) 44:20]

Chapter for Terce from the Book of Wisdom:
The Lord was in the covenant with him,[10] and in his flesh he made the covenant stand, and in temptation he was found faithful. [Ecclus (Sir) 44:20–21]

Chapter for Sext from the Book of Wisdom:
The Lord acknowledged him[11] in blessings and gave him an inheritance and divided his share into twelve tribes. [Ecclus (Sir) 44:26]

Chapter for None from the Book of Wisdom:
Saint James[12] was beloved by God and men, and his memory [f.129v] is a blessing. [Ecclus (Sir) 45:1]

Chapter for Vespers:
James[13] pleased God… **Look for it above**[14] [Ecclus (Sir) 44:16–17]

Another Chapter from the Book of Wisdom:
He[15] was pleasing and beloved of God, and he was removed from living among sinners. [Wis 4:10]

---

9. In the biblical text, this is Abraham.
10. In the biblical text, this is Abraham.
11. In the biblical text, this is Abraham.
12. In the biblical text, this is Moses.
13. In the biblical text, this is Enoch.
14. This is likely the chapter for vespers in this section: Ecclus (Sir) 44:16–17.
15. In the biblical text, this is not a reference to a particular individual but to a just person generally.

[CHAPTER 30]

Third Calends of January
[30.1] For the Translation and Calling of Saint James A Mass Published by the Lord Pope Calixtus

Jesus called...[1]

Ps.   *The heavens tell...* [Ps 18 / 19]

Or.   God, Whose Only Begotten chose Saint James to the order of the apostolate along the Sea of Galilee and Who gave him as an advocate to the Galicians, grant us, we beseech, that with his help, having left all earthly things, we may be worthy to acquire what is greater in the heavens, [through][2] our Lord...

Reading from the Book of Wisdom:

James[3] pleased God and was transported to paradise so that he might give repentance to the peoples.[4] He[5] was found perfect and just and became a conciliator in a time of wrath. [Ecclus (Sir) 44:16–17] The covenants of the world were placed with him[6] so that not all flesh would be destroyed. A great father[7] of a multitude of peoples and no one is found similar to him in glory who would keep the law of the Most High, and the Lord was in covenant with him. In his flesh he made the covenant stand, and in temptation he was found faithful. Therefore, in an oath, God gave him glory in his posterity such that his seed would grow like the dust of the earth so that the stars would exalt his seed and they would inherit from sea to sea and from the river up to the ends of

---

1. This is the *Jesus vocavit* text. See ch. 21.2, n. 11.
2. The word *per* ("through") was omitted from this standard formula.
3. In the biblical text, this is Enoch.
4. See ch. 19, n. 3 on this passage.
5. In the biblical text, this is Noah.
6. In the biblical text, this is Noah.
7. In the biblical text, this is Abraham.

LITURGY OF SAINT JAMES

  the earth. [Ecclus (Sir) 44:19–23] God recognized him in his blessings and gave him the inheritance and divided his share into twelve tribes. And He preserved for him men of mercy who found grace in the eyes of all flesh. [Ecclus (Sir) 44:26–27] He is beloved of God and men, and his memory is a blessing. [Ecclus (Sir) 45:1]

R. Herod sent... [Acts 12:1]
V. He, however, killed... [Acts 12:2]
  Alleluia.
  Jesus called...[8]
Seq. Let us give thanks and rejoice...[9]

Continuation of the Holy Gospel according to Mark:
  At that time, Jesus went along the Sea of Galilee and saw Simon and his brother Andrew casting their nets in the sea, as they were fishermen. And Jesus said to them: "Come follow Me and I will make you fishers of people." And they immediately left everything and followed Him. And He went a short way from there and saw James of Zebedee and John his brother, who were mending [f.130r] their nets in a boat. And He called them, and they left their father Zebedee in the boat with hired workers, and they followed Him. [Mk 1:16–20]

Off. Jesus went up...[10]
Sec. As we commemorate the brilliant solemnities of Saint James Your apostle and heap Your altar with gifts, O Lord, we beseech that they work a mortification of our vices and a vivification of virtues in us through Your generous blessing, through the Lord...
Pref. ...eternal God, and on this bright feast of Saint James...
Com. Jesus said to James...[11]

---

8. This is the *Jesus vocavit* text. See ch. 21.2, n. 11.
9. This is the *Gratulemur et letemur* text. See ch 26.6 for the full text.
10. This is the *Jesus vocavit* text. See ch. 21.2, n. 11.
11. This is the *Ait Jesus* text. See ch. 26.8 for the full text.

CHAPTER THIRTY

P.Com. Make us, we beseech, most merciful God, experience the patronages of Your beloved apostle James, You, Who grant us to celebrate glorious mysteries in his solemnities, through the Lord...

O God, Who adorned Saint James Your apostle with miracles, signs, and wonders on earth, grant us, we beseech, to be brought together in fellowship with him in the heavens, through the Lord...

[30.2] Pope Calixtus
Concerning the Office of the Octaves of the Translation of Saint James

The octaves of the *translation* and the calling of Saint James are celebrated on the seventh day, namely on the None of January,[12] since the octaves cannot be celebrated on the eighth day because of the feast of the Epiphany, which is celebrated then. Matins, however, should be sung with nine lessons on that day and the whole mass likewise, except that this Gospel must be read.

Continuation of the Holy Gospel according to Matthew:
At that time, the Lord Jesus was walking along the Sea of Galilee and saw two brothers, [Mt 4:18] James of Zebedee and John, his brother, in a boat with their father Zebedee, mending their nets, and He called them. And they immediately left their nets and their father and followed Him. And Jesus walked around all of Galilee, teaching in their synagogues, preaching the Gospel of the kingdom, and curing every sickness and every infirmity in the people. And His fame went out in all of Syria, and they brought Him all the sick people, seized by various illnesses and torments, and lunatics and paralytics, and He cured them. And many crowds followed Him from Galilee and Decapolis and Jerusalem and Judea and from beyond the Jordan. [Mt 4:21–25]

---

12. January 5.

[30.3] The Benedicamus[13] of Saint James Published by Master Anselm

Let the court of heaven rejoice.
>Let the day shine. [f.130v]

Let mother Church applaud.
>Let the day shine

In the victory of James.
>Let this day shine.

By the sword of Herod,
>Let the day shine,

He ascended to a seat in heaven,
>Let the day shine,

And obtained the joy of the heavens.
>Let this day shine.

He whom Christ the King in the world,
>Let the day shine,

Adorned with miracles,
>Let the day shine,

Was honored among the peoples.
>Let this day shine.

As the sun shines in glory,
>Let the day shine,

He gives in Galicia
>Let the day shine,

---

13. The Latin is *benedicamus* ("let us bless"). This element of the mass became manifest in the formula *Benedicamus Domino* ("Let us bless the Lord,") with a response *Deo gratias* ("Thanks be to God") as an alternative to the *Ite missa est* ("Go, the mass is ended") and its *Deo gratias*. Here the words *Benedicamus Domino* are in the penultimate stanza, with the *Deo gratias* worked into the final stanza.

CHAPTER THIRTY

And elsewhere signs.
   Let this day shine.

May he drive from us
   Let the day shine,
The harmful fires of evil,
   Let the day shine,
And give us the rewards of life.
   Let this day shine.

In the final danger,
   Let the day shine,
May he defend us from Zabulus,[14]
   Let the day shine,
And lead us to the abode of heaven,
   Let this day shine.

So that on a seat in the heavens,
   Let the day shine,
With immense and eternal joy,
   Let the day shine,
We may bless the Lord.
   Let this day shine.

In hating evils, [f.131r]
   Let the day shine.
In loving friendships,
   Let the day shine.
Let us say thanks to God.
   Let this day shine.

---

14. Latin *Zabulus*, from ancient Greek ζάβολος *(zábolos)*, a collateral form of διάβολος *(diábolos)*, with the meaning of "devil." See DuCange for more information. This is yet another name for the devil in the LSJ. See also ch. 1, n. 23.

[30.4] A Conductum[15] of Saint James, Published by an Ancient Bishop of Benevento[16]

O Saint James, it is your feast at its recurring time![17]
 Make very famous those who give honor to heaven!
He invites the people to celebrate his brilliant triumphs,

Let a boy repeat this standing between two cantors.[18]
 Make very famous those who give honor to heaven!
Behold, we sing, giving deserved thanks to God,
 Make very famous…[19]
Who granted you your ascension to the radiant heavens,
 Make very famous …
Defying the strong wounds of mortal flesh,
 Make very famous …
So that the perpetual enjoyment of life might come upon you,
 Make very famous …
Be mindful from where they contemplate the joys of your feast,
 Make very famous …

---

15. The "conductus" was technically a type of a rhythmic hymn, suited for processionals. Clearly here the term is used in the neuter *conductum* and not the usual *conductus*. It seems to be used for a "processional" here. We have left it in the neuter to maintain it as a potentially distinct form from its later flourishing as *conductus*.

16. AH 17:197–98. The first four stanzas of this hymn are also included in the additional folios at the end of the manuscript. See CCA 6.

17. In CC, above "Iacobe," in very small letters, is written *inclite*, "illustrious." These words are not found in S, nor do they fit the rhythm of the hymn. They could represent an alternative text for Saint James, i.e., "Illustrious Saint.…" In addition to the black notes on the staves, there are also red notes added for this hymn.

18. The placement of this instruction after the previous line may indicate that the choirboy is to sing the refrain after each verse.

19. The refrain is written out in the text for the first two verses only, after which only "Make very famous" is written out for the next six stanzas.

May you serve as creator to servants and pastor to students,
    Make very famous ...
For this reason, we bless the Lord and King of kings,
    Make very famous ...
Reader, read, and concerning the King
    Who rules all, say "Command, O Lord."

[30.5] A Conductum of Saint James, Published by Lord Fulbert, Bishop of Chartres[20] [f.131v]

On this day, let us give praises
With joy to the Son of the highest Maker.

Let a boy walking between two cantors repeat this:

    James, apostle most holy,
    Rescue us from evil things, most pious one.

This is a day more worthy than the others,
More famous than the others, shining from the sphere.

    James, apostle...[21]

On which day James ascends to the angels,
Gleams in heaven, and composes the music of Christ.

    James, apostle...

The one born of Zebedee and most dear
Gave signs most gloriously for the world.

    James, apostle...

---

20. As with the previous *conductum*, there are red notes in addition to the black ones on the staves, but only for the first verse and refrain. This hymn is found in AH 17:198.
21. The refrain "James, apostle..." likely refers to the verse that continues: "rescue us from evil things, most pious one" and was likely to be sung by the boy after each stanza.

*He gave solace to the blind and the lame,
He offered help to all people.*

James, apostle…

*Concerning the Last Judgment, therefore,
May he lead us to a seat in heaven.*

James, apostle…

Reader, read, and, concerning the King [f.132r]
Who rules all, say, "Command, O Lord."

[30.6] A Conductum of Saint James, Published by Master Robert, a Roman Cardinal[22]

Let our throng sing out to the Lord

Let the boy say this:
*With a joyful heart.
Let one celebrate the devout feasts of James*

Boy: *With a pure heart.
He performed as signs worthy miracles*

Boy: *Gentle as a lamb.
He was a light to the blind and a staff to the lame,*

Boy: *James the great.
He shines with signs in heaven and in the world*

Boy: *Now without measure.
He is resplendent in signs for the Galicians,*

Boy: *Happy champion.
He is the conserver and the protector of Spain,*

Boy: *Great and most bright.
May he protect us, and may we not be swallowed*

---

22. This hymn is found in AH 17:199. No information is available on Cardinal Robert.

CHAPTER THIRTY

Boy: *By bitter Orcus.*
Reader, read, and, concerning the King
Who rules all, say "Command, O Lord."

[30.7] A Conductum of Saint James, Published by Bishop and Saint Fortunatus of Poitiers[23]

Greetings, feast day! You will become venerated in all things.

Let the boy repeat this walking between two cantors

Let us rejoice! [f.132v]

On which James went up to the heavens, as he was worthy to do.
Let us rejoice!
He is the honor of the earth, the ultimate Thule.[24]
Let us rejoice!
This kingdom is suitable enough for the Galicians.
Let us rejoice!
He gives to the worldly lands many miracles.
Let us rejoice!
Whence, moreover, arises a singular love for the peoples.
Let us rejoice!
He, like the ancient Pharos,[25] sends out a light to the Indians.
Let us rejoice!
Spaniard, Moor, Persian, Briton love him.
Let us rejoice!

---

23. On Venantius Fortunatus, see ch. 2, n.122. This text is in AH 17:199–200.
24. The term *ultima Thile* for *ultima Thule* represents an outermost island or area. Here, given the context, it may apply to Galicia.
25. Pharos refers to "lighthouse," especially the lighthouse of Alexandria.

The orient and the occident hold him, as does Africa and the North.[26]
    Let us rejoice!
All honor militates for his praises,
    Let us rejoice!
And he roams the waves on the shore of the ocean,
    Let us rejoice!
And his virtue goes onward where no one can go on foot.
    Let us rejoice!

---

26. The Latin *Arctos* refers to the bear region or the north.

[CHAPTER 31]

[31.1] Adaptations for the Office of the Mass of Saint James, Published by Lord Bishop Fulbert of Chartres[1] And an Illustrious Man for Both Feasts of This Apostle To Be Sung [f.133r] by Whomever It Will Please

Singers among whom may be a bishop or priest dressed in robes, who should say this:
> Behold James is now here,
> Who is to be extolled with praises,
> Whose feast we celebrate,
> Whom with devoted minds
> We lift up with praises,
> Whom every people worships.

Other singers should respond:
> Tell all of us what kind
> Of person this James might be
> Whom you hold with such a grasp
> And with distinguished voices
> So that we may venerate him more dearly
> And love him with our minds
> And praise him more attentively
> And seek him out with prayers.

Others should respond:
> He is in reality James,
> Whom the Lord loves exceedingly,
> The retired soldier of Christ
> And the extraordinary standard bearer,
> Superior in military things,

---

1. For Fulbert of Chartres, see ch. 22.2, n.3.

LITURGY OF SAINT JAMES

Apostle of Galicia,
A most well-known pilgrim
And most worthy in honor,
Wondrous with miracles,
Magnificent in glory,
Whom every people, domestic
And foreign, seeks.

Others should sing:[2] [f.133v]
Alleluia in glory!
Praise be to God in all things!
Let the Church give thanks
Flowering with such a patron!
Let the court of heaven be glad!
Rejoice, heaven, earth, and seas!
And our little throng
Sing[3] *to God songs of praises.*[4]

Jesus called James…[5] **Let it be said in full.**
Let the kings and all peoples of the earth, let princes and all judges of the earth, youths and virgins, old with young praise the name of the Lord, for His Son… [Ps 148:11ff.][6]
Jesus called…**up to** "James"…[7]

---

2. While the Latin is *dicant* or "say," clearly it is in the sense of "sing," or "declare in song," as the notes are provided for what follows.
3. The Latin is *dic* ("to say"), where the context requires "sing."
4. The final word in the Latin is *carmina* ("songs"), followed by *eya*, which appears to be a musical extension of the last syllable of the word *carmina*.
5. This is the *Jesus vocavit* text. See ch. 21.2, n. 11. The directive to say it in full implies the existence of the abbreviated variants.
6. In the biblical text, "for His Son" is "for His name."
7. This is the first part of the *Jesus vocavit* text, to be continued here after the singing of the psalm. See ch. 21.2, n. 11.

CHAPTER THIRTY-ONE

> *Since it is good and pleasing to dwell as brethren in one God...* [Ps 132 / 133][8]
> And He gave...**up to** *"Boanerges."*[9]
> *Since they heard terrific thunder from the cloud on Mount Tabor: "This is My beloved Son..."*[10]
> *Which means "Sons of Thunder"*[11] [f.134r]

Ps. *The heavens tell...* [Ps 18 / 19]
> *Let the heavens and earth, sea and all the reptiles in them give praise, since the Lord...* [Ps 68:35–36 / 69:35–36][12]
> *Jesus called...***up to** *"of James"*[13]
> *So that he might send them to preach the kingdom of God...*[14]
> *And he gave...***up to** *"Boanerges"*[15]
> *One of them intoned from the heavenly places, "In the beginning was the Word..."*[16]
> *Which is "Sons of Thunder"*[17]
> *Glory be to the Father...*

---

8. The text is modified from the Psalm, where it is "How good and pleasing to live in unity as brethren!"

9. This is the second part of the *Jesus vocavit* text, begun before the singing of the psalm.

10. This is the *Iacobus et Ioannes tonitrum* text. See ch. 22.11. It is reproduced, as found here, attributed to Fulbert of Chartres, but without further commentary in AH 17:201.

11. This indicates a repetition of the ending of the *Jesus vocavit* text begun above.

12. The biblical text is "since God" rather than "since the Lord."

13. This again indicates singing the first part of the *Jesus vocavit* text. See ch. 21.2, n. 11.

14. This is a blend of Gospel verses: Mk 3:14 and 10:14; and cf. Lk 18:16.

15. This indicates singing the second part of the *Jesus vocavit* text after the singing of the preceding line.

16. This is based on wording of the first paragraph attributed to Jerome in ch. 20. The final quote is from John 1:1.

17. This indicates a repetition of the ending of the *Jesus vocavit* text begun above.

LITURGY OF SAINT JAMES

Let all peoples applaud with their minds! Let them rejoice in God in a voice of exultation, for the highest Lord and great King is terrifying![18]
Jesus called... **in full**[19]

[31.2] Bishop Fulbert of Chartres,[20] Concerning Saint James[21]

Immense King, pious Father, have mercy.[22]

Lord, have mercy.[23]

Savior, eternal God,[24] *have mercy.*

Lord, have mercy.

You Who hold all things in the palm of Your hand, have mercy.

Lord, have mercy.

Christ, Son of the highest Father, have mercy. [f.134v]

Christ, have mercy.[25]

You Who came down from the heavens, have mercy.

Christ, have mercy.

You redeemed Your creation.

Christ, have mercy.

---

18. Cf. Ps 46:2–3.
19. This is the *Jesus vocavit* text. See ch. 21.2, n. 11.
20. For Fulbert of Chartres, see ch. 22.2, n. 3.
21. This is the *Rex immense* text found in AH 17:201–2. It is also found in CCA 10.
22. Throughout, the "have mercy" is rendered by the transcribed Greek ἐλέησον *(eleison)*.
23. Throughout, the "Lord, have mercy" is rendered by the transcribed Greek *Kyrie eleison*.
24. The words here are rendered in CC by the transcribed Greek: *Soter* (Σωτήρ), *Theos* (Θεός) and *athanatos* (αθάνατος). We have translated the Greek words to English.
25. Throughout, the "Christ, have mercy" is rendered in CC by the transcribed Greek *Christe (Xr-e) eleison*. We have translated the Greek words into English.

CHAPTER THIRTY-ONE

Consoler, sweet love, have mercy.
    Lord, have mercy.
You Who have shone on James, have mercy.
    Lord, have mercy.
You Who spare us through his prayer, have mercy.
    Lord, have mercy.

King of all worlds, have mercy.[26]
    Lord, have mercy.
Holding all in a nourishing palm, have mercy.
    Lord, have mercy.
Spare those born, as they are given death, have mercy.
    Lord, have mercy.
Great Christ, gentle Lamb, have mercy.
    Christ, have mercy.
Son of God, salvation of matter, have mercy.
    Christ, have mercy.
O pious Son of Mary, have mercy.
    Christ, have mercy.
O illustrious Paraclete, have mercy.
    Lord, have mercy.
Consoler and loving One, have mercy.
    Lord, have mercy.
You, Who make the just James[27] *gleam, have mercy.*
    Lord, have mercy.

---

26. The remaining stanzas are entered below the lines of the first stanzas, using the same staves as the first set. The verses are presented as one would find the verses 1 and 2 in a modern hymnal. Whether they were to be interspersed as a second line to be sung immediately or postponed as a second set of stanzas as presented here, is unknown. They are not found in S.

27. In CC, the scribe adds below the line *vel Mariam,* "or Mary."

LITURGY OF SAINT JAMES

Glory to God in the highest, and peace on earth to men of good will! We praise You. We bless You. We adore You. We glorify You. We give You thanks because of Your great glory. Lord God, heavenly King, God the Father almighty, Lord and only Begotten Son, Jesus Christ, Lord God, Lamb of God, Son of the Father, You, Who take away the sins of the world, have mercy on us. You, Who take away [f.135r] *the sins of the world, accept our prayer. You, Who sit at the right hand of the Father, have mercy on us. For You alone are holy. You alone are Lord. You alone are the Most High, Jesus Christ.*[28]

[31.3] Verses of Bishop Fulbert of Chartres Concerning Saint James[29]

Two cantors sing: And the chorus adds:

You, Who called James on the Sea of Galilee...   ...e[30]
And Who chose him in his apostolic place...   ...e
You, Who showed him Your sun-like face on the mountain...   ...e
You, Who called him "Boanerges" along with his brother...   ...e
You, Who with vengeance killed Herod for his death...   ...e
You, Who endowed the people of Galicia with his body...   ...e
You, Who reign forever with the Father, pious King, to You be praise   ...e
With the Holy Spirit, also in the glory of God the Father.   *A...men.*
[f.135v]

---

28. AH 17:202.
29. AH 17:202.
30. The chorus here extends with flourish the last syllable of the line. In Latin each line ends with "e," but that is not the case in English. We show this with an ellipsis mark. In the manuscript, a red line below the notes indicates the length of this flourish. In the last line, rather than the last syllable being sung with a flourish of notes, the first syllable of "Amen" receives the flourish.

CHAPTER THIRTY-ONE

[31.4] Supplementary Adaptations of Readings from the Mass of Saint James, Published by Lord Bishop Fulbert of Chartres and an Illustrious Man[31]

Let the lector and cantor rejoice together:
> Let us sing to the Lord songs of glory!
> Let us cultivate these feasts today
> Of Saint James with rewards of heavenly grace!
> As the present divine reading taught,
> He wished to suffer the sword of Herod.
> For this James was worthy to enter heaven...

Lect. A reading from the Book, "Ecclesiastical History,"
Cant. In which the brilliant battles
> Of James are narrated exultantly;
> About proud Herod
> Over whom he triumphed
> Beautifully destroying
> His most dark threats.

Lect. He said, Herod sent in his bands to afflict[32] some from the Church and he killed James, brother of John, with a sword.

Cant. To the accumulation of his damnation,
> He beheaded the apostle,
> James, servant of God,
> Teaching the people true things.[33] [f.136r]

---

31. This text, found in AH 17:203–4, is based on Eusebius's *Ecclesiastical History* (Bk. 2, ch. 9, sect. 1–4 and ch.10, sect. 1). The Cantor adds a commentary on the reading, with notions from elsewhere, a few details of which seem based on the stories of Josias; for these, see Coffey and Dunn, *Miracles*, 110–17. Within the text, there are extracts from and references to Acts 12. We have not indicated the complex sources for these.

32. S has *affligeret* ("that he might afflict") instead of the *affligere* ("to afflict") of CC. Both manuscripts use these variants at times.

33. The Latin is *Vera* or ("true things") in CC, but S has *Verba* ("words") possibly for "words of God."

LITURGY OF SAINT JAMES

Lect. *Of this James, however, Clement of Alexandria also writes a story worthy of memory in the seventh book of his "Dispositions,"*
Cant. *So that he may be just in eternal memory,*
Lect. *Conveyed to him from the tradition of the elders,*
Cant. *So that another generation might know it.*
Lect. *Since certainly, he said, that also the one who had brought James to the judge for martyrdom was moved to penance.*
Cant. *When he saw the miracle, Josias took the rope from the neck of the apostle,*
Lect. *And he also confessed that he was a Christian,*
Cant. *And he confessed and did not deny Christ the Lord.*
Lect. *They were led, he said, both together to the punishment,*
Cant. *So that they might be worthy to receive the crown of glory.* [f.136]
Alleluia.
Lect. *And when they were being led on the road, he asked James to give him forgiveness,*
Cant. *The communion of saints and remission of sins,*
Lect. *But he hesitated a little.*
Cant. *James baptized him: In the mercy of the Father and of the Son and of the Holy Spirit.*
Lect. *"Peace be with you," he said.*
Cant. *"May the pious consoler offer you peace."*
Lect. *And he kissed him.*
Cant. *Oh, admirable kisses of divine love!*
Lect. *And thus, both were together beheaded.*
Cant. *And so they were worthy of triumphant crowns.*
Lect. *But then, he said, as divine scripture says, "Herod saw that it was pleasing to the Jews concerning the death of James,*
Cant. *Since those who have acted badly,* [f.137r] *exult in the worst things."*
Lect. *He added still more here, and he cast Peter into prison,*
Cant. *Handing him over to be guarded by groups of four soldiers.*

CHAPTER THIRTY-ONE

Lect. Without doubt, he wanted to punish him also, except that divine help was present, by which an angel helped him in the night,

Cant. And light shone in the small room of the prison.

Lect. Miraculously he broke the binding of the chains,

Cant. And the chains fell from his hands.

Lect. And he commanded him to go free to the ministry of preaching. And with Peter certainly these things were done, but the crime of the king perpetrated against the apostles did not suffer any delay in vengeance, but immediately the avenger was there with the divine right hand.

Cant. The Lord does not leave a crime [f.137v] without vengeance.

Lect. As the story in the Acts of the Apostles teaches us, when it said Herod went down to Caesarea and dressed in a brilliant regal garment on a solemn day, he sat before the tribunal and spoke sublimely to the people.

Cant. Oh, blind rich man! The day of his perdition is present and at hand, as time flies!

Lect. When the people called to him: "These are words of God and not of man." Immediately, it said, an angel of the Lord struck him, because he had not given glory to God.

Cant. From the sole of his feet to the top of his head there was no health in him.

Lect. And swarming with worms, he expired,

Cant. Who is consumed like putridity and like a garment [f.138r] that is eaten by a worm.

Lect. Praise and glory be to God,

Cant. ah...[34]

Lect. Peace, honor, and victory,

---

34. All the lines end with a word ending in *"a,"* which is continued by the cantor. The device does not work in English, because the lines do not end with a rhyme in "a" or another vowel that can be prolonged. We have simply used "a" written "ah", "o" written "oh", and "e" written "ee" throughout these musical extensions.

Cant. *ah…*
Lect. *Who sent Herod to Tartarus*
Cant. *ah…*
Lect. *For his evil*
Cant. *ah…*
Lect. *And sent James*
Cant. *ah…*
Lect. *To the heavenly seats.*
Cant. *ah…*
Lect. *With him may we also*
Cant. *ah…*
Lect. *Enjoy the starry joys.*
Cant. *ah…*

Both together:
    A…men.

[31.5] Holy[35]

Chor. Holy, Holy, Lord God of the heavenly hosts.[36] The heavens and the earth are full of Your glory. Hosanna in the highest. Blessed is He who comes in the name of the Lord.

Cants. [f.138v] Hosanna Who saves[37] and Who powerfully created all things in Your image.

Chor. *ah…*

Cants. To You Yourself praise honor and glory are fitting, O eternal King, unto the ages.

Chor. *ah…*

---

35. The title serves as the first of the three "holies" of the *Sanctus* (AH 17:205–6).

36. The Latin is *Sabaoth* ("heavenly hosts") leaving the word, as usual, in the Hebrew form.

37. The word Hosanna has as its stem the Hebrew word meaning "save."

Cants. You, Who were born from the bosom of the Father and arrived at the most high
Cants. oh...
Cants. To redeem the lost man by Your own blood,
Chor.   oh...
Cants. Whom the deadly one had deceived by iniquitous serpentine fraud through the tooth of a most rash wife,
Chor.   ee...
Cants. And Whom, being entangled in this crime, He had appropriately expelled from the light and border of paradise,
Chor.   ee...
Cants. Now deign to save
Chor.   ee...
Cants. From above, Jesus Christ,
Chor.   ee...
Cants. On high.

[31.6] Agnus Dei of Bishop Fulbert of Chartres

Cants. [f.139r] *Lamb of God,*
Chor.   *You, Who take away the sins of the world,*
Cants. *You, Who are pious and mild, merciful and sweet,*
Chor.   *Have mercy on us.*
        Lamb of God, You Who take away the sins of the world,
Cants. *Angelic bread of the saints, eternal life,*
Chor.   *Have mercy on us.*
        Lamb of God, Who take away the sins of the world,
Cants. *Be kind concerning our faults, offer us the gifts of virtues,*
Chor.   *Grant us peace.*

[31.7] The Benedicamus of Saint James, Published by a Certain Galician Teacher[38]

Let there be a canticle of happiness
To the King of eternal glory
Who gave the triumph of victory
To James today.

This apostle has adorned
Spain and the province
And has made that impious
People into the Church of Christ.

In the end, for the Son of God
Under the rule of Herod, [f.139v]
He acquired martyrdom for himself.
Let us bless the Lord.

For the madness of Herod,
Incited by pride,
Raged against the bulwarks of Christ
And despised His chosen ones.

In the accumulation of his damnation,
He beheaded James,
An apostle and servant of God,
Who taught the people true things.

Thus, he overcame the bands of the king
And wicked and violent things,
For he ascended to ethereal
Seats. Thanks be to God.

---

38. AH 17:206–7. It is also found in CCA 7 as *Regi perhennis glorie*.

CHAPTER THIRTY-ONE

Here Ends the First Book
May Glory Be to the Writer
And May It Be to the Reader also.
Amen.[39]

---

39. The incipit for Bk. II begins immediately, using varying colors of inks: "Here begins the second book of Saint James of Zebedee, Patron of Galicia, about His XXII Miracles. The attestation of Pope Calixtus." See Coffey and Dunn, *Miracles,* 1. See Illus., p. x above. It is surprising that in a codex of such importance the colophon and the incipit are crowded together in this way.

ADDENDA

Folios 185–96 of the *Codex Calixtinus*

[F.185R] [CCA 1] ATO, BISHOP OF TRIER[1]

Our happy phalanx applauds
On this day on which the champion
Of Christ rejoices without measure
   James in glory
   In the court of the angels.[2]

Whom Herod beheaded
And thus, Christ crowned
And enriched him
   In the heavenly country
   [In the court] of the angels.

Whose body is entombed
And is visited by many
And through which is given to them
   Well-being in Galicia
   [In the court] of the angels.

Therefore, celebrating his feast,
Singing his hymns,
And in giving honor, let us render
   Sweet praises to the Lord
   [In the court] of the angels.

---

1. This is the *Nostra phalanx*. Dreves (AH 17:207–8) suggests that the author is Hatton de Troyes. There is also a Hatton von Trier. We are not aware of this work being in any source prior to the CC.
2. The line in Latin is *Angelorum in curia* ("In the court of the angels"); the succeeding verses are simply *Angelorum* ("Of the angels"). We have supplied the missing three words in brackets.

[CCA 2] Master Albert of Paris[3]

Let Catholics rejoice together,
Let the heavenly citizens be glad
  On this very day.

Let the clerics apply themselves
To beautiful songs and chants
  On [this very] day.[4]

This is a praiseworthy day
And splendid with its bright light
  On [this very] day

On which James ascended
To the celestial palaces
  On [this very] day,

Winning over the sword of Herod
And the prize of the life received
  On [this very] day.

To the great Father of the family
Let us render the thanks of praise
  On this very day.

Let us give thanks to God.[5] [f.185v]

---

3. Albertus Parisiensis, canon (c.1127) and later a composer at Notre Dame in Paris (c.1146–1177). This is the *Congaudeant Catholici,* a *conductum* and his only known work, and it is considered the first work written for three voices.
4. The refrain is written *Die ista* ("On this very day") for the first and last verse; other verses simply give *Die*. The understanding is that the whole line is repeated and so has been supplied in brackets.
5. This line does not appear to be related to the preceding or following hymn.

ADDENDA TO THE CODEX CALIXTINUS

[CCA 3] Master Goslenus, Bishop of Soissons[6]

We give thanks as we celebrate the feast day
    That was distinguished by divine light.

This is the remarkable day of James
    Illuminated with signs that are worthy of him.

We beg of him that he lead us to the heavens
    As we sing his songs to Christ.

Lifting up grace from the heavens,
    May the faithful people, therefore, bless the Lord.

[CCA 4] Master Albetricus, Archbishop of Bourges[7]

To the honor of the highest King,
    Who holds all things together,
Let us celebrate, James,
    The solemnities of your death. [f.186r]

Along the shores of Galilee,
    You forsook your own things
And followed Christ and preached
    His realm.

You sought, in approaching Christ,
    Unknowingly then to sit,
But now you sit rather high
    In the twelve-fold court.

---

6. Jocelyn, Jocelin, or Gosselin de Vierzy (1126–52), bishop of Soissons from 1139. This sequence is known as *Gratulantes celebremus* (AH 17:208).

7. Alberich of Reims, c.1085–41, archbishop of Bourges from 1136. This is the *Ad superni Regis decus* text (AH 17:208–9).

You were the proto-martyr
  Of the twelve in the homeland.[8]
You hold the first seat
  Of the twelve in glory.

Make [f.186v] *us therefore be present*
  In the heaven without end
So that our mind may bless
  The Lord and King of kings.

[CCA 5] MASTER AIRARDUS OF VÉZELAY[9]

The yearly celebrations of joy[10]
Owed to you are to be
Given to you.
  The sweet organs
  Joined together
  Should resound.

And your eternal
Heavenly deeds
Are to be disclosed.
  The sweet organs...

These splendid things
Through all the ages
Should also be remembered.
  The sweet organs...

---

8. This refers to the Holy Land.
9. Apart from the mention in the CC, little is known about him. The abbey of Vézelay was the starting point of the Via Lemovicense, one of the four traditional pilgrim routes to Compostela according to Bk. V (Melczer, *Pilgrim's Guide,* 85).
10. This work, a two-part *conductum,* is the *Annua gaudia* text (AH 17:209.

So pious, so good,
Such valid teachings
Should be imitated.
> The sweet organs...

These sacred conditions
So florid and bright
Are to be loved.
> The sweet organs...

[CCA 6] An Ancient Bishop of Benevento

Saint James, your feast at its recurring time[11]
> *Make very* [f.187r] *famous those giving honor to heaven.*[12]

It invites the people to celebrate your brilliant triumphs.
> *Make very [famous those giving honor to heaven].*[13]

Behold, we sing and give deserved thanks to God,
> *Make very [famous those giving honor to heaven],*

Who granted to you to ascend to dazzling heaven.
> *Make very [famous those giving honor to heaven.]*

Look for it above.[14]

---

11. This is the *Iacobe sancte* text. This *conductum* may have had some polyphony added even in ch. 30.
12. This line is a refrain that is sung after each of the four lines of this prayer set to music.
13. The refrain is written out for the first line only. After that only the first two words are given, as indicated by the square brackets here.
14. AH 17:197–98. This *conductum* is included in ch. 30.4 with additional stanzas.

SERMONS AND LITURGY OF SAINT JAMES

[CCA 7] Master Gauterius of Château Renard Composed this Hymn[15]

Let there be a canticle of happiness
To the King of eternal glory,
Who gave the triumph of victory
To James today.

James has adorned
Spain and Galicia[16]
And has made that impious
People into the [f.187v] *Church of Christ.*

In the end, for the Son of God,
Under the rule of Herod,
He acquired martyrdom for himself.
Let us bless the Lord.

For the insanities of Herod
Incited by pride
Raged against the bulwarks of Christ
And despised His chosen ones.

In the accumulation of his damnation,
He beheaded James,
An apostle and servant of God,
Who taught the people true things.

Thus he overcame the bands of the king
And wicked and violent things,

---

15. This is included as the last piece in Bk. I (ch. 31.7) where it is attributed as: "The Benedicamus of Saint James Published by a Certain Galician Teacher." This is known as the *Regi perhennis glorie* (AH 17:206–7). It was necessary to place the Latin first line in the second line position for language flow.

16. Here "James" is substituted for "the apostle" in the text of ch. 31.7 and "Galicia" is likewise substituted for "province."

For to the ethereal seats
He ascended. Thanks be to God.

[CCA 8] Master John Legalis[17]

Let our voices resound
And thunder the praise
Of James to the Creator.

Let the cleric with the organ
And the people with the drum
    Sing to the Redeemer.

With the song due Him,
Let one sing to the Paraclete,
    That is, to the Consoler.

With this song without end,
Let us give praises
    To the Lord.

[CCA 9.1] Master Ato, Bishop of Trier[18]

R.   *While He was...*
V.   *For just as the crash of thunder resounds on the wheel of the earth, so also* [f.188r] *the preaching of Saint James went out to all the earth...*[19]

    Glory be to the Father and to the Son and to the Holy Spirit...[20]

---

17. This is the *Vox nostra resonet* text (AH 17:209). The author is unknown. The name, if taken at face value, would be John the Lawyer.
18. For Master Ato, see n. 4 above.
19. This responsorial and versicle are known as the *Dum esset Salvator*. See ch. 21.2, n. 11.
20. This and the following instances of "Glory be..." are written directly under the end of the last phrase in each verse.

[CCA 9.2] Another of Ato[21]

R. *To this James...*

V. *My soul is sad unto death.*
Glory be to the Father and to the Son and to the Holy Spirit...

[CCA 9.3] Another of Ato[22]

R. *James... of the virginal...*

V. *Pray for us with your continual prayer.*
Glory be to the nourishing Father and to the Son and to the Holy Flame.

[CCA 9.4] Another of Ato[23]

R. *O helper... [f.188v]*

V. *You, who help those in peril calling to you both on the sea and on land, plead with Christ and help us now and at the point of death.[24]*
Glory be to God, the most excellent nourishing Father, and to His highest and pious Son and to the Holy Spirit of Them both.

[CCA 9.5] Another of Ato[25]

Seq. *Give us a port at the Final Judgment*
So that with God, Who is without a beginning,

And with His Begotten One, Who is without an end,
And with the Paraclete that proceeded from both,

---

21. This is the *Huic Iacobo condoluit* text. See ch. 23.9 for the full text.
22. This is the *Iacobe virginei frater* text. See ch. 23.11 for the full text.
23. This is the *O adiutor omnium* text. See ch. 23.12 for the full text.
24. This is found at the end of Miracle 8: "You, who help those at sea or on land calling out to you in their peril, help us now and in the trial of our death" (Coffey and Dunn, *Miracles*, 30–31). In Miracle 8 the bishop is not named but is said to be returning from Jerusalem.
25. This is the *Portum in ultimo* text.

Addenda to the Codex Calixtinus

So that we, having been removed from the dark pit of Tartarus,
Having joined [f.189r] with the most holy choir of the angels,

Having been purged of vice and, having acquired joy
With you as the prize of life as a patron,

May enter with pious prayer
The garden of paradise.

[CCA 10] Bishop Fulbert of Chartres

Immense King, pious Father, have mercy.[26]
Savior, eternal God,[27] *have mercy.*
You, Who hold all things in the palm of Your hand, have mercy.[28]
Christ, Son of the highest Father, have mercy.[29]
You, Who came down from the heavens, have mercy.
You, Who redeemed Your creation, have mercy.[30]
Consoler, sweet love, have mercy.
You, Who have shone on James, have mercy.
You, Who spare us through his prayer, have mercy.

---

26. This is the *Rex immense* text. See ch. 31.2. Throughout, the "have mercy" is rendered in the Latin text by the transcribed Greek *eleison*, though consistently spelled *eleyson;* in this addenda version, the words "Lord" and "Christ" are omitted in the Latin text.

27. These words are rendered in CC by the transcribed Greek: *Soter, Theos* and *athanatos.*

28. Each line of these verses is written stacked one over the other as if in a column, under half the line of music. The first presentation of this in Bk. I, ch. 31.2 contains additional verses. The text is presented with the *Gloria* (normally sung after it).

29. Throughout, the "Christ, have mercy" is rendered in CC by the transcribed Greek *Christe (Xr-e) eleison.*

30. After this line, the notation *Ato prefatus* or "the aforementioned Ato" is added in rubrics. It is not certain if this is to indicate that the last three lines of the *Kyrie* are ascribed to him.

R. *Herod sent...*
He killed, however, [f.189v] *James, brother of John...* [Acts 12:1–2]

[CCA 11] Master Goslenus, Bishop of Soissons[31]

Alleluia
Jesus called James of Zebedee and John his brother and gave them the name "Boanerges." [f.190r]

[CCA 12.1] Gauterius, Mentioned Above[32]

Almighty Father, God, Creator to all, have mercy.
Christ, in the form of God, and Virtue and Wisdom of the Father, have mercy.
Sacred Breath from Both, bond and love, have mercy.

[CCA 12.2] Gauterius, Mentioned Above[33]

Let us bless the Lord.

[CCA 13.1] Master Droardus of Troyes[34]

Let us bless [f.190v] *the Lord.*

[CCA 13.2] Another of Droardus

Let us bless the Lord.

---

31. See above n. 6. This two-voice section is known as *Alleluia, Vocavit Ihesus Iacobum*. This is a variant of the *Jesus vocavit* text. See ch. 21.2, n. 11.
32. This is the *Cunctipotens Genitor Deus;* on Gauterius, see above, n. 15.
33. This and the next two entries are minimal *Benedicamus* texts. See ch. 30.3, n.13.
34. There is no additional information about Droard of Troyes.

ADDENDA TO THE CODEX CALIXTINUS

[CCA 14] Aymeric Picaud, Priest of Partiniacus[35]

1. *To the honor of the highest King, Who created all things*[36]
   We venerate and raise a shout of joy to the mighty works of James,
   Of whom the citizens of heaven rejoice in the highest court,
   Whose glorious deeds the Church recalls.
2. Above the Sea of Galilee, he set aside all things.
   After having seen the King, he did not want to return to mundane things
   But he decided to go and follow the One calling him,
   And he strove to preach His sacred precepts.[37]

---

35. The name "Aimericus Cancellarius" (Chancellor Aimeric) also appears below as a signatory to the letter ostensibly written by Pope Innocent affirming the veracity of the LSJ (CCA 16), as well as in the controversial appearance of "Aymeric Picaud from Parthenay-le-Vieux" in the body of that same letter. It also appears twice in Bk. V (the Guide) in ch. 5, "The Names of Those Who Restored the Road to St. James –Aimery–," and again in the heading to ch. 9, "The Characteristics of the City and the Church of St. James –Pope Calixtus and Aimery the Chancellor–." (Melczer, *Pilgrim's Guide*, 88, 119. See also 140–41.) The scholarship and questions about this person (or persons) and his (their) relationship to the LSJ is legion. For a discussion of these names/persons, see Stones, *The Pilgrim's Guide*, 1:18–22. For a review of scholarship about the role of this person (these persons) in the authorship and compilation of the LSJ, see Díaz y Díaz, *El Códice*, 64–69 and 85–88.

36. This is the *Ad honorem Regis summi* text (AH 17:210). For more information about the musical importance of this hymn, see David Hiley, "Two Unnoticed Pieces of Medieval Polyphony," *Plainsong and Medieval Music* 1.2 (October 1992):167–73.

37. The scribe has placed the final letter (-t) to the right hand margin for all of this stanza. There is at least one folio missing at this point. Herbers marked this loss by leaving a folio number omitted here. Whitehill presented a probable text for the remaining verses of the Picaud piece (Whitehill, 398–99). Although Whitehill does not say from where he made his transcription of this missing folio, it appears that he obtained it indirectly from the British Library, Additional 12213 (British Museum at the time of Whitehill's writing). We have added stanza numbers for ease of reference. Our translation of stanzas 3 to 11 use the text provided by Whitehill. The missing folio of CC

[Inserted text:]
3. He offered the faith of Christ to Hermogenes and Philetus,
   And he baptized Josias and offered strength to the sick man.[38]
   He once saw Jesus transformed by the divine will of the Father
   For Whom he accepted death from Herod and poured out his blood.
4. His body was buried in the land of Galicia,
   And those seeking out his body acquire a life of glory.
   He still shines throughout the world with divine miracles,
   As he once released twenty men from prison.[39]
5. The list of a sinner appeared deleted.[40]
   He restored one dead son of a mother to life.[41]
   He carried a dead person from Cize to his city —
   A twice-six-day journey — in one night.[42]
6. He brought back to life someone hanged for thirty days,[43]
   And he gave over an ass to a pilgrim from Poitiers,[44]

---

was still included prior to c.1325 when the British Museum manuscript was copied. It does not include musical notation for any of the pieces, but was likely made in Santiago de Compostela. Its text follows CC. For a complete description of this manuscript, see Stones, *The Pilgrim's Guide*, 1:109–13. In addition, a catch word at the bottom of CC f.190v matches the beginning of what would be CC f.191r as reflected in the British Library manuscript. The meter and the rhyme scheme of stanzas 3–11 match with stanzas 1–2.

38. This story is taken from the *Pasionario*. See Coffey and Dunn, *Miracles*, 110–17.
39. Bk. III, Miracle 1, Coffey and Dunn, *Miracles*, pp. 7–11. This and the following twenty-two lines each refer, in order, to the miracles of Bk. III of the CC. The summary lines here are so short as to be somewhat obscure.
40. Bk. III, Miracle 2, Coffey and Dunn, *Miracles*, pp. 11–14.
41. Bk. III, Miracle 3, Coffey and Dunn, *Miracles*, pp. 14–17.
42. Bk. III, Miracle 4, Coffey and Dunn, *Miracles*, pp. 18–22.
43. Bk. III, Miracle 5, Coffey and Dunn, *Miracles*, pp. 22–25.
44. Bk. III, Miracle 6, Coffey and Dunn, *Miracles*, pp. 25–27.

And he rescued Frisonus, who was wearing his armor from the sea,[45]
And he returned to a ship a bishop submerged in the sea.[46]

7. The apostle offered to a man the power of conquering the Turks.[47]
   He held afloat by his head a pilgrim who had fallen in the sea.[48]
   A healthy man jumping from a high arch was snatched from death.[49]
   A soldier touched by a shell was returned to health.[50]

8. Dalmatius was restored to health after his punishment.[51]
   A merchant discreetly escaped from a tower bent to the ground,[52]
   And he protected a soldier from those following him.[53]
   He liberated a sick man oppressed by demons.[54]

9. He restored to life one who had killed himself,[55]
   And he opened the closed doors of the oratory for a count,[56]
   And he appeared to Stephen, the servant of God, as a soldier.[57]
   A count was not able to harm a captive man with his sword[58]

---

45. Bk. III, Miracle 7, Coffey and Dunn, *Miracles*, pp. 28–30.
46. Bk. III, Miracle 8, Coffey and Dunn, *Miracles*, pp. 30–31.
47. Bk. III, Miracle 9, Coffey and Dunn, *Miracles*, pp. 32–34.
48. Bk. III, Miracle 10, Coffey and Dunn, *Miracles*, p. 34
49. Bk. III, Miracle 11, Coffey and Dunn, *Miracles*, p. 35.
50. Bk. III, Miracle 12, Coffey and Dunn, *Miracles*, p. 36.
51. Bk. III, Miracle 13, Coffey and Dunn, *Miracles*, p. 37.
52. Bk. III, Miracle 14, Coffey and Dunn, *Miracles*, pp. 38–39.
53. Bk. III, Miracle 15, Coffey and Dunn, *Miracles*, pp. 39–40.
54. Bk. III, Miracle 16, Coffey and Dunn, *Miracles*, pp. 41–44.
55. Bk. III, Miracle 17, Coffey and Dunn, *Miracles*, pp. 45–51.
56. Bk. III, Miracle 18, Coffey and Dunn, *Miracles*, pp. 52–54.
57. Bk. III, Miracle 19, Coffey and Dunn, *Miracles*, pp. 54–57.
58. Bk. III, Miracle 20, Coffey and Dunn, *Miracles*, pp. 57–59.

10. He humbly caused a crippled man to stand up on his legs.[59]
    He charmingly released a chained man thirteen times.[60]
    These are the sacrosanct divine miracles
    That James performed for the honor of Christ throughout the ages.
11. For this, let us cheerfully release praises to the King of kings!
    May we be worthy to live happily and eternally with him!
    Let there be an "Amen," and let us say solemnly, "Alleluia!"
    Let us, joined together, say over and over: "And onwards and upwards!"

[End of inserted text]

[CCA 15] [Fragment of a Mass for the Octaves of Saint James]

[f.192r][61]...He invited James and John.

Grant, we beseech, that through the merits of both of them whom You wished to make participants in His chalice, we may sit at the right side in Your kingdom, through the same...[62]

---

59. Bk. III, Miracle 21, Coffey and Dunn, *Miracles*, pp. 59–60.
60. Bk. III, Miracle 22, Coffey and Dunn, *Miracles*, pp. 60–63.
61. The CC material resumes here midway through a communion prayer. The missing text would have been: *Deus cuius filius ad bibendum calicem suum beatos filios Zebedei,...* "God whose Son [invited] Zebedee's sons [James and John] to drink from His chalice." The supplied text is from the "Mass for the Feast and the Octave of Saint James" (Vol. 1, 438) of López Ferreiro, *Historia de la Santa A.M. Iglesia de Santiago de Compostela*. From this point on, there is a marked change in the physical appearance and variety of the addenda material. Miscellaneous works rather than a continuation of the liturgical material in the style of chapters 21–31 seem to have been added, as if any material relative to St. James was simply inserted in a random manner.
62. We placed an ellipsis here on the assumption that there would be the usual formulaic ending "Christ our Lord. Amen," or some variant thereof.

ADDENDA TO THE CODEX CALIXTINUS

[CCA 16] Letter of Lord Pope Innocent[63]

Innocent, bishop, servant of the servants of God, to all the children of the Church, greetings, and apostolic benediction in Christ.

This is the codex, first edited by Lord Pope Calixtus, that Aymeric Picaud from Parthenay-le-Vieux[64] — who is also called Oliver of Asquins[65] from the villa of Saint Mary Magdalene of Vézelay[66] — and Girberga of Flanders, his companion, presented to Saint James in Galicia for the redemption of their souls. Attestation is given by our authority that it is most truthful in words, most fitting in delivery, foreign to anything heretical or apocryphal, and is among the authentic and precious ecclesiastical codices. We excommunicate and anathematize by the authority of God the almighty Father and of the Son and of the Holy Spirit, those who should perhaps disturb those bearing it on the route of Saint James or those who should steal or unjustly take it from the basilica of this apostle.

Be well.

I, Chancellor Aimeric,[67] affirm by signing with my hand that this book is authentic and true and for the honor of Saint James.

---

63. Pope Innocent II (born Gregorio Papareschi, d.1143, pope from 1130). As to the dating of the letter, two of the signatories (Aimeric of Burgundy and the younger Gregorio Papareschi, who was nephew of the pope) died in 1141.

64. Parthenay-le-Vieux is in the department of Deux-Sèvres, province of Poitou.

65. While the text reads *Iscani*, it is likely, from indications here and from proximity to Vézelay and its relationship with the pilgrimage route, to be the town of Asquins in the Bourgogne-Franche-Comté region, near Vézelay.

66. This likely refers to the Benedictine abbey and church of Saint Mary Magdalene in Vézelay.

67. Aimeric de la Châtre or of Burgundy was elevated to the rank of cardinal deacon of Santa Maria Nuova, Rome, by Calixtus II in 1120 or 1123. He was chancellor of the holy Roman Church from 1123 until his death in May 1141. For his relationship to Compostela, see Fletcher, *Saint James's Catapult*, 212–15, 219.

SERMONS AND LITURGY OF SAINT JAMES

I, Cardinal Girard of Sancta Cruce,[68] corroborate, by writing with my pen, that this book is precious and to the glory of Saint James.

I, Cardinal Guido Pissanus,[69] affirm that Lord Pope Innocent attested to this.

I, Cardinal Ivo,[70] do not take exception to approving that the authority of Lord Pope Innocent affirms this.

I, Cardinal Gregory,[71] nephew of Lord Pope Innocent, praise this codex as excellent for the honor of Saint James.

I, Cardinal Guido of Lombardy,[72] honor this codex as good and most noble for the honor of Saint James.

I, Cardinal Gregory of Iena,[73] similarly praise this codex as excellent for the honor of Saint James.

I, Bishop Alberic of Ostia,[74] as legate, proclaim this codex as legitimate and laudable in all ways and most precious for the honor of Saint James, of whom I am the humble servant. [f.192v]

---

68. Gherardo Caccianemice dal Orso was appointed by Calixtus II as cardinal priest of the church of the Holy Cross in Jerusalem in 1122 or 1124. He was chancellor of the holy Roman Church from 1141 to 1144. He was Pope Lucius II from March 1144 until his death in February 1145.

69. Guido Pissanus or Guido of Pisa was made cardinal deacon of the basilica of Saints Cosmas and Damian by Pope Innocent II in 1130 or 1132. He was chancellor of the holy Roman Church from 1146 until his death in 1149.

70. Cardinal Ivo was made cardinal priest of the basilica of Saint Lawrence in Damaso, Rome, legate in 1142, papal legate to the king of France, who died on his return in 1144 and was buried in the cathedral of Saint Peter in Trier.

71. Gregory Papareschi, raised to the rank of cardinal in 1134, d.1141; as in many cases, "nephew" does not ensure a blood relationship of any kind.

72. Unidentified. There were a number of cardinals by this name at the time.

73. Unidentified. There were several cardinals by this name at the time.

74. Alberic of Ostia (1080–1148) was born in Beauvais, France, became a Benedictine monk at Cluny and abbot of Vézelay from 1131 to 1138. He was made the cardinal-bishop of Ostia in 1138; as papal legate he was sent from Rome on various missions.

[CCA 17] A Miracle of Saint James,[75] Written Down by Alberic,[76] Abbot of Vézelay, Bishop of Ostia, and Legate in Rome

In the year of our Lord's Incarnation 1139, as Louis[77] reigned as king of France and Innocent[78] presided as pope, a certain man by the name of Bruno of Vézelay, from the town of Mary Magdalene,[79] was coming back from Saint James, and lacking money, he began to beg. Since he did not have anything with which he might buy a coin's worth of bread, on a certain day he was still hungry at about the ninth hour, and he was ashamed to beg. He was very distressed, and he implored with all his heart the help of Saint James and rested alone under a certain tree. While there, he slept a short time and dreamt that Saint James fed him some food. In fact, when he woke up, he found, near his head, ash cake[80] bread on which he lived

---

75. This miracle is written in the style and is dated within the parameters of the miracles of Bk. II. See Coffey and Dunn, *Miracles*, 64–65. While the current recto side of this folio has a script quite distinct from that of the previous folios, this verso folio is virtually identical to the first folios of the Addenda material. In fact, Díaz y Díaz, *El Códice Calixtino*, (153–54) describes the irregularities in the binding of folios 188–95, suggesting they originally had a different order.

76. See n. 74 above.

77. Louis VI, the Fat (1081–1137; reigned 1108–37).

78. See n. 63 above.

79. From the eleventh century it has been claimed that Mary Magdalene's relics were housed there. See Susan Haskins, *Mary Magdalen: Myth and Metaphor* (New York: Harcourt, Brace & Company, 1993), 98–100.

80. The exact term has not been located, but the Latin *subcinericium panem* certainly refers to a low-quality bread, baked in ashes rather than an oven, as evidenced by the base *cinericius* or "ash-like." Bread baked in this way *("khubz malla")* is mentioned in a tenth-century Arabic cookbook. In Nawal Nasrallah, *Annals of the Caliphs' Kitchens: Ibn Sayyār al-Warrāq's Tenth-Century Baghdadi Cookbook* (Leiden: Brill, 2007), it is described as "a simple bread of humble origin. It is baked in *malla*, a pit in which bread is baked in hot ashes and stones.... It is mostly baked by Bedouins and travelers.... This bread is a premonition of hard times to come, financially, because it is bread to eat only when pressed by necessity." (567)

for fifteen days until he came to his own region. On each day he would eat sufficiently from it twice, and every other day, he would find a full loaf of bread in his small bag. Oh, wondrous renewed deed of Elias the Prophet![81]

This was done by the Lord, and it is miraculous in our eyes. Therefore, let there be honor and glory to the King of kings. World without end. Amen.

[CCA 18] Alleluia in Greek

Alleluia
Jesus called...[82]
Jesus called James of Zebedee and John his brother and
    gave to them the name "Boanerges," which
    means "Sons of Thunder."[83]

Chorus: *Which means "Sons..."*[84]
Cantor: *Alleluia.* [f.193r]

---

81. In 1 Kgs (1 Sam) 17:8–16, the prophet Elijah asks a poor woman to feed him. She has only a small jar of meal but is able to make a cake to feed Elijah for many days without the meal running out.

82. This is the *Jesus vocavit* text. See ch. 21.2, n. 11.

83. This passage, beginning after "Jesus called," is in transliterated Greek letters: *"Efonisen ho Hyssus Iacobon tu Sebezeum ke Ioannin azelfon aptu, ke kale sen aptis onomata Boanerges pion pragma estin o yos tis vrontis."* Most of this would be generally comprehensible to a Greek speaker.

84. This indicates the repetition of the words: "which means 'Sons of Thunder.'"

ADDENDA TO THE CODEX CALIXTINUS

[CCA 19] [Dum Pater Familias][85]

Nominative:[86]

> *When the Father of the family,*[87]
> *The King of all,*
> *Gave provinces*
> *As a right of the apostles,*
> *James [received] Spain*
> *And shines as a beacon of morals.*[88]
>> *First among the apostles*
>> *To become a martyr in Jerusalem,*
>> *James is consecrated through*
>> *His honorable martyrdom.*

Genitive:

> *Of James, Galicia asks*
> *For gracious help.*
> *The glory of his body*

---

85. This is the *Dum Pater Familias* text (AH 17:213). We have used the first several words as the title. It is also known as the *Hymnus peregrinorum* or as "Canto de ultreia." See Illus., p. xiv.

86. On this new folio the script is quite different from previous folios, as is the musical notation. The poem uses the name "James" in the six cases of medieval Latin in the following order: nominative (used for the subject of a sentence: *Iacobus*), genitive (used to show possession: *Iacobi*), dative ("to whom" or "for whom" something is done, and also with some prepositions: *Iacobo*), accusative (object of a verb and of also with some prepositions: *Iacobum*), vocative (used for direct address: *Iacobe*), and ablative ("by which" something is done, in certain clause structures and after certain prepositions: *Iacobo*).

87. This also means "head of the household" and "patriarch of the family." It had legal implications as well.

88. The Latin here is *lux...morum*, literally "light of morals," and indicates that James has become a moral compass for the previously pagan land. The word *mos/moris* is used regularly in this sense in the CC. On the other hand, the word for Moors is *Mauri*, always written with the *au* stem. It is also a word that is used in the plural only.

Creates an extraordinary route,
And the frequency of prayers
Brings forth a pleasant melody.
  Lord Saint James,
  Good Saint James,
  Both onwards and upwards,
  God help us.[89]
 First among the apostles
 To become a martyr in Jerusalem,
 James is consecrated through
 His honorable martyrdom.

Dative:
 To James are freely given requests by
 All manner of people[90]
 For the sake of his relief.
 A pious soldier,
 A protection for all,
 Satisfies the prayers.
  First among the apostles
  To become a martyr in Jerusalem,

---

89. This small stanza, *"Herru Sanctiagu / Got Sanctiagu / E ultreia e susseia, / Deus aia nos"* is a mix of Germanic and Romance words that are understandable while presenting a number of difficulties. The first two lines are clearly Germanic and seem to be of Low German provenance. The word *Herr* is still used (without this spurious *"u"* ending) for "Lord" or "Sir" or even "Mr." in modern German. The word *Got* seems best translated as "good," though there are other possibilities dependent, in part, on the provenance of the word. The second two lines are clearly of Romance provenance, and their meaning is evident though the exact language is difficult to pinpoint, if, in fact, these words are actually from a particular language or dialect. See also ch. 26.6, n. 41.

90. The Latin is *parium* ("associates"), although the meaning does not convert to English. In addition, one can infer that petitions are offered to which James is able to respond satisfactorily, and thus "requests" is supplied here for context.

ADDENDA TO THE CODEX CALIXTINUS

    James is consecrated through
    His honorable martyrdom.

Accusative:
    Through this James, because of the miracles
    That are done by him,
    Anyone in severe danger
    May call to him;
    Anyone who hopes to be freed from bonds
    May have hope because of him.
        First among the apostles
        To become a martyr in Jerusalem,
        James is consecrated through
        His honorable martyrdom.

Vocative:
    O Saint James,
    Truly our strength,
    Remove our enemies from us
    And protect your own
    And summon the devout
    And make us pleasing to you.
        First among the apostles
        To become a martyr in Jerusalem,
        James is consecrated through
        His honorable martyrdom.

Ablative:
    Through propitious James
    We hope for forgiveness
    And for those things that we must

Earn from compliance[91] *and merit.*[92]
To the extraordinary Father
Let us give worthy praise. Amen.
    First among the apostles
    To become a martyr in Jerusalem,
    James is consecrated through
    His honorable martyrdom.

[CCA 20] [A Dicolos Tetrastrophos][93]

This ode is titled "dicolos tetrastrophos," that is, a song composed of two kinds of meters; from the fourth verse on, there occurs a replication of the meter. It is considered Sapphic, for it consists of three like verses — the first measure consists of a trochee, a spondee, a dactyl, and two trochees — and the fourth verse, an Adonius, runs with a dactyl and a spondee.[94]

    We have sacred signs that may be read,
    In which a window to the holy life
    Is made evident to the new minds, even to the true
        Israelites.

    In wandering gradually through the vastness of the desert,
    A happy place is found here for the Hebrews,
    Which they read as Elim, and for those who had gone forth, it was
        A sixth dwelling place.

---

91. The text inserts an alternative here: *vel ex officio* ("from service").
92. This notion of "earn" is implicit in the Latin *merito* or "deservedly."
93. While the introduction titles the work "A Dicolos Tetrastrophos," it is commonly titled by its first words: *Signa sunt nobis sacra* (AH 17:214–15).
94. This passage shows an acquaintance with complex classical poetic form. Its essence is that there are three lines of eleven syllables followed by one line of five syllables. The original complexity was for a language with an emphasis on vowel length rather than on stress. The commonality is the number of syllables.

ADDENDA TO THE CODEX CALIXTINUS

Springs numbering twice six flow there
Rising[95] up with their soft sound for the child.
The fruits of hope and the palms of honor stand
    Numbering seventy.[96]

Such a phenomenon expressed with matching figures[97]
Denotes the first and second order
Of the disciples who followed Christ
    In faith and cross. [f.193v]

Already, with God's help, the voice of these disciples,
Wondrous with the distinguished merits of virtues,
Goes out to the orb in obtaining the sweet glory
    Of the palms of victory.

The teaching[98] of these saints moistens the earth
Of the heart to be cultivated with the dew
Raining down[99] from above.
    Thanks be for the dew!

---

95. The words *id est recreare* ("that is, to recreate") are added in CC.

96. Cf. Ex 15:27. When Moses and the Israelites escaped from Egypt, their first camp was at Elim where they found twelve wells and seventy palm trees. Cf. also Exodus 3 and 33. The words *et due f* ("and two f") are added interlinearly. It is not known what the "f" represents. The "and two" is a likely reference to the idea that there were seventy-two rather than seventy disciples.

97. This is a pre-figuring of the seventy disciples. In the eastern tradition especially, there are considered to be seventy-two disciples as the interlinear note in the first instance of this piece indicates. In addition, there are twelve springs prefiguring the twelve apostles. The first order is the apostles, twelve in number, and the second order is the disciples, often seventy (or seventy-two) in number.

98. The Latin is *dogma* ("teaching"); in the second iteration of this work at the end of the addenda, the text reads *li[n]gua* or ("eloquence").

99. The words *vel influente* ("or flowing down") are added interlinearly.

SERMONS AND LITURGY OF SAINT JAMES

The sixth age has begun[100]
In which God comes to restore freely
And to call those of us who believe. Let us, therefore, keep watch
    In this welcome[101] time.

Among these believers, Saint James shines.
As a distinguished martyr and pillar of faith,
And as first in the choir of those slaughtered by Herod,
    He stands among the twelve.[102]

From this point onward, he is the honor of life and the embodiment of forgiveness,
Son of the greatest and highest Thunder,[103]
A supplanting star,[104] a wave of piety,
    A well-spring for pilgrims.

He is also given to the Spanish as a patron,
A shepherd, and bread set out for the traveler

---

100. The idea of the six ages of the world comes from St. Augustine's *De Civitate Dei,* especially in Bk. 22, ch. 30 (PL 41:801–4). It was treated by Bede in his *De Temporum Ratione,* especially in ch. 66–71 (PL 90:520–78). The first age was from Adam to Noah, the second from Noah to Abraham, the third from Abraham to David, the fourth from David to the Babylonian Captivity, the fifth from the Babylonian Captivity to the birth of Christ, and the sixth from the birth of Christ until the end of this world, with a seventh and eighth age of the world to come.

101. Several options are given interlinearly for *grato* ("welcome"): *Christi vel adapto vel allegato* ("'of Christ' or 'adapted' or 'mentioned'").

102. Slightly over a line and a half are expunged at this point. It appears that the scribe's eyes jumped to line 41, where he began copying, before noting his error.

103. A reference to James and John as "Sons of Thunder." There is an attempt, not entirely successful, to clarify here, repeating some of the words more clearly in the left margin, in particular *Filius summi Tonitrus et alti* ("Son of the highest and greatest Thunder"), however one must rely on the meaning to determine the correct endings.

104. A reference to James as a guiding light toward heaven, rather than to the North. The alternative *vel planeta* ("or 'planet'") is given interlinearly.

ADDENDA TO THE CODEX CALIXTINUS

On which travelers of meager diet
    Are restored.[105]

Thereafter he was for us a swift advocate,[106]
Seeking forgiveness from Christ the Judge.
Ask for us in the love of Christ[107]
    That we may live with you.

May there be belief[108] in the Father and the Begotten Christ
And also in the Gale[109] poured out from Both.
May the Threefold be in the Threefold [at the same time as] the
    One in the One.[110]

    A perpetual glory! Amen.[111] [f.194r]

---

105. James both guides and cares for pilgrims, even those with very little faith; pilgrims to his shrine will receive pardon. There is a mix of the physical and the moral here; the meager diet may refer to fasting as a form of penance connected to forgiveness. In the second presentation of the poem, the scribe evidently hesitates between the verb *reficio* ("to be refreshed/nourished") and *iustifico* ("to be justified/forgiven"). The best word in English is "restored."
106. James in heaven has access to Christ's judgment.
107. The manuscript adds *vel Trino* ("or 'of the Trinity'") as an alternative.
108. The word is "doxa," the transliterated Greek δόξα ("belief").
109. The Latin is *flamini* ("wind" or "gale") intensifies the idea of the "spirit" or "breath" in harmony with the thunder imagery.
110. The word *simul* ("together") is barely visible, and the *Unius* ("of One") may be just *Uni* ("for the one").
111. The last line of this stanza is stricken through, although it is a necessary and apparently correct last line. The bottom two-thirds of the folio are left blank.

[CCA 21.1] In theYear of the Lord's Incarnation MCLXIIII in Indiction XII[112] and Epact XXV: A Miracle of Saint James with a Resuscitated Boy[113]

God, through His saints, is marvelous and extraordinary;
    The Omnipotent One, powerful and alone, works wonders.
Still some of the saints of the Lord, by the power of the Mighty One,
    Can perform many signs and many powerful things.
And thus it is that James, filled with nourishing powers,
    Already shines as the pious standard bearer for all the world.
He stands as a pillar of virtue for the country and as a protector of the kingdom.
    He stands and comes through eternity as a help to pious prayers.[114]

In both the city of Clermont-Ferrand and[115] noble Le Puy,
    The bulwarks of Saint Florine[116] are known and celebrated.
A pilgrim, who was going from there to the threshold of Saint James,

---

112. This is the proper indiction year for 1164. The indictions are cycles of 15, with the year 313 being indiction 1, 314 being indiction 2, 327 being indiction 15, then 328 being indiction 1, and so forth.

113. The epact was a computation reflecting the relationship of the solar and lunar years, especially applied to the determination of the date for Easter. The formula is complex but this is correct for the year 1164. This date is from the calculations contained in Augustus de Morgan, *The Book of Almanacs* (London: Taylor Walton and Maberly, 1851), 2.

114. There is a stylized paragraph sign, presumably to indicate stanzas; we have divided the stanzas accordingly.

115. The text here gives a semantically equivalent interlinear alternative *vel tunc...vel tunc* for *tum...tum* ("both...and").

116. Sainte Florine is a town in the Haute-Loire region of France. The Latin is mistakenly *Sancti Florini* (masc.) rather than the expected *Sancte Florine* (fem.). It is about equidistant from Clermont-Ferrand and Le Puy.

Reported that a boy had been returned to life.
The one, whose spirit left the dead body,[117] was three years old,
And it was from the sunset[118] up until daybreak.
Consequently, the parents were not able to stop their tears
Or in pouring out prayers of entreaty to Saint James.
The following dawn, with his flesh ready to be prepared for interring,
They were lamenting with constant cries,
When the fortunate and always abundant grace of James
Raised the boy from there to a new life.[119]

Who can count so, so many commendations of praise
And gifts sent by these countless pilgrims?
Behold! The father of the boy related the deeds in the order they happened,
And he took the face cloth[120] as a token of proof.
This miracle was done by the Lord, Whose
Honor is in the saints. Perpetual glory! Amen.[121]
This was done by the Lord, and it is miraculous in our eyes. Amen.[122]

---

117. The Latin is *membra* ("members" i.e. "limbs" or "body parts").
118. The Latin is *sero solis* ("late hour of the sun").
119. This miracle is reminiscent of Bk. II, ch. 3, where a young man dies in the Montes de Oca and is resurrected by Saint James the next day. See Coffey and Dunn, *Miracles,* 14–17.
120. The Latin *sudariolum* often for handkerchief, here appears to be related to the preparation of the body. For descriptions of how "sudarium" was used to describe the burial facecloth or bonnet, see Olga Magoula, *Usage and Meaning of Early Medieval Textiles: A Structural Analysis of Vestimentary Systems in Francia and Anglo-Saxon England* (PhD diss., University of Birmingham, 2008), 64, 105–6, https://etheses.bham.ac.uk/id/eprint/954.
121. The "Amen" is struck through, and in the right margin the prose version that follows is written in the same hand as the text.
122. The Latin for this is in the right margin and is heavily abbreviated; there is, however, an unexplained "t" before the "a" that is clearly the abbreviation

[CCA 21.2] Another Miracle[123]
A Miracle of Saint James and the Twisted Face of the Son of the Viscount Known in the Land of Poitiers

There is all manner of pain and worthy retribution from justice,
> As all well-being is from the piety of God.

Happy is the one who has been worthy and standing in well-deserved safety
> When there is justice from the strong right hand of God.

A pilgrim, coming to the threshold of Saint James,
> Related such deeds with his companions as witnesses to them:

To many is known the castle by the name of Châtellerault[124]
> Standing twelve miles[125] beyond Poitiers.

Coming to this place, this pilgrim of Saint James,
> Returning for a fifth time, walked into an ambush.

And behold! The powerful son of the viscount[126] resisted the weapons.
>> However, he desired another person's wife. She was a pilgrim and she fled, prepared to die, and entered the river waters,
>> As she preferred to die rather than commit adultery.

---

for "amen." In addition, the entire sentence is circled with red ink, and a red ligatured "XE" is found below.

123. The Latin *Aliud Miraculum* is in the left margin.
124. A town in the north of the department of Vienne.
125. The distance from Châtellerault to Poitiers is, in fact, 39 km (24 miles).
126. Written above *vicecomitis* is *vel consulis,* meaning in Classical Latin, "consul," but in medieval Latin, "count."

ADDENDA TO THE CODEX CALIXTINUS

He offered her a pledge of safety, and she gave him fraudulent kisses,[127]
    Lest he touch her, and she might then die in the waters.
What a surprising thing! The woman, in the presence of the man and his companions,
    After suffering his force, obtained a monstrous compensation.
Certainly, a thing of wonder! A thing fearful to all!
    Soon they noticed an ugly blemish and hideous defect,
For this guilty man's tongue was drawn forward from his contorted mouth,
    And he was given only six days to live.
Such divine justice for pilgrims!
    Let this be an example of terror everywhere for evil people!
This wretch failed and never again will profit.
    From such a situation; the evil one fails, the good one profits.[128]
This was done by the Lord, and it is miraculous in our eyes.
    We praise You, God. These two signs resound:
One faith sings of three Persons as three Beings;
    The threefold Individuality always appropriated for the Three
One faith sings about the Three in one Being,
    And the Substance sings about the threefold Individuality of the Three.[129] [f.194v]

---

127. The words *in undys* or "in the waters" is added interlinearly.

128. This reflects the message in the first sermon of Bk. I by Bede (pp. 14–22), where he analyzes the Epistle of James about temptations, properly handled, as opportunities.

129. This last stanza is set apart in smaller script with larger margins. It refers to the Nicene doctrine of *homoousios* and *hypostasis,* in which there are three Persons in one Being.

[CCA 21.3] A Miracle of Saint James on the Liberation of Christians and the Flight of the Saracens from Portugal. This[130] is to Be Read on the Feast of the Miracles of Saint James on the V None of October[131]

Reading I:
> Behold, the wonders of God returned with the Maccabees,
>> And long-established signs arrived from heaven.
> The people of Hagar perished, and the just people triumphed everywhere![132]
>> Under King Afonso,[133] Miramirin[134] fell,
> And King Sancho[135] was also in the service of Saint James.
>> Like his father before him, he was a faithful friend;
> There now he has royal power and is a faithful vassal,
>> That is, of Saint James. He holds two kingdoms.
> As a confirmed promise, the son of the kingdom reigns with one scepter,
>> And in Seville, the king's hand is to attain victory.

---

130. The meaning is clear, though the word *hic* (masc.) has no antecedent and should likely be *hoc* (neut.).

131. October 3. The text, "This is to be read…October," is found in the left margin. (AH 17:216.)

132. The author compares the Maccabees (167–37BCE), who took back control of Judea, to the Christians retaking territory from the Moslem caliphates of the Iberian Peninsula.

133. Afonso I, king of Portugal (1139–85). The text uses "Alfonso."

134. Moralejo interprets the Latin *Miramirin* as a personal name, Miramolín (*Emir-almumenín,* or Abu-Yácub, second Almohad caliph). See Moralejo, 597, line 10.

135. Sancho I, king of Portugal (1185–1211). The text uses *Sancius.*

ADDENDA TO THE CODEX CALIXTINUS

Reading II:
> It is written in the gests[136] that King Almanzor[137] perished
>> By God striking him with dysentery.
> Now the son of Al-miramini[138] has also perished ignominiously,
>> A great king of the earth wanting to micturate.[139]
> And soon the abominable, secretly installed offspring of the previous one[140]
>> Died with the divine hand striking him.
> Divine signs and blessed praises resound,
>> And the Church sings a *Te Deum*.[141]
> You also, Calliope,[142] have been accustomed to narrate fittingly;
>> May you not be silent in praise of the great of Saint James.

Reading III:
> When the enemies pressed the Temple of the Lord in Jerusalem,
>> A wondrous battle array from heaven was seen in the air:
> White horses running and horsemen with gilded weapons
>> And with white garments, all in defense of the just faith.[143]

---

136. Various *chansons de geste* mention Almanzor.

137. Almanzor (c.938–1002) died from an illness, but only after becoming the leader of Al-Andalus, attacking León and Castilla, and even raiding Santiago de Compostela in 997. His ongoing infirmity (dysentery) is hinted at in the Pseudo-Turpin (Bk. IV, ch. 25) when Almanzor prays that his illness be cured but later reneges on his vow. See Poole, *Chronicle*, 87–88.

138. The CC adds *vel Admirati;* it is not clear whether this is an alternative name or an adjective ("admired").

139. The meaning of the Latin, *misciquitare,* is uncertain. However, the idea of dysuria (having difficulty urinating) seems a reasonable possibility, especially in view of the other ruler dying of dysentery.

140. We have adopted the abbreviated interlinear *vel* [p̶r̶i̶o̶]-*ris,* "or 'of the previous one,'" rather than the text's *priori,* "to the previous one."

141. The *Te Deum* or *Te Deum Laudamus* ("We praise You, God") is an early hymn of the Church.

142. The Greek muse of eloquence and epic poetry.

143. This imagery harkens back to the Maccabees reference in Reading I above (2 Macc 10:27–31).

SERMONS AND LITURGY OF SAINT JAMES

> Thus, the power of the Lord and the whole army of heaven
> > Continue the battles against the enemies of the faith.[144]
> Thence it is that many, but only those faithful who have been the worthy,
> > Have seen the great standard-bearer James.[145]
> It is because of this that the three feasts[146] of Saint James endure,
> > And the Church is made free,[147] if ever it was bound.
> On the feasts of James, there is a three-fold confession of praise,
> > A renewal of the heart by the mouth with proper faith at work.
> This opens the heavens for forgiving those bound by sin.
> > This is the renewal of life and the love of renewal.
> Therefore, the distinguished soldier of divine justice,
> > James, is able to live forever in Christ. Amen.
> > > This was done by the Lord
> > > And it is miraculous in our eyes.
> > > In the year of our Lord MCXC,
> > > In the era MCCXXVIII.[148] [f.195r]

---

144. The *Gesta Francorum* (written c.1100–1101) describes the soldiers' vision of St. George with white horses during the battle at Antioch during the First Crusade.

145. James has a military appearance in four of the miracles of Bk. II (ch. 4, 15, 16, and 19), but is only specifically astride a horse in ch. 4 and is not seen in battle in any of them. The siege (and fall) of Moslem-held Coimbra in 1064 predicted in ch. 19 is narrated in the *Historia Silense* (written c.1109–18), which tells of James's fighting alongside Fernando I. The fictional battle of Clavijo (844CE), in which Saint James is said to have first appeared as *Matamoros* (Moor-slayer), was recorded nearly 300 years later in the forged *Diploma of Ramiro I*.

146. The text adds in the margin: "that is of the passion, of the *translation*, and of the miracles; of the *translation* on the III Calends of January [December 30], of the passion on the VIII Calends of August [July 25], and of the miracles on the V None of October [October 3] for the pilgrim who was ordered to be killed."

147. The words *vel solvenda* ("or 'is to be freed'") are in the margin, as an alternative to the main text *solvitur* ("is freed").

148. Year of our Lord 1190; Spanish era 1228. On the Spanish peninsula, from the fifth to fifteenth centuries, the Spanish era was in use, which counted

ADDENDA TO THE CODEX CALIXTINUS

[CCA 22] Prayer of Master G.[149]

Adonai,[150] King of kings and Lord,
Alpha and Omega[151] of immeasurable light,
God speaking to us through a Man,
I acclaim You in Your name.

You, the Son of God, in restoring us
So that I may be free, just, and innocent,
Said that we are thus truly free,
If You have made us wretches free.[152]

From that comes the freedom of Your glory
That the service of Your justice[153]
Will justify me[154] tomorrow and today
With the chosen ones at the font of forgiveness.

To your servants you said, "Seek."
As to our requesting, we hear, "Request."
As to our knocking, You say the third time, "Knock."[155]
Your advice is an invitation to us.[156]

---

from 38BC. The AD *(Anno Domini)* system was adopted across the peninsula at various dates. To convert to the Spanish era one adds 38 to the AD date.
149. AH 17:217–18 suggests Walter of Chateau Renard. In the CC, the "Prayer of Master G." is written in red in the right-hand margin and is virtually illegible.
150. The Latin is *Adonay* for "Adonai" ("My Lord"), one of several Hebrew names for God.
151. "Omega" is rendered as "ω" using the cursive Greek form.
152. Herbers makes a comparison to Jn 8:36.
153. Herbers makes a comparison to Rom 8:21.
154. The text adds *vel nos* ("or 'us'") as an alternative.
155. Cf. Mt 7:7, Lk 11:9.
156. The Latin is the unknown *consultio;* however, *consultatio* results in "seeking advice" or at least by metonymy "advice."

Through Your divine title over time,[157]
You have visited us and the world.
Free me from the bond of sins
And confirm it with a sheaf of worthy grain.

After the years lived out with men —
Thirty-three with three months[158] —
Your death is the destruction of
Perpetual death, King of highest glory.

Through the distinctions of seven hours[159]
In which you drew to Yourself the people,
In redeeming us, Your servants,
May You cast Your eyes upon me.[160]

Because of this, may that singular mercy
Precede me in my misery.
To you I call through the hours of three days[161]
Four times ten[162] to be restored by You.

Through so many days, after
Spreading wide the gates of life to the innocent,

---

157. The first part of the word is blurred. We have used the word *etatis*, as did Dreves and others; however, rather than "of time," we have translated the expression as "over time."
158. Jesus is said to have lived thirty-three and one-third years.
159. The use of "seven" counts the hours on the cross including the starting and finishing hours.
160. The text adds *vel nos* ("or 'us'") as an alternative.
161. This may refer to the three days preceding the Resurrection.
162. Biblically, the number forty is often associated with periods of trial or probation, such as Jesus' time in the desert and the season of Lent.

ADDENDA TO THE CODEX CALIXTINUS

You arose from the dead after shattering the underworld,
Bearing the lamb forever[163] on Your shoulders.[164]

At the end[165] of the royal age,
The age of our army arises
So that we may be dressed with the cover of salvation
And be saved with the Son of God.

You made me,[166] Father. Through the Son,
As the Savior of the faithful, remake me.
Reward me[167] with the prize of the saints
So that there may be one measured dance for the Three.

Bring me with You, unity of the Father.
Pardon me, equality of the Begotten.
Rebuild me, charity of Both.
Splendor of the Three! Three-fold Identity!
    Here it ends

---

163. For *aeve*, DuCange gives "a long time," but it could be "forever" in this context.
164. Cf. Lk 15:5. The Latin is clearly *humis*, but a smudge above indicates a probable abbreviation of *er* for *humeris*.
165. The Latin is *mensuram* ("measure/extent"), but the sense is likely "end."
166. The text adds *vel nos* ("or 'us'") as an alternative.
167. The text adds *vel nos* ("or 'us'") as an alternative.

[CCA 23] Concerning the *Translation*[168] of Saint James Readings according to Pope Leo and Master Parucham[169]

Reading I:
Like a ray of the sun of justice,[170]
The first of the twelvefold militia,[171]
He, first, has field of victory
And is first cast on the lot of glory.

Civil discord moved the cruelty of the king[172]
Against the Church of Christ,
And James moved on to glory
Cut down by the sentence of Herod.

---

168. The text is faded and difficult to read; the context points toward this being the story of the *Translatio*. For this and other difficult readings, we have relied on Fidel Fita and Aureliano Fernández-Guerra, *Recuerdos de un viaje a Santiago de Galicia* (Madrid: Lezcano y Comp., 1880), 133–35; and Dreves, AH 17:211–13.

169. AH 17:211–13. These readings, in three columns, are difficult to read. Fita (*Recuerdos*, 133) describes the page as being "without numeration, faded, eroded by rubbing and from humidity. Its letters have been revived by my dear and wise friend, Mr. López Ferreiro, making use of chemical reagents." [Translation ours.] The restoration was aided by a perfectly regular meter and rhyme. The final name is blurred and has been variously read as *Parucham, Paricham,* or *Panicha,* among other possibilities.

170. Cf. Mal 4:2. The sun of justice is an epithet for Jesus; one of its rays, as used here, represents James.

171. Based on the twelve tribes of Israel. Cf. 2 Kgs (2 Sam) 2:12–17. Used here as a symbol for the twelve apostles.

172. Herod Agrippa, 11 BCE–44 CE, king of Judea from 41 CE. He ordered the beheading of James, Acts 12:2.

The seven[173] took him secretly from the land.[174]
They took his body and arrived at Joppa.[175]
There they caught sight of the boat by chance
And entered the boat and watched over the body.

Reading II:
The boat laden with its holy load,
Conducted by the steering of God,
At the farthest shores of Spain
Reached the port of the city of Iria.[176]

On a favorable day for the boat,
With psalms, hymns, and predictions,

---

173. In Bk. III, the *Translatio,* the story of the transferal of James's body from Jerusalem to Galicia is told in three separate ways. The first, slightly garbled, begins with a passing mention to the transport of his body, but with specific information about his disciples from the *Passio Iacobi;* the second incorporates the stories of the Seven Apostolic Men from the *Pasionario Hispánico;* and the third, ostensibly written by "Pope Saint Leo," tells of the disciples who accompany the body in the boat and after his burial. From the Prologue of Bk. III: "The apostle is said to have chosen nine disciples in Galicia while he still lived there. Of these disciples, seven went with him to Jerusalem and carried his body over the sea to Galicia after his martyrdom, while the other two remained in Galicia for the purpose of preaching." (Coffey and Dunn, *Miracles,* 70).

174. The text is largely unreadable; the best possibility for the two-syllable lacuna seems to be *terra* giving *ex terra* ("from the land"), which describes the story perfectly. This suggestion comes from Fita, *Recuerdos,* 133.

175. Latin had two forms for this city: *Joppa* and *Jope;* the accusative used here is *Ioppem.* Today it is called Jaffa in English and is the oldest section of the port city of Tel Aviv (Israel).

176. Iria (Flavia), an early settlement near the coast at the confluence of the Sar and Ulla rivers now in the municipality of Padrón, A Coruña, Galicia. "Flavia" was added in c.70CE, when the Roman emperor Vespasian granted its inhabitants Roman citizenship. In his honor, the town was called Iria Flavia. From the sixth century, there are bishops associated with Iria; the see was transferred from Iria to Compostela in 860. See López Ferreiro, *Historia de la S.A.M. Iglesia,* 1:218–30.

> Full of light, by chance,
> They came to rest in the port of Petronio.[177]
>
> A miraculous thing for such great glory!
> The center point of the sun in the space of the sky
> Raised the holy body from Iria
> Thence[178] where the church is now.

Reading III:
> Iria is called "twice streamed,"
> Either from the course of the banks of the Sar and the Ulla rivers
> Or from the rock and city of Petronia
> Or favor is away from Iria.[179]
>
> And the seven disciples, weeping,
> Being prudent,[180] went through places
> Asking about a hidden kind of place
> In which they might place the body of the apostle.

---

177. Padrón, Galicia, a few kilometers up the Ría de Arousa from Iria, has traditionally been considered the mooring point of the boat carrying Saint James's body. Its name comes from "Pedrón," or large stone. Several large stones in the area are related to the legend of Saint James. Under the altar of the church of Santiago is a monument from the Roman period, perhaps originally an altar to Neptune. Recent archaeology suggests that a large stone buried by an earlier channel of the Río Sar may have been the mythic stone of Bk. III's *Translatio*. See J.L. Jiménez, "Encuentran en Padrón restos del muelle milenario al que pudo llegar el Apóstol Santiago," *ABC Galicia*, 5/5/2018. See also ch. 17, n. 17.

178. The Latin is very faded. The suggestion is from Fita (*Recuerdos*, 133). The unanswered question is whether it means "from the place where the church is now" or "from there to where the church is now."

179. The author is clearly searching for the etymology of Iria. The Latin *sit* is fairly well visible, though the prefix is not. Fita suggests *absit* (*Recuerdos*, 133); we have chosen an affirming *insit*. The final word could be *gloria* or *gratia* or even another word. This is possibly one of the most problematic texts of the CC; thus, scholars have been forced to rely on alternative manuscripts to decipher it.

180. The best interpretation is from Fita (*Recuerdos*, 133) with *eubuli* rather than *inbuli* from the Greek, meaning "prudent."

ADDENDA TO THE CODEX CALIXTINUS

About twice six or twice eight miles
Distant from the flow of the Sar
There was discovered, by the will of God,
A place to bury the body with reverence.

Reading IV:
With the body buried in a marble casing,[181]
With fitting funeral rites, by divine favor,
They united with heaven to destroy the dragon
And to remove the harmful plague from the mountain.

The demon could not suffer the sign of the cross,
And he was divided and torn open through his stomach,
And holy water was sprinkled around the mountain,
And to this day it is called sacred.[182]

---

181. Tha Latin is *archis marmoreis,* as is also found in Fita (*Recuerdos,* 133). These (or similar) words have appeared connected to the Saint James tomb legend since their first known appearance in the sixth-century *Breviary of the Apostles.* (See Coffey and Dunn, *Miracles,* xxviii–xxx). The scholarship about this term includes: Manuel Díaz y Díaz, "El lugar del enterramiento de Santiago el Mayor en Isidoro de Sevilla," *Compostellanum* 1.4 (1956): 881–85; Casimiro Torres Rodríguez, "Arca marmórea," *Compostellanum* 2.2 (1957): 323–39, and "Notas sobre 'Arca marmórea,'" *Compostellanum* 4.2 (1959): 341–47; José Guerra Campos, "Notas críticas sobre el origen del culto sepulcral a Santiago de Compostela," *Ciencia tomista,* 88.279 (July–Sept. 1961): 417–74 and 88.230 (Oct.–Dec. 1961): 559–90; and Juan José Cebrián Franco, *Los relatos de la traslación de los restos del Apóstol Santiago a Compostela* (Santiago de Compostela: Instituto Teológico Compostelano, 2008).

182. The Pico Sacro is about 18km south of Santiago de Compostela above the Ulla River. The miracles of the dragon and the mountain plague are in Bk. III, ch. 1. See Coffey and Dunn, *Miracles,* 75–81.

Reading V:
    And what was previously called Illicinus[183] —
    "Seducing toward the crime of sin"[184] —
    What used to be inhospitable, once consecrated,
    Was hospitable and grazed because of its great bounty.[185]

    They had had hardly arrived from there to where the cattle were,
    When the cattle already felt the power
    And lost whatever fury they bore
    And willingly hastened to the yokes.

Reading VI:
    After this, the just discretion of God
    Determined that the three remain as colleagues
    As He steered the boat He had sent.
    Let Pope Leo be a witness to this.[186]

    The basilica was built over it,
    And the altar was placed above the tomb.
    People come here from the whole world.
    Here there is help for all prayers.

---

183. *Illicinus* is also known as Mons Sacer, Monsagro, Pico Sacro, and Mount Holy.

184. The second line gives the etymology of the name *Illicinus* from the first line. For more information about the etymology, see Coffey and Dunn, *Miracles,* 81, n. 49.

185. The author plays off two Greek words, which are transliterated into Latin: *axinus* and *euxinus.* These are applied to the Pontus or Black Sea, so inhospitable that it was a place of exile in the Roman Empire. Both Ovid and Boethius were exiled to the Black Sea. At times it was euphemistically called the hospitable sea.

186. Bk. III, ch. 2 is the letter of Pope St. Leo, narrating another version of the *Translatio* (Coffey and Dunn, *Miracles,* 85–88). For a history of the *Letter of the Pope Saint Leo,* see Manuel Díaz y Díaz, "La *Epistola Leonis,*" *Escritos jacobeos* (Santiago de Compostela: Consorcio de Santiago y Universidad de Santiago de Compostela, 2010), 133–81.

Here there are remedies for the languishing,
And forgiveness is given here to sinners.
Miracles are performed for them in Christ.
To Christ be always praise and glory!

Here the grace of Christ is about the three
As witnesses of the extreme glory
Through Whom victory is given to us.
Peace on the road! Honor in the country![187] [f.195v]

[CCA 24] [Your Justice Transforms]

Your justice is what transforms the earth and the heavens.
> Indeed, You, O Christ, are the very justice of the Father.

And justice in the flesh walked before the Father and shone with the cloud.
> And the justice has shone up to now on the members along its path.

Behold a humble monk, tested in the strength of his faith,
> Skilled in the art of glass and harmless in his conduct,

A pilgrim, he saw the thresholds of the apostolic city,
> And he came on foot in order to make glass.

He learned the steps, and his spiritual being could see.
> As his end was approaching, he related having seen these things:[188]

"Eight days passed in which I took no food,
> And I was anointed by monks, and I was almost about to be washed.

---

187. This last stanza is largely based on the text of Fita (*Recuerdos,* 133), as the text is badly faded. Neither Whitehill nor Dreves attempted to reproduce the text; Herbers and Xunta rely on Fita here.

188. Red lines in the right margin seem to indicate stanza breaks; we have followed these markings.

SERMONS AND LITURGY OF SAINT JAMES

I, a voice without a voice, moaning moans without the use of my chest
> Then asked for signs[189] from Saint James,

When suddenly, before the spiritual eye of my mind,
> Appeared a wondrous threefold vision in celestial light,

And so, he spoke in this way: 'And whom do you wish? I am James.
> John is here. He is my brother.'

"'You are healthy. Behold by whose glorious hand you are visited.
> The third person with us is the regal Mother of God.

Come. Behold a just generation soon to be my people.'
> Mirrored before us there was a monk,

Meanwhile both the underworld and paradise were seen
> In the manner of a middle and index fingers.

There was sulfur and fire and a spirit burning in pains.
> Oh, horror! A region of cauldron and heavy, stinking fire!

On the other side, there was an almost gleaming sun filled with full light.
> There was a life of salvation enjoying the gladness of the light.

From there, things seemed to go quickly and return quickly.
> A vision, but it appeared as great chaos on both sides."

Oldierius, in the convent of monks,
> Narrated and explained this faithfully to his brothers.

From there, he went to Clairvaux,[190] as well as to other holy places
> Like a fish that was chosen for swimming to his cloisters.

---

189. The Latin *inducias* is probably a scribal error for *indicia* ("signs").
190. The Cistercian abbey, located about 70 km southeast of Troyes, founded by St. Bernard in 1115.

The brothers of Oldierius, out of love for Saint James, said:
> "You came that you might make the windows of mystery.[191]
> You would take little bread and a small amount of food
> > If someone would give glass and lead for the windows."

Oh, happy vision giving such comfort
> In which the Mother of Christ appears with a word of well-being!

Oh, happy is the servant of the blessed Handmaid[192]
> And those whom the affection of the Mother sends before God!

May it be to the merit of the writer and apt for the one proposing it!
> All and a single and complete threefold praise to God! Amen.

[CCA 25] [Fragment on Historical Figures]

Charlemagne,[193] on the V Calends of February,[194]
Died in the eighth hundred and fourteenth year,[195]
First king of the Franks, Clovis, king of the Catholics,[196]

---

191. The Latin *misterii vitreas* ("windows of mystery") likely indicates "stained-glass windows" or could refer to the scenes depicted, i.e. the religious "mysteries".
192. Cf. Lk 1:38.
193. The Latin *Karole magne* is the vocative case ("O Charlemagne"), although the context is missing here. This short passage seems to be a fragment from another text.
194. January 28. February is preceded by *lors* and followed by *te;* the meaning is clear, but the context is insufficient for deciphering these two words.
195. Charlemagne (2 April 748–28 January 814), also known as Charles I. Bk. IV *(Chronicle of Pseudo-Turpin)* tells of Charlemagne's exploits in Spain.
196. Clovis (c.466–511) converted to Catholicism in 496 and was baptized on Christmas Day 508.

Teodomiro, the first of the bishops of Compostela[197]
By whom the letter was cleaned from stains, and mass was celebrated.[198]

[CCA 26] A Miracle of Saint James about a Cripple Who Stood up on the Feast of His *Translation*

It is read that tomorrow and today Christ gives salvation
    Spending three days casting out demons.
He also rightfully granted Saint James the curing of gout —
    To straighten legs[199] and to strengthen steps.[200]
Behold the praises at matins of the renowned *translation*
    He transformed this suffering Agrippa[201] so that he might afterward go by foot.[202]
For thirteen years that unfortunate Peter had crawled,
    Until, ever watchful, he saw a dove.

---

197. Teodomiro (d. 847), bishop of Iria after 818; he discovered (or confirmed) the tomb of Saint James.

198. This perhaps was intended as an add-on to the miracle of the sin deleted from the sheet of paper at Saint-Gilles. It is also similar to Miracle 2 of the *Miracles*. Two additional lines appear in the left margin: "Clovis, first king of the Franks / The first bishop of Compostela, Theodomirus." It is not certain if they are in addition to the similar lines in the text or perhaps a clarification or correction.

199. The Latin is *cures* likely for *crures,* as Herbers suggests (279).

200. The Latin *vel genu* ("or 'knee'") is found interlinearly as an alternative.

201. The Latin is *Agrupam,* but the miracle's recipient named below is "Peter"; this might refer to Marcus Agrippa, a Roman statesman, who suffered from foot problems that modern medicine has interpreted as gout.

202. *Pedes* is found alone, the preposition "by" is supplied from context.

Soon a boy, gleaming white,[203] was in that holy chapel of this gift.[204]

"'Touch my hand,' he said, and thus I was raised to my feet."

Thus, it is rightly believed that it was a simple age and the age of his prime

In which the nourishing spirit appeared for him to flourish again.

This happened in Compostela at the altar of Saint James at his[205] *translation,* as the ninth responsorial was being sung and his name would follow:[206] therefore, let the *Te Deum*[207] be started. This was done by the Lord through Saint James, and it is miraculous in our eyes. [f.196r][208]

[CCA 27] [The Spirit of Christ]

The spirit of Christ always shines with proportioned grace

And the apostolic pillar illustrates the faith.

The most brilliant virtue of pious James, who is found in the west,[209]

Continues everywhere as the pride and the honor of the world.

---

203. The Latin *albescens* ("growing white") refers especially to the dawn. The dove appears to morph into the gleaming white boy.

204. The text is not clear. Only *doni-e* at the end of the line offers a clue (some form of "gift/give").

205. The Latin is *iusius* or *insius,* probably an error for *istius* or *ipsius* ("his").

206. This is likely a reference to an imminent mention of James's name.

207. The hymn is the *"Te Deum"* or *"Te Deum laudamus"* ("We Praise You, God").

208. This folio was reinforced along the edge where it may have been tattered. For more information on this folio, see Díaz y Díaz, *El Códice Calixtino,* 187–95.

209. The word *hesperia* refers to the evening and the direction in which the sun sets; it was used to refer to Italy and Spain; at times the word *ultima* was added to clear any ambiguity when referring to the Iberian Peninsula. Here, the reference is clearly to Spain in connection with James.

His apostolic body is the virtue and the protection of the kingdom,
And his apostolic body is a pillar of the land.
Behold this blessed father shines with virtues everywhere.
After Peter, James is the blessed father everywhere.
The apostle is translated to the limits of the west,
And he radiates over the whole world from these limits of the west.
He gleams and performs all manner of favorable things with wondrous virtue.
This apostolic pillar does all these favorable things.
A citizen by the name of Peter, who was from the land
That Saint Giles[210] adorned, protected, and loved,
Came to the threshold of Saint James
With two witnesses of one voice with him.
One was Barnard, his uncle, who had witnessed the accomplished deed
And who commended it along with his weeping companion.
And then we were singing the divine praises on high,
With both choruses singing the laudatory *Te Deum*,[211]
With the bells resounding and the offices of the mass being carried out.
Peter, who had been called back to life, said:
"With the palm branches,[212] a pain had begun to make me sick in the evening,
And slowly it prevailed over my body

---

210. Saint-Gilles is in the department of Gard in France. Saint Giles is a favorite saint of the author. Chapters 3 and 5 of the Bk. II *Miracles* are similar to those attributed to Saint Gilles. The saint and the town bearing his name are cited several times in the *Veneranda dies* sermon (cf. ch. 17, n. 105) and have extended descriptions in Bk. V, ch. 8 (Melczer, *Pilgrim's Guide*, 98–102).
211. See above n. 141.
212. A metonymy for "Palm Sunday."

While I was keeping watch during the holy rites of the saint during the vigil of Easter,
And then death came, but life quickly returned.
Into the cold of the death of the flesh, but with a cloud descending,
At midnight life and well-being returned.
And what we call bells and you call bells[213]
While being struck during the vigil sounded in a classic triple manner,
I revived, with James granting and taking up my soul,
After I first cried out, 'Saint James, help.'"
As a sign of remarkable power and of well-being,
Here is this handkerchief,[214] with God Himself as witness,
To Whom be honor always, as it is through all the ages,
Who piously performs wondrous things though His saints.

[CCA 28] THE VISION OF A CERTAIN FOULQUES, A PILGRIM OF SAINT JAMES, THROUH GRACE TWELVE AND THIRTEEN TIMES[215]

A person named Foulques from Montreuil-sur-Mer[216]
Had come here to Saint James ten times.

---

213. The Latin gives *squillas* and *campanas*. The *squillas,* named for their resemblance to the shell fish, was generally used smaller bells, while the *campanas,* named for their place of manufacture (Campania, Italy), were generally larger bells, such as those in a steeple. However, it might also be a linguistic point since *campanas* is the Provençal word for "bell," while *esquila* is the Spanish word.

214. See above n. 120.

215. Only bits of the title (which is in rubrics) are legible: "... *legi...Iacobi... ...tredecies.*" The note in the right margin seems to be "ten" rather than "twelve," although the remaining bits of the title might indicate that it may have been "twelve" there.

216. Montreuil-sur-Mer is in Normandy in the department of Pas-de-Calais.

While he, therefore, was sleeping at Burgos, the nourishing James
> Appeared to him and visited him a fifth time to restore him.

"Greetings, brother," he said "I, the apostle that you seek, am here.
> You have been to my holy threshold thirteen times."

Then he gave a sweet drink to me[217] from a stone vessel
> Upon which I awoke.

In this way Saint James pointed out his trail in such a manner
> That he shone so that he might lift up the pilgrims.

In this was it showed, without doubt, that Compostela was already worthy
> By divine providence to hold the apostolic body.[218]

Now James, as witness, pointed out the city and his own tomb
> And he told these things to Foulques and pointed them out.

This was done by the Lord, and it is miraculous in our eyes.

[CCA 29] [JAMES, SAINT AND FATHER]

James, saint and father, you who are filled from the divine spring,
> Fill our hearts, prepare us sacred drinks

As you cast rays of celestial light in the heavens.
> With them may your light show the road to the pilgrims.

Indeed, as the Lord may goad us with a single wine,
> He gives a drink of tears and washes away the mire.

He measures the journey in tears as a measure of the roads traveled.
> An accessible spring gave the monthly purgation, and from it

---

217. The Latin *mihi me* ("to me me") is likely intended to be the intense form *mihimet*. ("to myself").

218. This is reminiscent of Bk. IV where Charlemagne sees a path of stars that ends in Galicia. While contemplating the night sky, Saint James appears three times to convince him to take an army to free his tomb from the infidel. Poole, *Chronicle*, 5–7.

ADDENDA TO THE CODEX CALIXTINUS

A fortuitous drink washes the soul and purges the darkness.
    There is a more felicitous sleep that sees as it watches. [f. 196v]

[CCA 30] [A DICOLOS TETRASTROPHOS][219]

We have sacred signs that may be read
In which a window to the holy life
Is made evident to the new minds even to the true Israelites.

In wandering gradually through the vastness of the desert,
A happy place is found here[220] for the Hebrews,
Which they read as Elim, and for those who had gone forth, it was
    A sixth dwelling place.

Springs numbering twice six flow there,
Rising up with their soft sound for the child.
The fruits of hope and the palms of honor [stand][221]
    Numbering seventy.

Such a phenomenon, expressed with matching figures,
Denotes the first and second order
Of the disciples who followed Christ
    In faith and the cross.

Already, with God's help, the voice of these disciples,
Wondrous with the distinguished merits of virtues,

---

219. This work is found in the AH 17:214–15, and above on f.193v (pp. 450–53). The notes on the wording are found there. The notes here are restricted to textual variants specific to this second presentation of the work in the CC. At the bottom of the folio in a relatively modern hand is written: *"idem ac fo 222 r et v"* or "the same as folio 222r and v."
220. The Latin is *hic* corrected from *hec*.
221. The Latin *stant* ("stand"), necessary for the meaning and the meter, is supplied here in brackets from the first presentation of the text.

Goes out to the orb in obtaining the sweet glory
>   Of the palms of victory.

The eloquence[222] of these saints moistens the earth
Of the heart to be cultivated, with the dew
Raining down[223] from above.
>   Thanks be for the dew!

The sixth age[224] has begun
In which God comes to restore freely
And to call those of us who believe. Let us therefore keep watch
>   In this time of Christ.[225]

Among these believers, Saint James shines.
As a distinguished martyr and pillar of faith
And as first in the choir of those slaughtered by Herod,
>   He stands among the twelve.

From this point onward, he is the honor of life and the embodiment of forgiveness,
Son of the greatest and highest Thunder,[226]
A supplanting star,[227] a wave[228] of piety,
>   A wellspring for pilgrims.

---

222. The previous version had *dogma* ("teaching") rather than *li[n]gua* ("eloquence").
223. The words *vel influente* ("or 'flowing down'") are added interlinearly here.
224. See n. 100 above.
225. The words *vel grato* ("or 'welcome'") are added interlinearly as a variant; the first presentation had several variants, including "of Christ," but had the "welcome" alternative in the text.
226. The Latin *vel sederis*, for *sideris* ("or 'star'") is given interlinearly as an alternative for *tonitrus* ("thunder") in the body of the text.
227. The alternative *vel planeta* ("or 'planet'") is given interlinearly as an alternative for "star."
228. The Latin is *undat* with a "t" added, making it a form that would fit only awkwardly here.

ADDENDA TO THE CODEX CALIXTINUS

He[229] is also given to the Spanish as a patron,
A shepherd, and bread set out for the traveler
On which travelers[230] of meager diet
    Are restored.[231]

Thereafter he was for us a swift advocate,
Seeking forgiveness from Christ the Judge.
Ask for us in the love of Christ
    That we may live with you.

May there be belief in the Father and the begotten Christ
And also in the Gale poured from Both.
May the Threefold be in the Threefold at the same time as the One in the One.
    A perpetual glory! Amen.

---

229. The Latin is *Hinc* ("Thence") for *Hic* ("He"); we have followed the first presentation here with "He."
230. The Latin has an interlinear *peregrini* ("pilgrims") as an alternative to "travelers."
231. This Latin is *iustificantur* and is corrected from *reficeamur* ("we are restored"); it is likely that the idea here is "restored," probably in the physical and spiritual sense. See above, n. 105.

BIBLIOGRAPHY

Acádemie de chant Grégorien. Gregorian Repertory. https://gregorien.info/chant/id/8720/0/en. Accessed 5/11/2020.

Acta sanctorum. Ed. Iohannes Bollandus, et al. Paris: Victor Palmé, 1863–1919.

Alfonso X. *Las siete partidas.* http://pensamientopenal.com.ar/legislacion/33312-vii-partidas-alfonso-sabio. Accessed 11/21/2020.

Anguita Jaén, José María. "Ensayo de interpretación de algunos términos inexplicados del *Liber Sancti Iacobi (Codex Calixtinus): 'cinnatores,' 'trebuchetum,' 'marsicias,'* etc." *Iacobus: Revista de estudios jacobeos y medievales* 1 (June 1996): 15–29; 2 (December 1996): 11–23.

—. "Más rubicundos que un elefante viejo fueron los apóstoles." *Ad Limina* 2.2 (2011): 15–28.

Asensio, Juan Carlos. "Tropos y prosas del Calixtino: Aspectos musicales." In *El* Codex Calixtinus *en la Europa del siglo XII: Symposium July 15–17, 2010,* 157–70. Madrid: Instituto Nacional de las Artes Escénicas y de la Música, 2011.

Bailey, Nathan. *An Universal Etymological English Dictionary.* London: N.p., 1724.

"Beatus Nicolaus." *Académie de chant grégorien.* https://gregorien.info/chant/id/952/0/en. Accessed 5/5/2020.

Bede, Venerable. *The Commentary on the Seven Catholic Epistles of Bede the Venerable.* Translated by David Hurst. Kalamazoo, MI: Cistercian Publications, 1985.

Bédier, Joseph. "La Chronique de Turpin et le pèlerinage de Compostelle." *Annales du Midi* 23 (1911): 425–50; 24 (1912): 18–48.

Biggs, Anselm Gordon. *Diego Gelmírez, First Archbishop of Compostela.* Washington, DC: Catholic University of America, 1949.

Blaise, Albert. *Lexicon latinitatis mediae aevi.* Corpus Christianorum. Turnholt: Brepols, 1977.

"Breviarium apostolorum." In *Prophetarum vitae fabulosae,* edited by Theodor Schermann, 207–11. Leipzig: Teubner, 1907.

Brundage, John A. "*Cruce signari:* The Rite for Taking the Sign of the Cross in England." *Traditio* 22 (1966): 289–310.

Cantus Manuscript Database. http://cantus.uwaterloo.ca/chant/186831. Accessed 5/5/2020.

Casimiro di Firenze, and Agnello Tramater. *L'ecclesiastico provveduto: Ovvero esortazioni familiari per tutte le domeniche, E Feste Principali Dell'anno.* Naples: Da' Torchi del Tramater, 1824

Cebrián Franco, Juan José. *Los relatos de la traslación de los restos del Apóstol Santiago a Compostela.* Santiago de Compostela: Instituto Teológico Compostelano, 2008.

Chrysostom, John. *Abecedario real e regia instrucçam de principes lusitanos.* Edited by Joam dos Prazeres. Lisbon: Gaume, 1692.

—. *Archieepiscopi Constantinopolitani opera omnia que exstant.* Edited by Bernard de Montfaucon. Paris: n.p., 1835. Vol. 6.

Codex Calixtinus de la Universidad de Salamanca [Facsimile]. Edited by Juan José García Gil and Pablo Molinero Hernando. Burgos: Siloé, arte y bibliofilia, 2011.

Coffey, Thomas, Linda Davidson, and Maryjane Dunn. *The Miracles of Saint James: Translations from the* Liber Sancti Jacobi. New York: Italica Press, 1996.

—, and Maryjane Dunn. *The Miracles and* Translatio *of Saint James.* New York: Italica Press, 2019.

—, and Terrence J. McGovern. "La Messe." In *A Middle French Translation of Bernard Gui's Shorter Historical Works,* edited by Jean Golein, 443–55. Lewiston, NY: The Edwin Mellen Press, 1993.

The Conflicts of the Holy Apostles, an Apocryphal Book of the Early Eastern Church. Translated from an Ethiopic MS. Translated by S.C. Malan. London: D. Nutt, 1871.

Corpus corporum. http://www.mlat.uzh.ch/MLS/. Accessed 5/9/2020.

Corrigan, Vincent. "Music and the Pilgrimage." In Dunn and Davidson, 43–67. New York: Garland Publishing, 1996.

Díaz y Díaz, Manuel C. "El lugar del enterramiento de Santiago el Mayor en Isidoro de Sevilla." *Compostellanum* 1.4 (1956): 881–85.

— "El texto y la tradición textual del Calixtino." In *Pistoia e il cammino di Santiago: Una dimensione europea nella Toscana medioevale,* edited by Lucia Gai, 23–55. Naples: Edizione Scientifiche Italiane, 1984.

—, María Araceli García Piñeiro, and Pilar del Oro Trigo. *El* Códice Calixtino *de la Catedral de Santiago.* Santiago de Compostela: Centro de Estudios Jacobeos, 1988.

BIBLIOGRAPHY

———. "El *Códice Calixtino:* Volviendo sobre el tema." In Williams and Stones, 1–10.

———. "La *Epistola Leonis*." In *Escritos jacobeos,* 133–81. Santiago de Compostela: Consorcio de Santiago y Universidad de Santiago de Compostela, 2010.

Dictionarium etymologicum latinum. Edited by Francis Holyoke. London: Felix Kingston, 1639.

Dionysius Cato. *Catonis Disticha.* Edited by Michael Manger. Augsburg: N.p., 1588.

Dioscorides, Pedanius. *The Greek Herbal of Dioscorides.* Edited by Robert T. Gunther. Translated by John Goodyear. New York: Hafner, 1959.

Dreves, Guido M., and C. Blume. *Analecta hymnica medii aevi.* Leipzig: Reisland, 1907.

Dunn, Maryjane, and Linda Davidson, eds. *The Pilgrimage to Compostela in the Middle Ages: A Book of Essays.* New York: Garland, 1996.

Eusebius of Caesaria. *Eusebius: Church History.* Translated by Arthur Cushman McGiffert. Nicene and Post-Nicene Fathers, Second Series, Vol. 1. Edited by Philip Schaff and Henry Wace. Buffalo, NY: Christian Literature Publishing Co., 1890. Revised and edited for New Advent by Kevin Knight. http://prenicea.net/doc4/40201-en-01.pdf. Accessed 5/5/2020.

Fábrega Grau, Angel, ed. *Pasionario Hispánico.* Madrid: Consejo Superior de Investigaciones Científicas, 1953–55.

Fabricius, Johann Albert, and Hermas. *Codex apocryphus Novi Testamenti.* 2nd ed. Hamburg: Benjam. Schilleri & Joh. Christoph. Kisneri, 1719. 2:516–31.

Fita, Fidel, and Aureliano Fernández-Guerra. *Recuerdos de un viaje a Santiago de Galicia.* Madrid: Lezcano y Comp., 1880.

———, and Julien Vinson, eds. *Le codex de Saint-Jacques de Compostelle: Livre IV.* Paris: Maisonnueve, 1882.

Fletcher, Richard. *St James's Catapult: The Life and Times of Diego Gelmírez of Santiago de Compostela.* Oxford: Clarendon, 1984.

Gaposchkin, M. Cecilia. "From Pilgrimage to Crusade: The Liturgy of Departure, 1095–1300." *Speculum* 88.1 (January 2013): 44–91.

Godefroy, Frédéric. *Lexique de l'ancien français.* Paris: Champion, 1971.

Grabois, Aryeh. *Illustrated Encyclopedia of Medieval Civilization.* New York: Mayflower, 1980.

Grant, Edward, ed. *A Source Book in Medieval Science*. Cambridge, MA: Harvard University Press, 1974.

Guerra Campos, José. "Notas críticas sobre el origen del culto sepulcral a Santiago de Compostela." *Ciencia tomista* 88.279 (July–Sept. 1961): 417–74; 88.230 (Oct.–Dec. 1961): 559–90.

Hämel, Adalbert. *Überlieferung und Bedeutung des* Liber Sancti Jacobi *und des Pseudo-Turpin*. Sitzungsberichte, Philosophisch-historische Klasse 2. Munich: Bayerische Akademie der Wissenschaften, 1950.

Haskins, Susan. *Mary Magdalen: Myth and Metaphor*. New York: Harcourt, Brace & Company, 1993.

Helmer, Paul, ed. *The Mass of St. James (Solemn Mass for the Feast of the Passion of Saint James of Compostela according to the* Codex Calixtinus). Ottawa: Institute of Medieval Music, 1988.

Herbers, Klaus. *Der Jacobuskult des 12. Jahrhunderts und der* Liber Sancti Jacobi. *Studien über das Verhältnis zwischen Religion und Gesellschaft im Hohen Mittelalter*. Historische Forschungen 7. Wiesbaden: F. Steiner, 1984.

—, and Manuel S. Noya. See *Liber Sancti Jacobi*.

Herwaarden, Jan van. *Between St. James and Erasmus: Studies in Late Medieval Religious Life: Devotion and Pilgrimage in the Netherlands*. Leiden: Brill, 2003.

Hiley, David. "Two Unnoticed Pieces of Medieval Polyphony." *Plainsong and Medieval Music* 1.2 (October 1992): 167–73.

Hohler, Christopher. "The Badge of Saint James." In *The Scallop: Studies of a Shell and Its Influences on Humankind*. Edited by Ian Cox, 49–70. London: Shell Transport and Trading Co., 1957.

Huglo, Michel. "Les Pièces notées du *Codex Calixtinus*." In Williams and Stones, 105–124.

James, Montague Rhodes. *The Apocryphal New Testament*. Oxford: Clarendon, 1986.

Jiménez, J.L. "Encuentran en Padrón restos del muelle milenario al que que pudo llegar el Apóstol Santiago." *ABC Galicia*, 5/5/2018. https://www.abc.es/espana/galicia/abci-encuentran-padron-restos-muelle-milenario-pudo-llegar-apostol-santiago-201805151803_noticia.html?sfns=mo. Accessed 3/24/2020.

Josephus. *Jewish Antiquities*. Translated by Louis H. Feldman. Loeb Classical Library. Cambridge, MA: Harvard University Press, 1930–65.

BIBLIOGRAPHY

—. *The Antiquities of the Jews.* Translated by William Whiston. Gutenberg Project: https://www.gutenberg.org/files/2848/2848-h/2848-h.htm#link192H_4_0001. Published first in 2009, and last updated in 2017. Accessed 5/10/2020.

Karp, Theodore. *The Polyphony of St. Martial and Santiago de Compostela.* Berkeley: University of California Press, 1992.

Lévy, Michel-André. *Louis I, II, III…XIV…: L'Étonnante histoire de la numérotation des rois de France.* Paris: Jourdan, 2014.

Lewis, Agnes Smith. *The Mythological Acts of the Apostles, Translated from an Arabic MS in the Convent of Deyr–es–Suriani, Egypt, and from MSS in the Convent of Saint Catherine on Mount Sinai and in the Vatican Library.* London: C.J. Clay and Sons, 1904.

Liber Sancti Iacobi (Ms. 2631). Repositorio documental Gredos: https://gredos.usal.es/handle/10366/128808. Accessed 6/13/2020.

Liber Sancti Jacobi: Codex Calixtinus. Edited by Walter Muir Whitehill, Germán Prado, and Jesús Carro García. 3 vols. Santiago de Compostela: Consejo Superior de Investigaciones Científicas, Instituto Padre Sarmiento de Estudios Gallegos, 1944. [Referred to as Whitehill.]

Liber Sancti Jacobi: Codex Calixtinus. Translated by A. Moralejo, C. Torres, and J. Feo. Santiago de Compostela: Consejo Superior de Investigaciones Científicas, Instituto Padre Sarmiento de Estudios Gallegos, 1951. [Referred to as Moralejo.] Rev. ed. and Spanish translation by María José García Blanco. Santiago de Compostela: Xunta de Galicia, 2014. [Referred to as Xunta]

Liber Sancti Jacobi: Codex Calixtinus. Edited by Klaus Herbers and Manuel S. Noya. Santiago de Compostela: Xunta de Galicia, 1998. [Referred to as Herbers]

Liber Sancti Jacobi: Codex Calixtinus de la Catedral de Santiago de Compostela. Facsimile ed. Madrid: Kaydeda, 1993.

Lipsius, Richard A. *Die Apokryphen Apostelgeschichten und Apostellegenden: Ein Beitrag zur Altchristlichen Literaturgeschichte.* Braunschweig: C.A. Schwetschke und Sohn, 1883.

López Calo, José. "Dónde y cuándo nació el *Códice Calixtino:* Aportaciones musicales a la solución de un viejo problema." In *El* Codex Calixtinus *en la Europa del siglo XII: Música, arte, codicolgía y liturgia,* edited by Juan Carlos Asensio Palacios, 71–107. Madrid: Gobierno de España, Ministerio de Cultura, Instituto Nacional de las Artes Escénicas y de la Música, 2011.

—, and Constantino Martínez. *La música medieval en Galicia.* A Coruña: Fundación Pedro Barrie de la Maza, 1982.

López Ferreiro, Antonio. *Historia de la Santa Apostólica Metropolitana Iglesia de Santiago de Compostela.* 11 vols. Santiago: Seminario, 1898–1909.

López Pacho, Ricardo. "El Culto a Santiago en el antifonario visigótico-mozárabe de la catedral de León." *Tierras de León: Revista de la Diputación Provincial* 38.107–8 (2006): 57–72.

Magistri Salernitani. Edited by Piero Giacosa. Milan: Fratelli Bocca, 1901.

Magoula, Olga. *Usage and Meaning of Early Medieval Textiles: A Structural Analysis of Vestimentary Systems in Francia and Anglo-Saxon England.* Ph.D. diss., University of Birmingham, 2008. https://etheses.bham.ac.uk/id/eprint/954/. Accessed 6/14/2020.

Malan, S.C., ed. *The Conflicts of the Holy Apostles, an Apocryphal Book of the Early Eastern Church. Translated from an Ethiopic MS.* London: D. Nutt, 1871.

Maitane d'Arnis, W.H. *Lexicon manuale ad scriptures mediae et infimae latinitatis.* Hildesheim, NY : Olms, 1977.

Melczer, William, ed. *The Pilgrim's Guide to Santiago de Compostela.* New York: Italica Press, 1993.

Morgan, Augustus de. *The Book of Almanacs.* London: Taylor, Walton, and Maberly, 1851.

Nasrallah, Nawal. *Annals of the Caliphs' Kitchens: Ibn Sayyār al-Warrāq's Tenth-Century Baghdadi Cookbook.* Leiden: Brill, 2010.

Nichols, Francis Morgan, trans. *The Marvels of Rome.* Edited by Eileen Gardiner. New York: Italica Press, 1986.

"Notre Dame de Pitié." *The Catholic World* 23 (April–September 1876): 117–28. New York: The Catholic Publication House, 1876.

Ovid. *The Art of Love.* Edited by Grant Showerman, Frank Justus Miller, et al. Loeb Classical Library 232. Cambridge, MA: Harvard University Press, 2002.

Pack, Sasha. "Revival of the Pilgrimage to Santiago de Compostela: The Politics of Religious, National, and European Patrimony, 1879–1988." *The Journal of Modern History* 82 (June 2010): 335–67.

Patrologiae cursus completus: Series graeca. Edited by Jacques Paul Migne. 161 vols. Paris: Migne, 1857–68.

Patrologiae cursus completus: Series latina. Edited by Jacques Paul Migne. 221 vols. Paris: Migne, 1844–64.

Peake, Harold. "Santiago: The Evolution of a Patron Saint." *Folk-Lore* 30.3 (1919): 208–26.

Pearson, A. Harford, ed. *The Sarum Missal: Done into English.* London: Church Printing Co., 1884.

Pérez de Urbel, Justo. "El antifonario de León y el culto de Santiago el Mayor en la liturgia mozárabe." *Revista de la Universidad de Madrid* 3.9 (1954): 5–24.

Plato. *Dialogues of Plato.* Translated by B. Jowett. New York: Charles Scribner's Sons, 1897.

Poole, Kevin. *Chronicle of Pseudo-Turpin: Book IV of the Liber Sancti Jacobi (Codex Calixtinus).* New York: Italica Press, 2014.

Pörtner, Rudolf, ed. "'Ad consultum veritatis attendite': Ein moralisch-paränetischer Rhythmus, in der Handschrift Leiden BPL 130 (um 1100)." In *Arbor amoena comis: 25 Jahre Mittelalterliches Seminar in Bonn, 1965–1990,* edited by Ewald Könsgen, 151–54. Stuttgart: Steiner, 1990.

Prado, Germán. *Música Codex Calixtinus.* See *Liber Sancti Jacobi,* Whitehill.

Pulsoni, Carlo. "Notes on Some of the Ethonyms in the *Veneranda dies.*" *Ad Limina* 1.1 (2010): 151–59.

Riesco Chueca, Pilar. *Pasionario Hispánico: Introducción, edición crítica y traducción.* Seville: Universidad de Sevilla, 1995.

Riese, Alexander, Franz Buecheler, and Ernst Lommatzsch, eds. *Anthologia latina: Sive poesis latinae supplementum.* Leipzig: B.G. Teubneri, 1894.

Robert, Ulysse. *Bullaire du pape Calixte II.* Paris: Imprimerie Nationale, 1891; rpt. Hildesheim: G. Olms, 1979.

—. *Histoire du pape Calixte II.* Paris: Alphonse Picard, 1891.

Romano Rocha, Pedro. *L'Office divin au moyen âge dans l'église de Braga: Originalité et dépendances d'une liturgie particulière au moyen âge.* Paris: Gulbenkian, 1980.

Ruiz Torres, Santiago. "New Evidence concerning the Origin of the Monophonic Chants in the *Codex Calixtinus.*" *Plainsong and Medieval Music* 26.2 (2017): 79–94. https://doi.org/10.1017/S0961137117000031.

Smith, Colin. "The Geography and History of Iberia in the *Liber Sancti Jacobi.*" In Dunn and Davidson, 23–41.

Stones, Alison, Jeanne Krochalis, Paula Gerson, and Annie Shaver-Crandell. *The Pilgrim's Guide to Santiago de Compostela: A Critical Edition.* 2 vols. London: Harvey Miller Publishers, 1998.

Suárez Otero, José. "Iria, Padrón, Santiago: Geografía mítica y realidad arqueológica." *Padrón, Iria y las tradiciones Jacobeas*, edited by Vicente Almazán, 245–72. Santiago de Compostela: Xunta de Galicia, 2004.

Tannahil, Reay. *Food in History*. New York: Stein and Day, 1973.

Temperán Villaverde, Elisardo. "El libro primero del *Códice Calixtino* de la Catedral de Santiago de Compostela: ¿Un propio de la iglesia Compostelana en el siglo XII?" *Compostellanum* 37.1–2 (1992): 63–150.

——. *La Liturgia propia de Santiago en el* Códice Calixtino. Santiago de Compostela: Xunta de Galicia, 1997.

Thompson, Daniel. *Materials and Techniques of Medieval Painting*. NY: Dover, 1956.

Torres Rodríguez, Casimiro. "Arca marmórea." *Compostellanum* 2.2 (1957): 323–39.

——. "Notas sobre 'Arca marmórea.'" *Compostellanum* 4.2 (1959): 341–47.

van der Werf, Hendrik. "The Polyphonic Music." In Williams and Stones, 125–36.

Villa-Amil y Castro, José. *Descripción histórico-artístico-arqueológica de la Catedral de Santiago*. Lugo: Soto Freire, 1866.

Wagner, Peter. *Die Gesänge der Jakobusliturgie zu Santiago de Compostela aus dem sog. Codex Calixtinus*. Fribourg: Universitäts-Buchhandlung, 1931.

Walther, Hans. *Proverbia sententiaeque latinitatis medii aevi; Lateinische Sprichwörter und Sentenzen des Mittelalters in alphabetischer Anordnung*. Göttingen: Vandenhoeck & Ruprecht, 1963.

Wallis, Faith, ed. *Medieval Medicine: A Reader*. Toronto: University of Toronto Press, 2010.

Whitehill, Walter Muir. See *Liber Sancti Jacobi*.

Williams, John, and Alison Stones, eds. *The* Codex Calixtinus *and the Shrine of St. James*. Tübingen: Gunter Narr Verlag, 1992.

INDEX OF BIBLICAL CITATIONS

Old Testament

Genesis
2–3 129
3:17–18 111
8:21 180
9:20–27 259
12:1 252
18:1 234
21:12 158
22:2 300
25:12–16 45
25–35 252
27:15–30 302
27–32 320
28:10–22 302
28:12–13 302
28:19 234
40:1–23 209
41:1–41 209
49 45

Exodus
3 453
4:13 109
15:9 99
15:27 453
16:1 46
Ex19:14–15 29
19:20 234
21:2 183
24:16 110
28:15–22 46
33 453
35:13 46, 103

Leviticus
20:26 303

Numbers
13:1–16 46
16:1–33 268

Deuteronomy
11:6 268
13:3 300
18:15 158

28:66 117
33:9 74
62:1ff. 325

Joshua
4:1–11 46

Judges
7:16–21 34

1 Kings (1 Sam)
2:3 186
2:10 160
2:12–17 189
2:22–25 189
4:4–11 189
4:17–18 189
17:8–16 448
18:31 46
21:1–9 162
21:1–16 20

2 Kings (2 Sam)
1:21 39
2:12–17 466
4:18–37 113
5 56, 57

4 Kings (2 Kings)
1:2 193
1:6 194
1:9 194
1:10 194
1:16–17 194

2 Chronicles
7:8 33

Tobit
13:11 289
13:14–15 289

Job
1:1 82
2:4 99
11:8–9 39, 299
31:40 111
40:20ff 132
40:23 132
41:1ff 132

PSALMS
  1:1 188
  1:3 20
  2:7 159
  4 333, 338, 357
  4:5 / 4:4 258
  9 356
  9:19 / 9:18 204
  9:25 / 10:4 184
  9:38 / 10:17 18
  11:6 / 12:5 118, 159
  11:9 / 12:9 32
  14:1 / 15:1 38, 145
  14:3 / 15:3 39
  15:5 / 16:5 184
  15:6 / 16:6 303
  15:9–10 / 16:9–10 159
  16:4 / 17:4 110
  16:8 / 17:8 181, 334
  17:11 / 18:10 159
  18 / 19 337, 371, 387, 389, 391, 394, 395, 398, 401, 405, 417
  18:2 / 19:1 45
  18:4 / 19:3 242
  18:5 / 19:4 121, 307, 320
  18:6 / 19:4 283
  18:7 / 19:6 140
  21 / 22 351
  21:15 / 22:14 43
  21:17–19 / 22:16–8 159
  23:8 / 24:8 186
  23:10 / 24:10 186
  25:2 / 26:2 22
  27:4–5 / 28: 4–5 276
  28:3 / 29:3 320
  32:8 / 33:8 187
  32:10 / 33:10 188
  33 / 34 165, 181, 337
  33:16 / 34:15 181
  33:22 / 34:21 165
  34:3 / 35:3 125
  34:10 / 35:10 300
  34:12 / 35:12 161
  35:4–5 / 36:4–5 188
  36:2 / 37:2 20
  36:3 / 37:3 76
  36:27 / 37:2 25

  38:9 / 39:9 199
  38:13 / 38: 12 338
  40:2 / 41:1 188
  40:2 / 41:1–2 253
  40:10 / 41:10 161
  42 / 43 351
  44 / 45 103, 109, 337
  44:2 / 45.1 109
  44:10 / 45:9 103
  44:17 / 45:16 383
  45:9–10 / 46:8–10 131
  46 / 47 338, 350, 418
  46:6 / 47:5 118, 159
  49:3 / 50:3 118, 160
  49:16–22 / 50:16–22 114
  50 xxxv, xli, xlii, xlviii, 18, 321, 324, 325, 327, 351
  51:9–10 / 52:7–8 138
  53 / 54 338
  54 / 55 338
  54:16 / 55:15 276
  54:23 / 55:22 76
  55 / 56 324
  55:12/ 56:12 293
  56 / 57 324
  60 / 61 338
  60:3 / 61:2 81
  61:10 / 62:10 272
  61:12–13 / 62:11–12 160
  62 / 63 325, 351
  63 / 64 338
  64 / 65 338
  64:5 / 65:4 143
  65 / 66 350
  67:13 / 68:13 39
  67:17 / 68:16 39
  68:22 / 69:21 159
  68:28 / 69:27 137
  68:35–36 / 69:35–36 417
  70:19 / 71:19 300
  71:3 / 72:3 39
  71:7 / 72:7 130
  73:13–14 / 74:13–14 74
  74 / 75 339
  74:11 / 75:10 181
  76:18–19 / 77:18–19 378
  76:19 / 77:18 307, 320
  76:19 / 77:18 307

INDEX OF BIBLICAL CITATIONS

79:4 / 80:19 179
79:8 / 80:19 179
79:20 / 80:19 179
80 / 81 350
80:11 / 81:10 180
82:2 300
83 / 84 338
83:8 / 84:7 238
83:11 / 84:10 147
84:9 / 85:8 180
84:12 / 85:11 43
85:8 / 86:8 299
88:27 / 89:27 159
88:28 / 89:28 159
89 / 90 325
89:8 / 90:8 300
91:13 / 92:12 20, 237
92 / 93 350
92:1 / 93:1 186
94 / 95 33, 120, 321, 334
94:2 / 95:2 33, 120
96 / 97 339
97 / 98 350
98 / 99 339, 350
99 / 100 350
103:24 / 104:24 185
104 / 105 322
104:18–19 / 105:18–19 109
105 / 106 322
105:17–18 / 106:17–18 161
105:20–21 / 106:20–21 28
105:21 / 106:21 28
106 / 107 322
108:5 / 109:5 161
109 / 110 355, 357
109:1 / 110:1 160
110:1–2 / 111:1–2 188
111:7 / 112:6–7 102
111:7 / 112:7 235
112 / 113 299, 329, 355
112:4 / 113:4 299
115 / 116:10ff. 356
115:12–13 / 116:12–13 137
116 / 117 330
118:54 / 119:54 257
118:99 / 119:99 186
118:165 / 119:165 120
125 /126 356

131:11 / 132:11 159
132 / 133 417
138 / 139 356, 383
138:6 / 139:6 186
138:11 / 139:11 35
138:17–18 / 139:17–18 365
138:17 / 139:17 8, 76, 181, 383
138:18 / 139:18 159, 186
144:18–19 / 145:18–19 126
145 / 146 330
146 / 147 331
147 / 147:12 331
148 326, 351, 416
150:1 143, 234

Proverbs
3:16 80, 147
8:34 33
9:1–3 182
11:6 136, 137
11:8 102, 136, 137
11:10 136, 137
13:1 110
18:3 215
18:10 45
20:4 114
20:10 273
23:31–32 260
28:9 18
31:4 259

Ecclesiastes
4:12 206

Wisdom
1:4–5 113
1:5 83
3:15 102
4:2 102
4:7 359
4:10 102, 229, 404
4:14 102
4:16–19 101
10:10 359
10:17 231
18:15–20 392
18:22 319, 355, 390
19:1 390
19:12–16 394

ECCLESIASTICUS (SIRACH)
1:1 17, 187
1:13 102, 190
2:14 19
11:30 142
12:13 126
15:1 189
19:2 260
24:11 184
24:23 20
31:12 136
31:14 136
31:19 136
32:1 259
34:27 278
39:4–5 92
44:16 229, 403, 404, 405
44:16ff. 295
44:16ff xxxix
44:17 297
44:19 297, 406
44:20 299, 300, 301, 404
44:21 300
44:22–23 301, 302
44:23 301
44:26 302, 404, 406
44:27 303
45:1 304, 404, 406
46:1 320, 326, 329, 341, 350, 387
46:1–2 320, 326, 329
48:13–14 317, 327
48:13ff. 401
48:15 318, 328, 342, 366
48:25 127
48:28 318, 328, 364
49:1–3 364
49:2 318, 328
49:3 341, 352, 356, 366
49:15 364
49:17–18 364
49:18 366
50:1 127, 359

CANTICLE OF CANTICLES
1:1 182
4:10 182, 404
8:6 188

ISAIAH
1:14 184, 280
1:16 25, 26
1:16–17 25
2:3 40
2:4 131
4:1 181
5:6 113
5:11–12 260
5:14 279
5:18–23 279
5:22 260
7:11–12 176
7:14 117, 158
8:7 50
9:2 127
9:6 127
11:1 117, 180
11:2 120, 183, 184
11:4 194
19:25 303
21:17–18 117
26:9 118
26:19 160
28:11 192
28:13 192
29:8 279
30:26 182
32:3 78
32:7 262
35:4–5 158
45:8 42
45:14 289
48:15 102
49:2 94
49:6 92
49:13 143
49:16–26 285
53:4 85
53:7 159
53:8 116
54:2–3 94
54:7 85
55:4 298
55:6 304
58:1 281
60:8 42, 294
61:1 186

INDEX OF BIBLICAL CITATIONS

62:2 120
64:1 109
65:12–15 277
66:2 120
66:24 133

JEREMIAH
4:22 187
13:19 116
14:8 117
14:9 334, 357
15:19 303
16:16 42, 74, 311
17:15 109
17:18 137
18:20 136
30:15 280
52:20 46

LAMENTATIONS
1:11 110, 122
4:4 110
4:7 42
4:8 43

EZEKIEL
1:15–19 116
2:1 30
3:26 113
16:43 197
23:25 264
36:11 159
36:23–25 118
37:14 118

DANIEL
3: 8–30 223
4:17 45
7:13 118, 159

HOSEA
4:8 58
6:3 118
14:6 235

JOEL
1:5 260
2:23 93
2:32 125

AMOS
8:11 108

JONAH
4:1–11 199
4:6–10 197

MICAH
4:2 40
5:5 130

HABAKKUK
3:11 283

ZECHARIAH
2:8 181
3:9 181
9:9 159

MALACHI
1:2–3 302
2:6 102
4:2 283, 466

OLD TESTAMENT PSEUDEPIGRAPHA

APOCALYPSE OF ZEPHANIAH
1:15–16 119

NEW TESTAMENT

Mark
1:16–20 343, 406
1:17 73, 140, 310
1:19–20 xv
1:29–31 312
1:34 206
2:14 51
2:25–27 162
2:26 46
3:12 206
3:13 40, 320
3:13–14 38
3:13–14ff. 23
3:13–17 319
3:13–19 366
3:13ff xxxix
3:14 417

Mark (cont.)
  3:14–15 40
  3:14–17 xvi
  3:16–19 51
  3:17 146, 211, 320
  3:18 40, 52
  3:18–19 41
  4:31 88
  5:21–42 xv
  5:21–43 47, 79, 164, 206
  6:3 52, 53, 232
  8:27 206
  8:36 278
  9:1–7 234
  9:2–3 164, 176, 297
  9:2–8 47, 176
  9:2–9 77, 146
  9:2–10 288
  9:2–13 xv
  9:34 258
  9:43 133
  9:45 xxv, 133, 289, 378, 404, 406
  9:47 92, 133
  10:14 417
  10:35–37 145
  10:35–37ff 201
  10:35–38 344
  10:35–40 222
  10:35–45 xv, 80, 378
  10:35ff xxxix, 395, 399
  10:37 338, 363
  10:38 177, 339
  10:39 107, 149, 202, 380
  10:40 150
  10:44 258
  11:15 273
  12:29–31 250
  12:41–44 293
  14 56
  14:22–24 xxxi
  14:32–42 xv, 206
  14:33–41 393
  14:34 85, 225, 347
  14:38 33
  15:21 48
  15:40 41, 208
  16:15–16 121
  16:16 186
  16:19 80

MATTHEW
  1:23 117, 158
  3:17 41, 211, 297
  4:1–22 208
  4:8 300
  4:17 297
  4:18 306, 407
  4:18–20ff. 291
  4:18–21 73
  4:18–22 47, 307
  4:18ff xxxix
  4:19 140, 310, 337
  4:21 337, 407
  4:21–22 xv, 71, 228
  4:21–22ff. 306
  4:21ff xxxix
  4:22 308, 337
  4:23 311
  4:24 312
  4:25 312
  5:1 39
  5:13 44
  5:14 38
  5:17 116
  6:9 190
  6:10 190
  6:11 190
  6:12 191
  6:13 191, 301
  6:33 75
  6:34 76
  7:2 272
  7:7 463
  8:14–15 312
  9:9–13 51
  9:18–26 47, 164, 206
  10:1–4ff 168
  10:1–15 385
  10:1ff xxxix, 402
  10:2 47, 51, 169
  10:3 52, 53, 170
  10:5–6 170
  10:7–8 170
  10:8 57, 86, 171, 183
  10:9 171
  10:9–10 171, 253, 254

INDEX OF BIBLICAL CITATIONS

10:10 171, 172
10:11 172, 173
10:12–13 173
10:15 173
10:16 9, 358
10:20 180
10:28 190
10:42 293, 310
11:11 209
11:27 149
11:28–29 230
11:29 298
12:38–42 176
12:50 52, 120
13:16 72
13:31 88
13:41 81
13:43 77
13:44 285
13:45 285
13:45–46 122
13:55 232
13:55–56 52
14:20 46
15:26 278
16:16 48
16:19 45
16:20 77
16:27 138
17:1–2 338
17:1–2ff 175
17:1–8 47, 77, 146, 234
17:1–9 288, 388
17:1–13 xv, 205
17:1ff xxxix
17:2 164, 175, 176, 297
17:3 176
17:4 176, 177, 221
17:5 77, 177, 185, 211, 297
17:7 178
17:8 178
17:9 178
17:19 88
18:22 186
19:21 254
19:28 146
20:16 175
20:18–19 221

20:19 221
20:20 221
20:20–21ff. 220
20:20–22 145, 366
20:20–23 222
20:20–28 xv, 80, 397
20:20ff xxxix
20:21 221
20:22 146, 148, 222, 224, 339, 366, 380
20:23 107, 137, 148, 149, 150, 223, 224
20:24 224
20:25 224
20:26 258
20:28 225
21:12 273
22:12–13 26
22:37–39 250
23:8 120
24:13 301
24:32 48
24:42 33
25:1–13 34
25:12 33
25:14–30 235
25:23 235
25:40 24
25:41 102
26:15 170
26:26–28 xxxi
26–27 56
26:33 198
26:36–46 xv
26:36–56 206
26:37ff xxxix, 197
26:38 47, 85, 197, 200, 225, 347
26:39 198, 202, 223
26:40 198
26:41 198, 199
26:42 199
26:43 199
26:45 199
26:46 199
26:66 161
27:19 99
27:56 208
28:19 170, 361

LUKE
- 1:35 185
- 1:38 473
- 1:78 284
- 1:79 284
- 2:14 130, 293
- 2:26 132
- 2:29–32 334
- 3:22 211
- 4:18 186
- 4:35 206
- 4:38–41 312
- 5:1–11 307
- 5:10 307
- 5:27 51
- 6:11–16 51
- 6:15 169
- 6:16 52
- 6:31 59
- 6:35 144
- 6:38 211, 272
- 8:40–56 xv, 164
- 9:3 253
- 9:25 278
- 9:28 xv, 77, 146, 164, 175, 234, 288, 297
- 9:28–36 xv, 77, 146, 164, 234, 288, 297
- 9:30–31 176
- 9:33 177
- 9:35 307
- 9:51–52ff. 179
- 9:51–56 xvi, 390
- 9:51ff xxxix
- 9:52 191
- 9:52–53 192
- 9:52–55 344
- 9:54 193
- 9:55 195
- 9:56 193, 195
- 9:62 310
- 10:1 54, 121
- 10:3 88, 358
- 10:22 149
- 10:23 72
- 10:24 109
- 10:27 250
- 10:38–42 76
- 11:0 463
- 12:31 75
- 12:35 29
- 13:19 88
- 13:24 145
- 15:5 465
- 15:17–18 110
- 16:19–31 19
- 16:22–25 21
- 17:6 88, 177
- 17:21 80, 150
- 18:16 417
- 19:1–10 292, 309
- 21:1–4 293, 310
- 21:18 303
- 22 56, 75, 222
- 22:19–20 xxxi
- 22:25–36 75
- 23:26 48
- 24:18 253

JOHN
- 1:1 41, 47, 307, 325, 417
- 1:14 78, 109
- 1:42 40
- 1:43–44 50
- 1:43–51 50
- 2:1–11 116
- 5:19 149
- 5:28 118
- 5:36–37 177
- 6:1 85
- 6:37 186
- 6:41 109
- 6:51 109
- 6:52 119
- 6:59 119
- 6:71 54
- 7:7 186
- 8:12 45
- 8:18 16, 177
- 8:25 94
- 9:1–3 161
- 9:1–12 160
- 10:18 225
- 10:30 150
- 10:41 84
- 10:42 84

INDEX OF BIBLICAL CITATIONS

11:27 48
12:24–25 138
12:26 140
12:31 82, 185, 297
12:43 135
13 56
14:2 224
14:6 126
14:12 86
14:23 117
14:27 132, 208
15:16 139, 243, 367
15:19 367
16:7 246
17:11 303
19:25 208
20:21 358
20:23 244
20:24–29 51
21:1–14 85
21:15 208

Acts

1:8 119, 141
1:12–26 xvi
1:13 51, 52, 170
2:5 16
2:9 16
2:17 118
2:21 125
3:6 169
3:19 297
3:22 158
5:1–11 254, 309
5:41 17
6 167
6:7 141
6:8 127
7 167
7:54 70, 125, 127
7:54–8:2 125
7:54–60 70
7:55 80
8:1 15
8:9–24 56
8:20 56
8:33 116
10 81

10:43 78
11 xxxix
11:27–28 108
11:27–28ff. 105
11:27–30 65, 396
11:28–30 108
11:29 113, 114, 116, 119
11:30 120
12 xxxix, 100, 215, 372, 421
12:1 97, 123, 150, 360, 387, 390, 392, 394, 396, 399, 401, 406
12:1–2 xv, 65, 108, 153, 288, 318, 320, 328, 329, 339, 341, 346, 350, 373, 396, 440
12:1–3 xvi, 31
12:1–10 66
12:2 387, 390, 392, 394, 396, 399, 401, 406
12:3 135, 215
12:3–4 100
12:3–7 166
12:3–10 166
12:5–18 100
12:19 126
12:19–22 100, 128
12:19–23 66
12:19–24 166, 396
12:20 130
12:21 131
12:22 131
12:23 132, 320
13:46 103, 193
13:47 92
14:21 231
15 258
19–23 66
21–23 345
23:6 212

Romans

2:6 138
2:21 114
5:2–3 147
5:3–4 17
5:10 298
5:20 169
6:5 148

ROMANS (CONT.)
6:23 138
8:9 86
8:18 16, 101
8:30 76
10:10 49
10:13 125
10:15 44
10:18 41, 307
11:25–26 193
11:33–34 186
12:17 304
12:19 138
13:10 116
13:11 24
13:13 261

1 CORINTHIANS
1:5 147
1:19 187
1:27–29 228
2:7–8 206
3:3–4 258
3:19 187
10:4 40
11:23–26) xxxi
14:12 192
14:15 33
14:21 192
15:34 24
15:53 77

2 CORINTHIANS
2:14–15 235
2:15 180
4:10 124
5:17 115
6:6 76, 189
6:16 117
8:21 304
11:2 53, 54
11:29 189
13:1 78

GALATIANS
1:19 52, 232
2:9 205
2:9–10 15
2:20 123

4:4–5 110
6:6 172

EPHESIANS
2:8 112
4:7–8 187
4:8 159
4:11 191
4:26–27 258
5:18 260
6:10–18 88
6:13 253
6:13–17 249
6:14 30

PHILIPPIANS
3:19 100, 135

COLOSSIANS
2:9 94, 184

1 THESSALONIANS
5:19–20 116

2 THESSALONIANS
2:8 194

1 TIMOTHY
2:4 40, 195
3:7 172
6:8 172
6:10 278

2 TIMOTHY
2:3–4 45
2:4 230
4:5 33

HEBREWS
1:2 303
7:19 112

JAMES
1:1 xxxix, 15, 326
1:1–12 365
1:1–14 14
1:1ff. 14, 317
1:2 16
1:3 17
1:4 17
1:5 17, 18

INDEX OF BIBLICAL CITATIONS

1:6 18
1:8 18
1:9 19
1:10 19
1:11 20
1:12 21
1:13 21, 22, 300
1:14 22
2:14–26 28
2:23 158
4:17 189
5:20 270

1 Peter
   3:14–15 190
   3:18 199
   5:8–9 131

2 Peter
   1:17 77, 211

1 John
   2:19 180

Jude
   1:1 53

Revelation
   2:1–29 41
   2:10 21
   3:1–22 41
   3:16 180
   5:6 181
   7:14 44
   12:1 46
   17:15 50
   21:12 46
   21:14 46
   22:12 138

GENERAL INDEX

A

A Dicolos Tetrastrophos. See *Signa sunt nobis sacra*
Aaron 46, 103, 319
Abagar V, of Osroene, king 169
Abiathar xvii, 162
Abiram 161
Abraham 20, 22, 45-46, 158, 161, 205, 234, 252, 286, 299-301, 404-5, 454
Achaia 62
Acts of Andrew 49
Ad honorem Regis summi xxvi, xliii, xliv, 441
Ad superni Regis decus xliv, 433
Adam 27, 109, 129, 160, 163-64, 252, 454
Afonso I, king of Portugal 460
Agabus 65, 105, 107-8, 110, 112, 396
Agatha, saint 8
Agnus Dei xxxiv, xlii, 361, 425
Ahaz 176
Ahaziah. See *Ochozias*.
Aimeric de la Châtre or of Burgundy. See *Aymeric Picaud*.
Airardus of Vézelay xliv, 434
Ait Jesus 380, 386, 390, 393, 395, 397, 399, 402, 406
Al-Andalus 461
Alberic of Vézelay, cardinal-bishop of Ostia xliv, 446-47
Alberich of Reims. See *Albetricus of Bourges*.
Albert of Paris xliv, 432
Albetricus of Bourges xliv, 433-34
Albineto, France 36
Alexandria xvii, 65, 124, 210, 413, 422
Alleluia Iacobe sanctissime 333, 357
Alma perpetui luminis 334, 357
Almanzor, 461
Ambrose, saint 4, 32, 270
Ananias 254, 309

Andrew, apostle 40-41, 47, 49, 62, 73, 121, 168-69, 227, 291-93, 307-8, 310, 337, 366, 385, 406
Angel of Darkness 22, 131
Annua gaudia xliv, 434
Annunciation 333
Anselm, saint xxiv, xxv, xlii, 2, 5, 36, 400-1, 408
Antioch, Turkey 65, 105, 108, 110-11, 115, 121, 193, 396, 462
Apostole Christi Iacobe 352
Arduin, soldier 37
Arian heresy. See *Arius*.
Aristobol, son of Herod 214
Arius 10; Arian heresy 10
Ark of the Covenant 104, 189
Arrats River, France 36
Ascension xvi, xxxvi, 11, 73, 115-16, 118, 154, 159-60, 164, 209-11, 375
Ato of Trier xliv, 347–49, 437–38
Aubiet, France 36
Auch, France 36
Augustine, saint, of Hippo xxv, xxvii, xxxviii, xxxix, 4, 12, 28, 120, 306-8, 454; Sermon of 306-13 (Chapter 20)
Aymeric Picaud xxvi, xliii, xliv, 441, 445
Aymericus the Chancellor xxvi, 441, 445

B

Bacchus 259, 261
Baptism 47, 184, 304
Barbadelo, Galicia 266
Bari, Italy 275, 276
Barletta, Italy 275
Barnabas 15, 65, 108, 115, 120-21, 258, 396
Bartholomew, apostle 41, 47, 50, 62, 121, 168-69, 276, 366, 385; basilica 276

Basilius 261
Basques 36, 240
Bede, saint xxiv, xxv, xxvii, xxxvii, xxxviii, xxxix, 4, 5, 11, 14-16, 20, 22, 36, 117, 144, 152, 215, 454, 459; Sermons of 14-22 (Chapter 1), 144-52 (Chapter 8)
Beelzebub 193
beggars 269-70
Benevento, bishop of xlii, xliv, 410, 435
Benevento, basilica of Saint Bartholomew 276
Bernard of Morre 37
Bernard of Clairvaux, saint 472
Besançon, France 37
Blastus 100, 128, 130, 166, 396
Bruno of Vézelay 447
Burgos, Spain 478

C

Caesarea 16, 66-7, 100, 126, 128-29, 166, 215, 372, 396, 423
Caligula. *See Gaius Caesar*
Calixtus, Blessing of 63 (Chapter 3); Letter of 1-10; Sermons of 23-62 (Chapter 2), 64-69 (Chapter 4), 70-84 (Chapter 5), 85-104 (Chapter 6), 105-43 (Chapter 7), 153-67 (Chapter 9), 179-96 (Chapter 12), 227-90 (Chapter 17), 295-306 (Chapter 19), 306-13 (Chapter 20)
Calliope, muse 461
Cana of Galilee 116, 169
Canticle of Simeon. *See Nunc dimittis*
Castilla, Spain 256, 461
Cathedral of Santiago de Compostela. *See Santiago de Compostela, basilica of*
Cephas. *See Peter, apostle*
Certe dum filii 366
Chaldeans 40

Charlemagne xxii, xxiii, xxiv, xxx, 473, 478, 515
Châteauneuf, France 258
Châtellerault, France 458
Cicero (Marcus Tullius) 87
Cize, Navarre 280, 401, 442
Clairvaux, France 472
Claudius Caesar, Roman emperor 65, 68, 105, 107-8, 112, 129, 215, 396
Claudius Lysias 157
Clemens servulorum gemitus 383, 390, 394, 399, 401
Clement of Alexandria xvii, 65, 124, 210, 319, 371–72, 422
Clermont-Ferrand, France 456
Cluny xxi, xxiii, xxv, xxvi, 1, 35, 323, 446
Columns of Hercules 217
Compline xxxv, xxxvi, 333-34, 357, 368, 381
Compostela, woman of 232-33
Cornelius 81
Cosmas and Damian, saints 38, 446
Creed xxxi, xxxiii, xxxiv, 378
Cupid 261
Custodi nos 334, 357
Cynics 171

D

Dacia 241, 289; Dacians 322
Damian, saint 38
Dathan 161
Day of Judgment 118, 275-76
Decapolis 312, 407
Deus qui diem festum 356, 381
Deus qui hanc noctem 334, 357, 368
Deus qui presentem 333, 368
devil 21, 74
Didymus 51; See Thomas, apostle
Diego Gelmírez xix, xxv, xxvi, xxvii, 1, 2
Dies irae 119, 134, 374
Dionysius Cato 258
Dioscorides, Pedanius 87, 236
Droardus of Troyes xliv, 440

GENERAL INDEX

Dum esset Salvator 77, 320, 323, 325, 328, 331, 343, 437
Dum Pater Familias ix, xxi, xlv, lii, 377, 449

E

Easter xxxii, xxxvi, 9, 34, 298, 361, 456, 477
Ecce sacerdos magnus 359
Edessa 62, 169
Egypt 28, 31, 142, 209, 252-53, 289, 360, 453
Egyptians 34-5, 241
Ekron. *See Accaron*
Elamites 16, 242
Eli 189
Elias 77-78, 176-78, 193-94, 317, 344, 366, 388, 390, 448
Elijah 295-96, 448
Elim 46, 103, 452-53, 479
Elisha, prophet 56, 112-13
Enoch 229, 295-97, 403-5
Ephesus 41, 62, 151
Epiphany xxxvi, 407
Esau 102, 302, 320
Espalion, France 38
Ethiopia 62, 289
Eusebius xvi, xvii, xxxix, xli, xlii, 16, 64-68, 112, 115, 119, 124, 128-29, 153, 169, 213, 215, 318-19, 331, 340, 345, 348, 350-56, 358, 360, 372, 383, 421; Sermon of 64-69 (Chapter 4)
Eve 129
Ezekiel 116, 159, 197, 209

F

Feast Days of Saint James xxii, 3, 36, 357-61
 January 5 (Octave of *Translation*) xxxviii, xxxix, xlii, 306, 407
 July 24 (Vigil of Passion) xxxviii, xxxix, xl, xli, 14, 23, 317-18, 321, 363
 July 25 (Passion) xviii, xxii, xxxvii, xxxviii, xxxix, xli, 3, 34, 70, 71, 85, 105, 144, 153, 168, 231, 318, 329, 369, 462
 July 26 (also Saint Josias) xxxviii, xxxix, xli, 64, 153, 168, 383
 July 27 xxxix, xli, 168, 175, 387
 July 28 xxxix, xli, 179, 389
 July 29 xxxix, xli, 197, 391
 July 30 xxxix, xli, 201, 394
 July 31 xxxix, xli, 205, 220, 358-59, 395
 August 1 (Octave of Passion) xli, 168, 398
 October 3 (Miracles) xxii, xxxvii, xli, 3, 71, 400-401, 460, 462
 December 30 (Calling and *Translation*) xxxviii, xxxix, xl, xli, xlii, 3, 71, 227, 231, 291, 295, 329, 403, 462
Feast of Miracles xli; See Feast Days of Saint James, October 3
Feast of Saint Josias the Martyr; See Feast Days of Saint James, July 26
Feast of Saint Peter in Chains; See Peter, apostle
Feast of the *Translation* of Saint James. See Feast days of Saint James, December 30
Felix per omnes 331, 352, 356, 403
Final Judgment. *See Last Judgment*
footwear 31, 75, 171-72, 253-55, 385,
Foulques, pilgrim 477–78
Frisians 240, 322
Frisonus, sailor 443
Fulbert of Chartres xxviii, xli, xlii, xliv, 321, 326, 341, 411, 415, 417-18, 420-21, 425, 439
Fulcher of Chartres 280

G

Gaius Caesar 65, 68, 129, 214
Galen 87

Galicia xviii, xxii, xxxviii, xliii, xlvi,
    23, 36, 41, 62, 64, 71, 73,
    85, 92, 105, 138-39, 141-42,
    144, 166, 179, 205, 216,
    220, 227, 229, 232-33, 238-
    40, 243-45, 264, 281, 283,
    285, 287, 289, 291, 295,
    300-301, 304, 306, 322,
    370-71, 376, 379-80, 387,
    408, 413, 416, 420, 427,
    431, 436, 442, 445, 449,
    467-68, 478
Galicians 32, 36, 70, 139, 231, 349,
    384, 403, 405, 412-13
Galilee 227
Galilee, Sea of xv, 47, 71-73, 85, 101,
    107, 141, 143, 164, 207,
    228, 283, 287, 291, 304,
    306, 308, 332, 403, 405-7,
    420, 441
Gascons 240, 257
Gascony 36
Gauterius of Château Renard xliv,
    436, 440
Gehazi 56; Gehazites 56
Gehenna 60, 101, 111, 135, 138,
    192, 277, 279. *See also hell,
    Orcus, Tartarus*
Gentiles 15, 49, 81, 86, 91, 95, 97,
    103, 108, 126, 140, 161,
    170, 193, 221, 298, 332,
    369, 385
Gethsemane xv, 206
Gherardo Caccianemice dal Orso.
    See Girard of Sancta Cruce
Gibraltar, Straits of. *See Columns of
    Hercules*
Gideon 34
Gilboa, Mountains of 39
Giles, saint 255, 267, 275, 476
Gelmírez, Diego. *See Diego Gelmírez*
Girard of Sancta Cruce, cardinal 446
Girberga of Flanders 445
Gloria xxxiii, xxxiv, xlii, 439
Gloriosissimam sollemnitatem 352, 371

Goslenus, bishop of Soissons.
    *See Gosselin de Vierzy, bishop
    of Soissons*
Gosselin de Vierzy, bishop of Soissons
    xliv, 433, 440
Goths 37, 240
Gratulantes celebremus xliv, 433
Gratulemur et letemur 374, 388, 396,
    406
Great Passion (Chapter 9) xxxix,
    153-67
Greeks 5, 40, 154, 240-43, 322
Gregorio Papareschi, cardinal 446.
Gregory I, saint, the Great xxv,
    xxxix, xli, 4, 201, 246, 291,
    306, 308-9, 311, 323, 327,
    333-34, 339, 345, 356-57,
    363, 366, 380; Sermons of
    201-4 (Chapter 14), 306-13
    (Chapter 20)
Gregory of Iena, cardinal 446
Gregory of Tours 3, 285
Guido of Lombardy, cardinal 446
Guido Pissanus, cardinal 446
Guy of Burgundy (Calixtus II) xiv,
    1, 37

H

Hagar 45, 158, 460
Hannah, mother of Samuel 159
Hebrews 28-9, 32, 35, 103, 193,
    452, 479
hell 22, 39, 58-60, 101, 107, 130,
    132-37, 140, 159, 164-65,
    186, 269, 272, 276-79, 297,
    299. *See also Gehenna, Orcus,
    Tartarus*
Hermogenes xvii, xix, 154-57, 212-
    13, 289, 319, 348, 372, 442
Herod Agrippa I xv, xvi, xviii, xliv,
    64-68, 72, 92, 97-100,
    106-8, 123, 126-33, 135,
    137-38, 141-42, 150, 153-
    54, 162-63, 165-66, 205,
    213-15, 218, 223, 229, 238,

GENERAL INDEX

288, 300, 307, 318, 320-21, 328-29, 331-32, 339-41, 345-47, 350, 354-55, 369-73, 376, 379-80, 386-87, 390, 392, 394, 396, 399, 401, 406, 408, 420-24, 426, 431-32, 436, 440, 442, 454, 466-67, 480
Herod Antipas, 213
Herod Archelaus 214
Herod II 214
Herod Philip II 68, 129, 213
Herod the Great 213-14
Hic est Iacobus dilectus 346
Hic Iacobus valde venerandus 346, 373, 390, 399
Hierapolis 62, 241
Hippocrates 87-88
Hophni 189
Huic Iacobo condoluit 438
Humbert, archbishop of Besançon 37

I

Iacobe pastor inclite 354
Iacobe Sancte xlii, xliv, xlv, 435
Iacobe virginei frater 331, 348, 353, 438
Iacobus et Ioannes tonitrum 326, 417
Iam locum celsitudinis 339, 345, 363, 366
Illicinus. *See Pico Sacro*
India xvii, 51, 62
innkeepers 4, 205, 262-68, 271, 275, 280-81, 360, 394,
Innocent II xxiii, xxvi, xxvii, xliii, xliv, 445-46
Iocundetur et letetur 334, 403
Iria Flavia, Galicia 232, 467, 468, 474
Isaac 46, 102, 158, 205, 300
Ishmael 45, 158
Isidore of Seville xviii, 15, 111
Israelite people 28, 30
Ivo, cardinal 446

J

Jacob 45-46, 82, 102-3, 205-6, 234, 252, 302-3, 320, 359
Jaffa, Israel 232, 467
Jairus's daughter 79
James, brother of Jesus 53.
James of Alphaeus 41, 48, 52, 62, 168, 169
James of Zebedee 9, 23, 41, 47, 51, 52, 64, 73, 85, 105, 136, 144, 168, 179, 291, 295, 306, 319, 321, 337, 343, 361, 363, 364, 366, 369, 371, 373, 374, 378, 385, 395, 406, 407, 427, 440, 448
James the Just xvi, 210
James the Lesser xvi, 14, 41, 167, 210
Jerome, saint xxv, xxvii, xxx, xxxvii, xxxviii, xxxix, xli, 4, 12, 120, 208, 306-7, 312, 325-26, 343, 359, 417; Sermons of 168-74 (Chapter 10), 175-78 (Chapter 11), 197-200 (Chapter 13), 220-26 (Chapter 16), 306-13 (Chapter 20)
Jerusalem xvi, xviii, xxi, xxiv, xxv, 2, 15-16, 46, 51, 62, 65, 71, 89, 92, 97, 105, 108, 110-11, 115, 118-19, 139, 141-42, 157-58, 166-67, 176, 179, 192, 195-97, 227, 229, 232-33, 237-39, 249-50, 253-54, 269, 281, 291, 312, 330-31, 349, 376, 390, 396, 407, 438, 446, 449-52, 461, 467
Jerusalemites 108, 141, 241
Jesus vocavit xlv, 9, 41, 319-20, 323, 325, 327-28, 338, 341, 353-56, 364, 371, 373, 378, 383, 387, 389-99, 401-2, 405-6, 416-18, 440, 448

Jews xxvii, 15, 38-39, 66, 81, 91, 95, 97, 100, 102, 117, 126, 135, 140, 153, 155, 157-58, 162, 166, 170, 186, 191-93, 205, 213-15, 218, 230, 242, 298, 303, 332, 340, 369, 372, 422
Jewish rebellion 167
Jocelyn or Jocelin of Soissons. *See Gosselin de Vierzy, bishop of Soissons*
John, apostle xv, xvi, 15, 41, 46-49, 62, 65, 73-77, 79-83, 85, 97, 108, 123-24, 144-46, 150-54, 164, 168-69, 175, 178-79, 191, 193, 195, 197, 200-202, 206-11, 216, 220-23, 227-28, 258, 289, 306-10, 318-20, 323-329, 337-39, 341, 343-46, 348, 350, 354-55, 363-64, 366, 370-71, 373-74, 377-78, 380, 385, 388, 390, 392, 396-97, 406-7, 421, 440, 444, 448, 454, 472; as John the Evangelist 70, 154, 223, 287, 295, 326
John Chrysostom, saint xxvii, xxx, xxxvii, xxxviii, xxxix, 218, 220; Sermon of 220–26 (Chapter 16)
John Legalis xliv, 437
John the Baptist, saint 7, 8, 209, 213, 275, 361
Jonah 40, 48, 197
Joppa. *See Jaffa*
Jordan River 46, 103-4, 132, 185, 297, 312, 407
Joseph, brother of Jesus 53
Joseph, son of Isaac, patriarch 142, 209, 364, 366
Josephus 66-9, 128-29, 214
Joshua 104
Josias xvi, xvii, xix, 125, 153, 162-63, 165, 168, 219, 318-19, 347, 351, 357-58, 364, 366, 372, 383, 386, 421-22, 442

Judaea 167
Judah, brother of James 52
Judah, tribe of 185
Judaites 56
Judas, brother of James 169-70
Judas Iscariot xvi, 41, 48, 54-56, 59, 78, 168, 170, 197, 262, 366, 385
Jude, brother of Jesus 53
Jude, apostle 54, 62, 170
Judea 15, 41, 67, 86, 94, 100, 113-14, 116, 119-21, 126, 128-29, 141, 154, 164, 166, 239, 312, 375, 396, 407, 460, 466

K

Kyrie xxxi, xxxiv, xlii, xliv, 361, 363, 418, 439

L

Last Judgment 80, 135, 137, 147, 187, 291, 303
Last Supper xxxi, 146, 307
Lauds xxxv, xxxvi, 324, 331, 350
Lawrence of Rome, saint 32
Lebbaeus, apostle. *See Lebtheus, apostle*
Le Puy, France 38, 275, 456; Basilica of Saint Mary 267, 275
Lebtheus, apostle 170
Leo I, the Great, pope xlv, 4
Leo, pope xxiv, xxvii, xxx, xxxvii, xxxix, 5, 466, 470; Sermon of 205–219 (Chapter 15)
León, Spain xl, xliii, 7, 256, 461
Leonard, saint 255, 275
leprosy 56-57
Letter of Pope Innocent II xxiii, xxiv, xxvi, xxvii, 445-46
Letter of Pope Saint Calixtus xiii, xiv, xxv, xxviii-xxix, xxx, 1-10
Levi, son of Alphaeus 51
Lord's prayer xxxi, xxxiv, 190-91
Louis VI, king 447
Lucca, Italy 275
Lucifer 21, 30
Lugo, Galicia 264

GENERAL INDEX

Lupa, queen 285
Lux et decus Hispanie 356

M

Macer, Aemilius or Floridus 87
Magnificat 333, 356
Mamre, Canaan 234
Marcus Agrippa 474
Marianne, wife of Herod 214
Martha, sister of Mary 76, 84
Martin of Tours, saint 3, 275; basilica 267
Mary, mother of James of Alpheus 52
Mary, mother of Jesus 8, 43, 52-53, 76, 84, 94, 115, 145, 208, 210, 237, 275, 299, 333, 400, 419, 447
Mary, sister of Martha 76, 84
Mary Magdalene, saint 8, 275, 447
Mary Salome, mother of the sons of Zebedee 52, 145, 208
Matins xxxv, xxxvi, 317-19, 326, 350, 357-58, 368, 404, 407
Matthew, apostle 41, 47, 50, 62, 168-69, 310, 366, 385
Matthias, saint 54
Maximus, bishop of Turin xxx, 4, 12, 261
Medes 16, 241
Mediterranean 95, 242
Minean Bridge, Galicia 264-65
Miracles in CC
  Ad honorem regi summi (CCA 14) 441-44
  embedded in Chapter 2 36-38
  Feast of xli
  of the ash-cake bread (CCA 17) 447-48
  about the resuscitated boy (CCA 21.1) 456-57
  about the twisted face (CCA 21.2) 458-59
  about the flight of the Saracens from Portugal (CCA 21.3) 460-62
  about the justice that transforms (CCA 24) 471-73
  about the cripple who stood up (CCA 26) 474-75
  about Peter the resuscitated boy (CCA 21.1) 456-57
  about the vision of a certain Foulques (CCA 28) 477-78
Mirecourt, France 37
Mirepoix, France 37
Misit Herodes rex 346
Monte Gargano 276
Montes de Oca, Spain 457
Montpellier, France 37-8
Montreuil-sur-Mer, France 477
Mont-Saint-Michel, France 276
Moses 28-29, 31, 46, 77-78, 103, 109, 112, 158, 176-78, 192, 234, 304, 388, 404, 453
Mount Bethel 103, 234, 302-3
Mount Sinai 28, 234
Mount Tabor 41, 47, 77, 101, 103, 107, 146, 164, 234, 288, 297, 303, 307, 326, 346, 370, 377, 379, 393, 398, 417
Myra, Turkey 7, 276

N

Naaman the Syrian 56
Naboth 20
Naddaver, Ethiopia 62
Nathaniel, apostle 50, 85, 276; See also Bartholomew, apostle
Navarre, Spain 36
Nebaioth, son of Ishmael 45
Nicholas, saint 7, 8, 276; basilica 276
Noah 259, 297-98, 403, 405, 454
None xxxv, xxxvi, 318-19, 328, 355, 381, 398, 404
Nostra phalanx xliv, 431
Nunc dimittis 334, 357

O

O adiutor omnium 330-31, 349, 356, 438
O Dei Verbum 216
Ochozias, king of Israel 193
Ode de Meung-sur-Loire. *See* Macer

509

Oldierius, monk 473
Ora pro nobis Beate Iacobe 352
Orcus 60, 133, 230, 262, 268, 277-78, 413. *See also Gehenna, hell, Tartarus*
Osroene, Turkey 169
Our Father. *See Lord's prayer*
Ovid 259

P

Padrón, Galicia 467-68
Palas del Rey, Galicia 264
Palm Sunday 476
Pamukkale, Turkey 62
Paraclete 73, 118, 246, 322, 419, 437-38
paradise 27, 31, 98, 187, 238, 425
Parthenay-le-Vieux, France 441, 445
Parthians 16, 241
Parucham, Master xlv, 466
Pasionario Hispánico xix, xxxix, 154-63, 467, 485
Passio Iacobi. See Great Passion and Short Passion
Passion of Saint James. *See Great Passion and Short Passion*
Passover 31, 34
Pateant aures 10, 382
Patmos, Greece 151, 223
Paul, saint 61, 65, 81, 115, 121, 125, 157, 167, 189, 205, 258, 260; as Saul 108, 120, 121, 167, 396; Feast of Peter and Paul 72, 361
Paul the Deacon 4
Pecham, John 180
Pelagians 17
Pelagius, monk 17
Pentecost xxxii, xxxvi, 9, 15, 62, 186, 361, 363
Pergamon, Greece 41, 87
Périgueux, France 257-58
Persia 62, 242
Peter, apostle xv, xvii, 15, 40, 46-48, 53-54, 56, 61, 66, 70, 73, 77, 85, 100, 121, 126-29, 135, 146, 164, 166, 168-70, 175-78, 186, 197-98, 206-8, 210-11, 215, 217, 221, 227, 254-55, 275, 291-93, 307-10, 312, 319, 323-24, 337, 340, 366, 372, 385, 388, 392, 422-23
 as Simon xv, 40, 47-48, 53, 56, 146, 168-70, 208, 211, 291, 319, 323-24, 366, 385, 392, 406
 basilica in Rome 267
 Feast of Peter and Paul 72, 361
 Feast of Saint Peter in Chains xxxii, xxxviii, 168, 358-59, 398
Petronia. *See Padrón*
Pharisees 125, 154, 158, 162, 176, 212, 218
Philetus xvii, xix, 154-56, 442
Philip, apostle 41, 47, 50, 62, 168-69, 366, 385
Philistines 189
Phinehas 189
Phrygia, Turkey 62
Piacenza, Italy 275
Pico Sacro, Galicia 469, 470
Pilate 99, 375; wife of 99
pilgrim blessing 247-49
pilgrim roads xxiii, 37, 59, 60, 247, 252, 257, 267-68, 269-70, 275, 360, 478
 Roman Way 59
 Via Lemovicense 434
 Via Tolosana 37, 255
 Via Turonense 275
Plato 171-72
Poitiers, France 61, 98, 245, 413, 442, 458
Portomarín, Galicia 264, 266
Portum in ultimo xliv, 438
Prince of Darkness 21
Prince of Hell 22, 107
Promised Land 31-32, 46, 103, 253
Psallat chorus 321, 326, 334, 357

GENERAL INDEX

Pseudo-Abdias xvii, xix, 125, 319, 372
purse 8, 58-59, 171, 247-49 (blessing of), 253, 268, 275, 278, 385

Q
Quintus Serenus Sammonicus 87

R
Redemptor imposuit 320, 323, 324
Regi perhennis glorie xliv, 426, 436
Resurrection 51, 86, 101, 115-16, 118, 136, 140, 148, 154, 164, 170, 176, 178, 205-6, 212, 221, 225, 243, 308, 375, 464
Rex immense 418, 439
Robert, cardinal xlii, 412
Rome xxi, xxvi, 32, 61, 65, 107, 254-55, 275, 446-47; basilica of St. Peter 267

S
Sabaim. *See Sheba*
Sabellius 10
Sadducees 212
Saint James, feasts of. *See Feast days of Saint James.*
Saint Peter in Chains, feast. *See Peter, apostle*
Saint-Côme d'Olt, France 38
Saint-Gilles, France 255, 258, 269, 275, 474, 476
Saint-Jean-d'Angély, France 275
Sainte-Florine, France 456
Salvator progressus pusillum 9, 343, 402-3
Salve festa dies 36, 349, 369-70 (Chapter 25)
Samaria 15, 41, 119, 141, 154, 164, 193, 239, 281, 330
San Michele Arcangelo, church of 276
Sancho I, king of Portugal 460
Sanctissime Apostole Iacobe 330, 373, 388, 394
Sanctissime O Iacobe 326, 341

Santiago de Compostela, basilica xiii, 8-9, 29, 61, 138, 139, 141, 232-33, 239, 243, 248-50, 256, 270, 281, 382, 445-56, 458, 470-71, 476, 478; tomb 230-31, 329, 470, 478
Sapphira 254, 309
Sar River, Galicia 468
Sardis 41, 241; Sardinians 241
Satan 21, 277
Saul. *See Paul, saint*
Scythia 171
Sedulius 228, 229
Serenus 87
seven spiritual gifts 180-81, 183, 187
Sext xxxv, xxxvi, 318-19, 328, 331, 354, 380, 398, 404
Shadrach, Meshach, and Abednego 223
Sheba 289
shells 249-51, 443, 477
Short Passion (Chapter 4) xxxix, 64-69
Sidonians 100, 128, 130, 166, 396
Signa sunt nobis sacra xlv, 452-55, 479-81
Simeon, saint 132
Simon, brother of Jesus 53
Simon Magus 56
Simon Peter. *See Peter, apostle*
Simon the Canaanite 40, 41, 168-69, 366, 385
Simon the Zealot, apostle 40, 48, 53, 62, 169
Simoniacs 56-7, 60, 278
Sinai 28, 110, 234
Sodom and Gomorrah 173, 385
Solomon 33, 206,
Saint-John-d'Angély, France 275
Saint-Léonard-de-Noblat, France 255; basilica 267
staff 31, 112, 156, 171-72, 247-49 (blessing), 253, 270, 385, 412

511

Stephen, saint 15, 70, 80, 121, 125, 127, 167
Stephen, saint, of Rieti 202-3
Strato's Tower 67
Syria 312, 407; Syrians 241; Syrian language 40, 173

T
Tartarus 60, 163, 192, 277, 278, 424, 439. *See also Gehenna, hell, Orcus*
Te Deum Laudamus 461
Tel Aviv. *See Jaffa*
Temple of Solomon 33
Teodomiro, bishop of Compostela and Iria xx, 474
Terce xxxv, xxxvi, 317-19, 327, 353, 364, 380, 393, 398, 404
Tertullian 151
Thaddeus, apostle 41, 48, 52-53, 168-70, 366, 385
Theophilus of Antioch, bishop 193
Thomas, apostle xxxi, 3, 41, 47, 51, 62, 85, 168-69, 366, 385; as Didymus 51
Titan 77, 282
Titus, Roman emperor 167
Tours, France 3, 267, 275, 285
Transfiguration xv, 41, 47, 77-79, 146, 175-178, 205-6, 288, 297, 379, 393
Triacastela, Galicia 266
Trinity xxxvi, 10, 30, 42, 50, 78, 94, 118, 120, 180, 184, 249, 336, 361, 375, 391, 455
Troy 261
Tudela, Navarre 36
Tui, Spain 36
Tullius 87

twelve tribes of Israel xvii, 15, 45, 104, 136, 146, 287, 466
Tyrians 100, 128, 130, 166, 396

U
Ulla River, Galicia 468-69
underworld 60

V
Valerian, Roman emperor 32
Venantius Fortunatus xlii, 61, 90, 98-99, 246-47, 285-87, 413
Veneranda dies xiii, xxviii, xxxviii, xlvii, 4, 205, 227, 240, 248, 319, 330-31, 360, 476; Chapter 17 227-90
Venite omnes Cristicole 334
Venus 88, 261
Vespasian, Roman emperor 167, 467
Vespers xxxv, xxxvi, 318-20, 329, 331, 333, 355-56, 367, 381, 398, 400, 403-4
Vézelay, France 59, 255, 269, 275, 434, 446-47; Church of Saint Mary Magdalene 445
Vigiliarum sacrarum 327, 364
Vindicianus, Helvius 87
Vitalis 261
Vox nostra resonet xliv, 437

W
Walter of Chateau Renard 463
William of Messina xxv, 2
William, patriarch of Jerusalem xxv, xli, 2, 331, 334, 348, 383
William, saint 255

Z
Zacchaeus 292, 309
zodiac 46

*Production of This Book Was Completed on
May 1, 2021 at Italica Press, Bristol,
United Kingdom. It Was Set in
Adobe Garamond Pro,
Charlemagne &
Luminari.*

* *
*

www.ingramcontent.com/pod-product-compliance
Lightning Source LLC
Chambersburg PA
CBHW021823220426
43663CB00005B/113